converSiNG
with angels
and ancients

conversing with angels and ancients

LITERARY MYTHS OF MEDIEVAL IRELAND

Joseph Falaky Nagy

Cornell University Press

ITHACA AND LONDON

Latin passages from Ludwig Bieler, ed. and trans., *The Patrician Texts in the Book of Armagh,* Scriptores Latini Hiberniae 10 (Dublin: DIAS, 1979), and Irish passages with translation from Cecile O'Rahilly, ed. and trans., *Táin Bó Cúailnge: Recension I* (Dublin: DIAS, 1976), are quoted by courtesy of the Governing Board of the School of Celtic Studies of the Dublin Institute for Advanced Studies.

Latin passages © Marjorie O. Anderson, 1991, are reprinted from A. O. Anderson and M. O. Anderson, ed. and trans., *Adomnán's Life of Columba,* 2d ed. (Oxford: Clarendon Press, 1991), by permission of Oxford University Press. Irish passages with translation © Máire Herbert, 1988, are reprinted from Máire Herbert, *Iona, Kells, and Derry: The History and Hagiography of the Monastic Familia of Columba* (Dublin: Four Courts Press, 1996), by permission of Four Courts Press.

First published 1997 by Cornell University Press.
First printing, Cornell Paperbacks, 1997.

Printed in the United States of America

Cornell University Press strives to utilize environmentally responsible suppliers and materials to the fullest extent possible in the publishing of its books. Such materials include vegetable-based, low-VOC inks and acid-free papers that are also either recycled, totally chlorine-free, or partly composed of nonwood fibers.

Library of Congress Cataloging-in-Publication Data

Nagy, Joseph Falaky.
    Conversing with angels and ancients : literary myths of medieval Ireland / Joseph Falaky Nagy.
        p.   cm.
    Includes bibliographical references and index.
    ISBN 0-8014-3300-2 (cloth : alk. paper). — ISBN 0-8014-8368-9 (paper : alk. paper)
    1. Mythology, Celtic.   2. Irish literature—To 1100.   3. Irish literature—Middle Irish, 1100–1500.   I. Title.
BL980.I7N34   1997
891.6'21093522—dc21   97-2192

Cloth printing   10 9 8 7 6 5 4 3 2 1
Paperback printing 10 9 8 7 6 5 4 3 2 1

contents

pReface

arly medieval Ireland inherited from the world of late classical antiquity the figure of the saint (*sanctus* in Latin, *noíb* in Irish)—a means of personalizing, localizing, and making more accessible the redemptive power that Christianity offered to its adherents. The institution of saints and the nature of their sanctity are among the most characteristic elements of the religion brought to Ireland in the fifth century. In the words of the historian Peter Brown:

> The rise of the cult of saints [in the era of the later Roman empire] was sensed by contemporaries, in no uncertain manner, to have broken most of the imaginative boundaries which ancient men had placed between heaven and earth, the divine and the human, the living and the dead, the town and its antithesis. . . . [This cult] designated dead human beings as the recipients of unalloyed reverence, and it linked these dead and invisible figures in no uncertain manner to precise visible places and, in many areas, to precise living representations.[1]

The commemoration of saints functioned for the Irish as a means of making space and time sacred in the new religious milieu. While sanctity was deemed an indisputable, universal fact, the saint was distinctly a local hero, the celebration of whose life and miracles added to the prestige and power of a territory, community, and extended family. Moreover, the saint, revered as such only in retrospect, was an index of the past, reviving the glorious sanctity of Christ and the apostles. Yet in aspiring to spiritual perfection, the saint of cult and legend also pointed ahead in time, living a life that anticipated death,

---

1. Brown 1981, 21.

and even experiencing heavenly visions while still on earth. Most important of all, the saints of Ireland, like Christian saints everywhere, were empowered and empowering patrons who could protect their devotees from day to day, and who were expected to stand by them on the Day of Judgment. Intercessors and mediators, saints bridged the gap between the sacred and the profane, the dead and the living, the familiar and the unknown.

There is, however, an Irish use of saints and saintly powers that constitutes an innovation in the history of Western Christianity. We shall see in the chapters to follow that the Irish saint mediated not only on a religious but also on a literary plane. The *noíb* could rehabilitate and sponsor the recording of a pre-Christian "native" past discredited in the eyes of a Christian present, sanction the literary preservation of some of the elements of that past, and discover the past anew for a present that had lost touch with its roots.

An Irish saint, as depicted in early Irish literature, is only as good as his or her word. Sanctity is grounded in the capacity of the saint's words to mean what they say—to invoke the power of what the words signify, and to signify unambiguously, at least from the perspective of the saint. This authority of the saint's utterance derives from God and is coveted by the saint's biographer, who of course urges us to accept his own word and rendition of the saint's words as authentic.

Mingled among the saint's reported words are the words of others engaged in saintly conversation. These other words, like the identities of the characters who speak them, are not incidental to the authority of the saint but provide a complement and counterpoint to it.

Among the others with whom saints like to talk are angels, those ubiquitous bearers of God's word who already dwell in the divine presence. Consorting with angels is, of course, not at all unusual for saints, but the extent to which Irish holy men and women keep angelic company is remarkable.[2] As the following introductory passage to an early Irish saint's life makes clear, saints and angels have a professional interest in common, in that both go about the business of communicating the divine to the rest of the world by means of miracles:

One of the poems of praise that David composed for the Lord, the Sixty-Seventh [Psalm], has this line at the end: "God is wondrous in his holy ones"—that is, he is to be praised through signs [or "miracles," *signa*] that he effects either through his angels or through the holy people who obey his commands. . . . Indeed, God's being "wondrous in his holy ones" is revealed in the sight of pagans, since he has given to those who promise [the reward of] Heaven the power to heal the sick, to revive the dead, to cleanse lepers, to cast out demons, to give sight to the blind, to make whole the crippled and the deaf,

2. See Stancliffe 1992, 102–10.

and the like—so that the magnitude of the signs may demonstrate the magnitude of the promises.[3]

While their sacred signifying reinforces that of the saints, angels are not the only extraordinary beings with whom saints long to talk. As we shall see, they characteristically strive to engage human relics of the dimly remembered past in conversation, figures who somehow or other live long enough to tell saints and their scribes of the old days, before the coming of Christianity to Ireland. Saints seek out such ancients, who reflect a mythological type with its roots in the pre-Christian past, not merely to convert them, but to converse with them. The older the ancient the more value is attached to his talk. Moreover, the more extraordinary the means of his survival or revival, the more interest is evinced by the saint in cultivating his company. Sometimes the saint makes that survival or the recovery of the ancient figure possible. If angels and what they have to say represent a body of Christian higher knowledge and offer a foretaste of the heavenly communion to come, this other order of conversational partner lets the saint explore a distinctly non-Christian past. The saint's knowledge of that past is thereby renewed and included in an ongoing process: preserving a body of cultural knowledge. Moreover, while the angelic dialogue is private and only indirectly translated into the public domain through the words and actions of the saint, this other kind of dialogue produces public monuments, in the form of texts, landmarks, or other objects that can operate as richly meaningful signs, independent of their creators and of the era in which they were created. Conversing with both angels and ancients can pull the saint—and the literature of which the saint is patron, protector, and even occasional practitioner—in dramatically different directions.

In this book we shall explore the centrality of these two types of dialogue to the glorious intellectual adventure that produced early medieval Irish literature between the seventh and thirteenth centuries. The conceit of talking alternately with angels and ancients shapes the saint's career, the "life" of the saint as text, and many of the outstanding works produced in Irish *scriptoria* in the centuries following the coming of Christianity and the establishment of a literate culture. In the ideological milieu of this culture, as we will discover, the one kind of dialogue motivates and supplements the other. From this

3. Óen didu dina molthaib sin dorigni Dabid don Choimdid in sechtmad psalm ar sescait as a forba hi fil in líne se .i. Mirabilis Deus in sanctis suis, id est, per signa laudabilis, quae siue in angelis suis, siue in hominibus sanctis qui eius iusionibus obsécundant, operatur. . . . At uero tunc mirabilis Deus in sanctis suis in conspectu gentium reuelatur, quando eis regna caelorum pollicentibus dedit potestam infirmos curandi, mortuos suscitandi, leprosos mundandi, demones ieciendi, cecos illuminandi, claudos et sordos sanandi, ⁊ caetera huiuscemodi, ut magnitudinem promisorum probet magnitudo signorum (Mulchrone 1939, lines 1998–2003, 2006–11). From the preface to the third part of the *Vita tripartita* of Saint Patrick (see p. 53 below).

interplay or dialogue among dialogues, texts emerge as the records kept by an eavesdropping literary tradition. Even if the words spoken in these dialogues are private, for the interlocutors' ears only, and therefore lost to posterity or only partially preserved, the fact that they were spoken serves as an etiology within texts, providing a raison d'être for their compilation and composition.

Even more fundamental to the early medieval Irish literary project than the particulars of these generating dialogues is the notion that the exchange of words is essential for the creation and understanding of texts. Literature, as its producers present it in early medieval Ireland, proceeds from talk and itself constitutes a kind of dialogue, among the characters and elements it features, between author and audience, and between the past it represents and the posterity to which it is consigned.

Needless to say, the framing of text in terms of conversation is a venerable device in the Western literary tradition, and in privileging it the early medieval Irish *literati* acknowledged their debt to the literate culture that they and their ancestors had embraced and cultivated. Yet the importance of dialogue to their literary project also resonated with the performative traditions of poetic composition and storytelling that predated the coming of Christianity to Ireland. These traditions continued to play a vital role in Irish cultural life throughout the medieval period, arguably outliving the literary tradition itself. The Old Irish word for story, *scél*, means 'news' in the plural (*scéla*), a verbal and narrative item of exchange in the never-ending round of questions and responses to be asked and heard in everyday life. The art of storytelling, as practiced by the early and modern Irish *scélaige* 'storyteller', and as tapped by the producers of the medieval Irish literary tradition, transforms *scéla* into *scél*. A report of particular circumstances and people addressed to a limited audience becomes a more universally accessible account that transcends the original circumstances of its telling.

The prototypical figure seeking to turn *scéla* into *scél* in the world of early medieval literature, listening to and participating in various conversations as well as undergoing and remembering experiences of note, is the saint. The narratives of extraordinary speakers and speaking featured in the corpus of early Irish hagiography—particularly in the lives of Patrick, Columba, and Brigit, who enjoy a venerable reputation as the three great saints of Ireland—constituted for the literary tradition that reproduced these marvelous events an arena for the testing of questions concerning language, communication, and cultural continuity that underlie not only the genre of the saint's life but the ambitious project of producing a literature in the vernacular.

JOSEPH FALAKY NAGY

Los Angeles

acknowledgments

much of the research that I conducted in connection with this book was funded by the Research Committee of the Academic Senate of the University of California, Los Angeles. I thank my colleagues in the Celtic Studies Association of North America who responded so helpfully to parts of this book which were presented in oral form. In particular I am grateful to Patrick K. Ford for all his keen advice and criticism. All translations from Irish and Latin are my own unless otherwise indicated in the notes.

My students—especially Karen Burgess, Paula Powers Coe, Angelique Gulermovich Epstein, Lawrence Eson, and Leslie Jones—have over the years provided me with brilliant and stimulating dialogue about matters pertaining to medieval Celtic literature. Their voracious interest in and dedication to the subject have always inspired me.

John Ackerman and Terence McKiernan of Cornell University Press have unstintingly provided me with their editorial wisdom and guidance. My copy editor Judith Bailey proved a model of patience and perspicacity. I am indebted to them.

I dedicate this book to my wife, Martha, and to my daughters, Ita and Emma.

J. F. N.

conversing
with angels
and ancients

Another characteristic is the backward look. Irish poetry is haunted by the revenant, the figure who has escaped death only to return and find that Ireland, under the Christians, has gone to Hell. But this note characterises not only the Pagans, but also the Christians themselves. . . . The Irish are like Orpheus, forever looking back at the Eurydice they are attempting to bring home from the Shades.

—Frank O'Connor, *The Backward Look*

introduction

Resurrecting the Truth

among the more important issues to have occupied the attention of Irish intellectuals of the early medieval period (seventh to ninth centuries) was the controversy over the proper dating of the movable feast of Easter. The tension between the system of dating still used by the Irish and the new system promulgated by the church in Rome, as well as by some Irish churchmen, generated debate, giving life and special meaning to concepts such as orthodox and heterodox, and old and new. Not surprisingly, the Easter question left its traces in rish literature, even in texts produced after the Roman system of dating and its proponents had generally prevailed. In the following scene from the *Vita Munnu,* an Irish saint's life written perhaps as early as 800 or earlier, two holy men stage the following contest concerning the matter of Easter:

Then, Saint Munnu said to the abbot Laisrén in the presence of all the people: "Now it is time for this council to be brought to a close, so that everyone may return to his home." Since they were still contending over the proper date for the celebration of Easter, Saint Munnu said: "Briefly, let us debate; but in the name of God, let us reach a decision. Three options are available to you, Laisrén: to throw two books in the fire, one proclaiming the old date for Easter, the other the new, and to see which one is saved from the flames; or to shut two monks, one of them mine and the other yours, in the same house, set the house on fire, and see which of the monks survives intact; or let us go to the grave of a deceased righteous monk, resurrect him, and have him tell us by which method of calculation we should arrive this year at the date for celebrating Easter." "We will not submit to the tests you propose. For we know that, on account of the magnitude of your achievement and sanctity, were you to say that Slíab Mairge [a mountain] should replace Mag Ailbe [a nearby plain], and Mag Ailbe should replace Slíab Mairge, God would immediately do this for you." (At the time, they were in Mag Ailbe, which is close to Slíab Mairge.) Then the people, agreeing with the saints, returned to their homes.[1]

Here, as is the case throughout medieval Irish literature, the search for the truth (that is, the correct date of Easter) is primarily a matter of delving into the past, where the "truth" can be found in its pristine form. The past, which is usually portrayed as having much to offer the present, is also seen as teetering on the brink of oblivion, although it is rarely beyond some means of recovery. The business of these saints, as of Irish men of letters in general, is to recapture the past and proclaim it.

This tale of the encounter between the forward-looking Laisrén, who favors the "new" system for dating Easter, and the backward-looking Munnu, who wants to preserve the "old" system, presents us with an inventory of modes by which the past is typically represented in medieval Irish texts. There are tests of authenticity to which the bearers of the literary tradition, at least in the realm of story, can subject assumptions about what truly "is" because it "was." The correct understanding of the past can be confirmed and actually expressed by means of a durable book, the tenacious survival of those who claim to know, or in the words of a person from the past brought into the present. Remarkably, the most effective, if not the most accurate representation of the truth of the past, at least according to this story, is the word of a truly holy man. Munnu's prayers, we are told, strike such a responsive chord with God that what he says is correct might as well be accepted as such. The past is what he says it is, by virtue of his saying it.

Also worth noting in this story is the option of reviving the dead as a way of getting to the heart of the matter. Generally in the world depicted in medieval Irish literature death does not strip the knowing man of knowledge, nor for

1. Postea sanctus Munna Lasreano abbati coram omnibus populis dixit: "Nunc tempus est, ut hoc consilium finiatur, vt vnusquisque ad locum suum redeat." Contendentes de ordine pasche, dixit sanctus Munnu: "Breuiter disputemus; set in nomine Domine agamus iudicium. Tres opciones dantur tibi, Lasreane; id est, duo libri in ignem mittentur, liber veteris ordinis et noui, ut videamus quis eorum de igne liberabitur; vel duo monachi, vnus meus, alter tuus, in vnam domum recludantur et domus comburatur, et videbimus, quis ex eis euadat intactus igne; aut eamus ad sepulcrum mortui iusti monachi et resuscitemus eum et indicet nobis, quo ordine debemus hoc anno pascha celebrare." Cui sanctus Lasreanus ait: "Non ibimus ad iudicium tuum; quoniam scimus, quod pre magnitudine laboris tui et sanctitatis, si diceres ut mons Marge commutaretur in locum campi Albe, et campus Albus in locum montis Mairge, hoc propter te Deus statim faceret." Erant enim illi tunc in campo Albe, cui imminet mons Marge. Postea consentientes populi cum sanctis, ad sua reuersi sunt (*Vita Munnu*, c. 27, Plummer 1910, 1:237; cf. c. 26, Heist 1965, 254–55). For comment, see Bieler 1986, 12:18–19; Walsh and Ó Cróinín 1988, 49–51. Richard Sharpe proposes the early date (1991, 334–38).

that matter does it strip the living of access to that knowledge. Indeed, as we shall see, the "dead," or those who should be dead but wondrously are not, tend to be the best informed and, in the right hands, the most obliging sources to tap.[2]

This search for faithful and effective representations of the past is motivated by the desire to integrate the past into the present, at least in the controlled environment of textual space, and to keep the present organically rooted in the past. Once the debate between Laisrén and Munnu is settled, everyone in attendance (the story claims) will henceforth be assured of the proper date of Easter and can celebrate it with full confidence in the correctness of the date. Underlying this tale, indeed the entire medieval Irish literary project to recapture the past, is the model of dialogue—in Irish, *acallam* or *immacallam*.[3] Through the sometimes private, sometimes public, exchange of utterances among speakers of various backgrounds and motivations, the discoveries that take place in the ever-narrowing space between relentless latter-day seekers of the truth and its elusive supernatural or ancient possessors are contained, verbalized, and even made the pretext for further adventures in the quest for the past. These contending dialogues, which we readers "overhear," purportedly provide the raw material out of which texts are created and authorize those texts as representations of venerable truths.

In medieval Irish texts, conversation requires at least two interlocutors, one of whom typically serves as the interrogator and "literary agent" through whose report we come to know of the dialogue in a textual form. The other participant, whose message is filtered first through his interaction with his dialogic partner and then through the text itself, virtually cries out to be interrogated, conveying a blend of the strange and the familiar, of the reassuringly authoritative and the heretofore unknown. This figure may be an angelic messenger from God, a surviving relic of the past, a revenant, or a denizen of some supernatural realm, Christian or non-Christian. Whatever mode his alterity assumes, the "other" comes bearing information that those with whom he speaks had thought was lost or inaccessible. What he brings to the conversation is news, but "old news" that casts both the past and the present in a new light. Moreover, this knowledge is never conveyed or captured in its totality; there is always the tantalizing prospect of a return visit, a resumption of the dialogue. The text we read, then, is to be understood as only a fragment of what was or could have been said.

A striking example of the importance of dialogue as a structuring and authorizing device in medieval Irish literature is the story told in the tenth- or

2. Knowledge is often an item of barter in the systems of reciprocal exchange between the living and the dead which obtains in other early medieval societies, as depicted in Geary 1994, 77–92.

3. These are the verbal nouns of *ad-gládathar* 'addresses, speaks to, converses' and *imm-acallatar* 'converse together', respectively (*DIL*, s.v.).

eleventh-century text *Suidigud Tellaig Temra* (Establishment of the hearth of Tara),[4] which concerns an inquest launched by the men of Ireland during the reign of the sixth-century king Diarmait mac Cerbaill. They are in search of the original boundaries of the royal seat, Tara, the sacred location at which the high kingship of Ireland, to which Diarmait has laid claim, is traditionally conferred and celebrated. To rediscover the lost boundaries will be in effect to restore and vindicate the Tara kingship, which this and many other medieval Irish texts place at the ideological heart of what was in fact a very complex society, resistant to the centralization and concentration of regal power. The men of Ireland, living in a Christian era, first turn to clerics and learned authorities, including the legendary scribe Cenn Fáelad. At this point the text refers briefly to the remarkable story of how Cenn Fáelad became a bulwark of the literary tradition.[5] Wounded in battle, he lost his "brain of forgetfulness" (*inchinn dermait*), an otherwise unattested brain within a brain which presumably induces loss of memory as a way of making room for new information or allows an editing of the remembered past, leaving out those elements that may be too burdensome or problematic to recall. "Consequently, he remembered whatever he heard of the lore of Ireland from that time to the present day."[6] It is this all-absorbing mind that, according to other texts, renders Cenn Fáelad a virtuosic scribe and the author of prized texts in a literary tradition that values the ability to capture and describe the past.

Yet Cenn Fáelad's store of *senchas* 'lore' does not extend far enough back in time to answer the questions about Tara. The sage therefore proposes collecting together the most ancient men of the island to see whether they have the answers.[7] They do not, but they suggest turning to Fintan mac Bóchra, one of the original settlers of Ireland, who has miraculously managed to live down to the present. Fintan is located and brought to the assembly, where he introduces himself as "knowledgeable about the visions, cattle raids, destructions, and wooings that have occurred since the Flood until now."[8] It is doubtless

4. Edited and translated in Best 1910. Valuable discussion of the text and its possible date are to be found in McCone 1990, 75–77.
5. The extant references to Cenn F(h)áelad mac Ailella, his legend, and his purported literary accomplishments are detailed in Mac Cana 1970, 62–66. See also the provocative analyses of the legend surrounding this figure in Chadwick 1942, 147–53; and Slotkin 1977–79, 437–40, 450. The "historical" Cenn Fáelad, designated *sapiens* in the Annals of Ulster (A.D. 679), is the subject of Flower 1947, 10–13; and McCone 1990, 23–24.
6. Conid cumain leis cach ní rochúala do senchas hÉrend o shin alle cosinndiu (Best 1910, 126).
7. One of these is the sage Tuán mac Cairill, featured in another dialogue that is clearly from the same mold as the following tale about Fintan. See Carey 1984a and 1984b.
8. Éolach ina fesaib 7 in táintib 7 ina toglaib 7 ina tochmorcaib do neoch dorónad díb ó dílind ille (Best 1910, 126). On Fintan and the figure of the informative antediluvian survivor, see d'Arbois de Jubainville 1903, 25–47; and Rees and Rees 1961, 113–15. According to a later strand of the literary tradition, Fintan conveyed ancient lore to Saint Patrick himself (Hennessy and Kelly 1875, 248–59). Mac Cana 1980a presents a thorough discussion of the traditional

not coincidental that what Fintan lists are the key events and even the customary designations of medieval Irish prose narrative genres. This survivor from the past is therefore a compendium of information that constitutes the stuff of literature.

Fintan does have the answers to the questions asked by the men of Ireland, and their dialogue is productive, ultimately resulting in the creation of the text that tells the story to us, its readers. Yet Fintan traces the information that makes this dialogue worthwhile back to an even earlier assembly of the men of Ireland, the setting of a dialogue in which Fintan received knowledge instead of dispensing it. The bearer of *senchas* on that occasion was "an angel of God or God himself,"[9] who explained the division of Ireland into five parts (the four provinces centered on the fifth part, which contains Tara) to representatives of the learned classes.

In giving centrality to dialogue, medieval Irish literature privileges a living exponent of speech who is sensitive to the needs and demands of interlocutors and audience, as well as to context. And yet, paradoxically, dialogue introduces speech into what is fundamentally and self-consciously a literary enterprise, creating a tension that frames, enters, and even exacerbates anxieties about the past which the model of dialogue is supposed to contain. Closure becomes all the more elusive when these elements and motives are speaking to one another and, indeed, warring against one another, albeit productively, as we shall see.

In the *Suidigud* text, the problem of achieving closure is intertwined with the search for suitable memorials by which to recall the information won through the ascending series of question-and-answer exchanges. Writing, the means of preserving the information that produces the text itself, is never explicitly mentioned, although the angelic interlocutor who comes to the men of Ireland is said to bear stone tablets. These Mosaic props, however, do not play a role in the story. A more lasting reminder comes from the berries that fall off the branch also borne by the visitor. These grow into the five trees that mark the partition of Ireland as conveyed in the conversation. Nevertheless, as Fintan points out, he has outlived all five of the trees. Now, in effect replacing them, he sets up a five-ridged stone at the assembly, meant to be a more permanent memorial.[10] Still, the most durable and trustworthy witness

---

nomenclature of narrative genres (including the *fís, táin, togail,* and *tochmarc*) to be found in medieval Irish literature.

9. Ba haingel Dé héside, nó fa Día féisi (Best 1910, 152).

10. This stone is clearly akin not only to the biblical memorial stones cited by McCone in his discussion of this tale (1990, 76) but also to the boundary markers or tombstones important in the early Irish landscape. These stones were often inscribed with writing in the pre-Christian *ogam* alphabet (Mac Niocaill 1969, 334; F. Kelly 1988, 204). It is worth noting that in the Latin of Romano-British inscriptions, the word *memoria* 'memory' also carried the meaning 'tombstone' (Jackson 1953, 622). Writing itself, according to a medieval Irish legal text, is like an "immovable rock" (*ail anscuichthe*) (trans. F. Kelly 1988, 163).

to the knowledge shrouded in the past is Fintan himself, who has miraculously survived since the time of Noah, his grandfather, and the Flood.[11] The knowledge that Fintan embodies, moreover, is neither static nor inflexible. The old-timer in the course of his many lives and through his encounter with the angelic visitor comes to know of the Christian God and the sacrifice of Christ. He is almost more Christian than the sixth-century audience to which he imparts his tale.

Unfortunately, however, Fintan's days as a living testimonial to the truth are numbered. He is a dying man at the end of our text, and his death's coinciding with its conclusion is a dramatic way to anoint the literary tradition (the text of the *Suidigud*) as his successor. The end of the featured series of conversations inaugurates a new kind of exchange, that between a text—the new Fintan, as it were—and its readers. Yet the details of his death and burial, that is, the makings of a memorial to Fintan the great communicator, are pointedly left unresolved:

> And thus did Fintan conclude his life and times, after performing penance and taking communion from the hand of Bishop Erc, son of Ochomon, son of Fidach. The spirits of Saint Patrick and Saint Brigit came so that they could listen to him. It is uncertain, moreover, where he was buried, but they [?] think that he was taken up in his fleshly body to a godly hidden place, just as Elijah and Enoch were taken to Paradise, where that long-lived ancient, Fintan mac Bóchra awaits the final rising.[12]

Has Fintan, therefore, not really departed? Is he only temporarily absent? The text, in its assumed role as voice of the past, wavers on this point. The dialogue is now no longer between the present and the past but between competing voices of the present advocating their various formulations of the past. The explanation offered, the text suggests, is not the only one to be found. This dissolution of the single authorial voice into an array of competing voices, an outcome by no means unique to this text, instills uncertainty in its readers about more than just the matter of where Fintan is buried or whether he really died. It leaves us with a stopgap, deferring certainty to the future, when Fintan will reappear. Like the mention of the five dead trees,

11. See Flower 1947, 6–9, 14–15, for a discussion of the strategies of cultural and historical recovery which underlie the story of Fintan and other medieval Irish narratives. Of considerable relevance here is the fundamental Irish legal concept, held in common with many other legal traditions, that the most reliable witness is a living human being who was present at and saw or heard the event in question (F. Kelly 1988, 203; Carey 1992, 1995a, 46).

12. Roforbastair tra Fintan a beathaid 7 sháegul fon indus sin, 7 dofarraid aithrighi 7 rochaith comaind 7 sacarbaigg do láim epscuip Erc meic Ochomoin meic Fidhaich, 7 dodechaid spirat Pátraic 7 Brigde co rabatar a fíadnaisi a éitsechta. Is indemin immorro cía baile in rohadhnocht, acht is dóig leo is ina chorp chollaigi rucad i nnach ndíamair ndíada amail rucad Ele 7 Enócc i pardus condafil ic ernaidi eiséirgi in sruthseanóir sáeghlach sin .i. Fintan mac Bóchra (Best 1910, 160).

whose life-span constituted a mere episode in the much longer life of Fintan, the textual drawing together of what some say about the ultimate fate of Fintan exhibits the lack of an important piece of knowledge and denies mastery of knowledge in its totality. The conclusion reveals the inability of the text to contain all the knowledge of the past, the body of lore from which Fintan regaled the men of Ireland in dialogue. Nonetheless, the text contains enough to make the past come alive for the auditors within the story and, presumably, for its readers.

The Origins of the Literary Tradition

In this book, we explore dialogic points of reference such as this epochal encounter in order to understand how they reflect on the cultural significance of the acts of writing and reading among the literati of early medieval Ireland. Our focus is etiological narratives in which literature is figured as a means of preserving what society needs to know from and about the past. In the body of texts to be considered are intricate, sometimes even self-defeating strategies by means of which medieval Irish men of letters, from the beginnings of their literary tradition in the sixth and seventh centuries to the watershed period of the twelfth-thirteenth centuries and beyond, traced the origins of the literature they produced. Arguably, no other vernacular corpus originating from the impact of Christianity upon a native European tradition offers such a spectacular wealth of reflexive analyses. In general, as we shall see, these "myths of origin" ground and explain the procession of literary production and transmission through the concept of an accessible, legitimating past, which speaks to the present by means of an ongoing tradition of verbal performances.

The self-consciousness of the medieval Irish literati reveals how an emerging written tradition attempted to find its own identity and authorize itself, assuming in the process various postures toward other modes of transmission, especially the ongoing oral tradition from which it distinguished itself. At times, literature depicts itself as emerging from oral tradition; at other times, it appears to be running alongside it, intersecting with it, running counter to it, or all the above simultaneously.

The legitimation of literature as a respectable, even superior, medium is never a simple matter, as scholars of other literary traditions have already amply demonstrated.[13] The more a written tradition nurtures notions of its

13. Some groundbreaking studies of the traditional conceptualizations of the instrumentality of writing in ancient and medieval literatures are Detienne 1967; Kelber 1983; Lerer 1991; Leupin 1982; K. O'Keeffe 1990; O'Flaherty 1988, 45–73; Stock 1983; Svenbro 1993; and Vance 1987. R. Howard Bloch, in his study of medieval literature as a form of ethnography (1983), declares the compulsively dictating Merlin of thirteenth-century romance to be "the

ability to control and impose closure on the materials that seem to be "entering" it, whether of purportedly oral, foreign, sacred, or ancient provenance, the more implicated the literary tradition may appear, even to its producers, in the modes of thought it claims to have rendered obsolete. The more literature attempts to present itself as an improvement on past media and even on what was transmitted through those media, the less efficient it may seem as a container of what its producers may well judge in the final analysis to be uncontainable.

Before beginning to sound the inner images of medieval Irish literature, let us review why medieval Ireland presents such a particularly fascinating case for the literary critic in search of the chinks in the armor of literary etiologies.

Although Ireland was never a part of the Roman Empire, the pre-Christian Irish clearly maintained contacts with Roman civilization by way of Romanized Gaul and Britain and even developed a form of writing, *ogam,* based on the Latin alphabet, which has survived on stone monuments in Ireland and western Britain.[14] Nonetheless, there is no solid evidence for the existence of a literature of ogam beyond inscriptions and messages, or for any body of "literature" other than oral, in pre-Christian Ireland.[15] There is, however, a considerable body of evidence that hierarchically organized castes of professional knowers and verbal performers—including poets, men of law, physicians, and certain craftsmen—existed in Ireland both before and during the Christian period.[16] Among these was the druid, whose associations with the pre-Christian religious tradition led to his early disappearance from, or perhaps his metamorphosis within, the Christianized Irish scene.[17] The poet figured prominently in the intellectual elite of early Irish Christian society, especially the most distinguished kind of poet, the *fili.* The poet functioned as the provider of praise to kings and other important members of society and

---

patron saint of letters within the Arthurian world" (1), whose "totalizing regard places him at once outside and at the center of the tale which he narrates and in which he participates" (5). It is perhaps not coincidental that the medieval myth of Merlin as described by Bloch is derived from the Celtic world, specifically, from the British tradition of Myrddin, whose commitment to oral communication, if not to written, is much in evidence in what we learn of him in extant Welsh tradition. (A survey of the literature associated with or featuring Myrddin is available in Jarman 1991. On the vatic aspects of Merlin/Myrddin, see Ziolkowski 1990.) Myrddin's Celtic cousin, the Irish Suibne, a figure clearly parallel to Myrddin, actually succeeds, albeit only fleetingly, in bridging the gap betwen oral and written tradition, as we shall see.

14. Ogam is the subject of McManus 1991.

15. Anthony Harvey (1992, 18–22) and Jane Stevenson (1989, 127–48; 1990) argue for the existence of a more widespread literacy and familiarity with Roman letters in pre-Christian Ireland.

16. Williams 1971; Williams and Ford 1992, 21–49; and Meid 1974 detail their functions and privileged status.

17. The "druidic" aspects of the medieval Irish poet, particularly in his interdependent relationship with kings, are explored in Mac Cana 1979.

also as storyteller and jurist.[18] In general, he appears to have served as the repository and disseminator of cultural truths, and poetry in oral performance was the paradigmatic medium for the expression of those truths. At least this is the conceit promulgated by the creators of medieval Irish literature, many of whom were *filid* 'poets' themselves. The centrality of poets and poetry to the collective formulation and reformulation of ideology is still to be readily observed in the Christian era, especially since at least the higher orders of poets appear to have joined forces with the church early on.[19] Perhaps the most important result of this alliance between native knower/performer and ecclesiastic was the creation of a literature in both Latin and Irish.

The beginnings of Christianity in Ireland are traceable to the fifth century and the arrival of the legendary Saint Patrick, who, however, may well have come on the heels of other missionaries.[20] The conversion of the Irish seems to have been remarkably bloodless. Medieval Irish hagiographic tradition makes precious few claims of saints martyred on native soil.[21] The early proselytizers, such as Patrick, appear to have been careful to establish good working relations with the more powerful members of the many kingdoms within which they operated.[22] Ireland, it should be pointed out, throughout most of its history was not a united nation but a complex weave of small-scale societies, which to a considerable extent "ran themselves" without too much interference from the kings who nominally ruled over them. These kingdoms, or *túatha*, were hierarchical coalitions of semi-independent social units based on kinship and clientage.

The extent to which Christianity affected everyday life in the Ireland of the sixth and seventh centuries remains unclear, but the spread of monasticism and the establishment of a network of politically and economically powerful monasteries during this period are indisputable.[23] It was in this monastic milieu, patronized by kings and powerful families (members of which often became clerics themselves) and most likely still very much in touch with cultural forces outside the monastery, that the literature explored in the following chapters took shape. For the bearers of this culture—monastic, yet thoroughly grounded in the secular world—proceeded to generate a body of

18. Mac Cana 1980a, 1–19, deals with the mastery over the art and repertoire of traditional storytelling which some texts treat as fundamental to the poetic function. On the legal expertise of the early Irish poet and the overlap between the professional domains of jurist and poet, see F. Kelly 1988, 47–49.

19. As concluded in Flower 1947, 3–5; Ó Corráin 1972, 74–77; and Mac Cana 1986, 60–64.

20. The earliest (that is, seventh-century) Patrician hagiography locates most of Patrick's missionary activity in the north of Ireland. Still, surviving legends about pre-Patrician missionaries and saints associated with the south of Ireland make for dubious historical sources, as argued in Sharpe 1989.

21. Clare Stancliffe (1982) examines the alternatives to "red" martyrdom formulated and produced in early medieval Ireland.

22. Mac Cana 1986 presents an overview of the proselytizing strategies apparently employed.

23. See Hughes 1966; Ryan 1972; and Bitel 1990.

literature in Latin and to give a literary form to their own native tongue. The Irish of medieval manuscripts is traditionally divided into three chronological stages: Old Irish (approximately 600–900), Middle Irish (900–1200), and Early Modern Irish (1200–1650). In the first two periods, between the sixth and twelfth centuries, Irish clerics, aware of their own heritage and keenly interested in the intellectual and institutional heritages of the Western church and classical civilization, produced a vernacular literature of remarkable diversity and heterogeneity, both antiquarian and attuned to contemporary issues. Theirs was a project dedicated in a truly catholic spirit to reconstructing from a seemingly discontinuous past a literary whole applicable to the present.[24] Historians have demonstrated the relevance of medieval Irish literary documents to the concerns and needs of their authors and their authors' patrons.[25] Yet, as we shall see, the aesthetics behind medieval Irish literature dictated that the text or its author make a convincing show of having captured at least some token of the past within a textual form in order to speak authoritatively about contemporary matters.

This literature grew, and today deserves to be read, in conjunction with the large body of texts in Latin which the Irish literati generated, both before and during the flowering of the vernacular literary tradition.[26] Hiberno-Latin literature does not form a separate stream, nor is it reasonable to assume that it was produced by a different kind of author for a different kind of audience. Perhaps the genre that thrived most vigorously in Latin was the saint's life, of which we have samples from as early as the seventh century and which successfully made the transition from Latin to Irish not long thereafter.[27] Featured in the Latin vita and Irish *betha* is the figure of the Irish saint, miracle worker and monastic founder, an embodiment of the religious and social factors that draw the audience of the life together. A key feature of the typical Irish saint, duly noted but barely explored by scholars of medieval Irish literature, is his dedication to writing and literature.[28] We shall discover that the saint often functions in his literarily figured life as a paradigmatic writer and that his struggles and triumphs represent for us the medieval Irish conception of how the acts of writing and reading transform culture.

---

24. This is essentially the assessment to be found underlying contemporary surveys of medieval Irish literature as diverse in other respects as Mac Cana 1980b, 12–17; McCone 1990; and Williams and Ford 1992, 11–117.

25. See, for example Ó Coileáin 1973; Ó Corráin 1987b; Ó Riain 1974; and Radner 1982.

26. The formidable surviving corpus of literature in Latin by Irishmen is enumerated in Lapidge and Sharpe 1985.

27. Introductions to medieval Irish saints' lives include McCone 1984b; Doherty 1987; and Sharpe 1991, 3–38.

28. J. Kelly 1979 provides a useful collection of references to books, reading, and writing in Irish saints' lives. A critical examination of medieval European attitudes towards the book is afforded in Gellrich 1985. On the functions of writing in various religious traditions, see Denny and Taylor 1985; Graham 1987.

Especially as we approach the works written in the twelfth century and later (the period of church reform and the Norman invasion of Ireland), we find that literature grows less and less certain of the existence of an audience appropriately receptive or sympathetic to representations of "ancient" truth. In the words of Proinsias Mac Cana,

> In fact one can hardly doubt that much of the vast output of late eleventh and twelfth-century scholars came as a reflex to ominous change, like the fighter betraying his inner distress by the very fury and volume of his counter-attack. It is significant that this wave of literary activity is predominantly compilatory in character: the great manuscript *bibliothecae* . . . which suggests not so much a creative urge as a conscious effort to regroup and consolidate the resources of native learning.[29]

Literature in this period was profoundly affected by changes taking place in the Irish church and by the gradual transferal of "secular" literary activity and its practitioners away from the realm of monasteries and churches into a more secular context. It has been said that as the literary experts moved out of their prestigious positions within the old monasteries and set up shop as professional men of letters, they became even more strongly attached to courts and powerful secular patrons. During this transitional period there also occurred a realignment between various traditional (or newly emerged) specialists in the verbal arts who had gone their separate ways when Christianity and literacy were introduced to Ireland. By the thirteenth century, the ecclesiastically sponsored literary world was a thing of the past, as Donnchadh Ó Corráin notes:

> On the whole, the reform was a triumph for the administrators and a disaster for Irish literature and general culture. The reformers destroyed the social, economic, and cultural base of Irish learning. Nothing replaced the greater monasteries with their schools and learned cadres, now robbed of their resources and their status. The monastic scholars moved out and joined with the praise poets to form the class of bardic poets of the later Middle Ages. The clerical lawyers, too, became secularized and most of what survives of vernacular law is due to late medieval secular families. Even the Irish script practically disappears in the thirteenth century. The disruption which followed the Norman invasion was, of course, responsible for much of this, but the reformer had laid the groundwork.[30]

I shall have occasion to note how these changes in literary culture and in the status of its proponents are reflected in some later texts.

29. Mac Cana 1984, 140–41.
30. Ó Corráin 1989b, 44, 47. Pádraig Ó Riain warns against assuming that all church reformers were unsympathetic to literary production and preservation (1994, 22–23).

Charting a Course

My study of the interrelated themes of text-generating dialogue and the literary recovery of the past begins in Chapter 1 with an exploration of the putative beginning of literature produced in Ireland, namely, the writings of the legendary bearer of Christianity to Ireland, the fifth-century Briton Patrick, son of Calpurnius. Specifically, I explore some of the central arguments in his so-called *Confessio,* a quasi-autobiographical attempt to assert and vindicate himself and his actions, apparently in the face of criticism from his ecclesiastical peers or superiors. Whereas the *Confessio* has been relentlessly mined for evidence about the historical Patrick, its possible contributions to the development of the Irish literary tradition—particularly Patrick's ingenious claim to authorial voice (based as it is on a professed novice's knowledge of literary expression) and his visionary experiences—have never been properly appreciated or explored. The *Confessio* clearly lies behind the image of Patrick and his mission which emerge from a very important and very early stratum of medieval Irish literature, namely, the pre-Norman lives of Patrick, an examination of which forms the core of the second chapter. These accounts, cultivating what has become the popular image of the missionary who single-handedly won Ireland to Christianity, constitute a profoundly influential formulation of the early Irish Christian vision of how a new order, including not only a new religion but also a new medium, came to replace, and yet also to recall, the old order of pre-Christian Ireland. Patrick's own account of his roles as both convert and converter, operating between the word of God and the human means of representing it, is perpetuated in these lives and in the perceptions of cultural change they reflected and fostered. Toward the end of the last chapter, I explore how the myth of the "Patrician" conversion of Ireland takes on a revolutionary new meaning in a vast literary work, the *Acallam na Senórach* (Dialogue of the ancients), a tour of the limits of literature as extraordinary in its own meandering way as is Patrick's *Confessio.*

Between these framing encounters with the "real" Patrick as reflected in his own writings and the larger-than-life Patrick of the *Acallam,* we shall meet other legendary figures, innovators who explore and challenge their cultural heritage and reactionaries who obstruct the march of Christian and literary time. Chapter 3 focuses on Columba, the sixth-century saint operating within a Christianized Ireland, whose major claim to literary fame rests on his epochal "reform" of poets and poetry during a unique trip back home. In Chapter 4, I assess the price paid by saints (and the literary tradition that honors them) for the power and privilege to transform culture by means of writing, examining stories featuring saints in chariots along with their shadowy and "expendable" companions. Then in Chapter 5, I conclude with a study of brigands, whose search for the social meaning of their lives curiously parallels and yet often threatens the work of saints, and whose tracking skills come to the aid of literary men searching for the lost heart of their tradition of performance and composition.

Over the last century, the extent to which medieval Irish literature reflects an oral tradition—including compositional techniques, stories, and elements of worldview deriving from the pre-Christian past—has received increasing attention.[31] In this journey through the subtexts of the Irish literary tradition, however, my focus is less on the realities of "oral" versus "literary" transmission and composition than on the literati's own perceptions of them. By the same token, the historical events and persons that may lie behind the texts, including the saints' lives, concern me less than the ideological truths these texts communicate. Especially in the wake of the wars fought by scholars of medieval Irish literature over the issue of its origins, we must keep in mind that it is often not in the best rhetorical interest of literature and its proponents to acknowledge its roots, and texts therefore bear very subtle if not unreliable witness to the circumstances and motivations that led to their inception. It should come as no surprise that, their assertions of the immutability of texts and the truth they contain notwithstanding, the bearers of a literary tradition continually tinker with or even rewrite their history in order to establish, update, or renew the right of the texts they produce to be read. Consequently, the variety of ways in which literary and oral tradition are described, related, and contrasted in these texts is impressively rich.

As I have said, the quest in medieval Irish literature for validating origins and literary authority is usually conducted and concluded, successfully or not, through dialogue. This premise of a dialogic nature doubtless made the performance of the medieval Irish text, whether read aloud or silently, all the more complex an experience for both reader and hearer.[32] Moreover, in many literary instances the assertion that the text is an outcome of an original dialogic performance *without* a "script" is clearly as important an element in the authorizing strategy as is the identification of the interlocutor(s) as supernatural or venerable. In other cases, the text is authorized by the presence of some oral-traditional genre "within" it which interacts with the text or with the reader's reception of it every time the text is read.

In the course of our travels in the interior of the medieval Irish literary world, however, it will soon become apparent that the distinction between

---

31. A shrewd evaluation of the scholarly positions on the nature and origin of medieval Irish texts is Ó Coileáin 1977–78. Along lines traceable to Flower's work, Hildegard Tristram (1989 and 1990) focuses on vignettes in the literary tradition's evolving construction of its own history. I explore the oral-written connection in medieval Irish literature in J. Nagy 1986, 1988, and 1989b.

32. Mary Carruthers points out that a dialogic element is already inherent in the act of reading as understood in late classical and medieval civilization: "Medieval reading is conceived to be not a 'hermeneutical circle' (which implies mere solipsism) but more like a 'hermeneutical dialogue' between two memories, that in the text being made very much present as it is familiarized to that of the reader" (Carruthers 1990, 169).

oral performance and written text, though both conspicuous and productive, is set up only to be mediated. The medieval Irish scribes appear to have been as wary of pat generalizations as any latter-day critic, skeptical of overly broad concepts such as "orality."[33] Moreover, if the "oral/literary" distinction does not hold, neither do the contrasts between "pagan" and "Christian" or "past" and "present" in reference to the components of this literature or the motivating forces behind it. The culture preceding the introduction of Christianity did not form a monolith any more than the culture that developed in its wake.[34] The scribal community of medieval Christian Ireland never generated a consistent policy on what to include in literary projects and what to exclude from them. Still, as Kim McCone has observed, the literature generated in this rich milieu self-consciously stages confrontations between what, for lack of better labels, we could call "native" and "foreign," "pagan" and "Christian," and "past" and "present" elements of culture.[35] On an ideological plane there are some important distinctions between various strands in medieval Irish literature, although these distinctions, like that between written and spoken, are often highlighted only to be dismantled or rendered invisible on a larger cultural "text." For instance, in a continuation of the biblical myth of the Tower of Babel averred in the early Irish treatise *Auraicept na n-Eces* (Poets' primer), we learn that Irish is definitely a separate language distinct from all others but that it was put together from the best elements of the premier languages.[36]

Analysis of the perceptions and postures that constitute the reflexivity of the early Irish literary tradition will take us into the semiotics underlying the quest for authority in these texts.[37] Certainly the *topos* of literary filiation (one text

33. While text-oriented scholars of oral tradition, such as Albert Lord in *The Singer of Tales* (1960) and later works (for instance, 1986), have always tried to locate the category of "oral" in a carefully documented context of performance, transmission, and composition, other scholars, such as Eric Havelock (1986) and Walter Ong (1982, 1986), have attempted to situate the distinction between "oral" and "literate/literary" at the heart of ambitious theories about human cultural and intellectual development. A striking corrective to drawing a theoretical "all-purpose" line between the written and spoken word is Svenbro 1993, a study of the politics of reading in classical Greek civilization, and of the insinuation of "voice" into "text" by way of the act of reading.

34. This thesis is forcefully argued in Fox 1988 in reference to the interaction of Christian and "pagan" cultural forces in late classical civilization. A similar argument is deftly applied to the Irish scene by J. P. Mackey (1992, 287), although Mackey's proposed model of "primal religion" is as leveling as the notion of "paganism" he wishes to replace. Herbert (1988b), Ó Cathasaigh (1984), and Ó Riain (1992b) provide sensitive discussions of the intermixture of elements and motives in early Irish Christian culture as reflected in the extant literature.

35. McCone 1990 is a virtuosic examination of how these dichotomies operate in medieval Irish literature, as well as in modern scholarship.

36. Ahlqvist 1983, 97–98. Ibid., 40–41; Poli 1986–89; Ó Corráin 1987b, 27–31; and McCone 1990, 36–37, provide commentary on this remarkable conceit.

37. Barbara Babcock has pointed out that reflexivity involves semiotics: it is a turning "inward," with the subject viewing itself as an object, that is, a sign (Babcock 1987, 236). Bernard

as indebted to another) is to be found in medieval Irish literature, but its creators were rarely content to authorize a text simply by invoking the concept of *auctoritas*, the rootedness of a work in earlier revered works, a validating quality to which classical and medieval texts typically aspire.[38] Again and again, we encounter in Irish literature the question what constitutes an authoritative representation, that is, a sign that genuinely communicates what *was* or what was once truthfully said? And who is authorized to interpret or create such signs, whether literary or not? Just as there are no simple answers to these questions, so the nature of literary authority is continually at issue, especially in accounts of how "new" elements, such as Christianity, were introduced into an existing cultural system of representations, precipitating a remixing and rematching of signs and the values attached to them. This interaction between the present legitimation of the text and the legitimations taking place within the text is graphically demonstrated in many of the stories examined in Chapter 2, tales in which monuments to pagan power are transformed into memorials to saintly miracles. Among the new signs is the sign of writing itself, in the forms of Latin and literary Irish orthographically based on Latin.

The definition of "sign" I use in this book is essentially Ferdinand de Saussure's: a sign is a relationship between a "signifier" (grounded in sensory perception) and a "signified" (to be distinguished from an actual referent).[39] The relationship that constitutes significance is culturally determined and meaningful only within a system of signs. That is, the relationship is arbitrary if viewed from outside the system of signs, but it is "necessary" when seen from within the system. This definition is hardly an imposition on the Irish tradition, inasmuch as the surprisingly "modern" understanding of signification which emerges from the texts evinces a keen appreciation of the conventionality of signs. Transactional terms of dialogue are systematically negotiated and affected, sometimes even drastically rearranged, by the often conflicting worldviews of those who use them.

Concluding the *Cattle Raid*

It may seem quixotic to seek ideological consistencies in a literature that is the product of such seemingly disparate strands and layers of literary tradi-

---

Merdrignac's work on Breton saints' lives (1985–86 and 1987) is a pioneering application of semiotics to a Celtic hagiographic tradition closely related to Ireland's.
38. Concerning medieval concepts of authority, see Miller 1986, 3–33; Minnis 1988, 1–39; and Carruthers 1990, 189–220. "In considering medieval views of textual authority, one needs always to keep in mind that *auctores* were, first of all, texts, not people. . . . There *is* no extra-textual authorial intention—whatever *intentio* there is is contained in the textual signs alone. All meaning develops from there" (ibid. 190).
39. Saussure 1972, 97–113. On the impact and implications of Saussure's theory of the sign, see Harland 1987, 11–19.

tion. The cultivation of heterogeneity can be a legitimating tactic, however, and signs that seem unrelated or even conflicting often add up to continuum, not chaos, in this literature. In the *Táin Bó Cúailnge* (Cattle raid of Cúailnge), as elsewhere, the issue of the origins of Irish literature as understood by the medieval Irish scribe interacts with larger cultural issues, and the interaction can lead to a reassessment of the concept of text itself.

The twelfth-century manuscript known as the Book of Leinster contains one of the recensions of the *Táin Bó Cúailnge*. Told in prose with verse inserts, the tale is clearly based to a significant degree on an oral tradition of stories about the heroes of ancient Ulster, particularly the youthful Cú Chulainn. It is also, however, clearly a literary work that acknowledges its kinship to other literary works and, given its length and ambitious scope, is rightly considered a literary experiment. The *Táin* is followed in the Book of Leinster by two famous closing statements, or colophons. The first is in Irish, as is the text it concludes: "A blessing on everyone who shall faithfully rehearse the *Táin* as it is here and shall not add any other form onto it."[40] This kind of attached blessing is by no means rare in medieval Irish literature, and variants of its sentiments can be found in other early and medieval literatures as well.[41]

To be noted are the connotations of the key word, *mebraigid*, translated here as "rehearse," a borrowing from Latin *memoria*. "Remembering" a text has a definite performative dimension in a culture such as that of medieval Ireland, in which texts normally were read aloud. Indeed, there is ample reason to believe that Irish literati viewed remembrance and speaking as mutually implicated or even as inseparable. Knowledge, especially a story about the past, is forgotten if it is not told. Consider the occurrence of the verb *mebraigid* in a Middle Irish place-name poem, *mebrugaid béoil oc búadaib*[42] "mouth, recall [the account just given] among excellent things!" And in a passage from a medieval prose tale, *crosáin*, oral performers usually characterized as threateningly sub-literary, are said to "remember" a mocking poem or song from hell (*conid iat na crosana sin ro mhebhraidhset*).[43] Remembering, as in *mebraigid*, is made manifest through the voice, but the object of remembering, at least in the case of the *Táin*, can be a text.

Thus, the Irish colophon characterizes the lengthy work that precedes it as

---

40. Trans. C. O'Rahilly 1967, 272. Bendacht ar cech óen mebraigfes go hindraic Táin amlaid seo ₇ ná tuillfe cruth aile furri (ibid., lines 4919–20).

41. A florid example of this kind of blessing upon the respectful user or transmitter of a story or its textual incarnation is contained in the Middle Irish text known as the *Altram Dá Tige Medar* (Fosterage of the house of two cups) (Dobbs 1930, 226, 228). This mode of closure is parodied in the Middle Irish *Aislinge Meic Conglinne* (Vision of Mac Conglinne) (Jackson 1990, lines 1332–49). On the forms of scribal commentary to be found in Irish manuscripts, see Plummer 1926.

42. E. Gwynn 1913, 46.

43. Harrison 1984, 144. On the figure of the *cros(s)án*, see Harrison 1989, 35–53.

intact, memorable, and performable. The wish is expressed that future generations of scribes and reciters will keep it intact, unencumbered by additions or emendations. Surely there is nothing here that challenges either the confidence of the producers of the literary tradition or the conceit of continuity between what they are doing and what was done in the past—or what oral storytellers still do—to convey that past to the future.

This colophon, however, is succeeded by another, which perhaps constitutes the commentary of the Book of Leinster scribe on the text and colophon he copied from his exemplar—a parting shot, as it were, that inserts the perspective of an authorial first person singular as boldly as the asides of the most intrusive Victorian novelist. Pointedly, this second colophon is in Latin, the language of Western medieval Christian culture and the written language on which the written form of Irish was orthographically modeled: "But I who have written this story, or rather this fable, give no credence to the various incidents related in it. For some things in it are the deceptions of demons [*praestrigia* (read: *praestigia*) *demonum*], others poetic figments; some are probable, others improbable; while still others are intended for the delectation of foolish men."[44]

This highly skeptical backward look, grounded in an act of writing that is not just rehearsing, wreaks havoc with the totality signed, sealed, and delivered into the future by the first colophon. The second colophon analyzes the text into heterogeneous bits, preeminently the "deceptions of demons," who figure as mascots for the scribe's campaign to invalidate the monolithic impression left by the text. Simultaneously, this campaign is an assertion of the I/writer's responsibility to stand aside from what has been produced and read it objectively. Clearly afoot here is an authorial strategy worlds apart from the first colophon's subsuming of the interpretative authorities of writer, performer, and reader or audience under the conceit of an unchanging text.

Nevertheless, the fundamentally different perspectives informing the two colophons are not altogether incompatible. As performable, "remembered" text, the *Táin* is sent off with best wishes to the rehearsals that will enable it to transcend time. Yet, as a written and therefore fixed text, the *Táin* is anchored in time and space, left behind by the oral tradition that putatively produced it. Such fixity leaves it prey to literary appropriation and (mis)interpretation, including the one that sees the illusory performances of demons behind the *Táin*.

The two colophons not only offer us contemporary commentaries on the text but also reflect the same perspectives that inform the medieval story of how the *Táin* was lost and then found in an earlier era. The tale, aptly dubbed

44. Trans. C. O'Rahilly 1967, 272. Sed ego qui scripsi hanc historiam aut uerius fabulam quibusdam fidem in hac historia aut fabula non accommodo. Quaedam enim ibi sunt praestrigia [*sic*] demonum, quaedam autem figmenta poetica, quaedam similia uero, quaedam non, quaedam ad delectationem stultorum (ibid., lines 4921–25).

by one scholar a "meta-legend," appears in abbreviated form in the Book of Leinster itself.[45] In this and other surviving versions of the story we are told that once in the not-too-distant past the poets and performers of Ireland, whose responsibility it had been to "rehearse" stories such as the *Táin*, realized or were forced to admit that they did not have a complete story of the famous cattle raid, retaining only fragments of it or nothing at all in their repertoire. According to the Book of Leinster version, the *Táin* had in fact been written down but then had been given away in exchange for a copy of the late-sixth-century Isidore of Seville's popular and influential compendium of learning, the *Etymologiae*.[46]

Not at all atypically of medieval Irish literature, the extant tellings of this story diverge in their explanations of how the *Táin* was ultimately recovered and textualized. Some variants say that it was the poem whimsically spoken to the tombstone of one of the heroes of the *Táin* by a poet in search of it which freakishly saved the day for the poetic institution. The poem, we are told, magically summoned up the dead hero, who then obligingly recited the story of the cattle raid for the surprised poet. And so the power and the honor of the praising poet and the revived hero, both oral performers here, are vindicated. The *Táin* of this version of the tale lives on intact into the future through acts of recalling and recounting, precisely as the author of the first colophon hoped it would.

In this version there is no need for ecclesiastical supervision or assistance to recover the tale and write it down again. Moreover, the means of restoring the

45. Best and O'Brien 1967, lines 32879–900. (The term *Metasage* was coined by Wolfgang Meid [1985, 127].) Other extant versions are to be found in texts edited in Meyer 1905b, 2–5, and in the late medieval narrative *Tromdám Gúaire* (The heavy hosting of Gúaire). Thurneysen 1921, 251–67; Carney 1955, 165–79; and Williams and Ford (1992, 89) supply citations, summaries, and translations of versions of this story and references to it. See also the allusion to Fergus (as speaking in death to the living) in one of the Middle Irish Triads (Meyer 1906b, 8).

46. Best and O'Brien 1967, lines 32881–83. James Carney (1955, 188) and Patrick Ford (1994, 255–56) maintain that these accounts envision not the recovery of a lost whole but the synthesis of elements of a story or several different stories into a new totality by means of literary composition. Clearly, the *Táin* as we have it does reflect literary sensibilities and ambitions. In all extant versions, however, the tradition bearers are depicted as decadent or incompetent and are exposed as frauds unable to supply their customers with what they request and expect to receive. We may reasonably assume, therefore, that the original audiences for this story would not have considered the production of a "total *Táin*" impossible for a competent and conscientious storyteller of yore. In the Book of Leinster the existence of a "lost" earlier version of the complete *Táin* which happened to be written down is posited as a motivating element in the tale. Moreover, in each extant version, it is the revivifying, and revived, act of oral performance that provides the poets with the "complete" and therefore canonically acceptable story. This outcome strongly suggests a traditional privileging of the oral over the written, even if the text does ultimately replace the performance. The loss of the *Táin*, vulnerable even (or rather, especially) in a written form, seems fitting punishment for the arrogant poets who have jealously appropriated tradition for their own selfish purposes by, among other means, writing. Analogous anxieties about writing as a tyrannical appropriation that violates a public trust are also to be found in ancient Greek tradition. See G. Nagy 1990, 168–69.

dead hero to life are totally secular, resulting in an epiphany that seems to have more to do with necromancy than with any Christian notions of communion with the souls of the dead.[47] These aspects of the story doubtless rendered both the voice of the dead hero and the text derived from that voice suspect to the more analytic, less catholic side of the collective scribal mind. The medieval reader and transmitter could also take offense at the implied ranking of oral performance ahead of writing or at the conceit by which a totality such as the *Táin* could be completely perishable in writing and then completely recoverable in oral performance. Viewed positively, the dead hero revived by eulogy can be said to fill a gap left by the transition from oral to written culture, and he fills it in with an admirably complete entity, namely, the entire story of the cattle raid. And yet, from a more jaundiced point of view, more skeptical of any sort of continuity between the past and the present, the dead hero may seem just another example of the *praestigia demonum*.[48] He is an illusion conjured up by the lies the demonically parasitical figure of the poet concocts, and what the poet or dead hero leaves behind, the telling of the story of the cattle raid, is not to be read and received as a whole but to be approached with caution, needing as it does the exorcism of critical analysis. It is as if, according to the author of the second colophon, the bits of story into which the *Táin* had disintegrated in the individual minds of the poets and storytellers had not been seamlessly put back together again in text at hand but had drifted apart once again before the reader's eyes.[49]

It was probably to counter precisely this kind of uneasiness that the story of the finding of the *Táin* was fitted with alternative versions according to which the dead hero was located and brought back to life only with the assistance of the saints of Ireland. These came to the aid of the poets by fasting against God until he produced the revenant with the story to tell. With this modification the dead hero and the text are certified as authentic through the collaboration between Christian holy man and Christianized native performer. This union works against the deconstructive demonization of the oral tradition and fills in the gap between text and performance and between churchman and poet.

I hasten to add, however, that literarily inclined ecclesiastics in medieval Ireland often were poets, and that the gap in question here existed more on

47. The motif of returning from the dead in order to correct a generation gone awry was available to the Irish literati in biblical tradition. See Luke 16:27.

48. McCone suggests that the author of the colophon, who spells *praestigiae* as *praestrigiae*, was directly or indirectly influenced by Isidore's proposed etymology for *praestigium*: Dictum enim praestigium quod praestringat aciem oculorum (*Etymologiae* 8.9.33), "It is called *praestigium* because it dulls the sharpness of the eyes" (1990, 149).

49. The myth of recovering the totality (or the proper sequence of episodes) of a tale of epic proportions is also to be found in classical Greek literature (as in the legend of the Peisistratean recension of Homer), as well as in Persian and Indian traditions concerning the origins of "canonical" texts of epic poems. See G. Nagy 1992a, 44–51; Davidson 1985, 103–16; Melia 1979.

an ideological than a historical level. As I noted, available evidence indicates that the Irish church and the higher poetic orders formed a working alliance early on, perhaps because poets saw possibilities in the innovation of writing as introduced by the church and its missionaries. Still, poets were associated with pre-Christian modes of divination and inspiration well into the Christian era (as evidenced, for instance, by the story of the finding of the *Táin.*)[50] Poets, moreover, although they embraced literacy, continued at least in theory to be characterized as performers and bearers of an oral tradition. Thus, a conspicuous gap persisted—and, curiously, even widened through time—between the figures of the poet and the ecclesiastic and between their concerns, at least in the realm of legend.

Myths of Origins

Stories that highlight transition and transmission, such as the story of the finding of the *Táin,* constitute a mythology of the Irish literary tradition, a narrative complex of protean motifs, patterns, and themes that express basic assumptions of the literati about their origins and their role in the greater scheme of things.[51] Mythology, as anthropologists and folklorists have come to understand it, is a cultural device for exploring the troubled and troubling aspects of a system of collective values and assumptions. Myths are not in the business of solving problems but of demonstrating and correlating them. It is therefore not surprising that these medieval Irish myths of literary origins are pervaded by problematic perceptions of writing and its relation to other modes of communication. Narrative elements, moreover, do not add up to a mythology unless we find them proliferating in multiforms that reflect an ongoing process of revising, fine-tuning, and adapting to new circumstances the themes meaningful to society and its tradition-bearers. These ubiquitous motifs and patterns are recycled by the producers of oral or literary story not simply because they are familiar and usable but because they convey messages that their audience wants to receive. The more grafted or marginal these recurring elements appear in the tales in which we find them, the more convincing the view that they are of compelling importance to the tradition that sustains them.

Many of the stories I will explore in this book come from Irish hagiography, particularly the saints' lives written in Latin and Irish between the seventh and twelfth centuries. My turning to hagiography as a source of information about

50. *Foillsigud,* the term for the revelation of the *Táin* to the poets in our texts, is the verbal noun of *foillsigid,* which has, according to the *DIL,* connotations of "super-normal revelation." There are various modes of enlightenment available to poets, such as the *imbas forosnai* mentioned in the Middle Irish *Sanas Cormaic,* usually known as Cormac's Glossary (Meyer 1912, 64). On these mantic techniques, see J. Nagy 1985, 25–26; T. O'Rahilly 1946, 323–25.
51. Cf. Scowcroft 1987, 81; and McCone 1990, 54–55, 64.

the authorizing strategies underlying the Irish literary tradition may seem unusual; the majority of those who study provenance and the interplay of the oral and the literary in early Irish literature focus on secular texts. Many Celtic scholars still consider saints' lives a separate kettle of fish, to be examined, if at all, apart from the "good stuff," such as the heroic sagas purportedly rooted in pre-Christian myth, or more sober, historically grounded genres such as law tracts, genealogies, and annals. Written traditions concerning holy Christian men and women, according to this point of view, offer insights into the nature of medieval Irish Christianity, some rousing propaganda for this or that church or monastery, pale reflections of secondhand saga themes, and possible means of corroborating information gotten from more solid sources, but little insight if any into the motivating forces behind the literary tradition. The author of a recent history of early Ireland issues the following astonishing dismissal: "Most of these Lives are less than edifying, being little more than a catalogue of miracles and wonders, some of them amusing, most of them ridiculous. . . . With few exceptions, the saints' Lives are a dismal swamp of superstition and perverted Christianity, dreary litanies of misplaced reverence and devotion."[52]

In fact, hagiography provides some of the earliest extant texts written by the Irish as "literature." The achievements and failures of the saint in the course of establishing and strengthening his reputation mirror how the hagiographer (probably the same literatus who was writing down the heroic tale, the law tract, and the annal) perceived his function as a recorder in a still relatively new medium of the fluid oral tradition that bound the past in which the saint lived to the present of the hagiographer. Furthermore, a problematic or even dark side to Irish saints' lives has barely been explored. Often enough, loose ends are left loose, contradictions are not resolved, and simmering tensions are allowed to boil over, leading into new episodes or opening up into altogether different lives or legend cycles. It is this open-endedness of Irish hagiography as story, the solving of narrative problems in ways that in fact only present newer or already existing problems in life as it is practiced or imagined, that makes this literature resemble a mythology in its own right, perhaps even more than does much of what passes for the remains of pre-Christian Irish mythology in literature. A primary goal of this book is to experiment with a deeper reading of the stories told and written about Irish saints, particularly Patrick and Columba, a reading that points up their fundamental connections with other, less explicitly Christian branches of the literary tradition.

Although what I am looking for are the ways in which literature was understood, justified, and grounded by the literati of early medieval Ireland, I take a distinctly folkloristic approach to these saints' lives, accepting as eminently

52. Ó Cróinín 1995, 210–11.

credible the typical claim of the hagiographer that he is setting down merely a part of a much larger orally (as well as literarily) transmitted story about his saintly subject. In other words, I treat the saint's life as a reflection of a collective tradition (even if the "collective" extends no further than the members of a particular monastic community or a network of such communities). I view any parallel, contrast, or intersection among saints' lives or other kinds of texts as a reflection of similar, diverging, or dialogic trends within an even wider collective tradition. This tradition may not have been shared by all segments of medieval Irish society, but certainly it was carried on by those communities—ecclesiastical as well as secular—that assumed the task of producing and perpetuating literature. Hagiographers and other writers working in a milieu so compulsively prone to reflect on itself invented by recycling and employing a *bricolage* that intuitively realized configurations already latent in their materials.[53] The profound thematic consistencies, as well as inconsistencies, among texts from many different sources which I adumbrate in the following pages constitute evidence, therefore, not only for extensive literary borrowing but also for a productive ideological substructure to medieval Irish literature and to the culture that in producing this literature reproduced itself.

53. This model of mythmaking was devised by Claude Lévi-Strauss (1962, 26–27).

1/ Rendered speechless:
the saint in his own words

A Patrician Dossier

The Book of Armagh, a manuscript penned around 800 by a monk named Fer Domnach 'Churchman' and two assistants, contains a number of Latin documents relating to Patrick, the fifth-century missionary saint of Ireland, and to the federation of churches and monasteries associated with the monastery of Armagh, which claimed him as its founder.[1] Whether in fact the ecclesiastical establishment of Armagh was founded by Patrick or had any special connection with him from its beginning is a point still debated by Patrician scholars.[2] Included in the book of Armagh are the so-called *Confessio,* a work attributed to Patrick himself; a life of Patrick written by the monk Muirchú in the latter half of the seventh century; an account of Patrick's missionary accomplishments compiled by the bishop Tírechán sometime in the same period; and the *Liber angeli* (Book of the angel), a seventh- or eighth-century text that details the privileges claimed by Armagh over the people, churches, and monasteries of Ireland.[3] Purportedly, this supremacy was announced to Patrick by an angel in a vision, and the *Liber angeli* dictated, or even written, by this supernatural emissary.[4] In addition, the Book of Armagh contains most of the New Testament, along with the

1. J. Gwynn 1913 is a diplomatic edition of the contents of this manuscript. The division of scribal labor it evinces is the subject of Sharpe 1982a.
2. Sharpe 1982c offers an overview of the history of Armagh and its connection with Patrician cult.
3. The edition of the *Confessio* I cite is that of Richard Hanson and Cécile Blanc (1978). Translations of excerpts are based on Hanson's (1983), with my own revisions. The lives, the *Liber angeli,* and various notes pertaining to Patrick included in the manuscript, are edited and translated in Bieler 1979.
4. The conceit is hardly unique. Koep 1952 is a study of this widespread motif of the divinely authored sacred book or writing that is handed over to a holy representative of humanity or a religious community.

fourth-century Life of Martin of Tours and the *Dialogi* (a sequel of sorts to the Life) by the Gaulish cleric Sulpicius Severus. One of the earliest and most influential saints' lives in Western Christian culture, Sulpicius's Life of Martin served as an inspiration for early Irish hagiography, including the various lives of Patrick.[5]

The Book of Armagh, with its carefully chosen contents, has been described as an aggrandizing dossier compiled and issued by members of Armagh's federation of monasteries, jockeying for privilege and prestige in the face of intense competition from other monastic networks, such as those centered on Iona and Clonard.[6] Armagh's apparently successful expansion of its ecclesiastical jurisdiction in the seventh through ninth centuries was probably linked to the political ascendancy of its patrons. These were in the first place the Airgialla, a federation of Ulster kingdoms in whose territory Armagh was situated, which became the dominant power in the province of Ulster. The patronage of Armagh then shifted to the Uí Néill, a powerful dynasty originally from what is known today as Donegal, which lay claim to the kingship of Ireland and came to dominate northern and central Ireland.[7]

Although the Patrician documents it contains certainly do not present an altogether homogeneous picture, the Book of Armagh offers an interpretation of the history of the Irish church and of its effects upon the Irish. Of central importance is the demonstration of venerability, not just of the documents themselves but also of the church of Armagh, its patron saint and protector Patrick, and the institutional forms of Christianity in Ireland. The venerability the book defines, seeks, and claims for itself and its literary subjects is a universally acknowledgeable and communicable power or authority. By virtue of its grounding in the events of the past, this authority can still compel those to whom it is communicated to act in accordance with it. Among the most insistently asked questions in these texts are whence does ecclesiastical authority come? Where does it reside as a kind of spiritual force? And perhaps most important, how is it communicated and made manifest?

These Patrician documents answer that authority came from God, and it came to rest in Patrick. In the course of time, Patrick delegated this authority to those to whom he entrusted the propagation and maintenance of the

5. Aubrey Gwynn (1966) has written on the popularity of the cult of Saint Martin in Ireland. See also Lapidge 1990, esp. 244–45. Stancliffe 1983 presents a thorough examination of the intellectual background to Sulpicius's hagiographic writings, which is also reflected throughout Irish hagiography.

6. Of course, there is more to the political subtexts of these Patrician documents than monomaniacal Armagh propaganda, as Catherine Swift (1994) shows in her examination of Tírechán's text (preserved in the Book of Armagh only) in particular.

7. Charles Doherty (1991, 68–69) provides a useful summary of what we know about the history of the rise of Armagh in the intertwined contexts of ecclesiastic controversy and Ulster politics. Herbert 1988a, 9–97, is the best available survey of some of the alliances and conflicts among monastic federations in pre-Norman Ireland, including the Easter and tonsure controversies and the roles played in ecclesiastical affairs by powerful dynasties such as the Uí Néill.

Christian faith and ultimately to his successors in the Armagh federation. Yet the communication of that authority from the past into the present remains a complicated and even problematic issue, for the divine authoritative message is transmitted through two separate codes or media. Not only do these at times appear to be in conflict with each other, but they also tend to fuse with the message and become infused with authority themselves, so much so that they become the instruments for the performance of miracles signifying authority and can even generate miracles by themselves.

These two media are speaking and writing. God and his witnesses, the foremost being Patrick, are envisioned as imparting the authoritative truth to Ireland through both their speech and their texts, communicative modes that, despite their common goal, are alternately contrasted and uncomfortably allied in the fulfillment of Patrick's evangelical mission. This alternation is symptomatic of a general unease felt by the bearers of the early medieval Irish literary tradition, the authors of the Patrician texts in the Book of Armagh included. Their anxiety centers on the nature of their own authority as writers and readers and on how their own bookish culture fits into the scheme of a universal Christian history and into the culture of early Irish society, both pre-Christian and Christian.

Patrick's *Confessio*

Already in his so-called *Confessio,* Patrick himself is probing the authority of writing, particularly his own. The work appears to have been well enough known to seventh-century Patrician hagiographers.[8] Nevertheless, the surviving lives shed scarcely any light on the event Patrick presents as the pivotal reason for producing this document, that is, an attack on his missionary and episcopal activities in Ireland, launched by his ecclesiastical colleagues back in his homeland, Britain. Inasmuch as the *Confessio* adumbrates a scan-

---

8. Of the eight extant copies of the *Confessio,* only the abridged text in the Book of Armagh survived in Ireland (see Grosjean 1958). Daniel Binchy (1961, 41–42) and Richard Hanson (1975, 1977) have discussed the nature of and possible reasons for the deletions in the text of the *Confessio* as presented in the Book of Armagh. "We can, I think, discern one master-principle in the omissions which we have been reviewing here, the desire to make the Patrick of the *Confession* fit the Patrick of later legend. The work was disappointing in that it provided no actual miracles, but it did provide visions, and these were all retained. For the rest, details disparaging of or contradictory to the Patrick of later legend . . . tended to be omitted. The epitomist of D [the text in the Book of Armagh] may have been the first student of Patrick who was determined to subordinate what Patrick said of himself to what later legend said of him. He certainly was not the last" (Hanson 1975, 95). Patrick is just as visionary in the abridged version but less implicated in (accusations of) possible misbehavior. There is, however, no compelling reason to believe that the abridgment was better known among Irish literati than the complete text. Indeed, the evidence would suggest that Patrick's early biographers used the latter. On the hagiographic use of materials from the *Confessio,* see Bieler 1952, 23–24; and Hanson 1977, 254–56.

dal, perhaps we should not be surprised that it is hardly acknowledged in the later vernacular literary tradition and that the version preserved in the Book of Armagh is a considerably "censored" one. Nevertheless, this remarkable work illuminates the background to some of the key themes and motifs in the early Patrician lives. While there may not be a direct link between the *Confessio* and these later traditions concerning the origins of Christianity and writing in Ireland, they share the same ideological terrain and deal in fascinatingly similar, occasionally contrasting, ways with the same issues.

The author of the *Confessio* presents the reader with a retrospective sketch of his life, the highlights of which are his term of slavery among the Irish, his escape, the revelations sent to him by God, and his accomplishments in converting the people among whom he formerly lived as a slave. Patrick takes pride in what he has achieved, but the twin purposes of the *Confessio* are to answer the criticisms of his fellow clerics, to whom he refers deferentially as *seniores*,[9] and to turn a shrewdly critical eye on himself and his evangelical career. His chosen designation for what he has written, *confessio*, clearly signals both the public and the private dimension of this statement in which Patrick asserts the rightness of what he has done in and with his life as a man of God, reveals the formative experiences of his inner life, and reasserts his authority by means of what has been described as an "examination of conscience out aloud, in public."[10] It is at the close that Patrick uses the title term, which in this context refers as much to his profession of faith as to his acknowledgment of failings:

> But I beg of those believing in and fearing God: whoever would deign to examine or accept this writing which the clearly unlearned sinner Patrick has written in Ireland, that no one ever say that it was through my own ignorance that I achieved or demonstrated anything pleasing to God. Rather, you are to think, and it is to be believed as most true that it was a gift of God. And this is my "confession" before I die.[11]

This "modestly" written *confessio*, we find, serves as a frame and explanation for a spoken *confessio* from his past, the divulging of which has raised doubts

9. C. 26, 37 (Hanson and Blanc 1978, 98, 110). On the significance of Patrick's use of the term, see Nearney 1949, 501–3.

10. Ibid., 506.

11. Sed precor credentibus et timentibus Deum, quicumque dignatus fuerit inspicere uel recipere hanc scripturam quam Patricius peccator indoctus scilicet Hiberione conscripsit, ut nemo umquam dicat quod mea ignorantia, si aliquid pusillum egi uel demonstrauerim secundum Dei placitum, sed arbitramini et uerissime credatur quod donum Dei fuisset. Et haec est confessio mea antequam moriar (c. 62, Hanson and Blanc 1978, 132). See also c. 61: Ecce iterum iterumque breuiter exponam uerba confessionis meae (ibid., 130–32), "Lo, again and again I will briefly set out the words of my 'confession.'"

The Pauline source of the concept of *confessio* is 1 Cor. 1:12, as Christine Mohrmann (1961, 4–7) points out. Peter Dronke (1981), however, has argued for a direct literary influence of Augustine's autobiography on Patrick's *Confessio*. Cf. Bradley 1983, 541 n. 27.

in church circles about Patrick and obliged him to take up the pen in his defense: "They discovered a matter, thirty years old, [to bring] against me: word[s] [*uerbum*] that I had confessed before I was a deacon. Out of the anxiety in a woeful soul, I confided to my dearest friend something I had committed once in my youth."[12] Patrick's youthful *uerbum* and its diffusion threaten to undermine his authority among his fellow ecclesiastics and perhaps even his converts. (Patrick in fact never specifies just what sin it was that he committed and later confessed.) In order to regain his authority, he must write out (as opposed to speak) a second, somewhat different kind of *confessio*, a public, not a private, statement. His strategy here is to attribute all of whatever authority he had and whatever authority his writing has to God.

To compose such a document, or any document for that matter, is not easy for Patrick. He expressed grave doubts about his ability to communicate in a written form, or, as Patrick sees it, to translate what he has to say into the learned Latin of writing:

And so I have long thought to write, but I have hesitated, until now, for I feared, not having read as widely as others, that I would intrude upon the language of men, who have thoroughly imbibed both law and sacred writings equally, and whose speech has not changed for the worse at all since their childhood but has grown closer to perfection all the while. For what I have to say has been rendered into an unfamiliar tongue, as can easily be proven by the distinctive flavor [*saliua*] of my writing, which also reveals the extent to which I am trained how to speak and I am educated. For it is said that you shall know the wise man by his tongue, as well as his sense, his knowledge, and what he teaches to be true.[13]

The *Confessio* is thus a professedly ill-at-ease textual assertion that Patrick possessed a "voice" of divine authority. His unusual reference to the quality of his writing as its *saliua* 'saliva' or, by extension, 'flavor', in possible anticipation of the shift of focus from *his* writing to the speech (*lingua*) of the wise man, reflects his attempt to inject as much as possible of the divine inspiration

12. Occasionem post annos triginta inuenerunt me aduersus uerbum quod confessus fueram antequod essem diaconus. Propter anxietatem maesto animo insinuaui amicissimo meo quae in pueritia mea una die gesseram (c. 27, Hanson and Blanc 1978, 100).

13. Quapropter olim cogitaui scribere, sed et usque nunc haesitaui; timui enim ne incederem in linguam hominum, quia non legi sicut et ceteri, qui optime itaque iura et sacras litteras utraque pari modo combiberunt et sermones illorum ex infantia numquam mutarunt, sed magis ad perfectum semper addiderunt. Nam sermo et loquela nostra translata est in linguam alienam, sicut facile potest probari ex saliua scripturae meae qualiter sum ego in sermonibus instructus atque eruditus, quia, inquit sapiens per linguam dinoscetur et sensus et scientia et doctrina ueritatis (c. 9, ibid., 78).

Mohrmann (1961, 9), finding Patrick's Latin unidiomatic and idiosyncratic, argues for taking Patrick's apologetic tone as real and not just rhetorical cliché, *pace* Nora Chadwick, in whose view Patrick was firmly in control of the Latin style of his time (1961, 23–29; see now also Howlett 1994, 116–21).

of his spoken language into a putatively hostile medium (the written word). Furthermore, Patrick, whose familiarity with the Bible is amply attested in the *Confessio,* may well have been referring in this expression to Christ's use of spittle as a projection of his divine power.[14]

It is this very familiarity with Scripture that gives Patrick the confidence to overcome his feelings of insecurity in the arena of belles lettres. By way of reference to the sacred text—specifically, Paul's imagery in his Second Letter to the Corinthians, the work from which Patrick derives the thematic framework of the *Confessio* as a whole—Patrick arrives at a strategically advantageous formulation of the relationship between spoken and written. This arrangement preserves the importance of the text in principle while artfully blurring its distinction from speech:

> But if what has been given to others had been given to me, I certainly would not have remained silent in repayment. Even if it happens to seem to some that I am trying to promote myself in this matter by means of my ignorance and hesitant speech, it has been written: stammering tongues will learn quickly how to speak of peace. And so how much more should we strive, we who are, it is said, a letter of Christ for salvation all the way to the ends of the earth, even if the letter is not polished.[15]

Patrick's reluctance to write, now equated with an unwillingness or inability to speak, is dissolved through a kind of literary glossolalia based on an implicit annexation of writing by speech. To write, then, is merely another way to speak. It is not to assume the onerous responsibility of individual authorship but potentially to become the mouthpiece of God or Christ. After all, Moses, who protests his "hesitant speech" (*tardiori lingua*) in the biblical passage (Exodus 4:10) Patrick pointedly cites in reference to himself, came to terms with his anxieties by becoming a scribal recorder of God's word. Since, according to Paul, we are all letters written by Christ, we should embrace the letter, but a new kind of letter, infused with the immediacy and vitality of the Spirit, not fixed or fixing, inanimate or impersonal, but liberating and even redolent of personality. And so, in presenting himself in written form, Patrick continues the paradoxical act of "living writing" begun by Christ himself. Patrick becomes his own letter, an immediate and compelling sign of divine authority, co-authored by the Divine Author.

14. David Howlett (1989, 100) sees Patrick's reference to *saliua* as emblematic of his subtle utilization of scriptural allusion in his writings.

15. Sed si itaque datum mihi fuisset sicut et ceteris, uerumtamen non silerem propter retributionem, et si forte uidetur apud aliquantos me in hoc praeponere cum mea inscientia et tardiori lingua, sed etiam scriptum est enim: Linguae balbutientes uelociter discent loqui pacem. Quanto magis nos adpetere debemus, qui sumus, inquit, epistola Christi in salutem usque ad ultimum terrae, et si non deserta (c. 11, Hanson and Blanc 1978, 80). Patrick's indebtedness to Paul's formulations in this and other passages is explored in full in Nerney 1949.

Visionary Speaking and Writing

Like Patrick in his *Confessio*, Paul in his Second Letter to the Corinthians is meeting a challenge to his personal authority by means of an exercise in authorship. In absentia, he finds that he can reassert his teachings in the hearts and minds of the Corinthian converts only through an epistle. This potentially treacherous medium, Paul acknowledges, needs to be backed up by the personal presence and speech of the author if it is not to lose its flexibility and appear either too strong or hollow (10:8–11). Writing and speech, moreover, are not the only media available for the propagation of divine truth. Letters, Paul says, should not even be necessary among Christians, who, in their common experience of finding Christ, become letters, written signs, to each other (2:1–6). Writing, as used in the Old Law, implies distance between the sender and the receiver, and also between the sender/receiver and the message itself. This separation, inherent in writing as a medium, is for Paul a kind of "death" that diminishes the strength of what is being communicated. With the experience of Christ, however, the believer should be able to dispense with the need for writing and, speaking in Christ, become an immediate form of sacred metawriting to his fellow Christians (2:7–18).[16]

Speaking in Christ is hardly the same as ordinary speaking. In the realm of normal discourse, such as debating with the rivals whose influence on the Corinthians he is countering, Paul or any other Christina is a fool, and whatever he says is boasting (11:21–23). Still, there is truth to this boasting, if only the boaster's awareness that experience communicates an authority that cannot be expressed through speech. The telling of such authorizing experience transcends human communication, just as the experience itself transcends bodily and spatial limitations: "I know a man in Christ who fourteen years ago was caught up to the third heaven—whether in the body or out of the body I do not know, God knows. And I know that this man was caught up into Paradise—whether in the body or out of the body I do not know, God knows—and he heard things that cannot be told, which man may not utter" (12:2–4).[17] This passage, the inspiration for the apocryphal "Vision of Paul" tradition that proved so popular in the Middle Ages,[18] presents a "twinned" apostle. He is both the man who experienced Paradise and the man who tells of it or, rather, tells of its inexpressibility. The writing Paul in effect calls on the authority of the caught-up Paul, of whom he speaks in the third person, to win and maintain the attention of his audience. What the visionary has experienced, he is beyond knowing. He himself becomes the visionary experience,

16. The influential Pauline images of the living letter and of writing as death are explored in Jager 1993, 63–64.

17. The translation is that of the Revised Standard Version.

18. Evidence for the influence of the "Vision" on Middle Irish literature is presented in Carey 1989; and Wright 1993, 106–21. A translation of a medieval Irish rendering of this text is available in Herbert and McNamara 1989, 132–36.

the true nature of which only God knows and the earthbound Paul who addresses the Corinthians cannot describe. Paul returns to this world with knowledge he cannot fully communicate. He is both the bearer of an unfathomable epiphany and its joyously frustrated would-be interpreter.

Taking his cue from Paul, Patrick in his *Confessio* attempts to discredit writing and even speech by recourse to personally experienced vision, to which conventional standards for judging the quality of discourse are inapplicable, but which nevertheless expresses an ineffable authority. A professed "fool" like Paul, he "boasts" of his life with its trials and hardships and of his persistence in his divinely assigned mission. Much of his early life, he tells us, was spent in slavery in Ireland, where he had been taken by pirates as a child. Having finally escaped by means of miraculous guidance, he returns to the safety of his home in Britain. There a series of transcendent personal experiences imbues Patrick with authority and renders him, the recipient of visions, an epiphany himself. Divine authorization is conferred in the course of three mystical encounters, the last two of which he describes thus:

And on another night—I do not know, but God knows whether in me or beside me—[there were] words [spoken] most skillfully which I heard but could not understand, except that at the end of what was said he uttered: "He who gave his life for you, it is he that speaks in you." Having been thus tested, I was exultant.

And a second time I saw in me the same one praying, and it was as if I were inside my own body, and I heard [him] above me, that is above the inner man, and there he was praying forcefully, with groans. Meanwhile, I was dumbfounded and astonished as I thought about who this person praying in me might be, but then at the end of what was said, he uttered that he was the Spirit. And, having been thus tested, I remembered the apostle saying: "The Spirit makes our weak prayer strong, for whether what we are praying for is fitting, we do not know; but the Spirit himself requests on our behalf with ineffable groans, which cannot be put into words" [Rom. 8:26].[19]

19. Et alia nocte—nescio, Deus scit, utrum in me an iuxta me—uerbis peritissime, quos ego audiui et non potui intellegere, nisi ad postremum orationis sic effitiatus est: "Qui dedit animam suam pro te, ipse est qui loquitur in te," et sic expertus sum gaudibundus. Et iterum uidi in me ipsum orantem et eram quasi intra corpus meum et audiui super me, hoc est super interiorem hominem, et ibi fortiter orabat gemitibus, et inter haec stupebam et ammirabam et cogitabam quis esset qui in me orabat, sed ad postremum orationis sic effitiatus est ut sit Spiritus, et sic expertus sum et recordatus sum apostolo dicente: Spiritus adiuuat infirmitates orationis nostrae: nam quod oremus sicut oportet nescimus: sed ipse Spiritus postulat pro nobis gemitibus inenarrabilibus quae verbis exprimi non possunt (cc. 24–25, Hanson and Blanc 1978, 98).

Note the absence of a verb in the main clause of the first sentence in this passage—a result of textual corruption, perhaps, or of authorial design to have the *uerbis* and *peritissime* hang, as it were, in a void.

Patrick, by so pointedly prefacing these dream narratives with visionary Paul's "I do not know, but God knows" ("nescio, Deus scit" [2 Cor. 12:2, 3]), signals his reentry into the ideological framework of Paul's Second Letter to the Corinthians, and specifically into the mode of "boasting" by which Paul articulates his own transcendent experience. Unlike Paul, Patrick does not claim to have been taken up into Paradise, but he is introduced to a divine voice, that of the Spirit, sounding from within. In the presence of this voice, Patrick develops an alter ego, a Patrick in the third person who mediates between the "I" of the *Confessio* and the Spirit who sanctifies him. Patrick's speech cannot convey the learned internal utterance or the groaning of the Spirit in full, any more than Paul could communicate in a first-person narrative what the "other" Paul learned in Paradise, or how he was transported there.

Yet what his inner self experiences and hears is not completely unintelligible to the earthbound Patrick. In fact, he can even communicate to his readers what he learns. In both cases, at the end of whatever was said, there is a bridge between the ineffable and the intelligible and communicable. Patrick does get the "punch line" underlying the utterance of the Spirit, hard to understand in the first case because it is so skillfully (*peritissime*) delivered, and in the second because it seems not to be speech proper but rather nonverbal groans.

It is worth noting that Patrick has to coin a verb to describe the speaking he finally understands: *effitiatus est* "he uttered" (?).[20] In his assertion of his ability to catch the gist of what he hears, however unique it is, Patrick removes himself and his discourse from the realm of the Pauline ineffable and returns to what at first seemed an uncomfortable position already staked out for himself at the beginning of the *Confessio:* the persona of the mediocre speaker and even worse writer, baffled by refined speech and now also by the groans of the Spirit. Yet, though he is baffled, these modes of communication do deliver their message, even or especially for a humble auditor like Patrick, who now spreads the message in his writing. The inner Patrick listening to the voice of the Spirit and the quoted voice of the Spirit itself pass along their authority to the speaking and writing "I" of the *Confessio*. While invoking the Pauline concept of justification through reference to an experience beyond words, Patrick comes down squarely on the side of language as a channel of divine authority and as the prime source of his own legitimation as a man with a sacred mission. God may know and understand all, but the author of the *Confessio* knows, and can communicate, a thing or two as well.

Furthermore, that which Patrick *heard* and understood as just enough to legitimate him in his own eyes must now be written up and thus made public in order for Patrick's reputation to be preserved. The text, therefore, is the ultimate destination of the comprehensible and communicable crux of what

20. Mohrman (1961, 11) discusses this curious lexical item.

the transcendent Patrick has to say, although the text, let us remember, is only a part of what was said.

Letters from an Angel

The complementarity of speaking and writing and the basic soundness of language as a medium for communicating the experience of receiving authority are already professed in the decidedly unecstatic vision Patrick receives before the two "experiment" with Pauline mysticism we have just considered.

Recounting what happened after he returned home from captivity, Patrick tells us:

> In a few years I was back in Britain with my parents, who took me back as their son and importuned me conscientiously that, now after my having suffered so many tribulations, I should never leave them. It was then that I saw in a vision of the night a man approaching, it would seem from Ireland, whose name was Victoricus, with innumerable letters, and he gave me one of these. I read its beginning that said "The Voice of the Irish," and as I was reciting the beginning of the letter, I thought I heard at the same time the voice of those who were [living] near the forest of Foclut, which is by the Western Sea, and this is what they exclaimed, as if from one mouth: "We ask you, holy boy, to come and walk among us again," and I was stung to the heart and rendered unable to read any further, and thus was I tested. Thank God that after many years the Lord accomplished for them what they were clamoring for.[21]

Here we see the prototype for the figure of Patrick's guardian angel Victoric(i)us or Victor, who features so prominently in Patrician hagiography. The *Confessio* does not specify just who or what Victoricus is, nor has the significance of the name been satisfactorily explained.[22]

. Significantly, unlike the divine voice in Patrick's subsequent visions, and unlike the mysterious messenger, perhaps one of the models for Patrick's

21. Et iterum post paucos annos in Brittanniis eram cum parentibus meis, qui me ut filium susceperunt et ex fide rogauerunt me ut uel modo ego post tantas tribulationes quas ego pertuli nusquam ab illis discederem, et ibi scilicet uidi in uisu noctis uirum uenientem quasi de Hiberione, cui nomen Victoricus, cum epistolis innumerabilibus, et dedit mihi unam ex his et legi principium epistolae continentem "Vox Hiberionacum," et cum recitabam principium epistolae putabam ipso momento audire uocem ipsorum qui erant iuxta siluam Vocluti quae est prope mare occidentale, et sic exclamauerunt quasi ex uno ore: "Rogamus te, sancte puer, ut uenias et adhuc ambulas inter nos," et ualde compunctus sum corde et amplius non potui legere et sic expertus sum. Deo gratias, quia post plurimos annos praestitit illis Dominus secundum clamorem illorum (c. 23, Hanson and Blanc 1978, 94–96).

22. Among others, Alfred Anscombe (1914), James Carney (1955, 411–12), and Nora Chadwick (1961, 27) have offered intriguing theories concerning the identity of Victor(icus) and the source of the name, but there is no scholarly consensus on Patrick's specific source for this figure or his name. See also Ó Raifeartaigh 1978, 26.

emissary, who calls Paul to mission work in Macedonia in Acts 16:9–10, Victoricus comes to Patrick *not* with something to say but with a packet of letters (*epistolae*) to read.[23] Yet we are once again in the realm of the inexpressible, it is important to note, for the number of letters cannot be calculated. The letter carrier reduces the innumerable to one—that is, the specific letter he gives Patrick to read—but all the other letters remain unreadable because they are inaccessible as well as without number. The single letter Patrick reads gives him authority, and what is more, writing about this writing (namely, the *Confessio*) reactivates that authority.

Victoricus's letters are, of course, no ordinary texts. Patrick, following Paul, has already internalized the letter, centering the text within the individual who follows Christ and attributing its authorship to Christ. Are these letters then representations of those whom Patrick will, or could, convert to Christianity? If indeed letter is meant to signify person, then the connection is realized by means of the speech that accompanies the letter. The *epistola* handed to Patrick, with the title "The Voice of the Irish," actually speaks to Patrick, beckoning him back to the land where he was a slave.[24]

This curious dream episode can be seen as well from another, even more compelling, interpretative angle. The letter, or Patrick's reading it *aloud*, acts as a cue for a "choral" utterance of such power that the reader is unable to read further, and the dreamer is awakened and torn away from his vision. The voice of the Irish disturbs the reception of the written message of authority, but it provides its own authorization. Patrick now knows what he must do, and God himself ultimately answers the voice, through the instrument of Patrick. He has read, heard, and dreamt enough to have a strong sense of mission, which he now transmits in the *Confessio*. Still, it is clear that he has by no means experienced all of what *could* be read or heard or dreamt.

And so we see that featured in each of the three visions or stages of a composite vision is an utterance of authority understood and communicable only to the crucial, albeit minimal, extent that it can effectively authorize the hearer. The chain of auditory mystical experiences is bracketed by encounters with texts: it is set off by a letter, and it finds its ultimate expression in Patrick's written *Confessio*. Yet, the bracketing texts, to be effective communicators, must be alive, accompanied by speech, that is, read aloud or infused with the *saliua* of the spoken word.[25] They are, moreover, limited to referring

---

23. The Pauline parallel is pointed out in Nerney 1949, 16.

24. Merdrignac 1985–86, 2:144–45, explores the relationship between writing and speaking in this passage and an analogous situation featured in a later Breton saint's life (the third Latin life of Tudual).

25. Of this episode Jane Stevenson remarks that when Patrick "holds the document in his hand, he *hears* the voice, or voices, of the writer, rather than *seeing* the words on the page. It is a way of reading far removed from our abstract appreciation of written data. Probably when Patrick read the Bible, he perceived it as the voice of God speaking directly to him, which may

to what is spoken. The letter, or that part of it which Patrick reads, proclaims or introduces the voice of the Irish, and the *Confessio* proclaims the utterances that communicate authority to Patrick. The miraculous speech that pervades the visions, which, by contrast, relies on no code other than itself, enjoys the luxury of self-reference: "He who gave his life for you, it is he that speaks in you." Patrick, while accepting Paul's conceit of the inexpressibility of experience that authorizes the subject and using it to diminish the claim on public discourse staked out by practitioners of learned standards of speech and writing, nevertheless expresses some of the inexpressible. He receives one of innumerable letters, he understands the tail end of what the ultraeloquent voice inside him has to say, and he translates the finale of the Spirit's lamentation into human speech. Thus communication within the visions and between those beings who appear in the vision and the audience of the *Confessio* occurs synecdochically, a part of the transmitted message having to stand for the whole. This part is, as it were, rescued from the rest of the discourse, which is beyond human communication, and the part becomes the cornerstone of what Patrick the writer has to say. His own means of communication, in fact, represent yet another synecdochic relationship. Patrick conspicuously protests his unfamiliarity with the conventions of refined and elegant speech, but he is obviously not totally unfamiliar with them. Just as what Patrick manages to read, hear, understand, and communicate in his visions is the key truth, so his modicum of education is, by implication, just enough for expressing what he needs to say. In the (written) words of one so bound by and yet also so aware of his own expressive limitations, the limitless becomes limited, and unquantifiable is quantified, and the ineffable is edited into a presentable form.

Calling upon Elijah

Patrick's experience is purely passive and receptive in the dreams examined so far, as well as in those that took place during his years of captivity, in which he hears a supernatural voice calling him to freedom.[26] In yet another vision recorded in the *Confessio*, experienced while he was still struggling to return home, Patrick himself actually speaks. The utterance does not come through a projected, "second" Patrick, like the inner man featured in one of

---

help to account for his very personal usage of the text and his passionate identification with St Paul" (Stevenson 1990, 17).

   Peter Dronke (1981, 29–31) proposes that the Victoricus episode and Patrick's other mystical experiences may derive from the scene of Augustine's climactic conversion experience in the *Confessions* (8.28–29). Stephen Nichols views this scene, in which Augustine is driven to consult Scripture after he overhears a child saying *tolle lege* ("pick up and read"), as exemplifying how, for Augustine, "the return of the oral to its written scriptural counterpart is a powerful imperative" (1991, 151). Of course, in Patrick's vision of the letters, the movement is *away* from the written.

26. C. 17, Hanson and Blanc 1978, 86–88.

the visions discussed above, but through Patrick the observer and victim of the vision and its narrator. And while the Spirit is said to be the ultimate source behind Patrick's utterance, it is Patrick who authoritatively says so, not the Spirit itself. Having told of his adventures with the pagans who took him away from his captivity only to subject him to more hardship, Patrick describes this memorable dream:

> Indeed, that same night [after an incident involving his captors], I was sleeping and Satan tempted me sorely, as I will remember as long as I will be in this body, and there fell on me what seemed like a great boulder, and none of my limbs had any strength left. And yet what inspired me, ignorant in spirit that I was, to call upon "Helias [Elijah]"? I saw the sun rise in the sky, and as I was shouting "Helias, Helias!" with [all] my strength, lo the splendor of that sun fell upon me and immediately freed me of all the weight [that was upon me], and I believe that it was Christ my Lord that saved me, and that it was his Spirit that shouted then on my behalf, and I hope that it will be so on the day of my affliction, as it says in the gospel: "On that day," assures the Lord, "it will not be you that speaks but the spirit of your Father that speaks in you" [Matt. 10:19–20].[27]

Patrick's "ignorance" in this case paradoxically prepares him not to be the vessel of a portion of a supernaturally authorizing message as in the other visions but to exclaim a powerful, ambiguous word. *Helias* is really a pun, playing on Elijah (to whom Christ called during his crucifixion [Mark 15:35–36; Matt. 27:47–49]) and Greek *helios* 'sun', and this wordplay (rather sophisticated and learned for one who professes to be so ignorant) actually succeeds in summoning the sun to Patrick's aid. Furthermore, Patrick's outburst, a mere fragment of speech, is identified in his dream analysis as the utterance of the Spirit. This, the later vision makes clear, is inexpressible as a totality, but here it is limited and communicable as the dreamer's exclamation. Once again, Patrick uses metonymy to bridge the gap between the inexpressible and the expressible. Except in this case, what Patrick *says*, as opposed to what he understands and records, is presented as a small but powerful portion of divine, infinite utterance. The point is thus made, as it is in the later visions featuring the voice of the Spirit, that the divine speaks through Patrick. His single, multivocal word compels with divine authority.

27. Eadem uero nocte eram dormiens et fortiter temptauit me Satanas, quod memor ero quamdiu fuero in hoc corpore, et cecidit super me ueluti saxum ingens et nihil membrorum meorum preualens. Sed unde me uenit ignarum in spiritu ut Heliam uocarem? Et inter haec uidi in caelum solem oriri et dum clamarem "Heliam, Heliam" uiribus meis, ecce splendor solis illius decidit super me et statim discussit a me omnem grauitudinem, et credo quod a Christo Domino meo subuentus sum et spiritus eius iam tunc clamabat pro me et spero quod sic erit in die pressurae meae, sicut in euangelio inquit: In illa die, Dominus testatur, non uos estis qui loquimini, sed spiritus Patris uestri quo loquitur in uobis (c. 20, ibid., 92–93).

Patrick Accused

Having demonstrated that his voice can on occasion be a fragment of God's, Patrick turns to the crisis brought about by the intimate confessional speech of his youth, the crisis that propelled him to write this public confessional document.[28] Significantly, he prefaces his vague words about the circumstances of the sin itself with the same quotation from Paul's letter he had used to introduce the vision of the elegant speaker, "I do not know, but God knows" ("*nescio, Deus scit*"), as if he were introducing another dream or were already in the realm of vision. In fact, the problematic episodes of his sin, his confession of it, and the improper and damaging dissemination of this information by his confessor-confidant take the form of yet another vision, once again featuring the interplay of spoken and written:

> And so, [after] the day that I was condemned by those I have already recalled and spoken of above, that night I saw in a vision of the night that there was honor-depriving writing [? *scriptum . . . sine honore*] against my face; meanwhile, I heard a divine message [*responsum*] saying to me: "With disappointment we have seen the face of the one [so] designated, with his name despoiled." It did not say, "With disappointment you saw," but "With disappointment we saw," as if to ally itself with him [that is, the person designated], as it says [in Scripture]: "He who touches you, it is as if he touches the pupil of my eye" [Zech. 2:8].[29]

As in his mystical encounter with Victoricus, a written message is delivered to a passive Patrick, and the significance of a text is announced by an accompanying voice, but there is nothing infinite about this message. It functions instead as an inscription or circumscription that "designates" disgrace, weighing as heavily on the dream face as does the stone on Patrick in the "Elijah" vision. Balancing out this nightmarish rendition of the theme of person as letter is the heard, totally comprehensible voice, an overwhelming "presence," even though it may simply be reading the inscription aloud. Although this voice seemingly subordinates itself to the writing by referring to the *scriptum*'s function of "designation," it comes into conflict with the writing by expressing sympathy for the person it condemns. The voice is clearly consonant with

28. In the Book of Armagh *Confessio* this vexing section is omitted (cc. 26–29, ibid., 98–102), the text resuming in c. 29 at *uidi in uisu noctis* ("I saw in a vision of the night"—see below). 29. Igitur in illo die quo reprobatus sum a memoratis supradictis ad noctem illam uidi in uisu noctis scriptum erat contra faciem meam sine honore et inter haec audiui responsum diuinum dicentem mihi: Male uidimus faciem designati, nudato nomine, nec sic praedixit: Male uidisti, sed: Male uidimus, quasi sibi se iunxisset, sicut dixit: *Qui uos tangit quasi qui tangit pupillam oculi mei* (c. 29, ibid., 102). On the connotation of the phrase *sine honore*, see Ó Raifeartaigh 1983/84, 29.

those of Patrick's other dreams, which are beyond reference to writing or even human speech. Thus the favorable spoken word of the vision opens up the constrictingly inscribed situation. In this capacity, the divine voice resembles the inspired voice of Patrick himself, which in the "Elijah" vision brings about the removal of the rock oppressing him.

Our understanding of this dream remains vexed. Whose face does Patrick see, with the inscription attached to it? At the beginning of the passage, he seems to be referring to his own. In that case, does not the writing indict him and strip him of authority? For if the face is Patrick's, then his fears that in writing out his confession he would expose himself to the ridicule of the learned have already been realized in this pejorative written designation. Yet Patrick analyzes the accompanying utterance as supportive of him. The seeming treachery of speech, speakers, and hearers which brought Patrick to this impasse in the first place is here balanced by the faithfulness expressed in the dream utterance, which proves treacherous not to Patrick but to the writing it objectively affirms but subjectively undermines. Nevertheless, the dream and Patrick's recounting of it hardly vindicate him.

Shortly after this dream narration, however, Patrick shifts the issue of culpability onto the figure of his accuser and perhaps even implies that the face he saw condemned with writing in his vision was that of his enemy, who would, for the purposes of Patrick's defense, make a more appropriate object for such opprobrium: "But I am more worried about my beloved friend, that we were allowed to hear such a message [*responsum*] about him."[30] Once the focus shifts to his accuser or, to put it differently, once Patrick's face is replaced with the face of the other, then the *responsum*, friendly when the face was still Patrick's, becomes troubling to hear.

Clearly then, the ambiguity of the face, the signified, reflects on the potential ambiguities of its signifiers, the written and spoken commentaries. In the context of this vision, however, Patrick manipulates the ambiguities of speech in his defense. When the *designatus* is Patrick, the utterance tilts toward him; when it is his accuser, the utterance tilts against *him*. This apparently intentional confusion in Patrick's discussion of his dream is by no means uncharacteristic of the *Confessio*, which often features what I call conspicuous displacement, a strategy for recapturing authority, which Patrick puts to good use in his project of self-vindication. We have already seen examples of this strategy in the synecdoche at work in Patrick's encounters with the authorizing voice. An incomprehensible totality of messages is displaced and replaced by a comprehensible part, *a* message, that adequately represents the totality and even the writer/speaker. Another key instance of displacement is the topical framework of the *Confessio*, that is, Patrick as the unlearned preacher,

30. Sed magis doleo pro amicissimo meo cur hoc meruimus audire tale responsum (c. 32, Hanson and Blanc 1978, 104).

wary of an alien and hostile medium but forced to exchange his "language" for the language of writing and in the process transforming this literary medium into something unique.

Let us recall, moreover, that Patrick enters the fray in order to prevent wrongful displacement from his God-given vocation. His life, as he presents it, is already a sequence of displacements, albeit of a sooner-or-later providential kind, first from his home in Britain to Ireland, and then from the comfort of that regained home to God's work back in Ireland. Displacement is amply evident, as well, in the visions that are the centerpieces of the *Confessio*. The voice that comes through Patrick and the writing that gives way to speech are prime examples. It is, Patrick says in the *Confessio*, precisely because he, the obedient recipient of God's word, is profoundly displaced and his voice is replaced, that he has authority to command the respect of his fellow Christians. This authority, however, based on the immediacy of speech, only barely fits within the confines of conventional writing.

The "Real" and the Legendary Patrick

However much the feisty author of the *Confessio* has to say about the relationship between speech and text, what he says tells us little, if anything, about the attitude of the fifth-century Christian missionaries toward the native oral tradition in Ireland. Still, the recurring themes central to the *Confessio* are, as we shall see in the next chapter, central as well to early Patrician hagiography and even to the self-authorizing procedures of medieval Irish literature in general. These themes include uneasiness with the written word as a repository of authorizing truth and a closer identification with speech; a perceived difference between the writing/reading and speaking/hearing of a message; a metonymic process of elimination which grants a modicum of control over the inexpressible; the advantages and disadvantages of displacement/replacement, and the obtaining of authority by means of being displaced/replaced.

In its focus on the *personal* struggle of Patrick to communicate his authority in writing and to translate the inexpressible or the numinously spoken into a public and written expression of authority, the *Confessio* may well have inspired the attempts of Patrick's early biographers to present the saint's career as a paradigm of the process whereby a pagan, preliterary, and (to the Christian world) unknown Ireland received "articulation" as a Christian nation.[31]

Comparing the *Confessio* with these accounts of his life, we find the saint's internal conflict projected onto a cultural scale or aligned with a cultural

31. Perhaps the most ambitious, albeit on occasion oversimplifying, study of the figure of Patrick as "culture hero" and of the Patrician legends as reflective of cultural clash and transition is Stefan Czarnowski's book *Le culte des héros et ses conditions sociales: Saint Patrick, héros national de l'Irlande* (1919).

tension comparable to Patrick's anxieties about his authority. The Patrick of these early lives (and later ones as well) propagates not only the Christian faith but also the written word, which transmits his authority and can even function as a weapon in the war against the pagan faith. His confidence in writing's ability to represent authority notwithstanding, Patrick is also a powerful speaker, whose utterances constitute more than mere readings of powerful texts and actually resist textuality.

2/ the return of the non-native: patrick's mission to ireland

Seventh-Century Lives of Patrick

*t*he Patrician anthology in the Book of Armagh contains, in addition to Patrick's own writings and a few other hagiographic items, the earliest surviving literary lives of the saint, namely, those of the seventh-century clerics Muirchú and Tírechán. Although we encounter much in the later accounts of Patrick's life which is not to be found in the Book of Armagh texts, the vast literary and oral legendary tradition centered on this saint already reveals its essential character in these two pioneering efforts. Muirchú's Life, which survives in sources other than the Book of Armagh, is structured as a biography, and even in the somewhat truncated form presented in the Book of Armagh, the text strikes the modern reader as much better crafted than its hagiographic companion piece. Tírechán's Life, which has survived only in the Book of Armagh, resembles more an itinerary than a life and lacks the authorial statement of intention characteristic of typical hagiography. The chronological and textual relationship between these two earliest Patrician lives remains unclear.[1]

Muirchú's prologue, in which he dedicates, justifies, and grounds his com-

---

1. More information on the texts is available in Bieler 1979, 1–43, from which I quote Muirchú's and Tírechán's lives. The translations, while my own, have been guided by Bieler's. Richard Sharpe (1988b) issues a salutary caution about some aspects of Bieler's presentation of the Patrician materials from the Book of Armagh.

   Most scholars consider Tírechán's composition too sketchy, incomplete, and downright "unbiographical" compared to other Irish hagiographic compositions to warrant the generic designation "life." See Swift 1994, 53–54, esp. n. 4. I use the term primarily for convenience but also as a reminder that Tírechán's text deserves to be taken as seriously as Muirchú's seemingly neater work.

position, is emblematic of the text to follow. Here and throughout, literary procedures are suffused with authorial reflection on how to apply those procedures to "new" material, that is, the data on Patrick available to Muirchú. The fledgling hagiographer uses various commonplaces available to an Irish writer of the seventh century and even resorts to apparent puns.[2] It is hard to resist the conclusion that in describing himself as a man out to sea, Muirchú is playfully alluding to his own name, which means "Sea Dog."[3] He also employs the standard modesty *topos* that Patrick had expanded beyond its topical limits in his own work. Once again, we encounter a putatively inexperienced author professing his inferiority to the many authorities who could far better express what the writer is about to say, though they have so far been unable to do so:

> For, my lord Áed [the bishop to whom Muirchú dedicates the Life, and by whom it may have been commissioned], certainly many have tried to draw up this story according to what their fathers and those who spread the word from the start [of Patrick's mission] have passed on to them. Yet, given the great difficulty involved in the work of putting together this story, as well as the diversity of opinions and the great number of uncertainties expressed by so many, they [the would-be biographers] have never arrived at a single fixed way of telling what happened. Therefore, I am not mistaken in that, as our people say, like boys who are brought into the amphitheater [for the first time], I have launched my childish rowboat of minimal abilities onto this most dangerous and profound sea of sacred story, with its boldly surging mounds of raging water amidst the most violent whirlpools lurking in unknown waters, tested and mastered by no vessel except one, that of my father Cogitosus. Lest, however, I be seen as making much out of little, I will proceed, with difficulty, to relate one at a time these few deeds of the many [performed by] Saint Patrick, [albeit] with [only] scant tradition, unreliable sources, a fading memory, a debilitated intelligence, and a vile style—but with a most reverent feeling of love, obeying the command of your sanctity and authority.[4]

2. Ludwig Bieler (1979, 193) describes some of these commonplaces (see also Howlett 1995, 250–53).

3. As noted in Mac Airt 1958, 72; Doherty 1991, 83. The medieval Irish love of such wordplay, especially Latin references to Irish names, is the subject of Herren 1976.

4. Quoniam quidem, mi domine Aido, multi conati sunt ordinare narrationem utique istam secundum quod patres eorum et qui ministri ab initio fuerunt sermonis tradiderunt illis, sed propter difficilimum narrationis opus diuersasque opiniones et plurimorum plurimas suspiciones numquam ad unum certumque historiae tramitem peruenierunt: ideo, ni fallor, iuxta hoc nostrorum prouerbium, ut deducuntur pueri in ambiteathrum in hoc periculossum et profundum narrationis sanctae pylagus turgentibus proterue gurgitum aggeribus inter acutissimos carubdes per ignota aequora insitos a nullis adhuc lintribus excepto tantum uno patris mei Coguitosi expertum atque occupatum ingenioli mei puerilem remi cymbam deduxi. Sed ne magnum de paruo uidear finguere, pauca haec de multis sancti Patricii gestis parua peritia, incertis auctoribus, memoria labili, attrito sensu, uili sermone, sed affectu píssimo caritatis

Muirchú's stylized anxiety, however, is less centered than Patrick's on the conventions to which he has subjected himself in the act of taking up a pen. Indeed, there are precious few literary models with which to compare what Muirchú is about to write. Cogitosus's Life of Brigit, also of the seventh century, is the only one he acknowledges. What Muirchú fears is the *innovation* of what he is doing, that is, collecting all the lore about Patrick circulating in oral tradition and putting it into a textual form for the first time.[5] This fear of innovation is ambiguously expressed in the prologue, and it is likely that the ambiguity is intentional. Is Muirchú concerned that what he presents is an impoverished fragment compared with the wealth of oral tradition, the product of "fading memory"? And that, compared with the authority of the *auctores* of written, Latin tradition, his own (oral) authorities or sources are "unreliable," in need of reinforcement from the authority of his dedicatee? Or perhaps the upsetting innovation is not the attempt to enclose the spoken textually but Muirchú's reliance (in the absence of a body of previously written literature) on oral tradition, perceived as rife with contradiction, shifting memory, and uncertain authority.

In Muirchú's statement of his intent and capacity as a writer, we confront dramatically contrasting views of the oral tradition and its relation to literature. Oral transmission preserves a vast, venerable "sea" of knowledge (to use Muirchú's metaphor), which flows from and through "those who spread the word from the start" and to which injustice is inevitably done by the condensation inherent in the act of writing.[6] Or, also according to the author,

---

sanctitatis tuae et auctoritatis imperio oboedens carptim grauatimque explicare aggrediar (Bieler 1979, 62.1–15).

As Bieler has pointed out (ibid., 62, note on lines 1–3), Muirchú's opening words evoke the beginning of Luke's Gospel (1:1–2), which similarly refers to the authority of those who saw, heard, or spoke of the subject of his account *ab initio*.

5. In a later passage, where Muirchú switches to a different strategy of presentation, he implies that what he is writing has been written before, at least piecemeal, and that the literary and oral "versions" of Patrician biography are compatible or *being made* compatible in his composition: "After so many miracles, which are written down elsewhere and which the world recounts faithfully" (Post uero miracula tanta, quae alibi scripta sunt et quae ore fideli mundus celebrat [2.4, Bieler 1979, 116.8–9]). Another reference to writings about Patrick's miracles can be found at 1.28.1, ibid., 100.25.

6. On the literary pedigree of Muirchú's trope ("subject" and "composition" as "sea" and "[little] boat," respectively), see Winterbottom 1976. Conceivably, Muirchú's usage is akin to the rhetoric of papal sermons. As Thomas Charles-Edwards notes, Leo the Great (fifth century) and Gregory the Great (ca. 600) employ the sea as a symbol of potential cultural resistance to the spread of Christianity, which missionary zeal transforms into a means for the even wider dissemination of the faith (1993, 11–12). Also part of the pedigree of the sea trope is a long-lived Indo-European mythological element, apparent, for example, in the Greek traditions concerning Nereus, the Old Man of the Sea, who, because he remembers all, is a "master of truth" (see Detienne 1967, 29–50). Similarly, in Irish tradition the inspiration for memorial, memorable, "truthful" utterance comes to poets from the watery deep. See P. Ford 1974. Ford notes also that Irish tradition makes it clear that knowledge and memory can turn against

spoken testimony is a virtually unchartable and impassable body over which to row the boat of authorial aspiration, which is best kept on its own literary waters.

Most likely, the ambiguity in this passage is at least in part a function of the author's probing the relationship between the oral tradition, carried on in Irish, and literature, written in Latin. Our impression of ambivalence and the suspicion that it is infused with the tensions between spoken and written language are reinforced by Muirchú's casting himself or his project in terms of a genre he locates in the native oral tradition of his day: "As our people say" ("iuxta hoc nostrorum prouerbium"). The proverbial image itself, boys being introduced into a public assembly presumably as fledgling orators, reiterates the issue of oral performance, whose power Muirchú is attempting to channel into his work.

Whatever the depth of Muirchú's understanding of his literary use of non-literary sources and of the complexities involved in writing down an oral tradition, the authorial strategy delineated in the prologue relies on a procedure familiar to us from the *Confessio* and typical of hagiography in general. The author of this life will not, cannot, record all that Patrick did, only a portion: "Lest, however, I be seen as making much out of little, I will proceed, with difficulty, to relate one at a time these few deeds of the many [performed by] Saint Patrick." Muirchú by his own admission presents a mere part of a still-unrecorded whole not only because a novice hagiographer is unable to comprehend it all but also because there is too much there for any human being to encompass and communicate totally.[7]

The "small" contribution of Muirchú to the saint's posterity is paralleled by the "scant tradition" (*parua peritia*) he mentions in the same sentence. *Peritia*, which in other texts is used synonymously with Irish *senchas*, means in the

would-be-possessors, as perhaps does Muirchú's account of the aftermath of Patrick's death, in which the armies of those trying to claim Patrick's corpse and thereby direct or even misdirect the "destined" course of Patrician posterity and tradition are driven back by an inlet turned into a raging sea (2.13.2, Bieler 1979, 120, and see 212, note on c.13). Compare the rising of rivers in the Middle Irish *Táin Bó Cúailnge* (C. O'Rahilly 1976b, lines 198–201, 1000–1026, 1158–64), and the fight between Achilles and the river Skamandros in Book 21 of the *Iliad*.

7. Ernst Curtius describes the popularity in early Western hagiography of the *topos* of *recusatio*, the profession of unwillingness to describe something characterized as indescribable or to enumerate what is supposedly innumerable (1953, 160). John 21:25 is an outstanding biblical precedent. There are several examples to be found in Irish tradition. Of the Westmeath saint Colmán mac Lúacháin (ca. 600), his twelfth-century biographer says: Ní coimsidh nech dechmad an neich dorigne-sim do aisneis acht mane tísad a aingel comaidechta nó spiratt a anma fèin ana churp doridhisi dia falsiugud, "No one can relate a tithe of what he did unless his guardian-angel should come or the spirit of his own soul should come back again into his body to make it known" (Meyer, trans., 1911a, 104, 105).

Latin of Irish writers both "tradition" and "knowledge of the tradition."[8] By implication, the "much" compared to which, or of which, Muirchú's work contains only "little" is all of *peritia*, which, according to Muirchú, has yet to be written down if it ever will be. Once again the author is measuring his literary product against the record of the spoken word and finding it relatively incomplete, although by no means necessarily inferior because of that incompleteness. The authorial hope is that textual limitation is in fact "economical" and even allows for a kind of literary control over materials that threaten to defeat or even overrun the mode of literature.

Muirchú's vessel does not venture out onto the unexplored territory of Patrician lore unmanned. At the helm is the author, who follows in the wake of the only extant Irish saint's life that verifiably antedates Muirchú's, namely, the Life of Brigit, whose author, Cogitosus, is honored with the designation "my father." In professing so vividly to be going out of bounds, displacing himself in order to fill a daunting gap, Muirchú elaborates on his framing metonymy. He has broken ahead of those who have tried to tell this story into a virtual no-man's-land where he doggedly follows the track of an isolated hagiographic explorer and father figure. Muirchú's own authority as a writer must live up to the challenges set by the aborted fragments of attempted lives of Patrick he has left behind, by Cogitosus's successful life of another saint, *and* by what lies underneath the project, the comparatively shifting currents of Patrician legend, which operates by rules radically different from those that obtain above its ever-changing surface.

Receiving the Call

The loneliness of his literary mission and the danger of deriving his authority from sources and media that exist in what is at best an uneasy harmony are paralleled in the picture Muirchú presents of Patrick's "literate" mission. After his miraculous rescue from captivity, Patrick undertakes years of study on the Continent, to which he had been called by his angel Victoricus, a far more ubiquitous and "vocal" personality than the mysterious Victoricus of the *Confessio*. Finally Patrick receives a summons to return to Ireland. It comes in a vision in which Victoricus himself declares to Patrick what in the *Confessio* is cued in with a letter and spoken by the Irish themselves in absentia: "The sons and daughters of the Forest of Foclut call to you."[9]

This direct oral communication, we should note, is addressed to a Patrick who has, Muirchú tells us, just finished an impressive thirty to forty years of text-based spiritual training with the learned Germanus of Auxerre.[10] This

8. See F. Byrne 1974, 138–39.
9. Vocant te filii et filiae siluae Foclitae (1.7, Bieler 1979, 72.5–6).
10. 1.6–7, ibid., 70.17–72.1.

seasoned monastic scholar is hardly the Patrick of the *Confessio*, who dwells on his lack of education and for whom every vision presents an internal crisis centered on his feelings of inadequacy as a learned, literate communicator. In Muirchú's account Patrick is almost being "held captive" in the continental realm of letters. The voice of the angel and the voices of Irish men and women to which the angel refers nudge him back into the arena of the now alien spoken word, which Patrick will come to dominate with the power of his text-based authority.

Yet before Patrick can set out for Ireland, a predecessor, it turns out, must be accounted for. Pope Celestine, Muirchú tells us, had already sent the archdeacon Palladius to convert the Irish. Having endured the arduous voyage, this first representative of Christianity in Ireland found a nation hostile to his message and left for Britain. It is only after he receives news of Palladius's death that Patrick is installed as bishop and heads out on his own voyage with a crew of fellow proselytizers.[11]

Patrick's epochal trip over the waters in the wake of an earlier attempt invites comparison with Muirchú's metaphorical formulation of his own voyage. The Life is itself, as we have seen, a crossing of sorts, from oral source to written document, in a rowboat no less. The gulf between these media, as the Life proceeds to show, is part of an even larger expanse between Christian and pagan, over which Patrick now travels in the narrative. In either case, to reach the other side of the "waters" means to lay claim and assert authority, in effect to invade hostile territory, although the invasion evolves into what is better described as an insinuating appropriation.

The two voyages, one literal and the other literary, are informed by some crucial attitudinal contrasts between Muirchú the native writer and the Patrick of hagiographic legend. The ominous precedent looming before the seaborne Patrick is not at all the shining example of success Cogitosus offers to Muirchú. Indeed, the figure of Palladius more closely resembles those who have tried but failed to accomplish what Muirchú now sets out to do. Furthermore, Muirchú, a Christian in a Christian country and a member of the universal church, all by virtue of Patrick's unprecedented triumph, always has *some* kind of literary precedent and community to fall back on, as well as an audience to address. Yet the hagiographer presents his own voyage as far more liable to disaster than Patrick's, which, he says, proceeded without any delay.

There is perhaps more to this difference than Muirchú's modesty and Patrick's overwhelming authority. For after all, Patrick crosses what Muirchú describes as *mare nostrum*, his, Muirchú's, and his audience's "sea." As one who has essentially become a stranger in Ireland, his years of captivity notwithstanding, the traveling Patrick of legend challenges an alien culture. Ahead lies a confrontation in which values and attitudes will tend to polarize.

11. 1.9.4, ibid., 74.9–12.

Muirchú, on the other hand, a Christian Irishman attempting to write what is supposedly only the second life ever written of an Irish saint, is trying to reconcile disparate cultures that, though they have drawn closer together by the seventh century, are still pointedly distinguishable, at least in literary contexts such as saints' lives. It is no wonder, then, that "Irish" waters prove rougher to cross for Muirchú than for Patrick and that the hagiographer makes a far more anxious seaman than his legendary subject. Once Patrick has crossed the ocean, however, his difficulties increase, and the deeper into Ireland he penetrates, the more closely they resemble those of his biographer.

The Pagan Yet Prescient Irish

Leaving Patrick en route on the Irish Sea, Muirchú shifts the focus of his story to Ireland, where certain of the Irish were raising a magical outcry against Patrick and what he would bring. These spoken words stand in contrast to the invitation mystically uttered by the children of the Wood of Foclut and delivered to Patrick by Victoricus:

In those days, when these events took place in the aforesaid region [Ireland], there was a certain great king, ferociously pagan, an emperor of barbarians reigning in Tara, which was then the capital of the kingdom of the Irish, by the name of Lóegaire, son of Niall, the founder of the royal dynasty [that reigned over] almost [all of] this island. This Lóegaire, moreover, had [in his court] seers and druids, fortune-tellers and magicians, and devisers of all manner of wicked art, who were able to know and foresee everything before it happened, by means of the technique[s] of paganism and idolatry. Two of these were preferred over the others, and their names were Lothroch, or Lochru, and Lucet Mael, or Ronal. Utilizing their magic art, these two would frequently prophesy of a certain alien practice in the future, like a kingdom with an unfamiliar, troublesome doctrine that would be brought over the seas from far away, dictated by the few but accepted by the many, to be honored by all, that would subvert kingdoms, kill resistant kings, seduce the masses, destroy all their gods, and with all the accomplishments of their art rejected, would reign forever. They also foretold of the one who would bring and urge this practice and prophesied in words like a little poem, often spoken by them, primarily in the two or three years preceding the arrival of Patrick. These are the words of the little poem, not very clear on account of the idiom of the language:

Adze-head will come, the end of his staff bent,
from his house, with a perforated head, he will chant abomination,
from his table, in the front of his house,
all of his household will respond to him, "So be it, so be it."

Which can be expressed more clearly in our words: "When all these things will come to pass, our kingdom, which is pagan, will not survive." Which did happen thus, afterwards, for with the overturning of the cults of idols after the coming of Patrick, the universal faith in Christ filled all among us. But enough of these matters; let us return to our topic.[12]

Thus, the voices of Ireland are clearly in conflict. The youth of the land, Patrick's angel reports, clamor in their untrained vigor for the new order, the religious culture and language he will disseminate, but the professional communicators learned in traditional knowledge raise their voices in visionary warning and studied mockery of Patrick's "chanted" words and the responses they elicit. Clearly, these men of "all manner of wicked art," particularly the *magi* 'druids' sense the imminent threat of a rival, whose voice may well drown out their own.

That the threat cannot be limited to any one cultural sphere is clearly indicated by what the druids say. Patrick's revolution, they unambiguously predict, will be *political* as well as religious and cultural. Kingdoms and their kings are in as much danger as the druids and other men of knowledge and communicative power who serve them. Reflected here is a keen awareness of the interplay of religion and politics, on the part of Muirchú and the Irish Christian community whose views he represents.

Underlying this interplay of "church" and "state" is the fundamental affinity, at least in theory, between the voice of political authority and the voice of religious authority, an affinity maintained as a basic social and cultural principle in Ireland both before and after the coming of Christianity. During the gradual conversion of Ireland in the fifth and following centuries, the Christian cleric displaced and to a significant extent replaced the professional pagan

12. In illis autem diebus quibus haec gesta sunt in praedictis regionibus fuit rex quidam magnus ferox gentilisque, imperator barbarorum regnans in Temoria, quae [tunc] erat caput [regni] Scotorum, Loiguire nomine filius Neill, origo stirpis regiae huius pene insolae. Hic autem sciuos et magos et aurispices et incantatores et omnis malae artis inuentores habuerat, qui poterant omnia scire et prouidere ex more gentilitatis et idolatriae antequam essent; e quibus duo prae caeteris praeferebantur, quorum nomina haec sunt: Lothroch qui est Lochru, et Lucetmael qui et Ronal, et hii duo ex sua arte magica crebrius profetabant morem quendam exterum futurum in modum regni cum ignota quadam doctrina molesta longinquo trans maria aduectum, a paucis dictatum, a multis susceptum, ab omnibus honorandum, regna subuersurum, resistentes reges occissurum, turbas seducturum, omnes eorum deos distructurum, et iectis omnibus illorum artis operibus in saecula regnaturum. Portantem quoque suadentemque hunc morem signauerunt et profetauerunt hiis uerbis quasi in modum uericuli [leg. uersiculi] crebro ab hiisdem dictis, maxime in antecedentibus aduentum Patricii duobus aut tribus annis. Haec autem sunt uersiculi uerba, propter linguae idioma non tam manifesta: "Adueniet ascicaput cum suo ligno curuicapite, / ex sua domu capite perforata incantabit nefas / a sua mensa ex anteriore parte domus suae, / respondebit ei sua familia tota 'fiat, fiat'." Quod nostris uerbis potest manifestius expraemi. "Quando ergo haec omnia fiant, regnum nostrum, quod est gentile, non stabit." Quod sic postea euenerat; euersis enim in aduentu Patricii idulorum culturis fides Christi catholica nostra repleuit omnia. De his ista sufficiant; redeamus ad propossitum (1.10, ibid., 74.13).

communicators whom Muirchú places in the king's court, even encroached on the king's own functions.[13] As we shall see, in later accounts the confrontation between conflicting voices of authority, between Patrick, the advocate of a text-based culture, and Lóegaire with his court of professional speakers, is transformed into a struggle for the very essence of social organization. It is fought between the principles of oral performance and those of textual preservation. In the end, Patrick prevails on the Irish to write down their laws, to translate social structure into a written form instead of leaving it in the memories and in the control of the bearers of oral tradition.

The poem of Lóegaire's magi, the initial salvo in a power struggle that will operate on several levels between Patrick and the pagan society toward which he is sailing, can be construed as both a traditional satire assailing a sighted enemy and a grudging admission of defeat before battle is even joined. These dual aspects of the *versiculus* are not necessarily incompatible. Satire as traditionally practiced in medieval Ireland can damage only insofar as it proclaims the embarrassing truth, which, when publicized, can discomfit the satirist as well as his intended victim. Almost despite itself, even the hostile professional pagan voice acknowledges the inevitability of the new epoch, as much as do the friendly voices of the youth of Ireland. The poem in fact even establishes a basis for rapprochement between the oral tradition as represented by Lóegaire's druids and the learned Christian tradition borne by Patrick, for the poem and the vision it communicates are in effect a rather accurate and witty translation into pagan terms of the Christian milieu. What is approaching, in other words, is not totally unknown or unknowable in native terms. Translation, albeit fragmentary, is possible. Furthermore, in Muirchú's present the poem can be translated from the original Irish into Latin, with which, in this case, the hagiographer identifies (*nostris verbis* 'our words').[14] The translator admits to the difficulties of translation and appreciation: "These are the words of the little poem, not very clear on account of the idiom of the language." Nevertheless, the translation is presented, the poem is paraphrased, and its gist is declared to be fatefully accurate. A possible communication link between pagan and Christian, and between Irish oral tradition and literature in

13. This point was made by the historian Wendy Davies (1982, 91).
14. An Irish version of this poem (with a continuation) is included in the earliest extant Irish Life of Patrick (Mulchrone 1939, lines 338–50). The bent staff is clearly the bishop's crozier. As for the "adze-head," Francis Byrne proposes the bishop's mitre as the referent instead of a style of tonsure, which is usually how it is interpreted, and, for the house with the perforated head or top, the priest's chasuble (F. Byrne and Francis 1994, 92–93).

Muirchú's opinion about the viability of translation can be compared with those to be found in a colophon in the Book of Armagh (Bieler 1979, 178.12–17) and in the Anglo-Saxon monk Bede's comments on the difficulties of translating an Old English poem into Latin in his Ecclesiastical History, 4.24 (eighth century). Arguably the contrast between the language of the poem (already rendered into Latin in the text) and the *nostra uerba* by which Muirchú seeks to render the poem clearer may be more a matter of "poetic language" versus "prose" than "Irish" versus "Latin."

Latin, is thus unearthed from the past and reestablished in the present of Muirchú's composition.

Significantly, this near breakthrough of the vernacular voice into the Life occurs not in the perfunctorily handled episode of Patrick's call to his vocation but in a scene featuring traditional performers and performance. While the *Confessio* was most likely a direct or corroborative source for the story of Patrick and the voices as told by Muirchú, an account in which the language of the visionary summons is not an issue, the story of the druids' prediction of the coming of Christianity was probably a living tale in the oral tradition of Muirchú's time. Here, then, is a passage where the metaphorical sea of unwritten legendry threatens to swamp the author's fragile craft, but where Muirchú's control over his materials, that is, his literary authority, becomes impressively evident. Without expressing any untoward sympathy toward the druids and the other pagan knowers and performers in Lóegaire's court, he manages to display the native wit with some modest pride and to demonstrate that it is translatable into the language of Christianity. Still, the freedom to translate without stripping the original of its unique authority perhaps vaguely alarms Muirchú and his audience, for he ends this section abruptly: "But enough of these matters; let us return to our topic."

Trying to Convert One's Master

Patrick in time responds to the challenge already laid down by Lóegaire's druids, but first, upon reaching Ireland, he sets out to settle what appears to be a private score:

It seemed to Patrick that nothing would be more perfect than to ransom himself first. So he headed north toward that pagan Miliucc, in whose household he had once been help captive, bringing him a twin ransom, terrestrial and celestial, so that Patrick might liberate [the soul of] the man whom he himself had previously served as a captive. . . . Patrick and his companions disembarked at Inber Sláine, hid their little ship, and went inland in search of a place to rest. The swineherd of a certain Díchu, good by nature albeit a pagan, who was living in the place that is now called Patrick's Barn, came upon them. Assuming that they were robbers or brigands, the swineherd left, told his master Díchu, and led him to the unsuspecting [intruders]. Díchu was planning in his heart to slay them, but when he saw the face of Saint Patrick, the Lord turned Díchu's thoughts to the good. Patrick preached the faith to him, and then and there Díchu believed in Patrick before everyone else. The saint rested at Díchu's house for a few days. But Patrick wished to go quickly so that he might visit the aforementioned Miliucc and present him with his ransom payment, as well as convert him to the Christian faith. So he left his ship with Díchu and journeyed through the territory of the Cruithni until he reached Slíab Mis. It was from this mountain that long ago, when he was there as a captive slave, Patrick had seen the angel Victoricus easily ascend into the sky, having left the imprint of his foot on the rock of the other [nearby] mountain.

Miliucc, hearing that his erstwhile servant was coming to visit him so as seemingly to impose upon him at the end of his life a practice that he did not wish to accept, surrendered himself willingly to fire at the devil's urging, lest he be made subject to his servant and the servant become Miliucc's master. He was immolated in the house where he had been residing as king, along with all of his gathered stock of possessions. Saint Patrick, on the other hand, standing in the aforesaid place on the right slope of Slíab Mis, where he, arriving full of grace, had his first view of the region where he had once served (a place where a cross still stands as a sign of his first view of that region), straightaway saw the burning funeral pyre of the king before his eyes.

Stupefied by the deed, Patrick was speechless for well-nigh two hours or three, sighing, groaning, and weeping, and then he uttered these words: "I do not know, but God knows, this king who surrendered himself to fire lest he believe at the end of his life and serve the eternal God, I do not know, but God knows, none of his descendants shall ever sit as a king upon his throne, from generation to generation, and in fact, his seed will serve [instead of being served] for all time." Having said these words, and praying and arming himself with the sign of the cross, Patrick swiftly headed back to the territory of the Ulaid, retracing the steps by which he had come, and returned to Díchu and Mag Inis, where he stayed for many days. He traversed this, his chosen and beloved plain, and the faith began to grow there.[15]

15. Ubi uissum est ei nihil perfectius esse quam ut semet ipsum primitus redemeret; et inde appetens sinistrales fines ad illum hominem gentilem Milcoin, apud quem quodam in captiuitate fuerat, portansque ei geminum seruitutis praetium, terrenum utique et caeleste, ut de captiuitate liberaret illum cui ante captiuus seruierat. . . . Et discenderunt in terram ad hostium Slain ille et qui cum eo erant in naui et absconderunt nauiculam et uenierunt aliquantulum in regionem ut requiescerent ibi, et inuenit eos porcinarius cuiusdam uiri natura boni licet gentilis, cui nomen erat Dichu, habitans ibi ubi nunc est orreum Patricii nomine cognominatum. Porcinarius autem putans eos fures aut latrones exiuit et indicauit domino suo du Dichoin et induxit illum super eos ignorantibus illis. Qui corde propossuerat occidere eos, sed uidens faciem sancti Patricii conuertit Dominus ad bonum cogitationes eius, et praedicauit Patricius fidem illi et ibi credidit Patricio prae omnibus et requiescit ibi sanctus apud illum non multis diebus. Sed uolens cito ire ut uissitaret praedictum hominem Milcoin et portaret ei praetium suum et uel sic conuerteret ad Christi fidem, relicta ibi nauis apud Dichoin coepit per terras diregere uiam in regiones Cruidnenorum donec peruenit ad montem Miss, de quo monte multo ante tempore quo ibi captiuus [erat] seruierat praeso uestigio in petra alterius montis expedito gradu uidit anguelum Victoricum in conspectu eius ascendisse in caelum.

Audiens autem Miliucc seruum suum iturum ad uissitandum eum, ut morem quem nolebat in fine uitae faceret quasi per uim, ne seruo subiectus fieret et ille sibi dominaret instinctu diabuli sponte se igni tradidit et in domu in qua prius habitauerat rex congregato ad se omni instrumento substantiae suae incensus est. Stans autem sanctus Patricius in praedicto loco a latere dextero montis Miss, ubi primum illam regionem in qua seruiuit cum tali gratia adue-

The tales of Díchu the first convert and Miliucc the obstinate heathen, which are usually coupled together in the lives of Patrick, were most likely part of the oral tradition to which Muirchú refers in his prologue.[16] This pair of episodes presents a paradigm of contrasting native responses to Christianity. Having broached the possibility of translating the druidic poem into Latin and, more generally, one culture into another, Muirchú at this pivotal juncture redoubles his efforts to frame Patrick's missionary expedition as a return voyage, the saint impelled by nostalgia and his sense of honor to revisit the home of his youth and there begin his work. Paradoxically, as this conflict of religions, cultures, and media builds in Muirchú's narrative, the representatives of the opposed sides seem to be drawing closer together. Not only can the utterance of one be translated into the language of the other, but the encounter between Christian and pagan is presentable as a reunion. The spirit of reconciliation that motivates the returning ex-slave at this point in his journey also informs the thinking of the author, who is striving, along with his audience, to come to terms with diverse forces, past and present.

To be taken into consideration are other, less altruistic factors in the saint's decision to return home: his discomfort at still being technically the slave of Miliucc and his wish to be released from bondage and so begin his mission with a "clean slate."[17] Patrick returns not only to save his master's soul but primarily to break their relationship formally and then reestablish ties with their roles reversed. Although Muirchú describes the planned conversion as a way of freeing Miliucc from the bondage of the devil, Miliucc understands that if he accepts Christianity, he will be immeasurably obligated to Patrick, becoming *his* (albeit spiritual) slave. To this legalistic attempt to appropriate control of both person and property, Miliucc responds by removing himself and his property out of Patrick's reach. The response bodes ill for the efforts

---

niens uidit, ubi nunc usque crux habetur in signum ad uissum primum illius regionis, ilico sub oculis rogum regis incensum intuitus. Stupefactus igitur ad hoc opus duabus aut tribus fere horis nullum uerbum proferens, suspirans et gemens lacrimansque atque haec uerba promens ait: "Nescio Deus scit, hic homo rex, qui se ipsum igni tradidit ne crederet in fine uitae suae et ne seruiret Deo aeterno, nescio Deus scit, nemo de filiis eius sedebit rex super sedem regni eius a generatione in generationem. Insuper et semen eius seruiet in sempiternum." Et his dictis orans et armans se signo crucis conuertit cito iter suum ad regiones Ulothorum per eadem uestigia quibus uenerat et rursum peruenit in campum Inis ad Dichoin ibique mansit diebus multis et circumiit totum campum et elegit et amauit et coepit fides crescere ibi (1.11.2–12.4, Bieler 1979, 76.22–80.20).

16. Both names, moreover, have *cú* 'dog' as their base. On *Miliucc* as a hypocorism of *Milchú* 'hunting hound', see *DIL*, s.v. *Miliuc*; and L. Breatnach 1987, 134 n. on section 19; Díchu or Dichú could be "Great Dog" or "Nondog". Although such dog names are not at all uncommon in Irish tradition, it is perhaps not coincidental that in the Tripartite Life Díchu sets his dog on the stranger, who calms it by quoting Scripture (Mulchrone 1939, lines 378–82). Patrick's meetings with nominal dogs may also foreshadow his later confrontations with "doglike" brigands, warriors, and kings, to be discussed hereafter.

17. McCone (1984b, 58–59) sees the desire to settle with Miliucc as a reflection of seventh-century ecclesiastical discomfort with the idea of slaves running away.

of both Muirchú and the growing literary community of which he is part to win a share in the authority of the oral tradition, a necessary source of knowledge and information upon which these literati are still dependent by their own admission.

The episode centering on the conversion of Díchu, Patrick's first convert, is the first attempt by missionary and pagan to understand and interpret each other's actions and motives correctly. No workable system of communication has yet been established, and the story is replete with ambiguous signs that can be "read" in more than one way or even misread. The *praetium* Patrick is bringing to Miliucc, for example, is meant to effect both the saint's total emancipation from his former owner and also Miliucc's own enslavement. Another ambiguous sign is the designation of Patrick's vessel as a *navicula* 'little ship,' an implicit reference to the even humbler *cymba* of Muirchú's prologue, reminding the reader yet again of the affinity between Patrick's mission and the literary work that frames it. Another ambiguous sign in the Díchu episode is Patrick himself. At first sight, he is taken for an invader, as to some extent he really is. But the sight of the saint's face gives Díchu the grace to interpret Patrick's arrival correctly, and he becomes a receptive host to a tired guest. Díchu himself sends out conflicting signals. He is a "good" pagan and so an object lesson in the importance of not drawing hasty conclusions.

Muirchú specifies that Díchu dwelled at the site of what was later to be known as Patrick's Barn (Saball Pátraic). This location is very important in Patrician topography, for it is, as we shall see, where the saint died, according to Muirchú and other authorities.[18] Yet as a "sign" of the saint and his death, Saball Pátraic presented an enormous problem for the Patrician ecclesiastical federation, and Armagh in particular, for if this sign were read totally and correctly according to the ideology of early Irish Christian culture, Armagh's authority would be irreparably undermined. The cult and prestige of any Irish saint were intimately associated with the ecclesiastical establishment that claimed his or her remains, which formed the basis of that establishment's authority to represent and speak or act on behalf of the saint.[19] Armagh, the chief foundation within the Patrician network of churches and monasteries, could not make this claim about Patrick, however, and never dared to try. This curious displacement of Patrick from where he should have died, as far as Armagh's and Muirchú's interests were concerned, is a problem we shall examine later. For now, it must suffice to observe that the ambiguous implications of Saball Pátraic and of Armagh itself as topical signs of Patrick's presence doubtless already loom at Patrick's arrival.

Despite all the potential for confusion and deadly misreadings, the encounter between Patrick and Díchu ends successfully for all concerned. Overcom-

18. The variant traditions concerning the site of Patrick's death and interment are set out in Sharpe 1982c, 40–44. See also Ó Raifeartaigh 1984.
19. Sharpe 1982c, 44.

ing a false start, Christian and pagan come to "understand" one another, and they enter into a mutually rewarding relationship. Salvation is granted in exchange for hospitality and, according to other, later versions of the story, land as well. The new convert transfers ownership of the site of Patrick's Barn to the saint. Furthermore, in the story as related in the Middle Irish Tripartite Life of Patrick (so called because it is divided into three sections), Díchu's welcome elicits a powerful poetic utterance of lasting authority in which Patrick declares that his spiritual gift to Díchu will extend to his descendants as well.[20]

Patrick's success with Díchu could be construed as an encouraging "dry run" for his approaching encounter with Miliucc. That Díchu is in fact the alter ego to the dark figure of Miliucc is suggested by his characterization as the employer of a swineherd (*porcinarius*), who is the initial link with the holy stranger, for although Muirchú says the slave Patrick tended sheep for Miliucc, other hagiographic sources claim that Patrick was his swineherd. The Tripartite Life self-consciously adds, however, that he *should* have been a shepherd, given his future vocation.[21]

Yet Miliucc is a "master" of a different sort from Díchu, and the climactic encounter that Patrick anticipates never happens. In the second of our pair of paradigmatic episodes, gone are the ambiguity of signs and a concomitant flexibility of interpretive attitudes and responses, a flexibility that in the previous episode made possible a breakthrough in intercultural communication. Instead, the approach of Patrick and the burning pyre are two unambiguous signs. Moreover, the possibility for subtler communication is swiftly erased. Miliucc understands Patrick's *praetium* 'ransom' for what it is, and he forestalls the impending dialogue in the most dramatic and conspicuous way possible, perhaps even a pointedly "native" way.[22] His reading of the "sign"

20. Mulchrone 1939, lines 387–94. The Tripartite Life (*Vita tripartita*), containing some Latin passages but predominantly in Irish, is the earliest surviving Life of Patrick in the vernacular. There are details in the Life that are not to be found in the surviving Latin lives. The gradual evolution of this text during the Middle Irish period has been detailed by David Dumville (Dumville et al. 1993, 255–58). See also F. Byrne and Francis 1994, 6–7.

21. Mulchrone 1939, lines 208–11. In the Tripartite Life another swineherd, Mo Chae, is converted by Patrick shortly after his encounter with Miliucc. Ibid., lines 421–27. The prominence of the figure of the swineherd (Irish *muc(c)aid*, Latin *porcinarius*) in the legends of Patrick would seem to indicate a Christian adaptation of the sacral significance attributed to swine and their guardians in pre-Christian Irish tradition (see P. Ford 1990b; Ní Chatháin 1979–80). Diego Poli highlights the functions of the mythological swineherd as a bringer or restorer of justice and as a "tracker" who can recover what has been lost or stolen (1992, 379–80)—terms certainly applicable to the legendary Patrick who "recollects" Ireland and returns to proselytize there. Like many other narrative motifs, the converted or converting (in the case of Patrick) swineherd may have been an emblem for the original medieval Irish audience of the ongoing evolution of traditional elements.

22. According to Whitley Stokes, who detects a vestige of Indo-European ritual in this episode, Miliucc's death is "more probably a case of suicide as a mode of vengeance . . . the object being that the ghost of the deceased may persecute the offender" (1890, 295n).

of Patrick's approach and his *praetium* is aided, we are told, by the devil. Thus Miliucc's prescience differs all the more dramatically from Díchu's divining of Patrick's intentions from his face, assisted, we are told, by God.

Patrick, while Miliucc is preparing his sardonic welcome, climbs a mountain and halts at a spot imbued with both personal and public significance. From Slíab Mis he sees the imprint of Victoricus's foot, which marks his past deliverance. Also to be found there today, Muirchú tells us, is a cross marking the spot where Patrick stood. The most affecting sign seen from this vantage point, however, is the blazing pyre of Miliucc, which reduces Patrick to dispirited stupefaction. After all, Miliucc's spectacular death represents an absolute rejection. Moreover, it leaves Patrick's debt unpaid and his lingering sense of subordination to his former master and all that he represents intact.[23]

In light of this spectacular failure to communicate, Patrick's stern curse on Miliucc's descendants reflects his need and that of the literary community promoting him to exorcize anxieties about their own authority. Miliucc, by opting for hell, has deprived Patrick of the power to control his spiritual destiny. Accordingly, in contrast to the spiritual blessing Patrick has just conferred on the sons of Díchu, the malediction against Miliucc's descendants specifically affects their worldly status. They will be deprived of a social position of leadership. Since the displacement of Miliucc Patrick has failed to achieve was political as well as religious in nature, this curse, the best the saint can do under the circumstances, is eminently appropriate.[24]

The starkness of the all-too-efficient signification in the story of Miliucc is indicated in Muirchú's prose itself. Having introduced the sentence in which Miliucc learns of Patrick's intent and takes action with, "audiens autem Miliucc" ("Miliucc, hearing"), the author opens the next sentence, in which Patrick enters the scene and witnesses his failure, with the parallel construction, "Stans autem sanctus Patricius" ("Saint Patrick, standing"). The one hears and acts immediately, to the extent of becoming a burning sign of his own defiance; the other sees the sign and is frozen into silence, as mute and immobile as the cross that will be erected on this spot.

Another stylistic device that functions within the language of this text to highlight the radical acts of communication taking place in the story being told is the author's rather conspicuous marking of Miliucc, a pagan sender who becomes his own message, and Patrick's already "significant" vantage point on the mountain where he receives yet another message (Miliucc's) and

23. Patrick's status as the subject or even the property of another is also evident in a different, more Christian mode. In the Middle Irish Life of Patrick from the Book of Lismore, when Victor orders him to die in Saball, as opposed to his beloved Armagh, he reminds him of his promise to Díchu (Stokes 1890, 18). Here, as in the Tripartite Life, Patrick responds by lamenting his perpetual subjugation to God's will. Mulchrone 1939, lines 2976–77.
24. On Patrick's curse as the hagiographer's comment on the political (mis)fortunes of Miliucc's people, the Bóinrige/Buanrige, see Dumville et al. 1993, 184–85.

prefigures a monumental sign to come (the cross), as *praedictus* 'aforemen-tioned'. The "aforementioning" of these polarized messengers and messages to which Muirchú alludes operates on two levels. It takes place within his narration, as Muirchú first refers to Miliucc and then to Slíab Mis. It also takes place within the narrative itself as prophecy, in the scene set in Lóegaire's court, when the king's druids warned of a fight to the death for authority. In a Middle Irish telling of Patrick's initial missionary adventures in Ireland, the druidic xenophobia that pervades Lóegaire's court and Miliucc's personal hostility toward Patrick are joined in a display of active virulence: "Neverthe-less, Miliucc came against Patrick with great hosts of pagans to prevent him from landing, for Lóegaire had enjoined the men of Ireland not to allow Patrick onto the land, for Lóegaire's druids had prophesied the coming of Patrick to Ireland."[25]

The Miliucc episode as related by Muirchú becomes all the more complex when we consider what Patrick finally says upon witnessing his old master's self-immolation. The statement consists of two sections, the first concerning Miliucc and the second his descendants, each beginning with a phrase we have heard before: "Nescio, Deus scit" ("I do not know, but God knows"). Is Muirchú's Patrick quoting from Paul's description of his visionary experience in 2 Corinthians, as is the Patrick of the *Confessio* (c. 24) when he speaks of the mysterious voice he heard in one of his nocturnal visions? The appearance of the phrase in this passage becomes all the more significant when we consid-er Muirchú's use of the visionary portions the *Confessio*. On the one hand, he incorporates into his narrative the key visions of the oppressive rock and the angel bearing a message from Ireland. On the other hand, he omits the two remaining, equally important extended mystical experiences, the sequential encounters with the spirit which Patrick introduces with this Pauline phrase. Is the crisis Patrick experiences on Slíab Mis an adaptation, perhaps to be taken in conjunction with the Díchu episode, of Patrick's encounters in the *Confessio* with a divinely authorizing voice that baffles him yet becomes his own voice? Note that upon seeing Miliucc's pyre, Patrick becomes *stupefactus* and finally gives way to sighing, crying, and moaning (*gemens*). In the *Confes-sio* passage featuring this external-internal voice, Patrick is similarly stupefied (*stupebam*), although not by what he sees but by the groans (*gemitibus*) he hears.[26] This stupefaction is clearly connected in each case with Patrick's profession of ignorance in the face of God's mysteries: "Nescio, Deus scit." Furthermore, in the sequence of the Díchu and Miliucc episodes, as well as

25. Sed tamen tanic Miliuc inaagaid cuslogu moraib dogéntib. conároléced he fothír, uair roforcongart Loegaire for firu Erenn. conaroslectis Patraic fothír, uair rothirchansatar adrúide doLoegaire tidecht Patraic docum nerenn (Stokes 1887, 2:448)—from the Middle Irish homi-letic Life of Patrick in the Lebor Brecc manuscript.

26. Et ibi fortiter orabat gemitibus, et inter haec stupebam et ammirabam et cogitabam quis esset in me orabat (c. 25, Hanson and Blanc 1978, 98).

within the Miliucc episode itself, pivotal acts of seeing and hearing or signs meant to be seen and signs meant to be heard alternate dramatically. The swineherd and his master Díchu see and then talk with Patrick. Miliucc hears of Patrick's imminence, and Patrick sees the pyre. Comparably, in the twin mystical experiences highlighted in the *Confessio* but seemingly ignored in this Life, these acts are juxtaposed: Patrick hears a voice of unknown origin, then sees a vision of his inner man (cc. 24–25).

These parallels invite a comparison between the "message" of the paired experiences of the *Confessio* and the "message" in the sequence of episodes that seemingly replace them in Muirchú's Life. In the encounters with vaguely familiar voice and vision, Patrick goes within himself and acquires a voice intelligible only in part, even to him. What he does comprehend and communicate is sufficient to establish his legitimacy as witness to God and as author. Similarly, in the episodes from Muirchú's Life in which Patrick puts this divine authorization into practice, the saint is once again encountering himself, if only in the sense of revisiting his past. I have already noted the irony underlying the scene in which Patrick, the former swineherd, meets that part of himself in a fellow *porcinarius*. Similarly, Patrick's tortuous affinity with his former master, his "outer man" who still owns him and whom Patrick wants to own in order to assert his authority, becomes all the more pronounced if we view the Patrick of early Irish hagiography as a projection of the Irish literary community's image of itself, and Miliucc as a symbol of their pre-Christian past, not altogether expunged from their present.

Is anything authoritative communicated to Patrick in the Díchu and Miliucc episodes, as there is in the "inner man" visions of the *Confessio*? After the confused initial communication between Patrick and Díchu's swineherd, the channels are opened, and Patrick's preaching wins a convert, the significant first of the many he will bring into the fold. This conversion in fact frames Patrick's entire missionary career, since it takes place at the site where, it is later revealed, he will die. In the pyre of Miliucc, by contrast, Patrick experiences an impasse, a message whose blankness is as baffling as the overwhelming fullness of the elegantly phrased utterance of the Spirit in the *Confessio*. There is, finally, nothing to say to Patrick, and no one to say it. It is Patrick himself who finally speaks, uttering a message audible to no one but himself and the audience of the story but authoritative nonetheless, a curse on what is left of Miliucc, his descendants. It is as if Muirchú or his sources had translated certain of Patrick's internal self-reflections from the *Confessio*, where the voice of authority speaks to and through the "I," into extroverted episodes of hagiography, where the saint's voice of authority is a "given" to be exercised in his relation with those who possess other kinds of authority.

Such a *Confessio*-based reading of the Miliucc episode certainly does not take away its sting. As the flames of the defiant king's pyre rage, neither the desired translation of the *praetium* from Patrick to Miliucc and authority from Miliucc to Patrick nor the concomitant transformation from slave to master and from master to slave can take place. Yet, perhaps not surprisingly, there is a variation on this story in which many of the same narrative elements are rearranged to affirm the potential for salvific communication, if not between Patrick and Miliucc, then at least between the saint and Miliucc's heirs. Tírechán in his collection of Patrician legends mentions Patrick's scaling of Slíab Mis, whence in Muirchú's account he views the crushing blow to his hopes, but not the proffered *praetium* or fiery suicide. Instead, Tírechán presents a kind of flashback:

> He ascended Slíab Mis in the territory of Bóinrige, where he had nurtured the son of Miliucc moccu Bóin, Gósacht by name, and the two daughters of the same man, when Patrick had been in slavery for seven years, and he instructed them sworn to secrecy for fear of the druid, their father. One night, however, the druid Miliucc saw flaming sparks pass from the mouth of the fool [? *fatuus*] Succet [an early name of Patrick's] into the mouth of his, Miliucc's, son, as a result of which his son's entire body was engulfed in flames, and from his mouth [the flames passed] into the mouths of his sisters. "Why," Miliucc asked Succet, "servant, did you do harm to my son last night?" Succet responded, "My lord, what did you see?" "You filled the mouth of my son with fire, and my son in turn filled the lips of my daughters, and they were all reduced to ashes. Their ashes revived many, and like birds they flew away with you and spewed out their vital parts." "They indeed spewed out their vital parts," responded Succet, "that is, their druidic home, for I put the word of my noble God in their mouths."[27]

Remarkably, the self-inflicted fire with which Miliucc expresses his control at least over himself and his possessions in the story as told by Muirchú is here transformed into a vivid expression of the authority of Patrick's word. In Tírechán's telling, to be consumed by the fire is to be reborn a new, saved being, "infected" with Christian power. Miliucc's son, Tírechán says, was actually ordained a cleric by Patrick.[28] In contrast to Muirchú's backward-

27. Ascendit autem ad montem Miss Boonrigi, quia nutriuit ibi filium Milcon maccu Buain, Gosacht nomine, et filias duas eiusdem uiri, quando erat in seruitute septem annorum, et docuit illos in taciturnitate cum iuramento pro timore magi. Sed alia nocte uidit magus Miliucc scintellas de ore Succeti fatui ignitas ascendentes in labia filii sui, et inflammatum est totum corpus filii sui, et de ore filii sui in ora sororum eius. "Cur," inquit, "o serue, malum fecisti filio meo in nocte quae praeteriit?" Respondit Succetus: "Domine mi, quid uidisti?" "Os filii mei replisti igne et filius meus labia filiarum repleuit et consumpti sunt omnes in cinerem et cinis eorum uiuificauit multos et quasi aues uolauerunt tecum et euomerunt uitalia sua frustra [frusta ?]." Respondit Succetus: "Frustra [frusta ?] uere euomerunt, id est domum magicam, quia dedi in ora eorum uerba Dei mei excelsi" (c. 49, Bieler 1979, 162.1–13; cf. Mulchrone 1939, lines 220–25; Stokes 1887, 2:392.4–17; Bieler 1971, 65–66).
28. C. 16, Bieler 1979, 136.21–23.

looking *pietas*, youthful rebellion inspirits Tírechán's tale. A slave foments revolt among his master's children, enabling them to slough off their pagan parental heritage one day. Miliucc's children bear no curse of servility and inferiority. Instead, they are the objects of Patrick's evangelical attentions and the future leaders of their people who rise above the errors of their ancestors. Although Patrick still fails to find in his former master a benevolent parent figure, he succeeds in robbing him of his role as father to his children, converts to whom Patrick has now become a spiritual father.

No doubt both narrative perspectives, the youthfully optimistic and the maturely resigned, reflect the ambivalence of these hagiographers toward their pre-Christian forbears, given even more significance in Tírechán's text in his identification of Miliucc not as a king but as a druid (*magus*).[29] In other words, Miliucc the master and father figure represents those whose supernaturally authoritative voices are to be replaced by Christian ones. Furthermore, Tírechán describes the Patrick who surreptitiously takes Miliucc's children away from him as a "fool" (*fatuus*) in the druid's household. This term may suggest in this context the other native orders of professional "knowers" and "communicators" who had far greater success than the more prestigious order of the druids in surviving in one form or another into the Christian era.[30] Conceivably, therefore, the struggle is being cast in terms not only of rival religions, social classes, and generations but also of different types of professional oral performers. The story in fact features both a conflict of wills and a test of kinds of knowledge and communication. With his druidic intuition, Miliucc divines the extraordinary activity of his *fatuus*, but the significance of his "vision" is beyond his understanding. The *fatuus* himself must explain to the druid what it means, and the meaning points to the strength of Patrick's voice and words, which have far more effect than Miliucc's, even on Miliucc's own children. In Tírechán's story, there is even a question-and-answer session by which Patrick demonstrates the superiority of his knowledge and authority over his master's. This kind of exchange is precisely what Muirchú's Patrick seeks and is chagrined to be denied.

29. See also c. 1 of Tírechán's account, Bieler 1979, 124.

30. The Irish word for fool, *drúth*, was conflated with the word for druid, *druí*, especially in later texts. *DIL*, s.v. 2 *drúth*; Harrison 1989, 29–31. Bieler in his edition of Tírechán's text proposes rendering *fatuus* as "prophet" (1979, 163, and see 232 n. on c. 49.2). Conceivably, *fatuus* could be a Latinization of Irish *fáith* 'prophet'. Williams 1979–80, 342–43, proposes a venerable pedigree for the Irish *drúth*, *óinmit* 'fool', and *crosán* 'lampooner' which places them surprisingly close to the much more distinguished figure of the *fili* 'poet' among the ranks of possessors of knowledge. See also Williams 1983. Practitioners of what were considered lowly performing arts were often associated with pagans and brigands in medieval Irish literature (McCone 1990, 220–32) and links may be found between the church and at least certain kinds of jesters and rhymesters. It is suggestive, for instance, that the term *crosán*, by which a class of lowly poets was designated, may well derive from *cros*, the Irish borrowed form of Latin *crux* (Harrison 1989, 37–39).

Yet a dialogue with a very different kind of speaker does frame Patrick's quest for recognition from the symbol of his pagan past in Muirchú's text, at least as it is arranged in some sources.[31] After we are told of Patrick's return to Díchu, his faithful first convert, and of his spreading the faith in Díchu's district, the subject of Patrick's relationship with his angel is revived:

Let our story return to what was said before. The angel [Victor] used to come to him the seventh day of every week, and Patrick would talk and enjoy dialogue with him, like one human with another. Already when Patrick was sixteen, a captive for six years, the angel came to be with him thirty times, and he enjoyed angelic consultation and dialogue before he left Ireland for the "Latins" [that is, before he escaped]. A hundred times during the day and a hundred times during the night he prayed. Once, while he was taking care of pigs, Patrick lost them, but the angel came and showed him where they were. On another occasion, the angel told him many things, and after he spoke with him, the angel put his foot upon a rock at Scirit on Slíab Mis and ascended before Patrick, and the traces of the angel's foot can still be seen on the rock. It was there that the angel spoke with Patrick thirty times, and it is a place of prayer where the prayers of the faithful obtain the most felicitous of responses.[32]

It is as if Patrick's failure to speak with Miliucc were being compensated by the excess of speech with the angel, just as in the past Victor, in finding the swine and performing various other miracles for his protégé, compensated for the difficulties and limitations Patrick suffered as a slave.[33] This pointed reference to the angel and the saint's frequent conversations with him also functions as a vindication of Patrick's divinely conferred knowledge, the "many things" that he learned from Victor, communing with him on the mountain

31. Bieler 1979, 201, note on A II 15. In the Book of Armagh the chapter detailing Patrick's relationship with his angel appears at the end of Muirchú's text.
32. Ad [pr]omissa iterum recurrat oratio. Anguelus ad eum in omni septima die septimanae semper uenire consuerat et sicut homo cum homine loquitur ita conloquio angueli fruebatur Patricius. Etiam in sexto decimo anno aetatis captus et sex annis seruiuit et per triginta uices conductionum anguelus ad eum uenerat et consiliis atque conloquiis fruebatur anguelicis antequam de Scotia ad Latinos pergeret. [Centies in die et centies in nocte orabat.] Aliquando sues custodiens perdidit eas et anguelus ueniens ad eum sues indicauit illi. Aliquando etiam anguelus illi loquens multa illi dixit et postquam illi locutus est pedem supra petram ponens in Scirit in montem Mis coram se ascendit et uestigia pedis anguelis in petra hucusque manentia cernuntur. Et in illo loco triginta uicibus ad eum et ille locus orandi locus est et ibi fidelium praeces fructum felicissimum obtinent (2.15, ibid., 80.20–82.11).
33. In some of the early lives, Victor helps Patrick to redeem himself from his pagan master by sending the boy's pigs on the track of a cache of gold. Bieler 1971, 68, 124. On the difficulties of dating these texts (the *Vita secunda*, *Vita tertia*, and *Vita quarta*, so called by the Irish hagiographer John Colgan who published them in his collection *Triadis thaumaturgae seu divorum Patricii, Columbae, et Brigidae acta* of 1647), and their relationship to the Lives written by Muirchú and Tírechán, as well as the Tripartite Life, see Bieler 1971, 1–39; and Byrne's discussion in F. Byrne and Francis 1994, 6–16.

like Moses with God. It is timely vindication, coming as it does, soon after the episode of Miliucc's disturbingly emphatic rejection of what Patrick has to offer. Similarly, Tírechán's variation, in which Patrick does succeed in manifesting his knowledge in Miliucc's household, is followed by a description of this mountain on which the angel had appeared and left his impression.[34]

The Victor of the Patrician lives is no mute letter carrier like his counterpart in the *Confessio*, and he leaves a permanent record of his presence. The footprints, revisited by a Patrick himself seeking dialogue, is still revered in the age of Muirchú and Tírechán. Here, even after Patrick's time, prayers continue to be answered, and a productive interaction between human and angel is maintained. This enduring sign of the rootedness of Christianity in Ireland stands in contrast to the spectacularly self-defeating referentiality of Miliucc's funeral pyre, which bears meaning only while it burns away all earthly traces of Miliucc.

The Saga of the Sons of Amolgaid

The transformative sign of the fire that emanates from Patrick's mouth, "burns" Miliucc's children, and eradicates their father's influence on them appears in another episode of Tírechán's Life. Notably, it is once again a story having to do with tracing authority to its source. Here, however, Patrick is led back not to the authorizing scenes of his youth but to the "voices of the Irish" that called him back to Ireland:

And he went inside the royal house, and they did not rise before him except for one man, that is, Erc, a pagan. Patrick asked him, "Why did you alone rise for me in deference to my God?" Erc told him, "I do not know why [*nescio quid*], but I saw flaming sparks ascend from your mouth into mine." The holy man asked, "Would you accept the baptism of God that I have with me?" He responded, "I would," and they proceeded to the spring called Loigles in Irish, called among us Vitulus Ciuitatum. When he had opened his book and was baptizing Erc, Patrick heard men laughing at him among themselves in light of what he had done, since they did not know what it was. He baptized several thousands of people that day.

Amidst the latter sentences of the ceremony of baptism, Patrick heard something: two noblemen chatting behind his back, and the one saying to the other, "Is it true that you said a year ago that you would come here around this time? Tell me your name, pray, and those of your father and your territory, and tell me where is your home." The other responded: "I am Énde, son of Amolgaid, son of Fiachrae, son of Echu, from the western regions of Mag Domnon and the Forest of Fochloth." When Patrick heard the name of the Forest of Foch-

34. C. 50, Bieler 1979, 162.

loth mentioned, he was overjoyed and said to Énde, son of Amolgaid, "And I will go with you, as I live and breathe, since the Lord instructed me to go [there]." Énde replied, "No, you are not coming with me, lest we both be killed." The saint, however, said, "On the contrary, you will never make it home alive unless I come with you, nor will you have eternal life, for it is on my account that you came here, like Joseph before the sons of Israel." Énde then said to Patrick, "Give my son baptism, since he is still young. I, however, and my brothers can't possibly profess our faith to you until we return to our people, for fear that we will be their laughingstock." And so Conall was baptized.

Then the six sons of Amolgaid, along with Énde and his young son who were contending with them, went before Lóegaire [the king of Ireland] for adjudication, with Patrick attending. They investigated the matter of their inheritance, and Lóegaire and Patrick decided that they should divide it among themselves into seven parts. And Énde said, "I sacrifice to the God of Patrick and to Patrick himself both my son and my inherited portion." It is for this reason, some say, that we are still servants of Patrick down to the present day.

The sons of Amolgaid and Patrick came to terms, backed by Lóegaire, son of Niall, along with the host of [their] people and [Patrick's] bishops, and set out for Slíab Aigli. Patrick, furthermore, paid in silver and gold a sum the equivalent of fifteen people, as he confirms in his writings, so as to guarantee that no bad man would impede them as they proceed directly across Ireland. For necessity compelled them to arrive at the Forest of Fochloth before the head of the year, in time for [Patrick's] second Easter [in Ireland], on account of the youths clamoring loudly, whose voices Patrick had heard from the wombs of their mothers, voices saying, "Come, holy Patrick, to save us."[35]

---

35. Et intrauit in domum regiam et non surrexerunt ante se nissi unus tantum, hoc est Hercus sacrilegus, et dixit illi: "Cur tu solus surrexisti in honorem Dei mei in me?" et dixit ei Hercus: "Nescio quid, uideo scintellas igneas de labiis tuis ascendere in labia mea." Sanctus quoque dixit: "Si babtisma Domini accipies, quod mecum est?" Respondit: "Accipiam," et uenierunt ad fontem Loigles in Scotica, nobiscum "Vitulus Ciuitatum." Cumque aperuisset librum atque babtitzasset uirum Hercum, audiuit uiros post tergum suum se inridentes ad inuicem de rei illius consideratione, quia nescierunt quid fecerat; et babtitzauit tot milia hominum in die illa.

Et inter caeteras babtismatis sententias . . . audiuit. Ecce duo namque uiri nobiles confabulabantur post tergum sibi, et dixit alter alteri: "Verum est quod dixisti a circulo anni qui praeteriit, ut ueniisses huc in illis diebus? Dic mihi nomen tuum, quaesso, et patris tui et agri tui et campi tui et ubi est domus tua." Respondit: "Endeus filius Amolngid sum ego, filii Fechrach filii Echach, ab occidentalibus plagis de campo Domnon de silua Fochloth." Cumque audiisset Patricius nomen siluae Fochlothi, gauissus est ualde et dixit Endeo Amolngid filio: "Et ego tecum exibo, si uiuus fuero, quia dixit mihi Dominus exire," et dixit Endeus: "Non exibis mecum, ne occidamur ad iuuicem." Sanctus quoque dixit: "Verumtamen numquam uiuus ad tuam regionem peruenies et tu, nissi unero tecum, et uitam aeternam non habebis, quia propter me uenisti huc quasi Ioseph ante filios Israel." Endeus autem dixit Patricio: "Tu filio meo babtismum da, quia tener est; ego autem et fratres mei non possimus tibi credere usque dum ad nostram plebem peruenerimus, ne inrideant nos." Conallus autem babtitzatus est. . . . Venierunt autem filii Amolngid sex ad iudicandum ante faciem Loiguiri, et Endeus contra eos

Since Tírechán sees Énde's action in passing his property over to Patrick as the reason why he and his audience "belong" to Patrick, it can be inferred that the hagiographer must have belonged to a church or monastery in Tír nAmolgada (the territory of the descendants of Amolgaid) which was part of the Armagh network.[36] If Tírechán is indeed speaking of the origins of his own ecclesiastical foundation, as seems likely, then his proudly declared identification with both Patrick and Énde in this episode would be all the stronger, rooted in a local as well as a religious context. The tale then would depict not only Patrick's but also Tírechán's "homecoming" and assert Patrician authority as it molds the very background of the hagiographer himself.

This account begins with incidents that set the scene for, and thus bring about, the crucial rediscovery, namely, Erc's conversion and subsequent baptism. Both are public events, but at the end of the second, a private voice breaks through when Patrick overhears the innocent bystander Énde's revealing words. The carefully executed change of narrative focus from Erc to the sons of Amolgaid encourages comparison, and what we find is a contrast very similar to that between Díchu and Miliucc in Muirchú's Life. The similarities between the two pairs of episodes, in fact, are so strong as to suggest either that they were formed from a common story pattern circulating within the oral Patrician tradition or that one is a literary reworking of the other. Erc, although "sacrilegious" and still a pagan, is nevertheless characterized as a decent man who knows enough to rise in the presence of a holy man. In the distinctly unfriendly environment of Lóegaire's court he is pointedly the first to be converted. We are thus reminded of Díchu, another good pagan who is able with the grace of God to override the swineherd's report of enemy invasion and respond favorably to Patrick's message. Of several people present at the saint's entry into the court, only Erc perceives the special, private sign (the mouth-to-mouth sparks) that binds him to the saint like a kindred spirit. Again Díchu comes to mind; he too is able to see the "sign" of Patrick's face,

---

unus et filius eius tener et Patricius ante illos, et inuestigauerunt causam hereditatis illorum, et iudicauit illis Loiguire et Patricius, ut diuiderent inter se hereditatem in septem partes. Et dixit Endeus: "Filium meum et partem hereditatis meae ego immolo Deo Patricii et Patricio." Per hoc dicunt alii quia serui sumus Patricii usque in praesentem diem. Foedus pepigerunt per manus Loiguiri filii Neill Patricius et filii Amolngid cum exercitu laicorum [et] episcoporum sanctorum et inierunt inter facere ad montem Egli, et extendit Patricius etiam praetium quindecim animarum hominum, ut in scriptione sua adfirmat, de argento et auro, ut nullus malorum hominum inpederet eos in uia recta transeuntes totam Hiberniam, quia necessitas poscit illos ut peruenirent siluam Fochliti ante caput anni pasca secunda causa filiorum clamantium clamore magno, [quorum] uoces audiuit in utero matrum suarum dicentium "Veni, sancte Patrici, saluos nos facere" (cc. 13.1–14.6, 15, Bieler 1979, 132.32–134.23, 134.29–136.6).

36. Tír nAmolgada includes modern-day Tirawley in County Mayo. On the extent of the Uí Amolgada territory, see Swift 1994, 73 n. 93. In drawing the connection between Tírechán and Tirawley, I am following Bieler 1979, 36.

and though he does not enjoy the almost physical intimacy granted Erc, his hospitality cushions the blow that Miliucc's refusal deals Patrick. Díchu, so generous, substitutes for the father figure Patrick had wished his former master would become.

In some respects, however, Erc is also reminiscent of Tírechán's Miliucc. Both witness the miracle of the fire issuing from Patrick's mouth, and both engage in dialogue with Patrick which produces an explanation for the freakish phenomenon. Intriguingly, when Patrick asks how he knew he should rise, Erc prefaces his response, a description of his vision, with an echo of the Pauline profession of ignorance in the face of the numinous: "Nescio quid." Thus Erc, who, according to the vision, is inflamed by Patrick's word to inflame others, actually formulates the vision, and his attitude toward it, in what have become, in the context of this body of literature, Patrician terms.

In one crucial respect, furthermore, Erc even resembles Muirchú's dark version of Miliucc. In his obstinate refusal to accept Patrick's authority, the former master produces, intentionally or unintentionally, a scene for Patrick to witness which functions as a "vision" of the type in the *Confessio*. The experience is humbling ("I do not know, God knows"), yet also empowering, although the power Patrick finally summons and expresses is purely destructive, cursing the descendants. Erc, by contrast, is exceptionally receptive to Patrick's vision-based and vision-inducing authority, but he also provides an occasion for an "audition" along the lines of the key vocational vision detailed in the *Confessio*. What he hears inspires Patrick to exercise his authority constructively, extending his missionary activities into the west of Ireland.

At Erc's baptism, as Patrick is reading the service, he hears derisory laughter from people he cannot see because they are standing behind him. Then he hears similarly disembodied conversation, although it does not remain anonymous. The crucial speaker identifies himself, and the Wood of Fochloth (Foclut), source of the voice of the Irish in Patrick's most important vision, is highlighted. This incident represents a striking rearrangement of the anxieties centered on communication which motivate the visions of the *Confessio*. In the latter work, it is Patrick's fear of the contempt of those more learned and literate than he which gives cogent meaning to his mystical encounters with divine letters and with the supremely eloquent Spirit. Here, at Erc's baptism, the mockery is directed not at his illiterate style but at his conspicuous and very proper use of a book, an object unknown to these Irishmen and representing to them an alien culture. Comparable is the embarrassment Énde anticipates should he and his brothers become Christians before they return home, that is, the derision of their countrymen. Thus the Patrick of the *Confessio* is vindicated in the Patrick of hagiography, who is far more learned in letters than those he is converting, at least in the eyes of his hagiographers and their audience.

Yet knowledge presents Patrick with a problem of communication almost as serious as ignorance. Now the question is not how to communicate authority within a literary mode but instead how to communicate a book-based authority to a culture that conveys authority through the spoken word. The visions of the *Confessio* offered a breakthrough in communication between the visionary speaker and Patrick the auditor. So too in Tírechán's episode, the invisible wall between Patrick and those talking behind his back cracks sufficiently to allow Patrick's voice into their conversation. A fragment of overheard "small talk" becomes the catalyst for a major missionary push westward, the fulfillment of a vision, and the tracking of an authorizing voice to its source. From the pack of innumerable letters the *Confessio* isolates the voices of the Irish calling Patrick from the neighborhood of the Wood of Fochloth; similarly, from a Babel of derisive unidentified voices, Tírechán's text singles out the mention of Fochloth by a specific speaker, who identifies himself. Furthermore, Tírechán presents the meeting with Énde and his brothers as a family reunion of sorts for Patrick and the beginning of a return "home." Patrick describes himself as a Joseph to an Irish version of the sons of Israel/Jacob. Once again, as in the twin episodes of Díchu and Miliucc, Patrick's missionary venture and, more generally, the quest for unification of the disparate strands of Irish society and culture under the Christian dispensation are framed within the metaphor of family, the members of which are attempting to adjust their relationships with one another, either by drawing closer or by respectfully drawing farther apart.

Remarkably, this familial and cultural adjustment comes about in the royal court, an arena that is still unfriendly to Patrick. Nevertheless, according to Tírechán, Lóegaire and Patrick are already willing and able to adjudicate together in the inheritance dispute that, presumably, brought the sons of Amolgaid to the court in the first place.[37] Equally remarkable is the division of the patrimony among all seven brothers.[38] We would have expected a "tilt" toward Énde, who has already made a commitment to Patrick and will donate his share of the inheritance to him. What Tírechán emphasizes in this scene, however, are consensus and compromise among disparate factions. The reordering of the "family" of Irish who summoned Patrick to Ireland and the maintenance of the family's continuity from generation to generation require difficult and delicate negotiations that Patrick and the Christian community he represents cannot oversee alone. Once the missionary joins forces with the king and the powerful men assembled in his court, critical mass is achieved, and the restructuring of the cultural family of Ireland begins. Patrick's trip to

37. The political implications of Lóegaire's seeming authority in the familial matters of the sons of Amolgaid are examined in Swift 1994, 72–76.
38. The importance of this passage for our understanding of early Irish inheritance custom is discussed in McCone 1984b, 57–58.

Fochloth is guaranteed by this convention composed of *all* the sons of Amolgaid and including both Christian and pagan forces. And the pagans, let us note, accept the payment Patrick did not have the opportunity to offer Miliucc, which gives Patrick the right to proselytize freely and exercise his authority. That the trip to the Wood of Fochloth is to conclude with Patrick's second Easter in Ireland is a further indication of the journey's significance as an extension or even fulfillment of the growing spirit of cooperation that was fostered in this episode set in Lóegaire's court, for Patrick's first encounter with the king of Ireland, by no means an amicable meeting, took place, as we shall see, at the first Easter.

Énde's reluctance to embrace Patrick's religion, all his evident goodwill notwithstanding, exhibits the same sort of concern for his public image which compelled Miliucc to make a fiery public spectacle of himself. Yet, unlike the jealous druid father, Énde happily gives his son along with his inheritance to the new order. His offering to the church, his "immolation" as it were of all that he holds dear, stands in stark contrast to the suicidally conspicuous consumption of Miliucc.

Given all the intimate links between the stories of Erc/Énde and Díchu/Miliucc, it should not come as a surprise when Tírechán tells us that Patrick is met in the territory of the sons of Amolgaid by hostile druids, one of whom goes up in smoke:

> Patrick crossed the river Muad, and lo, the druids of the sons of Amolgaid heard that a holy man had come to challenge them on their own turf. An innumerable multitude of druids congregated about the chief druid, named Recrad, who wishes to slay the holy Patrick. Recrad approached the [newcomers] with nine druids wearing white vestments, along with a druidic host. Patrick, Énde, and Conall, the son of Énde, saw Recrad from afar, as Patrick was baptizing an innumerable multitude. When Énde saw [the druids], he arose and grabbed his arms in order to drive the druids away, for the druids were some miles away from them, across an immeasurable river. Patrick sent Conall to the druids, so that they might identify Recrad, lest they accidentally kill someone else, and the youth stood beside the druid as a sign. And lo, the holy man Patrick arose and elevated his left hand to the God of heaven and cursed the druid, and the latter fell dead in the midst of his druids, burnt up before them all as a sign of his punishment. The crowd dispersed over all of Mag Domnon when they all saw this miracle, and Patrick baptized many that day. . . . And he blessed Énde's brother Fergus, son of Amolgaid, because it was in his field that Patrick had worked the miracle.[39]

39. Per Muadam uero uenit, et ecce audierunt magi filiorum Amolngid quod sanctus uir uenisset super eos in suas regiones proprias. Congregata est multitudo nimia magorum ad

As in Muirchú's account of Miliucc's death, so in this tale, the adversaries of Patrick *hear* of his arrival in their territory and act immediately. Also to be noted is that these are the druids of the returning sons of Amolgaid. It is presumably in part the reaction of these very magi which Énde took into account when he declined Patrick's offer of instant baptism. Even more so than the forestalled confrontation in Muirchú's Life, this is an encounter between alienated members of the same household or even between alter egos. These are the "good" sons of Amolgaid and their "bad" renegade druids, employees who seem in this episode to be attempting to usurp their employers' power as well as to repel the threat to their own authority. Comparable is the contest between the Christian former slave Patrick and his former master, the druid Miliucc.

The hostility between the two camps comes to a head while Patrick is baptizing converts, the same setting in which he and Énde met and talked in the first place. Except now, the voices that conflict with and threaten to drown out the voice of the baptizer are those of druids. In retrospect, the laughter and chatter of the sons of Amolgaid, among others, turns out to have foreshadowed this much more ominous interference closer to "home," that is, the Wood of Fochloth, the source of Patrick's summons to Ireland.

Patrick ignores the military response Énde attempts, choosing a less destructive and more devious strategy instead. He sends Énde's son Conall, who has already been "given" to Patrick, over to the party of druids, as if Conall were defecting or backsliding. Conall thus takes on the aura of a Christ figure, a mediator who in effect negates the forces of spiritual enslavement by allowing himself to be given over to them. Conall, already an item of exchange given by his father to Patrick, is now given over to the enemy as a guarantee, as the payment that Patrick could never give Miliucc. Furthermore, Conall is simultaneously operating as a spiritually kidnapped "son" that Patrick is returning to a pagan "father" figure, the chief magus. The druid Miliucc's struggle for control over his children comes to mind as a possible parallel.

Of course, Conall is not really given back. He infiltrates the hostile troop to point out the leader visually. The singling out of Conall and the subsequent

---

primum magum Recradum nomine, qui uoluit sanctum occidere Patricium, et uenit ad illos cum nouem magis induti[s] uestibus albis cum hoste magico; et uiderunt illum procul Patricius et Endeus filius Amolngid et Conallus Endi filius, quando babtizauit Patricius multitudinem nimiam, cumque uidisset Endeus, surrexit [et] arripuit arma, ut mago repelleret, quia ab illis erant magi trans riolum aquae nimium quasi . . . milia passuum. Missit autem Patricius Conallum filium Endi in obuiam magis, ut cognouissent illum, ne alium occiderent, et stetit iuxta magum filius in signum. Et ecce uir sanctus surrexit Patricius et eleuauit manum sinistram Deo caeli et maledixit magum, et cecidit mortuus in medio magorum eius, et exustus est ante faciem omnium in uindictae signum. Et dispersus est uulgus in totum campum Domnon, cum uiderunt omnes homines hoc miraculum, et babtizauit multos in illa die. . . . Et benedixit Amolngid filium Fergussum, fratrem Endi, quia in agro ipsius uirtutem fecit (c. 42.1–7, Bieler 1979, 156.12–28, 32–34).

identification of Recrad balance out an air of uncertainty that threatens to swamp not only the Patrician mission but the text itself, which features not only two *multitudines nimiae* 'innumerable crowds', one of them intensely hostile, but even a *riolus nimius* 'immeasurable river'. Indeed, Conall's crossing of this hyperbolized river and his indicating "who's who" among the druids for Patrick's benefit is comparable to Muirchú's crossing over the unknowable "sea" of shifting Patrician lore and rendering it manageable for his readers.

Conall is continuing the work begun by his father, Énde, who similarly rendered a dangerously vague situation specific, with the spoken sign of his casual remark about his home which sets him and his voice apart from the crowd Patrick is hearing. In both cases, a "private" sign, meaningful only to Patrick, makes possible a "public" sign, the performance or revelation of a miracle. The mention of the Wood of Fochloth, initially of interest only to Patrick, leads to the affirmation in Lóegaire's court of Patrick's mystical summons from Ireland. The private signal of Conall's standing beside the chief druid allows Patrick to perform his destructive miracle, which serves as a most persuasive public demonstration of the saint's authority.

Unlike Miliucc's self-immolation, which draws attention away from Patrick's return to the scene of his youth, the combustion of Recrad focuses attention on Patrick and his mission. In fact, like the fire that consumes Miliucc's children, these flames ultimately produce a host of converts, even if in this case the person actually burned is a lost cause. The saint's fiery power redounds especially on another son of Amolgaid, blessed because he owns the field where Patrick's authority has been so vividly demonstrated. Thus we are reminded that, after all, the territory on which the druids opposed Patrick's mission did not even belong to them but was the property of their employers, whom the druids had been trying to intimidate. Recrad, unlike Miliucc, disappears in a flash and takes no property with him. With the latter's death, in fact, the true owner of the land over which the druids were asserting their claim is delivered from pagan manipulation and freed to embrace the faith of Patrick.

Patrick, Disseminator of Signs

In sum, Muirchú's stories of Díchu and Miliucc, Tírechán's story of Miliucc, and the paired episodes concerning Erc and the sons of Amolgaid–all use a common pool of motifs to develop two themes concerning the transition from pagan to Christian culture which are fundamental to the hagiographic formulation of Patrick's mission and, more generally, to the medieval Irish perception of the change Christianity brought to Ireland. One of these themes is the problem of communication between Patrick and the Irish. In these tales new voices and signs are continually being asserted against intense interference from entrenched old voices and signs. The other theme is the familial nature of this struggle, in which it appears that each faction is intimately related to every other, and resolution implies a rearrangement of relationships and a concomitant redistribution of familial and social status.

It is instructive to observe how these themes operate together even more closely in the version of the conversion of the sons of Amolgaid presented in the Tripartite Life, where the character of Conall, hardly more than a pawn in Tírechán's version, emerges as the hero of a veritable medieval Irish bildungsroman:

> The sons of Amolgaid were involved in a contention over kingship. There were twenty-four long-standing families in the territory. They refused to accept as a king over them anyone with a nickname. Óengus [the most arrogant of the children of Amolgaid] had therefore given nicknames to all his brothers. Lóegaire, son of Niall, son of Eochu, the king of Tara, [agreed] to give judgment [in their case], along with his brother Éogan mac Néill.
>
> And so the sons of Amolgaid traveled to Tara in twelve chariots, although in writings concerning Patrick you can find it said that only seven went to judgment. They received the king's welcome. Óengus had been Lóegaire's fosterling at Tara, so he received a special welcome. Óengus asked the doormen not to let Conall, the son of Óengus's brother Énde the Crooked, inside the fort. Óengus very much feared Conall's skill in arguing his case. Óengus received what he requested from the doormen. And when Conall [arrived] outside, he heard the sound of Patrick's bell [being rung] at Tipra Pátraic near the fort. Conall went toward the sound. He greeted [Patrick]. "Cleric," he asked, "do you know what is the language of this [utterance] that I keep in my memory, *Hibernenses omnes clamant ad te pueri* [All the youth of Ireland cry to you], and so on? Two girls in our district uttered it while still in their mother's womb." "I was the one being called," said Patrick, "and I myself heard [that utterance] when I was on the islands of the Tyrrhene Sea, and I did not know whether the words were spoken inside or outside me. I will go with you to your region to baptize, teach, and evangelize." Patrick then asked about the reason why Conall had come, and Conall explained to him the situation and said that he had been barred from entering Tara. Patrick said to him, "Proceed now, the doors are open, and go to Éogan mac Néill, my faithful friend, who will help you. Discreetly grab his ring finger—that has always been a sign between us." And so it was done. "Welcome," said Éogan [to Conall], "what does Patrick wish?" "For you to help me," said Conall. Conall then proceeded to plead his case. "If," he said, "a case is won and property given on the basis of youth, I am the youngest. If, however, it is on the basis of my father's age, Énde the Crooked is the oldest here." To which Lóegaire responded, "[The right to] speech indeed to the

oldest, and conversation as well. If, however, property and valuables have already been given out to anyone, I will not seize them from him." They [that is, the sons of Amolgaid] left [Tara], with Patrick in their company. Patrick gave his chariot to Conall, so that his was the thirteenth chariot [in the company, the other twelve being those of his brothers].[40]

Clearly, the story has undergone considerable modification and elaboration in comparison to Tírechán's version, but it is still familiar. Erc's baptism no longer gives the context. Instead, Conall himself is an Erc-like figure who stands apart from his family as Erc stood apart from Lóegaire's court, the only one to respond to Patrick's authoritative "voice." In this case, the power of the saint's voice is symbolized not by sparks from his mouth, a visual sign, but by the ringing of his bell, an auditory sign. Like Erc, Conall converses with Patrick and offers him a mystical puzzle to solve. Interpretation of this puzzle again reveals the special link between pagan and Christian, namely, the cry from the Wood of Fochloth, which Conall has in his memory. What drives Conall to seek clarification from Patrick is the unintelligibility of the message. Conall's quandary, therefore, is the same as Patrick's in the visions of the *Confessio*: the supernatural communication is in a tongue he can hardly understand. I note in passing that, at least according the author of the Tripartite Life, the cry of the Irish to Patrick was in a language that the saint, unlike Conall, *could* understand. Thus, according to this line of thought, the cry is all the more the synecdochic breakthrough in communication that Patrick needs, both in his missionary work and in this particular vision from the

---

40. Bátar maicc Amalgada oc imchosnam immon ríge. Cethir chenél (.i.senchenela) fichet batar isin tír. Ro [fh]rithbruithset co ngabtais forru fer co foranmaim do ríg. Dubert dídu Oengus foranmand fora bráithre. Is he robu húalchu di chloind Amalgada, int Oengus. Fugellsat Loígaire macc Néill maicc Echach rí Temrac[h] ⁊ a bráthair .i. Eogan macc Néill. Lotar maicc Amalgada do Temraig in .xii. curribus, sed in libris Patricii inuénitur quod exierunt in iudicium tantum .uii.˙ fratres de eis. Fúaratar failti ocin ríg. Dalta int Oengus isin Temraig do Loígaire. Gaibthir failti sainriud fris and. Guidid Oíngus inna dorsidi arna tailctis isa ndún Conall macc a brathar .i. macc Endai Cruimb. Ro imeclaig Oengus trebairi [in gilla] oc tacru in fhír. Adcottai Oengus in sein óna doirsirib. A mbaí Conall fri les anechtar, rocúala guth cluic Pátraic o Thiprai Pátraic ocun dún. Téit Conall cuccai. Bendacha[i]s dó. "A chléirich," ol sé, "in fetar-su ced bélrae in so fil i foraithmiut lem-sa, 'Hibernénsés omnes clamant ad té pueri' et reliqua, ro gabsat dí ingin a broinn a máthar in nostris régionibus dicentés?" "Meisi dorógrad sin," ol Patraic, "⁊ rochuala-sa in tan ro bá i n-insib mara Toirén, et nesciui uturum in mé án éxtra [me] locuta sunt uerba. Et ibo tecum in regionem tuam babtizare, docére, euangelizare." Interrogat autem Patricius qua causa uenit Conall, ⁊ ro aisnéid Conall do Pátraic in fochun, ⁊ dixit naro léicet[h] isin Temraig. Cui dixit Pátricius: "Ingredire nunc inanuis apertis et adíi Eogan macc Néill, amicum mihi fidélem, qui té adiuuabit, capiens tú occulte mér tanaise a loetanán signum inter nos semper." Et factum est sic. "Fochen," ol Eogan, "cid as toisc du Pátraic?" Atrubairt Conall: "Fortachtaig dam." Toracart Conall iarom. "Masu ar oítid tra," ol sé, "is tacartha hitig rig ⁊ is gabthai ferann is mé as óam. Mású ar aís m'athar, as sinem and Endae Cromm." Quibus Loígaire respondit: "Erlabra dont shinsiur ém," ol sé, "⁊ acaldaim. Día tarta iṁ séotu ⁊ moíne du chach ní gataim airi." Lotar ass ⁊ Pátraic cum eis, ⁊ dorat Pátraic a charpatt do Chonall combu é in tres carpat dec (Mulchrone 1939, lines 1453–89).

Confessio. For Conall, seeking enlightenment and salvation from Patrick is therefore a request for translation. The haunted pagan asks the holy stranger to express the authority of a shared message in "native" terms. In the process, this authority expands beyond the privileged linguistic code and infiltrates the "native" code through which it will finally reveal itself.

Patrick happily obliges with the meaning of the message, activated, he explains, only now that the message has been shared, and he vows to respond to the message by "translating" himself, as it were, into the domain of its source. But Patrick obliges Conall even further and more immediately by interjecting himself and his authority into the familial dispute that brought Conall and his uncles, the proprietors of the Wood of Fochloth, to the king's court at Tara. For this shunned youth is the victim of his conniving uncle Óengus, who has deprived his brothers, including Conall's father, Énde, of eligibility for kingship by "overmarking" them publicly. To all of them he has assigned nicknames, denotations that, apparently, damage the public profile of each royal candidate or so delimit it that each is made unacceptable to his potential subjects. By helping Conall as he does and thereby undermining Óengus's authority to assign significance in pursuit of his own political ambitions, Patrick removes the burden of a restrictive code from the internal communications of the family, and of the territory he converts, while he introduces a new language, Latin, into their repertoire of codes.

The hagiographers, it is to be noted in connection with this enrichment of communication, particularly Tírechán, make repeated and marked mention of the books (written in Latin, of course) Patrick leaves in the territories he visits, in the hands of those clerics to whom he entrusts the spiritual care of his converts. In the kingdom of the sons of Amolgaid, Tírechán tell us, after the miraculous immolation of the chief druid, the dispersal of the other druids, and the baptizing of the multitudes, Patrick

> ordained holy Mucneus, brother of Cethiachus, and gave him the seven books of the Law, which Patrick left to Mac Erce, son of Mac Dregin. . . . And lo, a man came to them named Mac Dregin with his seven heathen sons, and he demanded the baptism of God from Patrick, and Patrick blessed him along with his sons. Of these he picked one named Mac Erce, wrote out an alphabet for him, and blessed him with a benediction suitable for a priest. The boy's father said, "It will offend me if my son leaves with you." Patrick said, "Not so. I will, however, give him into the care of Brón, son of Icne, and Olcán [two of Patrick's bishops]".[41]

41. Et ordinauit Mucneum sanctum, fratrem Cet[h]iachi, et dedit illi libros legis septem, quos reliquit post se Macc Erce filio Maic Dregin. . . . Et ecce quidam uir uenit ad illos nomine Macc Dregin cum filiis septem gentilibus et postulauit babtismum Dei a Patricio, et benedixit illum cum filiis et elegit unum filium ex ipsis, cui nomen erat Macc Ercae, et scripsit elementa et benedixit eum benedictione praespiteri. Et dixit pater filii: "Tedibit me, si tecum exierit filius

It is not implausible to see in the seven sons of Mac Dregin a replication of Tírechán's seven sons of Amolgaid, and to see in Mac Erce a duplicate of Conall, who is given to the church by his father, one of seven brothers, as a result of a chance encounter with Patrick at the baptism of an "Erc." Within this miniature version of the larger familial and religious drama that has just been played out in Tírechán's text, Patrick shows himself mindful of the family's integrity as he converts and claims its members. He seemingly does not take Mac Dregin's son, sacrificed to the cause of the church, far away from him. Yet by means of his arrangement Patrick also usurps the family's channels of authority. He reassigns the designated son to spiritual fathers, namely, the bishops to whom he is commended. And so, in Tírechán's text, Mac Erce becomes an heir to his clerical fosterers, rather than an heir within his "real" kin group. His stated inheritance, the seven books of the Heptateuch, is an encoded expression of the authority and continuity of his ecclesiastical family.

The motif of validation by means of sacred language brings us back to Mac Erce's alter ego, the Conall of the Tripartite Life, who by quoting Latin to Patrick assures for himself an inheritance and a place within both of his families, secular and ecclesiastical. The saint, pleasantly surprised, helps him find an authoritative voice with which to assert his rights articulately and effectively in the unfriendly environment of Lóegaire's court. But the key that makes Conall's public verbal debut possible is a far more intimate nonverbal communication. When the young man, following his Christian mentor's instructions, grabs the ring finger of Éogan mac Néill, this important member of the court recognizes a fellow friend of the saint. Once again, as in the stories of Erc and Énde, a privately shared sign leads to public performance. The youth, with Éogan's assistance, can now plead his case before the king, using the powers of persuasion his devious uncle so feared. Conall thus enacts within the hagiographic tale what Muirchú the hagiographer introduces as a metaphor for the venture of composing a saint's life, namely, speaking for the first time in an assembly. What Conall argues for, even more than a share of inheritance or the kingship of his land, is, as Lóegaire's response to his plea makes clear, dialogue. He wants the right to speak, to be heard, and to receive a response backed up with commitment both from his kinsfolk and the king of Ireland.

Such dialogue he has already received from Patrick, who also had to win the right to speak authoritatively in the king's court, in an episode we shall examine shortly. In fact, Conall's verbal battle for recognition, an intrafamilial challenge to authority, is a replay of Patrick's own contest in the court, which can also be described as the difficult but salvific return of an exiled son into

---

meus," et ait Patricius: "Non erit ita, sed illum Brono filio Icni commendabo et Olcano" (c. 42.7, 43.1–2, Bieler 1979, 156.28–30, 156.35–158.5).

the troubled bosom of his family. Furthermore, Conall's insistence on primacy whether inheritance goes to the oldest or the youngest has overtones of the argument that Christianity should enjoy preeminent authority either as the restoration of (or heir to) a belief and way of life more ancient than any other or as an altogether new religion that supersedes those practiced before.

Lóegaire rules in favor of Conall, presumably granting him the kingship of the territory of the sons of Amolgaid. The outcome is effected within a secular environment by a secular ruler, but in fact, it has been engineered by the representative of the new religious culture, who, we should recall, has stayed outside the court throughout the episode, affecting what happens inside it by remote control. Now, however, it is time for the familial rivals to return home, and Patrick travels with them, in his own voyage of return to the voices of the Wood of Fochloth. This time the "vehicle" for signaling Conall's newly won authority, the sign of the close bond between him and the saint, is Patrick's very own chariot, which allows his young protégé to travel in the same style as his brothers.

A Talk with a Deceased Sister

As in Tírechán's version of the story of Amolgaid's sons, the true obstacles to the new faith are encountered by those who struggle to accept or disseminate it, as they return to reclaim what they have left behind—be it home, familial inheritance, or kingship. The tensions spread out in Tírechán's account among the sons of Amolgaid and between them and their druids are concentrated in the Tripartite Life in the interactions between Conall and his uncle Óengus and between Patrick and Óengus. Here, the brothers are not salvageable as a group. One of them, the nicknaming Óengus, functions as an intimidating Miliucc or Recrad figure, possessed of a voice of formidable authority, and no mean manipulator of signs. This incorrigible opponent must be eliminated if Patrick's mission, which has become ineluctably intertwined with Conall's rise to power, is to succeed. To put it differently, his insistence on his own independent authority will lead, as in the case of Miliucc, to the last resort of self-destruction.

First, Óengus, unwilling to accept Lóegaire's judgment, tries to persuade two of his brothers to slay the interlopers Conall and Patrick, but to no avail. Then he himself attacks the traveling party with the assistance of two druids in particular, Réon and the already familiar Recrad/Rechred:

Réon declared that wherever he would catch sight of Patrick first, the earth would swallow Patrick up. That was reported to Patrick. "In fact, it is I," he said, "who will see him first." And when Patrick saw him, the earth swallowed Réon. "I will believe," he said, "if I am rescued." Then the earth threw him up so that he was up in the air, and he fell down, half dead. He believed and was baptized. Rechred was then snatched up and dropped, so that his head was broken upon a rock, and fire from heaven burned him up. This is the location of Ail in Drúad [Rock of the Druid]. There is a church near it, Cross Pátraic [Patrick's Cross] its name, to the east of Caill Fochlad. Tulach inna Drúad [Hill of the Druids] is the name of the place where the host of heathens had been [waiting for Patrick], to the west of Cross Pátraic. Glais Chonaig ["Stream of Conach") runs between them. Óengus said, "I will believe if my sister is awakened." This was Fedelm, daughter of Amolgaid, who had died a while back.[42]

Shortly afterward, a second encounter with druids brings us back to Tírechán's account of father and son's spirited defense of Patrick: "Énde saw the druids desirous of killing Patrick. He instructed his son, 'Go and guard Patrick, lest the druids slay him.' Patrick himself noticed them, and an ethereal fire burned nine of them up."[43]

In both confrontations as reported in the Tripartite Life, Patrick learns of the presence of the druids even though someone else in the story assumes that he will not find out about it so soon. In the first episode, the druid Réon expects to see Patrick first. In the second, Patrick's ally Énde sends his son ahead to protect the holy man. In being so remarkably quick to detect, Patrick avoids being turned into a sign of his opponents' power and instead turns *them* into signs of his power. Réon and Rechred become symbols of alternative responses to the Christian message. The first druid, entrapped in a mock burial, is "resurrected" by Patrick after he submits to the saint's authority. Rechred, to whom no lines are given in the Tripartite Life script, is raised only to be brought down without a word and is consumed by the same celestial fire that burns nine of his colleagues in the later episode.

Alongside this summary execution of those who advocate resistance to the new religion, we find our first instance, in the hagiographic narratives discussed so far, of a saved druid. Réon lives and becomes a Christian because, by playing into Patrick's hands and begging for mercy, he allows himself to function as a living sign of the power of the religion Patrick brings. Réon thus contrasts with Miliucc, who insists to the end on control over signs, including control over himself as a sign. The other druids are rendered mere static

---

42. Asbert Réon dú i n-aicciged Pátraic na sluicfed in talum. Atfes do Pátraic aní sin. "Is meisi ém," ol Pátraic, "citanaccigi." Ut uidit Patricius illum sloicsi in talam sís. "Creitfe," ol sé, má num anachair." Fóceirt in talam súas co mbuí osnaib gaíthaib, co torchair sís lethbéo. Credidit et babtizatus est. Focoisled dano súas Roechred, ⁊ dolléced anúas co mmemaid a chénn frisin ailich ⁊ no llosci tene di nim. Ata and Ail in Drúad. Atá céll ann, Cross Pátraic a ainm, fri Caill Fochlad anair. Telach inna [n]Drúad a ainm in phoirt i rraba buiden inna [n]geinti, fri Croiss Pátraic aníar. Glais Conaig etarru. Asbert Oengus: "Creitfe-sa dia tódúiscthar mo fiur," .i. Feidelm ingen Amalgada atbath ó céin (Mulchrone 1939, lines 1501–13).

43. Uidit Énda magos uólentes occidere Pátricium. Dixit filio súo Conallo: "Uáde et custodi Patricium né magi occiderent illum." Ipse Patricius sensit eos, et combussit ignis éthereus eos numero nouém (ibid., lines 1532–35).

witnesses to Patrick's authority. Even on such signs, as we have already seen, Patrick can build. The text tells us that his church, Patrick's Cross, is built near or on the sign of the Druid's Stone, where Rechred's head was crushed and his remains supernaturally incinerated.

The copious topographical information supplied in the conclusion to the account of the first encounter with druids serves to emphasize the translatability of what has just happened. The significant elements of the incident are mapped onto its location, which subsequently, as a field of signs, communicates the story to posterity. It is as if the river represents the rift between the two sides, which are symbolized by the church or cross and the druids' hill. These, however, are mediated by the presence beside the church of a rock named after a single, thoroughly defeated druid, a landmark symbolizing the defeat and appropriation of druidic authority.

Such detailed memorialization of event by means of place and place-name is by no means unique to Patrician hagiography. Indeed, it is one of the most widespread tendencies of medieval Irish literature. To be of lasting fame and value, according to the implications of this episode of the Tripartite Life and other works, the new religion must generate new place-names or at least somehow incorporate the existing place-name lore (*dindshenchas*) into its worldview. Thus, the transition in the text from the catalog of topographical "signs" to Óengus's specification of the sign he needs to witness in order to be converted is not as sudden or awkward as it might seem.

Óengus's request is an arresting variation on Réon's. Instead of asking that his life be saved, he asks Patrick to resurrect his sister and, by implication, as we shall see, the child in her womb, Óengus's nephew. The focus of attention in the ongoing saga of the sons of Amolgaid shifts from matters of religious conflict back onto the equally important issue of family reunion and reconciliation. Having deprived Óengus of his druids, Patrick is now challenged to restore his sister, and the challenge turns out to be not so formidable for a miracle worker whose career is in fact replete with resurrections:

> They proceeded to the grave in which was the dead pregnant woman, Patrick and Conall along the lower path to Cell Alaid, Óengus, however, by the upper path. They arrived at the grave. Patrick revived the woman along with her child in her womb, and they were both baptized in the Well of Óenadarc. . . . Revived, she preached to the crowds about the punishments of hell and the rewards of heaven, and in tears she begged her brother to believe in God through Patrick, which he did, and he was baptized. And on that day, twelve thousand people were baptized in the Well of Óenadarc.[44]

44. Lotar iaróm dond fherta i mboí in ben marb alachta, Pátraic ⁊ Conall íar conair thís, do Chill Alaid, Óengus immorro íarsin chonair úachtaraig. Recait in fert. Dodíusaig Pátraic in mnaí ⁊ a macc inna brú, et babtizati sunt ambo in fónte Óenadarcae. . . . Et suscitata illa

It should be noted that the raising of the dead woman and her unborn child occurs in the text of the Tripartite Life directly after Patrick baptizes the twin girls who, while still in their mother's womb, had issued the call Patrick heard in his famous vision, and whom he has finally rediscovered. Patrick tracks down the figures from his as yet unfulfilled past, the two women, in order to give them a new birth through baptism. The saint then retrieves an unfulfilled figure from Óengus's own past, his pregnant sister, so that she may "give birth" to the future by preaching the Christian message with particular immediacy. In both cases, the personified "past" *speaks* with a numinous authority, situated either before the beginning or beyond the end of the human life-span between womb and grave.[45]

The sign of resurrection is so powerful that it persuades Óengus to abandon his opposition to Christianity, at least nominally. It is important to recall that Óengus fought the new religion in the first place in order to protect his rights against those of his brother and nephew, who had joined forces with the advocate of the new faith. All told, Patrick first undermines Óengus's authority and then imposes his own authority on him through the terms of what can be described as familial discourse. The right to *acallam* 'conversation', won by both the "youngest" and the "oldest" of the family thanks to Patrick's intercession, provides them with the opportunity to plead their case successfully. This privilege is now extended to the dead as well, who speak forcefully to their kin not so much on their own behalf as on behalf of Christianity.

The parallel between Óengus and Tírechán's Miliucc runs deep in this episode. In his vision the druid sees Patrick destroying his son and daughter and then bringing them back to life—a process that, Patrick explains to him, signifies their conversion and turning away from their father and his pagan faith. Here, Patrick returns Óengus's sister and nephew from the dead, but as baptized proselytizers working on Patrick's behalf. Óengus's counterpart Mil-

---

predicauit turbis de poenis inferni et praemiis coeli, et per lacrimas rogauit fratrem suum ut Deo per Patricium crederet, quod factum est, et babtizatus est. Et in illo die .xii. milia babtizati sunt in fónte Óenadarcae (ibid., lines 1543–53).

45. The paradoxes in the story of the king Echu mac Cremthainn are even greater. Echu will permit his daughter to become a nun only if Patrick allows him to enter heaven without having to be baptized. Patrick at first balks at this unorthodox request but then relents. Echu leaves orders before he dies not to bury his body until Patrick arrives. The saint revives Echu and gives him a proper baptism. Ordered to preach on what he now knows about life after death, Echu does so with relish, and then, offered a choice between return to his earthly life or return to heaven, Echu opts for heaven without hesitation (Tripartite Life, ibid., lines 2067–113; noted in Bitel 1984, 15). In this case, the daughter can find her "true" (spiritual) father (Patrick) and her spiritual destiny only if Echu is permitted salvation without baptism. This omission is remedied by means of yet another, even odder temporal dislocation: the recovery of Echu from heaven itself, for the purpose of retroactively legitimating his entry. The raised Echu, who preaches to his daughter's generation and those yet to come, speaks from the perspective of one uniquely allowed to have his cake and eat it too.

iucc, despite the remarkable vision of life through death and the sobering challenge to his parental authority, does not join his children in the new order. As we shall see, Óengus, too, though he actually witnesses a demonstration of Patrick's revivifying power as well as the conversion of his kin, is only temporarily impressed.

In finding and baptizing the women whose voices from the womb so changed his life, Patrick takes on a surprising resemblance to Óengus, reunited with his pregnant sister who speaks to him of conversion. Of course, their resemblance quickly gives way to the underlying contrast of ambitions and goals, as the extraordinary summoning voices do or do not affect them. Nevertheless, this odd affinity is consistent with the sense of interconnectedness among the opposed parties which pervades the legendary picture of the conversion of Ireland.

A story confirming these impressions of both affinity and contrast between the figures of Patrick and Óengus is to be found in a number of sources. It is an anecdote about the young Patrick's reunion with his own sister under remarkable circumstances, which offers a fascinating permutation on the familial theme. Here it is from a Middle Irish homily on Patrick:

> Then the time of releasing Patrick from his enslavement approached, for the pagans customarily freed their slaves in the seventh year [of their service]. Since Miliucc did not think of [any other] way that he could detain Patrick, he bought a woman slave to give to Patrick in marriage. When on the night of the wedding they were placed together in their own dwelling, Patrick preached to the woman, so that they spent the entire night praying. Then in the morning of the next day Patrick noticed the white scar on her face. He asked her how she got it. She told him, "When I was in Nemthor among the Britons, I fell and struck my head [so hard] against a rock that death was near me. When my brother Succet saw the wound, he made the sign of the cross over it so that it healed completely at once." Then Patrick said, "I myself am your brother, and it was I who healed you." Then they gave thanks to God and fled into the wilderness.[46]

46. Rochomfocsig, tra, aimser thuaslaicthe Patraic adóire, arnochlechtatis nagenti saerad amogad isin sechtmad bliadain. O náimraided immurro Miliucc indus noastfad intii Patraic rochendaig cumail corusnaisc doPatraic hi. O rocuirtha hitech foleth aidche nabaindsi, isandsin pritchais Patraic don chumail corothochathitis innuli naidche ocernaigthe. Isinmatain iarnabaruch atconnairc Patraic ingelchrecht hindreich nacumaile. ocus roiarfaig di fochann inchrechtai. Atbert inchumal: "Intan basa inNemthur imBretnaib, darochar corusben mochend fricloich cumba focus bas dam. Otconnairc mobráthair .i. Succet, increcht, dorat ardhe crochi Crist tairis combahógshlan fochétoir." Ised atbert Patraic: "messi fén dobrathair, ocus isme roticc." Gníset insin atlugud doDia ocus tiagait isindithreb (Stokes 1887, 2:440, 442). See also the Tripartite Life, Mulchrone 1939, lines 229–34; and the pre-twelfth-century Latin lives edited in Bieler 1971, 66–67. In the tenth century (?) Latin Life of Patrick by Probus, it is Patrick's brother, not Patrick himself, who marries his sister (ibid., 195; on the dating and non-

It is while Patrick is in hiding with his sister in the wilds that he receives the call to leave Ireland on a ship sent for him.[47]

This account is yet another variant on the struggle for authority between Patrick and his nemesis Miliucc. It is also a veritable family romance, featuring the joyful reunion of lost members of a dissolved family or, in this case, the transformation of a "negative" familial relationship into a "positive" one.[48] Patrick's wife is, after all, Patrick's sister, who by her miraculous sign serves as a reminder of his saintliness. Accepting the domestic life Miliucc had prepared for him, as might have happened had his wife remained his wife, would have signified submission to the dominion of his master; the future Christian missionary would thus have ceded victory to the druid. Furthermore, had Patrick embraced his bride, his commission of incest, albeit unwitting, would have altogether betrayed the principles of family organization he would later use to the advantage of his mission. Fortunately, Patrick's preaching, his strong oral performance upon this occasion of the fortuitous recovery of his sister, allows the siblings to maintain the proper distance. Comparable is the sibling's sermon of Óengus's sister to her brother, in which she urges him to draw closer to her, by means of religious affiliation, and join the emerging familial consensus in favor of the new religion.

Like a tricksterish, tempting devil, Miliucc nearly sways Patrick from his divinely ordained course by reuniting him with his long-lost sister, in unwitting imitation of Patrick's miracles of resurrection and recovery. But the private sign Patrick astutely notices, the scar on her face, represents and injects into the story the true revelatory power behind the romance. Patrick had actually revived his sister in the past, and the scar remained as a token of her brush with death. Absconding with her out of Miliucc's reach, Patrick thus saves his own family from the perversions of the druid master, as he has saved Miliucc's.

Patrick's sister bears a sign that both identifies her and establishes an intimate link to the brother who revived her. This token of recognition, which establishes an affinity between Patrick and someone who should be a total stranger, is akin to the message in a foreign tongue which haunts Conall, Énde's idle mention of the Wood of Fochloth, and the act of holding Éogan mac Néill's finger. These privately communicative acts lay the groundwork for formally and openly "familiarizing" the old with the new, and for the trans-

Irish provenance of this life, see ibid., 39–40; F. Byrne and Francis 1994, 8–9). Possible echoes of classical literature in this story of reunited siblings are noted in ibid., 84.

47. Stokes 1887, 2:442.

48. I am adapting here the narrative model of the "family romance of neurotics," wherein the protagonist's bad parents or parent figures are revealed not to be his parents at all, and he is reunited with his true, good parents. See Otto Rank's Freudian study of the heroic biography pattern, Rank 1932, 69–82.

formation of Ireland into a Christian nation as formulated in these hagiographic sources.

Such intimate exchanges between Patrick and a solitary "other" need to be complemented by more public communications through which the authority of the saint is lastingly established. The encounter between the unbelieving Óengus and his sister is, unlike the meeting of Patrick with his sister, a public event, in which the sister functions herself as a sign for all to see and to interpret easily enough as an expression of Patrick's power. In contrast to the transparency of her sign, the scar on the saint's sister's face is meaningless without the private knowledge that brother and sister possess, even though the scar, like the resurrected sister, is a sign of Patrick's ability to raise the dead.

Moreover, Óengus's sister, brought back to life, is hardly a mute sign. Indeed, she has much to say, all of which confirms the worldview of Patrick and his religion. As we shall see, most of these miraculously revived figures from the past as featured in stories about Patrick and other Irish saints are brought back into the present not only as a spectacular demonstration of the saint's power, specifically the authority of his summoning voice, but also to talk in their own uniquely authorized voices to an audience either about the past or about the worlds they entered through death.

The utterances of the revived dead exhibit two kinds of immediacy to satisfy a secular audience demanding a sign of power, that of the revenant's direct speech and that of her/his experience. For what those who return from the dead describe, they, and sometimes they alone, know firsthand. Such first-person narratives bridge the various parallel gaps that the miracle of revival brings into focus, those between living and dead, present and past, and Christianity and paganism. Yet, we shall see, Patrick and the other saints who revive the dead occasionally risk undermining the authority of their own voices when they give the past a chance to speak. Sometimes the past threatens to overload the present with its own lore, a body of knowledge which expresses a worldview not always compatible with that of the present. Or the sheer force and volume of pre-Christian utterance, unlimited by the textuality by which Patrick's religion operates, can overpower the literary form into which its Christian amanuenses expect it to flow.

These problems, however, do not emerge in this episode of the revival of Óengus's sister. Her brothers, along with a host of other onlookers and listeners, are overwhelmed by what they see and hear, and they agree to submit to baptism. Yet Óengus's conversion turns out to be superficial:

Patrick headed south toward Fertae Locho Dáela. This was Óengus's territory. Patrick expected that he would gain possession of the land himself. Óengus came to him drunk, [however,] and refused to grant it him, for it was not from the heart that he believed, although he was baptized and avowed his faith. "By God's judgment," said Patrick, "it would be fair for your properties and off-spring not to be distinguished after your death. Your inheritors will be habitual beer-drinkers and kin-slayers on account of you."[49]

Once again, comparison with the combined stories of Díchu and Miliucc can draw out the significance of the saga of the sons of Amolgaid. Díchu, we recall, was the quintessentially generous host, who not only granted his own land to his guest but even embraced the stranger's religion. The besotted Óengus, in contrast, is the major beneficiary of his own feasting and refuses to share his possessions with Patrick, who lays down a curse upon him and his descendants similar to the one he pronounced on Miliucc and his progeny. The false convert makes a spectacle of himself in front of a scandalized Patrick. His insolence toward the representative of the new order, who seems to be taking away his power, is a public statement, like that of Miliucc, who reacts even more radically to avoid Patrick's annexation of his possessions. For such incorrigible enemies, Patrick provides the appropriate punishments of obscurity for the descendants of the threateningly conspicuous Miliucc and deadly discord among his heirs for the jealous family head Óengus.

There is perhaps even more to the scene. In Irish myths and rituals of kingship, which predated and survived into the Christian era, the royal candidate is transformed into a king and wedded to his land or the king renews his kingship in the context of a feast where he becomes intoxicated with a super-naturally proffered drink of kingship.[50] Inasmuch as Óengus has already been deprived of his kingship by Patrick and is now pressed for land, his drunken-ness may be interpreted as the final reassertion of his kingship. If it is, then the sign of inebriation does not achieve the desired effect. Óengus and his entire line are rendered ineligible for kingship, punished with the presented sign itself. They are trapped within the gesture of drunkenness and made victims of its ambiguity. As perpetual beer addicts, Óengus's descendants will be no celebrators of a kingship under their control. Rather, they will be exemplars of immoderation and lack of self-control.

A markedly different fate unfolds for Óengus's nemesis, the loyal Conall, and his descendants, as the story of this family is concluded in the Tripartite Life:

49. Luid fades do Fertai Locho Dáela. Oengusa in talam. Ro mmenair Pátraic congbail dó fesin and. Dananaic int Oengus i mmescai: do duaccai dó, ar nírpo ó chridiu ró creit cid in tan ro baitsed 7 foruisme creitim. "Mo débród," ol Pátraic, "ba cóir ceniptis árdda do chongbala-su 7 du chlainde post té. Bit coirmmgnáithi do chomarpai 7 bit fingalaig tríit" (Mulchrone 1939, lines 1560–66).
50. Máire Bhreathnach (1982, 256–59) discusses the king's inaugural drink and the ambiva-lent relationship between the king and the one who offers it to him.

"Arise, Conall," said Patrick; "you are to take the crozier." Conall said, "If it is the pious thing to do, I will do it for you." "Not so will it be," said Patrick. "You will bear arms to protect the heritage of your family, and you will be known as Conall Crozier-Shield. Ranks of laymen and clerics will come from you, and any one of your descendants whose shield bears the insignia of my crozier will not have warriors about him who are routed." Patrick did this for him.[51]

Here too we see ambiguity, but in this case, the combined ambiguity of Patrick's statement and of the sign works to the advantage of the recipient of Patrick's judgment. It is as if Patrick, by putting his request so vaguely, were initially testing Conall and the limits of his interpretative range, to see if he would be willing to take the ultimate step in submitting himself to the church, that is, to "take the crozier" and become one of Patrick's bishops. Conall assents to the ambiguous order as he interprets it. Even if the Tripartite Life is a macaronic text blending Irish with Latin, we nevertheless can savor the irony that Conall responds in Latin, recalling his first query of Patrick.

Upon receiving this reply, Patrick right away makes clear that he was actually referring to his own crozier, not to a crozier Conall would have as a bishop, and to his own authority, not to an independent authority that Conall would enjoy in that capacity. The crozier is to be a transferable or multi-referential sign of power for both Patrick and Conall, who will bear it in his name as one of the new Patrician nicknames for this generation of his family, and whose descendants will bear it on their shields. This emblem awarded to their paradigmatic ancestor by Patrick, unlike that foisted on him by his jealous kinsman, protects the descendants, instead of limiting them, and fosters collective action among members of the kin group, that is, those who fight alongside the bearer of the crozier-shield. The sign promotes amity, in contrast to the drunkenness assigned to the descendants of Óengus, which breeds dissension among them. The prophylactic ambiguity of the crozier allows it and the authority that it represents to operate not only on the ecclesiastical level but also on the putatively separate field of secular affairs, where Conall will carry on Patrick's work, building bridges between the ecclesiastical and the worldly.

Authority Put to the Test

In Muirchú's Life, the twin stories of Díchu and Míliucc open his account of Patrick's mission in Ireland and lead directly to what is presented

51. "Arddruig, a Chonaill," ol Pátraic, "gabáil bachla duit-siu." Conall dixit: "Si pium est tibi faciam." "Níbá ed bias and," ol Pátraic. "Bía-su fút gaisciud causa comarpsa dut cheniul, 7 bid tú in Conall Sciathbachall. Ordan loech 7 cleirech uait, et nách oen úait assa sciath i mbia toraind mu bachla-sa, ní soífetar óic imbi." Quod illi Patricius fecit (Mulchrone 1939, lines 1591–96).

as the most crucial and climactic encounter between Christian proselytizer and hostile pagan authority. This is in fact the same encounter that, in Tírechán's text and the Tripartite Life, sets the scene for the stories of Erc and the sons of Amolgaid. According to Muirchú, Patrick, having returned to Díchu after his disastrous attempt to win his freedom from Miliucc, takes the pagan bull by the horns: he decides to celebrate his first Easter as a missionary "in our Egypt"[52] in the territory of the king who resides at the ancient religious center of Tara in the most powerful kingdom in Ireland.

And so, having been frustrated in his personal mission to purchase his freedom as well as the loyalty of his former master, Patrick now sets out on a far more ambitious national campaign. The goal is the same, however, to annex a seemingly alien authority to the cause he espouses. In this case, the coveted power of what Muirchú presents as the greatest kingdom among the Irish does not reside in a particular individual such as Miliucc but in an institution. By celebrating Easter in Brega near Tara, Patrick makes a symbolic statement of an affinity that will soon become a reality.[53] And in linking what Patrick plans to do to the "Easter" of the Israelites in Egypt, which he equates with "our island," Muirchú reintroduces the liberation theme underlying the preceding episode of Miliucc. Patrick's planned celebration of Easter in sight of his enemies will proclaim his freedom from a constricting "gentile" culture and will signal his impending vindication in the home to which he has now returned. Conveniently for Patrick, and for the Christian community for whom Muirchú designed this analogy, Ireland is both his Egypt and his Israel, both captor or obstacle and the fulfillment of promise.

The voyage to this center of hostile power is explicitly compared with the voyage to Miliucc's home. Traveling by sea southward to Brega, Patrick, Muirchú notes, has Ireland on his right, whereas on the previous, unsuccessful trip to the north, it was on his left, all "ad plenitudinem ministerii" ("for the fulfillment of the ministry"). This phrase from the Book of Armagh appears in another manuscript as "ad plenitudinem misterii" ("for the fulfillment of the mystery"), again said in reference to the directional contrast between the two trips.[54] The implication of this phrase—namely that Patrick's journeys are the outward expressions of a spiritual message—affirms that the process of authoritative signification is central to Patrick's mission, as Muirchú delineates it. Patrick brings and generates signs and is himself a sign to Ireland. The challenge to the missionary and his latter-day hagiographer is to present these signs with an authority the Irish will recognize. In some respects, this is a "new" authority that Patrick must demonstrate, but in other

52. In nostra Aegipto (1.13.1, Bieler 1979, 82).
53. As Charles Doherty has noted (1991, 86–87), in having Patrick launch the "public" phase of his missionary campaign by celebrating Easter, Muirchú may well be alluding to the Easter controversies of his time (see pp. 1–2).
54. 1.14.1, Bieler 1979, 84, and note on line 5.

respects, it is an already recognized authority that Patrick must appropriate. Patrick's celebration of Easter in the powerful heart of enemy territory, like the attempt to convert his former master, exemplifies this double strategy.

Muirchú endows this episode with an important spatial dimension as a way of tagging key elements of the story. He describes (in Irish no less) the spot in Brega to which Patrick advances in this war of signs as a *fert* or *fertae* 'burial site'.[55] It is a symbolically appropriate place for the celebration of resurrection, and for the assertion of prestige and power, for both pre-Christian and Christian Irish culture, the *fert/fertae* was normally the resting place of a person of distinction and occasionally served as a boundary marker or a setting for public meetings.[56] In this case, the occupant of the grave is said to be one Fíacc, and his association with the site, says Muirchú, is attested not only in *fabulae* 'tales' but also in the words of a Ferchertne, "who had been one of the nine druid-prophets [*magis prophetis*] of Brega."[57]

This celebration on a noted gravesite is to be conducted by a reviver of the dead par excellence, the legendary Patrick who again and again uses resurrection as a sign of his power to convince unbelievers. Although Patrick does not revive anyone in this context, he does produce miraculous signs aplenty and undermines those of his opponents.[58] One of the first, as we shall see, to accept the message of Patrick's signs, submit to his authority, and even become one of his bishops is the poet Fíacc, a putative exponent of the pagan voice of authority whose name harks back to the individual for whom the *fert* or *fertae*, Patrick's missionary beachhead, was built. It is as if the saint, by staking a claim to Fíacc's mound, were absorbing the native power attached to it and to its resident, as well as signifying his own power over what it represents.[59]

---

55. 1.14.2, ibid., 84. On *fert/fertae* as an example of the "Celticisms" to be found in Muirchú's Latin, see Picard 1992, 361.

56. *DIL*, s.v. 1 *fert, fertae*; Charles-Edwards 1976a, 83 n. 3.

57. Qui fuerat unus e nouim magis profetis Bregg (1.14.2, Bieler 1979, 84.10). Fertus uirorum Feec or, in Irish, Ferta(e) Fir Féicc (Mulchrone 1939, line 435 and elsewhere) means "Mound of the Men of Fíacc" ("men" in the sense of "servants," according to Muirchú, [1.14.2, Bieler 1979, 84.9], but just as likely in the sense of "descendants"). Might Muirchú be punning on the loan-word *fert/fiurt* (from Latin *uirtus*) which means 'miracle'?

58. Other extant versions make more use of the resurrection motif, and to these I shall return. In the later Irish tradition concerning the (historically impossible) encounter between Patrick and the Viking king of Dublin, modeled on the meeting with Lóegaire, Patrick's ability to revive the dead forms the cornerstone of his missionary strategy. For text with translation, see Dumville et al. 1993, 260–61.

59. Within the context of the story, this second Fíacc is a "stronger" figure: alive, not dead; belonging to the future, not the past; a stripling, not an ancestor; a Christian, not an ancient pagan; and a "contemporary" poet who sings Patrick's praises (in the Old Irish composition known as "Fíacc's Hymn," for example [see n. 76]) not the subject of commemorative poetic composition (the ancient Fíacc mentioned by Ferchertne). And yet, as we shall see, from the perspective of the dedicatee and reader of Muirchú's texts, this latter Fíacc is himself an ancestral, commemorated figure.

Muirchú's interweaving of authoritative sources at this point, when Patrick's authority is about to be put to the ultimate test, is as notable as the use here of an Irish word for "burial site." In his brief description of the place, Muirchú invokes two conspicuously native and unliterary sources, namely, local stories and the testimony of a legendary druid and prophet. A not altogether friendly conjunction of separate authorities, Christian and pagan, is taking shape on this mound, and Muirchú reflects both the tension and the assimilation that result from the encounter in his own presentation of the event. The breakthrough of the native voice in this passage is framed by pointed authorial acknowledgments of Christian sources and models, both written and oral, for Patrick's actions as well as Muirchú's representation of them. These include the Old Testament, specifically the Book of Genesis, to which Muirchú's text refers the reader for the Paschal celebration of which Patrick's is presented as a replay, and the voice of the "prophet"—a biblical, not a pagan one—from whom the term used to designate Patrick's Easter, *sacrificium laudis*, is borrowed.[60]

In Muirchú's ensuing description of Lóegaire's court we are carried back to the scene of an earlier breakthrough of the native voice. It was in the same context, a royal assembly of druids and craftsmen, that Muirchú presented the poem that translated Christian culture into native terms in predicting the advent of Patrick, and which Muirchú translated into Latin. Now, the hagiographer is conspicuously attempting to translate the native situation itself into his biblical terms. Lóegaire is a Nebuchadnezzar, Tara is a Babylon, the assembled noblemen are "satraps," the convention at Tara is like the fateful feasts of Nebuchadnezzar or his son Belshazzar in the Book of Daniel.[61] Thus, by implication, Patrick is another Daniel. Later, in another specific reference to this biblical text, Patrick's protégé will emerge unscathed from an ordeal by fire arranged by Patrick and the druids; Muirchú will compare him to the three young Hebrews who were unharmed by the flames of the furnace into which they had been sent by Nebuchadnezzar.

This pervasive modeling of Patrick's encounter with Lóegaire and his druids on events in the Book of Daniel emphasizes the importance of signs and the ability to interpret them. For the prophet Daniel challenges the authority of kings and becomes even more authoritative than kings because he is able to interpret signs, both spoken (such as the dream that Nebuchadnezzar relates—Dan. 2) and written (the writing that appears on the wall during Belshazzar's feast—Dan. 5). As we shall see, Muirchú also draws an analogy between Patrick's duel with the druids and Peter's contest with Simon Magus. Curiously, however, he does not cite the obvious analogue of the wonder-working duel between Moses and the Egyptian priests.

---

60. Bieler 1979, 82, note on lines 13–14 (alternative version of 1.13.1), and 1.14.3, ibid., 84. The textual referent here, says Bieler, is Ps. 49:14. The prophet is therefore David.
61. 1.15.1–2, ibid., 84.

It is telling that Patrick is too busy producing signs in his contest with Lóegaire's druids to give any interpretation. That function is carried out by his opponents. This complementarity indicates that a kind of translation *is* occurring. Patrick produces signs that strike a chord with the druids with whom he is both competing and attempting to communicate.

The saint commences his celebration of Easter, which Muirchú pointedly arranges to coincide with the pagan feast of Tara, by lighting a bonfire on the plain of Brega. This act, Muirchú explains, is a direct violation of the pagan custom according to which the king is the first to kindle a light in recognition of the preeminence of his authority.[62] The Christian light illuminating the plain is a blow to the king's function as a source of light for his subjects. It is as if Patrick had learned a lesson from Miliucc's incendiary protest. Now, instead of being thwarted in his attempt to have authority transferred to himself, it is the saint who blocks the seemingly proper communication of authority by setting his own fire and becoming the distributor of a new light for Ireland. Of course, unlike Miliucc, Patrick does not destroy himself in this fire, even though, according to custom as described by Muirchú, it *should* have destroyed him. Anyone, we are told, who dared to light a fire before the king on the night of the feast of Tara was punished with death. Indeed, upon seeing the fire, Lóegaire sets out to slay the violator of custom upon the advice of his druids, who immediately interpret the sign of the fire correctly. If the king does not destroy the man who set the fire as soon as possible, they say, he and what he stands for will come to have dominion over them all.[63] Thus, Patrick's provocative Easter fire not only initiates communication, which will soon become a dialogue, but also draws the communicants closer together. The flame brings "the mountain to Mohammed" as it were.

A War of Words

Fearing the power of Patrick's signs and his ability to communicate with them, the druids do not allow their king to approach Patrick within the area illumined by his fire. Rather, they advise the king to wait until Patrick comes into their presence, where they themselves, as spokesmen both for Lóegaire and for the culture that endows king and druid with authority, will carry on the fight in direct communication with the alien (*sermocinabimur ad invicèm*).[64]

62. 1.15.3–4, ibid., 84, 86.
63. 1.15.5–6, ibid., 86.
64. 1.16.3, ibid., 88.3–4. Compare the account in the Tripartite Life: "We will plead in your presence" (tacermait in far fiadnaisi [Mulchrone 1939, lines 459–60]). The verb the druids use here to designate their upcoming exchange with Patrick, *do-accair* 'pleads', normally refers to legal argument (*DIL*, s.v. *do-accair*). Óengus mac Amolgada uses its noun form to describe

As the druids make clear, the primary signs to be used in the struggle will be verbal, despite the prominence of the fire and other nonverbal manifestations of power still to come. These signs are, by implication, relegated to the second order, "props" or aids to the powerful words spoken. Furthermore, the king is to judge the verbal contest. On the basis of their evaluations of the performances, Lóegaire and the rulers he epitomizes can ally themselves with either set of speakers and even use either ideology to legitimate their own authority.

Lóegaire, however, never really chooses. A figure reminiscent of the chronically resistant Óengus, he remains throughout on the side of his druids and finally pledges allegiance to the new religion only halfheartedly. After all, Lóegaire, like Óengus, is a king, and kingship as it functions in traditional Irish ideology both pre-Christian and Christian is sacral. It is therefore no easier for Lóegaire to adapt his authority to a Christian framework than for a druid to adapt his. Nevertheless, the cast of characters and the ground rules for the debate are now clear. There are to be two groups of speakers exchanging verbal and other signs and interpreting or undermining each other's signs, and an audience measuring the power of what each side communicates and gauging its effect within the audience's own sphere of authority.

Patrick, noticing the crowd that has gathered near his fire, goes into their midst. Even though they have come with chariots, he approaches humbly on foot, taking comfort from scriptural precedent: "Both aloud and in his heart Patrick chanted the verse of the Psalmist: 'Some may come in chariots, others on horseback, but we will walk, in the name of the Lord our God.' "[65] Patrick speaks powerfully to himself and to the readers or hearers of the Life, preparing for what is to come and, even more important, reflecting on the potential meaninglessness and arbitrariness of signification. By what he says and does, Patrick privately dismantles the trappings of prestige and power his enemies have brought to bear on him. Riding on chariots and horses is now a sign not of strength but of their weakness in relying upon empty gestures, just as going on foot indicates that he proclaims the might name of God.

When Patrick comes face to face with his opponents for the first time, moreover, he elicits from their company a public display of respect, despite the druids' prohibition of it. They had previously coached those assembled not to rise when Patrick arrived, lest they fall under his sway. It is as if in

---

what he fears his nephew will do in Lóegaire's court, "plead for his right" or "plead his case" ("oc tacru a fhír"). Mulchrone 1939, line 1466.

65. Huncque psalmistae uersiculum non incongrue in labiis et in corde decantans, "Hii in curribus et hii in equis, nos autem in nomine Dei nostri ambulabimus" (1.17.2, Bieler 1979, 88.12–14). The quotation is from Ps. 19:8. Muirchú may be following Evagrius's Latin version of Athanasius's Life of Saint Anthony, in which the same verse from the Psalms is recollected by Anthony in a successful attempt to strengthen his resolve in his struggle against demons (c. 39). The subject of Jerome's Life of Saint Hilarion utters this verse aloud as he dispels a demonic phantom chariot (c. 6).

Patrick's presence no sign could be merely perfunctory. Nevertheless, dis-obeying the druidic injunction, a man named Erc does stand, inspired by God.[66] Thus, even before the debate begins, at least one member of the audience has already made up his mind.

Here of course we recognize Tírechán's Erc whose story leads into the account of the sons of Amolgaid. Muirchú's Erc, having paid homage and delivered an almost preemptive strike in the public battle to come, has no further role to play, but Muirchú highlights his function as a sign bearer, even as a sign himself, by identifying him as the one whose "relics are currently revered in the city known as Sláine."[67] The relics preserve his memory into the present of Muirchú and his audience.

With this defection from the pagan camp noted, the contest starts in ear-nest:

> When they began their war of words, a druid named Lochru was insolent in the sight of Patrick, daring to belittle the catholic faith with reckless words. The holy Patrick, casting a piercing eye upon the druid saying such things, spoke confidently and loudly, with the same force as that with which Peter once spoke of Simon [Magus]: "Lord, you who can do everything and in whose power everything lies, you who sent me here, may this impious one who blasphemes your name be now lifted away and swiftly slain." After these words were spoken, the druid was lifted into the air and thrown back down, his brain was smashed on a stone, and he lay dead in plain view. The pagans grew afraid.[68]

For his abuse of language, Patrick's powerful words bring down upon the druid a spectacular death, reminiscent of the demise of one of his colleagues in a previously discussed episode of the Tripartite Life. While, strictly speak-ing, verbal exchange does take place, it is hardly the debate the druids had promised Lóegaire. Although Patrick does look at the person addressing him, as Muirchú makes very clear, Patrick does not deign to answer the blas-phemous speech directly, to enter into dialogue. Instead, he cuts off conversa-tion by interrupting what he views as an interruption. It is worth noting in this regard that in the Tripartite Life, the druid's opening salvo is actually presented as an interruption of diplomatic small talk: "Each asked for news of

---

66. 1.17.3, Bieler 1979, 88.
67. Cuius nunc reliquiae adorantur in illa ciuitate quae vocatur Slane (1.17.3, ibid., 88.16–17).
68. Incipientibusque illis sermonicinari ad inuicem alter magus nomine Lochru procax erat in conspectu sancti audiens detrachere fidei catholicae tumulentis uerbis. Hunc autem intuens turuo oculo talia promentem sanctus Patricius ut quondam Petrus de Simone cum quadam potentia et magno clamore confidenter ad Dominum dixit. . . . Et his dictis eliuatus est in aethera magus et iterum dimissus desuper uerso ad lapidem cerebro comminutus et mortuus fuerat coram eis, et timuerunt gentiles (1.17.5–6, ibid., 88.18–90.2).

the other, that is, Patrick and Lóegaire. Then Lochru came angrily and noisily, with contentious questions, to Patrick."[69]

Lóegaire is angered at the killing of his druid, who never did receive a proper response. He drops all semblance of impartiality and orders Patrick killed. The saint prays to God once again, asking that such speech and such speakers be muted, whereupon darkness descends on the assembly of the Irish, accompanied by an earthquake, "and they were laid low by this disaster in the presence of the king, on account," Muirchú emphasizes, "of what he said."[70]

Patrick has so far said nothing directly to Lóegaire, the druids, or the Irish, but he has already stripped them of their power and brought his own to bear on them, summoning aid from above. In this first, hardly civilized phase of the encounter, Patrick does not have to respond to anything they say. He need only keep open a channel of communication with God to stay in control of the situation. Those who speak ill receive nonverbal retribution, though brought by Patrick's righteous speech. Punished for his words, Lóegaire has lost most of his retinue, reduced to his wife and two others. The queen begs Patrick to spare her husband, and for the first time, the saint responds directly to speech addressed to him, although not with words but with an act of mercy. The thoroughly shaken Lóegaire accedes to his wife's request that he pay homage to Patrick, but his heart is not in the performance. Indeed, he attempts revenge shortly afterward, but this time he changes his strategy: "And after they had parted and the king had gone a short distance away, he called holy Patrick with false words, wishing to kill him by any means. Patrick, however, knew the thoughts of the wicked king."[71]

The duplicitous invitation escalates the verbal struggle. Now utterance may mask true intention instead of communicating it, and Patrick cannot simply dismiss it but must pay it heed. He counters the dangerous disguise of language with a misleading nonverbal sign. When the saint and his party appear before Lóegaire, it is in the form of deer, and thus they miraculously escape

69. Ro fiarfaig cach dídu scéla día cheli, .i. Pátraic 7 Lóegairi. Dodechaid Lochru co ro-sir 7 co engach, co cosnam 7 cestaib, fri Pátraic (Mulchrone 1939, lines 476–78).
70. Et prostrati sunt ab hac plaga coram rege ex suis sermonibus (1.18.4, Bieler 1979, 90.12–13).
71. Et postquam separauerunt ab inuicem paululum gradiens uocauit rex sanctum Patricium simulato uerbo uolens interficere eum quo modo. Sciens autem Patricus cogitationes regis pessimi (1.18.6–7, ibid., 90.19–21). Fortunately for the saint, even though he does respond to the king's devious summons, he knows the intent it masks. The Tripartite Life makes clear how he knows: "Not long afterward, the king called Patrick aside; he was planning to kill him; but it did not happen, because God revealed that plan to Patrick" ("Nírbú cían íar sin ró choggair in rí leis Pátraic for leith, 7 is ed ro imráid a marbad, 7 ní forchoemnacair. Forfhoilsig Día do Pátraic inní sin," Mulchrone 1939, lines 508–10). The same channel of communication that enables Patrick to screen out undesirable public utterances enables him to see through devious "private" speech, which means one thing to the speaker and something else to the hearer.

detection and death.[72] Here too, as in the story of the cursing of the drunken Óengus, the choice of sign has an especially pointed ideological dimension. In the Celtic mythology of sovereignty, sometimes the hero wins the kingship through success in a deer hunt. His prey, according to some tellings of this tale, is actually a supernatural being in disguise.[73] Thus, the ambiguity of signs permits Patrick to escape from the dangerous situation in which he has been placed by that very ambiguity, and the escape makes use of a traditional motif of particular significance to Patrick's royal opponent, who misses out on the proffered hunt.

The day after, Patrick, clearly having won the encounter of the previous night, carries the war of signs into the inner sanctum of a pagan society engrossed in celebrating its collective identity at the Feast of Tara:

> The next day, that is, Easter, when kings, princes, and druids were reclining at Lóegaire's table—for this day was the most important feast day among them—when they were eating and drinking wine in the palace of Tara, with some discussing and others pondering the things that had been done, holy Patrick with only five men came inside despite the closed doors, just as it can be read about Christ, in order to contend and to preach the holy faith in Tara before all the nations.[74]

The incidental sorting out of what is said and what lies behind speech ("some discussing and others pondering") hark back to the immediately preceding passage, where Lóegaire's words and thoughts were so dangerously far apart. We are now even deeper in the forbidding realm of ambiguity, where words are not to be taken at their face value, and saying and thinking are two different processes. But Patrick, having at first refused to engage in dialogue, has now come into Lóegaire's presence to redeem language. He will speak in no uncertain terms and preach with real power. In likening Patrick's bold invasion to the scriptural scene of the risen Christ among his disciples ("as it can be read about Christ"), Muirchú reminds us again that Patrick's power comes from his religion, which is based on as well as communicated through a written text. Once again, this medium is making its presence strongly felt in this preliterary culture through the voice of Patrick. And it is yet another indication of the merger of the hagiographer's voice with Patrick's that the biblical reference Muirchú makes here is functionally equivalent to the reas-

---

72. 1.18.7–8, Bieler 1979, 90.19–27.

73. Bromwich 1961, 442–53, presents some key instances in medieval Celtic narrative.

74. Sequenti uero die, hoc est in die pascae, recumbentibus regibus et principibus et magis apud Loiguire—festus enim dies maximus apud eos erat—manducantibus illis et bibentibus uinum in palatio Temoriae sermocinantibusque aliis et aliis cogitantibus de his quae facta fuerant, sanctus Patricius quinque tantum uiris, ut contenderet et uerbum faceret de fide sancta in Temoria coram omnibus nationibus, hostiis claussis secundum id quod de Christo legitur uenit (1.19.1–2, Bieler 1979, 92.3–7).

suring invocation of scriptural precedent Patrick uttered in the earlier episode. In fact, in the Tripartite Life account of Patrick's entry into Tara, it is the saint who prepares himself and the reader, by quoting Scripture: "It is not a 'candle under a bushel' that I will make of myself."[75]

Despite Patrick's professed intentions upon entering Tara, as described by Muirchú, the delayed debate does not commence right away. Instead, there is a replay of the motif of the man who shows courtesy to Patrick against druidic injunctions. Except now there are two such hidden devotees. The "finest poet" (*poetam optimum*) Dubthach moccu Lug(a)ir and his pupil, the "youthful poet" (*adoliscens poeta*) Fíacc, stand when Patrick enters. As in the case of Erc, Muirchú duly notes the survival of Fíacc's cult and relics down to Muirchú's own day.[76]

Dubthach's quasi-parental relationship with his pupil Fíacc evokes the model of the family, which, as we have seen in the stories of the children of Miliucc and the sons of Amolgaid, provides Patrick with a means of penetrating the cultural core of the society he is attempting to transform. Now, that is to say, it is a family of sorts, not just an individual, which publicly demonstrates allegiance to Patrick and the new religion. And this family of two generations has a conspicuously professional bent. Dubthach and Fíacc are *poets*, well versed in the arts of knowing and communicating. In Tírechán's version of the Miliucc story, we recall that Patrick turned the druid's children against him by teaching them in his capacity as a lowly "fool" (*fatuus*). In this scene of entry into Tara, Patrick appropriates yet another category of performer from the ranks of verbal artisans. This time, without uttering a single word, he persuades the premier poet of Ireland and his pupil to "defect" and, by implication, to devote their verbal craft to Patrick's cause.[77]

---

75. Niba coindel fó dabaich dogén dímm (Mulchrone 1939, lines 529–30).

76. 1.19.3–4, Bieler 1979, 92. See Richter 1994, 203–4.This is the poet to whom "Fíacc's Hymn," an Old Irish paean to Patrick, is attributed. See Stokes 1887, 2:404–10, 426 (another poem sometimes attributed to Fíacc and sometimes to another legendary poet, Nimíne Eices); on the "Hymn," see Kenney 1929, 339–40. According to the prose introduction to the "Hymn," Fíacc offers himself as bishop in place of Dubthach, so as to allow the latter to continue as a full-time poet: "The loss of me . . . is smaller to Ireland than the loss of Dubthach" ("Islugu moesbaidse ahErind," olFiac, "quam Dubtha[ch]," [Stokes 1887, 2:402]). Thus, according to at least this remarkable strand of the tradition, Fíacc is another of the many substitutes and stand-ins who dot the course of the legendary history of early Irish Christianity. His "sacrifice" allows old and new cultures to coexist productively, indeed, to merge in his person. After all, Fíacc himself clearly remains a poet. On his elevation to the episcopacy, see also the note in Book of Armagh (Bieler 1979, 176) and the Tripartite Life (Mulchrone 1939, lines 2219–36).

77. The genealogical subtext to the Dubthach story extends even into the reception of Muirchú's Life, which is dedicated to, and written for, Áed, bishop of Sléibte (Sletty in County Laois, Leinster), where Dubthach or Fíacc was supposedly the first bishop. Hence the story of Dubthach's conversion is designed "to flatter Áed" (Doherty 1991, 87), whose ecclesiastical establishment has become a part of—or, like a prodigal son, returned to—the Armagh fold. Ibid., 75–78; see Bieler 1979, 178. Moreover, it may not have been lost on Muirchú's

Signs Exposed, Transformed, Appropriated

At the feast of Tara, speaking and thinking, which, we have already seen, can produce dramatically different results, are intermixed in the festive milieu with eating and drinking. It is thus appropriate that the revelers speak to the newly arrived Patrick, but only to the extent of inviting him to eat and drink with them. Patrick knows the invitation is a trap, just as he recognized Lóegaire's false invitation, but given the rules of this verbal game, he cannot refuse without losing face.[78] The trap is set both in the words of offering and in what the words seem to offer, for the drink given to Patrick has been laced with poison by the druid Lucet Mael.

The saint, we have come to see, is always keenly aware of the public nature of his performance and of the potentially dangerous messages hidden in the performances of his opponents. Operating with this awareness, he spectacularly removes the "false" element from what has been given to him: "Holy Patrick, realizing how he was being tested, blessed his cup in the sight of all, and the liquid became like ice. After Patrick turned the vessel over, only the drop that the druid had put in it fell out. Again he blessed the cup, and the liquid returned to its natural state, and everyone was amazed."[79] Patrick's miraculous extraction of the secret poison from the seemingly harmless cup of hospitality turns a deviously delivered message of destruction into a token of his power recognizable by all. It also demonstrates his ability to manipulate the course as well as the objects of social exchange, whether edible or audible, to his own advantage. We have come far from the savage reprisals of the field of Brega. No longer simply eradicating the transmitters of hostile signs, Patrick is isolating and expelling that which is harmful in the signs themselves, which have become progressively more ambiguous, and saving what is harmless in them. Even some of the professional communicators/performers, the poets Dubthach and Fíacc, are now scheduled to be saved.

As if some common ground of communication has finally been established, a genuine dialogue between Patrick and his druidic opponent Lucet now finally begins:

---

audience that Áed, the recipient and reader of this textualization of the life of Patrick, is the spiritual descendant of a poet, an oral performer, who receives authority from the saint himself in a face-to-face encounter.

The further adventures of Dubthach, on the cusp between the old and the new order, are detailed on pp. 200–206. See also p. 236 n. 95, concerning a curious legendary twist given to the later relationship between Patrick and Fíacc.

78. 1.19.5, Bieler 1979, 92.14–16.

79. Vidensque sanctus Patricius hoc probationis genus uidentibus cunctis benedixit poculum suum et uersus est liquor in modum gelu et conuerso uasse cicidit gutta illa tantum quam inmisserat magus, et iterum benedixit poculum, conuersus est liquor in naturam suam et mirati sunt omnes (1.20.2, ibid., 92.21–94.1).

In a short while the druid said, "Let us perform miracles on this great plain." Patrick asked in response, "What kind of miracles?" The druid said, "Let us make it snow on the ground." Patrick said, "I do not wish to do anything against God's will." The druid said, "Well, I will do it, in the sight of all." Commencing with magical incantations, he made snow fall over the entire plain, reaching as high as [?]. All saw it and were amazed. Then said the holy man, "Now that we have seen it, get rid of it." But the druid said, "I cannot get rid of it until this time tomorrow." The holy man said, "So you are able to do bad but not good. Not so am I." Then, after Patrick blessed the entire circuit of the plain, the snow melted quicker than speech without the benefit of any rain, clouds, or wind. The crowds cheered and were profoundly amazed in their hearts. Shortly, after invoking demons, the druid brought the densest of fog down upon the plain, and everyone grumbled. The holy man said, "Expel the darkness." But the druid, as before, could not. The holy man then prayed and said a blessing, and suddenly the darkness was expelled, the sun shone again, and all cheered and gave thanks.[80]

While the verbal exchange featured in this passage can hardly be described as sparkling or even engaging, it is the first sustained conversation in the Life, and the longest Muirchú reports verbatim. The dialogue is punctuated by miracles (*signa*) that would be meaningless outside the given context of verbal give-and-take, unlike the previous signs reported in this section of the Life, which "overrode" discourse, such as the smashing of the impiously ranting druid against a rock. Yet the significance of the miraculous effects produced by the druid, unseasonable snow and fog, is in fact doubtful even within the context of the dialogue. As Patrick makes clear in what he says about them, these are not productive *signa* but aberrations. They actually work against the druid's purpose by alienating the onlookers, who mutter angrily and are grateful to Patrick for dispersing these obstructions. The druidically produced snow and fog may have been gauged to bear special significance for those in Lóegaire's court as well as the audience of the Life. In medieval Irish narrative the sudden descent of either unexpected snow or fog

80. Et post paululum ait magus: "Faciamus signa super hunc campum maximum," respondensque Patricius ait: "Quae?," et dixit magus: "Inducamus niuem super terram," et ait Patricius: "Nolo contraria uoluntati Dei inducere," et dixit magus: "Ego inducam uidentibus cunctis." Tunc incantationes magicas exorsus induxit niuem super totum campum pertinguentem *ferenn* et uiderunt omnes et mirati sunt. Et ait sanctus: "Ecce uidemus hoc, depone nunc." Et dixit: "Ante istam horam cras non possum deponere." Et ait sanctus: "Potes malum et non bonum facere. Non sic ego." Tunc benedicens per totum circuitum campum dicto citius absque ulla pluia aut nebulis aut uento euanuit nix, et exclamauerunt turbae et mirati sunt ualde corde. Et paulo post inuocatis demonibus induxit magus densissimas tenebras super terram in signum et mormurauerunt omnes. Et ait sanctus: "Expelle tenebras." At ille similiter non poterat. Sanctus autem orans benedixit et reppente expulsae sunt tenebrae et refulsit sol et exclamauerunt omnes et gratias egerunt (1.20.3–7, ibid., 94.1–17).

can signal an impending encounter with otherworldly characters.[81] Neverthe-less, within the interpretive framework Patrick articulates for his audience (and Muirchú articulates for the audience of the Life), these phenomena conceal more than they reveal, like the false words uttered by Lóegaire. With the vanishing of the fog, the sun shines once again, and, with the melting of the snow, "all cheered and gave thanks"; the very hearts of the onlookers are laid bare as they become receptive to Patrick's influence.

What the snow and fog hide most of all is the weakness of the druid, which Patrick elicits from him in the dialogue. In confessing his inability to dispel what he has produced, Lucet admits defeat, for these are special effects that the druid can impose on others but cannot control or remove at will. Lucet has to wait for them to "wear off" before he can get rid of them. Patrick, by contrast, not only generates his own *signa* but commandeers those of others. In this episode, he turns the demonically powered feats of Lucet into signs of both God's will and his own.

Patrick's Books, Druids' Books

Once he shows himself unable to manipulate even his own miracles, let along Patrick's, the druid loses control of the semiotic contest. He and his colleagues had been putatively directing this trial ever since they had detected Patrick's presence through the impudent sign of his fire. As the druidic posi-tion weaken, Lóegaire moves more into the center of the dialogue, acting as a referee rather than a partisan, and the conversation is resumed, this time among three speakers:

> Then, after all these things had been done in the sight of the king by the druid and Patrick, the king said to them: "Throw your books into the water and him whose books escape without being worn out we shall worship." Patrick re-sponded, "I will do it." The druid said, "I do not wish to undergo the test of water with him, for he holds water to be a god." Doubtless he had heard of the baptism with water administered by Patrick. And the king responded, saying, "Throw them into fire." "I am ready," said Patrick. But the unwilling druid said, "This man alternately venerates one year water, the next year fire as a god." "Not so," said the holy man, "but you yourself will go along with one of my lads into a partitioned and closed house, with my clothes on you and yours on my lad, and thus you will be subjected to fire and judged in the sight of the Most High." And this plan was settled upon.[82]

81. Instances are cited under Motifs D902.1 "Magic mist," D2143.6 "Magic control of snow," and F962 "Extraordinary precipitation" in Cross 1952.
82. His autem omnibus gestis in conspectu regis inter magum Patriciumque ait rex ad illos:

Within the ambience of miracle working established so far, Lóegaire's request is somewhat odd: to switch from out-of-season snow and overwhelming fog to books thrown in the water may seem almost anticlimactic. Still, the king's intervention is pivotal to the episode as a whole. Lóegaire is now the one proposing tests instead of the druids, and after Lóegaire, it will be Patrick's turn. Having learned what he needs to know from the telling verbal exchange accompanied by the spectacle of the wonderworking, the king, on behalf of the audience, shifts the focus of the contest onto another form of physically realized "voice," namely, writing. The Christian texts, whose durability Lóegaire wishes to try directly, have already, as I have noted, provided Patrick with both conviction and precedent in his duel with the magi. Now this source of authority is itself to be tested. Can it survive in water or in fire, environments as hostile as the pagan culture into which Patrick has introduced a religion based upon and distinguished by written authority? Patrick is confident that it can.

At this point it is important to recall just how central to Patrick's mission as depicted in the early lives the physical presence and dissemination of the written word is. In spreading Christianity among the Irish, Patrick is clearly shown fostering literacy as well.[83] I have noted that the saint regularly equips those he ordains with alphabets or other kinds of texts.[84] The importance of reading, however, goes beyond this relatively credible picture of the missionary disseminating literacy and literature.[85] Patrick in the Tripartite Life and elsewhere is also a miraculous channel of divine illumination through which the blind can see and the illiterate can read:

"Libros uestros in aquam mittite et illum cuius libri inlessi euasserunt adorabimus." Respondit Patricius: "Faciam ego," et dixit magus: "Nolo ego ad iudicium aquae uenire cum isto; aquam enim deum habet"; certe audiuit babtisma per aquam a Patricium datum. Et respondens rex ait: "Permitte per ignem." Et ait Patricius: "Prumptus sum." At magus nolens dixit: "Hic homo uersa uice in alternos annos nunc aquam nunc ignem deum ueneratur." Et ait sanctus: "Non sic, sed tu ipse ibis et unus ex meis pueris ibit tecum in separatem et conclaussam domum et meum erga te et tuum erga me[um puerum] erit uestimentum et sic simul incendemini [et iudicabimini] in conspectu Altissimi." Et hoc consilium insedit (1.20.8–11, Bieler 1979, 94.17–96.3).

83. Peter Brown remarks that the impression left by the Christian missionaries to Ireland, as portrayed in the early literature, was that they "brought books, not faces" (Brown 1982, 218). See also Lambert 1991, 162–63, where the symbolic significance of Patrick's literacy campaign is noted.

84. See, e.g., cc. 6.1, 28, 42.7, 43.1, 45.2, and 47.2, Bieler 1979, 126.31–35, 146.9–16, 156.28–29, 158.1–2, 21–24, 160.9–11, 12–13. On the meaning of *abgatoria/abgitorium* in Tírechán's text, see note on c. 6 (1), ibid., 217; Ó Cuív 1980; and Picard 1992, 362–63.

85. Tírechán's interest in the actual objects of literary heritage is doubtless related to his general interest in Patrician relics (an interest pointed out in Doherty 1991, 61). Tírechán's inventory, however, hedges in respect to the most powerful relic, the saint's body, concerning the whereabouts of which he and the tradition he represents express considerable confusion (cc. 54–55, Bieler 1979, 165), in contrast to the more definitive Muirchú (2.11, ibid., 120; see Doherty 1991, 84–85). As we shall see, Patrician traces do include some burial sites of figures whose encounter with Patrick makes them significant.

When the holy Patrick was born, he was taken to a blind, flat-faced youth for his baptism. Gornias was the name of this priest, and he did not have any water with which to perform the baptism, so he made the sign of the cross with the hand of the infant over the earth, and a spring of water burst forth. Gornias washed his face, and his eyes were opened, and one who had never studied letters read aloud the baptismal rite. And so God produced a threefold miracle for Patrick on that field: the spring of water coming out of the ground, the restoration of the blind youth's eyes, and the reading of the baptismal rite by one without knowledge of letters until then.[86]

Patrick's reliance on writings for the spreading of the new religion and his encouragement of reading provide an almost vindicating counterpart to the attitude of the "real" Patrick of the *Confessio*, who, as we saw, agonizes over his lack of reading and relies so heavily in his thinking and writing on the one book that he has read and knows thoroughly. Thus, the Lóegaire of Muirchú's Life, whom we last saw requesting of Patrick and the druid Lucet the testing of their books, plays into the saint's hands. Once the contest enters the realm of written signs, it is on Patrick's turf. In the Tara section of Muirchú's text, noticeably interlaced as it is with references and parallels to biblical situations, Patrick himself, as well as the other characters and situations, is a literary construct. He is clearly shown to derive a special authority from sacred literature, on the basis of his resemblance to biblical figures such as Moses, Daniel, Peter, and Christ.[87]

Lucet refuses to allow his own authority to be put to the test in this textual venue, where he senses he would be at a severe disadvantage, fighting on the enemy's terms.[88] Even in this intuition, however, Lucet demonstrates his

86. O ro génair iarom intí noemPatraic, iss ed rucad cusin macc ndall clarenech día baitsiud. Gorniass ainm int shacairt, ₇ nocho raibi husce ocai as ndénad in bathis co tarat airrde na cruiche di láim inna naíden tarsin talmain co rroímid topar husci ass. Lauit (.i. Gornias) faciem, ₇ ro eroslaicti a roisc dó, ₇ ro erlég in mbathais intí naro foglaind litri ríam. Dorigne Dia firt trédai ar Patraic isin maigin sin .i. in topur husci asin talmain, ₇ a roisc don mac dall, ₇ airlegend dó uird na baiste cen aithgne a litri có sin (Mulchrone 1939, lines 89–97; see also Stokes 1887, 2:392.18–24, 432.17–27).

87. Moses was celebrated in medieval tradition as a paradigmatic writer, particularly of the Law (McCone 1990, 95; Hennig 1949–51), and Patrick is explicitly compared with him in one of the hagiographic notes contained in Book of Armagh (Bieler 1979, 164.26–28; compare the Tripartite Life, Mulchrone 1939, lines 1295–99). One parallel the Book of Armagh author mentions is that the sites of both men's graves are unknown, although, confusingly, a following note states that Patrick's body was ultimately found (Bieler 1979, 164).

In Chapter 3 I examine a story from medieval Irish legal tradition in which Patrick is cast in the role of Mosaic lawgiver. As is true of Moses, the confusion or lack of knowledge concerning the whereabouts of Patrick's body accords well with his reputation as a disseminator of texts, which are usually read in the absence of their authors. On writing as a sign of absence, see Svenbro 1993, 145–59.

88. Clearly, I read Patrick's victories over druids as predicated on an assertion of more than simply "druidic" power in "druidic" terms, as these are characterized in the texts. Hence I

ineptitude in interpreting the devices of his Christian adversary. Neither water nor fire is "god" to Patrick, as the druid would know, Muirchú implies, had he not so thoroughly misunderstood sacramental signs, such as baptism. On a deeper level, the druid's problem is that he thinks the obstacle standing in the way of his side's triumph is the bias of the elements of water or fire and not the power of Patrick's text. Still, an avoidance of the written word of the Christian missionary is implied here. If it were only an ordeal by way of the elements which Lucet is resisting, then he would not have acceded to Patrick's proposal to prove his power in a burning house.

The contradiction and confusion in Lucet's understanding of the situation reflect not only on the druid but also on the hagiographer who is trying to have it both ways, setting up a triumph for Patrick and a literary pedigree for his rivals. The basic point being made here by Muirchú or by the tradition from which his stories derive is that the pagan knower/communicator fears the power of the ultimate Christian communication of knowledge, that is, Holy Writ. Books are the physical manifestations of the missionary voice of authority, objects that, from the Christian perspective, are far less trouble-some, far more manageable, and yet far more convincing than the natural phenomena Lucet summons with his voice and thereby renders into unnatu-ral and unwieldy signs. In line with Lucet's production of flashy miracles for Patrick to counter, Patrick in this situation could have been asked to create some spectacle. In fact, he is asked to produce his books, which are to be tested by the power of water and fire. Furthermore, at this climactically telling moment in the encounter between Christianity and paganism, when the Christian advocate's "trump card" is ironically introduced into the conflict by this on-again-off-again enemy Lóegaire, we are offered a tantalizing sugges-tion that the druids too had books to produce. These books never appear, however, and their existence is never actually acknowledged by the druids themselves. There is in fact no evidence to indicate that the pre-Christian Irish used writing to any significant degree in the transmission of traditional knowl-edge.

It is hardly a satisfactory explanation of this passage to say that Muirchú is simply wrong or naive about druidic literacy here. The discreet attribution of a written literature to pre-Christian performers and transmitters of lore founds Muirchú's parallel between the "old" and "new" cultures. His elusive myth of a pagan library forms part of a muted background to the hierarchy of values and media he is assembling in reconstructing the history of the conver-sion of Ireland.

There is also perhaps a personal element to the suggestive way in which Muirchú presents this curious test that never happens. Once again an episode

---

disagree with James Mackey's assertion that "Patrick can only outshine the druids by playing their own games" (1992, 295).

in Patrick's mission may well be reflecting what the hagiographer himself is attempting. For Patrick and Lucet, who are asked to try out how their books fare in water, are in the same vulnerable boat with Muirchú on a turbulent sea over which he admits he has little control. Muirchú at times proclaims his story confidently, like a spiritual son of Patrick, and shows no qualms about launching his document, but his anxiety in the prologue about the perils of the voyage and the scrutiny his vessel will receive likens him to his fellow Irishman Lucet, unwilling to have his "vessels" compete in an element that is antithetical to his authority. Compared to either "real" books or the oral tradition that supplies books with their information, the books of the druid and even Muirchú's own book seem insubstantial experiments. Nevertheless, they do exist at least imperfectly or in theory, and they represent a modest assertion of authorial control in the shadow of far greater authorities. We should note, however, that Muirchú's book was launched, but the druid's books were not, instead staying dry but unknown.

Patrick's Proxy and the Ordeal by Fire

After Lucet refuses to submit to any kind of book test, Patrick graciously refuses to press his advantage on his own territory and instead proposes an ordeal that tests the men themselves, not their signs. Instead of books, Patrick suggests that the users of books be put to the test of fire. Patrick will demonstrate his personal authority, not just the authority residing in and expressed through the written or spoken word, in order to beat the druids without taking any unfair "cultural" advantage. Also, to achieve what Patrick proposes for a test, will be to outdo Miliucc. Both of those who undergo the ordeal will have made themselves into incontrovertible signs of control over their own persons and dedication to their respective worldviews, but he who survives will be a unique sign that is not consumed in the act of signifying. He will be a sign that lives to tell the tale.[89]

Curiously, Patrick's test does not pit him directly against the druid. In a conspicuous double displacement, apparently acceptable to Lucet, Patrick sends "one of my lads" ("unus ex meis pueris") as his proxy and has the two representatives of opposing ideologies exchange clothing. Lucet wears Patrick's, and the boy, later identified by Muirchú as the saint's fosterling Benignus, wears the druid's. The saint is therefore not actually present in the house but only represented, as well as "misrepresented," by the druid in saint's clothing.

89. McCone (1990, 34) proposes the account in 1 Kings 18:20–40 of Elijah's challenge to the prophets of Baal in the presence of King Ahab as a source for this story. His worshippers pray that Baal will set alight a sacrificed bull, but he does not respond. Elijah's bull, however, bursts into a spectacular conflagration. Clearly the fire test proposed by Saint Munnu in his Life (c. 27, Plummer 1910, 1:237—see above) is analogous to that featured in this episode of Patrick's Life.

This displacement is a sign not of weakness but of the strength and continuity of the new culture Patrick is introducing. Even though he is housed in
the dry side of the wooden house, Benignus survives the conflagration, as the
saint himself would have. Muirchú compares him to the three Hebrew youths
cast into a fiery furnace for refusing to worship the false image erected by
Nebuchadnezzar.[90] An angel leads them to safety, and in their triumph the
youths temporarily take the attention of the reader away from the namesake
of the Book of Daniel. Similarly, Benignus "distracts" our attention from
Patrick in this episode.[91]

For the purpose of undergoing an ordeal, Patrick's protégé might as well be
Patrick, as the only other story about Benignus in Muirchú's composition
clearly indicates:

> By way of a brief account I will give the details of a certain miracle wondrously
> performed by the godly and apostolic Patrick, of whom we are speaking, while
> he was still alive, a miracle that we read of virtually only in connection with him
> and Saint Stephen. Once, when he had gone to a solitary place to pray at night
> and he saw, as he usually did, the wonders of heaven, Patrick, wishing to test his
> most beloved and faithful youth, said to him, "My son, tell me, I pray, if you are
> feeling what I am feeling." Then, without hesitation, the child, named Benig-
> nus, said, "Indeed, known to me is what you are feeling. For I see heaven
> opening up, with the son of God and his angels." Then Patrick said, "Indeed, I
> feel you are worthy to be my successor." Right away they went hurriedly to the
> usual place of prayer. As they were praying in the middle of the riverbed, the
> child said, "I can no longer bear the watery coldness," for the water was too
> cold for him. Then Patrick told him to go downstream. Benignus could not stay
> there long either, for, as he asserted, he found the water too hot. Not bearing to
> stand in that place for an extended while, he climbed up onto the bank.[92]

90. 1.20.13, Bieler 1979, 96.10–12. See Dan. 3.
91. Dáithí Ó hÓgáin has noted that the substitution of Benignus for Patrick creates a "rather
awkward situation" (1985, 9). He also suggests another biblical source (Luke 23:31) and
indicates a vestige of the legend lingering in the traditional green worn on Saint Patrick's
Day—said in popular tradition to signify Patrick and Benignus's/Benén's triumph (Ó hÓgáin
1985, 9–10).
92. Dominici et apostolici [uiri] Patricii, cuius mentionem facimus, quoddam miraculum
mirifice gestum in carne adhuc stanti quod ei et Stephano poene tantum contigisse legitur,
breui retexam relatu. Quodam ante tempore cum orationis causa ad locum solitum per noctur-
na spacia procideret, consueta caeli uidit miracula, suumque carissimum ac fidelem probare
uolens sanctum puerum dixit: "O fili mi, dic michi, quaeso, si sentis ea quae sentio." Tunc
paruulus nomine Benignus incunctanter dixit: "Iam michi cognita ea quae sentis. Nam uideo
caelum apertum et filium Dei et angelos eius." Tunc Patricius dixit: "Iam te meum suc-
cessorem dignum esse sentio." Nec mora, gradu consito ad [con]suetum locum orationis
peruenire. His [in] orationibus in medio fluminis alueo [constitutis] paruulus dixit: "Iam
algorem aquaticum sustinere non possum." Nam ei aqua nimis erat frigida. Tunc dixit ei
Patricius ut de superiori ad inferiorem descenderet. Nichilominus ibi diu perstare potuit. Nam

Patrick's protégé is again being tested, and this ordeal demonstrates his ability to share in the saint's beatific vision. Here is another of the intimate signs that establish a special bond between Patrick and whoever else is blessed with the knowledge of their significance. Benignus also shows himself able to put into words what Patrick is experiencing. His is the voice that renders the vision into an utterance and ultimately into a text about Patrick, that is, the episode in Muirchú's Life.[93]

This is a story about successful communication and the transference of authority, for Patrick names Benignus his successor. Furthermore, it stands in marked contrast to the cited story of Stephen; he has a vision like Patrick's, but his announcement of it is brutally drowned out by his unreceptive audience (Acts 7:55–58). Benignus emerges from the anecdote as a clearly worthy heir to Patrick, but it is also evident that he has only what authority Patrick shares with him. Or to put it in other terms, Benignus has authority only insofar as Patrick shares his signs with him or makes Benignus an instrument of his power.

The young man's limitations compared with his mentor's superior saintliness also become apparent in this episode, for the test featured here is in three parts, like the test by water and fire in the Tara episode, and Benignus, like Lucet's book, fails two of the three tests. He is ill at ease in Patrick's water, which is too cold for him, and in Patrick's "fire," which makes the water too hot for him.

The sharing of signs, which characterizes Patrick's relationship with Benignus, is not necessarily a gesture of communion. Almost as remarkable as the protégé's survival in the burning house, is the survival of Patrick's garment, which does not burn up with Lucet. The druid's garment, on the other hand, is burned off Benignus. Clothing does not confuse the protective power that Patrick summons to Benignus's aid. Had the saint's clothes saved Lucet, perhaps that miracle would have demonstrated Patrick's power just as forcefully, but the hagiographic tradition shies away from the implications of this audacious confusion. Lucet must burn. Patrick's garment marks out the druid for death instead of salvation.

Is the false gift of clothing Patrick's revenge for the false cup of hospitality offered to him earlier? The very premise of the test Patrick proposes would appear to be a hagiographic recycling of a Celtic narrative pattern concerning

---

se aquam [nimis] calidam sensisse testabatur. Tunc ille non sustinens in eo loco diu stare terram ascendit (1.22, Bieler 1979, 100.23–102.10, and for analogous incidents from other Irish saints' lives, see 207).

93. As a transmitter of Patrick's fame to posterity and as a junior member of the saint's retinue, Benignus is a fitting bearer of Patrick's writing tablets—the function assigned to him in a Middle Irish version of the story of Patrick's transforming his companions into deer, in which Benignus/Benén appears as a fawn and the tablets as a white bird (*én find*) on his shoulders (from the Lebor Brecc homily on Patrick [Stokes 1887, 2:458]; cf. pp. 87–88 above). I thank Karen Burgess for bringing this passage to my attention.

the dangers of hospitality and gift giving. Guests are lured to a deceptive feast by an enemy-turned-host, only to find that they are entrapped in an iron house with a fire lit under it. The guests, however, usually escape, much to the chagrin of their devious hosts.[94] As he enters the soon-to-be-destroyed house wearing Patrick's clothing, the doomed Lucet appears as an isolated figure, already stripped of his authority and of any rapport with his "audience," who were appalled by his previous miraculous stunts. The parallel with Miliucc's suicidal gesture is inescapable, particularly inasmuch as Lucet is enclosed in the fateful house with an adopted "son" of Patrick, who, according to Tírechán, fell in love with the saint when he once spent the night at Benignus's parents' house:

> After they awoke in the morning, and after Benignus's father had been blessed, Patrick was mounting his chariot, with one foot in it and the other still on the ground, when the boy Benignus reached out with his hands and grabbed Patrick's foot, shouting: "Allow me to go with Patrick, who is my real father." Patrick said: "Baptize him and put him in the chariot, for he is the heir to my kingdom." And so he became Bishop Benignus, successor to Patrick at the church of Armagh.[95]

Benignus, so utterly dedicated to Patrick, leaves his parents to follow his "real father," who shares his visions with him, confers his authority upon him, and even puts him through a test of fire. Another "son" who leaves his family to become Patrick's confidant and whom Patrick "burns" is Gósacht, the druid Miliucc's son. Admittedly, there are several other instances in Patrician hagiography of youths, both male and female, who abandon their parents and the religion of their parents in order to die for Patrick, literally or metaphorically, and who are thus translated into heaven or raised to ecclesiastical office. The ubiquity of the motif of the redeemed son or daughter notwithstanding, the parallel deaths of Miliucc and Lucet and the parallel trials of Miliucc's son and Benignus indicate a special kinship between the story of Patrick and his former master and the story of the ordeal at Tara. These parallels enrich the implications of substituting a representative of the next generation of bearers of knowledge and masters of communication to be tested against a represen-

94. The motif appears in both medieval Irish literature (for instance, the tale *Mesca Ulad* [Drunkenness of the Ulstermen]) and Welsh (the Second Branch of the *Mabinogi*). This particular correspondence (or borrowing) between the vernacular literary traditions is discussed in Mac Cana 1958, 16–23; Wright 1993, 189–206; and Ireland 1995, 449–51 (where the connection with the Patrician legend is noted).

95. Mane autem facto cum surgerent, conpleta benedictione super patrem Benigni Patricius currum conscendit et pedes illius diuerso alter in curru et alter super terram erat, et Benignus puer pedem Patricii tenuit duabus manibus strictis et clamauit: "Sinite me apud Patricium patrem proprium mihi," et dixit Patricius: "Babtitzate eum et eleuate in currum, quia heres regni mei est." Ipse est Benignus episcopus, successor Patriccii in aeclessia Machae (c. 5.4–5, Bieler 1979, 126.23–30).

tative of the older, pre-Christian generation. It is as if the culture Patrick engenders in Ireland were in effect appropriating its predecessor's future. Lucet and Miliucc burn to death, but Benignus and Gósacht, snatched from their forebears by Patrick, emerge from the conflagration of transition strengthened and transfigured.[96]

Children of the New Order

Patrick's transformative effects on the younger members of the Irish community he encounters extend even into the bosom of Lóegaire's own family. Perhaps the best-known hagiographic example of the sea change that representative members of a new generation undergo in response to the signs Patrick proffers is to be found in Tírechán's story of the two daughters of Lóegaire, in which the children are explicitly transported beyond the reach of both parent and druid. This tale, like the account of the duel with the druids at Tara, depicts the conversion of Ireland as a process in which dialogue alternates with demonstration. The girls' meeting with Patrick is clearly a multiform of Patrick's meeting with Díchu:

> And lo, the two daughters of King Lóegaire, fair-haired Ethne and red-haired Fedelm came in the morning to the spring to wash, as is the custom of women, and they came upon the holy synod of bishops with Patrick near the fountain. The girls had no idea whence the strangers came—of what kind they were, or from what people, or from what region they came—but they assumed that they were people of the *síd* [otherworldly dwelling], that is, of the earthly gods, or an illusion altogether. The girls said to them, "Whence are you, from where did you come?" Patrick said to them, "It would be better for you to declare your faith in our true God than to ask about our origins."[97]

96. E. M. Greenwood (1992) draws attention to the parallel between the protective power of Patrick's clothing and other instances of talismanic dress in medieval Irish literature. The sartorially coded transfer of authority between druid and Christian featured in this episode is reminiscent of the curious incident of clothes-swapping in the Life of Ciarán, the founder of the monastery of Clonmacnois, as well as in the Life of the founder of the monastery of Glen Dá Loch, Cóemgen (c. 32, Plummer 1910, 1:215; c. 28, ibid., 248–49). Shortly after Ciarán's death, Cóemgen visits Clonmacnois. Refusing to be disappointed, he shuts himself inside the church with Ciarán's corpse, which comes back to life and carries on a discussion with his visitor. When Cóemgen emerges, he is wearing Ciarán's clothing and the corpse has on Cóemgen's. So, we are told, did the two saints establish their friendship. I thank Máire Herbert for bringing this episode to my attention.

97. Et ecce duae filiae regis Loiguiri Ethne alba et Fedelm rufa ad fontem more mulierum ad lauandum mane uenierunt et senodum sanctum episcoporum cum Patricio iuxta fontem in- uenierunt. Et quocumque essent aut quacumque forma aut quacumque plebe aut quacumque regione non cognouerunt, sed illos uiros side aut deorum terrenorum aut fantassiam esti- mauerunt, et dixerunt filiae illis: "Ubi uos sitis et unde uenistis?" et dixit Patricius ad illas:

It was a woman, Lóegaire's wife, who initiated dialogue in the tense Easter encounter Muirchú describes, and here again it is the female contingent of the royal family which introduces the prospect of negotiation with the mysterious bringer of a powerful alien culture. The elder daughter, after Patrick's rebuke, proceeds to ask a flurry of questions about Patrick's religion, to which the saint replies with the recitation of an extensive creed. Thoroughly impressed with Patrick's verbal presentation, the girls ask not for further signs but for the real thing: the face of God, which they desperately desire to see. Patrick warns them that the price of such a vision is death, but this price they are more than willing to pay. And so, after being baptized and receiving communion, the daughters pass away to their eternal reward.

Patrick's encounter with Díchu, we recall, served as a contrasting prelude to his nonmeeting with Miliucc, the incorrigible pagan who makes himself into a sign of his antipathy toward Patrick and his religion. Similarly, Patrick's fortuitous encounter with the daughters of Lóegaire sets the scene for his meeting with druids. These pagans, however, turn out to be bearers of far more flexible signs than the one into which their stubborn colleague Miliucc turned himself:

They placed them [that is, Ethne and Fedelm], dressed, on a single bed, and their friends raised a wail and a great lament. The druid Caplait, who had fostered one of the girls, arrived and wept. Patrick preached to him, and Caplait believed, and his hair was shaven off [that is, he received the monastic tonsure]. His brother Mael came to him and said, "My brother now believes Patrick, but I will not; rather, I will convert Caplait back to heathenism." He spoke disparagingly to Mathonus [?] and Patrick. Patrick preached to him about the faith and he persuaded him to be penitent before God. Mael's hair was [already] shaven off in the druidic style, as can be seen on the head, called *airbacc giunnae*. From this incident comes the expression that is the most famous of all Irish expressions, "Calvus [the Latin equivalent of Irish *mael* 'without hair'] is like Caplait," since they both believed in God. The days of mourning the daughters of the king came to an end, and they buried them near the spring of Clebach and built a circular mound, in the likeness of a *fertae*, since thus do the Irish and pagans [bury their dead]. With us, however, it is known as a *re(i)lic* [burial site, borrowed from Latin *reliquiae*], that is, the remains of the girls. And [the site of] the *fertae*, along with the bones of the holy women, was offered to God and Patrick and to his successors in perpetuity, and he built an earthly church on that site.[98]

"Melior erat uos Deo uero nostro confiteri quam de genere nostro interrogare" (c. 26.3–4, Bieler 1979, 142.10–17). Following Picard 1991, 359–60, I am reading *aut deorum terrenorum* as a gloss on *side*.

98. Et posuerunt illas in lectulo uno uestimentis coopertas, et fecerunt ululatum et planctum magnum amici earum. Venit magus Caplit, qui nutriuit alteram, et fleuit, et illi Patricius

Although the druid foster father of one of the daughters is summoned to the scene by the traditional sounds of the lamentation for the dead, he falls under the spell of a new "genre" of oral performance, Patrick's preaching. The effect of the preacher's words, as well as Caplait's assent to them, receives expression through tonsure. Yet, as becomes clear, this sign is not altogether new. Caplait, like his brother Mael, already bears what is apparently a tonsorial mark of his druidic profession, attested in other sources as well.[99] Tírechán actually cites the Irish term for this haircut, *airbacc giunnae*, in yet another conspicuous breakthrough of the native voice into the Latin text.[100] Thus once again the Christianization of Ireland is represented as an improvement of existing signs and their authority by means of a translation or transformation of what is already present into the form it will take in the future. Druidic tonsure is replaced by the functionally equivalent clerical tonsure. Caplait, the shape of things to come, prefigures his brother Mael, who at first tries to reverse the flow of time with the power of his words (*verba dura*), spoken in an attempt to win his brother back to the pagan faith.[101] Mael too, however, falls under the spell of the newcomer's preaching and receives tonsure, or has his druidic tonsure redone, like his brother.

This incident, Tírechán tells us, gave rise to a lasting verbal monument, a saying which he translates into Latin as "similis est Caluus contra Caplait" ("Calvus [= Mael] is like Caplait"). In the Tripartite Life, the Irish form is given, with an accompanying gloss: "Cosmail Mael do Kaplait .i. ar is for óen ro chreitset" ("Mael is like Caplait, for they believed as one").[102] The episode, like the proverb, is a paradigm of the unanimity with which Christianity overwhelms and integrates the pagan Irish. The sisters act and speak as one in their quest to be united with God, and their fervor inspires druids to join with one another, as well as with the ranks of Christian clerics. There is a merger of

---

praedicauit et credidit et capilli capitis eius ablati sunt. Et frater illius uenit Mael et ipse dixit: "Frater meus credidit Patricio; sed non ego ita, sed reuertam eum in gentilitatem," et ad Mathonum et ad Patricium uerba dura dixit. Et Patricius illi de fide praedicauit et conuertit illum in poenitentiam Dei et ablati sunt capilli capitis illius, id est norma magica in capite uidebatur, *airbacc* ut dicitur *giunnae*. De hoc est uerbum quod clarius est omnibus uerbis Scoticis, "Similis est Caluus contra Caplit," quia crediderunt in Deo. Et consumpti sunt dies ululationis filiarum regis et sepilierunt eas iuxta fontem Clebach et fecerunt fossam rotundam in similitudinem *fertae*, quia sic faciebant Scotici homines et gentiles, nobiscum autem *reli*[*c*] . . . vocatur, id est residuae puellarum. Et immolata est *ferta* Deo et Patricio cum sanctarum ossibus et heredibus eius post se in saecula, et aeclessiam terenam fecit in eo loco (c. 26.16–21, Bieler 1979, 144.13–29). Cf. c. 42 in Patrick's *Confessio* (Hanson and Blanc 1978, 116) in which Patrick talks of the conversion of a young Irish noblewoman despite parental opposition.

99. The early Irish encoding of sacerdotal/supernatural status in terms of hair or the lack of it is the subject of J. Nagy 1981a; and Sayers 1991b, 179–82.

100. The possible meaning of this term is discussed in Joynt 1928.

101. It is noteworthy in this connection that these druid brothers, said to be in Lóegaire's employ, participated in a duel of miracles with Patrick at Tara, according to the Tripartite Life (Mulchrone 1939, lines 1032–39).

102. Ibid., lines 1162–63.

voices—those of the sisters and those of the druids in conflict—and a merger of signs, namely, *airbacc giunnae* and clerical tonsure. That this unanimity and univocality are the result of translation is indicated in both the Irish and Latin forms of the proverb. The name Caplait, it has been convincingly argued, is a form of Latin *(de)capillatus* 'shorn'[103]—that is, the borrowed *caplait* is parallel in meaning to Irish *mael*. In Tírechán's version of the proverb, Caplait is treated as a native name, and Mael is translated into Latin (Calvus). Thus the proverb is about the possibilities of harmonizing and mixing different codes. Mael or Calvus is the *equivalent* of Caplait. In the Christian system of signification, old signs are not necessarily stripped of their authority but can be invested with new meaning.

Tírechán extends this theme in his description of another lasting sign, the burial place of the daughters of Lóegaire. What the pre-Christian Irish called a *fertae* "we" call *reilic*. Tírechán, who despite what he has just said, proceeds to call it a *fertae*, stresses its function as a symbol of the authority of Patrick and his heirs. Once again, as in the case of Fert Féicc, where Patrick lit his Easter fire, the resting place of the dead becomes a landmark alive in the memory of the emerging Patrician topography.

Incorrigible Kings

We ought to note, however, that not all the gravesites left in the wake of the missionary juggernaut serve as beacons of Christian significance. Although some of Lóegaire's children and even some of his druids join the rush toward the new order, he himself does not experience a heartfelt conversion in either of the seventh-century lives. In Muirchú's composition, Lóegaire, angered by the death of his druid in the burning house, urges the killing of Patrick but is restrained by God himself from offering further resistance to the saint. The power of Patrick's voice is demonstrated one more time against the unruly crowd: "In response to the prayer of Patrick and his voice, the wrath of God descended upon the impious crowd, and many of them died."[104] The

---

103. J. B. Bury writes: "A moment's consideration will show that Tírechán cannot be right in supposing that this saw 'Mael is like to Caplait' arose out of the story which he tells. Both Mael and Caplait were magicians converted to Christianity and tonsured under Patrick's direction; in this they resembled each other; but how could such a resemblance become enshrined in a popular saying, unless there were some typical contrast to give it a point? . . . The clue lies in our hands. *Caplait* is a loan word from the Latin *capillatus* 'decapillated, shorn'; and a proverb declaring that the *mael* is like to the *caplait* proves that the two were not the same. The *mael* being the man with the native tonsure, the *caplait* was the man with a foreign tonsure, as his foreign names implies" (Bury 1905, 241; cf. Bieler 1979, 225–26, note on c. 26.19). If we accept Bury's intriguing analysis, then Tírechán's telling of the story, with its proverbial "punchline," emerges as a triumph of misreading, driven by the desire to graft the "native" (Mael) onto the Christian tradition. Compare Byrne's remarks in F. Byrne and Francis 1994, 102–4.

104. Ad praecem enim Patricii et ad uocem eius discendit ira Dei in populum inpium et perierunt multi ex eis (1.20.14, Bieler 1979, 96.16–17).

king, acknowledging that Christianity is the powerful wave of the future and that his pagan heritage is fast becoming a thing of the past, finally chooses the future: "It is better for me to believe than to die."[105] Yet by his obstinacy Lóegaire, like Miliucc (a fellow king, according to Muirchú), has identified himself too strongly as a relic of the old order to be allowed a significant role in the Patrician future. Says Patrick, "Since you have resisted my teaching and behaved scandalously toward me, no one of your seed will ever be king, although your own reign has been allowed to continue."[106] In Tírechán's text, the last time we see Lóegaire he is still acting like a loyal son of paganism, electing for himself the fate of a perpetual carryover from the past:

> "For my father, Niall, would not allow me to believe but would have me be buried on the perimeter of Tara, like a man standing in battle (for it was the custom of the pagans to be buried armed, with their weapons at hand), I the son of Niall and the son of Dúnlang [king of Leinster, the traditional enemy of the Uí Néill kings of Tara] face to face, because of the intensity of the hate as it exists [between us], until the day of *erdathe* (this, according to the druids, was the day of the judgment of the Lord) in Maistiu in Mag Lifi."[107]

Although it is a purely personal kind of escape that leaves one's descendants prey to Patrick's wrath, Lóegaire here has found a mode of existence free of Christian manipulation. His afterlife is situated neither in heaven nor in hell but in a landscape mapped out by tradition, where he serves as a boundary marker. Moreover, the hostility the interred and armed Lóegaire expresses is not only toward the Leinstermen but also toward the powerful system of signification Patrick has demonstrated.

In Muirchú's Life we find another example of a ruler who is neither converted nor killed but moves on to an interstitial existence as a register of lingering resistance to the new faith. In this case, however, the king's life beyond life is not so much an escape from the need to choose sides in the religious and cultural conflict as a punishment for having chosen the wrong side:

> I will not pass over a certain miraculous feat of Patrick's in silence. He was told of the most reprehensible activity of a certain British king named Coirtic, an ill-fated and cruel tyrant. For he was the most egregious persecutor and slayer of

105. Melius est credere me quam mori (1.21.1, ibid., 96.22).
106. Quia resististi doctrinae meae et fuisti scandalum mihi, licet prolonguentur dies regni tui, nullus tamen erit ex semine tuo rex in aeternum (1.21.2, ibid., 98.2–4).
107. Nam Neel pater meus non siniuit mihi credere, sed ut sepeliar in cacuminibus Temro quasi uiris consistentibus in bello (quia utuntur gentiles in sepulcris armati prumptis armis) facie ad faciem usque ad diem *erdathe* (apud magos, id est iudicii diem Domini) ego filius Neill et filius Dúnlinge imMaistin in campo Liphi pro duritate odi[u]i ut est hoc (c. 12.2, ibid., 132.25–30, and on the possible meanings of *erdathe*, see 218 n. on c. 12.2).

Christians. At first Patrick attempted to call him back to the way of truth by means of a letter, the salutary admonishments of which Corictic mocked. When Patrick was informed of how he had responded, he prayed to God, saying, "Lord, if it can be arranged, expel this perfidious one from this world and the one to come." Not much time elapsed before Corictic heard a musical performance in which the singer said that he, Corictic, should vacate his royal seat, an opinion that all of Corictic's most-beloved retainers boisterously seconded. Then Corictic, in the midst of the assembly, in their presence, turned into a fox and absconded immediately, so that from that day and hour he disappeared forever, like flowing water that passes away.[108]

Although Corictic is not an Irish king, and he is described in terms far more disapproving than those applied to Lóegaire, he too is an opponent who must be met and defeated on his own preliterate terms. The chiding letter has no effect. In this letter, I note in passing, we have one of the few overt links between Patrician hagiography and the genuine writings left by Patrick. There actually is a letter from Patrick to a King Coroticus which has survived, although not in the Book of Armagh.[109] This text outlives Coroticus/ Corictic, despite the negligible impact it had on him according to the legend, just as Muirchú the author will not "pass over" this story "in silence" ("non transibo silentio"). The wicked king, on the other hand, became a prisoner of his own reaction (or lack of reaction) to the saintly script, an exile who, unlike Muirchú, does indeed "pass away" (*transiens*), like running water, and is passed over by posterity, as well as drowned out, if not by the strictures of Patrick's writing, then by the concordant voices of a court performer and his audience. Unlike Miliucc, who by willfully and spectacularly removing himself from a world over which Patrick's authority is gaining control creates a disturbing sight for Patrick to ponder, Corictic simply ignores the signs of the times and is subsequently done in, ironically by a sign that he would presumably have acknowledged whether he was a Christian or not (the singer's performance in court). For all his self-condemning pagan stubbornness, Miliucc respects communication and the power it wields and conveys. Corictic

108. Quoddam mirabile gestum Patricii non transibo silentio. Huic nuntiatum est nequissimum opus cuiusdam regis Britannici nomine Corictic infausti crudelisque tyranni. Hic namque erat maximus persecutor interfectorque Christianorum. Patricius autem per epistolam ad uiam ueritatis reuocare temptauit; cuius salutaria deridebat monita. Cum autem ita nuntiarentur Patricio orauit Dominum dixit: "Domine, si fieri potest, expelle hunc perfidum de praesenti saeculoque futuro." Non grande post ea tempus effluxerat et musicam artem audiuit a quodam cantare quod de solio regali transiret, omnesque karissimi eius uiri in hanc proruperunt uocem. Tunc ille cum esset in medio foro, ilico uulpiculi miserabiliter arepta forma profectus in suorum praesentia ex illo die illaque hora uelut fluxus [a]quae transiens nusquam conparuit (1.29, ibid., 100.10–22).
109. The letter is edited in Hanson and Blanc 1978, 134–53, and translated in Hanson 1983, 58–75.

simply refuses to communicate or to respond to communication. Fittingly, he is rendered a figure as invisible as Patrick's letter was to him.[110]

The fateful ease with which Coríctic dismisses the written word of Patrick contrasts dramatically with the careful attention a different set of characters pays to another letter by the saint. This missive is sent to errant coworkers at the climax of a stray account (probably by Tírechán) preserved in the Book of Armagh, which features an array of familiar motifs:

> Patrick went from Mag Arthicc to Drummot Cérrigi and to Nairne Toisciurt and Ailech Esrachte. He was seen with eight or nine men, in Mosaic style carrying tablets with writing on them. The pagans called out against them as if intending to slay the holy ones, saying, "They carry swords in their hands with which to kill people. These objects in their possession seem by daylight to be of wood, but we think they are actually iron swords for the shedding of blood." The multitude wished to do harm to the holy men, but there was a compassionate man among them named Hercaith, of the line of Nothe, and the father of Feradach. He believed in the God of Patrick, and Patrick baptized him as well as his son Feradach. Hercaith offered his son to Patrick, and the boy went with him to study for thirty years. Patrick ordained him in the city of Rome and gave him the new name Sachellus. He also wrote out a psalter for Feradach, who also

110. Doubtless informing this legend is the account in Luke 13:31–33 of Christ's long-distance chiding of Herod, whom Christ refers to as a fox.

While Patrick condemns a king who disobeys him to the life of a fox in the wild, Brigit, a saint who, as we shall see, wields an authority that contrasts with the authority of Patrick, supplies a seemingly domesticated fox to a king bereft of his original one, only to allow the ersatz fox to run away after the slayer of the "real" pet fox has been released by the satisfied king. This story is told in the seventh-century Life of Brigit by Cogitosus (c. 20, Connolly and Picard 1987, 19–20). Brigit favors the wild fox, allowing him his "wildness" while bringing him closer to the realm of culture. Ciarán of Clonmacnois as presented in his Middle Irish Life is another saint who consorts with a wild fox—one that he rescues despite its having attempted to eat the book or tablet in or on which the saint practices long-distance dictation with his teacher (Stokes 1890, 120–21). Thus we can even find a wild fox who facilitates the exchange of writing—although in his act of consumption the fox demonstrates his inability to "digest" writing or its contents metaphorically and productively, by means of reading. In the semiotics of Patrick's miracle-working, on the other hand, a wild fox is a "decultured" man, fated to be lost to society entirely, at the prompting of the written and spoken word working in tandem.

Other hagiographic instances of the domestication of foxes are given in MacNickle 1934, 150–54. While the literary tradition itself does not draw attention to the contrast between the names, it is intriguing that the original name of Columba or Colum Cille 'Dove of the Church', a prominent saint who, like Brigit, represents a more acclimatized Christianity than does the newcomer Patrick (see Chapter 3), is said to have been Crimthann, a common name that means 'fox'. (See the list of the original names of famous saints contained in the twelfth-century Book of Leinster—Stokes 1890, 300–301; Grosjean 1934; see also Sharpe 1995, 243 n. 7.) According to another, roughly contemporary text preserved in the Lebor Brecc manuscript, the child Crimthann received the name by which he is better known from his coevals, who noted, perhaps mockingly, that, like "our dove from church" (ar colum bec-ni indiu on chill) he tended to join them only after participating in the chanting of the psalms (Stokes 1890, 301).

received from Patrick some of the relics of Peter and Paul, Lawrence and Stephen, all of which are now at Armagh.

And so Caetiacus and Sachellus proceeded to install bishops and ordain presbyters, deacons, and clerics in Mag Aí, without Patrick's advisement. Patrick blamed them for so doing and wrote them letters. Induced to penitence, they went to Armagh to undergo the penance of monks as two compliant children of Patrick. And he said to them, "Your churches will not be significant."[111]

Once again, whereas the Christian reader of signs can expose the falsehood of pagan signs or convert them to Christian meaning, pagans attach the wrong significance to Christian signs. The writings of the "Mosaic" new order conspicuously borne by Patrick and his retinue are seen as secret weapons of a dual nature, wooden by day and iron by night. Yet the apparent pagan misreading of Christian modes of communication, the most prominent of which is writing, is shown here as in other episodes to contain a kernel of acute observation. For the most powerful "weapon" Patrick can use to empower and control his flock is his writing. The psalter Patrick gives Sachellus, who is yet another filial offering made to the saint by an overwhelmed pagan father, persists as a powerful antique down to Tírechán's day. Like the relics of great saints imported from abroad, the books confer authority on Armagh. And when Patrick's protégé Sachellus, along with his equally errant colleague Caetiacus, seeks to pass on verbally in the act of ordination the power conferred upon him by Patrick without the saint's authorization, the sword hidden within writing is unsheathed. Patrick's chastising letter recalls the errant

111. Patricius uenit de campo Arthicc ad Drummut Cerigi et ad Nairniu Toisciurt, ad Ailich Esrachtae, et uiderunt illum cum uiris octo aut novem cum tabulis in manibus scriptis more Moysaico. Exclamauerunt gentiles super illos, ut sanctos occiderent, et dixerunt: "Gladios in manibus habent ad occidendos homines. Videntur lignei in die apud illos, sed ferreos gladios aestimamus ad effundendum sanguinem." Voluit multitudo nimia malefacere in sanctos; sed fuit uir misericors apud illos, Hercaith nomine, de genere Nothi, pater Feradachi. Credidit Deo Patricii, et babtizauit illum Patricius et Feradachum filium eius; et immolauit filium Patricio, et exiuit cum Patricio ad legendum triginta annis et ordinauit illum in urbe Roma et dedit nomen nouum Sachellum; et scripsit illi librum psalmorum, quem uidi, et portauit ab illo partem de reliquis Petri et Pauli, Laurentii et Stefani quae sunt in Machi.

Caetiacus itaque et Sachellus ordinabant episcopos, praespiteros, diaconos, clericos sine consilio Patricii in campo Aíi; et accussauit illos Patricius, et mittens aepistolas illis exierunt ad poenitentiam ducti ad Ardd Mache ad Patricium et fecerunt poenitentiam monachorum duo pueri Patricii prumpti. Et dixit eis: "Non magnae erunt aecclessiae uestrae" (Bieler 1979, 122.16–124.4).

Are these intimidating readable objects slabs of wood with ogam on them? And if they are, are the pagans projecting their own writing technology, and its power to bind and destroy, onto the newcomers, or is Tírechán making a connection between the introduction of ogam and the arrival of Christianity? In any event, it is relevant to note here that in Irish (and perhaps even Welsh) learned tradition, as in the Germanic lore of runic letters, a special connection is traced between writing, particularly its "hidden" powers, and trees/woods (Haycock 1990, 306).

proselytizers to the source of their authority, where they are punished for having strayed too far from it.

As in the cases of Miliucc and Lóegaire, both deprived of successful heirs, to misuse the process of signification or to use signs to express opposition to the new order is to be deprived of a posterity. Perhaps by implication the young clerics' presumption in acting without consultation was based on their confidence in the autonomy of the sacred word as written out by Patrick, that is, the text in Sachellus's possession. Paradoxically, more writing from Patrick reins in the transgressors, although face-to-face interaction and the stern voice of Patrick are required to finish the chastisement begun by the writing.

By contrast, in the story of Corictic the saint cannot enforce the message communicated in written form with his own utterance, since the British king is outside the range of his voice. Remarkably, however, the immediacy of speech hits home in Corictic's court through the medium of a poetic performance, which resonates among even the favored members of the king's retinue, who end up echoing the message themselves.[112] Although Corictic's actions are initially presented as offensive from a specifically Christian viewpoint, the poem of blame works in a "native" fashion. The verses arouse Corictic's people against him and have a physical impact on their subject. Here, then, is another memorable example of cooperation between Christian and pagan cultures and their respective modes of communication, the written letter and the oral poetic performance. Recall Muirchú's tale of how Patrick's advent is prophesied poetically or translated into a pagan poetic form, as well as the swiftly formed alliance between Patrick and the poets in Lóegaire's court, Dubthach and Fíacc. In these passages it is as if this native medium, poetic and oral, were neutral and capable of expressing either Christian or pagan values, or the poetic medium and its exponents were naturally attracted to the cause of one whose words are so strong. There is also a "divide and conquer" strategy at work here. Muirchú's Patrick does not alienate the entire community of oral performers but concentrates his hostility against the druids, while the poets actually come to the saint's aid with their craft, as in the episode of Corictic.

Like the miracles at Tara, the metamorphosis of Corictic into a fox is a sign of Patrick's authority, albeit a vanishing one, *and* of the authority of the poet who has proclaimed Corictic's unworthiness. Once again, words are effective when they produce significant visible results, that is, when they are made

---

112. Inasmuch as the situation is cast in terms of a failed written or private communication followed by a more public form of communication in a different medium altogether, we can perhaps adumbrate the inspiration for the story in the rhetorical stance of the "authentic" letter to Coroticus. This document, as Dumville has observed, presents itself as a successor to a previous, failed missive to Coroticus (Dumville et al. 1993, 188, 127). Moreover, the letter, like the poetic performance in the legend, addresses Coroticus's men more than Coroticus himself. "This, then, is at best an 'open letter'" (ibid., 118).

manifest or, sometimes, when they undo manifestations. Although the transformation itself is a public event, the fox is said to run away never to be seen
again. The *uulpiculus* is, after all, a creature of nature which does not belong
to the cultural realm, where Corictic the king was firmly ensconced before he
disregarded Patrick's word.[113] Thus the space previously occupied by the
human monarch Corictic is ultimately occupied not by a sign but by the
marked *absence* of a sign. His significance ultimately lies in the fearful fate of
being stripped of significance or being rendered hopelessly ambiguous. We
ask, as doubtless did the original audience, is Corictic finally human or animal? And so this king's fate ends up seeming not all that different from that of
Lóegaire, whose ambivalence is posthumously rendered a semantic ambiguity
and whose destiny it is to become a perpetual malingerer between kingdoms
and between Christian and pagan.

Recruiting on the Margins

While he freely exiles recalcitrant kings to the marginal zone of "nonpersons,"
Patrick finds recruits from among the ranks of those deprived of name or
social privilege, such as Conall, son of Amolgaid, who stood ignored outside
the dwelling of the king of Ireland. With the coming of Christianity, remarkable shifts take place inside and outside the social body, indicated, if not
actually effected, by Patrick's conferring, changing, or removing signs. He
invests, for instance, the reinstated Conall with his bishop's crozier, which
represents their joint authority.

Another such "outlandish" recruit for new Christian signification featured
in early Patrician hagiography is the brigand-king Mac Cuill, an extrasocial
tyrannus, as opposed to the social *tyrannus* Corictic.[114] In Muirchú's Life,
Mac Cuill's encounter with Patrick comes after the extended story of the
saint's trials at Tara:

> There was a certain man in Ulster in Patrick's time, Mac Cuill moccu Greccae.
> He was a very impious and savage tyrant, so that he was called Cyclops. . . . So

113. Although the fox and the wolf carry different semiotic charges in Irish tradition, it is valid
to bear in mind the strained, yet intimate relationship in medieval Irish tales between the figure
of the king and wolflike marauders to be found protecting, as well as preying on, the margins of
his realm. (I am grateful to Kathryn Lorenz for proposing this connection.) There is, for
example, the case of the tragic undoing of the kingship of Conaire at the hands of his feral
foster brothers in the Middle Irish *Togail Bruidne Dá Derga* (Destruction of Dá Derga's
hostel), on which, see McCone 1986; and J. Nagy 1985, 52–57, 142–46; text edited in Knott
1936. In Muirchú's account, it is as if Corictic goes to the opposite extreme of the continuum
that defines his kingship, extending from king within the social realm to canine warrior on the
margins, and drops off the continuum altogether.

114. Liam de Paor has pointed out that the mythological resonance of the name Mac Cuill,
also the name of a member of the primeval Túatha Dé Danann, makes the confrontation
between this figure and Patrick all the more symbolic (1979, 101, 120–21).

far gone in his impiety [was Mac Cuill] that one day, as he sat on a rugged hilltop in Druim Moccu Echach, where, sporting the basest symbols of cruelty, he would exercise his tyranny daily and wantonly slay passersby, he saw Patrick among them, radiant with the clear light of faith and glowing with a wondrous sort of diadem of celestial glory, walking down a proper road of life with his confidence in what he preached unshaken—and when he saw Patrick, Mac Cuill decided to kill him. He said to his henchmen, "Behold that seducer, a perverter of men comes, whose practice it is to concoct illusions with which to deceive and seduce many people. Let us go then and test him to see whether that god in whom he glories has any power."[115]

In this story, the boundaries of the social and cultural realm, on or beyond which our villain dwells, are shown to have their own system of signs. Mac Cuill is, if anything, overmarked. Not only does he have a nickname, but he bears signs of his monstrous behavior on his head, tokens to which his nickname (Cyclops) possibly refers.[116]

Patrick bears his own sign, the bright, diademlike light of faith that instantly identifies him to Mac Cuill. Himself a literal seducer who leads travelers astray, Mac Cuill judges Patrick to be a spiritual seducer, misleading people's minds and hearts with what the brigand considers false demonstrations of power, the *signa* that in his estimation are mere "illusions" (*praestigiae*). Mac Cuill and Patrick are thus both characterized as bearing significant signs that represent the dramatic changes, for good or bad, which brigand and saint can bring about in people's lives.

Like Lóegaire's druids, Mac Cuill sets out to engage Patrick in a dialogue of words and deeds in order to test the saint's power and that of his divine source of authority. The "icebreaker" in the conversation is a sign that Mac Cuill knows to be false: a brigand is slyly presented to the saint as if he were mortally ill. Challenged by the duplicitous Mac Cuill to heal the putatively sick man, the knowing Patrick archly declares, "It would be no wonder if he had been sick."[117] And the pagans find, to their horror, that the man is no

---

115. Erat quidam homo in regionibus Ulothorum Patricii tempore, Macuil m[oc]cu Greccae, et erat hic homo ualde impius saeuus tyrannus, ut cyclops nominaretur. . . . in tantum uergens impietatis in profundum ita ut die quadam in montosso aspero altoque sedens loco hi nDruim moccu Echach, ubi ille tyrannidem cotidie exercebat signa sumens nequissima crudelitatis et transeuntes hospites crudeli scelere interficiens, sanctum quoque Patricium claro fidei lumine radiantem et miro quodam caelestis gloriae deademate fulgentem uidens cum inconcussa doctrinae fiducia per congruum uiae iter ambulantem interficere cogitaret dicens satilitibus suis: "Ecce seductor ille et peruersor hominum uenit, cui mos facere praestigias, ut decipiat homines multosque seducat. Eamus ergo et temptemus eum et sciemus si habet potentiam aliquam ille deus in quo se glorietur" (1.23.1–5, Bieler 1979, 102.10–25).

116. On this and other physical markings associated with brigands in Irish tradition, see McCone 1986b, 21–22.

117. Nec mirum si infirmus fuisset (1.23.8, Bieler 1979, 104.6–7).

longer feigning sickness but is actually dead. Patrick's words make the hollow sign all too valid.

With Lóegaire's druids, the saint proved his ability to undo signs that, in the eyes of his opponents, betokened power. By taking away the false invalid's life, Patrick activates an inert sign constructed to deceive him; then he returns the man to life after Mac Cuill acknowledges Patrick's power. The dead brigand thus becomes a sign of the death of Mac Cuill's soul through sin and of its revival through repentance. In this instance, then, Patrick is defeating an enemy not by simply undoing his sign but by removing its ambiguity. The saint demonstrates his authority to the pagan brigands by making sure the corpse is a corpse and then raising the man from the dead.

This clarifying appropriation continues into the coda to the story, in which Patrick details to Mac Cuill what he, the now-repentant outlaw, is to do in order to obtain forgiveness for his sins. He is to leave Ireland in a rudderless boat, wearing minimal clothing and the "insignia of your sin on your head."[118] After drifting about on the sea, Mac Cuill, so conspicuously marked as a penitent, is found and adopted by two holy men on the Isle of Man, under whose instruction Mac Cuill becomes a noted cleric himself.[119]

Thus the signs of his cruelty and brigandage which Mac Cuill bore on his head are ultimately transformed under Patrick's supervision into an acknowledgment of his sinfulness and, ultimately, into clerical tonsure. In this story, the outsider, having come under Patrick's power, does not really move back into the social realm. Instead, he shifts to the different, more "positive" marginality of the holy man, who abjures the world of human conventions and social intercourse as vehemently as do brigands and other types of outsiders.[120]

The Origins of Armagh

Muirchú gives only one other instance of Patrick's raising the dead, a miracle with which he is particularly associated in other hagiographic accounts. It is to be found in the story of how the saint acquired the land upon which the monastery of Armagh was established. Here too, Patrick himself had slain the man he raises, and the context is yet another pagan's attempt to test Patrick's power and gauge his response to symbolic gestures.

Patrick, who is in search of territory, approaches a "wealthy and honorable man" named Dáire, who asks him, "'What land do you seek?' The holy man

118. Habens hoc insigne peccati tui in capite tuo (1.23.14, ibid., 104.24).
119. 1.23, ibid., 102–6.
120. The Christian figure of the *deorad Dé* 'exile of God' as well as the place of the non-Christian *deorad* and his displaced colleagues (the *cú glas* 'grey dog, wolf' and the *ambue*) within the taxonomy of early Irish social personhood are examined in Charles-Edwards 1976b. See ibid., 49, on Mac Cuill in particular.

said, 'I ask that you give me the hill named Druim Sailech, so that I may make something of the place.'"[121] Dáire bluntly refuses, although he does give Patrick some land nearby. Soon afterward, however, the deceitful Dáire retracts his grant with a sign that speaks louder than his words. He has a groom bring one of his horses onto Patrick's newly acquired land to graze. Patrick objects, "'Dáire has acted stupidly, letting brute animals disturb the little space that he has given to God.' Yet the groom did not listen, as if he were deaf, and, like a man who could not speak, he said nothing, not even opening his mouth, but departed, leaving the horse there for the night."[122]

In this scene, Patrick is confronted with two signs, each of which expresses hostility toward him. The first, the grazing horse, reveals the true intentions of Dáire, who in his conversation with Patrick seemed at least willing to coexist with the saint. The second sign, the seemingly deaf and mute groom, is a false sign, like the "corpse" Mac Cuill and his fellow brigands presented Patrick. Words, it is clear, have become cheap, and the time has come for nonverbal demonstrations of power.

Next day, the groom finds the horse dead, the saint having slain by remote control the sign of Dáire's ownership of the land. Upon being informed by the groom of the destruction of his property, the angered landowner, in the spirit of Lóegaire, orders Patrick killed but is then himself mortally struck down, either by the prescient Patrick (who has now dispensed not only with conversation but even with face-to-face confrontation) or by the virulence of his own words. The pretense put up by Dáire and his servant, that they are deaf and mute, renders genuine communication between them deadly in its consequences. Moreover, pretense becomes grim reality when Dáire is slain. Now he is truly deprived of all ability to hear or speak.

At this nadir in the relationship between Patrick and his current pagan opponent, it is once again the pagan woman who comes to the rescue, reestablishing a channel of communication. Dáire's widow realizes that her husband died as a result of his insult to the saint. Taking matters into her own hands, she orders that those who were sent to slay Patrick be recalled and that he be appeased. Verbal exchange is thus restored, but it is still oblique and devious:

> Two servants went to Patrick and, lying about what had happened, said, "Dáire is ill—let something be given by you by which perchance he may be healed."
> "To be sure," said Patrick. He blessed some water and gave it to them, saying, "Go and sprinkle some of this water on your horse, and then take the water

121. Homo diues et honorabilis. . . . "Quem locum petis?" "Peto," inquit sanctus, "ut illam altitudinem terrae quae nominatur Dorsum Salicis dones mihi, et construam ibi locum" (1.24.1–2, ibid., 108.1–7).
122. "Stulte fecit Daire bruta mittens animalia turbare locum paruum quem dedit Deo." At uero eques tamquam sordus non audiebat et sicut mutus non aperiens os suum nihil loquebatur, sed dimisso ibi equo nocte illa exiuit (1.24.3–4, ibid., 108.11–14).

[home] with you." They did so, and the horse was revived, and they took the water [home], and Dáire was brought back to life by means of the sprinkling of that holy water.[123]

Instead of showing the messengers that he knows what they are trying to conceal, Patrick perpetuates the deception and even complicates it. For he does not respond directly to their request, any more than Dáire had genuinely given Patrick the land. Patrick's response, in fact, would have been appropriate had the messengers' request concerned the slain horse. By offering to revive the horse instead of "curing" Dáire, Patrick, almost as if delivering a final slap at the offending pagan abusers of communication, substitutes the sign, the horse, for its sender, Dáire. The messengers, hardly deaf and dumb on this occasion, understand the substitution perfectly, and proceed to sprinkle the powerful sign of the holy water on both the horse and its owner, and thereby bring both back to life.

The story does not end there:

After all these things had happened, Dáire came to pay his respects to Patrick, bringing with him a wondrous imported bronze vessel of three measures' capacity. Said Dáire to Patrick, "May this bronze vessel be yours," and Patrick responded, "Grazacham." Returning home, Dáire said, "It is a stupid man who can say nothing worthwhile besides this 'grazacham' in thanks for such a wondrous bronze vessel of three measures' capacity." Dáire added to his servants, "Go and bring back to us our vessel." They left and said to Patrick, "We will take back the vessel." And still Patrick said, then as before, "Grazacham, take it," and they took it. Dáire queried them: "What did the Christian say when you took back the vessel?" "He said, 'Grazacham.'" "'Grazacham' upon its receipt, 'grazacham' upon its being reclaimed," said Dáire. "His expression is so useful. By virtue of these 'grazachams' his bronze vessel will be given back to him." This time Dáire went himself and brought the vessel to Patrick, saying, "Here is your vessel. You are a consistent and imperturbable man. In addition to the vessel, I will give you that portion of the land that you requested from me awhile back, as much of it as I have, and feel free to dwell upon it." And this became the city which is now called Armagh.[124]

123. Exieruntque duo uiri, qui dixerunt ei celantes quod factum est: "Ecce infirmatus est Daire; portetur illi aliquid a te si forte sanari possit." Sanctus autem Patricius sciens quae facta sunt dixit "Nimirum," benedixitque aquam et dedit eis dicens: "Ite aspargite equum uestrum ex aqua ista et portate illam uobiscum." Et fecerunt sic et reuixit equus, et portauerunt secum sanatusque est Daire asparsione aquae sanctae (1.24.7-9, ibid., 108.22-110.5).

124. Et uenit Daire post haec ut honoraret sanctum Patricium, portans secum eneum mirabilem transmarinum metritas ternas capientem, dixitque Daire ad sanctum: "Ecce his aeneus sit tecum," et ait sanctus Patricius "Grazacham." Reuersusque Daire ad domum suam dixit: "Stultus homo est, qui nihil boni dixit praeter 'Grazacham' tantum pro aeneo mirabili metritarum trium," additque Daire dicens seruis suis: "Ite reportate nobis aeneum nostrum."

In several important respects, this episode in the story of Dáire is a multiform of the previous one. Once again, Dáire does not take public speech seriously enough and reneges on his gift to Patrick. There is, as in the previous episode, a confrontation between the saint and Dáire's servants, which is reported back to the landowner. And this report elicits a reaction that is pivotal to the plot.

Of course, there are also significant differences between the two episodes, and as a sequence they depict progress in the communication between saint and pagan. In the story of the cauldron, it is Patrick's word, not Dáire's, that is initially "hollow," or at least seems so to Dáire, who considers the saint's response to the gift unsatisfactory. Before, Patrick had said Dáire behaved stupidly; now Dáire describes Patrick as stupid. Yet in his petulant response to Patrick's *grazacham*, Dáire once again revokes his gift and thus renders his own word suspect. Reciprocity breaks down despite continual attempts on the part of the pagans to converse with the saint. Dáire's servants hardly play deaf and dumb here. In fact, they return to Patrick eager to hear and report a response to what they have to say. Furthermore, Patrick does not deal with the problematic pagans by alternating between accommodation and retaliation. Rather, the solution lies in his resolutely maintaining the same attitude, and even saying the same word to them, despite the changing circumstances.

What is Patrick's *grazacham*, the expression that is so frustrating and yet ultimately satisfying to Dáire? It is most likely a phonetic transcription of the way Irish Latin speakers of Muirchú's day would have pronounced *gratias agimus* ("we give thanks"). If so, it is another example of the insinuation of a living voice into the hagiographer's literary text. Furthermore, this voice is all the more striking for speaking in Latin, as opposed to Irish. *Grazacham* is not only a blatantly spoken, not written, phrase that sticks out conspicuously in the text and offends the sensibilities of the well-schooled reader but is also meaningless to Dáire and his servants, who presumably do not understand Latin.

Patrick's utterance, however, has the power to persuade and to change hearts and circumstances, even if it strays from the standards of literary language or is downright unintelligible to its audience. *Grazacham* is empowered and becomes meaningful after it is used as a response to dramatically different situations. It becomes a projection of the speaker's own qualities, his consistency in the face of the inconsistencies of communication and communica-

---

Exierunt et dixerunt Patricio: "Portabimus aeneum." Nihilominus et illa uice sanctus Patricius dixit: "Gratzacham, portate," et portauerunt. Interrogauitque Daire socios suos dicens: "Quid dixit Christianus quando reportasti[s] aeneum?" At illi responderunt: "'Grazacham' dixit." Et ille respondens dixit: "'Grazacham' in dato, 'Grazacham' in ablato. Eius dictum tam bonum est; cum 'Grazacham' illis portabitur illi rursum aeneus suus." Et uenit Daire ipsemet illa uice et portauit aeneum ad Patricium dicens ei: "Fiat tecum aeneus tuus. Constans enim et incommotabilis homo es. Insuper et partem illam agri quam ollim petisti do tibi nunc quantum habeo, et inhabita ibi." Et illa est ciuitas quae nunc Ardd Machae nominatur (1.24.10–14, ibid., 110.5–22).

tors surrounding him. Both for the readers of the Life and for the pagans featured in this episode, a phrase severely handicapped as communication becomes the ultimate expression of Patrick's authority.

From this and other incidents we have considered, we can only conclude that words, whether spoken or written, do not make Patrick powerful. Instead, the speaking saint or the supernatural power inspiring his verbal performance makes the words instruments of his divinely sanctioned mission. In this important respect, Patrick as constructed in legend is not far from Patrick as he constructs himself in the *Confessio*.

The basis of dialogue between pagan and saint is at first threatened by the undervaluation of speech expressed in Dáire's broken promise and then the offence he takes at Patrick's *grazacham*. Another, equally serious threat to communication is the overvaluation of nonverbal signs, apparent in Dáire's overreaction to the death of the horse and in his revocation of his peace offering, the cauldron. These excesses, however, are checked, and a balanced understanding of what has been said and done spreads among all the characters of the drama, courtesy of Patrick. By the time their last verbal exchange occurs, so impressed is Dáire with Patrick that he grants him, in truth this time, the portion of land for which the saint had asked in their first encounter. And so, at long last, Patrick genuinely receives gifts that had been given to him, or that he had asked for, namely, the alternative parcel of land, the cauldron, and the hill of Armagh. This last gift, in which is rooted Patrick's lasting authority in Ireland, is obtained by means of the restoration of productive communication.

Patrick ascends to the heights of Armagh not by means of destructive displays of his power, such as those produced at Tara, but by means of what seems in comparison a ludicrously humble act. He triumphs by maintaining, no matter what the situation or reaction, his own "voice," which communicates in neither literary Latin nor Irish. To be effective in the mission of transforming Irish culture into Christian culture and of turning the voice of the Irish into a Christian voice, the proselytizing spoken word, even the humble *grazacham*, must be consistent and persistent, even more than it needs to be coherent, meaningful, or faithful to its written form.[125]

The prize won by Patrick, Armagh, or Ard Macha 'Hill of Macha', is

---

125. The story has lived on in oral storytelling tradition. In a version collected from Pádhraic Mac an Iomaire of Carna, County Galway, in the 1930s, Dáire has been replaced by Crom Dubh, a figure who typically plays the role of recalcitrant pagan in modern Patrician legendry, and *grazacham* with *Deo gratias*. To demonstrate the worth of his gratitude for Crom Dubh's gift of meat, "Patrick wrote the words 'Deo gratias!' three times on a piece of paper. Crom Dubh put the three quarters of beef on one side of the scales, and Patrick laid the piece of paper on which he had written 'Deo gratias!' three times on the other scale. The piece of paper weighed down that side of the scales, for it was much heavier than the three quarters of beef that Crom Dubh put in" (trans. in O'Sullivan 1977, 111; see also MacNeill 1962, 452–74; Ó hÓgáin 1985, 6–7).

located near the celebrated ancient capital of Ulster, Emain Macha 'Twins of Macha'. It is itself a powerful reminder of the pre-Christian heritage of Ireland, for Macha is a supernatural female who is a crucial figure in the pre-Christian mythology of Ulster as it is preserved in medieval literature.[126] Although the mythological aspect of the location is not mentioned at all in either Muirchú's or Tírechán's account, later sources point exultantly to the irony of founding Armagh on a site imbued with pre-Christian religious significance. That symbolic transformation and displacement are both at work in the story of Patrick's winning of Armagh is suggested by the story Muirchú tells of the saint's first visit to the hill as its new owner:

> Both Patrick and Dáire set out to inspect the wondrous and delightful offering of land. They ascended the hill and found a doe with its baby fawn lying there, on the site of where there is now the altar of the church to the north in Armagh. Patrick's companions wished to capture the fawn and kill it. The saint, however, did not wish for it to be killed and did not allow it to happen. Indeed, he himself held the fawn and put it on his shoulders. The doe followed him like the gentlest and sweetest of sheep, all the way to the place where Patrick released the fawn, in another glade, in the northern reaches of the area of Armagh, where even until today, according to those versed in tradition, some signs of Patrick's power persist.[127]

The wild animal, normally treated as prey, is here domesticated by the saint, whose intimate the fawn becomes, in the style of Benignus, the Irish boy who clings to Patrick. If not a veiled reference to the pre-Christian sacral connotations of Armagh, the deer is symbolic at least of the reticent pagans, such as Dáire, who are overwhelmed by Patrick's ability to communicate in a mode they come to understand, or whose power they sense. This element of the wild or the pagan, however, is not altogether absorbed into the Patrician juggernaut. The saint lets the fawn go near Armagh and settles on the land previously occupied by the animal, as if man and deer were exchanging residences. The glen where the deer is allowed to roam freely becomes home to signs of Patrick's miraculous power which persist down to Muirchú's era and are recorded in the memories of those versed in tradition (*periti*). At the

126. The pre-Christian background to Ard Macha and the significance of its proximity to Emain Macha are explored in Sharpe 1982, 48–59.

127. Et exierunt ambo sanctus Patricius et Daire ut considerarent mirabile oblationis et beneplacitum munus, et ascenderunt illam altitudinem terrae inuenieruntque ceruuam cum uitulo suo paruo iacente in loco in quo nunc altare est sinistralis aeclessiae in Ardd Machae, et uoluerunt comites Patricii tenere uitulum et occidere, sed noluit sanctus neque permissit, quin potius ipsemet sanctus tenuit uitulum portans eum in humeris suis, et secuta illum cerua uelut [mitissima] amantissimaque ouis usque dum dimisserat uitulum in altero saltu situm ad aquilonalem plagam Airdd Mache, ubi usque hodie signa quaedam uirtutis esse manentia periti dicunt (1.24.15–16, Bieler 1979, 110.23–112.4). On the connotations of the deer, see Lambkin 1987, 29–30.

epochal moment when Patrick obtains Armagh, the crowning symbol of his successful mission, a miraculous fusion occurs between human and animal, Christian and pagan. But the deer leaves Armagh and survives as a sign proliferating other signs, the subject of storytelling, in a place set apart from the ecclesiastical foundation Patrick has established. Patrick's animal protégé steers clear of Armagh, a place of writing, to which Muirchú, the recorder of past signs attempting to make literary sense out of the welter of tradition, professes his allegiance.

It would appear that the deer and Muirchú's written account of Patrick's accomplishments represent two separate modes of expressing and perpetuating Patrick's authority.[128] The hagiographer attempts to encompass the signs of power accessible through the other mode by mentioning them. Yet he does not go into detail, as if he suspected that the effort to incorporate into the text the power of something so immediate and still alive was doomed to failure.

Marked as it is by an uncharacteristic tenderness, the story of Patrick and the deer perhaps reflects a nostalgia for elements of the cultural past which were tolerated in the early days of Irish Christianity as Muirchú imagines them in the Life. The wild animal allowed to roam undisturbed by ecclesiastical progress is arguably emblematic of the positive side of the same past that produced the recalcitrant monarch Corictic. He too is consigned to a comparable isolation in the wilderness. Of course, release is not the same as banishment. And whereas we still hear of the deer in Muirchú's day, Corictic was never heard from after he was so radically demoted through the saint's curse. Nevertheless, both deer and profane king are left outside history as circumscribed by hagiography and remain unimplicated by that history.

Yet the deer is suggestive of more than mere pagan innocence. We should recall that the intense encounter between Lóegaire and Patrick was temporarily eased of its tension by the appearance of deer, that is, by Patrick and his company in the form of deer, escaping from the enraged king. In light of this story, it is possible to read the release of the deer of Armagh, which Patrick's companions had wanted to slay, much as Lóegaire had wanted to slay that other "deer," Patrick, as the saint's symbolic letting-go of a part of himself and of his style of signification and persuasion. To embark on the great collective project of Armagh, which culminates in the documents and claims collected in the Book of Armagh, is to give up the missionary's flexibility,

128. The Greek author Pausanias reported that a deer, sacred to the goddess Artemis, was found in latter-day Arcadia with a collar bearing the inscription: "Caught as a fawn when Agapenor [an Arcadian mentioned by Homer] was at Troy" (Pausanias 8.9.10, trans. in Levi 1971, 2:396). As the translator notes, "it was widely believed in antiquity that deer lived the longest of all animals" (ibid., n. 81). It is an intriguing coincidence that the witness to the past offered by Pausanias's deer, like that offered by the Armagh deer "tamed" in Muirchú's text, works together with writing as a "vehicle" for conveying a venerable account of the past (the *Iliad*, to which the inscription on the collar alludes).

freedom, and opportunity for dialogue in return for a relative fixity of relationships and communication.

The Canceled Dialogue of Patrick and Mochta

The account of the claiming of Armagh told in the Tripartite Life suggests in quite a different way that this monumental act and the culture it produced are predicated on a distinct, divinely mandated "tilt" toward a certain mode of persuasive discourse and an involuntary turning-away from another mode:

> Patrick returned to Fir Roiss, and settled in Druim Mór in the district of Ross above Clúain Caín. It is there that the angel came to him and said, "Not here was it granted for you to stay." "Then where?" asked Patrick. "Seek out Armagh in the north," said the angel. . . . Then Patrick went to Ard Pátraic to the east of Lugmag and tried to settle there. . . . Patrick would go west every day from Ard Pátraic, and Mochta [a local saint] would come east from Lugmag, so that they would meet every day for conversation at Lecc Mochta. One day, as they were there, the angel placed a letter between them. Patrick read the letter, and this is what it said:
>
>> "The devout cleric Mochta,
>> let him stay where he has settled,
>> while Patrick will go by the word of his King
>> and stay at gentle Armagh."
>
> So Patrick went after that to Armagh as instructed by the angel.[129]

Other than the story of Patrick's death, while I shall discuss shortly, and the story of Miliucc's suicide, this is the only instance in Patrician hagiography in which we see the saint's desire thwarted. It is, moreover, not simply a matter of human limitations in the face of a conflicting divine will. For example, in the famous tale of his fasting on the mountain Crúachán Aigli in the Tripartite

---

129. Luid dano for cúlu co Firu Ross, co torinscan congbáil hi nDruim Mór hi crích Ross os Chlúain Caín. Is and do dechaid int aingel a dóchum 7 dixit: "Ní sund rorath duit airisem." "Cest, cairm?" ol Pátraic. "Saig in Machai fothúaid," ol int aingel. . . . Is ed dochóid Pátraic íar sin do Ardd Pátraic fri Lúgmag anair, 7 folámadair congbáil and. . . . Ticed Pátraic anair cech día ó Ard Pátraic, 7 Mochtae aníar ó Lúgmag, co comraictis immaccaldaim cach día oc Licc Mochtae. Láa n-ánd tucc int aingel epistil eturru. Arléga Pátraic in n-epistil, 7 is ed ro baí hi suidiu: Mochta craibdech credal / bíid i n-airm i rragab: / téit Pátraic la bréithir a Ríg / i mMachai mín anad. . . . Dodechoid tra Pátraic íar sin don Machai, la breithir ind aingil (Mulchrone 1939, lines 2672–98). In the Latin Life of Mochta, or Mauchteus, the saints upon their angelically enforced separation bequeath their monasteries to each other (c. 7, Heist 1965, 396–97; noted in Doherty 1991, 59).

Life, Patrick holds out quite impressively against divine pressure, applying his own counterpressure until his demands are met.[130]

Rather, Armagh, like Miliucc, represents a reality that is in some important respects incompatible with the Patrician worldview and style. The absence of Patrick's remains from his chief ecclesiastical establishment is a fact that cannot be simply refashioned by the hagiographer to fit the saint's outlook and desires as he imagines them. This fact forms an integral part of the Patrician tradition, like the thwarted reconciliation with his pagan master.

Miliucc, the emblem of hard-core paganism and the "unredeemable" elements of the pagan past, deprives Patrick of the opportunity to speak with that past and master it fully. Instead of an opportunity for dialogue, Patrick is presented with a mute, flaming sign of bold defiance which leaves him speechless. In the story from the Tripartite Life, by contrast Patrick, feeling comfortable in the environs of Ard Pátraic, resists the future himself and turns a deaf ear to the angel's unambiguous direction to Armagh. This defiance is finally brought to a halt when a letter containing the word of the angel is thrust in Patrick's face, and he is forced to acknowledge the divine order by reading it aloud. Here, the sign that stops Patrick is a letter, which, unlike Miliucc's pyre, does not render him speechless but forces him to speak the words of another. These, moreover, are words that contradict the saint's own wishes.

In each of these cases, the authoritative voice of Patrick is tempered, and the saint is thwarted, sent back to Díchu or forward to Armagh, on his appropriate way. Within the context of the saint's life, this is displacement. In the context of the history of Christianity in Ireland, however, as reconstructed in hagiographic tradition, it is destiny.

The angel's delivery of the letter is clearly inspired by the vision described in the *Confessio*, in which the dream letter from Victoricus calls Patrick's attention to the voices of the Irish calling him back. The missive featured in the Tripartite Life episode is also associated with the spoken word. It is a translation into a literate form of the directive of the angel, which had already been delivered personally to Patrick once before. But no longer is the letter a device for evoking or memorializing spoken and heard communication that can and will happen again, as when Patrick reaches the Wood of Fochloth. It is now the final, authoritative form of words that have already been spoken. In fact, the letter, and the command it contains, interrupts and terminates the conversation (*immacallam*) in which Patrick was wrongly engaged. When the letter is literally interjected into the dialogue, Patrick can no longer speak freely to his dialogue partner Mochta, but is impelled to read out a message that will separate them beyond the range of conversation.[131]

---

130. Mulchrone 1939, lines 1289–1374. Tírechán sketches the legend (c. 38, Bieler 1979, 152).

131. The deference Patrick shows to Mochta takes on even more meaning when we consider

Throughout his mission Patrick relies on the authority communicated through his voice. This reliance is complemented by his dutiful dissemination of the written word and the authority contained in it. His voice, however, is finally restrained by a text and "contained" within the space it prescribes, namely, Armagh. It can hardly be coincidental that the reluctant writer of the *Confessio* who sees his face marked with a disapproving inscription in his dreams, is transformed in legend into a man driven, indeed forced, by the power behind the literate culture he espouses to found Armagh, which in time will conscript his voice of authority as its own.

Death Away from Home

Patrick, however, in a defeat of hagiographic expectations, did not die in Armagh. He died instead at Saball, on land given to him by his first convert, Díchu. This detail, which is not denied even by the most propagandistic of Armagh's hagiographers, would seem to deprive this monastic foundation of its potentially most valuable connection with the saint.[132] For the center of a saint's cult was normally the ecclesiastical foundation where he had died and been buried, where at the Last Judgment, he would rise from the dead and protect his devotees, who maintained his cult at its center, from the wrath of God. Muirchú and the author of the Tripartite Life solve this problem by explaining that, in fact, as part of the deal struck by the saint in accepting Saball as his final resting place, Patrick himself would be judging *all* the Irish

---

Charles Doherty's observation that Mochta is traditionally associated with County Louth, the homeland of the abbot of Armagh, Torbach (d. 808), on whose behest the Book of Armagh was written. "The Patrician dossier was certainly much more relevant to Torbach than personal antiquarism. As an outsider from Louth he was clearly justifying his right to be heir of Patrick at a time of intense and bloody political rivalry over control of the abbacy" (Doherty 1991, 58; cf. Bieler 1979, 49 n. 5).

On traditions concerning Mochta, said by Adomnán to be a British emigrant in Ireland, see Doherty 1991, 59; Sharpe 1990b; and Dumville et al. 1993, 54–57. The letter featured in our story is not the only one associated with this saint: one of his own letters, reminiscent of Patrick's style no less (ibid., 54), is briefly quoted in the notice on his death included in the Annals of Ulster (under 535 A.D., Mac Airt and Mac Niocaill 1983, 70). In the letter as quoted, Mochta is characterized as a *discipulus Patricii*. (On the significance of this entry, see Sharpe 1990b, 87–88.) He also plays a role in the tradition centered on Columba, whose impending birth, according to Adomnán, Mochta foretold (second preface, Anderson and Anderson 1991, 4). These details have led Dumville to characterize this saint as a figure with whom "prophecies and letters seem to be peculiarly associated" (Dumville et al. 1993, 57). Like the more secular ancients with whom the Patrick of later literary tradition consults (see pp. 317–21), Mochta appears as a venerable, almost anterior figure (with an amazing life-span of three hundred years, according to his Life, c. 19 [Heist 1965, 400]), to be approached for dialogue and knowledge about the past as well as the future. Liam de Paor has observed: "In the case of Mochta at least, we seem to have an example of the motif of the witness who reports an earlier to a later time" (1979, 97).

132. Here I am following Sharpe 1982b, 40–44, where the complexities and contradictions of the extant traditions concerning Patrick's death and burial are set out.

on Judgment Day. Hence the entire island is entitled to the saint's protection, not just those living in the vicinity of his burial site. Nevertheless, the displacement of the dying Patrick from Armagh remains a problem, and Muirchú does not avoid it. Indeed, he emphasizes it almost morbidly:

> After so many miracles, which are written down elsewhere and which the world recounts faithfully, as the day of his death approached, an angel came to him and told him that he was going to die. And so he sent a message to Armagh, which he loved above every other place, and ordered that several people come to him to escort him to where he wanted to go. Then with his companions he began the journey to Armagh, the place he desired to be, of his own free will. Beside the road, however, there was a burning bush that was not consumed by flames, like the bush that appeared to Moses long ago. In the bush was the angel Victor, who was wont to visit Patrick often, and Victor sent another angel to Patrick to prohibit him from proceeding to where he wished to proceed. This angel said, "Why are you setting out without benefit of Victor's counsel? In connection with this matter Victor summons you; abandon your trip and find him." And he left the road as he had been ordered and asked Victor what he should do. The angel responded, "Return to the place whence you started out (that is, Saball), and [if you do so] the four requests you made [of God] will be granted to you. . . . I tell you therefore to return thus, and dying [back at Saball] you will travel on the road traveled by your fathers."[133]

As in the story of Patrick's reluctant trek to Armagh in the Tripartite Life, the breakdown in communication between Patrick and his guardian angel Victor, whose counsel he had not sought, is signaled by the repetition of the act of communication by way of a proxy. Here, however, the proxy is not a letter but another angel, who converses with Patrick while Victor stands by as the burning bush, a mute sign of his presence.

The conflict between saintly nostalgia and the divine source of his authority is complicated by Muirchú's highlighting the biblical paradigm behind Patrick's crisis (Moses and the burning bush—Ex. 3:2–4). Instead of empowering Patrick to undertake new salvific adventures, as the epiphany did Moses,

133. Post uero miracula tanta, quae alibi scripta sunt et quae ore fideli mundus celebrat adpropinquante die mortis eius uenit ad eum anguelus et dixit illi de morte sua. Ideo ad Ardd Machae missit, quam prae omnibus terris dilexit; ideo mandauit ut uenirent ad eum uiri multi ad eundem deducendum quo uoluit. Inde cum comittibus suis iter carpere coepit ad Machi uoluntariae, tellurem cupitam satis. Sed iuxta uiam rubus quaedam arserat et non conbure[ba]tur sicut antea Moysi prouenerat. In rubo Victor erat anguelus, qui Patricium sepe uissitare solebat, et Victor alterum anguelum ad Patricium prohibendum ne pergat quo pergere cupít missit, et dixit illi: "Quare profisceris sine Victoris consilio? Quam ob rem Victor te uocat, et ad eum declina." Et ut ei iussum est declinauit et quid facere deberet interrogauit. Et respondens anguelus dixerat: "Reuertere ad locum unde uenis (hoc est Sabul) et datae sunt quattuor petitiones tibi quas petisti. . . . Reuertere igitur sicut tibi dico, et moriens ingredieris uiam patrum tuorum" (2.4–5, 7, Bieler 1979, 116.8–21, 116.29–118.1).

this fire reminds the soon-to-die saint of the limits of his power, and the continuing need for him to pay need to the voice of a higher authority. This necessary framing of Patrick's voice and actions within a hierarchy of authorities, including those of the angel and the hagiographic tradition that denies Patrick the burial site of Armagh, is already expressed in the sentence with which Muirchú opens this section: "After so many miracles, which are written down in other sources." Thus the crucial report of what the angel said to Patrick about his death *before* he died follows a pointed reference to what has been said *after* Patrick's death about his miracles, an account that is said to be available in writing.[134]

This is only the second time that Victor (or Victoricus) appears in Muirchú's narrative not as a speaker but as a visible sign. The previous instance was in the sequence of the twin stories of Díchu and Miliucc, where reference was made to the footprint left by Victor as he was breaking off his conversation with Patrick to ascend to heaven. Patrick, we recall, was passing within viewing distance of this angelic track on his way to the intractable Miliucc. The latter, a potential speaker turned into a mute sign of unreceptivity, is the first of several fiery markers Patrick encounters or creates in the course of his mission which map the boundaries of his authority.

Thus Patrick is either forced into founding the church of Armagh, according to the Tripartite Life, or, according to Muirchú, he is forced to dissociate himself from it in an important respect. He is not allowed to die or be buried there. There is a discontinuity as well as continuity between Patrick and Armagh, both the place and latter-day monastic culture over which Armagh claimed primacy.

The hagiographic tradition, however, as exemplified by Muirchú's work and the Tripartite Life, turns a potential weakness of Armagh's claim into a limitation of Patrick's own power. His displacement from or to Armagh is the result of a directive that the saint resists but finally obeys. His reluctance or his own desires in both cases make him less responsive or solicitous in his ongoing conversation with his angel Victor. This lapse in communication leads in both texts to a termination of the conversation by means of a third "party" who gives Patrick the order in no uncertain terms.

The breakdown of the dialogue with the angel is a serious matter, given the centrality of this exchange to the definition of Patrick's authority as formulated both by Patrick himself in the *Confessio* and by the hagiographic tradition. It is important to appreciate just how mundane for Patrick the conversations with his angel are, in the picture of his life drawn by Muirchú and other biographers. Already in the opening section of his account of the

---

134. The statement of course contradicts Muirchú's earlier implication that little had been written about Patrick's life (ibid., 62.1–6).

saint's life, Muirchú reminds us of Patrick's special communication link with the divine:

> After the many tribulations he experienced there [in Ireland], after the starvation and thirst, after the cold and nakedness, . . . and after the frequent visits of the angelic Victoricus, sent to Patrick by God, after the great miracles known to almost everyone, after the divine communications [to Patrick], of which I will quote one or two for the purpose of providing examples—"Well you should fast, for you are soon to return to your country," or "Lo, your ship is prepared" . . . —after all these things, as we said, which could hardly be enumerated by anyone . . . having left behind a tyrannical pagan, Patrick sailed to Britain.[135]

Noteworthy in this passage is the contrast between the "great miracles" of Patrick, which are declared to be public record, and the "divine communications," of which Muirchú quotes only "one or two," as if they were not as ingrained in common knowledge as the miracles or as if they were too numerous to list. It is in fact to the communications that Muirchú's summarizing qualification, "these things . . . which could hardly be enumerated," most immediately refers, by virtue of their being placed last in the list of things experienced by Patrick in captivity.

The angelic messages Muirchú cites are actually quotations from the *Confessio*. They are thus literary extracts, presentable outside of their conversational context. Even though they are words uttered by the angel to Patrick, these quotations markedly derive from a text, and so they form a contrast with the breakthroughs of living voice which, as we have seen, are strategically placed, usually in dialogic situations, in the Life. Indeed, the only other place where Muirchú includes any of the words spoken by an angelic visitor to Patrick is in the episode of Patrick's thwarted trip to Armagh, where the angel speaking is pointedly *not* Victor. Despite its celebrity and centrality to the Patrician mission, the dialogue between the saint and his usual angelic discussant therefore remains mostly private and confidential, outside the public, written realm of Muirchú's Life.

The "tyrannical pagan" Muirchú mentions, whom Patrick left behind, is Miliucc. We recall that it is arguably in connection with the traumatic outcome of Patrick's search for Miliucc that Muirchú elaborates on Patrick's angelic intimacies.[136] I suggested earlier that this extended reference to the

---

135. Post multas ibi tribulationes, post famem et sitim, post frigora et nuditates, . . . post frequentias angelici Victorici a Deo ad illum missi, post magnas uirtutes omnibus pene notas, post responsa diuina, e quibus unum aut duo haec exempli tantum gracia demonstrabo: "Bene ieiunas, cito iturus ad patriam tuam," et iterum: "Ecce nauis tua parata est" . . . post haec omnia, ut diximus, quae enumerari poene a nemine possunt . . . deserto tiranno gentilique homine . . . ad Britanias nauigauit (1.1.4–5, Bieler 1979, 66.31–68.11).
136. Ibid., 80.20–82.11.

angel partially recovers the figure of Patrick from the defeat handed to him by the defiant Miliucc, perhaps just as Victor, according to a story recounted in this passage, helped Patrick recover Miliucc's swine, which Patrick had lost. Indeed, in alluding to the angel's beneficence, Muirchú may be attempting to balance out his story of Patrick's failure to redeem himself from his master by alluding to an alternative tradition concerning how the relationship with Miliucc was concluded. According to some other early Latin lives of Patrick, the angel led the slave Patrick not merely to a herd of swine but to a cache of gold with which to purchase his freedom from Miliucc before leaving Ireland and his term of slavery.[137]

In the company of the angel, Patrick could always engage in privately empowering conversation. Yet, in his selections from the discourse between Patrick and Victor and in the way he presents those selections, Muirchú gives his readers only enough to certify Patrick's divine authorization. Otherwise, the interplay of their voices is either suppressed or unknown to Muirchú and his sources. The net effect of this metonymical representation is not a totality grasped but the portrayal of a rather stilted and stifling angelic voice speaking to and not with Patrick; the rest of the conversation, that unquantifiable portion which gave the saint so much pleasure, is left unheard. In describing the miraculous in Patrick's life, Muirchú pays far more attention to the public acts that people comprehend through the medium in which the hagiographer works than to the intimacies of angelic discourse.

The Cross by the Road

One of those "great miracles" that Muirchú includes in the latter part of his Life, shortly before his account of Patrick's death and burial, features a different type of conversation, involving a different type of supernatural being:

> Concerning his diligence in prayer. Whether staying somewhere or traveling, he was wont to chant all the psalms and the hymns, the Apocalypse of John, and all the spiritual canticles of Scripture daily, and he would also sign himself with the sign of the cross every hour of the day and night; for whatever cross he would see, he would stop his journey, stepping out from his chariot and reverencing it with prayer.
>
> Wherefore, on a certain day Patrick approached a cross which was situated near the road, but not seeing it, he passed it by. His charioteer did see it, however, and, after they had come to some hostel for which the charioteer had been heading, and as they began to pray before the meal, the charioteer said, "I saw a cross located near the road by which we came." Patrick left the hostel and,

137. Bieler 1971, 68, 124.

going back the way he had come, prayed. He saw a grave there, and he asked the dead person buried in that grave how he had died and whether he had lived in faith. The dead man responded, "I was a pagan in life, and here I was buried. But some woman from another region had a son who, having been long separated from her, died and was buried in her absence. After some days the grieving mother came to lament her lost son and in confusion thought that the grave of the pagan was that of her son, and she put the cross by the grave of the pagan." It was for this reason, said Patrick, that he did not see the cross, since it was in a pagan place of burial. And so the miracle emerged as greater by virtue of the dead person's speaking, the discovery of the man who died a Christian, and his being rewarded with the placement of the sign of the beloved cross beside him, its true destination.[138]

Patrick's *uirtus* 'miracle', the text emphasizes, is magnified in this incident not only because he once again raised the dead but also because the dead man spoke to him. This dialogue is conducted in public, or at least the saint's charioteer is present. This detail is pivotal to Tírechán's version of the story, as we shall soon see.

In some respects, it is helpful to consider the incident at the gravesite in light of another demonstration of Patrick's power over the dead, analyzed earlier. We saw in an episode in the story of the sons of Amolgaid the spectacle of Óengus's sister's revival and her attempt to win over her brother by means of a description of the afterlife. Her authority, as one who knows the beyond firsthand, is joined with Patrick's to produce an overwhelmingly persuasive

138. De dilegentia orationis. Omnes psalmos et ymnos et Apocalipsin Iohannis et omnia kantica spiritalia scripturarum cotidie decantans siue manens aut in itenere pergens, tropeo etiam crucis in omni hora diei noctisque centies se signans et ad omnes cruces quascumque uidisset orationis gratia de curru discendens declinabat.

Inde etiam in die quadam ingrediens crucem, quae erat iuxta uiam sita, non uidens praetergressus est. Hanc tamen auriga uidit, et ille dixit cum ad hospitium quoddam quo tenderat peruenissent et orare ante prandium coepissent, dixit, inquam, auriga: "Vidi crucem iuxta uiam per quam uenimus positam." At ille dimisso hospitio per uiam quam uenerat pergens orauit, et sepulcrum ibi uiderat, et mortuum in illo busto sepultum interrogauit qua morte abierat et sub fide uixerat. Respondit mortuus: "Gentilis uixi et hic sepultus fui. Quaedam etiam mulier in alia prouincia degens mortuum filium qui se longue separatus erat habuit et illa absente sepultus est; at post aliquot dies lugens mater omissum filium planxit et indiscreto errore sepulchrum gentilis hominis sui filii bustum esse putans crucem iuxta gentilem possuit." Et ob hanc caussam, ut Patricius dixit, crucem non uiderat quia sepulturae gentilis locus fuit. Et uirtus maior inde surrexerat, ut mortuus loqueretur et qui sub fide defunctus erat Christi scieretur et iuxta illum almae crucis fieret meritum signo in uero termin[i]o possito (2.1–2, Bieler 1979, 114.1–22).

A model for this story may have been the episode recounted in the fourth-century Life of Martin of Tours by Sulpicius Severus in which the saint invokes the spirit of a dead man to determine whether he truly was a holy man worthy of the flourishing cult centered on his grave. The voice of the dead man tells Martin that he was no saint but a brigand (c. 11; see Stancliffe 1983, 370). We should recall that Sulpicius's Life is contained in the Book of Armagh, a manuscript that also contains the only copy of Muirchú's Life to have survived in Ireland.

statement. In the tale currently under consideration, the dead man temporarily granted the gift of speech does not talk of his current existence, as did
the revived sister. Instead, his disembodied voice provides the reasons for
Patrick's curious oversight, which had been pointed out to him by his charioteer. With the restoration of his ability to communicate with the living, the
affable pagan in turn restores Patrick's reputation as an indefatigable and
unerring reader of signs, such as crosses encountered on the wayside. The
description of Patrick which sets the scene for this episode links his respect for
the ultimate Christian sign, the cross, with his knowledge of the literature of
the Christian faith, which he proclaims daily. He merges, as it were, its authority with that of his own voice, being not only an avid reader but also a
fervent reciter.

In contrast to the masses converted as a result of the resuscitation of the
dead sister and her child in the saga of the conversion of the sons of Amolgaid,
only one skeptic is persuaded by the corpse speaking from under the cross, the
saint's own charioteer. This miracle is seemingly performed for the benefit of
someone who is already a member of the Christian community, and it is
meant to solve an internal problem of perception and interpretation. Moreover, in this instance the revenant cannot be said to have any authority of his
own. Although he knows whereof he speaks and provides valuable information for the puzzled Patrick, by so forthrightly admitting to the inappropriate-
ness of the cross as his sign, he in effect confesses to his literal insignificance.

At first, the seemingly absentminded Patrick of this episode resembles the
Patrick who resists the repeated angelic message to head for Armagh or
the Patrick who proceeds to Armagh without consulting his angel first. In the
present episode, he seems to be once again missing a sign as commonplace in
his everyday life as are his conversations with Victor(icus). It turns out, however, that Patrick has been perfectly justified in not noticing the cross, since
the sign was misplaced, signifying the wrong "signified." It is thus as hollow
as the signs produced by the druids, which Patrick so easily dismantles. Re-
dounding to the saint's credit, at least according to the epilogue to this
episode, is the planting of the cross in the right spot, over the grave of the
previously unmarked Christian. Not only does the saint unscramble this odd
skewing of signification, but he reunites sign with its proper signified. He
rectifies the real mistake, which took place in the past, when the distraught
mother of the Christian put the cross on the wrong grave. Intriguingly, her
distraction was caused by the oral expression of her grief, her keening
("lugens . . . planxit"), which in Irish tradition, as in others, is a formalized
genre of oral performance with its roots in the pre-Christian past.[139] The

---

139. In the Old Irish Penitential, composed, according to Daniel Binchy, "not later than the
end of the eighth century" (appendix to Bieler 1963, 258), keening is counted as a sin
requiring substantial penance (5.17, ibid., 273). Compare the roughly contemporary Bigotian

interference and confusion caused by keening leaves her son unmarked as a Christian and renders the most authoritative Christian visual sign powerless and invisible, at least to Patrick. This is, however, a "happy fault," for her error accidentally brings about a vindication of Patrick's authority in the form of a memorable public dialogue between Patrick and a heathen of yore. Once again, women provide the link between the saint and natives who are unwilling or, in this case, unable to converse with him.

The voice of the helpful pagan restores proper signification for Patrick, the dead Christian, and the Christian community at large, which marks out its space, both physical and metaphysical, with the crosses to which Patrick so assiduously pays respect. But in restoring the significance of the cross, Patrick leaves the pagan out of the accounting, as the charioteer points out in Tírechán's account of the incident:

> [Having heard what the dead pagan had to say,] Patrick exited his chariot, grabbed the cross, and plucked it out of the heathen mound and planted it over the face of the baptized one. He then climbed back into his chariot and prayed to God silently. After he said, "Deliver us from evil," his charioteer spoke to him: "Why did you call upon the unbaptized man? For I feel sorry for a person who lacks baptism. God would have preferred that you bless him as if he were being baptized, and pour the water of baptism over the dead one's grave." But Patrick did not speak to him. I myself think he left the pagan alone because God did not wish for him to be saved. Let us now return to our account.[140]

The charioteer in no uncertain terms says Patrick has missed an opportunity to extend Christian mercy to the pagan and include him in the plan of salvation he brings to Ireland. Why didn't Patrick make the invisible cross a true sign by rendering the false signifier true, just as in a dramatic episode of Muirchú's Life Patrick deprived Mac Cuill's cohort of life in order to make the appearance of death a reality? Patrick's determination to ensure proper packaging without doing anything about the contents he had helped to reveal troubles the charioteer and perhaps even the hagiographer, who abruptly

---

Penitential, which condemns the commemorative *bardicatio* (translated by Bieler as "wailing") of women (ibid., 230).

140. Et exilít Patricius de curru suo et tenuit crucem et euellebat de gentili tumulo et posuit super faciem babtitzati, et ascendit super currum et orauit Deum taciter. Cum dixisset "libera nos a malo," dixit illi auriga illius: "Quid," auriga illius inquit, "cur appellasti gentilem non babtitzatum uirum? Quia ingemesco uirum sine babtismo. Melior erat apud Deum illum benedicere uice babtismatis et effundere aquam babtismi super sepulcrum mortui." Et non respondit illi; puto enim ideo eum reliquit, quia Deus eum saluare noluit. Redeamus ad historiam nostram (c. 41.3–4, Bieler 1979, 156.4–11).

Vernacular precedents for the figure of the charioteer who speaks his mind were pointed out by Binchy (ibid., 230, note on c. 41.4).

moves his narrative away from this episode.[141] By opting for a zealous realignment of sign with the intended signified, the saint cuts off communication with the pagan forever. Immediately afterward, Patrick withdraws into strictly private, prayerful conversation with God and then pointedly fails to respond to the charioteer's question. This breakdown of free and open dialogue, as in the stories concerning Patrick's ambiguous association with Armagh, accompanies an inscrutable divine will that ordains a conspicuous discontinuity. In this instance, the discontinuity is not in the relationship between Patrick and the future culture he establishes, but between the saint and the previous culture he helps to supplant.

Despite the potential for salvation and synthesis implicit in the purported conversation, the voice from the grave accidentally marked with the cross remains unredeemed, doomed to obscurity and silence. Living pagans can embrace and be embraced by the new order. Consider, for example, the *magi* Caplait and Mael, who survive the deaths of their fosterlings and become priests of the new religion. A dead pagan's acceptance into the community of saints, however, at least in this case, goes against God's will. Tírechán, it should be noted, merely speculates about the justification for this exclusion, offering no firm conclusions. Does such exclusion occur because the dead are not always deemed worthy of absorption into the new culture Patrick espouses? Or rather is it because their authority can be sufficient to threaten Patrick?

A False Prophet and a Genuine Swineherd

In Tírechán's text answers to these questions are perhaps provided within the sequence of episodes in which we find the story of the invisible cross. It immediately precedes the final chapter of the story of the sons of Amolgaid in which the climactic confrontation between Patrick and the druids of his shy converts takes place. Each of these consecutive tales features a Christian seemingly placed in jeopardy directly or indirectly by his equally Christian parent. Conall's father offers him to Patrick, who gives him a dangerous assignment; the unnamed Christian has no marker for his grave because of his mother's oversight. The tableau in the second tale in this sequence, Conall standing next to the chief druid to indicate his identity to Patrick, echoes the preceding tableau of the adjacent graves of heathen and Christian, with the Christian sign paradoxically marking the wrong grave. In the incident of the overlooked cross, the pagan is left in his mortal obscurity, and in the following episode, the druid is mercilessly eradicated, as if a dead but cooperative heathen can pose as much danger as a living but resistant druid.

141. Following Bieler, I am assuming that the *redeamus ad historiam nostram* belongs at the end of this passage (ibid.).

Other insights into the tale of Patrick and the misplaced cross are to be gleaned from a consideration of the two stories directly preceding it in Tírechán's narrative sequence. These also feature the pre-Christian dead and Patrick's control over them. The first story in this sequence shows Patrick disproving a pagan thesis that there is a close, sacred affinity between the dead and the places where they are buried:

Patrick went to a well in Findmag called Slán [Whole, Healthy], since it had been told to him that druids pay homage to this well and offer gifts to it as if it were a god. The well was square-shaped, with a square stone on its opening, and water would flow over the stone, that is, through the joints, like a royal trace [?]. The incredulous said that a certain deceased prophet had made a casket for himself underwater under the stone, so that he might purify his bones forever, for he feared being burned with fire. Hence they worshiped the well like a god. Now the background to this cult was explained to Patrick, and he, fired by the zeal of the living God, said, "It is untrue what you say, namely, that this well is the King of Waters" (for they had named it "King of Waters"). The local druids and pagans congregated at the well, along with an enormous crowd, and Patrick said to them, "Lift the stone. Let us see what is underneath, whether there are bones or not. For I say to you, there are no bones of any man down here, but only, methinks, a little of the gold and silver from your false offerings that has seeped through the joints of the stone structure." They could not, however, lift the stone. And so Patrick and his servants blessed the stone, and he said to the multitude, "Stand aside for a little while, so that you may see the strength of my God who lives in heaven." With his hands raised he lifted the stone from off the mouth of the well and positioned it just beyond the opening, and it has remained there ever since. And they found nothing in the well except water, and they all believed in God the Most High. A certain man sat apart near to the stone which Patrick had fixed in the ground, and Patrick blessed him, baptized him, and said to this person, whose name was Caeta or Cata, "Your seed will be blessed forever."[142]

142. Et uenit ad fontem Findmaige qui dicitur Slan, quia indicatum illi quod honorabant magi fontem et immolauerunt dona ad illum in modum dii. Fons uero quadratus fuit et petra quadrata erat in ore fontis (et ueniebat aqua super petram, .i. est per glutinationes) quasi uestigium regale, et dixerunt increduli quod quidam profeta mortuus fecit bibliothicam sibi in aqua sub petra, ut dealbaret ossa sua semper, quia timuit ignis exust[ion]em; quia adorabant fontem in modum dii. Et indicata est Patricio causa adorationis, et ipse zelum Dei habuit de Deo uiuo, et dixit: "Non uerum quod dicitis, quod rex aquarum fons erat" (quia dederunt illi nomen "aquarum rex"). Et congregati sunt magi et gentiles regionis illius et multitudo multa nimis ad fontem et Patricius ait illis: "Eleuate petram; uideamus quid subest, si ossa an non, quia dico uobis: sub ea ossa hominis non sunt; sed puto aliquid de auro et argento per glutinationem petrarum minime de uestris reprobis immolationibus"; et non potuerunt petram eleuare. Et benedixit Patricius et serui eius petram, et dixit Patricius multitudini: "Procul reddite pauliser, ut uideatis uirtutem Dei mei, qui in caelis habitat": et erectis manibus

Patrick undermines the reputation of the pagan landmark, only to construct it as a Christian one. Like the cross recovered from the mismarked grave, the stone covering the bogus object of pre-Christian worship is lifted up by Patrick, fixed in its new place forever, and memorialized in hagiographic tradition. To stunning effect, the saint exposes the emptiness of this sign of pagan life after death. There is after all no "prophet" behind the "royal trace" that emanates from the well. Furthermore, Patrick establishes a perpetual sign of "real" life after death in the person of Caeta. Here is a genuine individual standing by the stone, as opposed to the divinized human thought to be in the well, and a convert whose progeny "will be blessed forever."

There is a shift here, as in the story of the two graves, from a falsely signifying pre-Christian site to one of reestablished Christian signification. An important distinction, however, is that the site remains the same and presumably keeps or only then receives the name Slán 'Whole,' but it is rearranged and "converted" to Patrick's purposes of signifying the authority of the new faith and its proponents. The well is opened up, and what once lay horizontally, the stone lid, now stands erect. Moreover, the alignment between notable person and notable place is changed. In the native tradition centered on the Well of Findmag as reported by Tírechán, the location has become hopelessly confused with the legendary person associated with it. Because of the supposed presence of the sage, the well is itself treated as a royal person ("King of Waters").[143] Patrick pointedly disputes the anthropomorphic designation of the well as king. He insists that what makes it glow and produce a royal trace is not any numinous personal power within but the sacrifices offered to the well, that is, the results of the attribution of supernatural power to the site. The waters of Slán thus form a blank screen onto which pre-Christian assumptions about the sacred are projected. Indeed, Tírechán's description of the idolaters' understanding of the well's numinosity accords well with attestations recorded elsewhere of the archaic Indo-European concept of a fiery wisdom paradoxically residing in a body of water.[144]

The hagiographer presents this pre-Christian shrine as a literally and figuratively closed system of signification, interlocking person, place, and worshipers, a system that centers on a dead past and feeds on itself. For the more offerings made to the well or the dead man with whom it is associated, the more its water glitters and the more authoritative the cult becomes. Patrick opens the well to free the pre-Christian Irish, who cannot escape from it or

---

eleuauit petram ex ore fontis et ponebat illam e regione super ora fontis, et est semper. Et nihil inuenierunt in fonte nissi aquam tantum, et crediderunt Deo summo. Et sedit iuxta lapidem procul quem infixit uir quidam, cui benedixit Patricius, Caeta siue Cata nomine; et babtitzauit illum et dixit illi: "Erit semen tuum benedictum in saecula" (c. 39.2–7, ibid., 152.25–154.12).
143. Carney views *rex aquarum* as a possible reference to the mythological figure of Manannán, associated with the ocean and, specifically, the Isle of Man (1976, 185).
144. The Indo-European theme of "fire in the water" is described in Puhvel 1987, 277–83. P. Ford 1974 focuses on Celtic instances.

their preconceptions of sacred power by themselves. In addition, he replaces this closed system with an open, dynamic system of signification, through which a real life after death, a genuine everlasting future, is expressed.

The prophet that never was, a figment of the collective imagination, is said to have built his shelter in the waters in order to avoid fire.[145] Presumably, this is a reference to the fire awaiting intransigent pagans in hell. Doubtless another referent here is the fiery punishment Patrick regularly arranges for his druidic opponents. It is as if the prophet had anticipated the coming of Patrick, like his heathen colleagues, and built a shelter against the proselytizer's influence. But of course this prophet, Patrick demonstrates, never existed. Thus, within the repertoire, this tale balances out some of Patrick's more abrasive confrontations with pagans, such as the aborted encounter with Miliucc, who totally eradicates all traces of his existence with fire, so as to avoid the baptismal waters soon to be proffered by Patrick. Miliucc becomes a sign of pure negation which Patrick cannot dismantle. The pagan of the well, by contrast, purportedly fights fire with water and "becomes" the seemingly miraculous well, a sign of his continued life. In proving the traces of his existence false, Patrick renders a seeming sign of immortality into one of the Christian power to transform.

The episode that follows the tale of the well in Tírechán's text and directly precedes the account of the misplaced cross contrasts with both of the stories that frame it. It contains perhaps the most famous and discussed instance of resurrection recorded in Patrician hagiography:

> Saint Patrick traveled across the plains in the territories of Mac Erca in Dichuil and Aurchuil. In Dichuil Patrick came across a grave of wondrous size and stupendous in length, which his retinue was astonished to find extended a hundred and twenty feet long. They said, "We do not believe this business, that a man could have been this tall." Patrick responded, "If you wish, you will see him." "We wish it," they said, and so Patrick struck the stone near the head of the grave with his staff and made the sign of the cross over the grave, saying, "Lord, open the grave," and He opened it. And a large man arose whole and said, "Thank you, holy man for having raised me up out of many sorrows, if only for an hour." He wept most bitterly and asked, "May I walk with you?" They said, "We cannot allow you to walk with us, for men cannot look upon your face, for fear of you. But believe in the God of Heaven and accept the baptism of the Lord, and you will not return to the place where you were. And tell us whose [servant or descendant] you were." "I am the son of the son of Cas, son of Glas, and I was swineherd to Lugair, king of Irúaith. The war band [*fían*] of the son of Mac Con slew me in the reign of Cairpre Nia Fer, a hundred

---

145. Suggestively the word used for "shelter" is *bibliothica*, which in Hiberno-Latin sources (also spelled *bibliotheca*) typically refers to containers that preserve sacred Christian objects, particularly books. See Lambert 1991, 161–63; and Sharpe 1985.

years before today." He was baptized and made his confession to God. Having grown silent once again, he was restored to his grave.[146]

Unlike the previous miracle, in which a "grave" proved to be no grave at all, this demonstration of Patrick's power is aimed at convincing his own people, not an audience of unbelievers. The problem here is not that the onlookers give credence to a false sign but that they refuse to believe what signs seem to be saying. The gigantic grave and gravestone announce that here lies an enormous man, a superfluity of human dimensions, as opposed to the superfluity of human life-span which the glow emanating from the well was supposed to demonstrate.

Patrick's own ability to read signs of the past is in doubt here, as it is in the story of the misplaced cross, when the saint appears to overlook a sign and his charioteer believes what it seems to say. In the present story, Patrick maintains his flawless record of reading and interpreting signs and also vindicates the proportions of the pre-Christian past which his fellow Christians find hard to accept. Concomitantly, this ancient is not merely summoned to provide information and then dismissed to suffer his eternal punishment forever. Patrick baptizes the grandson of Cas, who, once converted, relapses into the silence of death. This cessation of dialogue, however, occurs only *after* the dead man has passed on authoritative information in acknowledgment of Patrick's voice, which evoked a "native" response in the first place and now inherits the knowledge of bygone matters the revenant has demonstrated.

Thus the life-restoring Patrick in effect re-presents the past to the contemporary Christian culture he has engendered. This culture balks at accepting its past, both its physical signs and its lingering presence, as well it should, given the skeptical orientation Patrick himself exhibits in the episodes preceding and following this story. Even here, the revived swineherd, despite his earnest

146. Et uenit sanctus Patricius per campos in regionibus Maicc Hercae in Dichuil et Aurchuil. Et uenit Patricius in Dichuil ad sepulcrum magnum magnitudinis mirae ingentemque longuitudine, quod inuenit familia illius et magno stupore mirabantur pedes traxisse centum uiginti, et dixerunt: "Non credimus hoc negotium quod esset homo longuitudinis huius." Et respondit Patricius et dixit: "Si uolueritis, uidebitis eum," et dixerunt: "Volumus," et percussit baculo suo lapidem iuxta caput eius et signauit sepulcrum signaculo crucis et dixit: "Aperi, Domine, sepulcrum," et aperuit. Et uir surrexit magnus sanus et dixit: "Bene sit tibi, o uir sancte, quod suscitasti me etiam una hora a doloribus multis," et ecce fleuit amarissime et dixit: "Ambulabo uobiscum?" Dixerunt: "Non possimus, ut nobiscum ambulaueris, quia non possunt homines uidere faciem tuam prae timore tuo. Sed crede Deo caeli et babtismum Domine accipe, et non reuerteris in locum quo fiebas; et indica nobis cuius es." "Ego sum Macc Maicc Cais Maic Glais, qui fui subulcus Lugir ríg Hirotae. Iugulauit me fian maicc Maicc Con in regno Coirpri Nioth Fer" (anno centesimo usque hodie). Et babtitzatus est et confessionem Dei fecit et resticuit et positus est iterum in sepulcro suo (c. 40, Bieler 1979, 154.15–33).

The story is discussed with an eye to possible sources and influences in Flower 1947, 5–11; Carney 1961, 142–52 (in which the connection with the story of the misplaced cross is noted); Szövérffy 1957, 48–96; Bieler 1975; and Ó hÓgáin 1985, 11–12 (which mentions a comparable legend from oral tradition in which the encountered ancient pagan is Conchobar, the king of Ulster featured in the so-called Ulster cycle of heroic tales).

request, is not allowed to travel with Patrick and his company, lest he prove to be more a repellent and threatening sign than a persuasive one. The pagan revenant is temporarily acceptable as a voice choked with contrition which speaks informatively of the past and of the Christian afterlife, but he cannot return in toto through a miracle that would go beyond translation of the past into the terms of the present and approach a potentially confusing equivocation.

Significantly, in a later life of Patrick, the revived swineherd, in his desire to escape his fate, even offers to carry Patrick's books but is sent back to his grave, albeit redeemed.[147] The representative of the pre-Christian past, who expresses himself through his voice, offers his allegiance to the expression of the ultimate authority behind the culture of the present: the book. But this realignment is not to be, at least for now. Rather, the walk of pagan together with Christian is deferred to the Christian future of the afterlife, when the swineherd and Patrick will meet again.

In sum, these three stories clearly form a set in Tírechán's text, presenting a gallery of signs that both reveal the pre-Christian past and presage the Christian future. The well, an empty sign of the falseness of pre-Christian worship, forms a pair with the cross that, as Patrick encounters it, represents a person who is not really "there." Interestingly, the only sign that really signifies what it appears to is the unbelievably enormous grave of the swineherd, seemingly the least credible of the signs or, at least, the only sign that evokes expressions of skepticism from onlookers. The *profeta* supposedly lurking in the well, as well as the pagan buried under the cross, were not where they should have been, but the gigantic son of Cas, the only person of the three featured behind the signs of these stories who is not characterized as displaced, is appropriately interred in a gigantic grave. It is as if the proper alignment of sign and signified were a necessary condition for Patrick to be able to communicate fully with the representatives of the past whom he must win over if he is to translate Irish culture into Christian terms. Semantic displacement can be the setting for partial or one-sided exchange. Because he is improperly marked with the cross, the pagan is allowed to answer Patrick's question, but he receives nothing from the saint in return and lapses back into his heathen anonymity. Or such displacement can provide the setting for the pointed absence of exchange. There is no one for Patrick to revive or to talk to in the well marked as sacred. The most productive situation for all concerned, however, takes place when a sign is vindicated. In the episode of the enormous grave, Patrick's authority and knowledge are reasserted, his audience is edified, and the swineherd is not only shifted temporarily from the category of the dead to that of the living, but his soul is permanently translated from hell

---

147. Bieler 1986, 18.358, lines 36–37. Preserved in a ca. 1200 English manuscript, this Life, according to Bieler, is based on Irish sources.

to heaven. Perhaps most important, information is obtained from the past and made part of the lore of the present. The saint's mission, it would appear from stories such as these, entails not only the conversion of Ireland but also the procurement of knowledge about the past from the dead, who open themselves up in dialogue with Patrick once the *correct* signs of their presence are duly acknowledged or even proven to be correct.[148] Even in the intensely agonistic world of early medieval Patrician legend, not all traces of the pre-Christian past are misleading.

148. The motif of Irish saints' raising the dead to find out about the past is examined in J. Nagy 1983b. Henken 1991, 56–64, presents Welsh hagiographic analogues. A tally of instances of the miracle of resurrecting or talking with the dead in Irish saints' lives is included in Bray 1992a, 92–93.

3/ the presence and
absence of columba

Adomnán's Apologies

Whereas Patrick and his mission as depicted in hagiography of the seventh and following centuries present the foundation of a dialogue between Christian and native tradition, the life of the sixth-century saint Columba (a Latin name meaning "dove") as portrayed by Adomnán in the late seventh century features a continuation and a ripening of that dialogue. Like Muirchú, Adomnán evinces a keen awareness that his composition represents a breakthrough. We readers are witnesses to the assertion of an Irish claim to the realm of universal sanctity in the person of Columba or, as he is known in Irish, Colum Cille 'Dove of the Church', and to the concomitant suffusion of Irish oral tradition about the holy man into the literary genre of the saintly vita, written in the language of the universal church.[1] Adomnán writes in his prologue:

No one, therefore, should think that I would write something counterfeit or dubious or uncertain about a man so praiseworthy as this. Rather, let him understand that what I know to have been handed down in the telling of elders and reliable and knowledgeable men is what will be narrated, and that it will be written down without any ambiguity. Or [what follows] comes from that which we have been able to find in writing from before our time, or from that which

---

1. To avoid confusion, I refer to the saint as Columba in my own text, even when the sources or traditions in question are in Irish. In translations, however, I follow the texts, using Columba for those in Latin and Colum Cille for those in Irish.

135

we, inquiring diligently, have learned by listening to certain knowing faithful ancients, who tell the story free of any doubt.[2]

Thus, paralleling Muirchú's Life of Patrick, Adomnán's Life of Columba depends for its very existence as a literary work on the same precarious mediation between local and universal and between oral and literary which, as we shall see, looms large in the saint's life. Columba's success or failure in reconciling these elements reflects on the success or failure of the Life itself.

The solutions Adomnán offers to the problems of incompatability jeopardizing the composition of the work and, by implication, the authorization of his subject as a genuine saint by now ring familiar:

> May readers not despise this pronouncement (which would have been impossible without divine help) of useful deeds and matters on account of some aspect of the base Irish tongue or on account of the persons' names or the obscure vocabulary of places and peoples, all of which, I suppose, would be worthless in the midst of diverse foreign tongues. We have, however, thought that the reader should be advised of how relatively few of the great many [of the saint's deeds] can be written out, if one wishes to avoid the readers' coming to loathe what they are reading. It seems to me that any reader will perchance observe how little of what could be divulged about this holy man has actually been dispersed among the common people, even in comparison to the few things which we are arranging in writing.[3]

The introduction of Irish matters, and even the Irish language, into the genre of the life, a supposed innovation for which Adomnán offers his humble apologies, is the intrusion of the same localized or "personal" voice that in its refusal to play by the rules of universal or literary convention wins a special,

2. Nemo itaque me de hoc tam praedicabili uiro aut mentitum estimet aut quasi quaedam dubia uel incerta scripturum; sed ea quae maiorum fideliumque uirorum tradita expertorum cognoui relatione narraturum et sine ulla ambiguitate craxaturum sciat, el uel ex hís quae ante nos inserta paginís repperire potuimus, uel ex hís quae auditu ab expertiís quibusdam fidelibus antiquís sine ulla dubitatione narrantibus diligentius sciscitantes didicimus (second preface, Anderson and Anderson 1991, 6). Translations of Adomnán's text are my own, with guidance provided by Anderson and Anderson 1991; and Sharpe 1995.

3. Et nec ob aliqua scoticae uilis uidelicet linguae aut humana onomata aut gentium obscura locorumue uocabula, quae ut puto inter alias exterarum gentium diuersas uilescunt linguas, utilium et non sine diuina opitulatione gestarum dispiciant rerum pronuntiationem.

Sed et hoc lectorem ammonendum putauimus quod de beatae memoriae uiro plura studio breuitatis etiam memoria digna a nobís sint praetermisa, et quasi pauca de plurimís ob euitandum fastidium lecturorum sint craxata. Et hoc ut arbitror quisque haec lecturus forte annotabit quod minima de maximís per populos fama de eodem beato uiro deuulgata disperserit ad horum etiam paucorum conparationem quae nunc breuiter craxare disponimus (first preface, Anderson and Anderson 1991, 2).

D. A. Bullough (1964, 127) points out the indebtedness of this passage to other hagiographic texts. See now also Sharpe 1995, 241 n. 2.

incontestable authority for Paul in the Second Letter to the Corinthians, for Patrick in the *Confessio,* and for Muirchú in his Life of Patrick. Native culture and the native tongue plead their case modestly in the court of Christian letters, but they do make an appearance, and Adomnán denies neither their independent existence nor their importance for understanding the life and accomplishments of Columba. Similarly, just as the native culture attempts to join the universal without surrendering its unique identity and authority, so the oral tradition is to be submitted in the Life proposed by Adomnán to the rules of form and closure dictated by literary tradition. The content of the text, however, will be only a metonymic representation of a totality that cannot possibly be circumscribed. This totality in its limitlessness asserts an essence beyond literary knowing.

Although the Columba of hagiography lives in an era when "pagans" are still to be encountered by the Christian holy man, the Irish-speaking world of the Life is already essentially committed to the new religion. Nevertheless, earlier traditions concerning the power of voice and the traditional conceptualizations of the authority behind voice are by no means gone from the milieu depicted by Adomnán. In fact, particularly in his Life of Columba and later hagiography centered on this saint, these conceptualizations are thriving. Furthermore, in this outstanding hagiographic case, the often hostile dialogue with druids, poets, and other representatives of the old order of communication, a dialogue putatively initiated by the figure of Patrick, is continued and even internalized within the not altogether consistent persona of Columba himself. Meanwhile, the inner dialogue between the saint and the source of his institutional authority so anxiously displayed in Patrick's *Confessio* is also to be found here, at times intersecting with the exchange between pre-Christian and Christian cultures. More prominent now in the interplay of voices and authorities, however, is the imposing reality of the text, which conveys the voice of divine authority and which, as a medium, can even co-opt the traditional voice.

Struck by an Angel

Perhaps the story in Adomnán's Life of Columba which best exemplifies the continuity of concerns it shares with the Patrician lives is the following curious anecdote about the saint's "run-in" with an emissary from God:

> Of the angel of the Lord who appeared in a vision to holy Columba while he was staying on the island of Hinba, an angel sent to command Columba to ordain Áedán.
> At another time, when the praiseworthy man was staying on the island of Hinba, on a certain night he saw in a rapture of the mind an angel of the Lord

who had been sent to him, with a glass book containing the rite of the ordination of kings in his hand. When the venerable man received the book from the angel's hand, he began to read it, as he was ordered to do by the angel. And when he refused to do what he was ordered to do in the book, namely, ordain Áedán as king (for Columba preferred Áedán's brother Éoganán), suddenly the angel struck the holy man with a whip in his outstretched hand, and it left a blue scar upon Columba's side that remained with him for the rest of his life. Then the angel said, "Know for certain that I was sent to you by God with this glass book so that you might ordain Áedán as king with the words that you have read in it, and that if you do not wish to follow this order, I will hit you again." And so after this angel of the Lord had appeared thus with the glass book in his hand for three nights in a row so as to relay this same order about the ordination of the aforementioned king, the holy man finally obeyed the word of the Lord and sailed to the island of Iona, where he ordained Áedán (who happened to go there about the same time) as king. Columba interspersed among the words of the ordination rite prophetic statements about what lay in store for the sons, grandsons, and great-grandsons of Áedán, and placing his hand over the head of the one he was ordaining, Columba blessed him.[4]

In a way reminiscent of Patrick's visionary experience with Victor and the innumerable letters he brings, Columba receives a written reminder of his mission contained in the pages of a glass book.[5] In this case, however, the

4. De angelo domini qui ad sanctum Columbam in Hinba commorantem insula per uisum apparuit, misus ut Aidanum in regem ordinaret.

Alio in tempore, cum uir praedicabilis in Hinba commoraretur insula, quadam nocte in extasi mentis angelum domini ad sé misum uidit, qui in manu uitreum ordinationis regum habebat librum. Quem cum uir uenerandus de manu angeli accipisset ab eo jusus legere coepit. Qui cum secundum quod ei in libro erat commendatum Aidanum in regem ordinare recussaret, quia magis Iogenanum fratrem eius dilegeret, subito angelus extendens manum sanctum percussit flagillo, cuius liuorosum in eius latere uestigium omnibus suae diebus permansit uitae. Hocque intulit uerbum: "Pro certo scias" inquiens, "quia ad té a deo misus sum cum uitreo libro, ut iuxta uerba quae in eo legisti Aidanum in regnum ordines. Quod si obsecundare huic nolueris iusioni, percutiam te iterato."

Hic itaque angelus domini cum per tris contenuas noctes eundem in manu uitreum habens codicem apparuisset, eademque domini iusa de regis eiusdem ordinatione commendasset, sanctus uerbo obsequtus domini ad Iouam transnauigauit insulam, ibidemque Aidanum hísdem aduentantem diebus in regem sicut erat iusus ordinauit. Et inter ordinationis uerba de filiis et nepotibus pronepotibusque eius futura profetizauit, inponensque manum super caput eius ordinans benedixit (3.5, Anderson and Anderson 1991, 188).

Michael Enright (1985a, 89–90; 1985b, 19–21) examines the echoes of 1 Kings 10:19–26 (the anointing of Saul as king by the prophet Samuel) in this passage: "The appearance of angel and book in the narrative is no mere magical reflex or literary conceit—on the contrary, both are present because Irish ecclesiastical culture of the period demanded that change be legitimated by one or the other" (1985b, 22).

5. Joseph Harris points out to me that glass makes for a rather unusual and problematic writing surface. Is the glassiness of the book a reference to the overlapping and subsequent opacity of texts in general, particularly the hard writ delivered by the angel? F. Byrne has

ordination conferred by the text applies not to the saintly reader but to a secular ruler whom Columba is to authorize in his royal office. The call to preach and baptize has now given way to a call to ordain a king. In Patrick's mystical experience, as we have noted, the letter acts as a cue for speech. Patrick hears writing spoken aloud as well as the voices of the Irish calling him. In this story about Columba, however, the text is not read aloud, unless by Columba himself, and the saint actually balks at what the text says.[6]

The saint's remarkable disobedience to the letter provokes a demonstration of the power of the bearer of the text. The angel reinforces the message and corrects Columba's deviation by means of both speech and physical punishment.[7] The blow of the scourge, moreover, leaves a lasting scar. Even such stern reinforcement of the message, however, has to be repeated on three successive nights before Columba is persuaded.

We should recall that the Patrick of hagiography, as opposed to the Patrick of the *Confessio*, is similarly not always happy with the angelic letters that he receives. Like Patrick in the story of the rude interruption of his conversation with Mochta, Columba is depicted as resisting the divine order delivered to him in written form. The presentation of the glass book is not even prefaced by any dialogue. Instead, the book is meant to replace dialogue, but it fails as a substitute. The angel must finally address Columba in order to accomplish his mission. And yet the failure of the glass book is avenged, for the disobedient reader himself becomes a readable text of disobedience. Columba will bear the scars of his encounter with the angel till his death.[8]

---

proposed that the designation *uitreus* refers to an enamel cover (1973, 255). In that case, the angel's glass book is akin to legendary classical- and medieval-era books with shining surfaces (made of substances such as emerald and gold), which are discussed in Speyer 1992, 78–81. The nineteenth-century editor of Adomnán William Reeves (1874, 287) pointed out a possible similarity between this glass book and an angelically delivered *codex candidus* 'white book' mentioned in Bede's Ecclesiastical History (5.13).

It may be significant that Columba is specifically identified with glass elsewhere in his legendry. There is the story of the monk Baithéne's vision of Columba and two fellow saints seated in chairs hovering above the ground. The chairs of the other saints are made of precious metals, but Columba's is made of glass—a feature he explains is an indication of his partiality for his people or of his human weaknesses (Stokes 1890, 302–3; Plummer 1910, 1:139; O'Kelleher and Schoepperle 1918, 120).

6. Columba's hesitation may also be related to a shift in the relationship between "church" and "state" which is signaled in the angel's decree. The innovative and biblical dimensions of royal ordination in Adomnán's time form the subject of Enright 1985a, 84–93, and 1985b, passim. Compare Sharpe 1995, 355–57, 358–59 n.

7. Lurking behind this incident of angelic abuse is Paul's mistreatment by an emissary of Satan (2 Cor. 12:7–10). In turn, perhaps it is the model for the blow a law-bearing angel delivers to Adomnán's body in an episode of a vernacular text that features the hagiographer as a saint in his own right, *Cáin Adomnáin* (Law of Adomnán). See Meyer 1905a, 22: *poculum arripuit 7 percussit latus eius.* There is also the reference to the supernatural beating doled out to Bishop Lawrence in Bede's Ecclesiastical History 2.6.

8. An array of other classical and medieval examples of the metaphorical relation between the surface or space of the human body and the book is presented in Curtius 1953, 302–47. The

Columba's personal preferences aside, there would appear to be genuine tension here between the saint and not only the content but also the medium of the message, a medium that can actually transform the receiver himself into yet another message, wearing the sign of a forced obedience to the law of the letter and relaying the power of the written word. The struggle in Columba's mind and heart between God's choice of Áedán and his own preference for Éoganán reveals a more fundamental conflict between personal and divine will, as well as the potential hostility between reading and speaking.

Keeping Conversations Private

Columba's permanent mark of resistance to a sacred text is paralleled by another disfiguring sign left on a rather different kind of culprit by Columba himself elsewhere in the Life:

> Another time, the holy man sharply reprimanded a certain student of his named Berchán, or Mes Loen, who was seeking wisdom. "Beware my son," he said, "that you not approach my room tonight as is always your wont." Berchán, after hearing this, disobediently went to the holy man's room in the still of the night while everyone else was asleep, and he could craftily peek in through the keyhole to see whether perchance some celestial vision were being made manifest to Columba, as indeed was the case. For in that same hour the room of the holy man was filled with a splendor of celestial brightness, from which the youthful transgressor, unable to look at it, ran away.
>
> The next day the holy man spoke to Berchán privately and scolded him with great severity, saying, "Last night, my son, you sinned before God, for you inanely thought that your disloyal, sly prying could be hidden from the Holy Spirit. Did I not see you coming to the door of my room then, and leaving afterwards? Had I not prayed for you at that moment, you would have died right there and then, struck down beside the door, or your eyes would have

---

motif of the scarring of the saint's body in the course of a supernatural encounter is also evident in Bede's account of the Irish saint Fursa's grueling vision (Ecclesiastical History, 3.19; cf. Heist 1965, 48).

Also worth noting in connection with the appearance of the glass-book motif in Adomnán's text, is the intrusion, shortly after the angelic visitation, of the only acknowledged extract from another composition in the text. Columba's prophecy concerning (and admonishment of) Áedán and his descendants, which follows the account of his royal ordination at the hands of the saint, is said by Adomnán (or, more likely, Adomnán's monastic editor) to be taken from Cuimmíne's (lost) account of Columba's miracles (Anderson and Anderson 1991, 188 n. 214). As Máire Herbert points out (1988a, 25), Columba's powerful utterance, with its reference to scourging, and the preceding episode with the angel fit together well. Moreover, the marking that changes Columba's body with new meaning and the alteration of his desires by means of coerced reading are paralleled by the editorial "grafting" of an admittedly "alien" extract onto the main body of the text—an extract, however, that proves congenial and productive within the text that absorbs it.

been torn from their sockets. But the Lord spared you on that occasion on my account. But know this: your face will bear a reproach when you are living back in your Irish home in luxury, for all the days of your life. This, however, have I been granted by the Lord by virtue of my prayer, that, since you are my student, you may perform a tearful penance before your death, and you will find God's mercy." And so all these things came to pass for Berchán, as were foretold in the prophetic words of the holy man.[9]

Most likely, what Berchán interrupts is one of the saint's noted dialogues with angels, to which Adomnán refers in another story, when a monk attempting to eavesdrop actually scares away the angelic participants in the "conversation" (*sermocinatio*).[10] These encounters, while informative, apparently are not meant for the monastic public at large, nor does the knowledge Columba acquires from them find its way into the manuscripts he and his scriptorial colleagues so assiduously produced. Yet, the Life makes clear, these conversa-

9. Alio itidem in tempore uir beatus cuidam suo sapientiam discenti alumno nomine Berchano, cuius cognomentum Mes loen, non mediocriter quadam denuntiauit die, inquiens: "Caueto, filii, ne hac sequenti nocte iuxta tuam semper consuetudinem ad meum appropinques hospitiolum." Qui hoc audiens contra interdictum ad domum beati uiri in noctis silentio aliis quiescentibus accessit, callideque explorans oculos e regione ad clauium foramina possuit, estimans scilicet, ut res probauit, aliquam intus caelestem uisionem sancto manifestari. Nam eadem hora beati uiri illud hospitiolum caelestis splendore claritudinis erat repletum, quam non sustenens intueri transgressor iuuenis ilico aufugit.

Quem die crastina sanctus seorsum dicens cum magna seueritate obiurgans haec ad eum profatur uerba, dicens: "Hac in nocte, filii, coram deo peccasti; nam tuae infitialis explorationem calliditatis a spiritu sancto celari uel abscondi posse inaniter putasti. Nonne ad mei hostium hospitioli té illa in hora approprinquantem et inde redeuntem uidi? Et nisi ego eodem momento pro té orarem, ibidem ante ianuam aut cadens morireris, aut tui de suís foraminibus oculi eruerentur. Sed tibi hac uice propter me dominus pepercit. Et hoc scito, quod in tua euernili patria luxoriose uiuens exprobationem facies tua omnibus patietur diebus uitae tuae. Hoc tamen a domino orans inpetraui, ut quia noster sis alumnus lacrimosam ante exitum agas penitudinem, et a deo misericordiam consequaris." Quae omnia secundum uerbum beati uiri ita ei postea contigerunt, sicuti de eo profetata sunt (3.21, Anderson and Anderson 1991, 212, 214).

10. 3.16, Anderson and Anderson 1991, 204, 206. In the *Amra(e) Choluim Chille*, an Old Irish poem eulogizing the saint, which dates perhaps to as early as the late sixth century and constitutes one of our earliest specimens of Irish, Columba is said to have "conversed with an angel" (fri angel n-acallastar [Stokes 1899–1900, 404]). The Middle Irish gloss on this passage in the twelfth-century manuscript Bodleian Rawlinson B.502 identifies the angel as one Axal (ibid.). Binchy explains the name as an Irish form of Latin *apostolus* (1958b). *Axal* appears in the text of the *amrae* itself, in a seemingly accusative plural form, *axalu* (Stokes 1899–1900, 172). Tellingly, one of the glosses supplied for this word (ibid.) is *immacalma* 'dialogues'. The explanation favored by the glossator, however, is that Axal is the name of the angel with whom Columba regularly spoke, as Patrick did with his own angel (Victor). He cites a passage from another poem, in which Axal is called the *angel acalma* 'angel of dialogue' (ibid.). It has been suggested that the angels who "flock" to Columba are to be envisioned in the shape of birds, perhaps specifically seagulls (Anderson and Anderson 1991, 204 n. 228). This interpretation would accord well with other aviary motifs in the saint's legendary dossier, to be discussed later.

tions can serve the valuable purpose of clarifying for the saint what is obscure in sacred Scripture. Shortly before Columba's death, Adomnán reports,

> he was heard to sing spiritual songs that had never been heard before. And he also saw many things hidden since the beginning of the world but made plainly manifest to him, as he himself revealed to a very few. Moreover, various obscurities of sacred Scripture appeared brilliantly plain and accessible to the eyes of his, the cleanest of hearts. He lamented that Baithéne his pupil was not present, who, had he perchance been there during the three days, could have written down the many mysteries unknown to other men concerning both the past and the future from the mouth of the holy man, as well as his insights into the books of Scripture. But this Baithéne, stranded on the island of Eigg by a contrary wind until the three days and nights of that incomparable, honorific visitation were over, could not be present.[11]

The mystical encounter Adomnán describes offers both miraculous sights and sounds, and it is an opportunity for transmission or composition. Columba learns new songs from the angels, or they inspire him to compose, while the darkness of Scripture is illuminated, as if text becomes vision accompanied by song in the ambience of the *sermocinatio*.

The kind of knowledge Columba acquires in these dialogues with the supernatural and the mode of acquiring it are actually described by the saint, as Adomnán records, in terms directly borrowed from Paul's Second Letter to the Corinthians, which, as we have seen, provided Patrick in his *Confessio* with the concept of a transcendent metawriting that authorizes and informs the divinely favored metareader:

> Luigbe, soldier of Christ, questioned the saint privately, "I would ask you to tell me whether these prophetic revelations are made manifest to you through sight or hearing or some other means unknown to humans." The holy man responded, "Concerning the very subtle matter about which you are inquiring, I can't tell you a thing about it unless you solemnly promise me, on bent knees in the name of God on high, that you will not talk of this most sacred mystery to anyone while I am still alive." Upon hearing this, Luigbe got on his knees right away, and with his face turned to the ground he promised fully all that Columba had ordered. The promise having been swiftly made, the holy man spoke thus

11. Carmina quoque quaedam spiritalia et ante inaudita decantari ab eo audiebantur. Sed et multa quaedam, ut ipse post coram paucís admodum professus est, occulta ab exordio mundi arcana aperte manifestata uidebat. Scripturarum quoque sacrarum obscura quaeque et dificillima plana et luce clarius aperta mundissimi cordis oculís patebant. Baitheneumque alumnum non adesse querebatur, qui si forte adesset illo in triduo uel de praeteritís uel de futurís deinceps seculís ab ore uiri beati quaedam plurima ab aliis ignorata hominibus misteria discriberet, aliquantas quoque sacrorum explanationes uoluminum. Qui tamen Baitheneus, in Egea insula uenti contrarietate detentus usque quo illi trinales illius inconparabilis et honorificae uisitationis dies et totidem noctes terminarentur, adesse non potuit (3.18, Anderson and Anderson 1991, 208).

to Luigbe when he arose: "There are some people, albeit very few, for whom divine grace makes it possible to see in all clarity the entire world rimmed by ocean and sky, all at the same moment, miraculously, as it were, in a single ray of sunshine, with the capacity of mind greatly expanded."

Doubtless so as to flee empty glory, the holy man seemed to tell of this miracle as if it happened to other chosen ones. That he was talking of himself, however, although obliquely, cannot be doubted by anyone who has read Paul, that vessel of election, when he speaks of his own visions. For he did not write "I know of myself" but "I know someone who was taken up into the third heaven." Although he seems to be speaking of someone else, no one doubts that he is talking about himself in a way that preserves his modesty. And so our Columba followed his example in what he said about spiritual visions as recounted above, words that Luigbe, whom the saint loved very much, was able to squeeze out of the holy man only after a great deal of importuning. So Luigbe himself testified in the presence of other holy men after the death of holy Columba. It is from these others, moreover, that we learned what we have already told about the holy man.[12]

Columba and Mongán

It is this same loving familiarity with esoteric knowledge that escapes the containment of writing or even human expression altogether which informs the character of Columba as he is depicted in an Old Irish text that seemingly brings him together with a figure from secular saga who is redolent with mythological associations, Mongán King of the Dál nAraidi of Ulster

12. Lugbeus, Christi miles, sanctum seorsum coepit interrogare, decens: "Quaesso mihi de hís talibus narres profeticís reuelationibus, quomodo si per uisum tibi an auditum an alio hominibus incognito manifestantur modo." Ad haec sanctus: "De qua nunc," ait, "inquiris ualde subtili ré nullatenus tibi quamlibet aliquam intimare particulam potero, nisi prius flexís genibus per nomen excelsi dei mihi firmiter promittas hoc té obscurissimum sacramentum nulli umquam hominum cunctís diebus uitae meae enarraturum." Qui haec audiens flexit contenuo genua et prostrato in terram uultu iuxta sancti praeceptionem plene omnia promisit. Qua statim perfecta promisione sanctus ad surgentem síc locutus inquit: "Sunt nonnulli quamlibet pauci admodum quibus diuina hoc contulit gratia, ut etiam totum totius terrae orbem, cum ambitu ociani et caeli, uno eodemque momento quasi sub uno solis radio mirabiliter laxato mentis sinu clare et manifestissime speculentur."

Hoc miraculum sanctus quamuís de aliis electís dicere uideatur, uanam utique fugiens gloriam, de sé ipso tamen dixisse, per oblicum licet, nullus dubitare debet qui Paulum legit apostolum uas electionis de talibus narrantem sibi reuelatís uisionibus. Non enim ita scripsit, "scio me," sed "scio hominem raptum usque ad tertium caelum." Quod quamlibet de alio dicere uideatur, nemo tamen dubitat síc de propria humilitatem custodiens enarrare persona. Quem etiam et noster Columba in spiritalium uisionum narratione sequtus est superius memorata, quam ab eo supradictus uir, quem plurimum sanctus amabat, magnís precibus praemisís uir potuit extorquere, sicut ipse coram aliorum personís sanctorum post sancti Columbae transitum testatus est. A quibus haec quae de sancto supra narrauimus indubitanter didicimus (1.43, ibid., 78, 80).

and son of the sea god Manannán mac Lir. The tale works by tantalizingly vague allusion and suggestion, as is appropriate for a text attempting in effect to ground its authority in a tradition of knowledge perpetuated by means of recondite speech.[13]

One day, when Columba is on the shore of a bay named Loch Febail along with his fellow monks, a young man approaches the saint from across the water, seeking *immacallam* 'dialogue'. When they meet, the youth lists for Columba some of the supernatural lands where he has traveled, and some of the beings, including the "living" and the "dead," with whom he has become familiar. For the final round of dialogue, however, in which Columba receives the juiciest bits of information, he dismisses his monks, and we the readers are also implicitly dismissed, since the text does not or cannot tell us what was said. What the text does coyly reveal, however, is that, according to some, the young man was the legendary Mongán.

It is notable that, in this account, unlike the ones from Adomnán's Life which I have examined, the knowledge imparted to the saint by means of extraordinary speech, a knowledge that subsequently does not find its way into the text, is clearly of a hybrid, if not outright non-Christian, nature. Furthermore, it is clear that we are witnessing here a meeting of different cultures equipped with media of contrasting contents. Also fascinating is the sanitized version of the story preserved in Maghnus Ó Domhnaill's *Betha Colaim Chille* (Life of Colum Cille), compiled in the sixteenth century from earlier sources, some of which are now lost. In this version the nature of the information obtained is altogether different, its literary inexpressibility even more apparent. Ó Domhnaill unequivocally identifies the young visitor as Mongán, and presents him as far more eager to learn of heaven and hell from Columba than to impart whatever information about pre-Christian other-worlds he may be privy to (and about which Columba in fact inquires). After the saint grants him a double vision of the afterlife, Mongán, who is asked to tell of what he has seen, admits that words fail him. Neither he nor the author of the tale attempts even a synecdochic representation.[14]

There is a compelling thematic link between the long-lived legend of Columba's encounter with Mongán, which results in a "blank" in the text, and a slight story told in Adomnán's Life. This episode features a visitor far less distinguished than Mongán, but it seems to be making the same point, even if

13. Meyer 1899; Grosjean 1927. For commentary on the tale, see Mac Cana 1975, 34–47; Carey 1984b, 100. James Carney (1976, 192) and now John Carey (1995b, 82–83) propose that the identification of the youth as Mongán in the earliest surviving version is extraneous. Even if it is, the coupling of two such acclaimed yet discreet bearers of esoteric knowledge accords well with their narrative personae. On the figure of Mongán, see J. Nagy 1987a, 13–24.

14. O'Kelleher and Schoepperle 1918, 78–82. The composition of, and sources for, this Life are detailed in Ó Fiannachta 1985; Sharpe 1990a; and Szövérffy 1957, 97–136. On Ó Domhnaill as a man of his time and the Life as a "distinctively Renaissance product," see Mac Craith 1990, 58–60.

serendipitously, about the potential incompatibility between writing and certain kinds of speech:

> One day, someone was shouting on the far side of the strait of the island of Iona. The holy man, sitting in his cottage propped up on wooden boards, said upon hearing the shouting, "The man who is shouting beyond the strait is not very smart, for today he will tip over and spill my inkhorn." Diarmait, Columba's attendant, heard what he said and for a short while stood by the door in anticipation of the grievous guest, ready to protect the inkhorn. But soon he left on account of some other business, and after he left the intrusive guest arrived and, seeking to kiss the holy man, knocked over and spilled the inkhorn with the rim of his clothing.[15]

It is as if this vignette and the Mongán anecdote were playing off the metaphor that appears in Muirchú's prologue, in which the act of writing or rendering textual what was previously or even inherently nontextual is compared to the feat of crossing over water against difficult odds. In these tales the voyagers are not writers but antiwriters, whose successful expeditions make writing all the more difficult for the writers whom they meet on land, who have presumably already made the voyage. Worth noting, however, is that, whereas the bungler from beyond the strait encounters a Columba well ensconced in his Scottish exile from Ireland, Mongán comes to a Columba still in Ireland, on the banks of Loch Febail, yet to make the voyage that will give him fame as the holy man of letters celebrated in hagiography.

The visitor in Adomnán's story, who, like Mongán, travels over water and with enthusiasm to see the saint, makes his impending presence "heard," and his clumsiness in regard to matters scribal (such as the care and maintenance of inkhorns) is announced by his shouting.[16] Diarmait, Columba's hapless companion, is no more capable of stopping the transmarine shouter from disrupting, with the best of intentions, Columba's work of writing than Columba's monks are able to overhear and document the good parts of his conversation with Mongán. There is to these intrusive figures something of the juggernaut, the unstoppable force of speech overwhelming or blotting out a literary attempt at containment. This force is perhaps equal to that of the unusually autocratic angel armed with glass book and whip.

15. Alia inter haec die ultra fretum Iouae insulae clamatum est. Quem sanctus sedens in tegoriolo tabulis subfulto audiens clamorem dicit: "Homo qui ultra clamitat fretum non est subtilis sensus; nam hodie mei corniculum atramenti inclinans effundet." Quod uerbum eius ministrator Diormitius audiens paulisper ante januam stans grauem exspectabat superuenturum hospitem, ut corniculum defenderet. Sed alia mox faciente causa inde recessit; et post eius recessum hospes molestus superuenit, sanctumque osculandum appetens ora uestimenti inclinatum effudit atramenti corniculum (1.25, Anderson and Anderson 1991, 52). For comment, see Picard 1985, 79.

16. To be compared with this story (as with that of the ill-fated poet Crónán, to be discussed shortly) is the episode featuring another distant shouter (quendam ultra fretum audiens . . . clamitantem) whom the saint prophetically chides for making noise when he should be performing penance before his impending death (1.27, Anderson and Anderson 1991, 52, 54).

In light of the indescribable and therefore untextualizable encounters with supernatural speakers and the intensity of Columba's subsequent infusion with power and knowledge as recounted in Adomnán's Life and other sources, the contrast between the story of the glass book and that of the disfigured Berchán becomes all the more pointed. Columba's rebellion against the written word would appear to be an understandable reaction to a very "ungeneric" medium of communication being introduced into the angelic *sermocinatio*. The punishment he receives, however, is precisely the one that is doled out to a third-party violator of the customary dialogue. It is hard to reconcile the implicit hierarchies of speech and writing operating in the two stories, just as it is difficult to reconcile the key facets of Columba's hagiographic personality, as we shall see.

Columba the Scribe

Columba is much more of a connoisseur and practitioner of the scribal craft than the Patrick of hagiography. Adomnán emphasizes Columba's love of literature.[17] Several of the miracles attributed to him have to do with books or the act of writing. For instance, in the following episode, the saint's great prescience makes him an ideal proofreader:

> On a certain day, Baithéne came to the holy man and said, "I need one of the brothers to go through the psalter which I have written with me and find the mistakes." Hearing this, Columba said, "Why do you impose this nuisance upon us for no reason? For in the psalter of which you speak there is neither superfluous letter to be found nor any letter missing, with the exception of an *I* vowel, which is the only thing missing."[18] And so, when the psalter was proofread, what the saint had said was confirmed.

In other episodes, books written by Columba miraculously survive prolonged exposure to *contraria elimenta* 'contrary elements', particularly water.[19]

17. Per annos xxxiiii insulanus miles conuersatus nullum etiam unius horae interuallum transire poterat quo non aut orationi aut lectioni uel scriptioni uel etiam alicui operationi incumberet (second preface, ibid., 6), "Having lived as an island soldier for thirty-four years, he was unable to spend even the interval of an hour without busying himself with prayer or reading or writing or some other kind of work." On the bookishness of Adomnán's Life and its subject, see Enright 1985b, 21.

18. Quadam die Baitheneus ad sanctum accedens ait: "Necesse habeo ut aliquis de fratribus mecum psalterium quod scripsi percurrens emendet." Quo audito sanctus síc profatur: "Cur hanc super nos infers sine cause molestiam? Nam in tuo hoc de quo dicis psalterio nec una superflua repperietur littera nec alia deesse excepta *.I.* uocali quae sola deest." Et síc toto perlecto psalterio sicuti sanctus praedixerat repertum exploratum est (1.23, Anderson and Anderson 1991, 50).

19. 2.8, 9, ibid., 104, 106.

The saint's devotion to texts is so great that according to later hagiographic tradition it is virtually a bookish hubris that leads to his banishment from Ireland. According to a tale told in sources much later than Adomnán's Life, the saint's unauthorized copying of a manuscript owned by another saintly literatus, Findén, leads to the issuing of a judgment by the high king of Ireland, Diarmait mac Cerbaill, according to which, just as a calf belongs to its mother, so too every copy of a book should stay with that book. Columba, however, refuses to return the copy, an action that leads to the cataclysmic Battle of Cúl Dremne, fought between the forces of the northern Uí Néill (Columba's kinsmen) and the southern Uí Néill, led by Diarmait. The high king's forces are routed, but Columba does not enjoy possession of his book without paying a heavy price. The saints of Ireland gather to condemn Columba for his role in the slaughter and send him into exile. Like the Patrick of the *Confessio*, Columba is not without his detractors.[20]

In this legend of illicit scribal activity and its consequences, Columba, much to his chagrin, is actually caught in the act of copying by a servant Findén sends to spy on his guest. With uncharacteristic cruelty Columba, one of the milder Irish saints, has a pet heron (*corr*) peck at the boy's eye through the keyhole, blinding it. The servant nevertheless has enough presence of mind to report what he has seen to Findén, who restores sight to the damaged eye. His miraculous recovery notwithstanding, this anonymous servant, with Berchán and Columba himself, is another disfigured obstructor of communication in Columban legendry.[21]

Saintly Oral Performances

Columba's commitment to the spoken word in his quest for knowledge and divine authorization is as notable as his pursuit of the written. He is not

20. O'Kelleher and Schoepperle 1918, 176–84; Breathnach 1926, 3; Kenney 1929, 435. A useful discussion of the legend is Lawlor 1916, 307–29, in which analogous legends are noted, as well as the tradition according to which Findén brought a better text of the Bible (perhaps even the Vulgate) to Ireland. On the multiplicity of saints named Findén (Finnian), see Ó Riain 1984. The story of Columba's appropriating a fellow cleric's book even survived into the repertoire of a modern-day Irish storyteller, Pádraig Eoghain Phádraig Mac an Luain (Mac an Luain 1985, 3, 74).

21. In the Irish Life of Ciarán of Clonmacnois, which establishes a close link between Ciarán and Columba, we find intriguing resonances. While studying with one of the saintly Findéns, Ciarán is asked for the book he is reading, the Gospel of Matthew, and he surrenders it—thus becoming known as Ciarán Half-Matthew, on account of his never having read through the complete text (Stokes 1890, 23–24, lines 4142–60; cf. Plummer 1910, 1:206 [c. 17]). An earlier multiform is to be found in the notes to the Martyrology of Óengus, in which it is Columba who importunes Ciarán, while he is studying with Findén, to surrender his (incomplete) copy of the gospel (Stokes 1905b, 202). This anecdote presents a saint who shares writing as opposed to appropriating it, as Columba does in the anecdote concerning his dispute with Findén. Elsewhere, Ciarán sends a heron to pluck out the eye of an interfering servant (Stokes 1890, 124–25, lines 4183–88), but this incident does not feature furtive writing.

only an eager auditor but also a notable performer, possessed of a powerful voice that some sources later than Adomnán present as trained in the techniques of *filidecht*, the vernacular poetic craft. Many extant Irish poems are attributed in the manuscripts containing them to Columba.[22] Literary tradition attributes the composition of verse to other saints, but no other saint has an established reputation as the author of so many poems.[23]

Adomnán makes no mention of the "creative" side of his subject, but he does describe Columba's voice as not only pleasing but also usable as a weapon against rival virtuosi of voice, such as Pictish magi:

> There is something else about which we ought not be silent, something that has been transmitted unimpeachably by certain authorities concerning the voice of the blessed man in psalmody. Incomparably raised on high, the voice of the venerable man could be heard in church amidst the voices of his fellow monks sometimes four furlongs away, that is, five hundred paces, at other times even as far away as eight furlongs, that is a thousand paces. Amazingly, at these times his voice did not exceed a normal human voice in its volume in the ears of those who were with him in church. Nevertheless, simultaneously, those who were over a thousand paces away from him could hear his voice so clearly that they could make out the syllables within the verses he was singing. His voice sounded the same in the ears of those both near and far. But it has been ascertained that this miracle of the blessed man's voice happened only rarely, since without the grace of the Holy Spirit it could not have happened at all.
>
> Nor should the story told about the incomparable magnification of his voice near the fort of King Bruide be left in silence. For once, when Columba himself with a few of his brothers was near the king's fort chanting the vespers according to custom, some druids [?] came to them and attempted to stop them as much as they could, lest the heathen masses hear the sound of the divine service coming from their mouths. When he realized what has happening, the holy man started singing the forty-fourth Psalm. Miraculously, his voice was raised up into the air at that moment, like formidable thunder, so that the king and his people were stricken with an unbearable terror.[24]

22. Bodleian Library Laud 615 contains a hefty anthology of poems attributed to Columba. See Meyer 1911b; and Sharpe 1995, 90–91, on this collection; and Meyer 1918, 385–96, for a sampling of the texts. Drawing on this manuscript and one other source, E. Gordon Quin (1981b) edited and translated a massive devotional poem of eighty-two quatrains supposedly composed by Columba. He dates the language of the poem to the eleventh or twelfth century (128).

23. In the commentary on the *Amra Choluim Chille*, a poem in praise of the saint composed for him by the chief poet of Ireland, we read: Ro aithnistar Aed do Dallan [ar ba filid dia ndernad ₇ file dos-gni] co mbad druine cech cetal in cetal-sa (Stokes 1899–1900, 282), "Áed (the high king of Ireland) commanded Dallán (the chief poet) that this poem should be stronger than every other poem," for, adds one manuscript, it was a *fili* for whom it was composed, and a *fili* who composed it.

24. Sed et hoc silere non debemus quod nobís ab expertís quibusdam de uoce beati psalmodiae uiri indubitanter traditum est. Quae scilicet uox uenerabilis uiri in eclesia cum

Columba's voice raised in prayer reaches those listening both near and far with equal clarity and immediacy, like a text that appears the same to whoever reads it.[25] The voice can penetrate and even co-opt the native, vernacular culture represented by the magi, drowning out their opposition and functioning as a convincing sign of the new religion's power, even more dramatic than Patrick's voice in comparable episodes. Furthermore, the voice is inspiring, of a power to make others raise their voices in powerful speech or song. One of those profoundly affected is Adomnán himself, who will not pass over the matter of Columba's voice in silence or allow the story of Columba and the magi to go untold. The saint's voice resonates in those who hear and echo it, even after his death:

> Not to be overlooked is the incident in which certain converted laymen, miscreants stained with blood, were saved from the hands of their enemies who had encircled the house in which they were singing songs in praise of the blessed man in the Irish tongue and commemorating his name, escaping unharmed from amidst the flames, the blades, and the lances. Miraculously, a few of them, who did not wish to sing those songs, as if they thought little of them, perished in that onslaught of their rivals. There are not just two or three people available to testify to this miracle, as required by law, but a hundred or even more.[26]

fratribus decantantis aliquando per iiii. stadia, hoc est d. passus, aliquando uero per octo, hoc est mille passus, inconparabili eleuata modo audiebatur. Mirum dictu, nec in auribus eorum qui secum in eclesia stabant uox eius modum humanae uocis in clamoris granditate excedebat. Sed tamen eadem hora qui ultra mille passuum lonquinquitatem stabant síc clare eandem audiebant uocem, ut illos quos canebat uersiculos etiam per singulas possent distingere syllabas. Similiter enim eius uox in auribus prope et longe audientium personabat. Sed hoc de uoce miraculum beati uiri non semper sed raro accedisse conprobatur, quod tamen sine diuini spiritus gratia nullo modo fieri potuisset.

Sed et illud non est tacendum quod aliquando de tali et inconparabili uocis eius subleuatione iuxta Brudei regis munitionem accedisse traditur. Nam ipse sanctus cum paucís fratribus extra regis munitionem dum uespertinales dei laudes ex more celebraret, quidam magi ad eos propius accedentes in quantum poterant prohibere conabantur, ne de ore ipsorum diuinae laudis sonus inter gentiles audiretur populos. Quo conperto sanctus xl. et iiii. psalmum decantare coepit. Mirumque in modum ita uox eius in aere eodem momento instar alicuius formidabilis tonitrui eleuata est, ut et rex et populus intolerabili essent pauore perterriti (1.37, Anderson and Anderson 1991, 70).

25. Compare the poem quoted in the commentary on the *Amra Choluim Chille*: Son a gotha Coluim cille / mor a binni os cach cléir, / co cenn cóic cet dec cémend / adbli remend, hed ba reil (Stokes 1899–1900, 176–77), "The sound of Columba's voice, great was its sweetness above any company: to the end of fifteen hundred paces—vastness of courses—it was clear." Intriguingly, Stokes says that "the Irish of this quatrain forms part of a piece ascribed in Laud 615 [a manuscript containing several poems attributed to Columba], p. 18, to Mongán" (ibid., 177 n. 3), a figure with distinctly pre-Christian connections who in the realm of legend, as we have seen, makes the acquaintance of Columba.

26. Sed et hoc etiam non praetereundum uidetur, quod eiusdem beati uiri per quaedam scoticae lingae laudum ipsius carmina et nominis commemorationem quidam quamlibet scelerati laicae conuersationis homines et sanguinarii, ea nocte qua eadem decantauerant cantica, de manibus inimicorum qui eandem eorumdem cantorum domum circumsteterant sint liberati; qui flammas inter et gladios et lanceas incolomes euassere. Mirumque in modum pauci

Here again we have the testing of a saint's authority in a burning house, as in the story of Patrick at Tara. In both cases, the saint is represented by a stand-in, and the house is also occupied by others whose death confirms the saint's power, as much as does the survival of their comrades. In the episode from Adomnán's Life, the "others" are not druids but, significantly, Christians who refuse to raise their voices in song.

Notable in this passage is Adomnán's specifying that the salvific songs in praise of Columba are in Irish, and that the fortunate performance in the house under siege, itself a commemoration of the saint of the powerful voice, potentially generates a great many performances of testimony. Also significant are the "miscreants" featured in the story, who sing Irish songs. Surely these must be former brigands, who, as we shall see, enjoy a special relationship with both poets and saints.[27]

The Columban Heritage

The marked association of Columba with speech and song even after his death lingers alongside his literary heritage. These details are juxtaposed in the Life, reflecting a delicate balance between Columba's commitments to two separate and seemingly not altogether compatible media. His writings, according to Adomnán, prove to be prophylactic relics, every bit as effective as the songs sung in his memory:

> Fearing imminent disaster [drought and famine], we settled upon a plan whereby some of our elders would walk around the recently plowed and sown field carrying the white tunic of holy Columba and the books penned by him, and they would lift up this tunic, which he was wearing when he died, and shake it three times, and they would open his books and read them on the "Hill of Angels," where once the citizens of the celestial country were seen descending to talk with the blessed man.[28]

---

ex ipsís, qui easdem sancti uiri commemorationis quasi paruipendentes canere noleurant decantationes, in illo emulorum impetu soli disperierant. Huius miraculi testes non duo aut tres iuxta legem sed etiam centeni aut eo amplius adhiberi potuere (1.1, Anderson and Anderson 1991, 16).

27. The figure of the brigand in this passage and another from Adomnán's Life is examined in Sharpe 1995, 253–54 nn. 45, 46, and 327–28 n. 258. Sharpe translates "quidam scelerati laicae conuersationis homines" in this passage as "men guilty of living the laic life," and he has demonstrated that laicus as used in medieval Irish hagiography often, if not usually, refers to brigands engaged in "pagan" cultic activities (Sharpe 1979, 81).

On protective hymns or loricae 'breastplates' attributed to Patrick, Columba, and other legendary saints, see Ní Chatháin 1976, 233–37. Of course, what protects the devotees in this story is commemorative verse, not necessarily a lorica.

28. Nos . . . inminentem plagam pertimescentes, hoc inito consilio fieri consiliati sumus, ut aliqui ex nostrís senioribus nuper aratum et seminatum campum cum sancti Columbae candida

This episode, which of course ends with the desired result of rain and successful harvest, breaks through from the "then" of the narrative of the saint's life into the "now" of the hagiographer's life. Prominently featured in the story is the remarkable act of reading on the site of the unreadable and unwritable dialogues between the holy man and the angels sent to him. Just as the tunic shaken in the air represents Columba and his protective authority brought back to life for the purpose of combatting the drought, so the reading of the book represents the passing-on of knowledge and authority from angel to saint. Yet, given the "bookishness" of the ritual representation, the angelic dialogue that comes to mind is that in which the glass book nearly becomes a substitute for verbal intercourse. Thus, at least in this case, Columba's authority as reader and writer does not simply coexist with the power of his voice beyond death but nearly annexes that power. Moreover, as the story of the glass book suggests, Columba's literary authority is not really autonomous at all, based as it is on a submission to the written word.

Adomnán's account of Columba's death features this same uneasy coexistence of his oral and his literary loyalties up to the time of his end and even beyond. The unheard-of songs sung by Columba during his final days as the result of a last flurry of angelic visitation are expressions of supernatural encounter which escape textualization. But then Columba has not given up his everyday scribal vocation even at this late, luminously transcendent stage of his life: "After [some prophetic] words, he descended from the hillock, returned to the monastery, and sat down in his cottage to write a psalter. He reached the thirty-third Psalm where it is written, 'Those who seek the Lord will not lack anything good.' He said, 'Here, at the end of the page, the work must cease. Whatever follows, let Baithéne write it out.'[29] Baithéne, who did not get to write down the divinely inspired songs, is commissioned by the dying Columba to complete the text he has begun. In finishing the psalter after Columba goes to his eternal reward, the fellow scribe gives closure to the saint's work and, in a sense, to the saint's life itself. It is literary work that goes on after Columba's death, but it is finite, just as the psalter, the work being copied, has a beginning and an end. The literary legacy left by the saint is certainly shown to be powerful and even indestructible, but it is not produc-

---

circumirent tunica, et librís stilo ipsius discriptís, leuarentque in aere et excuterent eandem per ter tunicam qua etiam hora exitus eius de carne indutus erat, et eius aperirent libros et legerent in colliculo angelorum, ubi aliquando caelestis patriae ciues ad beati uiri condictum uisi sunt discendere (2.44, Anderson and Anderson 1991, 172).

29. Post haec uerba de illo discendens monticellulo et ad monasterium reuertens sedebat in tegorio psalterium scribens. Et ad illum xxx. tertii psalmi uersiculum perueniens ubi scribitur, "Inquirentes autem dominum non deficient omni bono": "Híc," ait, "in fine cessandum est paginae. Quae uero sequuntur Baitheneus scribat" (3.23, ibid., 222).

In Paulinus's Life of Ambrose (early fifth century), we are told that the saint, close to his death, was visited by the Holy Spirit in the middle of dictating Psalm 43 to his biographer. Ambrose never finished his dictation (c. 42).

tive in the same way as the songs composed in Columba's memory, which generate testimony. It cannot be coincidence that the most conspicuous instance of literary "reproduction" in the hagiography of Columba, the story of his copying Findén's manuscript, hardly encourages confidence in the process.

Nor do the saint's writings directly save lives, as the songs do. Rather, they avert drought. Adomnán does tell a story in which the text produced by Columba wondrously survive destruction themselves:

> Many years after the passage of the blessed man to the Lord, a certain young man fell from his horse into the river called the Boyne in Irish and died. His corpse remained in the water for twenty days. The young man, who when he fell had a satchel made of skin containing books under his arm, was finally recovered after the aforesaid number of days, preserving the satchel between his arm and his side. When his corpse was brought out of the water and the satchel was opened, the page written by the sacred fingers of Columba, amidst the pages of other books that had not only been ruined but had rotted away, was found to be dry and not at all harmed, as if it had been hidden in a book box.[30]

One is reminded of resurrections of the dead performed by Patrick, who, as we have seen, can not only retrieve the dead but also tap into their store of knowledge. And yet, while the page survives in the water, the young man carrying (and reading) it, does not. Books, unlike the living voice, do not bring people back to life in Irish saints' lives.

The Hapless Poet

In Adomnán's Life, we read of the singing of songs passed on to the saint by angelic poets and the performance of Irish songs praising Columba by men not altogether representative of the church. In another episode, the saint's voice is raised in competition with that of his pagan sacerdotal counterparts.[31] Yet another conspicuous incident involves formalized oral performance, but here the saint pointedly refuses to play the role of audience in a context of traditional vernacular poetic composition:

30. Multorum namque transcursís annorum circulís post beati ad dominum transitum uiri, quidam iuuenis de equo lapsus, in flumine quod scotice Boend uocitatur mersus et mortuus, xx. sub aqua diebus permansit. Qui, sicuti sub ascella cadens libros in pellicio reconditos sacculo habebat, ita etiam post supra memoratum dierum numerum est repertus sacculum cum librís inter brachium et latus contenens. Cuius etiam ad aridam reportato cadauere, et aperto sacculo, folium sancti Columbae sanctis scriptum degitulís inter aliorum folia librorum non tantum corrupta sed et putrefacta inuentum est siccum et nullo modo corruptum, acsi in scriniolo esset reconditum (2.8, Anderson and Anderson 1991, 104).
31. 1.37, ibid., 70.

Another time, on a certain day, the holy one was sitting with his brothers near Loch Cé near the mouth of the river called Bos [Cow] in Latin, a certain Irish poet came to them. Upon the poet's departure after he had talked with Columba, the brothers asked the holy man, "Why did you not request of the poet Crónán who has just left that he sing something, according to the tradition of his poetic art?" The holy one answered them, "Why do you too engage in useless talk? How could I order a song of joy from that miserable little man who, now as he is being slain by his enemies, has rapidly reached the end of his life?" After he had said this, someone shouted from across the river, "That poet who just left you safe and sound, he was killed this hour by his enemies on the road." All who were then present marveled greatly, looking at each other astounded.[32]

We have seen these circumstances before. Again, Columba is in the company of his fellow monks on the banks of a body of water, a boundary zone, where a dialogue takes place between the saint and a visitor. This time, there is no blackout on the literary reporting of the exchange. Rather, the terminated dialogue conspicuously lacks the customary request for a poem, which would have allowed the encounter to develop into an occasion for oral performance. Columba has forestalled this usual outcome because he anticipates the imminent end of the performer's life and career.

In the story as text, there is no tantalizing hint of the absence or suppression of any important utterance. The literary production meshes successfully with the event and with what was said. It is as if Columba functions here as a representative of literary culture, to which the poet, crossing over, appeals for a hearing and perhaps even a transcription. Columba, however, does not elicit performance, nor does he allow the performer the satisfaction of performing. The saint and his biographer thus avoid, wittingly or unwittingly, the complicated matter of presenting an Irish poem in a Latin text and of transferring the oral into the written.

The exchange with the poet is dropped, but the saint continues the dialogue initiated by his fellow monks and scribes with a prophecy that proclaims closure. Indeed, it almost proclaims Columba's power to impose closure, although not upon the oral poem but upon the oral performer himself. The

---

32. Alio in tempore sanctus cum iuxta stagnum Cei, prope hostium fluminis quod latine Bos dicitur, die aliqua cum fratribus sederet, quidam ad eos scoticus poeta deuenit. Qui cum post aliquam recessiset sermocinationem, fratres ad sanctum. "Cur," aiunt, "a nobís regrediente Cronano poeta aliquod ex more suae artis canticum non postulasti modolabiliter decantari?" Quibus sanctus: "Quare et uos nunc inutilia profertis uerba? Quomodo ab illo misero homuncione carmen postularem laetitiae, qui nunc ab inimicís trucidatus finem adusque ocius peruenit uitae?" Hís a sancto dictís, et ecce ultra flumen aliquis clamitat homo, dicens: "Ille poeta qui a uobís nuper sospes rediit hora in hác ab inimicís in uia interfectus est." Omnes tum qui praesentes inerant ualde mirati sé inuicem intuentes obstipuere (1.42, ibid., 76). Stevenson notes Columba's seeming lack of interest in hearing the poet perform and suggests that the story may reflect a cultural or aesthetic divide between poet and saint (1995, 21–22).

rebuffed poet retreats back across the waves, only to be destroyed by his "enemies." His greatest enemy, however, would appear to be Columba, who does not even give Crónán the chance to live on through a composition in honor of the saint which could become a part of the tradition of song mentioned in the episode in which singing of or for Columba saves the singers. Poor Crónán is denied the fighting chance to save the life he might have had with such a song to his credit. Columba indeed appears here to be a singularly antitraditional nonaudience, acting as if the time immediately before the poet's death were not a good time to request a song that might immortalize the creator's subjects and his own craft.

Despite the thwarting of traditional expectations, the end of the story appears to restore the balance of power between saint and poet and between their respective media. The poet is now gone, never to perform again, but once more in Columban story, shouting is heard from across the water. It is speech that affirms the saint's prophecy of closure. Crónán, an anonymous voice announces, has indeed been killed. But this announcement reminds us that there is still plenty of voice to be heard from the "other side," and that Columba's own predictive utterance, or perhaps the poet's performance in its very marked absence, elicits further utterance, in a never-ending chain of production. This implied chain affirms the truth of the story of the talismanic songs sung by Columba's devotees. The poet has been terminated, but poetic voice and the dialogue of voices it engenders can apparently never be brought to a full stop.

In Praise of Columba

There are later accounts concerning Columba's relationship with poets which similarly focus on the issue of closure, whether of life-span, composition, or relationship. These tales constitute strong evidence for the continuing importance of the themes underlying the story of the ill-fated poet Crónán within the Columban tradition. The saint as he is depicted in literature written after Adomnán's work becomes in effect a patron of poets who both curtails and legitimates their art in the new, literary era of Christianity and whose own curtailment of life is celebrated, and his fame perpetuated, through a well-known and venerable Old Irish elegy that features a blend of oral and literary elements and techniques. Of this poem, known as the *Amra Choluim Chille* (Praise [?] of Colum Cille),[33] and of the history of its transmission, Daniel Binchy has said:

33. The text is edited and translated in Stokes 1899–1900; and Henry 1978, 191–212 (into Modern Irish). Certain passages are translated and discussed in Hull 1960–61. The most recent translation with commentary is to be found in Clancy and Márkus 1995, 96–128. *Amra* as an adjective means "wonderful, marvellous" (*DIL*, s.v. *amrae* I). As the designation for a poetic genre it is rare (see, for example, L. Breatnach 1989), and its precise meaning is unclear ("eulogy" (?), *DIL*, s.v. *amrae* II.d).

This ancient "rhetoric" came to be regarded as a quasi-magical incantation, rather like the Vedic hymns, in which every word had its peculiar virtue and any alteration would impair the efficacy of the whole. This theory would account for the remarkably uniform *textus receptus* in the various manuscripts and also for the elaborate verbal glossing, two features which are elsewhere found only in connexion with the "sacred" texts of the law.[34]

As part of the glossing, a considerable cycle of Middle Irish anecdotes accompanies the *Amra*. According to legend, these verses were composed on the occasion of Columba's saving the poets of Ireland from banishment. The expulsion of the entire profession was proposed at the Convention of Druim Cet by the men of Ireland, who were wearied by the arrogant demands of the poets.[35] The reputed composer of the *Amra* was the chief poet of Ireland himself, Dallán Forgaill:

> Then Dallán, the chief poet of Ireland, came to talk [*do acallaim*] with Colum Cille, so that when he was there, he recited to him the prologue [to the *Amra*]. But Colum Cille would not allow him to compose it any further beyond that point, so that he would have to finish it at the time of Colum Cille's death, for Colum Cille said that the poem would be [more] appropriate for a dead person, and Dallán should try to compose the poem on the spot [on the occasion of Colum Cille's death]. Colum Cille promised Dallán treasures and the benefits of the world for this poem of praise, but the only payment Dallán would accept was heaven for himself and for every one who would recite the poem every day, performing both sound and sense. . . . Three signs did Colum Cille [promise to] give Dallán which would indicate the time that he should compose [the rest of the poem]: a rider on a piebald who would bring the news of Colum Cille's death to Dallán; the first word that the rider would utter would be the begin-

34. Binchy 1958b, 164.
35. Adomnán's designation of the event is *condictum regum* 'a discussion among kings' (1.49, 2.6, Anderson and Anderson 1991, 88, 102; for other references to the saint's attendance, see 1.10–11, ibid., 32, 34). The Life states that Columba participated in the event, prophesying about Domnall, the high-king Áed's son, exhorting the imprisoned Scandlán, and miraculously dispelling diseases. No mention is made, however, of the issue of poetic license, which comes to the fore only in later accounts.
"Convention" is the usual modern English designation for what supposedly happened at Druim Cet. The Annals of Ulster (under the year 575 A.D.) refer to the event in Latin as a *con[uen]tio*; it is glossed in Irish *mordail* 'great assembly' (Mac Airt and Mac Niocaill 1983, 86). At the heart of these various characterizations the Scottish historian John Bannerman sees the institution of the *rígdál* 'royal assembly', as recorded, for instance, in early ninth-century annals—that is, an ad hoc occasion for the ratification of treaties between kings and kingdoms, which, in fact, is what tradition says happened at Druim Cet. According to Bannerman, the evolution of this historical event into a legendary cultural watershed for the Irish occurred by virtue of its connection with the popular Columba (1974, 157–70). The nature of this meeting, Adomnán's references to it, and Columba's role at it are also discussed in Sharpe 1995, 27–28, 272–73 n. 88, 312–14 n. 204.

ning of the praise poem; and Dallan's eyes would be given back to him during the time that he composed.[36]

Dallán has no more luck than Crónán in presenting a poem and its performance in person to the saintly object of his professional attention. The relationship and dialogue between performer and audience is disrupted once again by prophecy and death. This time, however, it is not the impending death of the poet but Columba's feeling that a poem of the kind Dallán has in mind would be appropriate only on the occasion of Columba's death, which will be clearly indicated to Dallán with prophetic signs. The saint marks the termination of his own life by deferring the poem, instead of anticipating the death of the poet by preventing the poem from "happening" as performance.

We should note that the poem is not altogether absent in the face-to-face encounter between poet and saintly patron. Dallán does give Columba a "preview," that is, a metonymic representation of the totality. Like Columba's still incomplete life, the poem goes only so far. Columba identifies himself with the poem by forbidding its continuation for now, and he makes it a means of achieving immortality for himself and Christian salvation for its composer and for all who perpetuate it in performance. Again, a primal poetic utterance opens up an unlimited chain of utterances that echo or respond to it, a discourse made possible because Columba does not cut off dialogue with the poet, even though he defers performance. In the story of Crónán, by contrast, the discourse continues *despite* Columba's cutting it off.

Columba agrees to payment for the poem in advance, in an exchange with Dallán which amounts in other versions of the story to haggling. The payment Dallán asks for and receives—eternal salvation to those who compose or recite it in return for the undying fame the poem will confer upon Columba—is high, as memorable as the poem being bought. Any future recitation of the *Amra*, Columba promises, will garner for the reciter what is in effect the Christian counterpart of the secular benefit that accrues to the subject of the poem.[37]

36. Tanic iaram Dallán ardollom Hérend in tan sin do acallaim Cholum Chille. Conid and ro gab in remfocul dó. 7 ni reléic Colum Cille dó a dénam secha sein co ndernad i n-amsir a éistecta ar asbert fri marb bas chubaid 7 is dochendaib ro thríall Dallán a dúain do dénam. Dorairngert trá Colum Cille do Dallán innmassa 7 torthe in talman ar in molad sa 7 ni ragaib acht nem dó féin 7 do cech óen no ngebad cach dia 7 dofucébad eter chéill 7 fhogur. . . . Trí comartha immorro dorat Colum Cille dó in tan dogénad .i. marcach eich alaid no innisfed dó étsecht Coluim Chille 7 in cetna fhoccul no ráidfed in marcach commad hé tosach in molta 7 a suile do lécud dó céin no beth ica dénam (from the glosses on the *Amra* supplied with the text in the late eleventh-century manuscript Lebor na hUidre, Best and Bergin 1929, lines 378–87).

37. A Middle Irish narrative example of the salvific power of the "performance" of the *Amra* is to be found in Grosjean 1937, 272–76. Clearly there is a link between these traditions and those centered on the composition of the famous Latin hymn *Audite omnes* about Saint Patrick. Supposedly, its author, his disciple Secundinus or Sechnall, tricked the humble Patrick

The Death of a Poet

Given the importance that Columba and the story itself place on the poem as memorial and the poet as memorializer, it would seem that the saint and his hagiographic tradition have undergone a dramatic change of heart from the rather frosty caution expressed in the story of the doomed poet Crónán. Arguably, the cycle of legends centered on the composition of the *Amra* represents what Binchy has called "the final confluence of the two streams,"[38] namely, the Christian and the pre-Christian, the literary and oral. And yet the Columba featured in these legends is still resisting "contemporary" and spontaneous performance. Moreover, in committing Dallán to the plan of composition outlined, Columba is fixing the performance of the poem and even attempting to fix the text itself, virtually removing compositional responsibility from the poet. Dallán's cue is to be the recitation from the back of a piebald horse of what is at least seminally a fixed, textualizable poem, with a clear beginning and clearly heading toward an end. Poetry is now no longer a flexible reaction to changing events but a prearranged reservation or a warm-up of something artistically cooked long ago.

The sign of Columba's death which most directly affects Dallán is the recovery of his sight, but only during the premiere performance of the *Amra*. The implications of this sign go against the traditional Irish ideology of poetry, in which blindness is no hindrance to poetry because it not only constitutes a transcendent mode of seeing but also emphasizes the oral basis of poetic discourse.[39] Is the implication then that Dallán's sight should be restored during the performance so he can read the poem, the glossing of which, let us recall, is the actual pretext for the preservation this story? If so, then this account of the creation of the *Amra*, while it represents an incorporation of the traditional poetic craft into the Christian worldview, also features a reformulation of that craft, as does the poem, and a strategic shifting of poetic authority away from the milieu of the poet to that of his saintly literate subject.

According to a striking account, Dallán's own demise is timed to occur after a performance in honor of yet another saint, Conall Cóel. In fact, the tale is a fitting complement both to the story of the fateful nonperformance of

---

into hearing the poem's first performance (Stokes 1887, 2:394–400). Perhaps this poet's success in making the subject of his poem receive it is a reflection on Patrick's lack of poetic "savvy" compared to Columba, or perhaps the saintly resistance is less effective because the poem is in Latin and therefore not as threatening a synthesis of potentially conflicting systems of communications and values as the *Amra*.

38. Binchy 1961, 18. On the ideological significance of this legendary meeting, see also Mac Cana 1979, 476.

39. The figure of the (wholly or partially) sightless poet in Celtic tradition looms large in Patrick Ford's analysis of the significance of legendary poets' physical defects (1990a, 37–40).

Crónán told in Adomnán's Life and to the account of the composition of the *Amra*:

> Dallán composed a praise poem for Conall Cóel, and the price that he demanded for it was that they be in the same place when they were raised from the dead. [Proximity to Conall would guarantee the poet's salvation.] Dallán was given what he demanded. Afterward, the blind one [Dallán] set out for a hostel. A student commented to the cleric, "Ugly is the blind one who has left, with his head sunk upon his breast." "It is bad news if he has indeed left," responded the cleric. He then arose and prayed to God, and it was revealed to him that it was true. Vikings arrived that night and destroyed the house in which the blind one was staying. His head was lopped off and thrown into the sea. The trunk of his corpse was brought to the cleric, but the head was not recovered, until the waves cast it up on land, at the same place where the trunk was. The cleric placed the head upon the trunk, so that you would have though that it had never been cut off. He was buried on the Island of Conall Cóel. This is [all] true.[40]

This is the only instance we have encountered so far of the normal poet-patron relationship, in which a poet offers a poem to a saint without interruption and is paid for it straightaway. Yet this performance, as much as Crónán's marked nonperformance, bodes ill for the poet, since soon after, the saint who is the subject of the poem divines the imminent death of the composer. Once again the poet comes to the saint across the waves, but this time the poet, not his poem, has been left incomplete. He is a corpse missing its head. Fortunately, the "deferred" head is miraculously transported on the sea to the saint, who manages to reunite the dismembered parts of Dallán's body, though without bringing him back to life. Still, this act constitutes payment for the poem. At the resurrection of the dead, Dallán will not only be in salvific proximity to his saintly patron but will also rise whole from the grave, thanks to Conall Cóel.

In his dealings with Columba, Dallán, having received the agreed-upon cues from him, completes the poem that will guarantee fame for the saint. In Dallán's dealings with Conall, it is the saint who, on receiving Dallán's

---

40. Molad dorinne Dallán do Chonall Chóel, ocus is he lógh ro chuindig fair, co mbeth a n-eseirghi a n-óenbaile, 7 tucad do in ní ro chuinnigh. Ocus ro imdigh in Dall ammach iarsin don tigh aiged, ocus adubairt dalta don clérech: Is granna ita in dall dochúaidh amach, 7 a chend for a ucht. Is olcc in scél sin, ol in clérech, masa amlaid itá. Atracht in clérech iarsin 7 ro guid in Cuimdid, 7 ro foillsiged do gob' fir. Tangatar goild insin oidqui sin, 7 ro airccsit in tech ir-raibi in dall, 7 ro benad a chenn de, 7 ro cuired in cenn isin fairgi, 7 tucad in chorp gus[in] clerech, 7 ni frith in cenn co ro laisit na tonna i tir hé i mbaili i raibi in corp, 7 tuc in clérech in cenn forsin corp, ocus dar lat nir' benadh de riam é, 7 ro hadnacht a nInis Cháil Chonuill, et uerum est (Stokes 1899–1900, 435–36).

"cues"—the trunk and later the floating head—reconstitutes the poet himself in preparation for both his immediate and ultimate disposition. Clearly Dallán has a fine working relationship with the saints he praises. Still, even though poet and saint interact to establish a heritage by which they will be remembered, each pursues his own line of work. The poet does not work miracles on behalf of or in place of the saint; the saint does not finish the poem for the poet. Both complementarity and professional respect characterize the relationship between them, and remarkably, each provides closure or definition for the other. The saint makes the poet into his, the saint's, own miracle, and the poet immortalizes the saint in his own composition.[41]

The lopped-off head of such a notable poet is able to "swim" in the water and to regain the unity of head and body, which was lost when the poet was alive. It is likely that this is a vestigial appearance of the universal "talking-head" motif, which was particularly meaningful symbol in Celtic and other Indo-European narrative traditions. The head that lives and speaks even after it is separated from the body is often that of a noted poet or possessor of knowledge (such as Orpheus in Greek tradition, or Kvásir in Norse), dwells or travels in water, and proves remarkably effective in righting a wrong or seeing some action through. Especially in Celtic traditions, the singing head is an emblem of the power of speech, which can live on and be effective even after the death of the speaker. Usually, the severed head comes alive and speaks in situations of intense, seemingly insuperable alienation between two or more parties or principles. Thus the division of the body into head and trunk is interpretable as an emblem of this troublesome dichotomy. Furthermore, the head's ability to exist as an independent totality serves to deflate the dichotomy and bring together the alienated parties or principles. This mediation reaches its climax in those instances where head and body are actually rejoined, thanks to the efforts of the head.[42]

The restoration of an original unity, the creation of a new, harmonious totality, and the transformation of a part into a whole are all possible outcomes in stories featuring the talking-head motif, and all in fact figure in the story of Dallán. His body is finally brought back together, at the same time as saint and poet are reunited. These two are cooperating now; they are not hostile or just unrelated to each other, as is the case with Columba and Crónán. Meanwhile, Dallán's poetry in praise of clerics such as Columba and Conall emerges as the "state of the art," a metonym of the poetic past, with

41. Of course, this relationship mirrors—perhaps magnifies—the traditional Indo-European poet-patron relationship. In ancient Greece, for example, the poet's memorialization of a powerful tyrant and the poet's own reputation last as long as the tyrant's power exists, or they are sustained in collective memory by the institutionalization of that power. G. Nagy 1990, 187–88, 225, 412.

42. The Indo-European, particularly Celtic, significance of heads is the topic of J. Nagy 1990b, 209–26.

the elements of the poetic craft objectionable to the new Christian culture deleted.

In the Middle Irish Life of Colum Cille, a fatefully decisive crossing once again forms the centerpiece of a story concerning the relationship between saint and devotee. This tale joins the growing repertoire of Columban legends in which we find figures going back and forth restlessly over a body of water: "On another day when Colum Cille was preaching to the crowds, a certain person went away across the nearby river to avoid listening to the word of God. The serpent struck him in the water and killed him instantly. His body was brought before Colum Cille, who made the sign of the cross with his staff over the man's chest, and he immediately arose."[43] Unlike the inimical magi who raised their own voices to drown out Columba's, the protagonist of this story tries to distance himself from the saintly voice simply by crossing the river. He stands in contrast to the loud enthusiast in Adomnán's Life, who audibly approaches Columba over water and disrupts scribal work.

Ironically, the medium of this skeptic's escape turns upon him when a denizen of the river takes his life. Crónán the poet goes to meet his death back across the waters after he is deprived of the chance to perform for Columba. This voyager's unwillingness to lend an ear to Columba's own kind of performance appears to seal his fate before he has even crossed over. He returns lifeless and mute from the waters, only to be brought back to life and made a sign of the authority of Columba's voice.

In these tales from Columban hagiography, bodies of water seem to possess the same significance with which the metaphorical sea is endowed in Muirchú's prologue to his Life of Patrick. To cross these waters is to make a statement of commitment to a culture or medium and to assert a mastery of authoritative voice. This assertion is usually brought into question in the course of the story. The noisy visitor from across the strait overwhelms the "voice" emanating from the inkhorn. The visiting poet's assertion of an authoritative voice is fundamentally disturbed, first by Columba's refusal to request a performance, and second by his unawareness of his impending death. The persistence of Dallán's head in swimming back to the rest of his body affirms the truth of his compositions. And finally, the skeptic's attempt to master Columba's voice by distancing himself from it fails in the very waters that create the distance. From his failure, however, emerges a remade man. This is a transformation for which we look in vain in the story of Crónán, but it glimmers as a possibility in the story of the death of Dallán.

---

43. Trans. Herbert 1988a, 261. Dia mboi tra Colum Cille i n-aroli lathi ic procept dona slogaib, luid aroli duine uadib darsin abaind bói i comfocus doib, na beth oc estec[h]t fri brethir nDé. Not-mbenand in nathir he isin usce co rus-marb fo cétoir. Tuccad a chorp i fhiadnaise Coluim Cille 7 dos-beirside croiss dia bachaill dar a bruinde cond-eracht fo cétoir (ibid., 238).

Donn Bó's Promise

That the prospect of a poetic return to life and specifically the talking-head motif are indeed lurking in the story of Dallán's death and that this story is relevant to the account of Dallán's meeting with Columba are virtually confirmed for us by the medieval tradition concerning the eighth-century Battle of Allen. Here a miracle attributed to Columba is performed on behalf of a figure eminently comparable to Dallán, a performer who is actually reduced to a singing head.[44]

Fergal mac Maíle Dúin, the king of the northern Uí Néill, sets out to battle against Murchad mac Brain, the king of Leinster. Fergal has in his entourage the entertainer (*airfitid*) Donn Bó, a famous musician and storyteller whose mother allowed him to accompany the king on his martial expedition only after the long-deceased Columba, as spoken for by the current abbot of the monastery of Iona, had guaranteed her son's return to her intact. On the eve of the battle, Fergal asks his premier performer to entertain him. Donn Bó says he cannot do anything that night, but he promises to perform for the king the next night, no matter where they happen to be. The battle goes against the North despite Columba's patronage, and Donn Bó's royal employer is slain. A Leinsterman who has gone onto the battlefield to fetch a souvenir comes upon the corpse of Fergal, and something unusual happens, as told in the Middle Irish text *Cath Almaine* (Battle of Allen):

> Then he heard something, a proclamation in the air over his head that said (for it was all heard): "A command to you from the King of the Seven Heavens: make music for your lord tonight, that is, for Fergal mac Maíle Dúin, even though you have all fallen in battle here with your artists, including the flute, horn, and harp players. Let neither terror nor weakness prevent you from performing tonight Fergal." Then the warrior heard whistling and sad music, and emanating from the closest tuft of rushes a droning that was sweetest music.
>
> The warrior approached it. The head said to him, "Do not approach me." "But who are you?" asked the warrior. "Not difficult to answer," said the head. "I am the head of Donn Bó. Last night I made the commitment to perform for the king tonight, so do not harm me." "Where is the body of Fergal here?" asked the warrior. "It is shining there on the other side from you." "Will you come with me?" asked the warrior. "You would be the best person by me to take me away," said the head, "but the grace of Christ to you if you would return me to my trunk." "I will do that, certainly," said the warrior.
>
> And he returned along with the head to Connal [where the victorious king was spending the night]. He found the Leinstermen drinking in his presence

44. The following summary is based on the text of *Cath Almaine* as edited in Ó Riain 1978.

that same night. "Did you bring a token back with you?" asked Murchad. "I brought the head of Donn Bó." "Place it upon the pillar yonder," said Murchad. The entire host recognized it as the head of Donn Bó, and they all said, "Alas for you, Donn Bó. Your form was lovely. Perform for us tonight, in the manner that you were performing for your lord just now." His face was then turned away, and a piteous drone rose on high, so that they were all lamenting and sorrowing.[45]

When the Leinster warrior returns Donn Bó's head to its body, they miraculously cohere and come alive, thanks to the intercession of Columba, who displays even greater power than his fellow saint Conall in the story of Dallán's death. And so the entertainer returns alive to his mother.

The key elements of this story from Middle Irish legendary saga are familiar to us from Columban lore. There is the deferred performance, which in this case finally does come about through a miracle. There is also the display of a communicative bond between performer and patron, whether saintly or secular, which endures despite death. Furthermore, here as elsewhere, composition and performance dedicated to Columba function as a marvelous demonstration of the saint's own power. The framing of the power of poetry and song within a field of Christian cues, such as the completion of the *Amra* upon the appearance of the prophesied tokens and during the period when Dallán's sight is restored, is even more pronounced in this tale. The deathly performance takes place only after a spectacular command from God is announced on the battlefield, a powerful utterance that generates yet another chain of utterances. After the performance ends, head is reunited with body by the intercession of Columba.

45. Co cuala ní, in n-escaire isin áer ós a chinn co n-epert, ar roclos uile: "timarnad dúib ó ríg secht nime; dénaid airfited do bar tigerna innocht .i. d'Fhergal mac Maíle-dúin, cia do-rochrabair sunn uile in bar n-áes dána etir cuislennchu ocus cornaire ocus cruittire; ná tair-mescad airfhuath nó écomnart sib d'airfited innocht d'Fhergal." Co cuala iaram int óclach in cúisig ocus in ceol sírechtach, co cuala dna 'sin tum luachra ba nesa dó in dord fiansa ba binne ceolaib.

Luid int óclach 'na dochum. "Ná tair ar m'amus," ar in cenn fris. "Ceisc, cia tú?" ar int óclach. "Ní ansa, mise cenn Duinn Bó," ar in cenn, "ocus naidm ronaidmed form irraír airfited in ríg innocht, ocus ná airchóitid dam." "Caide corp Fergail sunn?" ar int óclach. "Is é do-aitne frit anall." "Ceisc, indat-bér lem?" ar int óclach. "Is tú as dech lem nom-bera," ar in cenn, "acht ráth Críst dot chinn dianom-ruca, co tuca mé ar amus mo cholla doridise." "Do-bér éicin," ar int óclach.

Ocus impói int óclach ocus in cenn lais conice Connaill. Ocus fuair Laigniu oc ól ar a chinn 'sin aidche chétna. "In tucais comartha lat?" ar Murchad, "Tucas," ar int óclach, "cenn Duinn Bó." "Foraim arin uaitne út thall," ar Murchad. Tucsat in sluag uile aichne fair, corop é cenn Duinn Bó, ocus is ed roráidset uile: "Dirsan duit, a Duinn Bó. Ba cáem do delb. Déna airfited dúinn innocht, feib do-rignis dot thigerna imbuarach."

Impaigther a aiged dno, ocus at-racht a dord fiansa attruag ar aird, co mbátar uile oc caí ocus oc tuirse (Ó Riain 1978, 11–12, lines 139–64).

I later take up a hagiographic example of "the practice of taking home the severed heads of defeated enemies," noted in Sharpe 1995, 301 n. 175.

In this medieval account of the extraordinary death and life after death of a legendary performer, we once again see the celebrated link between Columba and the *áes dána* 'craftspeople', including distinguished poets such as Dallán and lowlier performers such as the *airfitid* Donn Bó. This musician-performer need not even compose a praise poem for the saint in order to receive his protection. All that is required is his mother's plea.

It is possibly significant that in the story of Donn Bó, whom the saint respects for his craft and not just because of a specific service rendered, the performer performs miracles, becoming his own "sign" (*comartha*) and wondrously fulfilling his own promise or prophecy. Yet here, as in the story of Dallán's death, the saint is still needed to pick up the pieces and put the vulnerable performer back together again. For the first time, however, the saint actually revives the performer, instead of only prophesying the performer's death or preserving his silenced remains.

The Saint, Poets, and the World

Saintly prophecy and preservation, particularly as featured in the stories of Crónán and Dallán, parallel the process of transcribing, transforming, rearranging, and textualizing oral performance—all of which the monastic scribal culture represented by saints such as Columba was in fact doing. What happens in the story of Donn Bó, on the other hand, opens up a wholly different realm of possibilities in the relationship between saint-scribe and poet-performer and in the teleology of performance as defined in the Christian era. Unlike his comrades on the battlefield, Donn Bó lives to tell the tale.[46] Our chief source for the story, however, does not leave us with an image of Donn Bó as the author of a record of the event. Nor, for that matter, is a single line of his quoted anywhere in the text. Paradoxically, performance, the "thing" performed, and the performer himself are fused or allowed to remain parts of a whole when Donn Bó's head becomes separated from his body and becomes a "performance piece." The life of Donn Bó does not result in the production of a text elicited by a saint, as does Dallán's. Rather, it continues indefinitely, with the saint's blessing, a career representing oral tradition that will not, should not, or cannot be recorded in a literary form.

Looking back on the Crónán episode from the perspective afforded us by the story behind the *Amra* and related legends, we note another advantage won by Adomnán's earlier, more cautious Columba in not eliciting a poem from the poet. Without a poem performed for him, the saint remains unobligated to the poet and free of the tangled web of reciprocity that the performance of a poem would have entailed. Columba himself remains free to utilize the power of his own voice, and the voices of others raised in Columban song have power and authority as well.

46. See Ó Riain 1978, xxx.

By pointedly not asking Crónán for a poem, Adomnán's Columba remains unimplicated in the prickly question of the role of vernacular poets in the Christian worldview. He also avoids the more immediate problem of the potential clash between literary and oral media, which the figure of the poet evokes with the same intensity so fiercely unleashed on Columba in the story of the glass book.

Significantly, this is not such a problem in Patrician hagiography, where the missionary saint of the fifth century is looking for allies and a common cultural ground from which to transform the native ideology and where poets—who, like Patrick, cultivate the authority of the truthful voice—are naturally attracted to the saint and the new religion he brings. In the later world of Adomnán's Life the battle has been won, and a reassessment or reframing of the poetic institution in Christian, literary terms is under way.

This reframing grows into an even more ambitious project in the later Columban tradition, as we can see from the stories already examined. The willingness of Columba and the literary tradition commemorating him to be implicated in the poetic institution grows considerably, arguably in proportion to the increasing dependence of that institution on the written word. Despite that dependence, the conceit, if not the reality, of the poet as performer and the poem as performance is stoutly maintained in the portrait of the poetic institution preserved in Columban legendry.

For example, in a late medieval poem that features a dialogue among Columba, Dallán, and Baithéne (Columba's monastic colleague), we find Columba graciously accepting the *Amra* from the grateful poet. Light-years away from the saint of Adomnán's Life, this Columba reacts to Baithéne's shock at his indulgence of Dallán by offering a resounding rationale for supporting poets, presented as professionals in need of making a living: "You and your poem are welcome; since it is time that it be recited, you shall have a reward without bestowal." Baithéne asks: "Is that not worldliness for you, Colum Cille, o cleric, to listen to the poets of Inis Fáil and to accept their poems?" Columba confidently responds: "Why should that be worldliness, o noble pure Baithéne, to purchase poetry—a prosperous course—since Christ himself purchased it? Christ himself purchased three fifties of poems [that is the Psalms] from David; he gave to him prosperity on the firm earth and heaven to his angelic soul."[47] Some quatrains attributed to Columba in Ó Domhnaill's Life, and possibly adapted from this poem,[48] continue in the same

---

47. Trans. Ó Cuív 1967–68, 168. Mo-cean duit is dat duain dil / a gabail uair is mithigh, / do-geba duais gan dail / ar ra-duain rena gabail. // Nach saegultacht duid-siu sin, / a Colaim Cilli, a chleirigh, / eisdecht filed Indsi Fail / issa nduana do gabail? // Cid ma budh saegaltacht sin, / a Baithin uasail igain, / cennach eigsi, reim go rath, / is Crist fein ar na cenach? // Do cenaigh Crist fein gu fir / tri chaoca duan o Dauidh, / tug do rath ar talmain tigh, / tug neam da anmain ainglidh (ibid., 168).
48. Cf. ibid., 166.

vein: "If every poem is a lie, then clothing and food are lies too, as are the whole world and even clayey man. To obtain the lie that is more lasting, I will give the lie that is more transient; [for] I am not taking anything blue, red, or fair green with me to the grave."[49]

According to the Columba of these verses, not only is there sacred precedent for listening to and paying for poems in the vernacular language and style, but there is a special kind of permanence to poetry. True, there is deceit, but it is no worse than that of the world itself, and poetic deceit is "more lasting" (*buaine*), if not simply "lasting." But, we may well ask, is this so thanks to writing? Do poems persist now in the same way that manuscripts and pages penned by holy men survive trial by water and fire?

Not only are poems lasting, says Columba, but the audience's relationship with the poet is an inescapable fact of life. There were poets (to be paid) in biblical times, there are poets to be heard in Columba's day, and thanks to the saint's efforts at Druim Cet, there will be poets in Ireland into the future. The poem, in the apologia expressed in these lines attributed to the saint, is the ultimate gift, and as such it is inherently deceptive but also productive of lasting effects. For a gift must always be reciprocated. Thus, the *Amra* does not disappear in part because a poem cannot disappear but, more important, because it generates or feeds into the relationship between poet and saint which has indeed proven to be lasting in Columban tradition.

In Ó Domhnaill's Life we find an anecdote that reflects another new development in the relationship between saint and poet. Here the poet-client relationship is not only assumed but apparently of a force rivaling the power of the saint himself:

Once Colum Cille went to cut wood for the church of Derry to the forest known as Fidbad. Men of knowledge [that is, poets] came to him seeking largess. He said to them that he had nothing to give them at the moment but that if they returned home with him, they would get something. They said, however, that they would not go and that if they did not get something then and there, they would satirize him. When Colum Cille heard the men of knowledge thus threatening satire, and he without anything to give them there, he was overwhelmed with shame—so much shame that those who were there saw smoke rise from his head, as well as a superfluity of sweat on his face. He put his hand to his face to wipe away that sweat, and a talent of gold was formed in the palm of his hand from the sweat. He gave that talent to the men of knowledge. And thus did God save Colum Cille's reputation for generosity.[50]

49. Masa brec gach dan suad, / is brec brat 's as brec biadh. / 's as brec an domhan uli, / 's as brec fos an duinecriadh. // Do cend na breice as buaine / do-ber brec as dimbuaine; / ni bía leam cum na huaidhe / gorm no derg no derg no deghuaine (O'Kelleher and Schoepperle 1918, 354).

50. Fect eli tainec C. c. do buain adhmaid docum eclaisi Doiri ar an coill darab ainm an

Curiously, the solution to Columba's quandary is not the destruction of the poets, impious enough to pressure a holy man. Surely that is what we would have expected in, say, Adomnán's Life, in which Columba predicts the poet's death instead of availing himself of the poet's services. In Ó Domhnaill's anecdote, by contrast, the poets' demands must be met, irrespective of their merits. Columba's divinely conferred power is revealed, but in a way that caters to the poets' extortion as well as to the saint's reputation for generosity.

Columba's gift to the poets in this story, gold derived from his sweat, is a truly intimate expression of the saint, an outpouring of his concern over how the poets might damage his reputation. Columba's dramatic giving of himself to the poets anticipates the establishment of an insoluble bond linking performance with payment and performer with patron in the story of the commissioning and payment of the *Amra*. In both cases, the saint pays in part to defer or avoid performance, thus exercising a control over the timing and spontaneity of poetry and its practitioners. Yet Dallán's distinctively open-ended payment, delicately extorted from Columba, is virtually the opposite of the worldly recompense won by the thuggish poets featured in Ó Domhnaill's episode, and it does more good for the poetic profession than any amount of gold ever could. For the payment given for the *Amra* extends far beyond the individual poet and the circumstances of composition, guaranteeing as it does the salvation of everyone who remembers the poem. Every time it is performed or recalled privately, Dallán's craft is rewarded, as much as Columba's fame is increased. In the story of the rapacious poets, the payment given them to forestall poetic performance stands as a reminder of the power and fame of the saint. The poets are satisfied, but the outcome redounds more to the reputation of Columba than to that of the poets. The selling of the *Amra* makes poetry into a powerful relic destined for eternal circulation and a validating sign of itself and its subject, but the saint's golden sweat disappears in the traffic of poets and patrons.

Columba's Poetic License

The encounter between saint and poets in the forest is replete with motifs that are traditionally associated with the institution of poetry in medieval Irish literature. Columba meets the bardic company not in a social set-

---

Fidbad, 7 tancutur daine eladhna cuige d'iarraid spreidhe air. Acus adubairt sesivn ríu nach raibe spreidh aige doib andsin, 7 da ndechdais leis don baile go fuigedh siad spreidh. Acus adubratar-san nach rachdais, 7 mvna faghdaís spréidh annsin fen úadh go cainfidís é. Mar docuala C.c. an t-aes eladhna ag bagar a cainte 7 gan ní aige doberadh se doib andsin, do gab nairí imarcach é, 7 do bi do mhéd na naire sin, go facaid a raibe do lathair an dethach do erigh dá chind, 7 do cuir allus imarcach dá agid, 7 do cuir a lamh fána agidh do bvain an allais-sin de, et dorindedh tallann oir don allus-sin ar a bois, 7 tuc sé an tallann sin don aeis eladhna. Et is mar sn do fhóir Dia naíre C. c. (O'Kelleher and Schoepperle 1918, 70).

ting, such as the conference of Druim Cet, but in the wilderness, where he is gathering wood. The marginality of this location, where, going by hagiographic clichés, an encounter with brigands would have been just as likely, underscores the potent "outsider" status shared and cultivated by both cleric and craftsman in medieval Irish society. Furthermore, the poets in the forest, who are presumably exercising their freedom to travel from one client to another, are presented to us in their less "civilized," more "natural" ambience. There is a distinctly extrasocial element to the medieval Irish poetic institution. It is an element that is intimately bound up with the destructive force of poetry, such as satire, with which the poets threaten Columba, as well as with the "hidden" processes of poetic inspiration.[51]

It is not only the circumstances of the encounter with the poets that are marked so as to highlight certain aspects of their craft. Columba's response to them is itself in poetic coin. Overheating and exuding an excess of liquid that results in the production of payment cannot but suggest certain key images associated in Irish tradition with the getting of poetic wisdom. One such image is the "Caldron of Poesy," a mental kitchen appliance in which the poetic composition is cooked and readied for consumption.[52] Another image conjured by the denouement is the bubble or drop of hot, inspiring liquid, which is featured, for instance, in the medieval and later folk accounts of the youth of the mythical poet-seer Finn mac Cumaill, upon whose thumb a drop falls from the cooked salmon of wisdom, with the result that he wins the gift of poetry.[53] Even the gold that results from Columba's pressure cooking is arguably a metaphor for poetic source or product, as the various connections traditionally traced in medieval Irish literature between treasure and poetry would seem to indicate.[54]

The Columba of post-seventh-century hagiography possesses solid credentials as a poet. In the Middle Irish Life of Columba, Patrick predicts of him: "Bid sui, bid fáith, bid file" ("He will be a sage, a prophet, a poet").[55] Hence, his power to counteract poets' threats in terms of their own discourse stems not only from his virtue as a man of God but also from his being at least in part cut from the same cloth as his sparring partners.

Immediately after the episode in Ó Domhnaill's Life given above we find its

51. The extrasocial, natural, and arcane aspects of the poetic institution as it is envisioned in medieval Celtic literatures are explored in J. Nagy 1981–82; 1985, passim; and P. Ford 1990a.
52. An early text featuring this caldron is edited and translated in L. Breatnach 1981; and Henry 1979–80.
53. A brief discussion of exudations of wisdom in Irish tradition is to be found in T. O'Rahilly 1946, 331–32 n. 5.
54. Relevant here is the traditional "alliterative and assonant reciprocal pair . . . *clú* 'fame' and *cnú* 'nut'; the latter word in the extended meaning 'jewel, trinket' represents the recompense for the poem conferring 'fame'" (Watkins 1976, 274).
55. Ed. and trans. Herbert 1988a, 224, 252.

multiform, a more extensive account in which the saint is pitted against yet another band of demanding poets:

> Colum Cille went confidently to a nearby spring, and he blessed and conse-
> crated it in the name of Jesus Christ. Then God performed a great good [*maith*]
> for him there, for he changed the water into wine for the space of an hour of the
> day. Subsequently, the name of that well was Maith. But Colum Cille was
> ashamed that he did not have any vessels in which to serve the wine to the
> entertainers and to everyone else besides. Then an angel revealed to him that
> three cups were hidden by men of old times long ago in the earthworks of an
> enormous [abandoned] fort nearby. And he found the cups in the place where
> the angel had said they were. There was another fort nearby to which he
> brought the band of entertainers and everyone else who was with him. He gave
> them a great feast of the wine, and so the name of God and the name of Colum
> Cille were glorified. Thus the name of that fort ever since has been the Fort of
> the Feast.[56]

Here, even more so than in the previous episode, Columba in a gesture of splendid magnanimity sustains the poetic prerogative by way of a conspicuous reference to the poetic craft. In this instance, however, the reference is "puri-fied" not by physical association with the saint himself but by being translated into Christian terms. To concoct the payment, Columba draws from a well, just as, according to tradition, poets draw their inspiration from a well of wisdom located in the otherworld.[57] But the wine that he makes of the water carries a marked sacramental connotation, so that in providing wine for his demanding "flock" Columba is reasserting his sacerdotal function.

The nature of the saint's gift, moreover, makes for a more intimate and genuine exchange between poet and patron than does the lump of gold, which, after it is given, does not necessitate any further contact beyond the

56. Teid C.c. go dochusach iarsin d'indsaighid tobair fhíruisce do bi 'san inadh sin, ⁊ do bendaig ⁊ do coisric a n-ainm Issu Crist e, ⁊ do-rinde Dia maith mor air andsin, uaire do claechlodh sé an t-uisce a fin do ré fedh uaire do lo; conadh "Maith" ainm an tobair-sin. Acus do bo nair le C.c. gan soithighe aige asa tibrad se an fin sin don cler ⁊ do cach arcena. Acus do foillsig an t-aingel dó go rabhatar cuirn, do folchatar sendaine aimser fada roimhe sin, a cladh na ratha romoíre bui laím ris; ⁊ fuair sé na cuirn san inadh adubairt an t-aingel a mbeith. Acus do bi raith eli do coír an inaidh sin, ⁊ ruc se an cliar ⁊ gach duine eli do bi faris les indte, ⁊ tug se fledh mor don fin-sin doib; gor moradh ainm De ⁊ C.c. de sin. Gonad "Raith na Fleidhe" ainm na ratha-sin ó sin alle (O'Kelleher and Schoepperle 1918, 72).

Comparable episodes featuring tense encounters between soliciting poets and a saint tempo-rarily low on supplies occur in the Irish Life of Saint Lasair (L. Gwynn 1911, 84) and the Tripartite Life of Patrick (Mulchrone 1939, 122–23), although these parallels lack the elabo-rate resolution to the Columban legend. In the incident from the Life of Lasair, the blind poet (*dalléiges*) Lugaid composes a genealogical poem about her after she miraculously feeds him and his colleagues. This outcome is, of course, reminiscent of the legend of the composition of the *Amra*.

57. See J. Nagy 1985, 279–80 n. 30, for references.

strictly professional. In the present story, Columba gives a gift that he and the poets must share, namely, a feast. This social gesture reculturalizes the abandoned space in which the saint finds the requisite vessels and even the poets themselves, who had refused Columba's offer to come home with him to Derry and enjoy his abundant hospitality there.

For the improvised feast to be a reality, for the poets to be paid, and for the honor of Columba as well as that of the poets to be rescued, the saint must first consult with an angel. This angel's replacing the poets as the focus of narrative attention in the hour of the saint's need mirrors the transformation of the well's contents into wine earlier in the same emergency, and the naming of the previously unmarked well. In a remarkable twist to the story, the two dialogues in sequence provoke further exploration of the setting in which the story unfolds. The divine messenger encourages Columba to unearth the valuables of the dead, which have been hidden in a nearby barrow for a considerable length of time. And so we see here a succession of exchanges involving Columba with, in turn, poet, angel, and the dead, the last of which, though they do not actually appear, make the most tangible contribution to the economy of both poet and saint. Albeit unwittingly, those who have secreted their treasure and themselves in the barrow prove as helpful to Columba as the angel. Together, the heavenly denizen and the denizens of the past make possible the final scene of conviviality and communion. This scene foreshadows the heavenly banquet that awaits Columba and the poets such as Dallán with whom he enjoys an affinity, and it realizes the ideal underlying the traditional poet-patron relationship, namely, collective life as a banquet, complete with generous hosts and duly reciprocating guests.

Another component of this final scene is the rediscovery of the past, perhaps as much the point of the story as is the glorification of the saint. From our latter-day perspective, this banquet does not take place in an anonymous spot beyond the social pale but in a location with a name derived from the circumstances that rendered the banquet possible, a name that lastingly encodes this place in tradition.

The Temptation of Columba

That the hagiographic terrain of Columban legendry serves as a laboratory for testing formulations of the institution of poetry in Christian terms is further indicated by the reappearance of several of the motifs examined above in one of the scenes played out at the convention of Druim Cet, when Columba formally assumes the role of patron of poets and recipient of their praise, after he persuades the men of Ireland not to banish poets altogether. The scene is described thus in medieval commentaries on the *Amra*:

Then the poets came to the assembly, bringing with them a poem of praise for Colum Cille. this type of musical composition was known as *aidbse*. It was an outstanding kind of music. . . . And they all performed that music for Colum Cille simultaneously. As a result, the cleric experienced a fit of pride, so that the air above his head was swarming with demons. This was revealed to Baithéne, who proceeded to chide Colum Cille. The cleric then lowered his head and did penance [for what he had done]. And when he raised his head, a great cloud of mist exploded from his head. The demons fled, scattered by that mist.[58]

The judgment [or trap] of vainglory that came to Colum Cille, on account of which Baithéne cited the writing of Basil in order to counter the vainglory: . . . Baithéne revealed to Colum Cille through [the writings of] Basil the fit of vainglory that overtook him at the convention, when the poets and musicians of Ireland came to entertain Colum Cille, as a result of which he became prideful and the air above his head filled up with demons. Then Baithéne read to him from the writing of Basil to reprove him, and after this incident he would not allow entertainers to come near him while he was alive, and he did not permit Dallán to compose his poem of praise for him while he, Colum Cille, was still alive. . . . The text of Basil forbade him to do any bad deeds, such as [allowing] the praise that the hosts composed for him to come between him and his God. Or he abandoned the works of God on account of the vision of the ruinous horde, and what dispelled it from him was the text or judgments of Basil.[59]

---

58. Táncatar íar sein na filid isin n-airecht ⁊ dúan molta léo dó ⁊ ocus aidbsi ainm in chiúil sin, ⁊ ba céol derscaigthech hé. . . . ⁊ i n-óenecht dognítis in ceol sin. Co tánic míad menman don chlereoch, corbo lán in t-aér húasa chind ó demnaib coro failsiged do Báithin sein ⁊ coro chairigside in clérech ⁊ co tuc clérech íar sein a chend fo choim ⁊ co nderna athrige ⁊ co túargaib íar sein a chend asa choim ⁊ co róemid ceo mór dia chind ⁊ co ro scaílit as na demna riasin céo sin (Best and Bergin 1929, lines 327–40, from the commentary on the *Amra* contained in the Lebor na hUidre manuscript; see also Stokes 1899–1900, 40, 42).

59. From the commentary in Rawlinson B.502 on the consecutive lines from the *Amra*, arbert Bassil brathu / argair[t] gnimu de adbsib airbrib aidblib, "he applied the judgments of Basil / he forbade works of *aidbse* amidst great hosts": In bráth diumussa dochuaid ind conid aire sen tuc Baethin testemain a Basil do throethad in diumais. . . . Nó ro mairnn Baethin tria Basil dosom in mbruth diummais rodan-gab isin mórdail dia tancatar cliara Hérenn dia airfitiud Coluim chille, co ragabh diumus de, cor'bo lan in t-aaer huas a chind do demnaib. Ro gab iarum Baethin testimain dó a Basil dia chursachad, ⁊ ni tharlaic-seom cuce na cliara post cein ba beo, ⁊ o shain ni tharat-som cetugud do Dallán im airchital do dénam do i mbethaid. . . . Nó no ergaired imme mala opera do denam in testimain tuc[ad] a Basil .i. ro ergair imme a menmain do bith inna Dia in molad doratsat na slóig fair. Nó ro ergart gnimu Dé de thaidbsin na n-immed nduaibsech, ⁊ is ed argart de seom sain .i. in testimain nó na bretha a Basil (Stokes 1899–1900, 180, 182).

Vernam Hull (1960–61, 246) offers an emendation of *argair gnimu* to *ar gair-gnimu* 'against vociferous performances', and takes this line as a continuation of the preceding one, hence: "He used Basil's judgments against vociferous performances." At least in Hull's reading, this portion of the *Amra* would then seem to be expressing the same oral/written dichotomy that underlies the legend told in the commentary.

These poets are not demanding a gift. Rather, they are offering an unsolicited gift, a performance of *aidbse*, which will entail payment. The saint is trapped just as he was in the forest with the demanding poets. The *aidbse* and the praise it conveys seduce him into an all-too-close relationship with poets or even into unseemly dependence on them. Fortunately, Columba's cloud, emanating as another burst of exasperated energy from his head, dispels the demons of his pride and the demons behind the pride-inducing element in the poets' performance. By thus exorcizing the demons that he oddly shares with the poets, Columba grants them a Christian, "spiritual" gift, as opposed to the secular gift of gold with which he had successfully concluded his interaction with them in the previously discussed story.

There are two key differences between the two stories featuring the motif of Columba's helpful exudation. First, in his confrontation with the extortionist poets the saint must act on his own, although monastic companions, who attest to the great heat emanating from Columba's head, are apparently present. By contrast, in the confrontation with the poets-as-sirens, Columba survives the ordeal only with the help of his companion Baithéne, who helps to bring him back to his ecclesiastical senses. Second, Baithéne assists Columba by introducing the powerful weapon of the written word, a text written by a church Father, which breaks the encomiastic spell. Here, perhaps, is the most dramatic example we have encountered so far of the conceit of a dichotomy between the Christian and the poetic ethos and also between the literary medium, the work written by Basil the Great, and the oral medium, the performance of *aidbse*. The song of the poets is strong because it is a collective expression, a choral rendition. The collective from which Columba strays under the sway of the poetic chorus, but to which he is brought back, is shown to be a readership.[60]

Once the struggle between saint and poet assumes a social dimension and is fused with the tension between oral and literary media, its outcome grows to cultural proportions. Columba's ambushes by poets in the woods far apart from the thoroughfares of society have no lasting repercussions and end with the maintenance of the status quo. Poets, these tales suggest, should be heeded and rewarded. The encounter between Columba and the poets at

---

60. Clearly this readership is grounded in the monastic classics. I owe to George Brown the useful observation that the fourth-century Cappadocian bishop Basil the Great, in this context as throughout medieval literature, was primarily associated with monastic life and discipline, and his writings (for example, the *Admonitio ad filium spiritualem*, ed. in Lehmann 1955) had a considerable effect on the development of Western monasticism (see Ryan 1972, 48–50). One of the more popular legends concerning this saint, attested in the earliest extant *Life* (fifth century) as well as in later literature, such as the so-called "Cambridge Songs" (a Latin anthology from the eleventh century), features Basil freeing a man from the grip of a hovering devil. The latter is made to drop to the ground a contract that committed the man's soul to hell (Ziolkowski 1994, 98–107, 268–69). Compare the story of Columba's freeing of a priest held by a demonic rabble (see below).

Druim Cet, however, is a "national" event that sets a precedent for all future poets and audiences. As a result of their fateful exchange, not only are a host of demons exposed and expelled from the poetic community and craft, but poetry and poets enter the new era in a censored and limited format. The demonically seductive is formally expunged from their utterance, and satire disappears from their professional behavior, as if the terms dictated by Columba to the poets at Druim Cet are, among other things, taking care of the problem raised in the totally separate legendry about his forest encounters. Furthermore, Columba limits the number of poets and the size of poetic retinues, so as to reduce the burden of maintaining poets for the population at large. Altogether, poetry and poets "after" Druim Cet are but a portion, far more manageable, of what they were "before." And in a development that is intimately connected with these others, the chief poet produces or will produce, at the time appointed by his saintly subject and patron, a poem made to Columban specifications, as opposed to the unwritten and outlawed *aidbse*.

As a result of the deliberations carried out at Druim Cet, poetry on the whole will now be compatible with writing, such as that of Basil, and no longer conceivable as a malady for which writing is the antidote. In other words, the enforced containment that makes the poetic institution endurable and even efficient for the people, not just the saints, of Ireland living in Columba's age is contingent on the ascendancy of text over performance, perhaps to the point of replacing it.

A Priest Rescued from Demons

Ó Domhnaill's Life adds an intriguing coda to the episode of Columba's great temptation at Druim Cet:

> The vapor scattered what there were of demons above his head in the air. Then all who were there at the convention, both layperson and cleric, saw the likeness of a man with a horrific shape fall before their eyes from the sky. For a while after his falling there was mist. Then he arose, was taken into the presence of Colum Cille and the king of Ireland, and asked for news. "I was a well-to-do priest of the Cenél Conaill [Colum Cille's own people]," he said, "and once I had a church built, with precious stones and crystal altars. I also had installed in it images of the sun and moon. As a result, pride and conceit sized me, so that demons came to me and took me with them high into the air, and for a year I was punished by them thus, on account of my pride. Then, when Colum Cille prayed as he just did and raised his head, the vapor that rose from his head at that time could have scattered all the demons of hell if they had been above his head. And as many as were there, he scattered them, and they let me go. For they could no longer hold me after the vapor from Colum Cille's head reached

them." . . . Later, Colum Cille blessed the priest, and he was a loyal man of God's and Colum Cille's after that.[61]

Again, the explosion of Columba's righteous indignation against his own weakness and against the strength of the poets' music produces as well as chastens. The saint fortuitously wins back from the forces of evil a fellow ecclesiastic who in some key respects resembles Columba himself. He too is of the the powerful dynastic lineage of the Cenél Conaill.[62] He too is a victim of pride and surrounded by demons. Also in both cases a man of God is turned away from the truth by putative representations of the truth communicated in distinctively nonliterary media: Columba is enchanted by what he hears about himself, and the errant priest is enchanted by what he sees, or by what he thinks is reflected of himself in what he sees.[63] Interestingly, his moral malady is more intensively narcissistic, since the representations that turn him inward are his own constructions. Columba's delusion or temporary acceptance of an alternative "truth" is brought about by unsolicited representations offered him by the poets. If, however, we take into account that the poetaster saint and the poets are involved in the same creative activity, then the poetic performance at Druim Cet and Columba's subsequent entrapment in it virtually constitute a self-projection for which the saint shares the responsibility.

Still, even with the resemblance between the unwitting rescuer Columba and the rescued cleric who can explain so lucidly how he was rescued, the former prisoner of devils is a marvelous "other" who literally drops from the

61. Do scáeil an detach sin a raibe do demhnaib os a cind san aiér. Acus do condaic a raibe 'sa mordail sin, itir laech 7 clerech, indamail duine a ndeilb ro-granna ac tuitim in a fiadnaise as an aieór. Acus do bi se tamall a nell tar eis tuitme do, 7 do eirig se iar sin, 7 tucadh a fiadhnaise C. C. 7 righ Erend é 7 do fiarfuidhed[h] scela de. "Sagart saidbhir do cinel Conaill me," ar se, "7 do cumdaigedh ecluss lium 7 do cuir me lecca loghmara 7 altóra gloinidhe san ecluis sin, 7 tuc me fo dera delb greine 7 esca do cur indte, 7 do gab dimus 7 med menman me trid sin, indus co tancatar na demhna cugam 7 gor tocbatar leo san aier a n-airde mhe, 7 ataim bliadhain 'com pianudh aca mar sin tre mo dímuss. Et an uair, umorro, dorinde C. C. an urnuidhe ud 7 do tocuib se a cend on a choim, do scaeilfedh an dethach do erich da cenn an uair sin abfuil do demhnaib a n-ifrend dá mbeidís os a cend; 7 ger mor a raibe and, do scaeil sí iad, 7 do lecetar mesi amach; oir nirb eídir leo mo congbail o do chuaidh dethach cind C. C. futha." . . . Do bendaigh C. C. an sagart iar sin, 7 ba hoclaech maith do Día 7 do C. C. é o sin amach (O'Kelleher and Schoepperle 1918, 356, 358; and see Stokes 1899–1900, 42, 50, 428–29).
62. Columba is said in Adomnán's Life to be the son of Fedelmid, a grandson of Conall Gulban, the eponymous ancestor of this branch of the Uí Néill—Conall being a son of the eponymous Niall (second preface, Anderson and Anderson 1991, 6). The importance of Columba's aristocratic background and family connections in his ecclesiastical career and in the unfolding of his legend is discussed in Herbert 1988a, passim; and Smyth 1984, 84–115.
63. Perhaps what seduces the priest in this story is some lingering form, or latter-day Christian reconstruction, of pre-Christian worship of heavenly bodies (as suggested in Stokes 1899–1900, 419). If the cleric's fall from grace is indeed a specific reference to earlier cult, then *aidbse*, the catalyst in the analogous account of Columba's own near seduction, seems all the more suggestive of pre-Christian practice.

sky and becomes an occasion for the confirmation of faith and the affirmation of Columba's authority. Primarily the priest is a storyteller, who, wakened from a deathlike state and returned to the realm of the living, tells of both the past and the otherworld, that is, his aery life with the demons. After his own oral performance, whose effects are markedly different from the poets', the priest, we are told, becomes a loyal member of Columba's retinue.

Basically, this sensational tale is a multiform of the revenant story pattern already familiar from Patrician hagiography. On more than one occasion, Patrick resurrects a dead person to hear of the past or the otherworld and to convince his fellow auditors of his authority and the power of the religion he preaches. In Columba's postmissionary era, however, firmly grounded in the Christian present, the "revenant" of Druim Cet is not a pagan but a fallen-away ecclesiastic.[64] Furthermore, in the Columban version of this story type, unlike the Patrician ones, the miraculous event is placed within the context of a debate about the poetic institution. It is because Columba has rid both himself and the poets' art of what is "traditional" but antithetical to the new religion and culture that the priest is released and given the chance to tell fellow humans, and posterity, about his curious fate.

It is eminently possible, if not probable, that the scenario of the recovered storyteller predates hagiography and is intimately connected with pre-Christian conceptualizations of the nature and sources of poetic inspiration.[65] In the Ireland of Patrick as portrayed in hagiography, the scenario is totally appropriated by and for the Christian saint in his struggle to have his voice heard. In the lore of Columba, on the other hand, a saint who lives in an era when Christian and poet can draw together (although warily) and the poetic institution can be "reintroduced" on at least some of its traditional terms, the resurrection scenario is reattracted to the poetic context and to the vernacular issues whence it may originally have derived. Let us note that the revenant of sorts, the rescued priest, appears both to the saint and to the poets, or even to the poets through the saint. Alternatively, and we shall see that there is no contradiction involved, the dialogue between the priest and Columba mirrors that between the poets, caught up in their own demons of representation, and the saint, who rids them and himself of their demons.

The Scandlán Affair

In the medieval traditions about Columba at Druim Cet, which, as I have indicated, go far beyond the rapprochement among rival conceptualiza-

64. This is not to say that Columba did not raise the dead, as did most other self-respecting Irish saints, following the pattern set by Martin of Tours and biblical role models. See, e.g., Adomnán's Life, 2.32, Anderson and Anderson, 1991, 140.
65. This thesis is argued in J. Nagy 1983b. Cf. McCone 1990, 199–200.

tions and authorizations of voice that Adomnán was attempting to arrange in the Life, the vain priest is not the only captive miraculously freed by Columba. One of the three reasons for Columba's decision to break his vow of exile and return to Ireland in order to attend the meeting of the men of Ireland at Druim Cet, besides defending the poets from an exile similar to that imposed upon him, has specifically to do with the liberation and revelation of a figure long hidden from social view in a deathlike state. According to what appears to be an extended interpolation in the Middle Irish Life which details the reasons why Columba came to the convention, the saint sets out after he hears of the terrible plight of one of Áed's hostages, Scandlán, the son of the king of the tributary kingdom of Ossory, who is confined to a closely guarded hut, where his pleas for adequate sustenance go unheeded.[66] After Áed refuses Columba's plea on Scandlán's behalf, a flash of lightning disrupts the assembly, and the prisoner is miraculously freed by an angel, who escorts him to the place where Columba is staying:

> They went thereafter to Derry. When the cleric at nocturns was passing west by the chancel screen, it was Scandlán who attended to his sandals for him, and Colum Cille asked: "Who is this?" "Scandlán," said he. "Have you news?" said Colum Cille. "A drink," said Scandlán. "Have you brought a blessing?" "A drink." "Tell me how you came?" "A drink." "Hesitancy of speech be on your successor always." "Do not say so," said Scandlán, "you shall have their dues, rents, and tribute forever." "May there be bishops and kings among your descendants," said Colum Cille; "One drink for you: a vat of ale big enough for three." Then he [Scandlán] raised the vat with both hands and drank it in one draught.[67]

Clearly operating in the story are conscious echoes of Patrick's encounter with Lóegaire, an earlier, pagan high king. The saint has in each case returned home to plead with the king at a "national" meeting, and the seemingly fruitless negotiations are stunningly interrupted by a cosmic display of power, such as the lightning bolt at Druim Cet, which humbles the saint's opponents. Also featured in both situations is the rescue of a beloved youth, functioning as a hostage, from life-threatening confinement. Patrick saves

66. Patrick Ford has suggested to me that the name's seeming derivation from the Latin borrowing *scandal* 'offence, cause of offence' (*DIL*, s.v.) gives added meaning to the role that the character named Scandlán plays in the legend of Druim Cet.

67. Trans. Herbert 1988a, 268. Do imdighsit iar sin co Doire. Tan boi an clerech im iarmerghe ic dol tar crann caingel siar, is e Sgannlan do frithoil a asa do 7 is-pert Colum Cille: "Cia so?" "Sgannlan," ol se. "Sgela lat," or Colum Cille. "Deoch," ol Sgannlan. "In tugais bennachtain," ol Colum Cille. "Deoch," ol Scannlan. "Indis cindus tancaduis," ol Colum Cille. "Deoch," ol Scannlan. "Dolma n-aithisg ar fher h'inaid do gress," ol Colum Cille. "Na habair," ol Sgannlan, "a cís 7 a cobach 7 a mbés duitsi do gres." "Espuic 7 righ dot' tshilso," ol Colum Cille. "Hendig duit," ol se, ".i. dabach trir do lind." Do togaib iar sin eter a dí laim an dabaig 7 at-ib ina endig (ibid., 246).

Benignus, who undergoes an ordeal for him in the burning house, and Columba saves Scandlán, a hostage to the high king for his father. Once rescued, the youth can assume his rightful inheritance, Benignus as Patrick's ultimate successor, Scandlán as the next king of Ossory.[68]

Of course, Scandlán is confined far longer than Benignus. Moreover, the Ossory prince does and says more after he is released than did Patrick's protégé, though what marks his speech so strongly is the very little he says. Like Patrick in the *grazacham* episode of Muirchú's Life, Scandlán becomes a man of one word or phrase. Indeed, he is nearly defined by it. Patrick's insistent *grazacham* finally earns him the respect of the pagan with whom he is engaged in long-distance dialogue, but had Scandlán not managed finally to say something beyond "a drink," he and his descendants would have been marked forever by terseness of speech, and nothing else. Fortunately, the commitment that Scandlán swiftly improvises to placate Columba earns a distinction for his lineage which balances out its verbal inadequacies.

Clearly Columba wants to hear from Scandlán a story about miraculous escape and adventure or at least a decent acknowledgment from one who has had such a special encounter with the supernatural. No such revelation is forthcoming, although in Scandlán's display of thirst it becomes clear to both the saint and the audience of this tale that his experience has made the prisoner rather exceptional. The dumb show of Scandlán's consumption of vast quantities in effect takes the place of the supernaturally induced recitation of "old" experiences which is the staple of Patrician revenant legends.

A story told in the Middle Irish Life of Columba offers itself as an analogue:

On another occasion, Baithéne left Colum Cille cooking an ox for the band of workmen. Among them was a former warrior of the men of Ireland, Mael Uma mac Baetáin. Colum Cille asked the latter how much he would eat when he was a fighting man. Mael Uma replied: "I used to consume a fat ox to satisfy my appetite when I was a warrior." Colum Cille ordered him to eat his fill. Mael Uma did his bidding and ate the whole ox. Then Baithéne came and inquired if the food was prepared. Thereupon Colum Cille commanded Mael Uma to assemble all the ox-bones in one place, and this was done. Colum Cille blessed

---

68. Possible biblical models for the miraculous freeing of prisoners, common in Irish saints' lives (Plummer 1910, 1:cxxxix n. 3), include Acts 12:1–19 (an angel releases Peter from his confinement—I thank John Carey for this reference) and 16:23–40 (Paul and Silas are freed by an earthquake—noted in Ó hÓgáin 1985, 60). Of course, in Irish hagiography the captivity is presented in terms of the Irish institution of the hostage (on which, see F. Kelly 1988, 173–75). A king is holding a person captive as a sign of his royal authority, but the prisoner happens to be a protégé of a saint, and so, the royal and ecclesiastical authorities collide. The issue at stake is arguably semiotic. When held as a *gíall* 'hostage', the protagonist is a sign of the king; when freed, a sign of the saint. The historical background to the legend of Scandlán's captivity and release is explored in Ryan 1946, 53–55.

the bones then, so that their flesh was restored on them and they were given to the workmen.[69]

From the veteran Mael Uma, Columba does get a story about "the past" and a testimony to the larger-than-life proportions of people of "the past," as does Patrick in Tírechán's account of the raising from the dead of the gigantic swineherd. Mael Uma is of course hardly a revenant, although as one converted to the monastic life from the secular, he is at least spiritually "revived" or "reborn." To be noted, however, is the insistent motif of resurrecting the dead, in this case, a dead ox.

Mael Uma's resemblance to Scandlán establishes an important connection between the lore of Druim Cet and the realm of *fénnidi* 'brigands', figures who are emblematic of the transition from childhood to adulthood in medieval Irish literature and who function as the representatives of the old order and oral tradition in later strands of the literary tradition. It is the wisdom of these fénnidi that Patrick and the scribal community spawned by Christianity tap in the thirteenth-century *Acallam na Senórach*, as we shall see later on. Surely therefore it is no coincidence that Mael Uma, Columba's hungry ex-warrior, appears in sources other than Columban legends as a *rígfhénnid*, chief of fénnidi. Furthermore, the appetite that proves Mael Uma's point and serves in place of Scandlán's making any point is an important feature of Oisín the fénnid's establishment of his "otherness" to Patrick in oral versions of the story of their encounter, which derive from the *Acallam* itself or the storytelling tradition behind this literary work.[70]

Thus the tale of Scandlán's liberation in medieval accounts of the meeting of Druim Cet is replete with motifs that indicate its kinship with stories of encounters and dialogues between saints and brigands or revenants. Central to the tale is an intriguing conflation: the figure of the ancient whom the saint revives to demonstrate the nature of the past blends with the figure of the dispossessed youth who is vindicated and restored to his rightful position in the hagiographic family romance we have seen in Patrician narratives. Given, however, the "death" and resurrection of Miliucc's children as envisioned by their father before their accession to his place of privilege, and the odd, dangerous placing of the king-to-be Conall next to the druid about to be slain

69. Trans. Herbert 1988a, 262–63. Fecht n-aill do Colum Cille for-fhacaib Boithín hé ic funi mairt don methil. Boi athlaech d'feraib Erenn accu .i. Moel Uma mac Boetáin esium. Ro iarfaid Colum Cille de cia mét a loingthi in tan ba hoclaech. At-bert Moel Uma: "No chaithind mart méth in sháith in tan ropsam oclach." Ro forcongair Colum Cille fairsium co ros-toimled a shaith. Da-roine Moel Uma airsium sin co nduaid in mart uli. Tanic Boithin iar sin cor iarfaig in ba herlam in essair. Ro forcongair tra Colum Cille for Moel Uma uli chnáma in mairt do thinol i n-oen baile, 7 da ronad amlaid. Bennachais Colum Cille iarum na cnamu 7 bói a fheoil fen impu iar sin co rruchta don methil (ibid., 239).

70. See Bruford 1986–87, 53–54. F. Ó Briain 1947, 36–37, cites some of the hagiographic instances of the cure of hungry individuals. On Mael Uma see Herbert 1988a, 285 n. on l. 460.

by Patrick, the convergence implicit in the Scandlán tale is perhaps not so unusual.[71]

In examining the legend of Scandlán at length, I may seem to have advanced beyond the theme of Columba's relationship with poets, but the literary tradition ties Scandlán to the poets by making them two of the three reasons why Columba decided to rescind his vow never to return to Ireland. Moreover, the story of Scandlán's return is yet another demonstration of the power of speech, in presence and in absence, which is the heart of the matter deliberated in the legend of Columba, the *Amra*, and the poets of Ireland. It can even be said that the details of Scandlán's imprisonment—deprivation, extreme confinement, and a kind of social death—all point to the ascetic rituals of poetic inspiration and composition to which Celtic traditions tantalizingly attest.[72]

In any event, someone as sorely deprived as poor Scandlán could be expected to have the kind of supernatural experience he does have, and Columba, as well as anyone else personally or professionally interested in good stories, such as poets, could be expected to be anxious to hear what happened. Scandlán, however, disappoints his would-be auditor and, in so doing, demonstrates the desirability of adding such information to the "pool" of tradition, even more unmistakably than cooperation would have done.

Worth noting for contrast is an alternative version of the story of Scandlán's release as told in the lengthy preface to the *Amra* contained in Rawlinson B.502, a twelfth-century manuscript, which is one of our earliest surviving sources for Irish vernacular literature, alongside the Lebor na hUidre and the Book of Leinster.[73] In this account, Scandlán's participation in dialogue is dramatically developed. Indeed, the refugee from royal injustice even manages to get a drink *and* tell his tale to Columba:

> As a dejected Colum Cille was going out through the door of the fort, he heard the cry of Scandlán, suffering as much as he was. . . . Then Colum Cille went to talk with him, and Scandlán said to him: "Go back, for the sake of Christ's suffering, and ask Áed to surrender me, for I am trapped by my obligations." The cleric went and asked Áed for him, but he was not given to him. "He will be released by matins tomorrow," said Colum Cille.
>
> "The madness of the crooked cleric yonder!" [said the queen,] "and the arrogance of his words." When she said this, she was washing herself. "It is you yourself who will be *corr* ['crooked' or 'a heron']," said Colum Cille, "outside at this ford until doomsday, with one wing broken, just as now only half of your

71. See pp. 57–58; 65–67.
72. Some of the more remarkable references in medieval Celtic literatures to the suffering or even "death" the figure of the poet must undergo for the sake of his craft are discussed in P. Ford 1987.
73. Stokes 1899–1900, 46–55.

hair is washed"—and so it happened—"and Scandlán will come to me by matins tomorrow."

. . . A great trembling of arms came over the encampment that night, with both thunder and fire in the evening, and by God's plan Scandlán was lifted past the encampment. He advanced, preceded by a shining cloud and followed by a dark one, until he came to Coirthe Snáma [that is, on the trail of Colum Cille].

He saw a boat there in front of him and a single man in it. "Who is there in the boat?" asked Scandlán. "Cuimmíne here," he said, "son of Feradach, son of Muiredach, son of Éogan, son of Niall" [that is, a descendant of Niall Noígiallach, like Columba, but in a rival lineage]. He had become an enemy of Colum Cille's after he had slain Coirpre Líath mac Lugdach Lámdeirg, despite his having been under Colum Cille's protection. "Give me passage and information," said Scandlán. "No," said Cuimmíne, until you make my peace with Colum Cille." "I will do that," said Scandlán. Cuimmíne bound him to do so.

They turned from there toward Ard mac nOdráin [where Colum Cille was staying]. It is then that Colum Cille arose for matins. Scandlán was there holding one of his sandals for him, in the manner that Colum Cille himself said he would.

"Who are you?" asked Colum Cille.

"Scandlán," he replied.

"News," said Colum Cille.

"A drink," said Scandlán.

A vessel reached the hand of Colum Cille, and he gave it to Scandlán.

"News," said Colum Cille.

"A drink," said Scandlán.

"Go out, Baithéne," said Colum Cille, "and bring his fill once again." It was brought, and Scandlán drank it.

"News," said Colum Cille.

"A drink," said Scandlán.

A third fill was brought to him, and he drank it.

"News," said Colum Cille.

And Scandlán then gave him his account.[74]

---

74. Hi tudecht do Colum cille fo dorus in duine immach fo dimbraig co cuala diucaire Scandláin ar meit na peine hi rabí. . . . Co ndeochaid Colum cille dia acallaim, 7 co n-erbairt Scandlán fris: "Heirg ar cessa[d] Issu Crist fort chii [leg. chúl], 7 nom-chuinnig for Aed, ar dorochar im fhiachu." Dochuaid in clerech 7 ro cuinnig, 7 ní thucad do. "Bid dilmain ria matain," ar Colum cille. "A mire in chorrchlerig út," [ar in rígan], "ocus sobcca a briathar!" 7 is amlaid bai 7 si ic folcud. "Tu fein bas chorr," ar Colum cille, "for ind ath-sa immuich co brath, 7 do lethsciath mbriste amal do lethfholt foilcthi"—7 doronad samlaid—"7 domruasa Scanlán ria matain." . . . Tanic armgrith mór hisin longphort in n-aidchi-sin etir toraind 7 tenid im fhescor, co tuargabad Scandlán tria lathar nDe sechtar na scuru 7 na longphurtu, 7 imrulaid iarsin 7 nel solusta remi, 7 nel dorcha 'na diaid, co Coirthi snama. Co facca in curach ara chinn 7 oenfer ann. "Cia fil isin churuch?" ar Scandlán. "Cummine ann," ar sé, "mac Feradaig, maic Muiredaig maic Eogain maic Neill." Bidba sede do Cholum chille iar marbad Coirpri Léith

After Scandlán reports his news and fulfills his promise to Cuimmíne, Columba and Scandlán hold a poetic dialogue in which the king-to-be pledges to the saint the allegiance and support of the kingdom of Ossory, and Columba acknowledges Scandlán's commitment and pledges in turn to favor Ossory and its kings if they prove steadfast. Then, as Columba is equipping Scandlán with a Gospel, as a talisman to protect him on his return home to Ossory, he notes the anxiety of the young claimant to the throne. Yet another poetic dialogue ensues, in which Scandlán confesses his great fear of his enemies and Columba confers his own staff (*bachall*) on Scandlán and his royal descendants and promises that it will protect him on the road home.

This detailed account, centering on a series of conversations, begins with the cry of Scandlán, which sets the story in motion. The crushing desperation of the prisoner's plight likens him all the more to the hagiographic type of the woeful dead person with whom a saint strikes up a conversation. Scandlán, however, still has the power to draw attention to himself by means of speech, unlike the dead whom Patrick must summon and to whom he must return the powers of speech.

The dialogue between Columba and the pleading prisoner Scandlán quickly gives way to a dialogue between the saint and the king. And then we overhear yet another exchange in which a third voice makes itself heard, that of Áed's queen. Her strikingly candid and biting remark reveals her to be the opposite of the typical Patrician queen or princess, whose characteristic function is to reestablish communication between the saint and her stubbornly resistant male relation (spouse, father, or brother). Still, in becoming the overt expression of her husband's relatively discreet hostility and thus the object of the saint's wrath, the queen does facilitate communication. Arguably, she is the scapegoat, and once her punishment is out of the way, Columba can resume normal relations with her husband Áed.

Scandlán, meanwhile, after escaping from his imprisonment, joins the ranks of characters who make dramatic crossings over water to converse with Columba. In Scandlán's case, he is confronted at the water's edge by a ferryman who turns out to be an old enemy of Columba's, a fellow layman whose conversation prepares Scandlán for his dialogue with the saint himself. It is with Columba that Scandlán agrees to speak as a proxy for Cuimmíne, as well as on his own behalf.

---

maic Lugdach Lamdeirg for a foessam. "Immurchor dam ⁊ eolus," ar Scandlán. "Ni tho," ar Cummin, "co nderna mo síd fri Colum cille." "Dogen," ar Scandlán. Nenaisc fair. Imsoat ass co hArd mac nOdrain. Is ann asraracht Columb cille dond iarmeirge. Scandlán conacab a lethassa immi feib asrubart fessin. "Cia so?" ar Colum cille. "Scandlán," ar se. "Scela," ar Colum cille. "Deog," ar Scanlán. [Tic] in ballan il-laim Coluim chille ⁊ dombeir dó. "Scela," ar Colum cille. "Deog," ar Scanlán. "Immach, a Baethin," ar Colum cille, "⁊ a lan aili do," ⁊ doberar, ⁊ ibid Scandlán. "Scela," ar Colum cille. "Deog," ar Scandlán. Doberar do in tres lán ⁊ ibid. "Scela," ar Colum cille. Ocus atchuaid Scandlan post iarsin a thairthiud do (ibid., 46, 48, 50).

Perhaps more than any of the various other dialogues featured in commentary on the composition of the *Amra*, the dialogue between Scandlán and Cuimmíne brings out the mediative function of such verbal exchanges, whereby common ground can be found and used as the basis for affirming old relationships or establishing new ones. For as the direct result of this encounter, Cuimmíne and Columba resolve their old feud. The dialogue between the escaped hostage and the incognito ferryman is also an opportunity to rehearse old stories, such as that of the killing of Coirpre Líath. Unfortunately, this tale, only alluded to here, has not survived, but what we know about Cuimmíne's victim suggests that he and Scandlán had much in common. Both were princes protected by Columba under adverse circumstances and finally elevated by him to their respective thrones.[75] For Scandlán to agree to plead for mercy on behalf of his counterpart's murderer is to enter into a pact with a stranger whose life was blighted by the same kind of violence that threatens Scandlán's own life. In the passage I have quoted, Cuimmíne is said to have offended the saint by slaying Coirpre while he was under Columba's protection; similarly, the incarceration of Scandlán, another of Columba's protégés, has violated the terms of hostageship guaranteed by Columba. With its implicit relevance to Scandlán's situation, the exchange between Cuimmíne and Scandlán appears as a frame for the central dialogue between Columba and Scandlán, a frame that concludes with Columba's assurance that Scandlán will be safe from his enemies.

The dialogue so recontextualized differs from the rather one-sided interchange between miraculously released prisoner and breathlessly interrogating saint which we heard before. In this telling of the story, which brings Cuimmíne into the interaction between saint and hostage, Columba is less insistent, responding to the request for a drink, and Scandlán does get around to telling his story. This variant, in addition to emphasizing the good that storytelling can do, as opposed to the harm its absence can cause, also features the undoing of a curse, on Cuimmíne, as opposed to the laying of a curse on Scandlán's descendants. In expanding the effects of dialogue between saint and a near-dead speaker to include the removal of a burdensome condition, this account of the dialogue falls in line with stories of conversations between living and dead in hagiographic and secular literature.

The final dialogue in the series of exchanges that constitutes the story of Scandlán serves to prepare the prince for his return to his kingdom and to provide him with the assurance that he may indeed assume his rightful responsibilities and privileges without fearing retaliation from the enemies who nearly left him dead in the hut. The conversation, in poetic form, focuses on the nature of the protection Columba can offer the understandably worried

---

75. Coirpre's story is recounted in Ó Domhnaill's Life (O'Kelleher and Schoepperle 1918, 218–20).

prince. Mentioned in the prose only and not in the accompanying verse is the saint's act of tying a copy of the Gospel around Scandlán's person to protect him during his upcoming trip to Ossory. This most literary of talismans fails to reassure the would-be traveler. Columba himself clearly does not view it as the best protection available, since, as the poetic dialogue begins, he offers Scandlán his staff or crozier, which will ward off all evil.

Despite the donation of this impressive and highly personal gift, Scandlán, as he confesses, still has qualms about going home. Columba continues to reassure him of a blessed future, and although Scandlán gives no indication that he has been persuaded, we the audience know that he did in fact reach Ossory and ascend the throne. Ultimately, it can be argued, the most powerful guarantee for Scandlán's safety is Columba's prophetic utterance within the dialogue, which is even more reliable than the attached Gospel or the staff. True, these are signs of authority with which saints' protégés are commonly invested in hagiography, but they pale in comparison to the immediate sign of saintly speech. Even if Basil's writings can return Columba to his clerical senses, they do not replace the voice of poets; so too the written Gospel itself must be superseded by more immediate and personal emblems of power if Scandlán is to make the transition from death back to life.

"Crooked Cleric"

At this point, with Scandlán's investiture still in mind, we return to the one hostile dialogue in the story of Scandlán, which brings about the divestiture of a character who, unlike Scandlán, is hardly beloved of Columba. The dialogue between Columba and the queen goes to the heart of the general problem of distinguishing proper from improper traditional discourse which underlies the deliberations at Druim Cet.[76] For in what she says and the reaction she elicits, the queen highlights a dark aspect of the poetic institution, which emerges only obliquely in Columba's interaction with the poets themselves. In accusing the saint of being "crooked" (*corr*), the queen implicates him in the same iniquity that makes poets and their poetry suspect in Christian eyes, and she also satirizes the saint, albeit not in poetic form. According to the commentary on the *Amra*, it is precisely the element of satire, among other "traits," which brought poets to the brink of exile and was banned by Columba. The queen-turned-heron is therefore almost a personification of a problem, an embodiment of satire, and her punishment and transformation is a grand theatrical expression of the saint's reform of poetic content and procedure.[77]

---

76. The legend of the queen-turned-heron was treated earlier in J. Nagy 1990a.
77. *Corrguinecht* is said to be one of the components of satire in an early law tract (L.

The poetic connection underlying the exchange between saint and queen is even more apparent in a variant of this episode, also preserved in the *Amra* apparatus, according to which the queen lashes out at Columba after he has blessed her stepson Domnall instead of her own son Conall: "'Excessive is the sorcery [*corrguinecht*] in which you are engaged,' [said the queen.] 'You yourself ought to be restless [*?For corracht*],' says the cleric. Whereupon she was turned into a heron [*corr*]. Thereafter her handmaid fell to insulting the cleric, and she was turned into another heron."[78] The irony of Columba's being accused of *corrguinecht* in the context of the meeting at Druim Cet and of the saint's encounter with the poets was doubtless not lost on the audience of these Columban legends. *Corrguinecht* is of the same pagan stock as the magic worked on the saint in the performance of *aidbse*, which exposed Columba's weakness.[79] And Columba, in giving his blessing to Domnall, is from the queen's cynical perspective simply attempting a Christian form of the flattery with which the poets nearly deprived Columba of his saintly authority. The queen is holding up a mirror to the saint and showing him and us just how inextricably bound he and the poets have become, or how inherently alike they are to begin with. Both possess authoritative, "magical" voices with which they attempt to sway the minds of kings, and both enjoy overwhelming reputations with which they nearly destroy themselves.

Columba throws off this accusation by turning it back on his accuser and taking what she says literally. Even in play words have multiple meanings and potentially deadly force. Columba, accused of being *corr* 'crooked' (as in *corrguinecht*), condemns her to a life of unrest (*for corracht*) and turns her into a *corr* 'heron'. The saint's shifting of his audience's attention from *corrguinecht* as the issue to *corr-* as allusion is analogous to Columba's and Baithéne's combating the immediacy and persuasiveness of *aidbse* with the text of Basil's writings. The pun on *corr*, perhaps meant to suggest a bookish wit, counteracts the virulence of the queen's spontaneous insult and effectively changes the subject.[80]

Breatnach 1987, 114). Hence the queen is perhaps accusing Columba of the same kind of malignant power he is expunging from the poetic order in order to make it more acceptable to contemporary, Christianized society. If her accusation has any basis, it strengthens the saint's identification with poets.

78. "Romor in chorrgainecht for a tai." "Is cet duitsiu," ar in clerech, "bith for corracht." Conid annsin ro soad-si hi cuirr. Co ra gaib a hinailt iarsin for athissigud in clerig, co ro soad sede dano hi cuirr n-aile (Stokes 1899–1900, 40).

79. References in the literature to *corrguinecht* in the sense of 'sorcery' are cited in *DIL*, s.v. See also Scowcroft 1995, 142 n. 78.

80. Perhaps Columba in meting out this punishment is pointing out a genuine feature of *corrguinecht*, which consists, according to a late gloss on an early law tract, of "being on one foot and with one eye open while doing the *glám dícinn* [a satirical composition or ritual]," (beth for lethcois for lethlaim for lethsuil ag denam na glaime dícinn [*CIH*, line 1480; see L. Breatnach 1987, 140, note on *corrguinecht*]). Standing on one leg is certainly evocative of long-legged birds such as the heron (cf. Ó Cuív 1961–63, 338).

The aid of a third party comes here not to Columba, who has no need of Baithéne or Basil in devising the pun, but to the queen, whose handmaid carries on the verbal fight against the cleric, with similar results. She too becomes a victim of the wordplay. And in contrast to the earlier revelation of the true demonic nature of both Columba's pride and the *aidbse*, and its expulsion into the air resulting in the purification of the poets and their craft, the queen and her attendant are "disguised" as herons and grounded at Druim Cet, to serve as perpetual signs of their own foolishness and the saint's authority. Recall the earlier passage: " 'It is you yourself who will be a heron,' said Colum Cille, 'outside at this ford until doomsday, with one wing broken, just as now only half of your hair is washed'—and so it happened."

Featured as they are in the outcomes of parallel incidents, the demons expelled from Druim Cet and the herons bound to it appear as inverse images of what is wrong with poetry from the Christian perspective espoused in Columban hagiography. The problem with poets and the poetic institution is the potential for the immediate and spontaneous presentation of voice to deceive, seduce, or wound with invective. Curiously, however, this dark, distinctly performative side of poetry is described in the *Amra* legend in metaphorical terms that suggest its limitlessness. The demons dispelled are seemingly innumerable, and are not captured or gathered in one place to be kept out of harm's way. Nor is any terminus given to the longevity of the heron-women, who are granted a conspicuous immortality as well as being condemned to animal form. To what extent, we may well ask, can Columba, or the Christian literary tradition he represents, control the creatures they have created or released?

According to the alternative version of the story of the heron(s) quoted earlier, the queen's insult is not directed at what Columba does, supposedly *corrguinecht*, but at what he is. She calls him a *corrchléirech* 'crooked cleric'. Here too, the saint takes the accusation and renders it into a ricocheting pun. The *corr-* of the abusive appellation becomes *corr* 'heron', and the accuser becomes a heron herself.

In fact, the pun may already be at work in this case in the original accusation, since the Columba of hagiography is in a way a "heron-cleric." The heron or crane (a similar bird also designated *corr*) plays a prominent role in more than one episode of Columban legend. I have already noted that it was with his savage pet heron (*corr*) that the saint attempted to protect himself from the prying eyes that viewed him copying a manuscript. A less violent and more sentimental bird appears in another Columban tale, which is already to be found in Adomnán's Life:

Another time, when the holy man was living on the island of Iona, he summoned one of the monks and instructed him thus: "On the third day after the dawning of this one, you ought to be waiting in the western part of the island, sitting on the seashore. For from the northern region of Ireland, after the ninth hour of the day, a guest crane [*grus*] will approach, thoroughly exhausted, having been driven by the winds on lengthy travels through the air. It will come to rest before you, falling on the shore with its strength nearly spent. You will lift it carefully and compassionately, and you will take it to the nearby dwelling, where you will feed the well-received bird for three days and nights, ministering to it solicitously. Later, rested and its strength fully restored after three days, and not wishing to stay among us as a pilgrim anymore, it will return to the dear region of Ireland whence it came. That is why I so diligently commend the bird to you—because it comes from the land of our fathers."[81]

Of course, the prophecy is borne out, and the crane returns home safely.

The remarkable treatment accorded the bird is more than a reflection of Columba's kindness toward animals. Having the crane treated like a human pilgrim or guest is the opposite of what he does in the legend of Drum Cet, namely, treat a human being as a *corr*. In both cases, however, I would argue that the bird functions as a projection of the saint himself (who after all bears an aviary name). In the Druim Cet anecdote, Columba is designated a heron by virtue of the queen's insulting appellation, or by virtue of Columba's exploiting its ambiguity. In Adomnán's Life, the saint's concern for the bird, as well as the description of it as a pilgrim in exile from Ireland like Columba himself, implies the identification between crane and saint. Moreover, the heron serves as a reflexive symbol or extension of Columba in the affair of the copied manuscript.

Yet the crane pilgrim, like the queen who becomes a heron, is also definitely unlike Columba, and even represents what Columba is *not* or what he no longer has. Unlike Columba, the bird, after it is brought back from the brink of death by starvation and exhaustion, will return home to Ireland. The saint makes clear in the story as it is told by Adomnán that the crane is to be saved and nourished because it "comes from the land of our fathers." The bird is a synecdochic token of the home and the past that the saint has abandoned. As if he were stricken with crippling pangs of nostalgia or too alienated from this symbolic aspect of the crane to deal with it directly, Columba does not welcome and care for the visitor himself but has a fellow monk do the work.

81. Alio namque in tempore cum sanctus in Ioua inhabitaret insula, unum de fratribus aduocans síc conpellat: "Tertia ab hac inlucescente die exspectare debebis in occidentali huius insulae parte, super maris oram sedens. Nam de aquilonali Euerniae regione quaedam hospita grus uentís per longos aeris agitata circuitus post nonam diei horam ualde fessa et fatigata superueniet, et pene consumptís uiribus coram té in litore cadens recumbet. Quam misericorditer subleuare curabis, et ad propinquam deportabis domum, ibidemque hospitaliter receptam per tres dies et noctes ei ministrans sollicite cibabis. Et post, expleto recreata triduo, nolens ultra apud nos perigrinari, ad priorem Scotiae dulcem unde orta remeabit regionem plene resumtís uiribus. Quam ideo tibi síc deligenter commendo, quia de nostrae paternitatis regione est oriunda" (1.48, Anderson and Anderson 1991, 86).

In Ó Domhnaill's version of the story, however, the exiled saint finally does encounter the *corr*, which refuses to take nourishment until it sees Columba and has a private conversation with him:

The monk brought the crane (*corr*) with him to the place where Colum Cille was, and upon approaching the saint, the crane bent her knee and bowed her head as a sign of obedience to him, and she made its happiness clear in his presence. Right away the bird ate food from his hand, and she was inseparable from him from then on, as long as she stayed in that place. She would go with him to church and to every other place where he himself would go. After three days, the crane came to Colum Cille screaming, screeching, and beating its wings. The monks asked him why she did that. This is what Colum Cille said in response: "She is saying goodbye to me, and she is now going to go back to her own home, but she is full of grief and sorrow over the tragedy of her leaving me, as she fears [?] that she will not see me ever again [or "until Judgment Day"]. And it is fitting for her to feel that way, since I too am full of grief and sorrow over her departure." He then lamented grievously, saying that it was more pleasant for the little crane than for himself, in that [?] she had permission to return to Ireland. The crane then parted from Colum Cille, and he left her with his blessing. Then she rose in the presence of all and turned her face toward Ireland, and they watched her fly away until she was out of their sight.[82]

This dialogue between human and bird is but a continuation of an earlier dialogue that took place at a wrenching point in Columba's life, when he was setting out on his exile from Ireland:

Then they [that is, Colum Cille and his party] took the boat across Loch Febail to the place where the loch flows into the ocean, to a place now called the White-Headed Waves [Tonda Cenanda]. It was not just the people of his country that were afflicted with grief over the departure of Colum Cille but also birds and brute beasts, as the following attests. The seagulls and other birds of Loch Febail accompanied the boat on both sides, screaming and screeching on

82. Tuc an manuch an corr les iar sin mar a raibe C.C., 7 ar techt do láthair di, do fhill a glún 7 do crom a cend a comartha umhla dó, 7 do rinde luthghair imarcach 'n-a fiadnaise, 7 do caith si biad as a laimh fen fo cedoir, 7 nir delaigh si ris o sin amach an fad do bí sí sa mbaile; 7 do bidh sí faris inha shella, 7 do teigheadh si leis do eclais 7 in gach inadh eli a tégedh se fen. Acus a cend an tress lai iar sin, tainicc an corr a fiadnuisi C.C., 7 do bí sí ag screduigh 7 ac screchaigh 7 ag bualad a sciathán fa ceile; 7 do fiarfuidheatar na manaigh de cred fa nderna sí sin. Frecrais C.C. iad 7 assedh adubairt: "Ag gabail cheda agam-sa ata sí," ar sé, "7 rachaid sí ar a haiss dá duthaigh fen anoss, 7 ata sí lán do tuirse 7 do dobrón tre na olcus le beith ag delughadh rim-sa di, 7 mar ata adhail aice nach faicfe sí misi go brath arís. Et is cumáin disi sin," ar C.C., "oir ata tuirse 7 dobrón mor orum-sa ina diaidh-se." Acus do cai sé go ger iar sin 7 assedh adubairt sé, corb aibhne don cuirr bicc sin ina dó fen trian a ced do beith aice dul ar a hais co hErinn arís. Ceiliubruis an corr iar sin do C.C. 7 do lécc sen a bendacht le; 7 do eirich sí as fiadnaise caich uile an uair sin, 7 tuc a haghaidh docum na hErenn; 7 do batar san gá feithemh co ndechaidh sí as a n-amharc (O'Kelleher and Schoepperle 1918, 270).

account of the tragedy of Colum Cille's leaving Ireland. He understood their utterance as an expression of that sorrow, just as he would have understood such utterance from humans. So great was Colum Cille's nobility and his love for his native land that he was no more perturbed by the prospect of parting from his countrymen than he was by the prospect of parting from the seagulls and the flocks of the other kinds of birds of Loch Febail. And so he composed the following quatrain:

> The seagulls of Loch Febail
> before me and behind me;
> they are not coming with me in my coracle,
> alas, sad is our parting.

And it is a demonstration of the truth of this story that a crane left Ireland and went to visit Colum Cille on Iona in Scotland, as Saint Adomnán recounts it.[83]

The dialogic framework of the relationship between Columba and the *corr* indicates both their separateness and their affinity. In Ó Domhnaill's Life, the crane is a bird for Columba to converse with and listen to, but in what it says and feels, it mirrors Columba's own plight and emotional turmoil. So too the poets at Druim Cet compose an "image" of Columba that is nearly convincing, and Áed's queen hurls insults at the saint which are not altogether without foundation. Herons/cranes represent a part of Columba from which he must distance himself and yet which he treasures and loves and to which he is in a unique position to lend an ear. And in the figure of the *corr* the heartfelt issues of poetry, native tradition, and Ireland itself come together most dramatically, elements of Columba's hagiographic persona and ambiguous, even hostile, realities over which he attempts to exert authority from a carefully chosen distance.

Here then we have pinpointed the connections within Columban legendry which make meaningful Columba's puzzling act of turning his hateful accusers into creatures belonging to his favorite species. The *corr* is akin to the poets performing *aidbse* and to the spiteful queen in that all three reflect key

---

83. Is andsin do chuiretar an long ar siubal ar fedh Locha Febuil cusan inadh a teid an loch isan bfhairge moír re n-abortar na Tonda Cenanda aniugh; ⁊ ni hedh amhain do bi cumha no tuirsi ar daínibh a tire fen a ndiaidh C.C. acht do bi cumha ar énuch ⁊ ar ainmindte eccíallaidhe 'na diaidh. Acus do derbad an sceoil sin, do batar failenda ⁊ énach Locha Febuil dá gach taeb da luing ag imthecht dó ⁊ iad ag screjaigh ⁊ ag screchadh ar a olcuss leo C.C. d'fhagail Erind. Agus do tuigedh se-siun a n-urlabhra ag denam na tuirsi sin, amail do tuicfedh se ó dainibh hí; ⁊ do bi an oiret sin do daendaigecht ⁊ do gradh ag C.C. ar a tír ⁊ ar a athardha duthchusa fen nach mor gur mo an tuirse do bi air ag delugadh rena dainib ina in tuirse do bí air ag delugad re failendaib ⁊ re hénlaithib locha [Febuil]. Gonadh andsin dorinde se an rand-sa: Failenda Locha Febhail, / romham acus am deghaid, / ni tegaid leam am curuch, / uch is dubach ar ndegail. Et do derbadh an sceoil sin, do cuaídh corr ar cuairt docum C.C. ó Erinn a nAlpain go hI, amail mebhruighes Adhamhnan naem air (ibid., 194–96).

aspects of the saint himself, and yet they also constitute dangerously independent entities upon which Columba imposes limits and boundaries, although with mixed success. The herons of Druim Cet will live forever, poets continue to ply their craft, sometimes even resorting to satire, and the pilgrim crane is, after all, not a pet but a wild creature that must return to its unfettered life, as both saint and bird recognize.

Important for us to note in the matter of herons and cranes is the similarity between the accompanying or visiting *corr* that crosses water noisily either with Columba or toward him and the various transmarine poets, speakers, or noisemakers we have seen in this chapter. The voyages of all of these performers constitute statements about the power of speech and Columba's ability to control or check that power. That *corr* and poet are no strangers to each other is further demonstrated by one of the most conspicuous appearances of the heron in early medieval Irish literature outside Columban hagiography. There is an account of the legendary poet Aithirne according to which he owned three herons from the otherworld, who functioned as a vivid symbol of the poet's notorious stinginess. Each would loudly and rudely discourage potential guests from visiting the house of the birds' master.[84] Clearly, the birds express the dark side of Aithirne's craft, his antisocial attitude and unwillingness to accept social control. It was this dark side that brought about the dangerous alienation of poet from client and the social and cultural crisis leading to the meeting of Druim Cet. Columba's herons, on the other hand, reflect the brighter side of the profession, the mediation between past and present, human and nonhuman, and "noise" and speech, mediation that is also the business of Columba himself.

Perhaps the most striking remark made by the wandering crane to Columba, according to Ó Domhnaill's report, is that she is saddened by the prospect of not seeing the saint again in their lifetimes. Is the human or the crane fated to live longer? More likely the bird, given the Irish folk belief in the preternaturally long life-spans of herons.[85] The herons of Druim Cet, we recall, are condemned to make their plaintive noises at that site until doomsday. It would appear that herons—some flying to Columba from his past and others sent flying off into the future—are travelers through time as well as space.

This transcendent dimension of the birds' journey makes Columba's dialogues with them all the more significant. As creatures freed of the restrictions of time, they are potential preservers of past lore, or preservers of present lore into the future, as they are in the legend of the herons of Druim Cet. And while we do not find traditional stories explicitly passed on in any of the Columban *corr* legends, the bird performs precisely this function in an epi-

84. Thurneysen 1918, 398–99.
85. Folkloric examples of long-lived herons/cranes are given in Ross 1967, 286.

sode of the early modern Irish recension of the *Acallam na Senórach* (Dialogue of the ancients), which primarily features a lengthy exchange between Patrick and ancient survivors from the heroic past.[86] The time traveler Oisín—the hero who is brimming with lore himself—encounters a lone heron, whom he asks to tell her story. The bird identifies herself, claiming to be more than two centuries old, and proceeds to tell the tragic tale of how she was changed into a heron as a result of her animosity toward a sexual rival. The bird, in exchange for the tale she has told, requests a story from Oisín, and he happily obliges her. Thus the encounter between the heron and the old hero turns into a genuine dialogue that enriches the narrative tradition.

Still, the herons/cranes that Columba encounters in hagiography are not *so* old, even if they do bring back memories of Columba's years in Ireland. And the herons that Columba fashions out of the queen and her maid are designed to bear his authority into the future. The temporal "shallowness" of Columba's birds is in fact consistent with the agenda of many Columban legends, particularly those clustered around the meeting of Druim Cet. Patrick, both in the earliest strands of the hagiographic tradition and in later secular variations, is shown raising the dead in order to establish communication between the past and the Christian present. Columba, who represents a later development of Christian culture in Ireland, already has a Christian past from which he is not alienated, and he is involved in renovating Christianized native culture, especially the poetic institution, so it can endure in a future that is to be all the more Christian and all the more literate. Hence the figures summoned or restored to their previous status by Columba, including the poets rescued from exile, are hardly pristine pagans restored to life, nor is there any pressing need to send them back to the grave or away to their respective eternal rewards in heaven or hell. Rather, they live on in this world, in some cases even outliving Columba, after they have been rehabilitated according to the sensibilities of Columba's scribal culture.

Columba and the Kings

In Columba's day as depicted in hagiography, the saintly struggle is no longer to appropriate native signs for Christian meanings, as it was for the trailblazing Patrick. Native and Christian signs and meanings can now reflect each other and intermingle, as in the text of the *Amra*, provided they are framed within the forms that saintly scribes can copy, comment on, and control. Yet that frame is not always assured; as in the episode of the glass book, it can turn against the saintly scribe himself, threatening to rob him of his authoritative voice, his most important instrument of social and cultural change.

86. Ní Shéaghdha 1942–45, 3:84–110.

We should not overlook what tradition tells us was the third reason why Columba came to Druim Cet, if only because it is probably closest to the circumstances of the actual meeting, in which the historical Columba may well have taken part.[87] The saint, supposedly, was called upon to mediate between the conflicting claims of the men of Ireland, as represented by Áed mac Ainmirech, and the men of Scotland, as represented by Áedán mac Gabráin, to the northeastern Irish kingdom of Dál Riata, from which the kingdom of Dál Riata in Scotland had derived. In fact, according to the majority of sources, it is not Columba himself who devised an acceptable arrangement whereby the resources of the Irish kingdom were fairly divided. Rather, he is said to have delegated the arbitrating to his protégé Colmán mac Coimgelláin, himself of the Irish branch of the Dál Riata.[88]

By the terms of the agreement, the Dál Riata are to belong fully neither to Scotland nor to Ireland. It is as if the solution to the problem were to make the Dál Riata, the forebears of the kingdom of Scotland, resemble Columba, who is similarly "torn" and balanced precariously between the two lands separated by ocean.

The division of his loyalties is rarely realized more dramatically than in his coming to the meeting of Druim Cet and thereby jeopardizing his oath never to "see" or "touch" Ireland again:

> Wondrous to say that Colum Cille actually did return to Ireland, even though he had pledged that he would leave Ireland, never to trample on her soil again, never again to see her men or women, and never to partake of her food and drink again.
>
> He fulfilled his pledge completely, for there was a sod of Scottish earth under his feet throughout the time that he was in Ireland. Moreover, there was a piece of cerecloth over his eyes, and a cap pulled down on it besides, as well as the hood of his cloak over all that. Thus he saw neither Irishman nor Irishwoman, just as he had vowed before. . . . He brought a full supply of food and drink from Scotland so that he would not have to consume any Irish food or drink while he was there.[89]

---

87. The historical "reality" behind the tradition of the convention involving the Dál Riata (both their Irish and Scottish branches) and the Uí Néill, is explored in Bannerman 1974, 157–70.

88. Stokes 1899–1900, 132; O'Kelleher and Schoepperle 1918, 196–98, 366.

89. Is ingnadh a radha co ndechaidh C.C. a n-Erind aris ⁊ gur gell se ac fagbail Erend dó, nach sailteoradh se uír Erend coidhce, ⁊ nach faicfedh se a fir nó a mna coidhce, ⁊ nach caithfedh se a biadh nó a deoch go brath.

Do comaill C.C. co himlan sin; oir do bi fod d'uír na hAlpan fan cossaib an fad do bi se a n-Erind, ⁊ do bi bréid cíartha tar a suilib, ⁊ do bi birrét ar a muin sin anúas, ⁊ do bi atan a cochaill tarrsa sin amuigh. Is amlaid sin nach b-faca se fir nó mna Erend mar do ghell se remhe sin. . . . Et ruc lon bidh ⁊ dighe a hAlbain less ar cor nach caithead se biadh no deoch na hEirend an fad do beith se indte (O'Kelleher and Schoepperle 1918, 342, 344).

Standing on his own piece of earth throughout and refusing sustenance that would obligate him to those who provide it, Columba as presented in this passage from Ó Domhnaill's Life serves as a human model for the political independence, or interdependence, he indirectly arranges for the Dál Riata.

The poetic agenda of the meeting resurfaces in the detail of Columba's blindness during his stay in Ireland. Columba blindfolded resembles his poetic counterpart, the poet Dallán, whose name means "Blind One." And if the *Forgaill* element in the poet's name is indeed from *Forgell/Forgall* 'testimony, authority',[90] then the similarity between the two figures is all the greater. Certainly both poet and saint are deeply involved in the business of guaranteeing and testifying. Columba strives to preserve his protégés and maintain agreements reached under his aegis, and Dallán assures both the continued livelihood of poets and the everlasting fame of their patron Columba.

Still another aspect of the physical isolation and self-enclosure of the temporarily returned exile Columba suggests an affinity between the seemingly separate problems of protecting the Dál Riata and the poets. Columba's mode of conducting and presenting himself is a way for him to keep his word and also to maintain at least the appearance of standing apart or even hiding from the contentious parties, the men of Scotland and the men of Ireland, along the lines of the impartiality that the Dál Riata aspire to win for themselves. Perhaps Columba is similarly concealed in the company of the poets. After he falls under the spell of their performance and is chided by Baithéne, we are told in the words of a commentary on the *Amra*, that Columba "tuc . . . a chend fo choim," and then after he repented, "co tuargaib iar sein a chend asa choim," as a result of which the demon-dispelling cloud burst from his head.[91] While these phrases could be translated as "he lowered his head" and "he raised his head," the argument can be made for translating them literally, as "he put his head in his cloak" and "he raised his head out of his cloak,"[92] in light of the attested image of a veiled Columba at Druim Cet, as well as the importance of Columba's cloak as a device for mystical revelation in Ó Domhnaill's version of the story of Mongán's meeting with the saint.[93]

The implication of this incident, then, would be that in listening to the poets perform, Columba is letting down his guard as a mediator and giving in not only to his love of praise or poetry but also to his love of Ireland. Columba's heart, however, may belong no more to Ireland than to Scotland, just as the musical performance of *aidbse* is tempered although not replaced by Basil's writings, and just as neither the men of Ireland nor the men of Scotland are entitled to all of what the Dál Riata have to offer. The conflict at Druim Cet is not only between media or between nations but also between

90. P. Ford 1987, 48.
91. Best and Bergin 1929, lines 337, 338–39; see also Stokes 1899–1900, 42.
92. I thank Patrick Ford for pointing out this ambiguity to me. See *DIL*, s.v. 1 *coim*.
93. O'Kelleher and Schoepperle 1918, 80–82.

two kings, Áedán mac Gabráin of Scotland and Áed mac Ainmirech of Ireland, each of whom has a special relationship with Columba, the mediator in their struggle. Recall that the saint's association with and protection of Áedán were not of his choosing but were obligations imposed by the angel and his glass book. The relationship, however, as it is depicted in hagiography, develops without any significant disruption after its rocky start. Columba's relationship with Áed, on the other hand, is even more of a given. They are kinsmen, both members of the powerful royal lineage of Cenél Conaill. It is this unforced and unprescribed relationship that actually holds more tension. Columba must rescue Scandlán from Áed, whose wife satirizes the saint.

Áedán, whom in Adomnán's Life Columba consecrated king (an innovation in the concept of kingship and the church's role in society), certainly appears a liberal and modern monarch compared to the reactionary Áed, who generally appears in the Druim Cet legend as ungenerous and resistant to the changes Columba suggests. And while Columba takes cognizance of Áedán after he reads about him in a supernaturally written glass book, Áed starts paying attention to Columba only after they speak face to face. The king of Ireland, like his wife, is finally thwarted by authoritative voices, the saint's and even his own.

The schema underlying the legends of Druim Cet is, however, not as simple as "Áedán is to Áed as clerics are to poets," for Áed wants to be rid of the poets as much as the other men of Ireland do. In the web of relationships underlying these tales, the poets are the "odd men out," not unlike Columba, who is careful not to choose sides. And it is because they are anomalous that the poets succeed in making the transition from the past into the future, under Columba's supervision. By the end of Columba's visit, by contrast, Áed's authority is in considerable doubt.

Getting Bells

Another contrasted pair of characters who figure in the lore of Druim Cet and whose lives as they are affected by the saint evoke the same issues relating to poetry which pervade so much of this body of narrative, are the half brothers, sons of Áed, Conall and Domnall. An interpolation in the Middle Irish Life gives a story of their encounters with Columba:

> Now Áed mac Ainmirech was told of Colum Cille's coming to the meeting, and he became very angry with him when he heard, saying that he would take vengeance on anyone from whom Colum Cille received respect or honor in the assembly. Then they saw Colum Cille approach the gathering, and the company of theirs which was nearest to him was that of Conall mac Áeda, the latter a son worthy of this king, Áed. When Conall saw them, he incited the rabble of the

assembly upon them, so that thrice nine of them were taken and injured. Colum
Cille asked: "By whom were that band set upon us?" He was told that it was by
Conall. Colum Cille cursed Conall, and thrice nine bells were rung against him,
so that someone said "Conall is getting bells," and because of this he is given
the name Conall Cloccach. And the cleric took from him kingship and sovereignty, and banished his sense and intellect save only for the length of time he
was defecating.

After that, Colum Cille went to the company of Domnall mac Áeda. Domnall
immediately rose before him and welcomed him, kissed him on the cheek, and
seated him in his own place. And Colum Cille granted him many blessings: fifty
years in the kingship of Ireland, battle victory during that time, and every
utterance of his to be fulfilled. A year and a half would be the duration of his
final illness, and he would receive the body of Christ every Sunday during that
time. . . . [Here follows the story of the queen, who, angered at the taking of
kingship from her son Conall, insults Columba and is turned into a heron.]

Colum Cille said to Domnall that they should go together to speak with Áed
[about the poets and about Scandlán's release], and fear of conversing with the
king overcame Domnall, so that Colum Cille said: "Do not be afraid, for the
Holy Spirit will protect you from him." They went together then to parley with
the king [*do agallam an rig*].[94]

The figures of Conall and Domnall, as depicted here, constitute hagiographic types, strikingly analogous to similar figures of Patrician legend. Conall, who leads a collective attack on Patrick only to be recognized and publicly
named as a miscreant, resembles the wayward ruler Coirtic in Muirchú's
Life, who scorns Patrick's authority and is subsequently rejected by his
people, stripped of his kingship and even his humanity, and turned into a
creature of the wild.[95] Domnall, who pays respect to Patrick in the public

94. Trans. Herbert 1988a, 266–67. At-cuas immorro d'Aod mac Ainmirech Colum Cille do
toigecht docum na dala ⁊ ro fergaided co mor fris e o't-cuala ⁊ do raid cebe occa fuigbed cádus
na anoir isin airec[h]tus conaithfead fair. At-conncatar iar sin Colum Cille docum na dala ⁊ ba
he airec[h]t ba nesa do dib .i. airecht Conaill meic Aodha, mac dingmala don rígh eiside: .i.
d'Aod. Amal at-connairc Conall iad ro greis daoscar-shluag in arec[h]ta futhaib co rus-gabtha
⁊ co rusbristea tri naonmair dib. Ro fhiarfaig Colum Cille: "Cuich o'r laiti cucaind in lucht so?"
Ád-cuas dó conad o Conall. ⁊ do escain Colum Cille Conall ⁊ ro benta tri noi ceolain fair conad
as-pert araili duine: "Fo-geib Conall cloga." Conad do sin ata Conall Clogach ⁊ ro ben an
clerech righe ⁊ airechus aire ⁊ a ceill ⁊ a inntlecht acht frisin re no beit ag imtealcad a cuirp.

Do cuaid Colum Cille iar sin co hairecht Domnaill meic Aoda. Atracht Domnall fo cétoir
riam ⁊ do fer failti fris ⁊ do rad poig dia gruaigh ⁊ do rad e 'na hinad fein ⁊ ro fhagaib Colum
Cille briathar imda do .i. caoga bliadan a righe nErenn do ⁊ cathbuaid do frisin re sin ⁊ gach
briathar at-berid do comullad ⁊ bliadan co leith do isin galar a n-eibelad ⁊ corp Crist do
caithem do gacha domnaig frisin re sin. . . .

Atbert Colum fri Domnall dol doib immaille do agallam Aoda ⁊ do gab imecla Domnall am
agallaim in righ ⁊ ad-bert Colum Cille: "Ni ba himecal duit, ar biaid in Spirat Naom ocat
imdeghail aire." Do-cuadar immalle .v. do agallam an rig (ibid., 244–46).

95. See pp. 104–9.

assembly despite the king his father's injunction against such behavior, parallels Dubthach, the poet in Lóegaire's court who recognizes Patrick's authority despite the king's orders and is rewarded by the saint accordingly.[96]

Given the charged context of the twin stories of the half brothers—the meeting where the fate of poetry in Ireland was decided—it is doubtless no accident that in the stories featuring figures analogous to Conall and Domnall, the power and perspicacity of poetry and its practitioners are on display. Corictic is driven out of the human realm by a poet who performs in his court, and Dubthach is very pointedly designated a poet. Furthermore, the attack on Columba and his retinue launched by the excessively loyal son Conall and his retinue is a dark variation on the well-intentioned but even more deadly "attack" on Columba by the poetic company. In both cases, the saint needs to be enlightened by his companions about the nature of the attack or the identity of the attackers. And Columba's counterattack relies on the strength of a clerical sign or medium, a bell or book, which when "activated," bell rung or book read, brings about the displacement of the guilty party, Conall or the demons.

The remaking of Conall, which caps the reform of the rules of poetic behavior and repertoire brought about by Columba, drives home the same theme about the dangers of challenging the power of saints over communication that underlies the story of Corictic. This is the king, we recall, who disregards Patrick's letter and is subsequently banished into the wilderness as a fox through the combined power of saintly anger and poetic performance. An even more dramatic example of the consequences of attempting to "drown out" a saint's message is the legend of Suibne, purportedly a king of the Dál nAraidi of eastern Ulster in the seventh century. An extensive body of poetry in Middle Irish is attributed to this figure, whose tale is told in a twelfth- or thirteenth-century prose composition framing most of these poems.[97]

Suibne's saintly nemesis is the cleric Rónán, whose attempts to build a church in Suibne's kingdom are met with fierce resistance. In his haste to stop Rónán, the enraged Suibne goes forth naked and throws the saint's psalter in the water, whence it is later rescued by a friendly otter. Suibne also thwarts Rónán's attempts to negotiate a truce among the forces drawn up to fight the Battle of Mag Rath, and in an attack on Rónán's retinue he grazes the saint's bell with his spear. In punishment for all these acts of violence, Suibne is cursed by the saint. The malediction renders him senseless and at one with the creatures of the wild. Curiously, a side effect of the curse is the poetic inspira-

96. See p. 89.
97. *Buile Shuibhne* (Madness [or Vision] of Suibne), edited and translated by J. G. O'Keeffe (1910 [ed. and trans.], 1931 [ed.]). That the legends concerning Conall and Suibne share crucial features (including the element of the saint's curse leading to madness) has been noted by Pádraig Ó Riain (1972, 182–85).

tion of Suibne, for during his life as a madman living in nature, he reputedly composes the poems for which he is famous in tradition. His talent is coupled with exceptional wisdom, of value to both layman and cleric. He is in fact "adopted" by another saint, Moling, after he demonstrates his knowledge of canonical hours. The arrangement to which they agree allows for an extended dialogue between them, with minimal disruption of their respective modi vivendi. Suibne is to continue to wander the wilds, provided he comes back to Moling's church every evening and dictates what he has experienced and what he has composed. This fruitful interaction comes to a tragic end, however, when Moling's swineherd slays Suibne after his wife falsely accuses the madman of having molested her. In the verse he composes near death, Suibne seems almost to regret even the modest rapprochement with human society and sanity through which he had been bound to Moling, and, ultimately, to his death.

Suibne's story brings out the positive features of the divine punishment inflicted on miscreants such as himself, Corictic, Conall, and Áed's queen. Those who mock the symbols of saintly power and pointedly disregard or denigrate the media through which saintly authority is communicated, are, on the one hand, rendered *productive* signs of the saints, values, and media that they have attempted to oppose. As such, they become authoritative themselves. On the other hand, the success of their recasting as signs of the new culture rests on their being cast as signs of the native culture and its media as well. They are recycled signs, which give out dual messages. Thus, the herons of Druim Cet remind their auditors of the power of Columba in perpetuum, but they "work" as Columban signs because, according to tradition, herons have supernaturally long life-spans. The *corr* is reframed or recycled to suit Christian literary purposes, without its traditional import being erased, just as in the *Amra* traditional poetic diction and technique are put at the service of clerical culture and textualized.

The mad or bestialized king (Corictic, Conall, or Suibne) is a graphic sign of saintly control over the forces that threaten the saint, but the sign in its madness or bestiality perpetuates the behavior and attitude that threatened the saint in the first place. And at least in the cases of Corictic and Suibne, the offense consists of denying the written word its authority. The punishment brings about a realignment between written, which has been undervalued, and spoken, which has implicitly been overvalued. Corictic, who ignores the letter written by Patrick, is finally driven over the brink by an oral performance, and Suibne, who tries to destroy a psalter, acquires an amanuensis. The madness or wildness with which the sign is invested, however, precludes a pat balance between written and spoken. Corictic, who is never to be seen again, is an errant sign, beyond our reach, whereas Suibne, who is seen again, arouses antisocial feelings and suspicions that lead to his death.

As for Conall, who "gets bells," he is henceforth circumscribed with these symbols of clerical authority, as his nickname indicates, and his madness, like Suibne's, is made marginally acceptable to society in that his reason returns periodically, when he is relieving himself. In the medieval Irish monastic milieu as well as in many other cultures, this bodily function was considered particularly dangerous to the physical and spiritual well-being of the person performing it.[98]

Conall is not cast completely outside the pale, just as he is not exposed to the utter risk of witless defecation. Furthermore, the body imagery here probably also applies to society, which Columba is putatively protecting from the likes of Conall, and which, in the madman's brief returns to sanity, is afforded some contact and common ground with this not-altogether-errant sign.

In other sources we learn that Conall became the royal fool (*rígóinmit*) in Domnall's court. The "good" son of Áed, therefore, becomes the keeper of the "bad" son, and Columba's protégé plays patron/audience to the performer that Columba's opponent becomes. Conall's adeptness in verse making and his preternatural wisdom are on display in his only appearance in a medieval saga concerning his half brother Domnall, the *Cath Maighe Rath* (Battle of Mag Rath). Congal Cáech, an Ulster king fighting an unjust war against Domnall, who by now is the high king of Ireland, encounters Conall on the battlefield and asks for a quatrain revealing who the victor will be. The fool obliges with verse that foretells Congal's death, although Congal corrects certain details of the prediction.[99]

Thus, in punishing Conall for his impiety, Columba simultaneously improves on his voice, making it into that of a prophet and poet. Similarly, in the case of Domnall, Columba's blessing refines his protégé's voice, making it into an instrument whose utterances are always true and giving its possessor the confidence to speak to his father about Scandlán and the poets. In none of

98. "Privies and urinals, they are dwellings for demons" (fialtige 7 fual-tige, it adbai do demnaib indsin), says one Middle Irish monastic rule, which goes on to detail what the cautious monk may or may not do while availing himself of such facilities (E. Gwynn 1927, 74).

99. Marstrander 1911b, 240. At least one of the motifs featured in the legend of Druim Cet lives on in the further adventures of Conall Cloccach as portrayed in this Early Modern Irish text. The fool is said to be the sole survivor of the force sent by the king of Scotland to the battle. In the fashion of Scandlán, Conall can only ask for a drink when the king asks him for news. Only after three drinks can he speak, proclaiming that the king will see no one else returning from the battlefield. Having delivered his news, Conall dies (ibid., 242–43).

Conall Cloccach is featured prominently in the (as yet unedited) Early Modern Irish text *Imtheachta na n Óinmhideadh* (The fools' adventures), alongside another holy fool, Mac Dá Cherda (see Ó Coileáin 1973, 91–95; and Harrison 1989, 30–31, 72–73).

The Annals of Ulster mention another son of Áed named Conall, Conall Cú 'Dog', who escaped from the Battle of Slemain in 602 (Mac Airt and Mac Niocaill 1983, 100). Ó Cuív suggests that this "canine" survivor (said to have been suckled by a dog) is a multiform of his brother Conall Cloccach (1964–66, 183–87).

our sources, however, does Domnall actually contribute to this or any other dialogue. Whether cursing or blessing, the Columba of the legends of Druim Cet is putting his stamp on all he meets, the sons of the king, Áed's queen, the poets of Ireland, Scandlán. And the performances as well as the writings that emerge from this epochal confrontation carry forth and celebrate what has been ratified, echoing with the voice of Columba himself.

Continuities in Columban Legend

This Columba of the *Amra* tradition and later medieval hagiography is clearly descended from the Columba of Adomnán's Life, who can be heard near and far, and whose sanctity has inspired songs that live on and preserve the lives of their singers. And the Columba of the poets who is nearly seduced by their music but is brought back to reason by a stint of reading is recognizable in the Columba who is battered by glass book and angelic whip into accepting the divine choice for the kingship. In the images of Columba, both earlier and later, we see a man of letters who has a past to look back on, listen to, and draw on, even if he is in exile from it. This is a past that, precisely because it is distant, is willing to engage in dialogue, unlike, say, the self-destructive Miliucc of Patrician lore. It is also a past that is still very much a part of Columba himself.

The Columban past is ineluctably associated with Ireland, the love–hate object of Columba's perpetual homesickness; with native culture, which he both preserves and cajoles into a "better" representation of itself; and with oral tradition, which uneasily coexists, barely circumscribed and perpetually productive, with the literary tradition Columba perpetuates. Unlike the Patrick of hagiography, Columba is so in touch with his past that he himself can absorb it, both in the seventh-century Life, which includes stories of events that reflect posthumously on Columba, and in the later lore of Druim Cet, such as the account of the convention interpolated into the Middle Irish Life, in which Columba emerges as a quasi-ancient with whom conversation is sought by a younger generation: "When Colum Cille had been thirty years in Scotland, longing seized the men of Ireland to see and speak with him before his death. They sent a message to him asking if he would go to speak to them at the Convention of Druim Cet."[100] This stance of Columba's is made possible by a relative shallowness in the concept of the past operating within these various narrative traditions concerning the saint. After all, "native" or "old" here is no longer necessarily "pagan." Furthermore, as we have already

100. Trans. Herbert 1988a, 265. O ra boi Colum Cille tricha bliadan a nAlbain ro gab inmalle firu Erenn ima fhaicsin ⁊ ima imacalluim a nAlbain ro gab inmalle firu Erenn ima fhaicsin ⁊ ima imacalluim ria ndul ar ceal. Do-cóass uaidib ara cend dia ndeochad dia n-acallam go mordail Droma Cet (ibid., 244).

seen, the agenda of the meeting of Druim Cet is, despite what is said in the quoted passage, not so much the linking of archaic and current as the devising or retooling of media and mediators for the purpose of relaying the proceedings to future generations, hungry for poetry as well as eternal salvation.

The stories of Druim Cet and the hagiographic figure of Columba provide powerful alternative models for understanding and communicating in literary terms the relationship among the past, present, and future of tradition. These models provide a balance to the less catholic, more possessive ones that inhabit Patrician legendry, where displacement and metonymy are touted as instruments for ensuring the present's control over the past, instead of ensuring the survival and growth of the viable elements of the past into the future.[101] We shall see that both sets of models and perspectives, the more agonistic Patrician and the more accommodating Columban, extend in their literary applications well beyond the realm of hagiography.

101. Given the different values and effects attached to the strategy of displacement in the two hagiographic traditions, it is fitting that, according to a tradition already recorded in the Book of Armagh, Columba was the person who found Patrick's missing, or displaced, corpse (55.2, Bieler 1979, 164; compare the bizarre tale told in Ó Domhnaill's Life of how the saint's corpse came to rest beside those of Patrick and Brigit [O'Kelleher and Schoepperle 1918, 420, 422]). Within the Patrician legend the guest-starring Columba thereby effects a satisfying closure and finds the missing piece of the saintly puzzle. Within the Book of Armagh, on the other hand, the statement of Columba's intervention and discovery contradicts an immediately preceding note that compares Patrick with the similarly missing Moses.

4/ necessary sacrifices: saints and their doubles

The Prologue to the *Senchas Már*

So far, I have been seeking medieval Irish formulations of the relationship between the written and the spoken primarily in hagiographic texts. The literary interest in this relationship, however, as well as the tendency to formulate it in terms of saints and their saintly accomplishments, extends well beyond the realm of religious legends. As we will see in this and the following chapter, even literary genres that may seem far removed in subject matter and procedure from the saint's life are just as focused on the question of origins and authority, and they engage in and expand upon the same ongoing cultural dialogue about the relative authority of written and oral modes of communication.

The most puzzling and least explored body of literature left to posterity by the Irish literary tradition is the law tracts, constituting an enormous corpus that ranges from poetic texts in archaic Irish to late medieval commentary.[1] Key questions concerning the provenance and use of the law tracts remain unanswered. The accepted scholarly wisdom until recently was that at the heart of this corpus lies a transcription of legal lore that had been passed on orally in metrical form by the Irish jurists (*brithemain*) until, coming in contact with Christian written culture, these professionals, closely related to the *filid*, committed their tradition to writing to memorialize and reauthorize it by means of the new medium. Now, however, students of Irish law tend to emphasize the modeling of many legal texts and principles on Christian, particularly biblical, materials, and to note that monastic men of letters, not just the hypothetical pre-Christian, illiterate *brithemain*, were perfectly capa-

---

1. A helpful introduction and guide to medieval Irish law and law tracts is F. Kelly 1988.

ble of composing legal or other kinds of poetry in the putatively oral, "archaic" style, referred to in manuscripts as *roscada*.[2] While the outcome of current scholarly deliberations and contentions concerning these texts remains uncertain, it is clear that there are to be no simple answers to the question of origins in the field of Irish law.

Insufficiently, if at all, appreciated by Irish legal scholars, however, is the fact that the bearers of the literary tradition of the law tracts were themselves vitally interested in this issue and have left fascinating clues about their own tentative answers to questions of origin. Their perspective was, of course, hardly disinterested, since the authority of the texts they produced, copied, and used, was grounded, in the fashion of ancient and medieval cultures, in what could or did become the commonly accepted conceptualization of how they came into being. As we shall see, the writers of at least some law tracts shared much with the hagiographers, for most likely they all belonged to the same literary and monastic culture. Moreover, legal texts, as much as saints' lives, reflect a lively concern with the relationship between the text and that which it attempts to represent and with the closely connected and equally problematic relationship between the present and the past.

A prime example of this self-consciousness of the legal literary tradition is the *Senchas Már* (The great [compendium of] lore). Underlying this monumental compilation of legal texts is a story according to which the laws contained therein were originally written down at the dawn of Christianity in Ireland.[3] Indeed, according to this story, the legal record happened to be written down as an outcome of the epochal confrontation between Patrick and Lóegaire at Tara, which, as we have seen, forms a key episode in the Patrician biography. Told in the so-called Pseudohistorical Prologue to the *Senchas Már*, this literary myth of origins has been dated to as early as the early eighth century.[4]

2. See, for example, McCone 1990, 41–46, 84–106.
3. *CIH* 339.1–342.39, 874.35–876.27, 1650.1–1657.9; cf. 527.14–529.5 (from an eighth-century text known as *Córus Béscnai* [Arrangement of law]; on the dating of this text, which is included in the *Senchas Már*, and its relationship to the Prologue, see Binchy 1975–76, 23–24; and McCone 1986a, 21–25). The nature and organization of the *Senchas Már* compilation, which represents in effect a legal "school," are examined in F. Kelly 1988, 242–46. An exploration of the relationship among the extant versions of the Prologue, along with an edition of these materials, is to be found in Carey 1994. Related material is also to be found in the later nonlegal text *Comthóth Loegaire* (Conversion of Lóegaire), preserved as an interpolation (of the twelfth or thirteenth century) in the Lebor na hUidre manuscript (Best and Bergin 1929, lines 9732–820; the text has been edited and translated by Plummer [1883–85] and Stokes [1887, 2:562–67]). Important contributions to our understanding of this story concerning the Patrician canonization of legal lore are to be found in Binchy 1975–76; Carey 1990; and McLeod 1982; but most of all in McCone 1986a. The following translations of excerpts from the (Prologue to) the *Senchas Már* are based on McCone's, to be found in 1986a. See now also Carey 1994.
4. McCone 1986a, 23–26.

Upon the arrival of Patrick and Christianity, the men of Ireland meet with their king, Lóegaire. Asked what would be the most troublesome result of accepting the new faith, they point out the difficulty of reconciling their custom of meting out death to murderers with the Christian doctrine of mercy. Were Patrick's religion to prevail, there would be "no control over reavers" anymore ("ni bia comus for fogluib"),[5] and the social fabric would come apart. As if to determine whether Patrick himself is aware of the ramifications of his doctrine, the men of Ireland and their king set up a test case. Lóegaire offers a free choice of reward to anyone who is willing to slay a member of Patrick's retinue, so that Patrick's reaction to this act of outright murder might be gauged. The offer is accepted by one Núadu Derg, said to be a brother, as well as a hostage, of Lóegaire's. (In fact, there is no other extant reference to a brother of Lóegaire or a son of Niall—Lóegaire's legendary father—known as Núadu, nor is there any discernible reason why a king would be holding his own brother as a hostage, when the point of keeping hostages was to give a king leverage over families or kingdoms other than his own.)

The price this shadowy Núadu exacts for committing the heinous deed is his freedom and appointment as the leader of Lóegaire's cavalry. Assured of receiving what he has requested, the hired assassin casts his spear at Patrick's retinue and thus slays Patrick's charioteer, Odrán, at random. Or, says the Prologue, Núadu was actually aiming at Patrick or the charioteer, who was trying to fix the chariot while Patrick was waiting inside it.[6] According to one version of the Prologue, the saint, incensed at the insult, assumes a stance in which the arms are outstretched so as to form a cross, a *crosfigill*.[7] In response to the powerful sign, all hell breaks loose at Tara, very much along the lines described by Muirchú in his account of the Easter encounter between Patrick and Lóegaire.[8] The text remarks parenthetically at this point that an earthquake generated by this outburst of fury tilted the site of Tara in a sign that has been passed on to posterity.

Patrick finally relents and restrains the cosmic forces he has unleashed after the men of Ireland offer him his choice of judge in the matter of reparation. The saint has no trouble picking an arbiter. Without hesitation he chooses Dubthach moccu Lugair, described in the text as a *fili* 'poet' and a "vessel full

5. *CIH* 875.8 (corresponds to Carey 1994, 11). See also *CIH* 1656.1; and Best and Bergin 1929, line 9748–49.
6. Et rogabustar a sleigh a cetoir ⁊ docuaid d'indsaighi na cleirech, ⁊ tarluig in sleig fuitib ⁊ romarbustar odran aru patraig. No goma inu carpat nobeth in clerech and ⁊ odran oc corugud in carpait, ⁊ goma cuigi bodein noberud int urcur (*CIH* 340.1–3), "He took his spear right away and went to seek Patrick. He threw the spear among them and slew Odrán, Patrick's charioteer. Or, the cleric was perhaps in the chariot, and Odrán fixing the chariot, so that it was at that one [Odrán? Patrick?] that he aimed the cast" (cf. Carey 1994, 31).
7. *CIH* 340.4; Carey 1994, 31–32.
8. See p. 87.

of the grace of the Holy Spirit."[9] Notably, there is no indication in any of our sources for this story that Patrick and Dubthach had met previously, though in Muirchú's Life Dubthach is noted for being the only one to rise in deference to Patrick, against the orders of the king, when the saint first enters the court of Tara.[10]

His prestige as a vessel of the Spirit notwithstanding, Dubthach expresses considerable misgivings about judging this case. Should he rule in favor of Patrick and issue a death sentence for the murderer, the poet laments, he may offend the God of mercy. Should he spare Núadu, he may anger Patrick. The saint reassures Dubthach, blessing his mouth and enjoining him to speak as the spirit moves him, and he does. A poem attributed to Dubthach follows in the text, accompanied by a prose explanation of what in fact he declared as his judgment in this inspired poem. The poet's decision is described as a "compromise between mercy and punishment."[11] Núadu is to be executed, but Patrick is to save his soul.

This, however, is not the end of the story. Since, the text continues, these days no one is able to guarantee heaven for anyone as Patrick could in the good old days,[12] today the *tíachtain* 'compromise' is based on the principle of compensation. In other words, a murderer pays compensation to the relatives of the victim, and only if he is unable or unwilling to do so is the criminal slain.

The test case of the punishment of Odrán's slayer Núadu is thus settled, apparently to everyone's satisfaction. Patrick then summons the men of Ireland to a "dialogue" (*immacallam*).[13] At this meeting, they are told of the saint's miracles, particularly of his slaying the impious living and raising the worthy dead.[14] Thoroughly edified, they acquiesce in Patrick's evangelical juggernaut, and then the epoch-making command toward which the story has been leading is given. Lóegaire, in the wake of his subjects' conversion, orders that the whole native tradition of oral performance, particularly poetry and law, be reviewed, edited, and "canonized," as it were, so that whatever is acceptable within a Christian milieu may be kept and, implicitly, whatever is unacceptable be purged.

Codifying Tradition

That there is much to keep, if indeed not the entire body of traditional law and lore, is evident from the existence of the likes of Dubthach, a pagan

---

9. Lestar lan do rath in spirta naim in sin (*CIH* 340.11; see also 875.22; Carey 1994, 11).
10. See p. 89.
11. Tiachtain iter dilgud ⁊ indechad (*CIH* 341.27; Carey 1994, 29).
12. Uair nach fuil comus nime ac neoch inniu amail roboi in la-sin (*CIH* 341.28–29; Carey 1994, 29).
13. *CIH* 341.34.
14. Marbad na mbeo ⁊ beougud na marb (*CIH* 341.35–36).

vessel of the Holy Spirit. As the Prologue puts it, "The natural law extended to many things not covered by the law of the letter,"[15] that is, the law as formulated by literate Christian culture. And so, in response to Lóegaire's command, the verbal arts of Ireland are put on display: "It is then that each of the men of art of Ireland came to demonstrate his craft in the presence of Patrick and all the chiefs of Ireland."[16]

At this point in the story the most dramatic type of "progress" is set in motion. For these performances representative of the "natural law" of the past are not simply heard and remembered. Now they are to be preserved and fixed in a new way. A committee of nine is formed, consisting of three clerics, including Patrick; three poets, including Dubthach; and three kings, including Lóegaire. Their task is to supervise the commitment of the just-performed tradition to a written form, and this editorial process results in the *Senchas Már*.

Having grounded the collection he is introducing in the very beginnings of the literary tradition of the Irish, the author of the Prologue proceeds to take us even further back in the history of transmission:

> Before Patrick came, the right to speak was not given to anyone except three people: the chronicler, for recounting and storytelling; the man of art, for composing praise and satire; and the man of law, for issuing judgments by way of pronouncements [*roscada*] and maxims [*fásaige*]. But since Patrick came, each of these kinds of speech is under the yoke of the man of the white language—that is, of the Bible.[17]

In pagan times, the text continues, judgment was jealously kept in the hands of poets. Their pronouncements, however, proved too obscure for lay folk, and after a particularly obfuscating exchange between a senior and a junior Ulster poet—a verbal duel celebrated in a nonlegal text known as *Immacallam in Dá Thúara(i)d*[18] (The dialogue of the two sages)—Conchobar, the exasperated king of Ulster, proclaimed: "Plainly, from now on there will be a portion [of speech] for everyone, except for what is properly theirs [that is, poets'], which will not go to all. Otherwise, everyone will get a share."[19]

15. Rosiacht recht aicnid mar nad rochat recht litri (*CIH* 342.8; Carey 1994, 12; see also *CIH* 875.40, 1656.16–17, and 528.28 [from the law tract *Córus Béscnai*]).

16. Is and sin tarrcomlad cach aes dana la herind co tarfen cach a ceird fia patraic ar belaib cacha flatha la herind (*CIH* 341.40–342.2; Carey 1994, 12; see also *CIH* 875.33–35, 1656.9–10).

17. Co tainic patraic tra ni tabarta urlabra acht do triur i nerinn: fer comgne fri asndeis ⁊ scelugud, fer certa fri molad ⁊ air, Breithem fri breithemnus a roscadaib ⁊ fasagaib. O tainic immurgu patraic, is fo mam ata cach urlabra dona fiib-so do fir in berla bain .i. ina canoine (*CIH* 342.23–25; Carey 1994, 12; see also *CIH* 876.10–13, 1656.31–34).

18. Edited by Stokes (1905a).

19. "Is menann," ol conchobar, "biaid cuit do cach and-som onniu; acht inni bus duthaig

This contextualizing of the composition of the *Senchas Már* by way of reference to the incident of the *Immacallam in Dá Thúara(i)d* invites comparison between the canonizing *immacallam* held at Tara, which completed the task of redistribution begun by Conchobar, and another famous conference in Irish legend, the Convention of Druim Cet. This meeting, we recall, similarly brought together clerics, poets, and kings, and is also presented within tradition as a continuation of the process carried forward in Conchobar's landmark decision.

According to the Columban legend of Druim Cet, one of the three problems solved was an excess of poets, whose demands had become so great that the Irish decided to expel all poets from the island. Our sources emphasize that the same threat to the continuation of the poetic tradition in Ireland had been posed earlier, at the time of the *Immacallam in Dá Thúara(i)d,* when the Irish lost their patience with the obfuscation of poets. At Druim Cet, Columba's compromise reduced the number of poets. From then on, there was to be only one chief poet in each kingdom, with a severely reduced retinue. Furthermore, Columba, according to legend, exorcised the poetic institution, removing its demonic or pagan elements and the poison of satire, that is, the wherewithal of poetic extortion.

While both Columba's decision at Druim Cet and Patrick's at Tara are viewed within their respective literary contexts as of a piece with the Ulstermen's earlier attempt to control and make the best use of poets, it is important to note a striking difference between the effect of the earlier, pre-Christian decision and those of the later, Christian ones. Conchobar, in proclaiming that the lore and craft of poets are to be distributed among the men of Ireland, chops up this body of knowledge and disseminates it. He also implicitly democratizes the poetic institution, opening it up to nonpoets, and thereby unwittingly creates the crisis that comes to a head at Druim Cet, where the problem is not that poets are unclear but that it is too easy to become a poet, and there are too many of them. So too at the Tara conference presided over by Patrick and his committee of nine, clarity is no longer at issue. Rather, what is required is the Christian editing of *senchas*—sorting the "acceptable" from the "unacceptable"—into a form controllable by the man of letters, that is, the cleric. Limits must be imposed, and in the myth of the writing down of the *Senchas Már,* the attempted textualization of oral lore is symbolic of this necessary process of limitation and control.

As if to highlight the contrast with the aftermath of Conchobar's decision to parcel out poetic lore, the author of the *Senchas Már* Prologue portrays pre-Patrician oral performance as restricted, to three kinds of performers/practitioners, just as it was restricted in the time of the two sages and

doib-som de nis ricfa; gebaid cach a drechta de" (*CIH* 342.31–32; Carey 1994, 13; see also *CIH* 876.19–20, 1657.1–2).

their *immacallam* by virtue of the obscurity of poetic expression. Yet, with the writing down of the *Senchas Már,* performance and the lore it transmits are not said thereby to be parceled out among the men of Ireland. Rather, in the era of Patrick, our author says, the limited number of performers is increased by only one, to whom, however, the rest are now bound. This is the "man of white language" ("fer in bérla báin"), that is, the Christian literatus.

Thus writing is an act of appropriation not just of the past by the Patrician present but also of the voice of an elite group of professional knowers by an even more exclusive group, whose voice is in fact writing. The *Senchas Már,* then, irrespective of what it really is, represents for the author of the Prologue both a bringing together of traditional knowledge and a relocation of its authority. Mercy is shown to *senchas* 'lore' and it is spared for posterity, but in a form that renders it the exclusive property of its new preservers. *Senchas* thus shares a common fate with Núadu, the murderer of Patrick's charioteer, who is slain in body but whose death, viewed from a Christian perspective, appears a granting of eternal life and even a means of co-opting the murderer into the community of saints.

This seemingly rosy picture of the rapprochement of past and present in the codification of *senchas* notwithstanding, some aspects of the story told in the Prologue hint at a more problematic view of the processes of transmission and transition lying behind the creation of the text. In the legalistic world of the Prologue, containment and a hierarchical integration of society are the desiderata, and the breakdown or crossing of boundaries, as well as individual enterprise, potentially endangers the well-being of both society and individuals. Hence, the sequence of *tíachtain* 'compromise', at which Dubthach arrived, inspired by the Holy Spirit, and of *immacallam* between Patrick and the men of Ireland results in a clear set of relationships and a body of written-out rules regarding them. Earlier in the story, the desired Christianization and restructuring of Ireland are nearly derailed when Lóegaire and the men of Ireland meet pointedly apart from Patrick in their own *immacallam.*

Furthermore, the plot to slay a member of Patrick's retinue hinges on the king's dangerously liberal offer of a choice of reward to the slayer. Núadu, who accepts the offer and asks for his release, proceeds to commit the crime without any assistance, freed of the restrictions or "containment" of hostageship. Ironically, the freeing of hostages is typical saintly practice. Recall, for example, the story of Columba's liberation of the wretched Scandlán.[20] In this case, however, it is not the saint but the hostage himself or the saint's enemies who accomplish his release.

The ominous motif of isolation appears yet again in the charioteer's death: he falls victim to the ambush because he is outside his chariot, trying to adjust

---

20. Other hagiographic instances of rescue from hostageship or slavery are cited in Bitel 1990, 167–69.

it. The most dramatic instance of "being out on a limb" is, however, yet to come. Patrick chooses but one man, Dubthach the poet, to adjudicate. This singling out of a vessel of the Holy Spirit is, as I have noted, paralleled by the singularity of his behavior in the episode of Muirchú's Life in which Dubthach is the only one in the court of the king of Ireland courageous and inspired enough to pay respect to Patrick. In the story as told in the Prologue to the *Senchas Már,* Dubthach seems keenly aware that he is caught in a potentially desperate game.

It is in his isolation, however, that Dubthach, with a little help from the Holy Spirit, breaks through the impasse between individual and collective action and intention. His poem, the composition and innovation of one poet, becomes the policy of a people. It is the expression of a *tíachtain,* literally a 'coming (together)' of God and man, which unites past with present and attempts to bring the murderer back into the fold by making him a citizen of heaven or by reconciling him to society through payment of compensation. The writing down of native tradition under Patrician imprimatur is carried on in the spirit of this same *tíachtain,* which assures that nothing of value is lost as a united Ireland proudly advances into the age of letters.

This confidence in literary retention stands in bold contrast to the conceit of the typical saintly life, according to which what is written down is a humble synecdoche of a miraculously abundant past. The final impression left by the Prologue, which introduces what purports to be a thorough collection of law texts, is of completion, restoration, and fulfillment. This message is projected in the figure of the writing commission, a microcosm that successfully contains the macrocosm, a representative body that produces a representative text. The theme of a unified totality is also apparent in the inclusive schema of the four, no longer just three, masters of authoritative utterance, who embody a perfection that supposedly was already evolving in pre-Christian times.

Old Law and New

Another kind of perfection communicated by the unfolding story is of a distinctly Christian variety. That is, we see here the fulfillment of the "old" or natural law, the *recht aicnid,* by means of the new, or at least by means of a new way of storing and disseminating law. This process of completion harks back to the purported relationship between the Old and New Testaments, and as Kim McCone has pointed out, the figure of Dubthach, the native vessel of the Holy Spirit, is modeled at least in part on the Hebrew prophets, who, according to Christian tradition, anticipated the coming of Christ.[21] We

21. McCone 1990, 98. The syncretistic strategy at work in this story is also discussed in Gerriets 1991, 30–31. Wormald places this Irish "Old Testament" formulation of their past in

should observe, however, that the old law and lore are in no way presented here as already textualized, like the Old Testament, or even as textualizable before the conversion of heart, mind, and culture brought about by Patrick. In fact, it is precisely the performative nature and contextual function of *senchas* in pre-Patrician culture which are emphasized. Law, in the case of the judgment of Dubthach, is generated, revealed, and dramatically proclaimed in response to a specific set of circumstances, not retrieved out of a preexisting canon.

Furthermore, the juxtaposition between this living tradition and its divinely inspired supplement, *recht litre* 'law of the letter', the contrast underlying the process that supposedly resulted in the writing of the *Senchas Már*, disquietingly conjures up Paul's privileging of an unwritten covenant informed by the Spirit over writing, which brings only death (2 Cor. 3:6). As we have seen, the Patrick of the seventh-century lives of Muirchú and Tírechán, as if taking his cue from Paul, virtually never achieves a breakthrough in his evangelical mission by way of powerful reading or writing. It is the authority of his voice which he must demonstrate to those he is trying to convert. Only later does writing back up this oral performance, as, for instance, in the episodes from the seventh-century Patrician lives in which the saint regularly equips those he has converted and ordained with writing manuals.[22]

In a hagiographic instance when Patrick does try to achieve his goal by writing rather than speaking, the episode in which he sends a chastening letter to the tyrant Corictic, the effort proves a resounding failure. Corictic simply ignores the letter. What is required to dispose of him is public denunciation by a poet, which, presumably in conjunction with Patrick's simmering ire, transforms Corictic into a fox.[23] In this story, alike in some important ways to the account we have been examining from the Prologue to the *Senchas Már*, the poet's voice is allowed to replace Patrick's in a contention between the saint and a tyrannical secular ruler, just as Patrick and the men of Ireland turn to Dubthach for a pronouncement in the matter of Núadu's crime. Worthy of note in this regard is the pointedly nonverbal reaction of Patrick to the assault on his person and authority. The *crosfigill*, the figure of a cross, into which he forms his body, while it is certainly effective, is hardly as productive as Dubthach's verbal sign.

The parallels between the two accounts invite us to see in the *Senchas Már* Prologue an implicit ranking of the values of speaking and writing along the lines suggested by the Corictic episode, even though the sequence of events

---

the wider context of an early medieval *topos* of barbarian peoples as latter-day Hebrews who legitimate their legal system by means of Mosaic acts of writing (1977, 130–35). The significance of the Pauline concept of "natural law" in early Irish legal tradition, particularly as reflected in this story, is the subject of McLeod 1982.

22. See pp. 96, 107.

23. See pp. 104–9, 193–95.

by which those values are tested differs. In the Prologue, writing, that is, the writing down of the *Senchas Már* by the commission of nine, follows and voluminously fills out the immediate ad hoc and ad hominem utterance of Dubthach. In the story of Coirtic, however, direct speech accomplishes what written indirect speech could not.

In any event, the model for what happens in the story of Dubthach's judgment cannot simply have been the standard exegetical understanding of the relationship between the Old and New Testaments. Would the Irish men of letters in their quest to understand their own culture in biblical terms have been willing to go so far in heterodoxy as to privilege the Old Testament with the power of the spoken word, to the detriment of the New?[24] If that strategy is indeed what produced this legend, then it would appear that the Irish formulation of native culture in biblical terms went hand in hand with a formulation of biblical history in native terms.

Another scriptural resonance, perhaps as important for establishing the authority of the text to its readership as the prophetic status of Dubthach, is the centrality of the motif of Christ-like sacrifice. For Patrick to be mollified, for the native and Christian laws to be reconciled, and for Ireland to be saved through conversion, Núadu must be slain. His death, however, makes possible his everlasting life, as well as the everlasting life of the now-Christian Irish. Before Núadu's execution, death as punishment was both physical and spiritual. Now, execution can only affect the body. Indeed, since the end of the age of reviving saints, even execution, we are told, has become a rarity, replaced by a system of compensation.

The Self-Effacing Charioteer

This Christological dimension to Núadu is, however, considerably complicated if not downright opposed by his being actually culpable, a Judas-like murderer who slays the innocent charioteer for a price. In fact, the true sacrificial lamb might seem to be the charioteer. Indeed, Odrán meets the fate that could have been Patrick's if Núadu's shot was indeed random or meant for the saint.

In regard to neither Núadu nor Odrán do our texts make the analogy to Christ explicit. The closest we find to such typologizing is in a telling of another Patrician story, which, Binchy has observed,[25] is possibly one of the key sources for the story told in the *Senchas Már* Prologue, since it too features the slaying of the saint's charioteer Odrán as the result of mistaken

---

24. Carey (1990) argues that Dubthach as "type" refers more to the (putatively preliterate) patriarchs than to the Old Testament prophets, and that the Patrick of this etiology is more Mosaic (as one who introduces a written law) than Christlike.
25. Binchy 1975–76, 22.

identity. According to the pre-Norman Latin Life of Patrick (the so-called *Vita quarta*),[26] Failge, the ancestor of the Uí Failge (who gave their name to modern-day Offaly), swears revenge on Patrick for destroying the idols Failge worshiped. Patrick's associates conceal this threat from him. One day, the saint declares to his charioteer that he wishes to travel in a certain district. Odrán knows it is in Failge's domain and knows of Failge's threat. He devises a ruse to protect Patrick; he asks that, just for one day, the saint act as charioteer and allow Odrán the luxury of being driven around. Patrick consents, and Failge mistakes the charioteer for the saint and slays him with his spear. Upon committing the deed, Failge falls dead. The account concludes triumphantly: "With a martyr's crown [Odrán] went to the Lord, for he gave his life for his brother according to apostolic precept."[27]

The variant of this story preserved in the Tripartite Life elaborates on the theme of the charioteer's laying down his life for his fellow man, not just for Patrick but even for his own murderer. When Patrick sees that Odrán has been felled by a spear, he responds with a curse on Failge, but before Patrick can mention the miscreant's name, the dying charioteer interrupts him and interpolates the name of a famous tree located in Offaly. Patrick acquiesces, granting his servant's last wish, through which the virulence of his saintly curse is transferred from its original target to a hapless tree.[28]

We learn elsewhere in the Tripartite Life that Odrán was himself from Offaly.[29] In light of this detail, his final act takes on the appearance of an expression of solidarity with a fellow countryman, or possibly even a kinsman. That Odrán and his slayer in the Prologue to the *Senchas Már* similarly have something in common is suggested by their mutual interest in horses. Núadu, we recall, asks to be put in charge of the cavalry.

This affinity between Odrán and Failge is also detectable in another telling of the story, in another pre-Norman Latin life of Patrick, the *Vita tertia*, as well as in the version to be found in the Middle Irish Life of Patrick preserved

---

26. Bieler 1971, 106.
27. Cum corona martirii ad Dominum migravit quoniam iuxta apostolicum praeceptum animam suam pro fratre posuit (ibid.). In the list of chapter headings which is included with the *Vita quarta* in the single manuscript in which it has been preserved (see ibid., 3–4), the victim of Failge's assassination attempt is said to be Benignus, or Benén (ibid., 50: de martyrio Benigni discipuli eius et morte Folge persecutoris; also noted in F. Byrne and Francis 1994, 106). While, as Bieler points out (1971, 50 n. on line 2), this identification is probably the result of scribal error, it is a reasonable mistake. Benignus, we recall, was the successor to, and a close companion of, Patrick, and he was nearly sacrificed as a substitute for Patrick in the burning house at Tara. Moreover, Tírechán places the scene of Benignus's passionate profession of loyalty to Patrick in the latter's chariot, as he is about to leave the home of Benignus's family and continue his mission. As Patrick accepts Benignus as his fosterling, he proclaims: Babtizate eum et eleuate eum in currum (c. 5, Bieler 1979, 126), "Baptize him and lift him into the chariot." As intimate, successor, substitute, and subordinate, the legendary figure of Benignus is eminently qualified to play the role of Patrick's charioteer.
28. Mulchrone 1939, lines 2574–85.
29. Ibid., line 3135.

in the Book of Lismore.[30] Here, Failge is indeed punished after his murderous deed, but in a strikingly convoluted way. As soon as the charioteer dies, Failge's soul leaves his body and, we assume, journeys to hell, while a devil possesses Failge's mortal shell. No one notices the change until, some time later, Patrick comes calling on Failge. The servant who goes to fetch Failge finds a mere pile of bones. This exposure of the false Failge is duly announced to Patrick as he waits at the door, but it is no surprise to the knowing saint, who once again demonstrates that he cannot be fooled by false signs. Thus, both Odrán and Failge are characterized in this version of the story as temporary impostors, whose charades are in fact preludes to incontrovertible death. Odrán assumes the role of Patrick before he is slain; a demon assumes the "role" of Failge and then, surprised by Patrick, leaves behind Failge's mortal remains. Furthermore, as if there were an innate tendency in the story for dual formations to develop, the figure of Failge, toward whom Odrán evinces such sympathy in the version of the story told in the Tripartite Life, is split in two as a result of his encounter with the charioteer. There is a "before" and an "after" Failge, one human and the other supernatural. Another development along these lines is evident in the tradition recorded at the end of the story as told in the Tripartite Life, that the inhabitants of the territory of Uí Failge of today are descended not from the "bad" Failge but from one Failge Ross, a scion blessed by Patrick, and clearly a (more palatable) doublet of the murderous Failge.[31]

To Raise or Not to Raise the Dead

What is most remarkable about the fate of the charioteer in all the versions of the story is that Patrick clearly does not have the slightest intention to do what he does often enough in other, analogous situations. He does not restore his charioteer, the victim of pagan persecution, to life. Typically, the Patrick of hagiography, with solid precedent set for him in the gospel accounts of Christ and earlier saints' lives, does not hesitate to exercise his saintly authority most dramatically by reviving the dead.

This aspect of Patrick's miracle-working is already conspicuous in the seventh-century stratum of Patrician legend, as we have seen. His ability to raise the dead continues to receive considerable attention in later sources, such as the Life by the twelfth-century Anglo-Norman Jocelin of Furness, who puts the count of those revived by Patrick at thirty-three and who quotes from a letter attributed to the saint: "He has given to me, the Lord to the lowly one, the power of performing signs among a barbarous people (the like of which deeds are not recorded even of the great Apostles) in such a way that I might

30. Bieler 1971, 157–58; Stokes 1890, 13.
31. Mulchrone 1939, 130. CF. F. Byrne and Francis 1994, 106, on the two Failges.

bring back to life bodies that had dissolved into dust many years ago."[32] It may well be to Patrick's appropriation of the dead by resurrecting them that one of Lóegaire's druids, Matha, refers: "The druid predicted to Lóegaire that Patrick would steal the living and the dead from him."[33] We should note that the prediction is made not in a life of Patrick, but in an eighth-century law tract incorporated in the *Senchas Már,* which echoes some of the formulations of the past we have seen in the Prologue.

Among the dead or near-dead revived by Patrick, we recall, are his own sister, a man feigning death whom Patrick actually slays only to bring him back to life, the sister of a pagan who demands that she be returned to him along with her unborn child as the condition for his accepting the new faith, and perhaps the most intriguing of Patrick's revenants, the dead who are brought back to life because the saint wishes to obtain esoteric information from them and to find out who they are. In almost all these cases, the revived dead serve Patrick as signs of his miraculous power and the authority of what he preaches and are rewarded for their semiotic service. They are allowed to live out their lives; they are converted; or their souls are dispatched to heaven.

In only a single instance does Patrick bring a corpse to life only to let it lapse back into death without changing its physical or moral status at all. This defeat of our expectations occurs in the account of Patrick's overlooking a cross on a pagan's grave, already to be found in the earliest extant stratum of Patrician hagiography.[34] It is important to note that even in this rather untypical tale, raising the dead still has to do with creating and empowering signs. For with what the revived pagan has to say, Patrick can attach the cross (the signifier) to the proper signified (the grave of the deceased Christian), thus restoring his reputation as one who pays every cross its due. In Tírechán's account of the episode, it is Patrick's charioteer who points out to him, almost on our behalf as readers of Patrician hagiography, that the saint's behavior in this case seems to go against generic norms. Could not Patrick have simply saved the soul of the helpfully informative pagan, in addition to putting the cross where it belongs? To this question as put by the charioteer,

32. My translation, based on the text as given in Carney 1961, 138: Dedit mihi Dominus exiguo uirtutem faciendi signa in populo barbaro, qualia, nec â magnis Apostolis leguntur facta, ita ut in nomine Domini Dei nostri Jesu Christi resuscitarem à mortuis corpora in puluere a multis annis resoluta (c. 79).

In the *Historia Brittonum* attributed to Nennius (ca. 800), Patrick is said to have raised nine persons from the dead (c. 54). Perhaps the most immediate model for the figure of the revivifying Patrick that we already see in seventh-century Irish hagiography is the Martin of the fourth-century Sulpicius Severus's Life and Dialogues. Martin not only raises the dead (Life, c. 7, 8; Dialogues, 2.4) but is characterized as outstanding, particularly in comparison to the eremitical saints of the Near East, by virtue of his ability to raise the dead (Dialogues, 1.24, 2.5).

33. Dorarngart-side in drai do Laegaire getad Padraig biu 7 marbu aire (from the *Córus Béscnai,* CIH 527.28).

34. See pp. 124–28.

neither Patrick nor Tírechán has a definitive answer. Here, as in the version of the story of Odrán's death told in the Tripartite Life, the figure of the charioteer is associated with a jarring shift of signification and a shift in expectations. In this case, however, he notices the shifts and points them out, whereas in the Failge episode, where the virulence of Patrick's curse is transferred from intended target to arboreal bystander, it is the charioteer who brings about the play of signs, switching tree with saint's enemy.

Partners Separated

In coming back to the rather somber hagiographic tale of the two graves, we may seem to have come a long way from the cheery picture of reconciliation presented in the Prologue to the *Senchas Már*. Yet the distance is shortened when we consider that we are still in the company of a figure that played a key role in the legal legend. Past could not have been wedded to future, nor would the *Senchas Már* have been written, had Patrick not been tragically cut off from his charioteer. On the other hand, in this episode of the mismarked pagan, Patrick himself cuts off communication not only with the past but also with his charioteer, who becomes here something of a problem for the saint. It is the charioteer who points out the saint's seeming oversight at the beginning of the story, and then at the end embarrassingly brings up the question of the pagan's salvation. By ignoring the question Patrick suppresses the thorny issue altogether, just as he dispatched the pagan back into the hell of his heathendom.

As different as the two stories appear on the surface, in both Tírechán's Life and the Prologue to the *Senchas Már* the figure of the charioteer is associated with issues of life and death and with the concept of justice as promulgated by the new order of Patrick and the church. Furthermore, both narratives feature what can be called "twinning" between a pair of antithetical characters, that is, the two dead men buried alongside each other and, in the other account, Patrick's charioteer and his murderer. The members of each pair share a parallel fate, dying together or one shortly after the other, and even seem interchangeable, at least in the case of the two dead men of Tírechán's episode, although in the final analysis they prove separable in a decisive way. Moreover, in each case, one member of the pair, the pagan whose burial site Patrick's charioteer notices and the charioteer himself in the other story, *must* remain obscure, dead, or even doomed. Meanwhile, the other member of the pair is translated into the Christian community. In one story, it is the dead man whose grave is finally marked properly with the cross, and in the other, it is the miscreant Núadu Derg, who loses his life but whose eternal soul is conspicuously saved.

This structural similarity between the two narratives is not coincidental. Indeed, it is indicative of a generative pattern underlying the other, equally intriguing stories extant in literary tradition involving Patrick's charioteer. There are two other such stories, besides those we have already examined, in Patrician hagiography. One is to be found in Muirchú's Life, directly after the episode of the mismarked graves. The seventh-century hagiographer's inclusion of this second story involving the charioteer at this point in his narrative has the effect of drawing as much attention to this figure as does Tírechán's text, which, though it does not contain this story, elaborates on the role of the charioteer in the episode of the mismarked graves. Here is what Muirchú has to say about the further adventures of the Patrick and his driver:

> Customarily, Patrick would not travel from Saturday night until Monday morning. One Sunday he spent the night on a field in honor of the sacred time, and it rained heavily during a storm. Although the entire country was devastated by the heavy downpour, it stayed dry in the place where the holy bishop was spending the night. . . . Patrick's charioteer approached and told of having lost track of his horses (whose loss he lamented as if they had been beloved friends), since he could not search for them in the obscuring dark. This stirred the compassion of the holy father, and he said to the tearful charioteer: "God, a prompt helper of helpers, will assist in hard times; you will find the horses you bewail." Thereupon, pulling up his sleeve, he lifted his outstretched hand, and, as if they were lights, his five fingers lit up the area, so that by the light of the extended hand the charioteer could find the horses that he had lost, and cease his weeping. The charioteer, however, did not speak of this miracle until after Patrick's death.[35]

The ever-ready Patrick's solution to the desperate situation of the loss of his means of transportation constitutes an ersatz resurrection. He brings back the horses his charioteer had been lamenting as if they had died, and with the return of the animals the charioteer ceases his weeping and groaning (*gemitus*). This motif of overwhelming bereavement is another link between this and the preceding episode in Muirchú's text, which features a mother who is so distraught that she cannot identify her son's grave. Grief over the loss of a loved one creates in both cases a serious impediment to the saint's progress.

---

35. Consuitudo autem illi erat ut a uespera dominicae noctis usque ad mane secundae feriae Patricius non ambularet inde. In quadam dominica die honore sacri temporis in campo pernoctans grauis pluia cum tempestate accederat, sed cum grauis pluia in tota patria populata est in loco ubi sanctus episcopus pernoctabat siccitas erat. . . . [Accedit] auriga, memorat equos amissos, quasi amicos caros planxit, quia illos quaerere tenebris arcentibus uissum non poterat. Inde pietas Patricii patris pii mota est et flebili aurigae dixit: "Deus in angustís, [in] inoportunitatibus adiutor prumptus adiutorium praestabit et equos quos ploras inuenies." Exhinc manum spolians manica extensam eleuauit et quinque digiti sicut luminaria ita proxima quaeque inluxera[n]t et per lucem extensae manus equos quos amisserat auriga soluto gemitu inuenit. Sed hoc miraculum auriga comes usque ad Patricii obitum absconderat (2.3, Bieler 1979, 114.23–116.7).

The charioteer himself is in no physical danger in this episode of the missing horses, but his anxiety about their well-being is noticeable.[36] The public discovery of the miraculous recovery is deferred till after Patrick's death, as if its single witness, the charioteer, were silenced. This motif appears in stories about Saint Columba, who, as we have seen, on occasion forbids witnesses to his miracles or angelic dialogues to divulge them until after his death,[37] but is virtually nonexistent in Patrician hagiography, save for this one instance.

Thus, a twinning of sorts takes place in this rain-drenched Patrician episode between the charioteer and his horses, who are shown to be inseparable. Yet they are also set off by the correlated dichotomies "present versus absent" and "keeping silent versus speaking," for when the horses are absent, the charioteer speaks effectively, but when the horses are returned, the charioteer turns mute.

This motif of the strategically timed silence of Patrick's charioteer, of his seeming peripheral even though, it turns out, he clearly has something important to tell or do, also appears in the story of Patrick's most important dialogue of all. In the Tripartite Life's account of this pivotal event in Patrick's career, the conversation takes place on top of the mountain Crúachán Aigli in Connacht, between the saint and an angelic emissary of God. The dialogue is brought about by Patrick's fasting in protest against God, and it results in ridding Ireland of noxious birds and God's granting key concessions to the insistent Patrick. With what he wins on the mountain, including the exclusive right to judge all the Irish on Judgment Day, Patrick's position as the Irish Moses and Christ all in one is firmly established.[38]

According to both the Tripartite Life and the far more cursory account of the climb up Crúachán Aigli told by Tírechán,[39] Patrick's apotheosis does not come without a price. His elevation forms a sequence with the death of his charioteer (in this episode called Totmael), which our sources tell us happened directly before or after Patrick went up. The saint buries his servant, builds a monument to him, and declares that he will return to this spot at the end of the world.[40]

---

36. It should be pointed out that *auriga* also has the meaning "groom," as is indicated in the text of the medieval *Vita tertia* of Patrick, where it is not the *eques* of the landowner Dáire who allows a horse to graze on land given to Patrick (as in Muirchú's telling of the story) but his *auriga* (Bieler 1971, 176). This trespassing horse, we recall, is slain and then revived by Patrick.

37. For instance, 3.6, 7, 16 (Anderson and Anderson 1991, 190, 192, 204, 206).

38. Mulchrone 1939, lines 1289–1374. See also the Life by Probus (Bieler 1971, 212–13). Máire MacNeill (1962, 71–84) offers a survey of the legendry and ritual practices centered on Cruach Phádraig, one of the most important and popular pilgrimage sites in medieval and modern Ireland.

39. Mulchrone 1939, lines 1388–89; c. 38, Bieler 1979, 152.

40. A story is told about Saint Mochta of Louth in his Latin Life that provides an intriguing variation on the pattern evident in the Patrician legend under discussion. According to his Life, Mochta, while fighting demons alongside Patrick and fasting on Crúachán, reconstitutes and

Why does the hagiographic tradition as represented by these two texts tie the demise of the charioteer to what is the most important event in Patrick's evolution into the saint of the Irish?[41] It is as if the victory won on Crúachán Aigli against both the winged forces of evil and the forces of divine authority demanded some form of sacrifice from the victor. For the new, improved Patrick descends at the expense of the shadowy charioteer, to whom the saint expresses his undying commitment, even gratitude.[42] Patrick will come back to the grave of his servant and witness the resurrection of one who, as we recall from the accounts of his death, could be mistaken for Patrick himself. The saint will come back, however, only at the end of the world, when the charioteer's resurrection, instead of being the public miracle it would have been in Patrick's day, will be just one among a multitude of miraculous signs of the end of the world. As in the story of the recovery of the horses, the charioteer is designated Patrick's silent partner, but now his dormancy takes on an eschatological dimension, not being simply confined to the span of Patrick's life.[43]

---

brings back to life the shattered remains of his disciple Fintan, who had been thrown down by demons (Heist 1965, 398). Is this *discipulus* an upgraded version of the sacrificed Patrician charioteer, who represents a (re)integrated cultural "body" precisely because he is *not* revived?

41. In the Life by Probus, the charioteer is actually buried on Crúachán Aigli (Bieler 1971, 212).

42. Kim McCone compares Totmael's fate to that of Lot's wife in Genesis; the charioteer in this Patrician legend constitutes an "early Irish example of a companion's liminal immobilization on the way to an ascetic eminence reserved for his master alone" (McCone 1990, 188).

43. Tírechán in passing mentions yet another terminated charioteer of Patrick's, one Boidmal or Bodmael (17.2, Bieler 1979, 137), whose death and burial validate the extent of Patrick's authority (specifically, his ownership of a tract of land).

The motif of the sacrificed companion persists in the modern oral legendry centered on Patrick's encounter with God on Crúachán Aigli (see MacNeill 1962, 80–81, 502–4, 546; and Melia 1978, 536–40, on both the Irish and an analogous Breton tradition). In modern tellings, however, the victim is identified as Saint Benignus, who is Patrick's successor and "alter ego" in earlier hagiographic tradition. According to the oral legend, the "folk" Benignus—modern Beannán or Mo Bheannán/Mionnán—or an otherwise named companion (Patrick's "boy, cleric, or driver"—MacNeill 1962, 80) is sent ahead to the peak as a scout and is found dead. Or he is left behind while Patrick ascends, but neglects his duty or even covets Patrick's bell, as a result of which he dies (and, at least in one telling, is resurrected by the saint). Patrick raises the stone of Mionnán (Leacht Mionnáin) in his memory, and it marks the first station in the pilgrimage. In light of the dioscuric theme running through the stories having to do with Patrick's relationship with his charioteer, it is suggestive that the victim-companion is sometimes one of two youths in Patrick's company, the other of whom survives the ordeal.

Doubtless there is a connection between the driver and/or companion seemingly sacrificed and perpetually memorialized at Crúachán Aigli and the immortal guardians (*cométaidi*), arguably recycled pre-Christian divinities, appointed by Patrick to protect the people of Ireland in his absence until Doomsday, mentioned in the Tripartite Life (Mulchrone 1939, line 1376) and discussed in Mac Cana 1988, 323–27. One happens to have been left at Crúachán Aigli, where his bell can still be heard, even though he himself cannot be found (róclunetar guth a chluic ₇ ní fogabar, Mulchrone 1939, line 1378).

The Guidance of the Driver

It would appear, then, that the story of how the *Senchas Már* was written down starts with the death of a figure who regularly dies and stays dead under similar circumstances elsewhere in Patrician hagiography. Moreover, the charioteer's death, alongside its Christological overtones, poses a challenge to some of the expectations we acquire as readers of Patrician hagiography about what Patrick can or is willing to do for the dead. Patrick, or the tradition that traces itself back to Patrick, refuses or is unable to bring back the charioteer. Such muting or suppression fosters the same unease so bluntly expressed in what the charioteer says to Patrick in Tírechán's account of the incident of the two graves. The Prologue to the *Senchas Már* as well as the many Patrician stories in which the dead do come back to life exude confidence about the prospects of recovering the past through a Christian, literary tradition. It is the saint's own trusty charioteer, however, who indicates the limitations of that recovery. Working within the text, either as commentator or as corpse, either as an interpreter of signs or as a sign himself, he undermines the reader's confidence in the text's ability to enclose and "revive" all that it claims it can.

Why is it the saint's charioteer who rocks the saintly and literary boat or at least points out that it is rocking? The Indo-European mythological heritage of the Irish, as recycled by the literary tradition in order to carry new meanings, seems to present some answers to this question. For the role of the charioteer in ancient Greek and Indic epic traditions is often that of alter ego to the hero riding in the chariot, but also anti-ego, either authoritatively offering prudent instruction to the impetuous hero or bringing out the dark, destructive side of the hero's character.[44] Such charioteers are certainly to be found in medieval Irish literature as well.

Easily the most famous relationship between hero and charioteer in Irish saga is that between the Ulster warrior Cú Chulainn and his driver, Lóeg. In the texts that emphasize the relationship, such as the Middle Irish *Serglige Con Culainn* (Wasting sickness of Cú Chulainn) and the *Táin Bó Cúailnge*, Lóeg's alternating identification with and distance from Cú Chulainn are

---

44. This weave of alterity and affinity is often further complicated by the fact that the charioteer is a god in disguise. Alf Hiltebeitel has discussed the complex role the god Krishna plays as charioteer to the hero Arjuna in the Indic epic *Mahābhārata* (1976, 102–9, 255–66), and the parallels that exist between this tradition and the various stories featuring the interplay of the Irish hero Cú Chulainn and his charioteer, especially in the *Táin* (1982). In his survey of the Indo-European narrative figure of the charioteer, Hiltebeitel, following Stig Wikander, has drawn attention to the figure's dark side, as evinced, for example, in the sinister machinations of the battle-inciting Norse god Odin in his stint as charioteering impostor in the second book of Saxo's History of the Danes (ibid., 109–12). In the *Iliad* (23.280), as is pointed out in Sinos 1980, 49–52, the mirroring relationship between the heroes Achilles and Patroclus, one of the most famous friendships in Greek epic tradition, is articulated by Achilles himself in terms of the hero and his charioteer.

elaborately explored.[45] In the *Serglige*, it is his charioteer whom the ailing Cú Chulainn sends into the otherworld of Mag Mell to inspect it before the hero accepts the invitation to go there himself to fight a battle on an otherworldly king's behalf and win the love of the king's fair sister. Lóeg's role as a not-altogether-at-ease "stand-in" for Cú Chulainn is made clear in his exchange with the woman who escorts him to the otherworld: "'Alas, that it is not Cú Chulainn who is in your shape here now,' Lí Ban said. 'I would prefer if he were the one here, too,' replied Lóeg."[46]

When he returns to Cú Chulainn, still lying in his bed suffering the after-effects of an earlier encounter with supernatural women, Lóeg tells of his experiences in the otherworld, in the fashion of those many characters whose metaphysical travels render them indispensable storytellers. This account has a startling effect on the hero, who gets up, converses easily with Lóeg, and is renewed in his mind by what the charioteer has to say. It is as if the charioteer brings back for the hero a revivifying cure, in the form of news from the otherworld; he has rescued him as, Cú Chulainn's wife, Emer, charges, his fellow Ulster heroes, for all their heroism and high social status, had not been able or willing to do.[47]

The motif of the charioteer's supplying the hero with valuable firsthand information about his destination is replicated in the "childhood deeds" section of the *Táin Bó Cúailnge*, in the episode in which the young Cú Chulainn goes on his first foray beyond the bounds of the province in the king's chariot, driven by the king's charioteer, Ibar. Although he expresses a good deal of hesitation about doing what the youthful hero proposes, Ibar nevertheless does drive him and answers Cú Chulainn's questions about the unfamiliar terrain: "So he told him the name of every chief fort between Temair and Cennannas. He named, moreover, their meadowlands and their fords, their renowned places and their dwellings, their forts and their fortified heights."[48] In addition, Ibar provides his charge with the necessary information about the magical capabilities of the opponents he meets, so that Cú Chulainn can

---

45. On the difficulties of dating the *Serglige*, consisting of two fused recensions (from between 800 and 1100) preserved in the eleventh-century Lebor na hUidre and a later copy, see Dillon 1953, xi–xvi.

46. "Appraind ₇ bith appraind nach hé Cú Chulaind fil it richt indossa," or Lí Ban. "Bád maith limsa dano combad hé no beth and," for Láeg (ibid., lines 148–50).

Perhaps Lóeg's playing proxy for the incapacitated Cú Chulainn in the *Serglige* is ultimately in line with the practice of the Celts who invaded Greece in the third century B.C. as described by Pausanias: "When the Gaulish cavalry were in battle, the grooms would stay behind the ranks and make themselves useful with new mounts when a horse or rider fell, but when a man was killed the slave would mount the horse in place of his master" (10.19.6, trans. in Levi 1971, 1:456).

47. Dillon 1953, lines 347–50.

48. Trans. C. O'Rahilly 1976b, 144. Adfét dó dano ainm cech prímdúne eter Themair ₇ Cenandas. Adfét dó chétamus a n-íathu ₇ a n-áthus, a n-airdirci ₇ a treba, a ndúne ₇ a n-arddindgnu (ibid., lines 700–702).

defeat them.[49] We should recall in this regard that Odrán the driver had knowledge that even Patrick did not: he knew that Failge meant to kill Patrick and that Patrick's route would take him into Failge's territory.

And so we see that the Irish *arae* 'charioteer' can be a possessor of key information as well as a guardian of balance and containment within a given situation. Whether the danger takes the form of an invitation to the otherworld, a young warrior's brash ambition, or a recalcitrant pagan's death threat against a saint, the charioteer can neutralize, temper, or even absorb it. In the words of an Old Irish "mirror for princes" known as the *Audacht Morainn* (The testament of Morann), "Let [the king-to-be] observe the driver of an old chariot. For the driver of an old wheel-rim does not sleep. He looks ahead, he looks behind, in front and to the right and to the left. He looks, he defends, he protects, so that he may not break with neglect or violence the wheel-rims which run under him."[50]

The Wily Sidekick

There is, however, a devious side to the knowledge and utility of the charioteer, which is on display, for example, in the role Lóeg plays in the death of Cú Chulainn's dearest foster brother and most powerful opponent, Fer Diad, in the earlier recension of the *Táin*. Hard pressed by his adversary, Cú Chulainn asks Lóeg "to urge him on when he was overcome and to praise him when he was victorious fighting against his opponent. So his charioteer said to him: 'Your opponent goes over you as a tail goes over a cat. He belabours you as flax-heads are beaten in a pond. He chastises you as a fond woman chastises her son.'"[51] Having proven his potential as a satirist, Lóeg watches Cú Chulainn redouble his efforts against Fer Diad, who, however, continues to stave off the Ulster hero, and more *gresad* 'shaming' from the charioteer is required, producing a dramatic result: "Then, Cú Chulainn swelled and grew big as a bladder does when inflated. His size increased so

49. Ibid., lines 733–54.
50. Trans. F. Kelly 1976, 8. Ardosécath arid sencharpait. Ar nícon-chotli are senfhonnith. Remi-déci, íarmo-déci, tair sceo desiul sceo túaithbiul. De-éci, im-dích, im-dídnathar, arna bó co foill na forráin fonnath fod-rethat (ibid.).

  Philip O'Leary (1986, 1) briefly considers some of the more general implications of this passage, particularly in connection with the metaphor of the "driver of an old chariot." Hiltebeitel surveys some of the philosophical applications of the concepts chariot/charioteer/charioteering in Indian tradition (1982, 92) and even suggests a metaphysical subtext to the chariot featured in the Irish tale of the spectral chariot (ibid., n. 2), to be discussed later.
51. Trans. C. O'Rahilly 1976b, 207. Asbert Cú Chulaind íarom fria araid ara ngresad an tan ba ráen fair et ara molad in tan ba ráen riam og comracc fri Fer Diad. Is íarom aspert a ara fris: "Tét an fer tarat amail téti bott tar catt. Nodnigh an fer amail neghar coipp i llundai. Notcúra an fer amail cúruss ben boídh a mac" (ibid., lines 3082–87). O'Rahilly's translation is fine-tuned in Mac Cana 1992, 77 n. 21.

that he was bigger than Fer Diad."[52] At this point, Lóeg tips the balance altogether by supplying Cú Chulainn with his secret weapon, the *gae bolga*, which only Cú Chulainn and his supernatural fosterer know how to wield: "'Look out for the *gae bolga!*' cried the charioteer and cast it to him downstream. Cú Chulainn caught it between his toes and cast it at Fer Diad into his anus."[53]

In an earlier episode of the *Táin*, Cú Chulainn again uses the *gae bolga*, sent to him by Lóeg, against an almost equally difficult opponent. In this case, however, the hero is severely hampered by an attack against him while he is fighting the warrior Lóch. The attacker is the Morrígan, a supernatural female with whom Cú Chulainn enjoys an intense love-hate relationship.[54]

Lóeg the *arae* and the *gae bolga* together save the hero's life in these two situations. Yet Lóeg hardly seems to deserve the sort of credit paid to the charioteer Odrán, who saved Patrick's life not by means of a spear but by absorbing the spear meant for Patrick. For the sinister *gae bolga* and its devious use in single combat (*fír fer*, literally 'truth of men') raise troubling questions about the fairness of Cú Chulainn's victory over Fer Diad and Lóch.[55] A virtually self-propelled spear that sneakily enters from behind and below is hardly a standard item in the arsenal of Irish saga heroics. Furthermore, it is instrumental in the two problematic "kills" in Cú Chulainn's heroic career, that of his beloved foster brother Fer Diad and that of his own son, Condla. In these cases Cú Chulainn slays a warrior who is virtually his equivalent in strength and skill and who is also his close kinsman.[56] As Eric Hamp has pointed out, the name Fer Diad itself refers to this affinity. It means "one of two," the other being presumably Cú Chulainn.[57] Hence, the problem faced by the hero in these stories is not limited to the tragic clash of obligations which brings him to kill his foster brother or his son. Also at issue is the difficulty of demonstrating an independent heroic identity against a figure who is clearly his match, the "other" of the "two."[58]

Against such an opponent Cú Chulainn must reveal and use a unique gift that marks him as exceptional. That gift is the ability to use the *gae bolga*, a skill that the female warrior Scáthach taught only to Cú Chulainn, though she

52. Trans. C. O'Rahilly 1976b, 207. Ra lín at ₇ infisi amail anáil i llés. Forbrid a méd co mba móam oltás Fer Diad (ibid., lines 3093–94). On the praise and blame doled out by charioteers, see Hiltebeitel 1982, 99–104.
53. Trans. C. O'Rahilly 1976b, 207. "Fomna an gaí mbulga!" ol in t-ara. Dolléci ndó lasan sruth. Gaibt[h]i Cú cona ladair ₇ imambeir do Fhir Diad a timt[h]iracht a chuirp (ibid., lines 3095–97).
54. Ibid., lines 1874–2030.
55. What constitutes a "fair fight" (*fír fer*) in medieval Irish literature is the subject of O'Leary 1987.
56. The tale of Condla's death is edited in van Hamel 1933, 11–15.
57. Hamp 1982.
58. Another "twin" relationship, between Cú Chulainn and Conall Cernach, is discussed briefly in P. Ford 1977, 8.

also fostered Fer Diad and Condla and instructed them in martial arts.[59] In this regard, the name Scáthach 'shadowy, like a reflection' takes on a special meaning.[60] This trainer of warriors passes what she knows and what she can do on to her young charge, rendering him her heroic projection, or herself his shadow. This relationship with a backgrounded, occasionally foregrounded, shadow or reflection in turn resembles the hero's relationship with his charioteer.

Saving Fergus mac Léiti's Face

A vivid example of the *arae*'s power to act as a mirror to the hero in the chariot, holding up a reflection of his past sins and virtues and even manipulating the problems inherent in his heroic existence, is to be found in the story of the death of Fergus mac Léiti, which in its earliest form is preserved in Old Irish legal commentary.[61] This Fergus is clearly akin to the other Ferguses who loom as kingly and ancestral figures in Ulster saga, including the formidable Fergus mac Róich, one of Cú Chulainn's chief fosterers, who plays an important role in the *Táin*, as well as in the story of how the *Táin* was recovered by the "modern" generation of poets, saints, and scribes.[62]

Fergus mac Léiti, king of Ulster, receives from supernatural benefactors the ability to travel under the surface of any body of water, with the exception of Loch Rudraige. This he is told never to enter, although it is in his own territory. It is, however, no easier for Fergus to resist a taboo than for any other hero, and accompanied by his charioteer, he breaches the boundary set between him and what should rightfully be his to traverse. After diving into the forbidden waters, he encounters a "horrid aquatic creature" (*peist uiscide uathmar*):

> At times it would stretch itself out, and at other times it would draw itself together, like a smith's bellows. As Fergus gazed upon it, his mouth was trans-

59. C. O'Rahilly 1976b, lines 3088–89; van Hamel 1933, 15.
60. The connotations of this name as well as those of the name Aífe, assigned in the Ulster cycle to a closely related figure, are pointed out in Meroney 1958b, 257.
61. This text is edited and examined in Binchy 1952.
62. See pp. 17–20. Ruairí Ó hUiginn (1993, 36–37) surveys the common ground between the two Ferguses. There are other significant parallels: the careers of both heroes are marked by lingering dishonor (Fergus mac Róich's failure to protect the sons of Uisliu, leading to his departure from Ulster; Fergus mac Léiti's facial disfigurement) and banishment (Fergus mac Róich's exile from Ulster; the injunction against Fergus mac Léiti's entering Loch Rudraige). Even more striking, both figures are characterized as survivors who return to tell the tale: Fergus mac Róich comes back to life to recount the cattle raid of Cúailnge, and Fergus mac Léiti, as we shall see, expends his last breath announcing to the Ulstermen that he is the "survivor" (*tiugba*) and victor in the fight with the lake monster. The value of the survivor as a source of story is indicated in another Irish word for "survivor," *sceola(ng)*, literally 'news bringer', from *scél* 'story' (*DIL*, s.v. *sceola*).

formed, extending as far as the back of his neck. In fear he returned to shore and asked his charioteer, "How do I look to you?" "You look bad," he said, "but it is nothing that some sleep couldn't cure." Thereupon the charioteer put him to sleep in the chariot, and Fergus slept.

While he slept, the charioteer went to the wise men of Ulster who were in Emain Macha and told them about the king's adventures and about what had happened to him. The charioteer asked them whom they would take as king after Fergus, for it was not easy to have a king with a blemish in Emain Macha.

The counsel of the wise men of Ulster was to have the king come to his house and to be shielded from all manner of riff-raff, lest some fool or jester should taunt him in the face with his blemish, and that he should always be washed while lying on his back, lest he see his reflection in the water. And thus was he guarded for the next seven years.[63]

In the long run, however, this precaution proves as ineffective as the taboo against Loch Rudraige. A slave woman whom Fergus castigates pays him back in kind by pointing out his blemish to him. Humiliated, Fergus returns to the depths of Loch Rudraige, where he fights a marathon battle with the monster and finally emerges with its head to proclaim "I am the survivor,"[64] only to sink back among the waves, dead.

What we see in the story of Fergus contrasts with the situation featured in the *Serglige Con Culainn,* where the hero's proxy goes forth into the alien world to reconnoiter for him and returns with both a story to tell and a cure for the *serglige* 'wasting sickness'. In the account of Fergus's tragic adventure the charioteer is pointedly left behind, and the hero goes forth on an adventure that only he can undertake. When Fergus returns, he tells no story, and his ability to fulfill his heroic and kingly duties is as impaired as Cú Chulainn's ever was, in or out of his sickbed. Fergus, like a warrior drained of his defining energy, falls asleep after he reemerges on shore, and his physical marking renders him a highly problematic king.

The monstrous epiphany Fergus encounters on his solitary quest is argua-

---

63. Based on the translation in Binchy 1952, 42–43. Ala nuair rosraiged [read *no-s-riged*] in uair naib nosnimairced [read *do-s-n-immairced*] amal bolg ngobenn. La diuderc do fuire rosiapartha a beoile doa dib culadaib ⁊ doluid as for tir ar omon ⁊ asbert fria araid cia cuimacci [read *co-m-acci*]. is olcc do gne ol int ara acht nib [read *niba*] lia. berthi cotlud dit. la sodain danalaig int ara ina carpat ⁊ contuil. cein contuilsium teit int ara calleicc co gaotha ulath batar i nemain macha ⁊ inset [read *in-fét*] doaib imthechta in rig ⁊ a mbui fair. friscomarca(i)r doaib cia ri(g) nogebdais tara eisi ar nibud tara eisi ar nibud urusa ri co nainim i nemain. Ba si comairle gaoth nulad in ri do tuidecht dia tig ⁊ glanadh ara cinn o cach doescurslua(i)g arna beth druth na hoinmid ann arna toirbeitis a ainme [read *ainim*] ina inchaib ⁊ folcad faon do do gres arnach aiced [read *arnach acad*] a scath i nuisciu. dognith iarom a imcomet co leir co cend .vii. mbliadan [read *mbliadnae*] (ibid., 38, with Binchy's suggested emendations given in brackets).

64. Isbert friu meisi is tiugba olse (ibid., 39).

bly a mirror image of the warrior, specifically in his more frenzied aspect. Here is a monster that expands and contracts, like the traditional Irish hero in the heat of his battle fury.[65] What is more, the bellowslike monster later proves a ferocious opponent, almost as hard to kill as Fergus himself.

The hero king, having seen this nightmarish image of his own darker side in the lake that should be his but has been declared off limits, mirrors the mirror image. His face grows distorted, the mouth stretching out like the monster itself. Normally, a hero such as Cú Chulainn experiences *ríastrad* 'distortion' when sufficiently roused to arms, but such physical expansions and contractions threatening the closure of the body are temporary, brought to an end by the closure imposed on heroic energy by the "body" of social relationships, which are threatened as well as protected by the warrior caught up in his distortion. Yet in the case of poor Fergus, who has confronted such a powerful alter ego image, the condition sticks and therefore makes him subject to satire, the verbal mirror that now can be held up to him at any time by those who want to disrupt the status quo for their own ends. It is no doubt significant that Fergus sees his reflection in the water, the element in which he encountered the overwhelming image of himself in the first place, as the climax to an exchange of insults. The revelation comes as the confirmation of cutting comments received from a slave, someone on the margin of society, the zone where satirists lurk. Fergus is in fact as marginal as the slave. The defect in his public image, once spoken of aloud, invalidates his kingship and distances him from the center of social power.

It is the charioteer who first encounters this new, revealed Fergus and whom the hero asks to shed light on his appearance. The *arae* is handed the opportunity to satirize, to point out the inadequacies of his chariot companion, but of course he does not do so, except in a very gentle and ambiguous way. His tact is a tribute to his loyalty, but it also catapults him into the inner circles of authority within Ulster society. The charioteer becomes, after Fergus falls asleep, a member of the council of elders, announcing the crisis to them and urging them to decide how to handle it. Here, as in the passage from the *Audacht Morainn* quoted earlier, the figure of the charioteer is intimately associated with the business of kingship, although in neither case is there any question of his taking on a king's responsibilities. The charioteer only carries and manipulates an image of the ideal king, or a saddening image of the king as he really is. Perhaps needless to say, this expressive function can be carried out only if the *arae* remains distinct from the king. The charioteer is a *sign* of the king, or kingship, or a producer of signs that represent kingship, but not the king himself.

---

65. On the distortions experienced by heroic warriors in Irish tradition, see J. Nagy 1983a, 40; and Henry 1982.

Semiotics in the Chariot

In the same way, Lóeg, Cú Chulainn's charioteer, is himself a sign, or generates signs (sometimes satirical) of his heroic passenger. This is the true significance and power of the charioteer. He controls the "message" the hero conveys, just as he conveys messages relayed to or about him, and he is in a position to manipulate these communications. The underwater monster, by contrast, functioning as an evil mirror image of Fergus's charioteer, is both like the hero and capable of distorting the heroic message, fatefully changing Fergus's appearance into a more accurate reflection of his sinister martial side.

Although Lóeg has no role in the story of the demise of Condla, in which the dark side of Cú Chulainn's heroism is revealed, the charioteer's importance in the account of the death of Fer Diad ties him closely to the function of the *gae bolga*, a sign of the hero which is communicated in a most deadly and morally dubious fashion. First, Lóeg is asked to goad Cú Chulainn with verbal praise and blame, modes of discourse through which the two warriors can be distinguished and hierarchically ordered. Having performed the service of setting Cú Chulainn apart from his opponent, Lóeg finally introduces the weapon that does literally to Fer Diad what Lóeg's satire did metaphorically to Cú Chulainn, that is, cut, pierce, and penetrate. The *arae* and the weapon he introduces, an object that only he and Cú Chulainn can handle, come in a violently decisive way between the twinned, equally matched warriors locked in fruitless combat.

It is not as if Lóeg undercuts the principle of "twinness" here. Rather, he substitutes his intimacy with Cú Chulainn for that between the hero and his foster brother, a relationship that has become unworkable within the network of alliances that has evolved in the story. Lóeg in this manner rescues Cú Chulainn, despite or perhaps even by means of his "dark" or "demonic" and satirical mirror image. The charioteer not only passes on to the young man the knowledge he needs to survive beyond the boundaries of his society, whether outside Ulster or even outside this world, but also gives the hero the necessary "push" to make the difficult decisions that establish his adult identity. This praise and blame can unleash powers, such as those embodied in the *gae bolga* or in the wild challenge to Emain Macha at the end of the "boyhood deeds" chariot ride, which can explode existing social relationships and assumptions and even the ethos the hero embodies. For explicitly in the slaying of Fer Diad and implicitly in that of Condla, Cú Chulainn loses a part of himself and of his past: "All was play and sport until I met with Fer Diad at the ford. I thought that beloved Fer Diad would live after me for ever."[66]

---

66. Trans. C. O'Rahilly 1976b, 208. Cluichi cách, caíne cách / co Fer Diad isin áth / indar limsa Fer dil Diad / is am diaid no biad co bráth (ibid., lines 3139–42).

In these encounters with the "other" who threatens to usurp the identity of the hero, the ultimate arbiter of difference is death. Simply put, one hero survives, and the other does not. In the *Táin*, I have noted, it is the charioteer who introduces the mortal weapon that separates the men from the boys. In the story of the death of Cú Chulainn, as recounted in both the Middle Irish and the Early Modern Irish versions,[67] we see that the charioteer himself can play the role of the other who must finally part from hero, alive or dead.

According to the Middle Irish version of the tale, Cú Chulainn's downfall in battle is brought about by means of an elaborate trap, through which he is gradually separated from his weapons, his charioteer, and his horses through the power of satire. Pairs of men engaged in combat are arranged on the battlefield, and as Cú Chulainn encounters them, a satirist (commissioned by the hero's enemies) goads him into separating the warring members of each pair. Every time he does so, by slaying both warriors, the satirist demands of him his spear, which Cú Chulainn finally surrenders each time by killing the satirist with it. The weapon obtained, it is launched at its owner, with the prophecy made by the attending magicians orchestrating the attack that the spear will kill a king. The victims, however, are first Lóeg, and then the Líath Macha, one of Cú Chulainn's chariot horses. When their prophecies are challenged, the magicians vindicate themselves by claiming that Lóeg was after all the king of charioteers, and the Líath Macha the king of horses.[68] In the end, Cú Chulainn's spear, obtained by his enemies a third time, finds its mark in its own master, and Cú Chulainn dies shortly thereafter.

Lóeg's death, while not the last in the series, signals the total breakdown of the teamwork that characterizes and distinguishes hero and charioteer. After he is deprived of his charioteer, Cú Chulainn declares, "I will be both warrior (*eirr*) and charioteer (*arae*) today."[69] On the equine front, when the Líath Macha is hit, it abandons the chariot harness and the other horse to return to the lake whence it first came to Cú Chulainn, but later the Líath Macha returns to defend its dying master against his enemies. According to the Early Modern Irish version, the Líath Macha is found afterward on the battlefield by the Ulster hero Conall Cernach, who will soon avenge the slaying of Cú Chulainn. He enjoins the horse to become *his* chariot horse, but the Líath Macha refuses, running away to the lake of its origin and drowning itself therein.[70] When the hero is finally struck with his own spear, his other horse, the Dub Sainglinn, also bolts and retires to *its* lake but, unlike the heroic Líath

---

67. The earlier extant version is contained in the twelfth-century Book of Leinster (Best and O'Brien 1956, lines 13762–14295; trans. in Tymoczko 1981, 38–83). The later version is edited in van Hamel 1933, 72–133 ("It is Early Modern Irish and dates, at its very best, from the fifteenth century," ibid., 69).

68. Best and O'Brien 1956, lines 13997–14001, 14023–26.

69. Conid and atbert Cu Chulaind bam eirrse 7 bam ara isind lathiusa indiu (ibid., lines 13979–80).

70. Van Hamel 1933, 117.

Macha, is not said to return for a last stand. Thus, just as *eirr* and *arae* are irrevocably separated from each other by death, so too the paths their horses take in the ensuing chaos diverge, and their destinations and identities, previously so inextricable, emerge as separate.

Still, Cú Chulainn does die in the end, as did Lóeg. In a most unusual development, however, the hero, according to the Middle Irish account, returns as a ghost to the women gathered around Emer, his wife, lamenting his death. He comes in a spectral chariot (*síaburcharpat*) and utters a *síaburchobra(e)* 'spectral speech' in which he prophesies the coming of Patrick.[71] Clearly he is still functioning as both warrior and charioteer, having absorbed both roles normally played by a pair, just as he bridges the gap between life and death and between the past, to which he belongs, and the future, which he predicts. Cú Chulainn, the dominant member of the pair *eirr* and *arae*, ends up playing the role of an "undead" bringer of information from the beyond, while Lóeg remains pointedly absent, having substituted for Cú Chulainn and thus bought time for his master in his last battle.

The diverging fates of Cú Chulainn and Lóeg in the Middle Irish version of the death tale contrast strikingly with those featured in the later version of the story. Here, Cú Chulainn is killed and stays dead, but Lóeg and one of the two horses, the Dub Sainglinn/Sailind, live to tell the tale:

> As for Emer, she would be on the rampart of Emain Macha every day looking out upon the field [waiting for Cú Chulainn to return] and listening for news [*scélaibh*]. Not long was the maiden thus when she saw a lone horseman coming over the plain of Emain towards her, and slowly and dejectedly did he approach. Fear overtook the queen at the sight, and she saw that it was Lóeg. "Truly," she said, "it is Lóeg and the Dub Sailind yonder, having left Cú Chulainn and the Líath Macha dead upon Mag Muirthemne under great quantities of gore and masses of blood; alas that is not Cú Chulainn and the Líath Macha who are approaching us."[72]

Once again, as in the *Serglige,* a woman laments the substitution of Lóeg for Cú Chulainn, but in this as in the previous case, it is precisely because it is possible to substitute the charioteer for the warrior that information is trans-

71. Best and O'Brien 1956, lines 14176–97. The *síaburchobra* is contrasted in the text with what is called the *béochobra Con Culaind* "living speech of, or about, Cú Chulainn," his self-eulogizing premonition (ibid., lines 13845–74).

72. Imthúsa Eimire uero, do bí sí ar foradhmúr na hEmhna gach laí ac feithim in muighe uaithe 7 ac éistecht re scélaibh. 7 ní cian do bí inn ingin in tan sin, co facaidh in t-áenmarcach tar mag na hEmhna dá hindsaighi, 7 is mall ainéscaidh táinic. Do ghabh crith 7 egla in ríghan aga faicsin, 7 do aithin gurob é Láegh do bí ann. "Is fír sin," arsi Emer, "is é Láegh súd 7 in Dúbh Sailind súd ar fágáil Con Culainn 7 in Liath Macha do fágbáil marbh ar Mag Muirthemne fo linntibh cró 7 fo cháebaibh fola, 7 dursain nach hé Cú Chulainn 7 in Liath Macha táinic d'ar n-indsaighi" (van Hamel 1933, 114–15).

mitted and the news of Cú Chulainn's death can be relayed to his loved ones, as well as posterity.

We should note, however, that Lóeg's function here as the survivor of a collapsed pair and the bringer of knowledge is not predicated on any supernatural ability to survive death or return from beyond the grave. He is very much the "mortal" member, who disappears from view in this text as soon as he returns to Emain Macha with the news. The same can be said of the Dub Sainglinn. It returns home, unlike the Líath Macha, who, as we have seen, stays on the battlefield only to reject a substitute master and destroy itself.

In sum, the charioteer in these tales about Cú Chulainn acts not only as a foil to the hero but also as his projection, through whom the hero can reconnoiter unfamiliar territory and establish links with strangers friendly and hostile. The *arae* can even serve as a mirror image that reflects the mortal or undesirable aspects of the hero, for he can satirize the hero in an especially acute way, holding up to him a most unflattering image of himself based on intimate knowledge. Moreover, in saga as in hagiography, the figure of the charioteer and the activity of charioteering itself serve as vehicles for posing a range of profound questions concerning similarity, differentiation, and convergence. How do narrative characters engaged in a common activity or aiming at a common goal keep, or fail to keep, their identities apart? How or where do dramatically contrasting characters or functions find common ground? And how are seemingly identical characters/functions to be differentiated? The capacity of the charioteer in narrative to frame such issues as well as mediate between opposed cultural forces most likely originates in the working, as well as perhaps the social, relationship that would hold between the one driving the chariot and the one being driven in it, not to mention the cooperation and coordination required of the horses drawing the chariot. Needless to say, the charioteer could continue to operate on a symbolic level in the realm of narrative even after real chariots and charioteering ceased to be realities of everyday life.[73]

Indo-European Twins

The usefulness of the figure of the charioteer as a means of exploring the complementarity of the categories of "similar" and "different" comes into

73. The mixture of hierarchy and familiarity in the working relationship between Irish hero and charioteer, including details such as Cú Chulainn's calling Lóeg *popa* '(foster) daddy', and aspects of the relationship as it operates in Indian epic tradition are reviewed in Hiltebeitel 1982, 92–94; Mac Cana 1992, 87–88. Barry Raftery (1993) and James Mallory (1992, 147–51) present surveys of the rather nebulous historical background to the frequent references to chariots, charioteers, and chariot horses in early Irish heroic tale and hagiography. See also Greene 1972; Piggott 1986; Koch 1987, 257–62; and Ó Cróinín 1995, 49. In contrast to what can be ascertained concerning the British and continental Celts, there is in fact very little archaeological evidence for the existence of chariots in ancient Ireland.

play in other Indo-European traditions as well. Significantly, he is often one of twins, or on occasion, both twins are known for their charioteering skills or horsemanship. The divine Aśvinau of Vedic tradition as well as Castor and Polydeuces, the Dioscuri of Greek mythology, are characterized as chariot drivers and lovers of horses, or even as horselike themselves.[74] In one medieval Irish account, Emain Macha, the "capital" of the Ulster of heroic saga, is said to have been named after the twins of the supernatural woman Macha, who was forced to race against the king's chariot horses and gave birth after she won.[75]

Within the pair of fabled twins as displayed in Irish and other storytelling traditions worldwide, there is usually a dominant and a recessive member. The recessive one may be associated with plebeian activities in contrast to his more aristocratic brother or may be mortal, whereas the dominant other is immortal.[76] Such alternation reminds us, of course, of the relationship between charioteer and hero, who often appear twinlike, if not actual twins. This commingling of charioteering and dioscurism in Indo-European traditions is most likely a result of their mutual association with the paradoxical theme of similarity through difference or difference through similarity.

The seemingly requisite death of Patrick's charioteer in preparation for or in the wake of Patrick's elevation to his unique position of everlasting authority; the charioteer's marked attachment to his horses, evident in Muirchú's tale of the rainstorm; and his continually being simultaneously paired and contrasted with Patrick or some other character—all these attest to the bricolage of the hagiographic tradition, wherein the dioscuric myth and the mythological figure of the shadowy charioteer are recycled to express a very "contemporary" set of problems. In both the story of the original writing down of *senchas* and the hagiographic account of the death of Failge, Patrick and his charioteer are indistinguishable in the eyes of their enemies; yet, in other circumstances they are very clearly marked as separate. Even more intriguing is that

74. Ward 1968, 11–15; Frame 1978, 132–52.
75. The story and the possible identities of these mysterious twins are the subject of Bruford 1989.
76. Ward 1968, 20–24. See also Lyle 1985, 3–4, 9; J. Nagy 1987a, 19–24. At work in some of these instances of contrasting twins in traditional story is the intersection of two of the "Epic Laws of Folk Narrative" as formulated by the Danish folklorist Axel Olrik: "Further, we might observe that wherever two people appear in the same role, both are depicted as being small and weak. In this type of close association, two people can evade the Law of Contrast and become subjugated instead to the *Law of Twins* (*das Gesetz der Zwillinge*). The word "twins" must be taken here in a broad sense. It can mean real twins—a sibling pair—or simply two people who appear together in the same role. . . . If, however, the twins are elevated to major roles, then they will be subordinated to the Law of Contrast and, accordingly, will be pitted against one another. This may be illustrated by the myths of the Dioscuri. One is bright and one is gloomy; one immortal and the other mortal. They fight over the same woman and eventually kill each other" (trans. Jeanne P. Steager, Olrik 1965, 135–36). Olga Davidson (1994, 142–55) presents a case study of "dioscurism" in relationships between narrative figures who are not siblings.

Odrán is also brought into dioscuric relationships with those enemies, to whom he is actually related, as in the story of Failge, or with whom he shares common interests and ends. In the *Senchas Már,* Odrán and Núadu Derg, who wishes to lead the king's cavalry, both like horses, and both end up serving as Christlike sacrificial victims.

With his various connections, the charioteer emerges as a "twin" to Patrick and what he represents, and also to those who oppose Patrick in pre-Christian Irish society as it is hagiographically envisioned. As such, he is an impressive mediator figure, but he also poses something of a threat to the Patrician order in the way that he makes mediation too easy. There are, for example, associations between the figure of the charioteer and certain performance genres and information-gathering activities that the new culture insists are unacceptable. These include satire, which, as we recall, had to be removed from the poetic institution; keening, which the charioteer performs in Muirchú's account of the lost horses; and in the case of Lóeg, reporting on his travels in the otherworld.

The figure of the charioteer, while useful as a sign of continuity, nevertheless needs to be fine-tuned within the realm of saintly legend, and an element of discontinuity is introduced into his literary dossier. Hence he is sacrificed for the cause of saving Patrick's life, dying in the same kind of deceptive attack that Lóeg encourages Cú Chulainn to make and yet from which he temporarily protects Cú Chulainn in the story of the hero's death. The latter-day "literary" charioteer, meanwhile, must also die for the purpose of magnifying Patrick's sanctity and promoting the new Christian, literate culture. Very much the recessive twin, Odrán dies and stays dead, contained within his grave and, so to speak, in the pages of the *Senchas Már,* the writing of which is predicated on his death.

Finding the Bastard's Father

The potential damage the saint's charioteer could wreak as a point of entry for a sinister side of native culture is intimated in a story outside the Patrician hagiographic canon, in the Latin Life of Ailbe,[77] who, because he supposedly spread Christianity even before the arrival of Patrick, poses a threat to the monopolizing reputation of *the* missionary to the Irish. In fact, the dilemma featured in the story constitutes an implicit struggle for authority between Ailbe and the "newcomer" saint.

Patrick, at the beginning of the tale, is faced with an unpleasant problem. One of the holy women in his retinue has borne a child, and even Patrick

---

77. C. 30, Heist 1965, 125; c. 23, Plummer 1910, 1:55; translated in de Paor 1993, 235. The Life as preserved in the so-called Salamanca Manuscript (Heist 1965) is perhaps as early as 750–850 (Sharpe 1991, 390, 329). On the episode about to be discussed, see Sharpe 1989, 392.

cannot divine who the father is. The woman meanwhile refuses to cooperate with the saint in his search for the answer. There is only one person in Ireland, Patrick's angel tells him, that could find out, the senior saint Ailbe.

Here we have a classic shift in the saintly quest for authoritative information from angel to ancient, contrasting with the situation featured in the Tripartite Life, where Patrick's protracted dialogue with another ancient, Mochta of Louth, is rudely interrupted by an angel's interposing a letter between the interlocutors.[78] Ailbe is consulted, and he has all the men in Patrick's retinue summoned to one place, only to detect through his holy powers that one of Patrick's people is missing from the assembly, his charioteer (*auriga*), who lingers alone in the field. After the *auriga* is compelled to join the crowd, Ailbe proceeds to baptize the baby and orders it to walk over to its father. The miraculously walking infant ambles over to the charioteer and declares, "Hic est pater meus." The exposed *auriga* confesses, and the miracle redounds to Ailbe's credit.[79]

Aside from the instances in which the charioteer dies while Patrick triumphantly lives on, this is the only case in Patrician legendry in which this figure is so dramatically set apart from Patrick, with the saint at the center of an assembly of his chosen retinue, and the *auriga* having stayed behind by himself. Similar isolation of a member of the pair "charioteer and hero" has, in the stories concerning Cú Chulainn and Lóeg we have examined, potentially grave consequences, such as the isolations or even the slaying of one of them.

The *auriga* is apparently not punished for his transgression, but the kind of sin he has committed arouses Patrick to an unparalleled pitch of fury against a seduced woman in another story, having to do with Patrick's very own sister, which we shall examine later. It is as if Patrick were incapable of punishing the tricksterish charioteer himself. Although they are physically and morally separated in this episode, perhaps saint and *auriga* are still too "close," as hero and charioteer, a dioscuric pair, for Patrick himself to renounce his companion and sever the relationship.

Another aspect of the story may also help explain why the charioteer gets off so lightly. In coming to Ailbe and laying his problem at the elder saint's feet, Patrick is symbolically deferring to another saint's authority and acknowledging his own junior status. As the putative prime saint of the Irish, he makes such acknowledgments rarely (for example, in his *immacallam* with Mochta of Louth). There is another acknowledgment of seniority and lineage

---

78. See pp. 118–20.

79. This story is reminiscent of the account given in the ninth-century *Historia Brittonum* attributed to Nennius of how the attempt of the British king Vortigern and his corrupt daughter to embarrass the visiting Saint Germanus by accusing him of having sired a child by her, backfires: the infant, empowered by the saint, speaks and identifies Vortigern as his father by incest (c. 39).

in this episode as well: the infant, who moves and speaks by divine inspiration, identifies his father. This miracle, managed by the pre-Patrician saint and carried out by the wonder child, who has just been baptized into the Christian fold, helps to reincorporate the *auriga* into that fold instead of intensifying his isolation as the one accused. We are reminded here of the punishment of Núadu Derg, who, once he is identified as the wrongdoer and punished, is not expelled from but embraced by the communion of saints. Similarly, the figure of the miraculously speaking child brings to mind the poet Dubthach, who is also authorized by a saint to proclaim the truth in a criminal procedure and who delivers a keenly prescient verbal performance. Perhaps relevant in this regard is the well-established motif in Celtic legendary tradition of poets who spectacularly demonstrate their verbal skills while still in their infancy.[80]

The baby's act of addressing his father would seem to signal a rapprochement between a baptized new generation and a potentially disruptive anterior force, just as the junior Patrick's turning to the senior Ailbe for help with a problem seemingly brings together inconsistent views of the origins of Irish Christianity. The narrower question of who has precedence and authority, Ailbe or Patrick, is fused with the much wider dilemmas of evaluating good and bad behavior, collective and individual action, and older and younger traditions.

Doubtless, the hagiographers who display Patrick and other saints so prominently in chariots and with charioteers were as aware as we are of the traditional resonances of this tableau, and even of its anachronism. The saints of Ireland are the "new" heroes, who, like the "old" heroes, go about in chariots and have close relationships with their charioteers. If so, then casting the charioteer in the role of the embraced sinner who has broken the Christian moral code of chastity in a way that arguably harks back to "pagan" behavior, is as pointed a comment on the relationship between the past and the present as is casting the charioteer in the role of honored sacrificial victim in the story of the death of Odrán.

While the charioteer signals a troublesome past for the Christian reader, the Christological overtones make for an even more complex reading of the ubiquitous figure of the *auriga*. The child who is born under mysterious circumstances, without a father it would seem, becomes a source of edification for the doubting onlookers and a manifestation of divine grace. Surely "Hic est pater meus" echoes the Gospel account of the identification of Christ as *meus filius* by God the Father when the young man is baptized in the Jordan.

Of course, the figure of Christ mediates between the "distant" divine parent and humanity, which is alienated from God. Christ comes from and

---

80. For instance, poetic art personified, according to a Middle Irish text, comes into this world as a precociously speaking baby (Radner 1990, 172–77).

returns to the father and proclaims his intimate relationship with him. So too the wonder child of this story from the Life of Ailbe proceeds miraculously to his father, who had previously been obscured, and makes a public statement about him. This "product" of the new Patrician society, unsanctioned but innocent and baptized, reenacts the story of salvation, to the greater glory of that society. Once again, a family romance with a happy ending unfolds in the presence of the evangelizing Patrick.

Yet this story of the charioteer is to be found not in a life of Patrick but in the Life of Ailbe. What is more, the wonder child, while junior in status as Patrick is in comparison to Ailbe, receives his authority from the older saint, becoming his agent and a renewed manifestation of the old saint's power, in the same way that Dubthach is deputized by Patrick to speak on his behalf. Furthermore, the *auriga*, while a "father" like Ailbe, is Patrick's man, and he is the newcomer in the Christian assembly called by Ailbe, just as Patrick is the new missionary on the block already peopled by Ailbe and other pre-Patrician saints. Therefore, the proposition "Ailbe is to Patrick as the child is to the charioteer" holds true as much as does "Ailbe is to Patrick as the charioteer is to the child." It is precisely such simultaneous similarities and differences that the narrative devices of dioscurism and the figure of the charioteer serve to express. In this atmosphere of ambiguity, Patrick is separated from the bad egg within his retinue (the charioteer) and yet also even more inextricably bound up with him.[81]

A similar mixture of Patrician vindication and implication develops in a story about Saint Brigit (from the Old Irish Life of this Leinster figure) in which we find the same pattern that informs the story we have just examined.[82] Once again, the public determination of paternity, which is at the heart of this story pattern, is brought up in a narrative situation that deals with the touchy question of how Patrick interacts with saints whose own authorizations are potentially incompatible with his own.

A woman accuses Brón, a cleric in Patrick's retinue, of being the father of her child. Brón denies the charge. Patrick turns to Bishop Mel of Leinster for help in resolving the dispute, and Mel advises him to consult Brigit. She, however, will not perform miracles in his presence out of deference to his superiority, and so Mel arranges for Brigit to confer with Patrick's retinue in his absence. The saint turns to the *infans* and asks it to identify its father. The baby says it is not Brón but a deformed man lurking about the periphery of

81. This is not the only instance in which a "pre-Patrician" saint mediates between Patrick and an offender connected with horses. See the story of how the slayer of Patrick's horse was saved by Ciarán of Saigir, a native son who is said to have been deputized by Patrick to lay the groundwork for Patrick's own conversion efforts (cc. 3, 13, Plummer 1910, 1:218, 222; c. 8, Heist 1965, 349; cc. 2, 12, Plummer 1922:1, 103, 106; cc. 1, 10, ibid., 113, 117).
82. Ó hAodha 1987, 14–15. This macaronic Old Irish/Latin text is dated by its editor to the ninth century (ibid., xxiii–xxv).

the assembly.[83] Thus, the cleric is vindicated and Brigit's power spectacularly revealed to Patrick, albeit not in person.

The guilty party here is not described as Patrick's charioteer, but, like the *auriga* in the Life of Ailbe, he is keeping his distance from the assembly (as is Patrick, for a different reason). Once the miscreant is brought in and identified as the father, the cleric Brón, whose dishonor threatened the honor of Patrick himself, is vindicated. Patrick, however, is still left outside, framing as it were the whole miraculous performance, which could not have taken place with his witnessing it. Arguably, Patrick brings about the miracle by virtue of his marked absence. Thus Brigit's miracle serves to heighten Patrick's own authority as well her own, just as the secret father stands out all the more despite his nonattendance.

There is, then, at least a structural affinity between the roles played by Patrick and the figure of the father. If, furthermore, we compare this lecherous wrongdoer to the charioteer featured in the story from the Life of Ailbe, then his physical deformity takes on significance. He is, in other words, hard pressed to maintain a low profile in this or any other situation, try as he may.

Saint Brigit under or in Control?

Brigit's shyness is not only a way of expressing embarrassed deference or an incompatibility of her authority with Patrick's but also a strategy for preserving Brigit's authority from Patrician encroachment. It is important to appreciate the extent of Brigit's power and reputation among Irish women saints. Supposedly the sixth-century founder of a monastic foundation, Brigit is traditionally counted as one of the three great saints of Ireland, the other two being Patrick and Columba.[84] She and her monastery of Kildare present a striking alternative or even pose a threat to her male colleagues and their own ecclesiastical establishments.

What is more, the cult of Brigit is the most spectacular example of the transformations effected by the medieval Irish hagiographic tradition, whereby pre-Christian divinity or divine trait becomes Christian saint or typical saintly behavior. There are incontrovertible references in medieval Irish literature to a pre-Christian divinity Bríg or Brigit, who is obviously the inspiration

---

83. Quidam homo qui in extrema partae concili velut ultimus deformisque (ibid., 15). See Stokes 1890, 43 (the Middle Irish Life in the Book of Lismore), in which the culprit is said to be a "duine duthair deroil" "a base [?], insignificant man."

84. Richard Sharpe (1991, 14) and others have pointed out that it is most likely not coincidental that the four earliest saints' lives that have survived from Irish tradition (all of them seventh-century compositions) are those of Brigit, Patrick (two extant lives), and Columba. The ideological grouping of these saints derives in part from the delicate political balance among the three powerful monastic federations associated with them.

for much of the cult of Saint Brigit.[85] That medieval Irish literati were aware of the continuity behind the syncretistic figure of Brigit and the problems she posed as such is indicated by the discontinuities that map out her life as documented in hagiographic tradition.

Remarkably, the authority of Brigit, according to her early Irish Life, stems from a male's misreading or misapplication of sacred text. When Brigit went to Bishop Mel to receive the veil of a nun, he became so "intoxicated" with the sanctity in his presence that he read the ritual for ordaining a bishop over her.[86] Thus, Brigit is unique among Irish holy women in being a fully accredited bishop. The heady power that made her such an anomaly subverts "proper" reading (specifically, Mel's reading of the appropriate service) as well as male domination of the ecclesiastical hierarchy.[87]

Among Irish saints, Brigit is remarkably unliterary in her range of interests and miracle-working powers. Yet, a story from a Middle Irish Life of Brigit tells how she became the patroness of students or "sons of reading" (*meic léiginn*).[88] While tending her sheep, Brigit sees the scholar Ninnid running by and asks him to stop and pray for her. He says that he would be happy to, but that he is rushing to heaven, which will close if he is not there on time. Still, he will stay and pray for her, provided that she promises to pray for him, for her prayers, it is understood, will guarantee him entrance into heaven no matter when he gets there. By the power of Brigit's intercession, Ninnid predicts, thousands will be saved. The saint agrees, and they become fast friends, with Ninnid serving as Brigit's priest, ministering to her religious needs. She becomes the protectress of all similarly harried students of book-learning.

Scholar and woman saint clearly have something to offer each other, but what Brigit proposes and Ninnid accepts constitutes a curious deferral or even negation of the closure of death. It is through his learning, we assume, that Ninnid has ascertained the time of his death and salvation, to which he is hurrying when he meets Brigit. The saint's prayer affords Ninnid, and an indefinite number of other anxious souls, much more flexible access to heaven. It also gives him a lease on his clerical life, drawing Ninnid back from the grave *and* from the scholarship that had dictated his course of action. Thus, Brigit's patronage of students is not so much a reinforcement of the principles

---

85. On the uniqueness of Brigit among Irish saints, see Ó Riain 1995, 150–56. Bray 1992b is a study of some of the pre-Christian aspects of this figure, specifically the fire symbolism associated with the cult of Brigit. Stancliffe (1992, 98) proposes a complementarity between the figures of Brigit and Patrick in hagiographic tradition.
86. Ó hAodha 1978, 6; Stokes 1890, 40 (the Lismore Life).
87. It is significant that in the Tripartite Life a case involving Mel serves as a turning point in the history of the etiquette of ecclesiastical gender relations. Rumor spreads that Mel and his sister, who are cohabiting prayerfully, are in fact involved in an incestuous affair. When Patrick investigates, holy brother and sister vindicate their reputations by means of miracles, but Patrick nonetheless declares that, to avoid even the hint of scandal, henceforth all saintly men and women should live separately (Mulchrone 1939, lines 980–94).
88. Stokes 1890, 46–47.

of the literate culture through which they are being processed as a liberating alternative powerful enough to frame that culture or to open up the boundaries that it imposes upon itself and the culture at large.

In the account of Brigit's consecration as a bishop, the saint unwittingly "steals" a power, and a text, to which normally only men are entitled, and in the tale of her encounter with Ninnid, she offers life and a more flexible "reading" of fate to a scholar about to become an obituary notice. This usurpation of text-based male authority is reenacted yet again, albeit discreetly, when only she can solve a problem that threatens the integrity and purity of Patrick's retinue of clerics. Brigit's pointed threat to male control does not, however, go unchecked altogether. We already learn, for instance, in Cogitosus's Latin Life of Brigit, the earliest extant saint's life written in Ireland, that Brigit cannot actually exercise the powers of a bishop but leaves such matters to the holy man Conleth.[89] Similarly, though Ninnid puts his salvation in Brigit's hands, he becomes her spiritual guide and provider. Moreover, Brigit's miraculous outdoing of Patrick can be performed only in his absence, and in the service of Patrick's own interests.

It adds considerably to our understanding of the symbolism of charioteering to observe that the problem of fitting Brigit into a system of authority dominated by men of letters is contained on two separate hagiographic occasions within the space of a chariot. In one case, Brigit is the subordinate figure, if not actually the charioteer, in the vehicle, and in the other case, she is the "hero" who must be transported and guided.

One of these two episodes, which is already attested in a ninth-century source, takes place early in Brigit's saintly career.[90] Her father, fed up with her annoying penchant for giving away his possessions to those in need, takes her in his chariot to sell her to the king of Leinster as a slave. In the version of the story told in the later Middle Irish Life, the father specifically tells Brigit that she should not interpret his taking her in a chariot as homage to her; it is simply a necessary step in getting rid of her.[91] When he goes inside the king's residence, he gives his sword, a valuable heirloom, to Brigit for safekeeping, only to find upon his return, much to his ever-mounting chagrin, that she has given the sword away to a leper. The king of Leinster, meanwhile, decides that a person of such sanctity would make an inappropriate slave.

Brigit's father, who, not unlike Patrick's nemesis Miliucc, balks mightily at

89. There is no serviceable modern edition of Cogitosus's text, which is to be found in John Colgan's compilation *Triadis thaumaturgae* (Louvain, 1647), pp. 527–42; for more information about editions and commentary, see Lapidge and Sharpe 1985, 102. The text has been translated by Seán Connolly and Jean-Michel Picard (1987; see preface, c. 5 [p. 11] for the passage cited), and by Liam de Paor (1993, 207–24).

90. Ó hAodha 1978, 4 (from the Old Irish Life of Brigit).

91. Ní ar anoir ná ar charaidh duit dot-berur isin carput, acht is dod breith dot reic (Stokes 1890, 39). "It is not out of honor or friendship toward you that you are being taken in the chariot, but so that you may be transported to your sale."

his children's leanings toward the new order, does not succeed in keeping his prized possession within his chariot. Nor does he manage to dispose of the "problem" of Brigit by treating her as property that is his to keep or give away, even though she does stay inside his chariot throughout the episode, honored or not. Her donation of her father's sword to the leper is reminiscent of another instance of her generosity toward lepers, when she actually gives her own chariot to them.[92] At least her father still has the status symbol of the chariot to which he may return after he leaves the king's residence.

A more successful symbolic containment of Brigit within the space of a chariot occurs in a story in which she is brought under control not by her father but by the clergy. Furthermore, the means of control is to be found not in the chariot itself, which can prove to be an arena for unpredictable struggles for authority, but in the person of the charioteer. The story, attested in various early lives, begins with Brigit's accepting a dinner invitation issued by a Leinsterman who, as the saint soon divines, is still a pagan, although a good man.[93] She refuses his food as impure. Upon discovering Brigit's attitude, her host declares that, although in the past he had refused to convert for Patrick's sake, for hers he is willing to do so.

Brigit is delighted, but she is disappointed to find that there is no deacon in her company who can baptize the new convert. She sends word to Patrick, asking him to dispatch one of his deacons. He does so, giving her in addition a piece of advice, from one missionary to another. Henceforth her charioteer should always be a deacon, so that she will be prepared for this kind of situation.

In this story, Brigit again proves to be an alternative authority figure, achieving success where Patrick had encountered only failure.[94] Yet, as in the stories that detail her relations with Bishop Mel and the scholar Ninnid, it becomes clear that Brigit must still depend on male clerics, who help to maintain the balance between Brigitine and male, literary, Patrician authority. Specifically, the cleric whose job it is to facilitate the breakthroughs Brigit achieves is assigned to Brigit's chariot, serving the double function of driver and baptizer. His most important task, however, is to be a living sign of Patrick, controlling the course of Brigit's saintly activities both literally and metaphorically. The charioteering deacon becomes the go-between in the

---

92. Ó hAodha 1978, 12–13. Compare the miracle recorded in the Life of Áed mac Bricc, a saint who, as we shall see, is closely associated with Brigit (c. 14, Heist 1965, 172).

93. C. 40 of the so-called *Vita prima* (trans. in Connolly 1989, 23–24). See also the Old Irish Life (Ó hAodha 1978, 15); c. 43 of the *Vita quarta* (Sharpe 1991, 154–55, and see n. 79).

94. Brigit is not the only "difficult" woman to be encountered around a chariot in hagiography. In the Latin Life of Brendan of Clonfert, the young saint, left in the chariot to keep an eye on it by Erc, his holy mentor, meets a *puella regia* who asks him to let her come up onto the chariot and play with him. After she ignores his command to go away, Brendan strikes her with his whip, and she finally does leave. The eager young saint is punished by Erc for his harshness (c. 4, Heist 1965, 325–26; c. 5, Plummer 1910, 1:99–100).

delicate relationship between the two potentially competing saints.[95] This is a mediator who presumably will tilt toward the Patrician side of the continuum, but we have encountered ample evidence to suggest that charioteers are not always to be trusted, any more than signs remain firmly in the control of those generating them.

In Patrician legend, the charioteer can substitute for the saint himself. In Brigit's case, the charioteer is a substitute for someone else (Patrick or the male ecclesiastical culture he champions). What is more, his presence makes her status in her own chariot as ambiguous as it was years ago in the chariot of her father. In the Brigitine tradition the struggles over authority between male and female saint, between Patrician and non-Patrician groundings of Irish Christianity, and even between father and offspring, either take place within the actual space of a chariot or center on the figure of the charioteer, his multiform, or simply the other person in the chariot besides the dominating male in charge. Similarly, in the variants of the story of the murder of Patrick's charioteer as told in legal and hagiographic traditions, the assault on the saint's authority and his right to replace the old cultural order unleashes its fury on the charioteer. Yet, either before or after his death, the victimized driver demonstrates, alongside his twinlike affinity with the saint, an ambivalence toward his victimizer and his victimization, ranging in manifestation from an impressive willingness to forgive his killer and sacrifice himself to kinship ties with the opposition. In fact, the charioteer can himself manifest in his behavior the cultural forces that elude saintly control and must be brought to light and checked. The saint's *auriga* appears to play a role comparable to that of the mirrorlike charioteer in the Cú Chulainn story cycle. He is the saint's double, bringing out both the best and the worst in him and mediating between the saint and worlds that he himself will not or cannot contact.

Travels with Áed mac Bricc

Perhaps nowhere in hagiography do chariot and charioteer serve more dramatically to define saintly heroism and authority than in the Latin Life of

95. Perhaps a similar kind of rapprochement, or even domination, is achieved in a story told elliptically in Irish in the Book of Armagh, concerning Fíacc, the poet-bishop of Sletty and son of Dubthach (Bieler 1979, 178; see pp. 82, 89). Sechnall, one of Patrick's bishops, criticizes Patrick for owning a certain chariot. Patrick sends the chariot to Sechnall without a human charioteer but accompanied by angels. After three nights, Sechnall sends it on to an ecclesiastical colleague, Manchán, who in turn sends it to Fíacc. Fíacc refuses to accept it until the chariot circles his church three times and an angel-charioteer declares, "This is for you from Patrick, since he knows of your weakness" (Is duitsiu tucad ó Pátricc ó rufitir du lobri). The insistence of Patrick's offer (to a "weak" poet-cleric no less), the problematic ownership of the chariot, and its ultimate delivery to a Leinster church that was an outpost of the Armagh federation in Brigit's traditional territory—all suggest that the story concerns more than just Patrick's kindness to sickly clerics.

Áed mac Bricc, a saint of the southern Uí Néill and "one of the few Irish saints the basis of whose fame is personal and general, rather than monastic."[96] As we shall see, his Latin Life is rife with miracles that highlight his riding in a chariot and his control over his not-always-obedient charioteer.[97]

Áed's earliest attested and perhaps most important claim to fame is his intimate connection with Brigit. At least as early as the eighth century, Áed enjoyed the reputation of being a healer of headaches, and he is credited with having cured Brigit of this malady.[98] His intriguing method is described in a story told in Áed's Life.[99] A man comes to the saint complaining of his overwhelming headache, of which he asks Áed to relieve him. Áed explains that the only way he could cure the headache would be by taking it on himself. The man importunes him, and so Áed, in an outstanding display of compassion, assumes the headache himself and nurses it for the rest of his life. The Life goes on to note that Áed also cured Brigit of a bad headache and will do likewise today for those who pray to him.

Arguably, Áed's willingness to take the oppressive ills of others on himself is akin to the altrustic urge associated with the figure of the charioteer and the act of charioteering. This is precisely the kind of voluntary sacrifice Odrán makes for Patrick. For Áed to take up Brigit's burden is for him to become her replacement, to whom she is obliged, for it is thanks to him that she can continue to function unhampered as the Brigit of hagiographic tradition.

The one other extant story that links the two features the miraculous production of a book.[100] Áed comes to Brigit requesting a copy of the Gospels, for he has none. Brigit and he pray together, and Áed finds the desired book in her *sinus* (a Latin word that can mean either 'lap' or 'bosom'). In other episodes of the Life, as we shall see, it is Áed's *sinus* that is featured, where his charioteer is ordered to place his head lest he witness the miracles the saint is performing. The blessed *sinus,* here as elsewhere in medieval Irish hagiography, is one of the more active sites of the saint's authority; others place their heads there as a gesture acknowledging the saint's power and their willingness to "know" only as and what the saint wishes. The *sinus* is a productive zone, whence emerges knowledge that enlightens the devotee and

96. Kenney 1929, 393. Of Áed (whose name, common in Irish, means "fire"), Charles Plummer says: "Mythologically he seems to show traces, not perhaps very distinct, of a fire or solar deity or hero, and it is not out of harmony with this that he appears as a tamer of animals, a healer of disease, and a releaser of captives" (Plummer 1910, 1:xxviii; cf. McCone 1990, 165).
97. The recension preserved in the Salamanca Manuscript (Heist 1965, 167–81) appears to be the earliest extant version, perhaps composed as early as 750–850. See Sharpe 1991, 390, 329. It is the source of the narratives here examined unless otherwise noted.
98. The story is to be found in the Old Irish Life of Brigit (Ó hAodha 1978, 9–10) and the Latin Life of Áed, c. 17 (Heist 1965, 173). See also the episode in Brigit's *Vita prima*, c. 29 (trans. in Connolly 1989, 20). The eighth-century Reichenau Manuscript includes a hymn invoking the aid of Áed in curing a headache (Stokes 1890, 324; Kenney 1929, 393–94).
99. C. 17, Heist 1965, 173.
100. C. 21, ibid., 174.

authorizes the saint. In this case, the saints authorized are Brigit, who is otherwise only rarely associated with books and book learning, and Áed, who obtains the requisite book. Even more intriguing is that Brigit produces a book for someone who takes on her headache, just as Patrick and company produce a book, a memorial volume as it were, when Odrán takes on a death perhaps meant for Patrick.

With this seeming parallel between the Áed-Brigit and Odrán-Patrick relationships in mind, we can return with fresh insight to the story of Brigit's only other documented encounter with someone marked as a reader, namely, Ninnid the cleric. Here too the principle of transference is at work. Brigit asks a reader speeding toward salvation in heaven to defer that salvation in order to pray with and for her. He agrees on condition that she pray for him and others, thus spreading her own right to salvation among her devotees. As a result, Ninnid becomes Brigit's priestly confidant, her "mirror," who, as a representative of male literary culture, exerts control over her, although Brigit in return asserts her own authority, becoming the patroness of readers like Ninnid. It is notable in this regard that Brigit's deacon-charioteer is valuable to her not only because as a male he is authorized to baptize but also because as a reader he can proclaim the sacred texts that need to be read at the ceremony of baptism and other ritual occasions. And he can proclaim them better, presumably, than could Bishop Mel, whose misapplication of reading resulted in the productive problem that is Brigit.

Therefore, in the case of the female saint, the charioteer or his analogue reads on behalf of, or thanks to, the holy passenger in the chariot. In the case of Patrick and Odrán, it is the passenger and not the charioteer who is marked as the reader or writer. Even so, the saint's literary activity is predicated on the charioteer's sacrifice.

His request from Brigit notwithstanding, the Áed of the Life is hardly characterized as a bookish saint, on the order of Columba. Indeed, as the Life says, "while he may have been the teacher of multitudes, he himself, as the experts say, was not taught by literature or a teacher, but by the Spirit of God."[101] This statement comes directly after a story the hagiographer tells to illustrate his point that God always accompanied Áed. In this tale, the saint feels God's presence in, or perhaps under, his chariot (*currus*). As he is trying to cross a forest in the province of Leinster, Áed's vehicle is lifted up above the trees and flies across the wilderness.[102]

101. Qui dum plurimorum magister esset, ipse vero, ut periti dicunt, nec litteris nec magistro eruditus est, sed Spiritu Dei (c. 19, Heist 1965, 173). A similar characterization follows a story that shows Áed actually coming between a reader and his text. According to the variant accounts, Saints Cainnech and Brendan of Birr spot the young swineherd Áed's saintly potential when he interrupts them while one of them is writing a Gospel in a sylvan retreat, or while they are reading the Gospel under the trees, or while they are having a private conversation (cc. 2–3, ibid., 168; see Sharpe 1991, 316–17).
102. C. 19, Heist 1965, 173.

This is hardly the only instance of this particular miracle in the saint's Life. On another occasion, Áed, attempting to cross another impassable forest in his chariot, tells his charioteer to put his head in Áed's *sinus* and not to look up until he is told. When he hears the tops of trees hitting the chariot wheels, the *auriga*, overcome by curiosity, opens one eye just for a little while, and is suddenly blinded in that eye. Afterward, Áed chides the disobedient charioteer and restores sight to the blinded eye. Saint and charioteer arrive at their destination without any further difficulty.[103]

Here we have two remarkable demonstrations of what a saint can do with a chariot. It can become not only yet another sign of his saintly authority and power but also a vehicle for overcoming barriers of space and time. When it is so used in the Life of Áed, the saint must wrest the *currus* from the control of its driver and exert a control over the charioteer which pointedly subverts the normal business of charioteering. The *auriga* should not be in the chariot with his eyes closed, but he runs the risk, as do Columba's companions on occasion, of becoming privy to a special, almost private empowerment of the saint which is too strong to bear, "see," or communicate. The saint usurps the driver's role, in contrast to the Patrician charioteer who usurps the saint's role for a day, only to be sacrificed on his behalf. Áed, the saintly *auriga*, exercises an authority that is not to be seen, at least not by his charioteer, although it can be written up and proclaimed in the genre of the Life.

To be compared with the furtive insight afforded Áed's charioteer is the intimacy that develops between Patrick and his charioteer in the account of the miracle of the retrieval of the horses in Muirchú's Life. In both cases, a "Columban" limitation is imposed on the *auriga*, implicitly in the case of Patrick and explicitly in the case of Áed. This limitation constitutes another expression of saintly control. It is a variation on a theme also evident in the story of Odrán, where a charioteer is sacrificed; in Tírechán's story of the two graves, in which the saint refuses to answer his driver's question; and in the episode from the Life of Ailbe which features the miraculous revelation of the charioteer's secret crime.

God speeds the passage of time for Áed and yet also maintains the delicate thread of relationship between past and present, all by way of the chariot, in yet another story featuring the vehicle's aerial mode. Áed intuits that a wealthy man in the province of Munster, to whose spiritual needs Áed had promised to attend, is in his death throes. The saint hurries to reach the sick man's bedside before he expires. The trip in the chariot, however, proves

---

103. C. 36, ibid., 178. The charioteer is also told to cover his eyes in the bosom of the saint or the folds of his garment during the performance of a miracle in c. 42 (ibid., 179), and in the Latin Life of Crónán, c. 20 (ibid., 279). Compare the uses of Columba's *coim* 'cloak' in the story of his encounter with the poets at Druim Cet and in Ó Domhnaill's account of his meeting with Mongán (see p. 191). See also an incident in the Irish Life of Colmán mac Lúacháin (Meyer 1911a, 68).

difficult, for there is no level road through the forest. Áed orders his charioteer to put his head in the saint's bosom or lap (*sinus*), and the chariot is borne through the air in the hands of angels, all the way to the home of the devotee, who by this time has died, unbeknownst to Áed. The saint sends a boy to inquire whether he should come to the man, whom he assumes to be alive, or the man will come to him. The corpse is miraculously revived on the arrival of the messenger, and the man insists on going to Áed, since the saint must be tired after his arduous journey. Áed asks him the question that saints, as we have seen, sometimes pose to revenants: Does he want to stay alive or return to the heavenly reward whence he had been summoned back? The Munsterman chooses heaven. He receives communion from Áed and dies again.[104]

A marginal comment in the manuscript draws a connection between the miracle of the swift chariot and the miracle of the revived man: "As his chariot was lifted into the air, so too the dead man was revived."[105] Although the angelically driven chariot does not get Áed there in time to converse with the man before he dies the first time, the miracle establishes a momentum that reverses time and brings the dead back to life to speak with the living. The polite exchange that takes place after Áed arrives, a conversation in which it is decided that the revenant will come to the saint, not the saint to the revenant, reestablishes Áed as the magnetic center of attention and authority in the situation. It also reinforces the statement that, just as Áed's chariot can traverse space by virtue of his holy power, so the dead can walk to Áed.

Furthermore, the scenario of the extraordinary trip and arrival of a rider in a chariot, the news of which brings the sick or dead man at the terminus of the journey back to life, is quite reminiscent of what happens in the *Serglige Con Culainn*,[106] except that it is the charioteer himself who makes the trip and conveys his own news to his master, the ailing Cú Chulainn. In this episode from the life of Áed, however, the charioteer is once again, as in other chariot-related miracles involving this saint, pointedly deprived of an active role in the miracle of conveyance.

Saving the King's Horse

Áed's most spectacular performance as saintly charioteer comes about in response to an emergency on Áed's own turf in northern Leinster, which, as the story begins, stands in imminent danger of invasion by the king of Mun-

---

104. C. 11, Heist 1965, 170–71. In the version given in Plummer 1910, 1:37, c.7, the miraculous ride in the chariot is omitted.
105. Quomodo currus eius in aera est levatus, et quomodo mortuus est resu[s]ci[ta]tus (Heist 1965, 171 n. 1 on c. 11).
106. Cú Chulainn revives after receiving his charioteer's report on the otherworld (Dillon 1953, lines 229–32).

ster and his army.[107] The local king importunes Áed to talk with the Munstermen, who are his kinsmen on his mother's side. The saint sets out in his chariot. Though it loses a wheel, the chariot continues on its way without any difficulty.[108] At the army camp, Áed demands that the Munstermen cancel the invasion. The king's obstinate refusal to do so provokes a terrible demonstration of the power of Áed's wrath. The king's favorite counselor is struck dead, and his two favorite chariot horses are swallowed by the earth. The king, now willing to relent, sends a messenger after Áed. When the saint returns in his chariot, he drives it over the penitent king three times and predicts that as many times as the king allowed him to drive over him, so many of the future kings of Munster will be from his line. The king agrees to withdraw his forces but requests in return that Áed restore the counselor and the two horses. The saint does bring back the king's friend, who in classic revenant fashion has become a talking advertisement for the saint's authority and takes the king to task for his obstinacy. Of the two horses, however, Áed agrees to restore only one. The other remains underground, at a spot whence a spring erupts, producing what the text says is called in Irish Loch Gabra 'Lake of the Horse'.[109]

In this tale, a veritable showcase of the motifs associated with heroic and saintly chariots and charioteering, the dioscuric element is clear. As Áed sets out to encounter the invaders, one wheel is lost, but the chariot goes on. Later, the king loses his beloved counselor, and though he is not said to have been in a chariot at the time he was slain, the counselor is brought into association with the chariot horses, yet another pair subject to the saint's wrath. Within each set of animate "twins," human and animal, a rift develops in the wake of the saint's arrival and departure in a chariot. The counselor becomes an advocate of concession to the obdurate king, while one horse comes back to life and the other does not.

Yet it is precisely in their alienation that twins cease to be mere duplicates and become each other's complementary mirrors. The counselor, on being revived and thus marked as more than a simple mortal, serves to remind the king of his erstwhile uncooperative attitude toward the saint. Meanwhile, the horse that stays underneath signals the dark, destructive aspect of the saint's power, the positive aspect of which is signified by the other member of the team that has become Áed's sign.

Áed is no idle witness to the revalidation of these relationships. Rather, he is

---

107. C. 5, Plummer 1910, 1:36–37. See also cc. 8–9, Heist 1965, 169–70.
108. The same miracle, we note, is attributed to Brigit, as early as Cogitosus's Life, c. 17 (trans. Connolly and Picard 1987, 18), as well as, elsewhere in his Life, to Áed once again (c. 49, Heist 1965, 181).
109. Compare a miracle in the Latin Life of Laisrén, in which the saint raises two horses at the behest of a recalcitrant *regulus* 'king', who in turn is blinded and then healed by the saint (c. 16–17, Plummer 1910, 2:134–35).

very much in control of what happens to these various pairs. Indeed, Áed is the impresario who stages both their coupling and their separation. In the case of the wheels, he shows that he can proceed even with one of the pair missing, and in the cases of the animate couples, he reduces or separates them in order to impose his will. Moreover, as we will see again in some Patrician legends, the saint's running over his opponent with his chariot, as well as depriving his opponent of a team for pulling his own chariot, embody the quest for control of native institutions so characteristic of Irish hagiography. Such nearly lethal use of a chariot is all the more symbolically effective in that it is, as we shall see, most likely a pre-Christian narrative motif.

Running over the king and depriving him of one of his horses are not purely punitive acts, nor is the royal counselor, the king's "other half" who experiences an even closer brush with death, to be left dead. Because the king allows himself to be run over, the punishment leaves an impression for the future, securing the kingship for at least some of his descendants. Perhaps, as in the Patrician and Columban traditions, the saint's prophecy about the success or failure of the descendants of those with whom he is dealing is a way of demonstrating control over figures who are not altogether controllable in the present of the narrative. Furthermore, with the fulfillment of the penance of allowing a chariot to drive over him, the king lives to see a compromise arranged between him and the saint. There will be no war against Áed's people, but the counselor is returned and partial glory for the king's line is assured.

The king's mock death, his marking with the traces left by the saint's chariot, betokens a resilience that parallels the reversible fate suffered by his friend. As a result of these death-defying ordeals, the working relationship between society and the church and the continuation of a peaceful present into what seemed to be a troubled future are assured. Thus, also bearing in mind the prominence of the horse, the chariot, and the theme of revival or salvation, we are brought back to the outcome presented in the Prologue to the *Senchas Már*, where the would-be horseman, Núadu, who aspires to be the leader of cavalry, is executed after he has wreaked havoc near a chariot (the murder of the charioteer Odrán). Núadu's death, which is emphatically reinterpreted as salvation of the soul, leads to rapprochement and even textual certainty in the relationship between church and society. And yet, in both stories, a key player not only dies but stays conspicuously dead. In one account, it is the shadowy charioteer, and in the other it is a chariot horse, a victim whose consignment to a lake resonates with the fate of one or both of Cú Chulainn's horses in the tale of that hero's death.

If Patrick's lack of interest in Odrán's revival is part of a syndrome in Patrician legend of suppressing the figure of the charioteer in his capacity as a reference to the thornier or darker aspects of the transition from pagan past to Christian present, then what of the horse that remains underground, at a location that becomes a lake named after the horse? We should note that Áed's Life breaks its linguistic code in order to identify the place-name in Irish. As we have seen, such rupture in other Latin lives signals a breakthrough of the native voice into the Christian discourse of the text. Such mixing of codes in some cases highlights a synthesis of native and Christian perspectives and in other cases marks a division between them which resists facile mediation. Surely in this case what is highlighted in the outcome of the story and yet stays buried and out of reach is the capacity of the horse (in Celtic and other Indo-European traditions) to represent sovereignty.[110] Those manifestations of kingly power that are unacceptable in a Christian society where saints and the literati who celebrate them lay claim to the highest authority are not so much undone as kept underfoot, like the chastised Munster king who survives the ordeal of Áed's chariot.

Retribution and the Charioteer

In this episode from the Life of Áed and in other narrative instances in which a twinlike partner literally or metaphorically "goes underground," the hagiographic tradition is exploiting a flexibility inherent in the dioscuric pattern, whereby twins demonstrate difference as well as similarity. If there is innovation, it is the freezing of this flexibility in time and space. One of the horses swallowed by the earth is left there, just as Patrick's charioteer is never resurrected and his good question about the justice of leaving the mismarked pagan condemned is never answered.

By splitting up pairs of twins and clearly defining their differences, Áed exerts control over kingship, including the powerful pagan authority of which the horse is a traditional sign. Significantly, Áed achieves this triumph in the absence of any reference to his charioteer. When the *auriga* is present in the Life, the lines of opposition tend to be more penetrable, as if the saint's driver were mediating by virtue of his mere presence. Distances evaporate, the dead come back to life, time proves less compelling than it first seemed, and even if the charioteer is told not to peek, he does, and he is not permanently punished.

Two episodes involving Áed's charioteer, each centered on a death, highlight the quality of mercy which the figure of the charioteer almost unwittingly introduces for discussion, as in Tírechán's tale of the two graves. In one of the stories from Áed's Life, one man slays another in proximity to the chariot and the *auriga* inside it.[111] Shocked at what he has witnessed, the charioteer, almost in imitation of his saintly master, curses the killer, declaring that his hand should fall off in punishment for the crime. The hand does fall

---

110. The equine dimension to Indo-European kingship is described in Puhvel 1987, 269–76.
111. C. 32, Heist 1965, 177.

off. Áed then congratulates the charioteer on what he has done. Not only has he brought divine vengeance down upon the wicked, but he has actually given the sinner the chance to save his soul, "for when man wishes to punish, God does not."[112] In fact, Áed intuits, God will give the murderer one more year of life to do penance.

This story has much in common with the account of how the *Senchas Már* came to be written. This time it is not the charioteer who is slain, but he could have become an unintended victim of the assault that took place near the chariot, just as Patrick might have been the victim of Núadu's spear cast. And the curse of Áed's charioteer and its aftermath become, as explained by the saint, a case study of how Christian mercy works. Similarly, the sacrifice of Odrán, Patrick's charioteer, echoes the salvific death of Christ, and his murder serves as a test of Christian equanimity. Furthermore, each story introduces a limitation or synecdoche of punishment. According to the worldview that Patrick supposedly brings to Ireland, execution can affect only the body, not the soul, which is saved and sent to heaven. Or in the Áed episode, it is the hand that receives the brunt of the punishment the entire body deserves, and less serious (corporeal) human punishment takes the place of far more serious (spiritual) divine punishment. Like his counterpart in the Patrician legend of the two graves, this charioteer, whose well-aimed curse holds up a punishing mirror to the offender as devastingly as satire, can intervene, albeit unwittingly, on behalf of those whom the saint-hero might just as soon destroy or ignore. And it becomes clear from stories such as those about the unveiling of the *auriga*'s libido and the nearly dire consequences of his insolent curiosity that the charioteer mediates so successfully between "saint" and "sinner" because he has much in common with both sinner and saintly master, whose authoritative voice or appearance he even borrows on occasion.

In the other story from the Life of Áed which centers on the theme of mercy in a matter concerning the charioteer, his authority as a sign of the saint, whom he represents as much as he does those whom the saint himself cannot, is vividly commemorated—almost.[113] Also noteworthy in this story is how the *auriga*'s significance and the tragic loss of his life dim the saint's own authority, as if, without his "twin," he were suddenly at a loss as to how to control the situation, until he receives the classic hagiographic mode of (re)authorization, the visit from an angel.

Nine marauders slay Áed's charioteer in Slige Assail in Meath. A saddened Áed goes away and is met by an angel who declares: "Had you not quickly left the scene of shed blood, the earth would have swallowed those nine men, and a fiery tower would have been kindled there, which would have remained unextinguished till Judgment Day [added in another version of the Life: "as a

---

112. Enim homo vult vindicare, Deus non vult (ibid.).
113. C. 40, Heist 1965, 178.

sign of vengeance"]. Even so, those nine savage men will die the worst possible death, nine days hence."[114] Perhaps significant here is the characterization of those who committed the crime as *viri crudeles* 'savage men'; the man who committed the murder so disrespectfully and dangerously close to Áed's chariot was similarly characterized.[115] These "savage men," furthermore, do the deed on a road associated in early Ireland with a famous near-victim of highway robbery, the traveler Assal, who found the road as he attempted to escape from *díbergaig* 'brigands' on horseback.[116] Despite their seemingly disruptive ways, reavers, as we will have other occasions to observe, have a special affinity with the king of Tara, in whose domain the charioteer is slaughtered (Meath).

And so we are brought back to the figure of Núadu, who commits an act of murder with the king's sanction, and aspires, we recall, to be one of Lóegaire's main military officers, the leader of his cavalry. The killing of Patrick's charioteer by this mysterious renegade "brother" of the king is accompanied by a spectacular cosmic display of divine wrath, an earthquake and the opening of hell. And had Áed "stuck with it" in the story of his charioteer's death, there would have been an even more dramatic and more lasting sign of punishment, and of the death of a saint's *auriga*, set in place, a tower of eternal flame to last till Judgment Day.[117]

The most curious aspect of this legend is that, what could have happened to mark the spot where the charioteer died did not happen after all. What does happen is a defeat of expectations, both ours and apparently those of the angel, who seems to be chiding Áed for having fled the scene of the crime. Once again, hagiography does not allow the figure of the charioteer to reach his full potential as a sign of the saint's authority, or his own, as if such completion would be somehow unacceptable or too hard to handle.

Even though the story ultimately steers away from the lastingly remarkable, it bears a strong resemblance to the other instance in the Life when the earth swallows up the living on Áed's behalf, namely, the account of the miracle of Loch Gabra. Both incidents take place in or near Meath, the putative center

---

114. Nisi cito veneris de loco illo sanguinis effussi, illos novem viros deglutisset terra, et turris igneus ibidem esset accensus, qui inextingibilis permaneret ad diem iudicii. Tamen morte pessima nona die peribunt illi novem viri crudeles (ibid.). The addition (in signum vindicte) is from c. 29, Plummer 1910, 1:43, in which telling of the story the victim is not specifically identified as Áed's charioteer.

115. C. 32, Heist 1965, 177.

116. The lore of Slige Assail is to be found in E. Gwynn 1913, 280; and Stokes 1894–95, 454. Intriguingly, Assal was heading on the eve of Samain for the Feast of Tara, a celebration and renewal of the kingship of Tara, and was traveling at night, although, we are told, it was dangerous to do so at this time of year on account of the ubiquity of supernatural beings. Here, as elsewhere in medieval Irish literature, brigands are associated with otherworldly forces, especially malevolent ones.

117. There is a somewhat similar eschatological connection between Patrick and *his* charioteer, whose grave Patrick promises to visit in the Last Days (see pp. 214–15).

of Ireland associated with the fabled kingship of Ireland, and both feature the motif of the saint's going away from what appears to be an unwinnable struggle, only to be informed that the struggle is hardly lost. In one of these stories, a royal horse, one of a pair, is left in the ground at the source of what is to become a lake. In the other, brigands slay a charioteer and might have been engulfed by the ground under a lasting display of fire emanating from the earth. The equine lake and the proposed tower of fire built on the remains of the *viri crudeles* and on the blood of Áed's *auriga* would thus appear to be homologous signs. And yet, in the past recorded in the Life, the miracle of Loch Gabra did happen, whereas the *turris igneus* 'fiery tower' remains unrealized. That which the lake contains and represents is compatible with its simultaneous function as a sign of saintly authority. Apparently, however, the fire of the would-be miracle would have fused together too much—saint, charioteer, and brigand—to work as a sign in the world of hagiography, where the resultant synthesis would have been unacceptable.

Driving with a Vengeance

So far, we have seen the saint's authority expressed both on behalf of and against his charioteer, and by means of or within the space of the chariot itself. Clearly, the motif of charioteering is a vehicle for the definition and exploration of saintly power and for the sorting out of the elements of society toward which the saint is sympathetic or antipathetic. As these processes unfold in the hagiographic literature, ambiguities and ambivalences abound, problems that the charioteering motif is traditionally equipped to control, what with its dioscuric implications. Sometimes the charioteer functions as a shadowy twin to both the saint himself and the opponents toward whom he heads in his chariot. In this dioscuric capacity, the *auriga* mediates between the cultural forces and epochs that must be bridged if the saint is to be in ideological charge, but as a result he can become overcharged with significance, particularly of the "old," traditional kind, and thus must be laid to rest and kept dormant. And so we find the driver under the tombstone, piously placed there by the grieving saint, who, his loss notwithstanding, can drive his own chariot.

As an added benefit for the audience of saints' lives, the death of the charioteer, usually presented as self-sacrifice, carries Christological overtones that, given the dioscuric reverberations, redound to the saint's credit as well. Yet what the saint suppresses or sees sacrificed in the person of the charioteer is also a part of his own authoritative public personality. For the saint, as a person and a cultural image, is native too (with the fascinating exception of Patrick), and the occasionally threatening knowledge wielded by the charioteer is a reflection of the saint's own. Alternatively, it is a vestige of the knowledge possessed by the figures who traditionally occupied the place in the chariot which the saint now claims as his. The loss of the *auriga* is an attempt to solve the conflict inherent in the figure of the saint as he or she develops in Irish Christianity.

That the vindictive saint riding forth in his chariot against, and occasionally over, enemies in a clearly polarized struggle of wills and authorities is to an extent fighting an internal battle as well, comes across vividly in two other episodes from Patrician hagiography, each of which features Patrick engaged in the violent act of driving the chariot over an offender who is submitting himself to the saint's mercy. Áed mac Bricc, perhaps the charioteering saint par excellence, drives the chariot over the repentant Munster king, for whom this dangerous ceremony of submission assures modest success for his line. In the Patrician legends, on the other hand, those who go under the chariot are figures closely associated with Patrick, and the driving over, instead of representing acquisition and the spread of the saint's control, serves to reestablish order within the saint's ranks. In each case, in fact, the saintly fold is increased, but against the wishes and outside the control of Patrick. In all three instances, therefore, driving over someone in a chariot is a means of letting someone else get away with something. It is the price to be paid for a compromise, and the victim is the scapegoat in a deal struck between the saint and forces or circumstances he cannot master.

In one of these Patrician tales featuring punitive driving, the saint actually turns against a member of his own family, in a bizarre distortion of the family-romance pattern of conversion and spiritual revival which recurs throughout seventh-century Patrician narrative. In this episode from the Tripartite Life, Patrick's sister Lupait, who has borne a child out of wedlock, is confronted by her angry brother, who repeatedly runs over her in his chariot, until she dies—but not before she persuades Patrick to spare the lives of her lover and their child. Patrick assents but curses them to lives of sickness. And so the saint's bastard nephew Áedán has the chance to grow up, becoming a saint in his own right.[118]

The tale brings to mind the tradition recorded outside Patrician hagiography, and discussed earlier in this chapter, in which Patrick's charioteer (absent from the story just told) is the guilty seducer. The *auriga*, however, is not said to be punished for his sin, whereas Lupait pays a high price for her indiscretion.

Patrick's sister, we recall, is featured in other episodes of Patrick's life. She is the first person he ever brought back to life, when they were still children, and

118. Mulchrone 1939, lines 2774–87 (noted as a possible example of foundation sacrifice in F. Byrne and Francis 1994, 12). The story would appear to be cast from the same hagiographic mold as the conception of Saint David in Welsh tradition. On the David legend and other instances of a story pattern featuring a fallen or raped nun and her holy child, see Bray 1985–86, 82–83.

the mark she bears on her forehead makes it possible for Patrick to recognize her on their putative wedding night.[119] This secret sign, whose significance only Patrick and his sister know, conveys the intimate relationship between the two, siblings and almost husband and wife. Their intimacy notwithstanding, they would be strangers to each other were it not for that sign, a reminder of Lupait's death and resurrection. What is more, Patrick of the Tripartite Life, alienated from the sinful Lupait, actually ends up destroying her with a harshness usually reserved for his bitterest enemies. Thus the relationship between Patrick and his sister features a paradoxical combination of familiarity, which allows for resurrection and later recognition, and alienation, which sets the stage for the antinomian prospect of Patrick married to his own sister and actually allows the realization of the grim scenario in the present story. As she alternates between the roles of beloved intimate and agent provocateur, Patrick's sister approximates in function the shadowy twin that haunts the Patrician lives. Does her resurrection early in life through the power of her brother then stand out as an apparent exception to the tendency for twinlike figures in Patrick's career to stay dead? Perhaps, but then this is the only revenant "managed" by the saint whom he not only brings back to life but also dispatches. Patrick undoes the resurrection he brought about, when Lupait, no longer representing Patrick's authority, acquires a lover and child who will develop his own saintly reputation.[120]

This last-mentioned detail is no mere genealogical coda but the net result of what happens in the story. Submitting to the chariot, Lupait is not only executed for her crime but wins a future for her offspring, sacrificing herself for the welfare of Colmán and Áedán. Against them, Patrick's wrath is moder-

---

119. See pp. 76–77.

120. In the Book of Armagh, we learn of another son of Patrick's sister, Lommán (Bieler 1979, 166, 168; mention is also made of other nephews, ibid., 168). Left behind by Patrick to guard the boat in which they had come to Ireland, Lommán, like a second-generation Patrick, proceeds up the river Boyne and encounters Foirtchernn, the son of a British woman and the grandson of Lóegaire. The young man is won over by Lommán when he comes upon him reading the Gospel aloud, and Foirtchernn's mother, who arrives in search of her son, is delighted to meet a fellow Briton. Foirtchernn's father actually greets Lommán in British, revealing that his own mother (that is, Lóegaire's queen) was British as well, and embraces the new faith. Like the story of Patrick's attempt to meet with his old master, Miliucc, this legend frames the history of the introduction of Christianity in terms of nostalgia and reunion, albeit with a more successful outcome than the story of Miliucc. As in Patrick's encounter with the daughters of Lóegaire, the women in the hagiographic family romance play a vital role in opening the channel of communication between cultures, thereby saving their own souls and those of their menfolk, just as Lupait, however compromised, can persuade Patrick not to destroy her son. Telling details in the Lommán legend include the contrasting media and languages: Foirtchernn is impressed by Lommán's reading a text in a foreign language, but Foirtchernn's mother and his father, the latter by virtue of his having had a British mother, can actually converse with Lommán, in a tongue foreign to the Irish but familiar to the evangelizing saint and these women.

ated, although not only does he take life from the sister whom he rendered the living dead, but he reduces her lover and their child to a state of deathly life (perpetual illness).[121] So, her fall from grace notwithstanding, the figure of Patrick's sister falls in line with the heroic charioteer Odrán, the murderous Núadu, and even the tricksterish *auriga* of Saint Áed—all of whom "must" die, but through whom mercy and prolongation of life are granted to Patrick (in the case of Odrán), a sinner (in the case of Áed's charioteer), or even the native oral tradition altogether (in the case of Núadu). Lupait's death is the basis of a compromise by which lives are spared and a saint's future assured.[122]

Patrick's chariot ride over his own sister, then, is a case of turning the chariot against a "female" version of the charioteer, a figure who should reliably follow and reflect Patrick's authority but is implicated in other authorities that threaten the saint's. Lupait is also comparable to Brigit in her father's chariot, a female passenger in the male bandwagon who should be under control but finds a way to subvert it. Running over Lupait destroys her, but it does not stamp out her "line," which is in fact saved by her torture, just as the Leinster king's submission to Áed's chariot (another case of a man's faring better than a woman in the face of a saint's wrath) is turned into a partial blessing to be conferred on the miscreant's progeny. It is as if punishment by means of the chariot were a less permanently destructive course of action to take in a situation where some kind of punitive response is necessary. The act of driving over someone with a chariot, therefore, is less an expression of the rider's inability or unwillingness to extirpate a problematic figure or issue than it is of the victim/issue's durability. The immediate "problem" may be ground into the dust, but its implications live on, even productively. In this connection it is worthy of mention that, whereas Patrick is denied the saint's right to be buried at the center of his cult (Armagh), the remains of his fallen sister, some early sources say, were interred at Armagh, reinforcing the con-

---

121. Lupait's status as a sacrificial victim is perhaps echoed by her very name. *Lupait/lipait,* according to Early Modern Irish glossators, means "pig" or specifically "November bonham" (*banba samna*), and is used to designate the pig sacrificed on the eve of Saint Martin's Day, November 11 (*DIL,* s.v. *lupait*). Cf. F. Byrne and Francis 1994, 70.

122. A comparable story is told of the Leinster saint Molaisse of Lethglenn, whose sister is impregnated by one of the monks in Molaisse's community and offers to die in place of her lover. According to the early Irish text in which this tale told, she is saved from hell by the prayers of the offending monk. In a curious parallel to the story of Patrick and the two graves, the deceased sister's grave raises the issue of saintly perspicacity and the confusion of "pagan" and "Christian." Molaisse does not see, or refuses to acknowledge the existence of, the angels commuting to and from his sister's grave. When the visiting saint Fursa notices them and asks who is buried there, Molaisse claims it is an "idol" (*ídal*) and a "demon of a nun" (*demon caillige*). Were it not for Fursa's intervention, Molaisse's misreading of her grave, like Patrick's ignoring of the cross, would have gone unchallenged (Pokorny 1913).

nection of this church with its putative founder.[123] If Patrick's body cannot be claimed, Lupait's body is the next best thing, increasing the number of resident Patrician memorabilia that assure the importance of Armagh in the times to come.

The other episode from Patrician hagiography which features the motif of penance by chariot employs a different cast of characters. Here too, however, a previous history must be taken into account if we are to appreciate the pathos of the situation. In fact, the Tripartite Life, our source for the story of Lupait's demise as well, lays out this history before telling the story of Patrick's exercise in chariot-borne fury.[124] In the course of his missionary circuit throughout Ireland, Patrick meets with a local king in northern Ulster. At the site of their encounter, the sound of an infant is heard emanating from the ground. The earth is dug up, and they find a grave smelling of wine and containing the body of a woman who had died of an illness. She had been brought over the sea to Ireland (presumably in slavery) and had not lived long enough to give birth to her child, who is still alive in her womb seven days after her death. "Bad is that" (*olc sin*), declares the king upon finding the wondrous survivor. "Let that be his name—Olcán," declares his druid, and Patrick baptizes the baby boy.[125] When the child grows up, Patrick installs him as bishop of the Dál Riata of Ulster.

We have already seen a pregnancy disrupted by death but brought to fruition by the miracle-working Patrick in the extended account of the conversion of the sons of Amolgaid, when the "bad" brother requests the return of his deceased sister along with her unborn child as his condition for becoming a Christian.[126] In that legend the woman is revived along with her child, and she becomes a powerfully convincing sign of Patrick's authority and the source of revelations about life beyond death. In the episode currently under discussion, only the child returns to the world of the living, and his emergence out of the grave is not explicitly attributed to the grace or strength of Patrick. In fact, it is the baby's own ability and will to survive as well as the power of his voice to resonate from the realm of the dead into that of the living which are crucial. Yet, although the baby's crying in the grave is what sets the story in motion, the wondrous event is ultimately characterized in olfactory terms, the smell of wine emanating from the grave, instead of aural terms. The unearthed infant, unlike those wondrous babies whom saints empower to speak about their paternity, has nothing to say. No precocious words identify or glorify the attendant saint. Furthermore, he is assigned a characterization

---

123. Both sources (the *Vita secunda* and the *Vita tertia*) state at the beginning of their accounts of the saint's life that Patrick has a sister named Lupita (Lupait), and that her remains are in Armagh (Bieler 1971, 51, 118).

124. Mulchrone 1939, lines 1869–79, 1900–36.

125. Tírechán tells us that Olcán was fostered by Patrick (c. 48.3, Bieler 1979, 160.32).

126. See pp. 74–76. Once again Patrick resurrects a pregnant woman.

that is hardly reassuring, and the king and his druid give him a name before Patrick baptizes him and brings the infant under his control. Olcán is "processed" into a social identity with a remarkable degree of cooperation among parties that in most other hagiographic instances would be polarized rather than harmonized under such circumstances. In the story of the revived mother and son, for example, the pagan son of Amolgaid who demanded the miracle is a hoarding king who ultimately listens to his druids rather than heed the power evinced in the miracle.

Therefore, Olcán constitutes another pointed deflection of generic expectations, like the charioteer whom Patrick will not revive. And in this case, the going against the grain of saintly miracle actually raises questions about the extent of Patrick's control over the "bad" situation and the remarkable "bad" person who emerges from it. Olcán does become a full-fledged member of Patrick's church, both controlled, as a protégé, and controlling, as a bishop, within the new culture. Yet, as we shall see, he is also a problem waiting to resurface.

Our text has more to say about Olcán. First, however, we are told of Patrick's difficulties in the Ulster kingdom of Dál nAraidi, caused by the resistance to the new religion offered by King Sárán ('Disgrace'), one of the twelve sons of Cóelbad. Once again the pattern of the dynastic family composed of scions who are divided in their response to Patrick recurs, for some of the brothers are receptive to the new order. This recurrence is another link between this sequence of events tied together by the figure of Olcán and the stories centering on the similarly conflicted sons of Amolgaid, which feature the miracle of the baby born out of the grave. After Sárán expels Patrick from land he had claimed for the church, the saint curses him, denying him both heaven and earth, and moves onto territory supplied him by Conlae, another, more sympathetic son of Cóelbad.

At this point Olcán reenters the story. Sárán, having engaged in *brat* 'plundering', activity associated as much with outlaws living on the margins of society as with tyrannical kings who wield their power unjustly, brings his captives through Bishop Olcán's territory in Dál Riata. The cleric takes pity on the tyrant's prizes, who are wailing pitifully, and asks Sárán to release them. The king refuses to do so unless Olcán guarantees him afterlife in heaven. The bishop responds that he cannot do so, since Patrick had explicitly denied heaven to Sárán. Refusing to accept Patrick's as the last word on the subject, Sárán presses his case, threatening to slay not only his captives but all the bishop's men (stating clearly, however, that he would not harm the bishop himself) and promising to be a scourge to all "adze-heads" (*tail-cinn*—that is, clerics) of whom the adze-head par excellence is Patrick himself. Olcán, faced with an impossible situation, relents and promises heaven to the devious king.

The compromised bishop then heads off to see his superior and patron

Patrick and submit himself to his mercy. The saint, having already heard about what his bishop has done, is furiously heading to meet Olcán himself. When they confront each other on the road, Patrick impulsively gives the order to his charioteer, "The chariot over him!" ("In carputt taris"). The role of the *arae* 'charioteer' in this story, however, is not to be a passive one. No, he says to Patrick, "I do not dare go over a bishop."[127]

Rebuffed, Patrick does not go so far as to take hold of the reins himself, but he does not give up altogether. He curses Olcán's establishment, proclaiming that it will never be of much account and instead will be racked by disaster, and so, the text hastens to add, it came to pass. The saint also declares that the remains of Olcán's ecclesiastical territory will be inherited by a "little boy" (*macc becc*) of Olcán's following (identified as one Mac Nisse) and by someone who has not yet been born, Senán of Inis Cathaig. Appearing to relent somewhat, Patrick finally says to Olcán, "Your reputation will be noble in heaven,"[128] seemingly acknowledging that Olcán retains a rightful claim to heaven, even if he did give it away to one markedly undeserving. The remark also hints of Patrick's own ambivalence toward Olcán, who, if nothing else, exhibited considerable compassion and bravery in standing up to Patrick's authority. The episode ends, however, with a statement muddying the impression that Olcán is bound for heaven. The text reads: "The sin of Sárán, then, was transferred upon the bishop Olcán at this point."[129]

Patrick's response to the embarrassing situation and the deflection of that response are reminiscent of what happens in Muirchú's account of Patrick's failed final encounter with his master Miliucc. There, too, Patrick sets out with a clear sense of how to settle a score and assert his authority but ends up helpless in the face of circumstances that take Miliucc out of Patrick's control. All the saint can do is curse Miliucc's descendants, making sure that the future does not reflect what has turned out to be an unchangeable past.

Similarly, in the story of Olcán's punishment, Patrick knows perfectly well how he wants to respond to this challenge from among his own flock, but he is prevented from seeing his revenge through. Patrick can direct his wrath only upon Olcán's monastery and his descendants, in one of the few instances when the saint's wishes are thwarted. Remarkably, it is not Olcán who resists. Unlike Miliucc, he humbly awaits Patrick's judgment. Rather, it is the saint's charioteer who refuses to obey Patrick's order. Once again his is the voice of mercy, as was Odrán's, raised on behalf of his own slayer. In this case, moreover, the charioteer also brings up the issue of propriety. For it is one thing to run over your sister and quite another to run over one of your bishops.

In the charioteer's objection we hear the same note of skepticism about Patrick's criteria for inclusion in and exclusion from the ranks of the saved

127. Ní lomur, ol int ára, a dul tar epscop (Mulchrone 1939, lines 1927–28).
128. Bid huasal du airliud hi nnim (ibid., line 1935).
129. Chin Sárán tra, iss ed rolaad for epscop Olcán sund (ibid., lines 1935–36).

which we heard in his unanswered question at the site of the two mismarked graves. And on whose behalf does the charioteer speak? Olcán, marked from birth as problematic ("evil" or "bad"), fuses in his person the two cultures that both clash and merge in the epic of Patrick's missionary adventures: torn alive from the dead, found by a king, named by a druid, and fostered by a saint, he is an ambiguous construct eliciting ambivalence, at least from the team of Patrick and the charioteer.

The hapless Olcán is a living sign of saintly power, which must, however, ultimately be discarded if the power it signifies is to be maintained. He is therefore a kindred spirit to the revived, helpful pagan whom Patrick sends back to hell but whom the charioteer would prefer to see saved. Even more remarkable is that Sárán forces Olcán to realize his full potential and usurp Patrick's authority, to become as it were a second Patrick, not just his projection, as any of Patrick's foster sons or bishops might be, but actually equipped with the power to overrule Patrick's word.

The senior saint thus rushes to the meeting with his fosterling in order to eliminate a rival or even substitute, with whom, seen in this light, the charioteer, another potential replacement for Patrick, shares a special bond. Driving over the competitor, who is both mirror and counterpoint to Patrick, as a way of asserting control over this threat from "below" is considerably complicated here by dissension within the space of the chariot "above," and this disagreement duplicates the breakdown in relationship between the saint in the chariot and his fosterling dangerously located outside it.

Thanks to the disobedience of the driver, Patrick does not destroy what he himself helped to revive and shape into his own image. Still, he does blight Olcán's future in a sad twist on the family romance in which Patrick plays a role disturbingly close to that of the restrictive parent Miliucc, who attempts to deny heaven to his "offspring." The blighting, however, is a matter of transference, inasmuch as Olcán's own person is not to be touched. And so this arrangement stands in direct contrast to the fate of Lupait, whose suffering of the ultimate punishment decreases the intensity of the punishment transferred onto her lover and child. This transference in the case of Olcán and his posterity, moreover, constitutes a passing-on even further of something that has already changed hands, namely, the "guilt" (*cin*) of Sárán, which, the text tells us, Olcán has taken on, either in granting Sárán heaven or by the will of Patrick. In either case, Olcán's assumption of a pagan's load of sin becomes a way of minimizing the undoing of Patrick's word. Olcán, then, did not really become Patrick in giving heaven to Sárán. Rather, he became Sárán himself, in an almost Christ-like, scapegoat fashion. We should recall that, before the text informs us of this transference of guilt, Patrick declares that Olcán, for all the wrong he has done him, will be praised in heaven.

In his apparent capacity for identifying with another and thereby taking over what is undesirable, Olcán resembles Áed mac Bricc, the collector of other people's headaches. Áed's penchant for absorbing physical malady is a specialization of the plays of transference that he and his charioteer act out. Similarly, Olcán's destiny as both receiver and conduit of fateful transference is realized before the wheels of a chariot occupied by a bickering team of saint and charioteer.

It would appear from this hagiographic example as well as from the account of the punishment of Patrick's sister that the motif of riding over the object of wrath has to do with ongoing relationships in need of modification. In each case an intimate, well-established relationship comes under strain that divides it into "before" and "after" phases. Even the Loch Gabra episode from the Life of Áed mac Bricc would seem to affirm this analysis of the motif, in that Áed is *returning* to the Leinster king, whom he has already met although hardly grown intimate with, when he punishes him with the chariot.

Yet another bit of background to the story of Olcán leads to a future condition, but this detail casts the events in an even more ambiguous light than did the information about Olcán's miraculous origins. The figure of Mac Nisse, the *macc becc* 'little boy' mentioned in Patrick's curse as the one who would inherit Olcán's territory, is mentioned in a somewhat garbled passage placed in the narrative immediately after the story that introduces Olcán.[130] All that is certain in this passage is that Mac Nisse was a student of Patrick's, that for a wrong that he did to the saint's sister Mac Nisse lost his hand (as the result of Patrick's curse?), and that the cairn where this happened is named after the hand. John Colgan, the seventeenth-century editor of the Tripartite Life, explains in a note on this passage that Mac Nisse's crime was seducing Patrick's sister or niece.[131] The punishment inflicted on Mac Nisse, the loss of his hand, evokes the story of Áed's charioteer, in which he saves a miscreant's soul by depriving him of a hand, as opposed to his life. The hand in both situations is that which is punished in synecdochic representation of its owner. Its loss makes possible a prolongation of life or even salvation of the soul. In the case of Mac Nisse, as in the case of the second horse, which is not unearthed by Áed, the scapegoat is memorialized down to the hagiographer's day in the form of a place-name and place that contain the sacrificed object.

Etarcomol in Overdrive

The linked accounts of Lupait's death and the near-execution by chariot of Olcán provide us with valuable insights into the Patrician myth not only because they constitute remarkably embarrassing breakdowns of the saint's authority but also because they are among the few instances in hagiography of

130. Et ro lég Macc Nisse Condiri a shalmu ic Pátraic, et indignátus sororem illius male[di]xit cédens fratrem tribus uicibus .uii. enim die trúncata est manus ipsius. Is de atá Cárn Lama (ibid., lines 1880–83).
131. Cited in Stokes 1887, 1:163 n. 1.

the outright borrowing of a specific narrative motif from the secular heroic tradition. For Patrick is not the only injured party to have used his chariot as a vehicle of revenge in medieval literature. We shall see that Fergus mac Róich, the foster father of Cú Chulainn, former king of the Ulstermen, and the most powerful ally of the Connacht queen Medb in her invasion of the province of Ulster as chronicled in the *Táin Bó Cúailnge,* lashes out in a similar way in one of the episodes of that famous text, at no less a figure than Cú Chulainn himself.

The parallel between this incident from saga and the two hagiographic episodes goes much deeper than the level of detail. The story from the *Táin,* like the two Patrician tales, is a study in negotiating the similarity and the difference between members of twinlike pairs. It is also a lesson in the difficulties involved when one member mediates between the other member and the world outside the potentially closed system formed by the pair, including those polarized realities between which the twins were destined to mediate in the first place.[132]

The story of Fergus's tantrum appears in the earliest extant recension of the *Táin.*[133] Medb, the leader of the forces invading Ulster, tells Fergus to visit Cú Chulainn, who is protecting the province, and propose an arrangement whereby Cú Chulainn will match his skills against one opponent at a time in a set duel, instead of attacking them helter-skelter as he has been up till now. The impetuous young warrior Etarcomol, a foster son of Medb and her husband Ailill, insists on accompanying Fergus so as to gain a glimpse of the much-talked-about enemy, despite the older warrior's misgivings. The arrival of these two is announced to Cú Chulainn by Lóeg, his charioteer, who sees them first. Lóeg says Fergus's sword, seemingly carried in its scabbard across his thighs, is as long as a boat's rudder,[134] but his master corrects him. The scabbard is empty, for the hero's sword had been spirited away by Ailill's charioteer.[135]

Fergus and Cú Chulainn engage in a meeting marked by harmony and generosity, despite the strain in their relationship brought about by the raid into Ulster and Fergus's role in it. After Fergus leaves the scene of their conference, an agreement having been concluded with Cú Chulainn, Etarcomol stays behind and taunts the hero, who warns him to depart lest he be too sorely tempted to violate the youth's protection as guaranteed by Fergus: "But for your being under his protection, I would have sent back your distended loins and your dismembered body behind your chariot to your en-

132. The mythic function of twin mediators, "weak" in comparison to other kinds of mediator figures, is a recurring theme in the anthropologist Claude Lévi-Strauss's studies of Native American narratives (see, for example, 1985).
133. C. O'Rahilly 1976b, lines 1287–1387, the version I follow unless otherwise indicated.
134. Ibid., line 1305.
135. Ibid., lines 1306–10.

campment."[136] Etarcomol does leave, but then, reflecting aloud to his charioteer, decides that he cannot wait until the next day to be the first to engage in single combat with Cú Chulainn, as he claims to have told Fergus he would be. He turns back and challenges Cú Chulainn, who continues to restrain himself, even to the point of shearing off the increasingly aggressive youth's clothes and then his hair as warnings to him. Etarcomol, however, cannot let go of his idée fixe, and finally in exasperation Cú Chulainn slices him in two.

When Fergus sees Etarcomol's chariot return with only the driver, he returns in fury to Cú Chulainn. "You think my club is short," he says to his fosterling.[137] And as if to prove that his proverbial club is not short, three times Fergus drives over Cú Chulainn, who, while protesting his innocence, submits meekly. The chastised Cú Chulainn then convinces Fergus of the correctness of his behavior by calling upon Etarcomol's charioteer to corroborate his story. "He said that he would not go away till he carried off my head or left his own head with me. Which would you prefer, Fergus my foster father?"[138] Forced to admit that Etarcomol's arrogance made what happened inevitable, Fergus disposes of the body in a remarkable way: "Then Fergus put a spanceling band through Etarcomol's heels and dragged him behind his own chariot to the camp. Whenever Etarcomol's body went over rocks, one half would part from the other; when the path was smooth, the two parts would come together again."[139] Medb is aghast at Fergus's treatment of her fosterling: "'That was not kind treatment for a young hound, Fergus,' said Medb. 'It is no source of annoyance to me,' said Fergus, 'that the mongrel should have waged battle with the great hound for whom he was no match.'"[140] Etarcomol is buried, and a monument with an *ogam* inscription is placed on his grave.

One of the several striking aspects of this story is the definitiveness with which the survivors, as well as the text of the *Táin* itself, dispose of the remains and the memory of Etarcomol, one of Cú Chulainn's many victims. He is the first to fall under the arranged terms that set the scene for the rest of the story until the Ulstermen recover from the debility that prevented them from joining the "Hound of Ulster" in the defense of their province. Even the language of the text reflects the starkness of the end of Etarcomol: "Cladar a

136. Trans. ibid., 162. Manipad do shnádud immorro, roptís do renga rigthi ⁊ do chet[h]ramain scaílte ricfaitís úaim dochom in dúnaid i ndegaid do charpait (ibid., lines 1330–31).

137. Trans. ibid., 163. Is garit mo lorg latt (ibid., line 1363).

138. Trans. ibid., 163. "Asrubairt," ol Cú Chulaind, "ní regad co rrucad mo chend-sa nó co fárcbad-som dano a chend lem-sa. Cia de bad assu lat-su, a popa Fhergus?" (ibid., lines 1373–75).

139. Trans. ibid., 163. Atnaig Fergus íarom id n-erchomail tria a dí pherid ⁊ berthi i ndead a c[h]arpait fadessin don dúnud. In tan ba réid, conrictís affrissi (ibid., lines 1378–80).

140. Trans. ibid., 163. "Ni boíd ind imbert moíthchulióin sin, a Fhergus," ol Medb. "Ní tocrád dam dano in at[h]echmatud," ol Fergus, "do glieid frisin coin móir nád n-argarad" (ibid., lines 1382–84).

fhert íarom. Sátir a lia. Scríbthair a ainm n-ogaim. Agair a gubae" ("His grave was then dug, his memorial stone fixed, his ogam inscription written, and his lamentation performed").[141] The prose is terse and unambiguous, unlike the teasing verbal pyrotechnics of his encounter with Cú Chulainn and its imme-diate aftermath. In all its other appearances in the text, ogam is written by Cú Chulainn, warning the invading forces not to proceed or challenging them.[142] In a way, Cú Chulainn is the author of Etarcomol's inscription as well, or at least he is certainly responsible for its being written. It constitutes yet another warning to those who would cross the boundaries, both territorial and behaviorial, guarded by this formidable warrior. The "markedness" of Etarcomol's death and its association with writing, specifically with writing as a termination of the initiative displayed by a troublesome figure, echo the proscriptive death of Patrick's charioteer. These alternately ignominious and glorious ends resonate with other forms of closure imposed on figures who represent failed mediation between pagan and Christian or whose mediation is tolerable only if it is contained within the grave or in writing, such as the texts brought together under the title of *Senchas Már*.

That the figure of Etarcomol himself is an attempt at mediation is indicated by his very name, composed of the prefixed preposition *eter* 'between' and the noun *comal* 'pact'. He is the issue of agreement between members of pairs engaged in tense games of alternating cooperation and antagonism. These pairs consist of Fergus and Medb, on whose behalf Fergus has agreed to protect the youth, and Fergus and Cú Chulainn. Also, Etarcomol enters his own pact, giving his word to Fergus that he will not make trouble during the conference with Cú Chulainn. And with an eye to the analogy between Fergus and Patrick, both of whom use their chariots as blunt instruments to reassert their authority, we note that Fergus's mission in this episode is to arrange for a new relationship, as workable and minimally destructive as can be managed between the invaders of Ulster and its designated protector. Etarcomol, his name notwithstanding, jeopardizes Fergus's and Cú Chu-lainn's mutually beneficial plan by "jumping the gun" and forcing Cú Chu-lainn into disregarding both the new terms of hostility and his private agreement with Fergus not to harm Etarcomol.

Cú Chulainn's remarkable restraint in the face of Etarcomol's taunts is a tribute to his good faith in this new era ushered into the story by Fergus and exercised in the display of forbearance toward Etarcomol. This embodied

141. Ibid., lines 1385–86.
142. Ibid., lines 225–26, 339–40, 827–29. There is an instance of ogam not inscribed by Cú Chulainn in the Book of Leinster recension in the section featuring the Ulster exiles' recollec-tion of Cú Chulainn's *macgnímrada* 'boyhood deeds'. The youthful Cú Chulainn reads a warning left by some enemies of Ulster. C. O'Rahilly 1967, lines 1070–73. I note in passing that in this recension's account of Etarcomol's demise, no mention is made of his burial or of the inscription (ibid., lines 1565–1695).

pact, however, works against his own fragile safekeeping and ends up fragmented. At first, Etarcomol is pared down to the bare essentials, his clothing and hair removed by Cú Chulainn's deftly diplomatic thrusts. Then he is finally split in two, like the two poised sides in the conflict themselves. Fortunately, as interpreted by both Cú Chulainn, who submits to Fergus's chariot, and Fergus, who listens to Etarcomol's charioteer, the incident of Etarcomol's death does not set back the relationships that have been established. Instead, it leads to an affirmation of those relationships and of the superiority and uniqueness of Cú Chulainn in comparison to all other warriors featured in the *Táin*. These are the facts that endure in the story. Ironically, Etarcomol in death proves a far better guarantee of them than he did in life. His skeptical probes, which threatened the delicate balances being achieved give way to the silent testimony of his inscribed tombstone.[143]

Yet, before arriving at the secure terminus of Etarcomol's grave, the reader is subjected to the bizarre scene of the halves of the cheeky warrior being dragged along by the chariot, at times coming together and at other times coming apart, depending upon the smoothness or the roughness of the ground. The image of Etarcomol's body in grisly flux evokes the precariousness of his status as a mediator and as a young man trying to prove himself, as well the precariousness of the relationships between Cú Chulainn and the invading forces, between Cú Chulainn and Fergus, and between Fergus and Medb. Etarcomol's body settles down only after the terse exchange between the angry and surprised foster mother and the warrior she holds responsible, whose authority has in Medb's eyes been brought into question as a result of his charge's death. Their dialogue, however, neatly resolves the discordant perceptions. Medb calls Etarcomol a *maethchuilén,* literally 'soft pup', leaving unspecified just what kind of "dog" or warrior Etarcomol was, beyond his youth. Fergus, on the other hand, derogates the dead young man as an *athechmatud* 'mutt' and compares him invidiously to the *cú mór* 'great

---

143. Arguably, the role of Etarcomol in the *Táin* and that of Archilochus, Nestor's son, in the funeral games episode of the *Iliad* are analogous, reflecting an underlying Indo-European thematic cluster. Both are brash young men whose lives and careers pivot on a wily act of circumvention in a chariot. Specifically, Antilochus executes a devious maneuver on the racecourse as he negotiates the turn marked by a *sēma* 'tombstone', 'turning point', as well as 'sign' more generally (G. Nagy 1992b). Andrew Ford has noted the impermanence or paradoxical indecipherability of this *sēma* as well as of most other purportedly imperishable memorial *sēmata* mentioned elsewhere in the poem, and he traces this skepticism concerning the permanence of signs to the performing poet's misgivings about the project of textualizing his performance—the production, as it were, of his own *sēma* (1992, 131–71). The conceit of disjunction between grave marker and who or what actually lies in the grave is to be found in our texts as well, for instance, in the Patrician legends discussed on pp. 124–28. The conceit as it operates in Irish tradition raises many of the same questions concerning the validity of writing/literature as a representation of the past as those that Ford adumbrates in Homeric discourse. In the Etarcomol episode as well, it is ironic that the first inscribed death is that of a hero whose behavior hardly amounts to a paradigm of heroic behavior for ages to come.

hound' whose standing as a warrior Etarcomol disputed unsuccessfully.[144] And so Cú Chulainn's rash challenger, the shadowy "twin" who stings him with satirical comment and aspires to be another Cú Chulainn, is thoroughly disposed of and dismissed, as one whose departure from life is emphatically inscribed both literally and metaphorically, as a "dog" that had metaphorical potential but lapsed into abject dog-ness.

While the usual cordiality of Fergus's and Cú Chulainn's dealings with each other is presumably restored by the end of this episode, the tension between foster son, who is fighting off an invasion of Ulster single-handedly, and foster father, who is assisting the invading forces, remains unsettled and unsettling. Similarly, the conflict between Cú Chulainn and the men of Ireland is channeled and formalized by way of the arrangement Fergus proposes and Cú Chulainn accepts, but in no way lessened in its intensity. Etarcomol himself, as his name indicates ("mutual agreement"), is a conduit of communication and behavior between the two greater warriors. Hence for Cú Chulainn to violate Etarcomol's protection is for him to risk slighting Fergus's honor in the same way that it was slighted by the Ulster king Conchobar when he brought about the death of Noísiu, yet another threatening youth whose safety Fergus had guaranteed.[145]

Etarcomol's usefulness is, however, not limited to representing Fergus to Cú Chulainn. His posthumous mistreatment at the hands of the chariot-driving Fergus, a process characterized by repetition, the body alternately splitting and coming together, is, after all, an extension or duplication of the repetitive punishment by chariot, being driven over three times, inflicted on Cú Chulainn. Of course, the Hound of Ulster, unlike Etarcomol, is alive at the time and survives. Another detail that brings together the figures of Cú Chulainn and his rival is the mode of chastisement Cú Chulainn employs as a last resort before he finally slays Etarcomol outright, namely, shaving off the insolent challenger's hair. Cú Chulainn undergoes the same kind of humiliation in another tale, concerning his encounter with perhaps his most formidable opponent, Cú Roí.[146] Therefore, Etarcomol mirrors the warriors on either side of the line of communication which he both represents and endangers.

That the Cú Chulainn–Fergus connection is key to the episode is also suggested by the sexual subtext that provides material for much of the explicit or implicit satire it contains. For Fergus, great warrior and male of renowned dimensions,[147] to be caught with only a wooden sword in his scabbard or, in

---

144. C. O'Rahilly 1976b, lines 1382–84.
145. The earlier literary telling of the story of Deirdriu, the consort of Conchobar, and her elopement with Noísiu was edited and translated in Hull 1949. Maria Tymoczko (1985–86, 155–58) analyzes the threat posed to Conchobar's kingship by Noísiu and his brothers.
146. Best 1905, 22.
147. Fergus's sexuality and his accomplishments as a progenitor are detailed in Ó hUiginn 1993, passim.

Cú Chulainn's words, with an "empty rudder" is to be exposed as highly vulnerable to sardonic quip and even stripped of the authority that would give pause to younger warriors such as Cú Chulainn. Indeed, when Fergus discovers what has happened to Etarcomol, he clearly reads Cú Chulainn's actions as based on an assumption that Fergus's power is not what it used to be, and in his words to this effect he arguably alludes to the not only hidden but stolen sign of his authority by which Cú Chulainn and his charioteer first identified him in the episode: "You think my club [*lorg*] is short." A *lorg* can be of wood or metal and so it can be taken as a reference to the "real" sword/fake, wooden sword in Fergus's sheath, as well as to his male member.

Given Etarcomol's role as a double projection, it is not surprising that the exchange of insults between Cú Chulainn and Etarcomol foreshadows this later sexually charged exchange between Cú Chulainn and Fergus. Of the defender of Ulster Etarcomol says, "You are merely a handsome youth with wooden weapons."[148] Thus Etarcomol plays Cú Chulainn to Cú Chulainn's Fergus, purporting to point out the inadequacy of his martial equipment and the hollowness of his reputation. In response, Cú Chulainn threatens to have Etarcomol's "distended loins" (*renga rigthi*) sent back along with his dissected body to the camp of the enemy.[149] This threat is later realized in Etarcomol's halving and the gruesome public joining and splitting of his parts in the track of a chariot. This emasculation enhances the virile reputation of Cú Chulainn, whose own *lorg* is clearly neither short nor wooden. On the other hand, riding over Cú Chulainn—a more stylized, less direct way to emasculate—cannot conceal the fact that Fergus's sword is indeed missing and that his reputation remains in jeopardy.

Saintly and Heroic Passengers

This sexual element is certainly present in the Patrician legends featuring punishment by chariot as well. Patrick drives over his sister Lupait because she has been unchaste, and Olcán, over whom Patrick nearly drives in the other legend, is *olc* because of the unusual circumstances of his birth, and his loss becomes the gain of Lupait's seducer, Mac Nisse. Sex generates problems and questions about the future of a "current" set of hierarchically arranged relationships in all these narrative instances. Who is more virile, the young Cú Chulainn or Fergus, his senior? Cú Chulainn or his coeval, Etarcomol? What is the status of the soul and cult of Patrick's sister as a "fallen woman," and what is the ecclesiastical status of her lover and the offspring of the illicit

148. Trans. C. O'Rahilly 1976b, 162. Maccáem tuchtach amne co ngaisciud do [fh]id (ibid., line 1327). He is saying that Cú Chulainn is a child, specifically, the boy Sétanta (not yet named Cú Chulainn), playing with toy weapons of wood as described in the "boyhood deeds" section of the *Táin* (ibid., lines 415–17).
149. Ibid., line 1330.

union? Can a child born of a dead woman become Patrick's bishop, and can the besmirched Mac Nisse fill the gap created by the cursing of Olcán? All these dilemmas have to do with generational competition and transition, fundamental issues that we find vividly highlighted in these stories.

Not to be overlooked in the Etarcomol episode is the pivotal role played by charioteers in the sequence of events leading to Fergus's displays of his chariot-borne authority. It is Lóeg who announces the arrival of Fergus and Etarcomol, although it is Cú Chulainn who informs the charioteer of the absence of Fergus's sword. Here and elsewhere, the hero tends to engage in one-upmanship with his charioteer in matters of knowledge and estimation.[150] On the other side of the confrontation, Fergus's embarrassingly absent weapon remains in the safekeeping of another charioteer, Ailill's. Etarcomol's own charioteer is the recipient of another kind of secret, his master's declaration of his intention to fight with Cú Chulainn, a plan of which Fergus remains unaware. It is thanks to this intimate knowledge that the charioteer is able to vindicate Cú Chulainn and verify his version of what happened. Finally, Fergus's assertions of seniority over the two younger warriors, driving over Cú Chulainn and dragging the remains of Etarcomol, are actually carried out by his charioteer. All these drivers, then, form the reference points within this story of an intragenerational conflict (between Cú Chulainn and Etarcomol) that is resolved in the course of being interwoven with an intergenerational conflict (between Cú Chulainn and Fergus) that refuses to go away.

Additionally, the charioteers of this story are the recipients or purveyors of information vital to the reputations of the warriors whom they transport, and masters of the "vehicles" of the warriors' reputation and authority. The *arae* 'charioteer', it would appear, provides a solid, discreet support for the *eirr* 'chariot warrior' and his social class as it asserts its hierarchical superiority and fends off both external and internal threats to its stability. The proposed etymologies of these key words, *arae* from *are-sed-s* 'the one who stays' and *eirr* from *en-ret-s* 'the one who attacks', reinforce our sense of the charioteer's role as "back-up" to his, more mobile, partner, as well as pivot for his wide-ranging activities.[151]

In his additional capacities as confidant and eyewitness, the *arae* becomes privy to secrets whose revelation could, and sometimes does, upset the delicate relations among warriors. Sometimes warriors attempt to suppress these embarrassments with the aid of their chariots and charioteers. Etarcomol is

---

150. For instance, in the story of how Cú Chulainn wooed his wife, Emer (*Tochmarc Emire*), Lóeg relies for his understanding of the riddling and punning exchange between Cú Chulainn and Emer on glosses supplied by Cú Chulainn (van Hamel 1933, 32–42). In the *Táin* Cú Chulainn estimates the number of soldiers in the invading army after Lóeg admits that he cannot (C. O'Rahilly 1976b, lines 316–29).

151. Campanile 1989.

precisely such an embarrassment, and courtesy of charioteers and their chariots, he is promptly and ignominiously disposed of. Similarly, the *auriga* of Patrician hagiography is privy to the saint's secrets and to his occasionally embarrassing private experiences, such as missing the cross on the way—not to mention the driver's being intimate with a woman in the saint's retinue. Remarkably, in the story of Olcán, Patrick's charioteer can even defy his master and refuse to participate in a ritual reassertion of the saint's authority. In refusing to drive the chariot over a bishop, the *auriga* suddenly takes center stage, demonstrating even more potentially threatening control over the situation than does Etarcomol's charioteer when he vindicates Cú Chulainn. In the latter case, the driver speaks only after Fergus has already subjected Cú Chulainn to the humiliation of being under a chariot.

And so we see that legends concerning some of the most serious challenges to Patrick's authority, such as the story of the assassination attempt on the saint which results in the death of Odrán or the stories of Patrick's punishment of his wayward sister and the errant bishop Olcán, not only prominently feature the saint's chariot and his charioteer but resemble events from heroic tales which similarly revolve around this mode of transportation, that is, the death of Lóeg in place of Cú Chulainn and Fergus's chastising of his seemingly disrespectful foster son. The parallelism, however, is limited, and the linking motif is differently realized in each hagiographic instance. Unlike Cú Chulainn, Patrick does not proceed to his death after that of his charioteer. Indeed, the slaying of Odrán signals the saving of Patrick's life and even, in the Prologue to the *Senchas Már,* to a new epoch for all Ireland. And whereas Fergus's ride over Cú Chulainn inflicts no serious harm, Patrick's punitive charioteering either brings death (Lupait's) or is halted before anything happens. What saves Olcán from the wheels of Patrick's chariot is the institutional authority of the church, which protects bishops even if they have done wrong, or the doctrine of mercy, or simply the disobedience of Patrick's charioteer.

If, as seems likely, the Patrician tales in these instances echo heroic saga, then the hagiographic tradition is revalidating the figure of Patrick and what he represents by reference to the "old" narrative tradition and the venerable figures featured in it. Yet the hagiographers also inscribe these tales with a difference that sets Patrick and his authority apart from secular tale.

These charioteering ties that bind the literary figures of Patrick, Cú Chulainn, and Fergus together make all the more suggestive the accounts to be found in medieval literature concerning the return from the dead of these two Ulster heroes, and of their productive encounters with Patrick himself (in the case of Cú Chulainn) or with Christian, literary "moderns" (in the case of Fergus). It is unlikely that the choice of these two particular Ulster figures to represent the heroic past is unconnected with the parallels Patrician legendry has constructed between their subject and these heroes. Our sense of a connection gains strength from the fact that in one of these accounts of revival, the dead hero returns by way of charioteering. As we have seen, this is a medium not only for reestablishing the authority and uniqueness of the "hero" riding in the chariot but also, at least in the Christian context, for communication and negotiation of competing authorities across boundaries of time and space.

The Prophetic Cú Chulainn

I have already noted that at the end of the earlier account of Cú Chulainn's death, he is said to have appeared after his slaying in a *síaburcharpat* 'spectral chariot' to the women who had tried to dissuade him from going forth to battle. He delivers to them a *síaburchobrae* 'spectral speech'.[152] In this poetic utterance, addressed apostrophically to Emain Macha, the capital of Ulster as the province is portrayed in heroic narrative, Cú Chulainn first prophesies the coming of Patrick, who will settle nearby at Armagh, close to Emain Macha. Then, he describes his existence as that of a vengeful, chariot-borne revenant: "I will attack many men like a murdered man, I will ride about a very long ride, I was crushed too soon."[153] Finally, he tells of the coming of Christ, who will save humankind, and of the ominous portents that will be made manifest during the last days of the world.[154]

Cú Chulainn's prophecies reinforce his own role as a precursor of Patrick, whom the hero describes as a protector of Ulster far more powerful and lasting than he himself ever was. His miraculous epiphany casts Cú Chulainn as a reflection of Christ himself, who, like the Ulster hero, dies young and then miraculously appears to his female devotees, revived by his own supernatural power.[155] In the performance of his síaburchobrae, the Ulster hero is transformed from a potential foreshadowing of the profoundly authoritative figures of Christian tradition-to-come into a self-conscious and verbal sign,

152. Best and O'Brien 1956, lines 14176–215. Trans. Tymoczko 1981, 67–72.
153. Trans. Tymoczko 1981, 68. Dofias mór fer mar fer mart. Forriadam réim n-erchían ar ba rom ron traethad (Best and O'Brien 1956, lines 14188–90).
154. Whatever the pre-Christian sources for the image of the epiphanic and prophetic Cú Chulainn in a supernatural chariot might have been, biblical parallels may have influenced its literary formation. Elijah, for example, is taken up to heaven in a fiery chariot (2 Kings 2:1–18), and the inspired chariot-borne apostle Philip converts his driver and then miraculously disappears (Acts 12).
155. See Matt. 28:1–10; Mark 16:1–11; Luke 23:55–24:11; John 20:11–18. Referring to the annalistic dating of Cú Chulainn's death to A.D. 2, John Kelleher has observed: "The choice of date—like 33 A.D. for the death of Conchobar—was clearly to associate these heroes with Christ. Thus the lives of Christ and Cú Chulainn overlap by one year—to which may be added that each has a life-span divisible by three; each has a divine father but is known as the son of a mortal father; each dies for his people, erect and pierced by a spear. By such manipulations the preeminence of the Táin was again asserted, but at the cost of blurring the other intended associations" (1971, 121–22). A caution against an overreading of Cú Chulainn as Christ is issued in Ó Cathasaigh 1993, 126–28.

transcending not only the void between death and life but also the void between "inside" and "outside" the narrative tradition. Cú Chulainn can now not only frame his own narrative tradition but articulate salvation history from the Christian perspective. It is as if the hero were now as informed by and about the literary, Christian ideology as are the literati who preserve the stories about him, such as this one, in a written form.

This remarkable heightening of Cú Chulainn's authority, which was always based on his ability to perceive, know, and communicate his perceptions, and the concomitant dissemination of his authoritative statement are predicated on his dying and coming back to life as a voice from the past and a presence that can still be as destructive as he was in life, and on his being ensconced in his chariot. The connection between the utterance and the chariot in this episode is brought out by the marked presence of the compound element *síabur* in the terms applied to the vehicle in and through which the revived Cú Chulainn appears (the síaburcharpat) and to the prophetic statement he makes to the women (síaburchobrae). The semantic field of *síabair/síabur* 'supernatural being, specter' overlaps considerably with those of other words denoting otherworldly creatures, such as *sírite* 'sprite', which is the designation other characters use to describe Cú Chulainn in narrative situations where he is being chided or taunted.[156] *Síabair* and *síabraid* 'distorts, transforms', furthermore, appear in our texts in reference to Cú Chulainn's famous battle fury, which renders him *ríastarthae* 'distorted, magically transformed'.[157] Hence *síabur* as used in Cú Chulainn's death tale refers specifically to the fundamental "nonhuman," ambiguous nature of this hero, said in some sources to be the son of the pagan god Lug, and in others denied an identity as an Ulsterman.[158] The division of Cú Chulainn's nature is intensified in death to the extent that his characteristically marginal or outsider status within his pre-Christian society becomes a vantage point closer to that of the latter-day, literary preservers of the tradition than to the vantage point of the tradition bearers depicted within the Ulster cycle of stories (that is, druids and poets).

If we conceptualize the encounter between the revenant Cú Chulainn and the Ulsterwomen as a dialogue, then his síaburchobrae can be viewed as a delayed response to the pleas of the women for the living Cú Chulainn to stay at home and so thwart the unfolding of his, and the narrative tradition's, destiny. And in the voice of the responding Cú Chulainn we hear of the

156. *DIL*, s.v. *síabair*, and *sírite* (b).
157. *DIL*, s.v. *síabair*, *síabraid*, *ríastartha(e)*, and *ríastraid;* and Sayers 1991a, 52–54. On *síabair* and *síabraid*, see also R. Breatnach 1990, 39.
158. C. O'Rahilly 1976b, line 2109. According to the *Táin* and other sources, Cú Chulainn and his father are not prey to the condition that characterizes the Ulstermen, their recurring *cess* 'debility' (ibid., lines 216–17). As Ó Cathasaigh (1993, 124) has pointed out, however, the *Táin* also contains a passage in which Cú Chulainn is identified as an Ulsterman (C. O'Rahilly 1976b, lines 421–22).

ongoing completion of past, unfinished business, the bloody vengeance the revenant claims to be pursuing. Even more so, we hear what the Ulsterwomen would have heard as an announcement of the future from the future to the past. In this respect the síaburchobrae forms a stark contrast to the various declarations of what *was* and of what would have been lost to posterity forever were it not for these declarations, voices from the past which punctuate the hagiographically mapped landscape of a present interested in its past. Cú Chulainn, now a specter from the future, enters the world of a narrative tradition that purports to present the past and smashes its basic assumptions with a powerful statement of what is and is not lasting. Significantly, the herald of this statement rides in a chariot. Moreover, the representative of the past now redesigned to speak for the future appears to be a chariot warrior alone in his chariot, referring pointedly in his síaburchobrae to the death and absence of his charioteering foil: "Lóeg, with his incitements, has died."[159]

The Spectral Chariot

The síaburcharpat, as Cú Chulainn's "time machine" for authoritative travel across temporal as well as spatial boundaries and as a platform for utterance which places his own authority within a modern ideological framework, is a conceit that reappears even more spectacularly in the Middle Irish text preserved in the earliest extant collection of vernacular Irish literature, the late eleventh-century manuscript Lebor na hUidre (Book of the dun cow). This text is the *Síaburcharpat Con Culainn* (The spectral chariot of Cú Chulainn).[160] Here, however, we find none of the ambiguity that casts a numinous haze on the returned Cú Chulainn in the coda to the story of his death. It is made absolutely clear in the *Síaburcharpat* that the chariot and the rider(s) in it are completely under the control of Patrick, who actually made the chariot and drives it, as it were, by remote control. Says the conjured Cú Chulainn to his latter-day interviewer: "It is Patrick who fashioned it so that it might be the best."[161]

159. Trans. Tymoczko 1981, 69. Atbath Loeg iruilled (Best and O'Brien 1956, line 14194).
160. This text has survived in three manuscripts, including the Lebor na hUidre (Best and Bergin 1929, lines 9221–565, with the ending supplied by the twelfth- or thirteenth-century Interpolator). For the other two extant versions, see Meyer's transcription of the text from MS. Egerton 88 collated with that preserved in another British Museum manuscript (1910c, 48–56). There is no twentieth-century edition/translation of this text in print. (See Crowe 1871; and Zimmer 1888 for earlier attempts.) Consequently, scholarly examinations of the text are few and far between. See, however, Corthals 1992 for the fascinating suggestion that the text contains a reference to its own oral recitation or performance. Thurneysen, who provides a summary, dates the text to no earlier than the tenth century (1921, 567–71). Unless otherwise indicated, cited passages are from the text preserved in the Lebor na hUidre.
161. Is Patraic ro cruthaigestar / conid hé as dech (Best and Bergin 1929, lines 9510–11).

Rarely do we see a revenant become such a thorough advocate for the saint that summoned him. But then, few revenants carry the narratological and ideological weight of the celebrated Cú Chulainn, who, as we have seen, can even be recast as a pagan version of what Christ or Patrick will be and do much more powerfully. In the *Siaburcharpat* the pre-figure actually meets and is then thoroughly appropriated by and made subject to the anticipated figure. If this is dialogue between the past and the present (and Cú Chulainn is more than once said in the text to be engaged in an *acallam*),[162] then the past as conveyed in the chariot knows precisely what the present wants to hear. And as we shall see, it delivers that information without rocking the chariot redesigned by saintly intent.

The opening scene is one we have witnessed before. Patrick is engaged in the tricky business of trying to persuade Lóegaire, the king of Ireland, to convert to the new religion. The monarch emphatically lays down a condition: "I will not believe in you or in your God until you awaken Cú Chulainn for me, complete with all the glamor ascribed to him in stories, so that I may see him and speak with him in my presence here—and then I will believe in you."[163] Previously, in Muirchú's Life of Patrick, we saw Lóegaire or his representatives take offense at competitive, threatening signs produced by Patrick, such as the Easter fire, or engage in a contest of signs to see whose are more lasting and more real. The druids are unable or unwilling to produce the requisite signs, their books, for testing by the elements against Patrick's, according to Lóegaire's proposal. It is at this point, we recall, that the balance of power between the contesting parties shifts, and Patrick becomes both the proposer of tests and, as before, the more authoritative contestant. In the ultimate test, as arranged by Patrick, clerics and druids try out the durability of their own bodies as signs.

Elsewhere we have seen that the meeting between Patrick and Lóegaire can be played out in the reverse order as well, a personal, life-threatening encounter followed by an indirect textual encounter. In the Prologue to the *Senchas Már*, the hostile sign of resistance to Patrick's new regime, the slaying of a sign or "stand-in" of Patrick, gives way to the merciful Christian embracing of native traditions as they are contained in written form. This shift in attitudes

---

The antecedent of *hé* may be Patrick instead of the chariot, in which case the translation should read: "so that he is the best."

An even more fearsome chariot, with a murderous, sword-wielding spectral driver inside it, is summoned by Saint Cainnech to destroy an uncooperative king. The saint, however, revives the king, who experiences a change of heart (c. 32, Heist 1965, 190; c. 27, Plummer 1910, 1:162–63).

162. Best and Bergin 1929, lines 9232, 9282, 9283 (*comaccallaim*), 9284, 9295; and lines 9226 and 9306, in which we see forms of *ad-gládathar*, the verbal noun of which is *acallam*.

163. Noco chretiubsa duitsiu nách do Dia nó coro dusce Coin Culaind damsa fó míadamla feib adfiadar i scelaib conid n-acur ⁊ conid n-arladur ar mo bélaib sund is air sain no cretiubsa duitsiu (ibid., lines 9224–27).

and signs, we recall, takes place by way of an oral performance that constitutes a breakthrough in representation, namely, the judgment of God delivered through the mouth and medium of a traditional poet.

Lóegaire's request to Patrick in the *Síaburcharpat* is a third variation on the pattern of direct encounter and indirect, ultimately literary representation which leads in Patrician legend to the Christianization of Irish tradition. In order to convince the king of Ireland of the authority of Christianity, the saint must reproduce, not simply represent, the native tradition, metonymically in the person of Cú Chulainn as he is recorded in the old stories.[164] Lóegaire's request entails in effect his own transformation into an authoritative witness to that tradition, a conduit of information from the past to the present, by virtue of Christianity. Lóegaire is to take the place of the revenant as the chronicler of a past that is made present for him, and him alone, inasmuch as he is to be the only one present at Cú Chulainn's first appearance:

A messenger came from God to Patrick and told him that they should go the next day onto the rampart of the rath of Tara, and that Cú Chulainn would come to them there. And so afterwards Lóegaire came to talk with Patrick after Cú Chulainn had appeared to Lóegaire in his chariot. Patrick asked Lóegaire, "Did anything appear to you?" "Something certainly did," responded Lóegaire.[165]

The meeting with Cú Chulainn is as intimate an experience for Lóegaire as Patrick's encounters with his angelic messengers are for him. The complementarity of these two kinds of meeting with two very different kinds of interlocutor is explicit in this passage. Furthermore, these two meetings or dialogues sustain and form the substance of yet a third, and the most important and most public of the three, the dialogue between Patrick and Lóegaire.

Whereas one of these dialogues is perfunctory (that between Patrick and his angel), the others are to be the stuff of story. It becomes clear, however, that introducing into the dialogue between the saint and Lóegaire the news of what went on between Lóegaire and Cú Chulainn is initially not an easy matter: "'Something certainly did appear to me,' said Lóegaire, 'but I do not

164. In making this demand, Lóegaire is in effect giving the saint the opportunity to do what Lóegaire's druid, according to an Old Irish legal tract, warns him Patrick will do: "It was Corc son of Lugaid who first bowed before him. He was in hostageship with Lóegaire. Lóegaire, then, refused Patrick on account of the druid Matha son of Umor. He, the druid, had prophesied to Lóegaire that Patrick would rob him of the living and the dead" (trans. McCone 1986a, 22). *Corc mac Luigdech cetaroslecht do bai side a ngiall la Laegaire. Frisbruig di Laegaire fri Patraic daig in druad Matha mac Umoir. Dorarngart-side in drai do Laegaire getad Padraig biu ⁊ marbu aire (CIH 527.26–28).*

165. *Tic techtaire iarom on Chomdid co Patraic co tairistis co arna bárach for dua na rátha .i. na Temrach ⁊ ticfad Cu Chulaind a ndochum and. Is iar sin iarom luid Lóegaire do acallaim Patraic iar taidbsin Con Culaind dó ina charput. Asbert Patraic fri Loegaire innut tarfás ní. Domarfhás immorro for Loegaire* (Best and Bergin 1929, lines 9229–33).

have the power to talk about it, unless you bless and consecrate my mouth.' 'I will not bless your mouth,' said Patrick, 'until I get my wish. I will, however, bless the air that comes out of your mouth so that you can relate the vision that was shown to you.'"[166] Noteworthy here is Patrick's curiosity about what happened to Lóegaire, his desire to hear him describe what he saw, which is as intense as, if not identical with, the desire of the audience or readership of the story itself. Equally noteworthy is Lóegaire's craftiness, which, however, is no greater than Patrick's. Having been put in the unique position of being able to represent the past from direct experience, the king requests that he be empowered and "cleared" by Patrick as a legitimate channel of information about the past, without committing himself to Patrick's new order.

In his request for authorization from Patrick, Lóegaire resembles the figure of Dubthach from the *Senchas Már,* yet another mediator who engages in dialogue with Patrick, but who is assigned to encounter the future, not the past that Lóegaire desires.[167] Dubthach is exceedingly reluctant to be empowered to speak about the way things should and will be, since he fears that as a result he will belong to no one's order and will be an outcast hated by Patrick or by God as well as by the men of Ireland. Lóegaire, by contrast, proves more than happy to talk of what he now knows firsthand, so long as he can remain uncommitted in the struggle between Christian and pagan.

Indeed, such a vivid demonstration of the past as Lóegaire has witnessed, even if it was brought about by the power of Patrick's religion, could conceivably serve as a countersign to the Christian future Patrick proposes. To give Lóegaire carte blanche to speak might have proven as counterproductive to Patrick's goals as the unthinkable act of lending his authoritative signs to Lóegaire's druids or ensuring that the druid's own signs hold up instead of dissolving before Patrick's ability to read others' signs correctly.

In this way the story of the spectral chariot arrives at an impasse. Lóegaire now has something we and Patrick very much want to know, but for the saint to validate him as a communicator of vital information and to play the role of audience would be to jeopardize the position of superiority from which Patrick deals with Lóegaire and the recalcitrant cultural forces he represents. For Lóegaire's spoken recollection of Cú Chulainn would be no guarantee of his fidelity to the new order.

The solution hit upon by the saint is ingenious, based on a distinction that

---

166. Domarfás immorro for Loegaire, 7 nim thá cumac día aisnéis mani sénasu 7 mani chosecra mo gin. Ni senubsa ol Patraic do ginsu conom raib mo ríar. arsenub immorro in n-aér dotháet as du ginsu co n-écis in tadbsin tarfás duit (ibid., lines 9233–37).
167. As McCone has pointed out, the situation in the *Síaburcharpat* in general distinctly resembles that presented in the Prologue to the *Senchas Már:* "The scheme of saint, helper-hero and king here essentially replicates that of saint (Patrick again), helper-poet (Dubthach) and king (Lóegaire again) in the legal sphere" (McCone 1990, 201).

will serve as yet another device in the literary Patrick's attempts to negotiate a working relationship between native and Christian culture. He refuses to sign Lóegaire's mouth but agrees to sign the air Lóegaire exhales as he speaks. Thus, it is the medium through which Lóegaire conveys his precious knowledge about his vision of the past, the air that carries his words, a medium that also physically passes forth from Lóegaire to his listener, which receives saintly empowerment—the speech, but not the speaker. What Lóegaire says, therefore, has a life, and a loyalty, apart from Lóegaire himself. The utterance is saved for posterity and becomes the public domain of the literary tradition that transmits the tale, without being at all open to interpretation as a token of Lóegaire's own salvation.

Hence the situation in this text presents all the sharper contrast with the Prologue to the *Senchas Már,* in which Patrick blesses Dubthach's own mouth, not just his utterance. This sanctification of the speaker as well as his speech suits the intentions of the author of the Prologue, who seeks to validate not only a text (the *Senchas Már*) but also the various higher classes of performers and bearers of cultural information. The author of the *Síaburcharpat,* as we shall see, is more interested in grabbing precious visions of the past for the written tradition, even if they come through unauthorized channels, and is not concerned with validating the tradition-bearers of old or their patrons, such as King Lóegaire.

With Patrick's blessing of the air, Lóegaire commences his account of what he saw. Straightaway we learn, to our surprise in light of what we had been told before, that the king was in fact not alone in his strange encounter. He mentions asking Benén, the Benignus of the Latin lives of Patrick, about the various phenomena that accompany the grand entrance of Cú Chulainn and Lóeg in their chariot. (Benén explains, for example, that the devastating wind emanates from hell, which had been opened to allow Cú Chulainn to leave.)[168] And so, Patrick's ubiquitous protégé, heir and alter ego acclaimed in hagiographic tradition, is, it turns out, present with Lóegaire, experiencing the vision, and even "present" in the speech that, by Patrick's fiat, has been effectively divorced from the speaker. Both for Lóegaire, in the experience itself, and for us the readers, in reading the speech-rendered-text, Benén proves a helpful glossator to whom one can turn for explanations of disorienting details. His presence makes possible yet another framing dialogue (like that between Lóegaire and Patrick), which makes sense of and puts into perspective the anticipated dialogue between Lóegaire and Cú Chulainn.

But, we may ask, does Benén really belong in this scene? And why was he not mentioned before in the story? First, we should note that his presence at this stage in Lóegaire's test of Patrick's authority parallels his introduction into the ultimate test of the saint's and the druids' powers as it is featured in

168. Best and Bergin 1929, lines 9238–44.

Muirchú's version of the story of Lóegaire's encounter with Patrick. There too, it is pointedly Benén and not Patrick who, rather surprisingly, enters with the representative of paganism into a situation in which, as in this case, the distinction between cultures becomes blurred as death is faced and overcome for the sake of saving souls. This situation is the test undergone in the house that is set on fire and from which Benén will emerge unscathed, even though he is dressed in a druid's mantle. Sending a substitute to represent him in the arena of religious contention is an indication of the strength of Patrick's hand in the game he is playing. The saint's choice also reflects the ubiquity afforded him by the transferable power that allows Benén not only to stand in for him but also ultimately to replace Patrick, to assume Patrick's mantle as his successor. Furthermore, in neither Muirchú's Life nor the *Siaburcharpat* does Benén encounter merely his counterpart, that is, a secondary player in the drama such as a servant or pupil on the other side. He meets the authentic article, the druidic archenemy in the one case, and, in the other, Cú Chulainn in the flesh.

As for why Benén's presence is noted only in Lóegaire's account of what happened and not before, the answer lies in the blessing Patrick gives the account and in its appropriation by the saint from the speaker. Benén's presence in it serves as a reminder of its authorization and confers an imprimatur on the account, standing as it does apart from Lóegaire. This function is complemented by Benén's service as glossator within the account.

The king gives Patrick an elaborate description of the chariot warrior as well as the chariot, charioteer, and two horses that complete the picture. Having come face to face with a vision of his traditional past, Lóegaire no longer needs the interpretations of Benén and can put the scene in his own words. This assertion of Lóegaire's own native powers of description and interpretation, even if they are displayed in speech that is no longer strictly Lóegaire's own, reaches a climax with his concluding gloss on the scene: "It *seems* to me that it was Cú Chulainn and his charioteer Lóeg that were there, along with the Dub Sainglenn and Líath Macha under the yoke of the chariot."[169]

That Lóegaire is withholding total credence in what he has seen and experi-

---

169. Dóich limsa bad hé Cu Chulaind ⁊ Lóeg a ara no beth and ⁊ Dub Sainglend ⁊ Liath Macha. no beth fón charpat (Best and Bergin 1929, lines 9278–80).

Cecile O'Rahilly includes this description among several in the Ulster cycle which form a type of "run." "These passages of semirhythmical and alliterative prose are found in what may be called 'identification scenes': a watcher describes the approach of a chariot-warrior who is identified for him by his interlocutor. . . . There can be little doubt that such passages had been memorised by the scribe and formed as it were part of his equipment" (1976a, 194). If, then, in the description of the spectral chariot we are dealing with a (preliterate or literary) traditional narrative genre (also exemplified by the description of Cú Chulainn and his chariot edited and translated by C. O'Rahilly in 1976a, a text that is preserved free-standing in the Book of Leinster), then Lóegaire is obtaining, and Patrick is granting, permission for the performance of something requiring more virtuosity than a straightforward personal-experience narrative.

enced becomes clear in his response to Patrick's attempt to force the issue of allegiance at the conclusion of Lóegaire's description:

> "And so do you believe in God, now that Cú Chulainn has come to speak with you?" "If it is Cú Chulainn I saw, it seems to me a short time that he spent conversing." "God is able, and if it is he [Cú Chulainn] who was over there, he will come back to talk with you."[170]

Patrick may have succeeded in divorcing Lóegaire's speech from Lóegaire, but the king in turn questions the validity of the evocation of the past arranged by Patrick and by God, and he challenges it sufficiently strongly to make even Patrick talk of it conditionally. For Lóegaire, what casts doubt on his vision experience is that it lacked a sufficiency of dialogue. This induced image of Cú Chulainn lacked his own speech, which, implicitly, would have demonstrated the truth or falsehood of what Lóegaire was seeing.

Seeing, then, is not believing. The vision must have a voice, one that is willing to converse. And for a voice to verify effectively, it cannot be stripped of the speaker, whose own, powerful identity needs to be maintained. Patrick's co-optation of the past is thus challenged. And so, when Cú Chulainn makes a return appearance through the power of God, Lóegaire is no longer accompanied by Benén alone but also by Patrick himself. Representation and appropriation of other voices will no longer do as means of converting hearts and minds. Patrick (and we, the readers) must be there for the vision, just as Lóegaire's narrative of the first appearance has called forth the text's own narrative of the second.

Of course, Lóegaire's reclaiming of the link between voice and speaker is hardly a defeat of the cultural forces Patrick espouses. For the more direct involvement of Patrick in the reception of the vision now to be accompanied by speech means the appropriation of the dialogue of voices itself. As a result of Patrick's meeting the ancient hero face to face, the narration no longer consists of a report delivered by a not altogether reliable witness but is carried on by the "voice" of the text itself. With Patrick present, the epochal dialogue becomes a three-way affair, our latter-day textual access to it assured by the presence of the saint. But without Patrick there to participate, who knows what Cú Chulainn and Lóegaire might have said to each other?

Upon reappearing this time, Cú Chulainn approaches Patrick, Lóegaire, and their respective companies. In his chariot with his charioteer, he performs his famous feats, which constitute his traditional calling card. His first words, however, are addressed to Patrick ("He went to speak with Patrick"),[171] and they form a brief poetic plea for his soul's salvation:

170. In creti Dia fodechtsa a Loegairi ol Patraic úair dodeochaid Cu Chulaind dot acallaim. Mása é Cu Chulaind atconnarc is garit limsa ro boí ic comaccallaim. Is folaid Dia ol Patraic mas éseom ro boí and dorega dot acallaimsiu afrithisi (Best and Bergin 1929, lines 9281–84).
171. Dolluid Cú Chulaind do acallaim Patraic (ibid., line 9295).

> I beseech you, holy Patrick,
> that I may follow you.
> Carry me with your believers
> to the Land(s) of the
> Living.[172]

The hero's reference to heaven as "the Land of the Living"(Tír na mBéo) generates some ambiguity, since that designation could serve as the name of a non-Christian otherworld.[173] The referent of Tír na mBéo, however, is absolutely clear in this context, as is the Christianized orientation of the once-proud Cú Chulainn himself. His orientation is immediately apparent to Lóegaire, who, as we shall see, harbors suspicions about the authenticity of what he is now not only seeing but also hearing. Perhaps the suspicions arise because the revenant-performer, without even being asked a question, is so totally dedicated and responsive to the new, saintly interlocutor in the three-way dialogue. In the words of Kim McCone, "Once again Cú Chulainn appears with all the outward trappings of glory, but his words soon reveal a broken man."[174]

Having given Patrick his due and having made a plea on his own soul's behalf, Cú Chulainn turns to Lóegaire and right away makes the point that, at least from Patrick's perspective, the whole reason for arranging this encounter is to convert Lóegaire:

"Believe in God and Saint Patrick, Lóegaire, lest a wave of earth cover you. For it is no specter [*síabair*] who has come to you, but Cú Chulainn mac Súaltaim.

> It is right for every strong person to have a world:
> Not hidden is the earth of either the silent or the champion;
> heaven is the earth of every saint;
> the drone of a specter . . .
> over the earth of every kind [of person] in turn do you drive."

Cú Chulainn was [then] silent, and Lóegaire did not speak.

"Who rides Brega? Who sits on its slopes? Who guards its fords? Who avenges its women? Who makes love to its girls?" [asked Cú Chulainn].

"What is it to me or to you to inquire about these things?" said Lóegaire.

[Cú Chulainn responds with another poem, in which he insists the person who he was in the past is now really there with Lóegaire, and ends with:]

172. Ateoch a nóem Patraic / itt arrad iteó. / romucca lat chretmecho / hi tírib na mbeó (ibid., lines 9297–9300). This stanza clearly forms a traditional poetic *dúnad* 'closure' with the last stanza of the longer poem Cú Chulainn is about to chant: Ateoch a nóemPatraic / it arrad nom theig / romfhuca lat chretmecho / is tir immaréid (ibid., lines 9532–35).
173. See Dumville 1976, 81–82. The multivocality of Celtic terms for the otherworld is the subject of Mac Cana 1976; and Sims-Williams 1990.
174. McCone 1990, 200.

"Believe in God and Patrick, Lóegaire, for it is no specter who has come to you, but Cú Chulainn mac Súaltaim."

"If it is Cú who is here, then tell us some of your great exploits."

"Well enough."[175]

In fact, the dead hero's warning to the king is in vain, for at the end of the story Lóegaire agrees to become a Christian only after he is actually overwhelmed by the wave of earth with which Cú Chulainn had threatened him. It is as if Lóegaire can never fully accept what the hero urges upon him, here or later in the dialogue. Cú Chulainn advocates, and Lóegaire resists, a religion that demands belief in the fundamental reality of what Lóegaire is privileged to see.

The original readers of the *Síaburcharpat* may well have sympathized with Lóegaire, not so much in his balking at becoming a Christian as in his hesitation in acknowledging the supernatural didact (who insists he is no *síabair*) as the Cú Chulainn of tradition. Although he may not be a "specter" in the sense of an apparition evoked by pagan magic, Cú Chulainn, as noted above, is indeed a *síabair* in a more specialized sense. Furthermore, the chariot in which Cú Chulainn is transported to Lóegaire is designated in the title of the text and in the story of the hero's death a *síaburcharpat*. Lóegaire would thus be quite justified in evaluating what he is hearing as the "drone of a specter."[176]

What the Cú Chulainn produced by Patrick is asking of Lóegaire goes beyond embracing Christianity or suspending normal expectations about life, death, and the "pastness" of the past. In being asked to believe in God, Patrick, and the validity of *this* Cú Chulainn, Lóegaire is expected to accept a new Cú Chulainn, less fantastic than the *síabair* of story. And he is being asked to accept yet another disjunction, not between speech and the speaker but between traditional image and "the real thing" and between the real passenger in the chariot and the spectral vehicle by which he is communicated to his audience.

Even if the chariot conveying Cú Chulainn to the reader is an artifice, it still refers to those realities of Lóegaire's life which form a bridge between his fin-

175. Creit do Dia 7 do náemPatraic a Loegairi ná túadaig tond talman torut ar ní síabrae rodatánic is Cú Chulaind mac Sóalta ar is bith cach rúanaid recht ná talam cach ciúin celar cach triúin talam cach naib nem ar is dord síabrai cen midisiu is bith cáich ar úair immáredisiu. Boí Cu Chulaind ina thost 7 ni arlasair Loegaire. Cía rét Brega a Loegairi cia suides a fantu. Cia aires a n-áthu. Cía aithet a mna. Cia charat a n-ingena. Ced duit-siu 7 damsa or Loegaire a n-airfaigidside. Ro boí tan a Loegairi bá messe immátheged immatimchellad immidamthellech. Ba mesi alau cúrad cartais glonnaib arddaib immananaigtís ro boí tan a Loegairi. Ba messi dothéged a margressa noruíned a márcongala. Bá messi in Cú Chulaind cathbúadach gnússachtach gesechtach rigderg roíglethan rogellach no bíd ar Maig maínech Murthemne. Creit do Día 7 do Phatraic a Loegairi ar ní siabrai dotánic acht Cu Chulaind mac Soalta. Mássa Chú fil and or Loegaire adfét dúnd día márgnímaib. Ba fír són a Loegairi, or Cu Chulaind (Best and Bergin 1929, lines 9301–17).

176. Dord síabrai (Best and Bergin 1929, line 9304).

de-siècle world of the pre-Christian past and the epic world of Cú Chulainn. The hero speaks with the king as one hero in a chariot to another. "Who rides over Brega [in Lóegaire's kingdom]?" is the risen hero's opening gambit for winning the trust, and the response, of the skeptical king. Lóegaire, however, rebuffs the revenant, questioning aloud the relevance of such topics: "What is it to you or to me to inquire about these things?" Lóegaire in effect questions the value of the small talk as a means for determining whether this is the real Cú Chulainn or not.

The hero's subsequent response to Lóegaire's request for an accounting of *margníma* 'great deeds' is met with a vote of no confidence: "If your deeds were as you describe, they were those of a [mere] chariot warrior, not of a Hound."[177] Undaunted, Cú Chulainn, struggling to obtain recognition of his heroism, goes on to define what his "dogness" is and isn't: "I wasn't just a dog for guarding calves. I was the dog that guarded Emain Macha."[178]

Curiously, after this formulation of how Cú Chulainn is a *cú* 'dog'—an element in his heroic composition as important as his being a *síabair* in battle and a hero in a chariot[179]—Lóegaire responds in a way that indicates not only that he is satisfied with the evidence he has heard but also that he has dropped the canine criterion for determining whether he is talking with the real Cú Chulainn or not. He is now happy to acknowledge the truth of what he is seeing and the authenticity of the being with whom he is speaking through the metaphor of charioteering: "If those deeds were indeed as you recounted them, then one would think them to be the deeds of a chariot warrior."[180]

The chariot metaphor now operating at full potential in the dialogue between living and dead, Cú Chulainn then drives home the point: "True . . . mine were indeed the feats of a chariot warrior. I *was* a chariot warrior. I was a charioteer. I was the driver of a big chariot."[181] At least in this self-aggrandizing rhetoric, the hero's charioteer has been obliterated. As I noted of the story of the death of Cú Chulainn, having to serve as his own charioteer signifies the impending glorious demise of the hero. Now, in death, Cú Chulainn is still claiming the role of charioteer for himself.

And yet the hero has not forgotten the contribution made by his erstwhile partner in heroics. Cú Chulainn ends his retrospective self-portrait: "I was

177. Manus fil samlaid na gnima sin feib adrímiu batár gníma erred latsu níptar gníma con (ibid., lines 9323–24).
178. Nipsa causa ingaire gamna. Basa cháusa ingaire Emna (ibid., lines 9328–29).
179. In a famous episode from the "boyhood deeds" section of the *Táin*, Cú Chulainn is given his name as a sign of his new role as the substitute "guard dog" of the smith Culann (C. O'Rahilly 1976b, lines 598–604).
180. Manus fil na gníma sain feib dodrímiseo bátár gníma erred latso (Best and Bergin 1929, lines 9330–31).
181. Bá fir són a Lóegairi ol Cu Chulaind bátar gníma erred limsa. Bása eirrsea. Bása aura. Bása ara carpait máir (ibid., lines 9331–33).

good when satirized. I was better when praised."[182] This is a compact formulation of how he, the hero in the chariot, is molded into the figure of tradition by expectations and assumptions that "drive" him, and by his goading charioteer, whose job, as we have seen, included critiquing the hero's performance. Cú Chulainn's statement would also seem to refer to the more hostile kind of pressure at work in the death tale, emanating from outside the chariot, which devious enemies attempt to upset with the threat of satire.

The image the chariot communicates, the Cú Chulainn of tradition, is a function of such public utterances of praise and blame. The only one in this scene to utter them, however, is Cú Chulainn himself, who is acting as both his own charioteer and his own eulogist. Lóeg, we recall, is putatively there, but he remains pointedly silent. Cú Chulainn, the revived performer and proselytizer, has taken away the reins of his charioteer, while the chariot itself has taken possession, as it were, of the process of representing the hero. And the chariot, we learn from Cú Chulainn, is no neutral device. It is owned and operated by Patrick, not simply a revived reality like the horses or Cú Chulainn himself:

> These horses, Lóegaire,
> run the course victoriously;
> it is Patrick who revived them,
> so that they may be fast [again].
> This chariot you see
> in front of the horses,
> it is Patrick who fashioned it
> so that it might be the best.[183]

The featured dialogue is therefore not only made possible by the chariot but located within the metaphor of the chariot, which frames the interlocutors. Cú Chulainn rides in a chariot, an extension of Patrick's power, and Cú Chulainn addresses Lóegaire as if he were a fellow chariot-borne warrior.

A threat Cú Chulainn employs in trying to sway Lóegaire features the punishment that was realized in the story of the charioteering Saint Áed's encounter with the recalcitrant Munster king and his counselor: "[Believe,] lest a wave of earth cover you."[184] In that tale, it was horses that were swallowed by the earth, while the counselor was struck dead as punishment for the king's disobedience. In the *Síaburcharpat*, it is the royal figure himself who will be temporarily buried after he obstinately refuses to believe in Pat-

---

182. Basa maith frim aír. Basa ferr fri molad (ibid., lines 9337–38).
183. Ind eich seo a Loegairi / retha [*leg*. rethait or rethach?] rith co mbúaid / is Patraic dodrathbeogastar / condat e ata lúaith. // In carpat so atchisiu / i ndegaid na n-ech / is Patraic ro cruthaigestar / conid hé as dech (ibid., lines 9504–511).
184. Ná tuadaig tond talman torut (ibid., lines 9301–2, and cf. lines 9536–37, where this warning is reiterated).

rick despite Cú Chulainn's plea. The punishment of Lóegaire in this text is reminiscent of his fate as recorded by Tírechán, according to whom the king was buried in a pagan manner, as a talisman protecting his kingdom from invasion.[185]

Unlike Tírechán's Lóegaire, the Lóegaire of the *Síaburcharpat* is retrieved from the ground, as is one of the two miraculously buried horses in the story from Áed's Life. One member of the equine pair is, however, left behind in the ground as a silent memorial. We may ask, does Lóegaire leave someone or something behind? Arguably, he leaves his pagan self and the mode of memorialization such burial implies in Tírechán's account. Surely Lóegaire is one of the most divided figures in hagiographic or hagiographically based literature, vacillating between his pagan and Christian options for expressing kingly authority, a blend of deviousness and bewilderment. That he can appear in these accounts as either a "good" or a "bad" figure attests to the ambiguity Lóegaire embraces as a modus vivendi in the often dichotomous world of Patrician story.

Yet Lóegaire is not the only one in the *Síaburcharpat* rescued from what may be pagan posterity but is Christian ignominy. For a transposition of the dioscuric pattern we saw in the Áed episode has taken place in this text, as is evident from the passage telling us what happens to the king and to Cú Chulainn: "The earth came over Lóegaire, while heaven is said to have been granted to Cú Chulainn. Then, finally, Lóegaire believes in Patrick."[186] Thus, while Lóegaire comes up out of the ground, Cú Chulainn is elevated even further in the scheme of things, all the way to heaven. Lóegaire thereby parallels the horse that stays underground, a sign of rebellion and resistance which becomes a sign of saintly control. And like the king in the Áed episode, who is edified by the return to life of his comrade, Lóegaire is swayed by the translation into heaven of the resurrected hero of old whose presence he had specially requested.

In light of the stories examined in this chapter, it should come as no surprise to find such dioscuric patternings attendant upon the marvelous chariot ride in the *Síaburcharpat*. Indeed, the extended poem Cú Chulainn utters in the presence of Lóegaire and Patrick after he has been accepted as authentic is itself a "twinned" composition, consisting of a putatively pagan story of heroic adventure followed by a Christian retelling. This is the same

185. On the variant traditions concerning the fate of Lóegaire, see MacEoin 1968. Perhaps a template behind Patrick's punishment of Lóegaire in the *Síaburcharpat* and other instances of the premature burial of saints' enemies is the fate of the biblical Korah, who challenges Moses' authority in the desert and is swallowed by the ground (Numbers 16). Compare also Best and Bergin 1929, lines 9738–40, from the Middle Irish account of Lóegaire's conversion, in which not only does the resistant druid (*sic!*) Lóegaire fall into the earth but dogs defecate on his head.

186. Dodeochaid talam tar Loegaire adfiadar nem do Choin Culaind. Ro chreti trá Lóegaire do Patraic iarom (ibid., lines 9539–40).

kind of repetition with variation that structures the evolving relationship between Lóegaire and Cú Chulainn. The hero first appears passively to Lóegaire, cutting an impressive, traditional, but aloof figure. Then in the course of their second encounter, which includes dialogue, Cú Chulainn presents a finer-tuned version of himself, still the dog and chariot warrior par excellence, but less spectral—and impressively up-to-date in his worldview. Likewise, the story the hero tells starts out as a full-blown account of the wonders and difficulties of raiding in the otherworld. And yet this story turns out to be of no account compared to its sequel, a voyage to hell undergone by the hero's soul: "All that I suffered of tribulation upon land and sea, Lóegaire, was easy compared to a single night with an angry demon."[187] While the Cú Chulainn of the first story in the first half of the poem is left swimming in the ocean without a boat, carrying a load of his companions on his back, a protector of his people as memorably awash in the sea as the talismanic Lóegaire is fixed under earth, the Cú Chulainn of the second, following story is rescued from his damnation by the wondrous chariot designed by Patrick, a vehicle that will proceed to take him to his eternal reward.

What Cú Chulainn performs may actually be confirmation of the worst of Lóegaire's suspicions concerning the authenticity of what he is seeing and hearing, since, in the context of the extant literature of this period, the poem is patently unconventional. It is in essence a narrative poem, a creature most rare in Old and Middle Irish literature, particularly in the Ulster cycle, and arguably as much a creature of the literary tradition as the chariot that conveys its author.

And yet it is to the period of the eleventh and twelfth centuries, the milieu of the earliest manuscript in which the *Síaburcharpat* is preserved, that we can trace the first literary documentations of the genre of the Fenian *laíd* 'lay'.[188] This is a narrative poem centered on characters from a different heroic cycle, the Fenian, which becomes literarily dominant in later centuries. The early extant examples of the Fenian lay, which flourished during the early modern period, may well be the tip of an iceberg of a repertoire that had accumulated in oral tradition but had not yet surfaced in literature. So it is possible that Cú Chulainn, licensed within the confines of the Patrician chariot to appeal to the native sensibilities of the nonliterary Lóegaire, gives voice to a genuine oral performative genre.

In any event, something new is being introduced into the literary tradition by the professed nonspecter in the spectral chariot. The symbol of the past ushers in a reinvigorating blast of "real" performance, or he heralds the shape of literary things to come. As in the Prologue to the *Senchas Már*, Lóegaire

187. An ro chesusa d'imned a Lóegairi / for muir 7 tír. / bá ansa damsa óenadaig / la demon co n-ír (ibid., lines 9439–42).
188. Gerard Murphy (1971, 18–22) describes Cú Chulainn's poem as "a clear forerunner of the Fionn type of ballad" (21). Compare Mac Cana 1989, 130–31.

witnesses the unfolding of a literary history that involves the conversion of both souls and media. In the *Síaburcharpat*, however, the changes can occur only with the benefit of the perspective afforded by riding in a hijacked chariot, which has been made a product and a sign of the authority of the new order taking shape, and by hearing what the rider in that chariot has to say, even if it is scripted.

The Price Devotees Pay

My analysis of the charioteer, especially when dead or mute, as a linch-pin in the symbolic process whereby a literary present acknowledges an oral past derives from a consideration of the roles charioteers play in stories about life-or-death confrontations involving them or the heroes they convey. This involvement of the figure of the *arae* or *auriga* in the writing of a literary prehistory is also indicated in ways that take us beyond the realm of chariots and charioteering. For instance, Odrán, the name of Patrick's charioteer in the Prologue to the *Senchas Már,* designates other legendary figures who play similar roles. This name, formed from the adjective *odor/odur* 'brown (like an otter)' (cognate with English *otter*), and other "otter" names such as *Do-burchú, Dobrán* 'Otter', and *Mael Doburchon* 'Devotee of Otter' are not rare, but we can hardly dismiss as coincidental the thematic connections among characters so named in the surviving literature.[189] In fact, we find an otter "type" operating in the realm of hagiography, a recurring figure characterized by a self-sacrificing nature and supreme devotion to a saint.

An outstanding example demonstrates the intensity of this devotion in a Middle Irish anecdote featuring the Leinster saint Moling:

> Once, as Moling was in the Taídiu [a waterway he himself had constructed], he saw Mael Doburchon, son of Cellach, coming towards him, looking for his horses. The house of Mael Doburchon was a guesthouse for the many. Moling was good to him because Moling was his spiritual mentor. He greeted Moling. "We are on a search, cleric," Mael Doburchon said. "On a search for Christ, that is," said Moling. "Enormous was the deed of the Jews," said Mael Do-burchon, "crucifying Christ—we would try with all our might to save him."

189. On the meaning of *odor* see also Thurneysen 1946, 74. An examination of otters and figures with otter names featured in narrative is contained in J. Nagy 1985–86, 124–27 (following the lead of the intuitive, if erratic, observations on "otter" figures in Chadwick 1942, 125–41; see now also F. Byrne and Francis 1994, 106). There is, for example, the indubitably aquatic holy man Odrán who is said to swim to his isolated island retreat (in the Middle Irish notes on the Martyrology of Óengus, Stokes 1905b, 228). Given that *odor* as a color word is also associated with cows, as in the celebrated manuscript title Lebor na hUidre (Book of the dun cow), it is possible that the name Odrán refers to the dun color of cows, not otters. Compare the bovine name of Cú Chulainn's charioteer, Lóeg/Láeg 'Calf'. Nonethe-less, the preponderance of the nominal evidence points to the otter behind *odor,* as we shall see.

Moling then went into the midst of a thicket of blackthorn and put his cowl upon a stake in the middle of the thicket. "If that cowl were Christ, how would you save it?" Mael Doburchon took off his clothes and went into the thicket so that he reached the cowl and held it in his two hands. "It is thus I would have saved Christ," said Mael Doburchon, with streams of blood coming out of his extremities. "That was memorable," said Moling. "You will be rewarded by Christ. The denizens of hell will never be able to shed your blood, and demons will not contend for your soul. Go, monk," Moling said, speaking to the cowl [?], "on the search with Mael Doburchon." The cowl [?] went ahead and landed on the haunches of the horse, thus pointing out where it was, so that Mael Doburchon could take his horses home.[190]

Like Patrick's charioteer, the hospitaler Mael Doburchon expresses his identification with his beloved living saint and with Christ, the object of his saint's devotion, by means of an act of self-destruction that makes him into a Christlike paradigm of sacrifice. Mael Doburchon's demonstration is said to be *amra* 'memorable' and, like the *Amra* composed by Dallán for Columba, it demonstrates the extent to which the native or secular, as represented by the hospitaler, can coexist creatively with the Christian.

Mael Doburchon's flaying himself alive clearly derives from the same kind of emotional reaction to the news which features in the medieval account of the death of King Conchobar in the Ulster cycle of heroic tales. Upon hearing of the death of Christ at the hands of the Jews, the aging king commits the remnants of his heroic energy to venting his rage, but in his agitation an old wound opens up, and Conchobar dies.[191] In the story of Mael Doburchon, ideology and goals are even more dramatically redirected. A man in search of traces of his horse(s) is told to seek Christ instead, and since Christ cannot be met in the flesh in this life, Mael Doburchon is yet again redirected. Now, he is to seek and obtain a cowl, an emblem of the saint, who, by imitating Christ, represents him in this tableau.

190. Fecht do Moling issin Táidin conaccca Mael doburchon mac Cellaig chuice for iarraid a each. Tech n-aiged sochaide tech Mail doburchon. Ba maith tra fria Moling intanrud fobith issé rob anmchara dó. Bendachaid do Moling. For iarraid atam, a chleirig, ar Mael doburchon. For iarair Críst ón, ar Moling,. Is mor in t-echt sin dorónsat Iudaide, Críst do chrochad. Dobermais ar cumang oca thesarcain, ar Mael doburchon. Gaibte (.i. teit) Moling iarum a medon muine. Amal bud hé Críst tra i cochull cindus donesarta? Srethis (.i. curis) Mael doburchon a étach de, ⁊ dosrala in muine seocho cona dib lamaib co rocht in cochall, co mbói etir a dí láim. Is amlaid sin donesairgfind sea, ar Mael doburchon, Críst, ⁊ ro badar sreba fola assa indaib. Amra sin, a Mail doburchon, ar Moling: rot-bia a lóg la Críst. Ní theilgfit fir ifirn fuil assat co brath, ⁊ nocho taicerat demna fria t'anmain. Eirg, a manaig ut, frissin certan forsin iarraid la Mael doburchon. Gaibthe roime in certan co furim for di lis na ngabra ait ir-raba, conda-ruc Maeldoburchon leis a eochu dochum a thigi (from the notes on the Martyrology of Óengus, Stokes 1905b, 152; see also Meyer 1893, 188–91).
191. The various Middle Irish versions of the story of how Conchobar died are edited and translated in Meyer 1906a, 4–19. See also Corthals 1989.

Clearly, this tale pivots on a shift in the protagonist's search for a meaningful goal, from "horse" to "Christ." In that shift the convert and reader are given a lesson in representation and in how the same message can be read into different forms of representation. Mael Doburchon's religious attention is redirected from Christ to Moling, the cowl becomes an extension of the saint, and the metaphor of Moling as Christ is matched by the metonym of the hood as Moling. The sign of the cowl goes itself in search of the missing horse and, having found it, becomes actually attached to the animal. The tale thus unites seemingly different meanings and different modes of representing them.

This fusing of contrasting orders of signifiers and signifieds is hardly as epochal as, say, the transformation of *senchas* into text which is featured in the Prologue to the *Senchas Már*. And yet, like that moment of literary creation, the "rediscovery" of Christ, the cowl, and the horse in this legend of Moling is based on a foundation sacrifice of sorts, the near-death of Mael Doburchon on his quest for the cowl. It can hardly be coincidence, moreover, that the alternative and alternating poles of meaning between which the seeker seeks and almost loses his life in this story, as in the Patrician legend of the charioteer in search of his missing team, are "horse," that perennial symbol of pagan cult, and "Christ," represented in the Patrician tale by the saint, to whom the lamenting charioteer comes in despair and who consoles and revives with Christlike compassion.

The message implicit in the story of Mael Doburchon emerges even more clearly when we consider the parallels between this tale and that of another of Moling's remarkable charges, the *geilt* 'madman' Suibne, whose madness, as we saw, confers poetic inspiration upon him as well as misery.[192] Suibne does not come to Moling with an eye to recovering anything so specific and tangible as a horse, but he too, like Mael Doburchon, is redirected. Moling enjoins him to wander as much as he likes, provided that every day he returns to Moling's dwelling to dictate the poems he has composed and the adventures he has experienced to the saint.[193] This arrangement harks back to the miracle that undoes the damage Suibne has done to the library of another saint, Rónán, who curses him with madness. The saint's psalter, which Suibne had impulsively thrown into the water in defiance of the saint, is retrieved by a helpful otter.[194] The animal's unexpected intervention in the cause of preserving a precious text prefigures what Suibne himself will be doing for Moling in his latter days, that is, retrieving cherished experience and inspiration derived from the wilderness and offering them up for literary preservation.

192. As told in the twelfth-century text *Buile Shuibhne* (see pp. 194–95). On the figure of the madman (*geilt*) as exemplified by Suibne, see Ó Riain 1972; and J. Nagy 1982 and 1996.
193. J. O'Keeffe 1931, lines 2133–39. On the affinities of this premise with others highlighted in other texts of this period, including the *Acallam*, see Ó Riain 1974, 173–74.
194. J. O'Keeffe 1931, lines 55–58, 99–100.

Mael Doburchon's shifting his search from lost horses to the "lost" but risen Christ or the more tangible "lost" cowl, a sign of both saintly and Christian authority and protection, is parallel to Suibne's submission of poems to Moling's pen, and the otter's return of the psalter unharmed. In all three cases, cooperation is achieved among previously unrelated beings and forces, and the transmission of a message in a literary or at least "tangible" and emphatically Christian mode of signification takes place.

Yet Suibne dies under tragic circumstances in Moling's household, and in his dying words he regrets having established communication with the saint and the culture he represents. The story of Mael Doburchon gives no hint of such a dramatic change in the fortunes and feelings of those participating in the linking of native and Christian cultures. In fact, Mael Doburchon's actual death is not at all required, as either a precondition or a consequence of the rapprochement. In this regard, yet another saint's companion with an otter name proves a closer analogue to Patrick's charioteer, whose death, we recall, is literal and not just figural.

Odrán's Burial

On the whole, the Middle Irish Life of Columba is an unremarkable text, lacking the detail of Adomnán's earlier account of the saint's career. There is one episode in this Life, however, which stands out as a stark instance of the foundation sacrifice in medieval Irish literature.[195] Arriving in his exile from Ireland on the isle of Iona, where he is to establish his primary monastery, Columba chooses what would appear to be a decidedly "native" as opposed to Christian course of action:

> Then Colum Cille said to his company: "It would benefit us if our roots were put down into the ground here," and he said to them: "Someone among you should go down into the soil of the island to consecrate it." The obedient Odrán rose up and said: "If I be taken, I am prepared for it," said he. "Odrán," said Colum Cille, "you will be rewarded for it. No one will be granted his request at my own grave, unless he first seek it of you." Then Odrán went to heaven.[196]

---

195. Vestiges of foundation sacrifice in modern Irish folklore, including the belief that burying of horse heads underneath the floor makes for more resonant acoustics, form the subject of Ó Súilleabháin 1945. This legend of Columba's brother and its kinship to other Celtic narratives featuring human sacrifice are mentioned in passing in Robinson 1913, 195–96, and Carey 1995a, 55–56 n. 35.

196. Trans. Herbert 1988a, 261. At-bert Colum Cille ind sin rá muntir: "Is maith dún ar fréma do dul fó thalmain súnd," 7 at-bert friu: "Is cet díb nech écin uaib do dul fo úir na hinnsi-se dia coisecrad." Atracht suas Odran erlattad 7 is ed atbert, "Dianam-gabtha," olse, "is

We learn from other sources that the cemetery on Iona was named after this monk, Reilic Odráin.[197] According to Maghnus Ó Domhnaill's Early Modern Irish account of this incident, Columba dictated the sacrifice on Iona after he had expelled druids who were attempting to drive him away.[198]

It may seem that the motivation behind the curiously unspecified dispatching of Odrán lies more in pagan than in Christian culture. This widely disseminated motif of foundation sacrifice appears elsewhere in Celtic narrative traditions, for instance, in the episode in the *Historia Brittonum* attributed to the British monk Nennius (ca. 800) in which the "fatherless" child Ambrosius, later in tradition to be identified with Merlin, is nearly sacrificed by the tyrant Vortigern in his quest to build a fortress on a mountain.[199] Of course, in addition to its folkloric subtext, the voluntary death of Odrán also carries Christological overtones, as does the charioteer Odrán's giving his life on behalf of Patrick. In recognition of his sacrifice, Columba gives Odrán the honor of being in effect the intercessor between the saint and his future devotees, as Christ the Son is the intercessor between imploring humanity and God the Father. Yet Odrán's triumphant Christlike resurrection, either now or in the final days, is neither staged or anticipated in this legend as preserved in literary sources. Indeed, as the tutelary spirit of the Iona cemetery, Odrán passes into posterity as very much a "deceased" member of the community.[200]

---

erlom lem sin." "A Odrain," ol Colum Cille, "rot-bia a lóg sin .i. ni tiberthar a itghe do neoch icom ligesi mina fortsa shirfes ar thús." Luid iarum Odran docum nime (c. 52, ibid., 237).
197. "The sacrificial victim, Odrán, is commemorated at Reilic Odráin in Iona, site of a church dating from the end of the eleventh century. Nothing can be discovered about the origin of the legend, but it may be suggested that its propagation was connected with the enclosure of the *reilic* and the building there of a church or shrine" (Herbert 1988a, 197). Information about the cemetery site (Réilig Òrain in Scottish Gaelic), the figure after whom it is named, and the legend concerning him is presented in Sharpe 1995, 65–71, 277–78 n. 100, 360–62 n. 365. On the religious and cultural functions of cemeteries in medieval Irish monastic culture, see Lucas 1986.
198. O'Kelleher and Schoepperle 1918, 200.
199. Cc. 40–42.
200. Could it be that in this obscure tradition concerning a sacrificed brother of Columba's we have not only an analogue to the troubled relationship between Patrick and his sister as depicted in the Tripartite Life and elsewhere, but also to the even more mysterious tradition of an "old" or "other" Patrick, upon whose missionary failure or demise the "new" Patrick entered the Irish scene and proved successful? The duplication of Patrick, evident in a variety of sources (see T. O'Rahilly 1957), is at least partly a way to reconcile the legend of Patrick's missionary activity (to which the only surviving contemporary attestations are Patrick's own writings) with the report (to be found under A.D. 429 in the chronicle compiled by Prosper of Aquitaine in the fifth century) of the mission of one Palladius, sent by the pope to Ireland to be its first bishop (on the significance of Prosper's noting this mission, see Charles-Edwards 1993). Already in Tírechán's text, we are told that Palladius was also known as Patrick and suffered martyrdom, and that his work was carried on, with greater success, by his namesake (c. 56, Bieler 1979, 164, 166). Just as Columba builds his famous monastery on the corpse of a sacrificed colleague, the "second" Patrick builds his successful mission on the groundwork established by his failed alter ego and predecessor.
Another Patrician substitute worth mentioning here, a figure upon whose death the perpetu-

Furthermore, it is intriguing that in Ó Domhnaill's account, Odrán's death follows the "exorcizing" of the druids that infested Iona before Columba's arrival. Even more telling is the sometimes humorous treatment this story receives in Scottish Gaelic oral tradition. This development may actually be a vestige of an earlier way of telling the story, the implications of which are too disturbing to be included in a written life of the saint. According to versions collected from nineteenth-century storytellers, Columba is continually thwarted in his attempts to build his church on Iona, until he learns through supernatural means that someone must be buried under the ground before the building can be erected.[201] The saint asks for volunteers, but the only man willing to go under is his own brother, Dòbhran 'Otter' or 'Beaver', from *dobur* 'water' or 'dark', as in Irish *doburchú* 'otter'.[202] Dòbhran agrees to be buried in a chamber on the condition that he be dug up in a week's time. The condition is accepted. When the exhumed Dòbhran raises his head out of the hole a week later, the gaze from his eyes turns the tips of a certain kind of plant red, and Columcille, realizing that something dangerous is afoot, has him reburied. Dòbhran stays down, but the tip of the plant has remained red ever since. According to a variant of the story collected in nineteenth-century Nova Scotia, it is not the brother's gaze but what he says that sends him back to the grave. As he is being excavated, he proclaims, "Hell is not as bad as people say,"[203] at the hearing of which Columcille orders the dirt to be thrown back into the hole.

It is fitting that we find the most explicit manifestation of the potentially disruptive nature of the saint's shadowy companion in folk legend, as opposed to the literary accounts I have dealt with in this chapter. For the disruption that threatens stems in part from the anxieties of the bearers of literary culture

---

ation of the Patrician cult is predicated, and whose words live on after his death, is Sechnall or Secundinus (whose name, appropriately enough, means "second"), whom Patrick installs as bishop when he himself leaves the country (Mulchrone 1939, lines 2816–17), and whom he allows to compose the famous Latin hymn *Audite omnes* in his honor only because Patrick knows Sechnall will soon die: ar is hé cétna epscop dochóid fó úir nErend "for he was the first bishop to go under the ground [that is, to die] in Ireland" (ibid., lines 2867–68; on Sechnall's hymn, see Kenney 1929, 258–60; and Andy Orchard's discussion, edition, and translation (1993, 153–73).

201. Hyde 1915, 198.

202. *DIL*, s.v. *dobrán*, 1 *dobur*, 2 *dobur*, and *doburchú*. The sinister and mysterious nature of otters as they are depicted in Irish and Scottish Gaelic traditions is explored in J. Nagy 1985–86. An Irish oral legend about a particularly vicious otter (*dobharchú*) is noted in Tohall 1948, 129.

203. Cha n'eil an iorron chomh dona agus a tháthar ag rádh (Hyde 1915, 198). The story (with the protagonist named Oran) is already attested in the Highland travelogue of Thomas Pennant in the late eighteenth century: "To the surprize of all beholders, Oran started up, and began to reveal the secrets of his prison-house; and particularly declared, that all that had been said of hell was a mere joke. This dangerous impiety so shocked Columba that, with great policy, he instantly ordered the earth to be flung in again; poor Oran was overwhelmed, and an end for ever put to his prating. His grave is near the door, distinguished only by a plain red stone" (text in Youngson 1974, 172; see Crawford 1933, 465). Note the persistence of the motif of Oran/Dòbhran's presence being marked by red.

concerning the compatability of oral and literary traditions. The untrammeled speech of Dòbhran from the grave poses an even graver danger to Christianity and the delicate cultural balance of ideologies, secular and religious or pagan and Christian, than the most baleful utterances of druids and other enemies of the new faith, since here the speaker, a Christian no less, speaks with the unimpeachable authority of the dead, who can only speak the truth.[204] Before the earth is shoveled back over him, the Dòbhran of oral story, who is the saint's own brother, enjoys the unique privilege of coming back to life on his own. It is remarkable that Dòbhran can return without saintly intervention or interference in the "natural order" which usually makes such communications beyond the grave possible in hagiographic literature. We know of nothing he has done which merits him this distinction, but whatever empowers Dòbhran, his performance from the grave, which departs so violently from the standard scenario of saintly legend, warrants the genuine burial of this troubling figure.

Brendan's Disposable *Crosán*

And so, in this story the oral tradition has preserved more successfully than the literary tradition an important subtext underlying stories concerning saints and their odd, eminently or even necessarily expendable companions,[205] such as charioteers, quasi-twins, siblings, wild men, and otters, perhaps because the oral tradition is in fact what these stories are really about. This subtext, however, is hardly lost in the literary versions, as we have seen. It is most certainly palpable in a medieval tale about another saint, Brendan (Old Irish Brénainn) of Clonfert, which brings together the elements of substitution, central to the "myth" of Patrick's charioteer, and the quest for new meaning, notably on display in the tale of Moling's devotee Mael Doburchon. We also find in this story the Christian rephrasing of native or pagan practice and motivation which makes the tale of Columba's sacrificed monk hagiographically palatable but is pointedly undone in the folk version.

Brendan, according to the Latin and Middle Irish versions of his Life, is about to set out with his monks in a coracle to find the Christian Isle of the Blessed across the ocean when he meets a man who wishes to be taken on

204. Worthy of note in connection with the Dòbhran legend is the idea to be found in early Welsh poetry, and possibly in other Celtic sources, that undergoing a premature or mock burial provides contact with other, not necessarily "demonic," supernatural forces, including the sources of poetic inspiration (P. Ford 1987, 41–48). A previously unnoted analogue is to be found in an Irish oral legend collected in modern times, according to which King David composes the Penitential Psalms as a way of magically lifting himself out of the grave in which he had been buried alive in punishment for his adultery (Ó Súilleabháin 1970, 260).

205. Aguirre 1990, 208–11, offers an explanation for the necessary presence (and subsequent absence) of such figures in light of the hero's "spiritual quest" and psychological development, with special reference to the Middle Irish *Immram Curaig Maildúin* (Voyage of Maeldúin's coracle).

board at the last moment.[206] He is identified in the text as a *crosán*, a lowly type of poet-entertainer, and he expresses the hope that he may prove to be of some use on the voyage.[207] In fact, early on in their travels, when Brendan and company arrive at the Isle of Ravenous Mice, one of the many wondrous and dangerous highlights of their trip, the crosán proves his worth. Brendan explains that the mice are hungry for human flesh and that it is the performer's fate to be eaten by them in place of Brendan or his crew. The crosán happily accepts what is described as a martyrdom, and those remaining on the boat see his soul ascending to heaven after his body is thrown to the mice.[208]

The crosán's death saves the members of the expedition, but it does not get them to their destination. After many other adventures, Brendan's coracle arrives at an island whose inhabitants are playing sleep-inducing music. Sure of having reached their goal, the saint and his crew receive a wax tablet from the inhabitants of the island on which is inscribed a disappointing message. This is in fact not the island for which they have been looking, the tablet reads, and they should return home and reexamine Scripture in order to be better able to locate the Isle of the Blessed. When Brendan returns home, his foster mother, Ita (Íte), chides him for having attempted to reach so sacred a place in a vessel made of the (impure) skins of dead animals, instead of a boat made of wood. Brendan sets forth again, having reread Scripture and built a new boat, and ultimately finds what he seeks.[209]

It is important to view the episode of the crosán in the wider context of Brendan's two voyages, the first of which turns out to be a quest launched without sufficient literary preparation, a failure inscribed on a wax tablet which issues instructions for the future. Ita's explanation for the failure, pointing to Brendan's use of skins instead of wood as the medium of conveyance, suggests that there existed an implicit native agenda behind Brendan's search

---

206. Plummer 1910, 1:136–37 (Latin); Plummer 1922, 1:53–54; Stokes 1890, 111–12 (Irish).

207. Harrison 1989 offers a thorough examination of the figure of the *crosán* in Irish literary tradition. In Brendan's Latin Life, the sacrificial victim is said to be a *preco* 'herald' (c. 72, Plummer 1910, 1:137). The figure of the medieval herald, his association with performers, and his Indo-European roots are discussed in Bullock-Davies 1978, 39–43. On the Indo-European figure of the herald and analogous performers in Celtic tradition, see Williams 1979–80, 314–19.

208. Compare the story of the *crosán* who goes on pilgrimage with reformed brigands, the Uí Chorra, and in death becomes a speaking bird, in the Middle Irish *Immram Curaig Ua Corra* (Voyage of the coracle of the Uí Chorra) (van Hamel 1941, 101–2). Although in both this case and that of Brendan's *crosán* the marginal crew member offers himself in a Christ-like fashion and is not simply thrown overboard, clearly the story pattern underlying these medieval Irish religious tales owes something to the biblical legend of Jonah (as told in the Book of Jonah). This kinship is especially clear in a variant on the pattern to be found in Ó Domhnaill's Life of Columba (O'Kelleher and Schoepperle 1918, 196).

209. Plummer 1922, 1:63–64. See also Plummer 1910, 1:136 (c. 71); Heist 1965, 328 (c. 10); and Stokes 1890, 110. In Plummer 1910, 1:136, the incident of the sacrifice of the crew member takes place as the beginning of the second voyage.

for knowledge of life in perfect harmony with God. In one of the pagan Irish divinatory practices evidenced in medieval literature, the seeker of supernatural knowledge lies on the skins of freshly slain animals in order to obtain the desired information.[210] And so we may ask, is Brendan's leather-bound quest confused or discomfitingly syncretistic in its method? In any event, it needs to be rethought, as well as invested with the authority of writing. The success of the quest also hinges on the sacrifice—or purging?—of a representative of oral tradition, a figure whose role in the story is to absent himself almost as soon as he is introduced. The performer, along with the mixed messages being sent out and received by Brendan and his fellow voyagers, has been discarded, becoming the cornerstone for a more successful outcome in line with Christian and literary orthodoxy, that is, finally attaining the Isle of the Blessed. Like the other seemingly insignificant, disreputable, or "old-fashioned" figures we have met in this chapter, the crosán finds his moment of glory in an act that simultaneously expresses both the affinity between him and the saint who manages his destiny and the unbridgeable gap that separates them.[211] In stories of the expendable companion, this disquieting gap is hastily covered over, like the grave of a sacrificed victim, as the literary tradition builds on and appropriates the authority of the oral. Despite the cover-up, traces of what was, and of what was said, pointedly remain and await decoding.

210. T. O'Rahilly 1946, 324–25; J. Nagy 1985, 140, 281–82 n. 36.

211. There is another, even more curious collocation of saint, voyage, oral performer, and animal skin in the Early Modern Irish Life of Molaisse. The latter goes to hell equipped only with a cowl made of badger skin and a small strip of the same kind of skin in his hand in quest of the drúth 'fool' Manann the Leprous. Molaisse succeeds in calling the fool out of heaven (O'Grady 1892, 1:21). The name Manann, derived from the place-name Mana (Isle of Man) or *mana* 'omen', suggests the name of Manannán, one of the prominent figures in the pre-Christian Irish pantheon.

Fíacc of Sletty, the author of a famous hymn about Patrick in Irish (see pp. 89, 236 n. 95 above), is, like Brendán's crosán, a "doomed" man. While the crosán became food for mice, Fíacc, says the Tripartite Life, was nibbled at by a beetle nearly to death [Mulchrone 1939, line 2862]). This gruesome torture constitutes the ascetic practice of the great Ita as well (Stokes 1905b, 42, 44; see Bray 1992c, 30–31). In fact, once the process of eating Ita is stopped by her well-meaning colleagues, who kill her voracious bug, she declares in anger that none of them will succeed her—that is, that her monastery will pass from the hands of her fellow holy women into those of monks. Thus, the foundation of Ita's monastery and cult is radically altered once Ita is saved from an impending death that she would have happily embraced. Her anger abates, however, once she is granted the miraculous privilege of nursing the Christ child. While nursing, or being "eaten" in this more honorific way, Ita composes her famous poem about the experience and the privilege (edited and annotated in Quin 1981a).

This recurring connection between death or duress and poetic composition is doubtless a reflection of the "shamanic" aspects of poetry to be found in Celtic traditions, as well as throughout the world's oral traditions. On this pain-and-poetry nexus, see P. Ford 1987; Melia 1983; and J. Nagy 1981b.

5/ tracking down the past

Gold in Louernius's Wake

We have seen that the charioteer's role in the drama of the conversion of Ireland and the shift of power from an oral to a literary elite culture is predicated on his traditional association with the hero he transports in the chariot. The charioteer can function as his shadowy twin, representing both what the hero is and what he is not. Subsequently, the *auriga* can be substituted for the saint as a sacrificial victim in crises of transition which demand at least partial shedding of the old to accommodate the new.

Other aspects of the traditional characterization, however, make the charioteer eminently suitable as an operator in the ideological conceptualization of the origins of the literary tradition. For instance, the "king" of charioteers, Lóeg, is said in the *Táin Bó Cúailnge* and elsewhere to have "three virtues of charioteering," ("teóra búada aradnachta"), all of which go to the heart of what is expected of an *arae* at least as he is depicted in narrative: "leaping over a gap, straight cleaving, and casting of a rod."[1] William Sayers, whose translations of these terms I am quoting, glosses the third of these "gifts" thus:

> It is suggested, then, that *immorchor ndelend* [casting of a rod] may refer to the use of the charioteer's wand both to sight a straight course . . . , perhaps with reference to the stars and prominent landmarks, and to hold the team on this course. The exceptional aspect of the gift possessed by Láeg would be the ability

1. Teóra búada aradnachta . . . léim dar boilg 7 foscul ndírich 7 imorchor ndelind (C. O'Rahilly 1976b, lines 2211–12). This triad, as used in the texts of the *Táin* and the *Mesca Ulad* (Drunkenness of the Ulstermen), is the subject of Sayers 1981. The translation of *foscul ndíri[u]ch* (straight cleaving) is not certain.

287

to conduct the chariot on a perfectly straight course over a long distance—between the points named in the text, perhaps even from the journey's start to its finish.[2]

The paradigmatic charioteer, then, is single-minded in his purpose and method, transporting himself and the hero to their destination in the most direct way possible and not letting obstacles such as "gaps" stand in his way. The Middle Irish text *Mesca Ulad* (Drunkenness of the Ulstermen), one of the two surviving tales in which these three virtues are mentioned, features the spectacular consequences of such directness and "drive" when they are displayed on the level of heroic story:

> Every hill over which they [the Ulstermen traveling in their chariots and led by Cú Chulainn and Lóeg] passed they leveled, so that they left it in low glens; every wood through which they passed, the iron wheels of the chariots cut the roots of the great trees, so that it was open country after them; the streams and fords and pools which they crossed were fully dry bare stones after them for a long time, and for long periods, from the quantity which the cavalcades carried away with their own bodies out of the contents of cascade, ford, and pool.[3]

It should be noted, however, that the Ulstermen do not reach their destination at the end of this wild ride. Instead, they find themselves far off course, in the lair of enemies. Cú Chulainn knows where they are, but his charioteer does not. The hero offers to lead his fellow warriors out of the hostile territory as soon as possible, but they refuse the offering. Having left such conspicuous tracks, they feel honor-bound to make their presence felt further, and not to render what they have done simply a "fox's track" (*slicht sinnaig*).[4] Thus the impact of the hard chariot driving on the landscape of the story is no demonstration of efficiency; it is an advertisement for the presence of the Ulstermen. This devastating sign of their intrusion is left, according to the text, as one of the "proofs of the story," along with stone columns erected by the charioteers to shelter their horses from a sudden snowstorm.[5]

We recall from the Life of Saint Áed, discussed in the previous chapter, that his charioteer's ability to reach his destination despite distance and obstacles is put to the test on various occasions. Yet on these occasions, he is found wanting, and Áed takes over the reins, making the chariot go in ways that are

2. Ibid., 1981, 166.
3. Cach tailach dara tictís múrtís co fáctais ina fóenglenntaib. Cach fidbad dara tictís no thesctaís rotha íarnaide na carpat fréma na ralach romór comba crích machairi da n-éis. Cach sruth ⁊ cach áth ⁊ cach inber dara tictís ba lecca lomma lántirma dara n-éis ra hed cían ⁊ ra dréchta fata ra mét na bertís a n-echrada ra n-irglúnib na hessa ⁊ na hátha ⁊ na hinbera assa corpaib fodéin (Watson 1941, lines 269–76).
4. Ibid., lines 333–37.
5. Ibid., lines 306–12.

beyond the skills of even a Lóeg. Significantly, when Áed puts the chariot in flight, he prevents the charioteer from seeing anything at all and thus assumes his function altogether, not only driving the horses but surveying the terrain, or the air in this case, as well. After the saint appropriates the function of the charioteer, stripping him of his identity as thoroughly as the charioteer is elsewhere stripped of his life, the juggernaut of saintly mission goes on to transcend in power and efficiency even the "drive" that marks virtuosic charioteering. Áed effortlessly goes over the obstacles, such as forests and vast distances, instead of plunging through them destructively.

The ability of the exemplary charioteer to reach his goal in a straight line and overcome all obstacles, an ability coveted and taken over by the figure of the saint, who proceeds to outdo his driver, is closely connected to the charioteer's ability to see "straight," the ability suppressed by Áed, and to make "straight" judgments and estimates. It is on account of these traits that the charioteer is held up as an example to the prince who is instructed in the Old Irish *Audacht Morainn* to act like "the driver of an old chariot."[6]

The perspicacity of the charioteer, compared to that of his passenger, is very much an issue in the stories about Patrick's driver. A harmonious exchange between saintly power and charioteer's intelligence comes about in the story of the loss and recovery of the horses, in which the *auriga* is literally and figuratively left in the dark as to the whereabouts of his animals.[7] He is not, however, totally without resources, for with his performance of lament he attracts Patrick's attention and sympathy. The illumination the saint provides casts light on the terrain the charioteer could no longer master and makes possible the continuation and completion of the journey.

In the account of the overlooked cross, by contrast, the perceptions of saint and charioteer are directly at odds over the visibility of the cross and the worthiness of the pagan who speaks to Patrick from the grave. While not as blatant an act as Saint Áed's covering his driver's eyes, Patrick's refusal to respond to the charioteer's question points out a gap (hard to leap with a chariot!) not just between perceptions but also between interpretations of signs, even of signification itself. True, Patrick's authority as a reader of signs is vindicated, as I have already discussed, but saint and charioteer hardly achieve a unanimity of readings.

A similar difference in knowledge and interpretation is featured in the story of Failge's assassination attempt, but here it is the charioteer who incontrovertibly knows more than the saint.[8] Patrick in fact rarely appears more passive than in this story. It is the insightful and active charioteer who knows

6. See p. 218. The wisdom of the charioteer is matched in Greek and Indic traditions by that of the chariot builder, who creates by means of paradigmatic "joinery," like the poet, who artfully "joins together" words (G. Nagy 1979, 297–300).

7. See pp. 213–14.

8. See pp. 208–10.

of Failge's threat, who knows the territory Patrick wants to enter, and who recognizes the danger that lurks therein. He craftily arranges a deceptive sign that means one thing to Patrick, who knows he is not the charioteer but thinks he is switching roles in order to satisfy the charioteer's whim; another to Failge, who "reads" the false Patrick as the real; and yet a third to the charioteer himself. The tale demonstrates that the charioteer who is a master of direction can work through indirection as well.

This "indirection" also pertains to the aftermath of the charioteer's driving, for while the *arae* must vigilantly look about, above, and ahead in search of signs of the road and the direction he wishes to take, his chariot leaves behind its traces, which, as the passage quoted from the *Mesca Ulad* makes clear, are signs of presence, representing both metonymically and metaphorically the nature and status of those riding in the chariot. Thus, the charioteer is as busy producing signs that are left behind for residents, fellow travelers, and posterity as he is reading signs that take him to his destination and the outcome of his adventure.

Often the signs left by the chariot's horses and wheels are conspicuous and easy to read. In the *Mesca Ulad,* for example, the Ulstermen are almost proud of the tracks they have left in the wrong territory and refuse to render them meaningless or harder to read by immediate departure. In another medieval Ulster tale, *Fled Bricrenn* (Bricriu's feast), which features a competition among the prime Ulster heroes to see who stands above the rest, the warrior Conall is mocked for the larger-than-life trail his chariot leaves behind, a devastation that is unmistakably his.[9] And in a virtuosically descriptive passage in the *Táin Bó Cúailnge,* a vengeful Cú Chulainn and Lóeg proceed to decorate themselves and their chariot with gear and customized designs that mark them as who and what they are, including a "sign of his charioteer-ness" on Lóeg's head to distinguish him from his master.[10] Properly attired and marked, they attack the whole host of Ireland assembled to ravage Ulster. The hero and his charioteer leave behind them ditches that mark off the provinces of Ireland, as a warning for their occupants to respect the boundaries and refrain from invasion. Here then the track of the chariot not only leads to the vehicle and those in it, but reestablishes the political and territorial order that is continually threatened in the story.

The potential significance of the tracks left by the chariot, chariot rider, or charioteer and the hermeneutic challenge they occasionally pose to those whose business it is to read or produce signs are vividly illustrated in an anecdote preserved in the observations of the Greek historian Posidonius on the Celts, as cited by Athenaeus (first century B.C.):

9. Best and Bergin 1929, lines 8489–94.
10. C. O'Rahilly 1976b, lines 2185–334.

Posidonius, again, when telling of the wealth of Louernius, father of Bituis who was dethroned by the Romans, says that in an attempt to win popular favour he rode in a chariot over the plains distributing gold and silver to the tens of thousands of Celts who followed him; moreover, he made a square enclosure one and a half miles each way, within which he filled vats with expensive liquor and prepared so great a quantity of food that for many days all who wished could enter and enjoy the feast prepared, being served without a break by the attendants. And when at length he fixed a day for the ending of the feast, a Celtic poet who arrived too late met Louernius and composed a song magnifying his greatness and lamenting his own late arrival. Louernius was very pleased and asked for a bag of gold and threw it to the poet who ran beside the chariot. The poet picked it up and sang another song saying that the very tracks made by his chariot on the earth gave gold and largesse to mankind.[11]

Here we see demonstrated the institution of prestation and counterprestation underlying the poetic institution among the Celts and many other peoples, whereby "poem" calls forth "gift" from patron, which in turn calls forth yet another "poem," and so on. Tellingly, the process is located here in the wake of a chariot, the movement of which induces performance and the tracks of which contain or "mean" the poet's reward. Furthermore, the interpretation of the tracks in these terms constitutes even more performance. The tracks and what they contain are translated into a verbal form by the poet, whose coming late to Louernius's party is turned from a disadvantage to an advantage, just as following alongside or after the chariot gives him signs to play with poetically and the inspiration to interpret them profitably. The chariot rider and charioteer look ahead for the signs that lead them to their destination, while they leave behind tracks for a poet to render into a lasting performative tribute.

Although the leap from Posidonius to medieval Ireland is considerable, it is tempting to link the implications of the Louernius story with the secondary meaning of both of the Irish words for "track," *slicht* and *lorg* 'recension' or 'version of a text'.[12] Literature can indeed be construed as a trail left in and by the past, textual performances elicited by and containing in a transmuted form the "gold" scattered behind the predecessors of textual performers and the great persons of the past. Such a formulation of the origins of native literature accords well with what we have seen in the *Síaburcharpat*, wherein

11. From the translation in Tierney 1960, 248, of Athenaeus 4.37, text in Tierney 1960, 225–26. Compare Strabo 4.2.3, and Tierney 1960, 203 (commentary). J. E. Caerwyn Williams (1979–80) compares the Celtic "parasites" of classical ethnography, such as the encomiast described in the cited passage, with the oral performers of medieval Ireland and Wales and (following Tierney 1960, 251) with the figure of the herald in other Indo-European traditions.
12. *DIL*, s.v. 1 *lorg* (b) and *slicht* (b).

the chariot of Cú Chulainn, now a mode of conveyance under Patrick's control, leaves posterity a textualized performance. The formulation even casts the story told in the Prologue to the *Senchas Már* in a new light. The metaphorical trace left by Patrick's charioteer, the difficult question of what do with his murderer, engenders a reexamination of what is contained in the past and the packaging of what is salvageable under the new order into a textual form.

A metaphorical reading of "track" would also allow us to interpret the odd casting of the saint's charioteer in the role of seducer (which we saw in the Life of Ailbe) as yet another demonstration of how the charioteer both notes and produces signs. For *slicht* and *lorg* may well have come to mean "track" and "recension" by way of also meaning "offspring."[13] In leaving a woman of Patrick's retinue with child, the charioteer is extending his impression beyond the path on which he drives his chariot. Let us recall, however, that the child born of this illicit union, like the texts indirectly produced by the chariot/charioteer, does not function in the story as a sign of the charioteer's importance. All these "tracks" are annexed by the authority of the saint, and while they may still convey the past, they "speak" as meaningful signs only by the power of the saint and the literary culture he represents. The bastard sired by the charioteer can identify his father and point to him, but first he must be adopted by the saint.

As one who both notes and generates signs, the charioteer is clearly in a position to function as a sign himself. And signify he does, in his capacity as a shadowy twin to the hero/saint in the chariot, and as a reflexive sign enforcing, undermining, and controlling the significance of his passenger. This power is evident in the Ulster cycle when Lóeg goes in place of Cú Chulainn (in the *Serglige*) or when the presence or absence of his charioteer constitutes a comment on Cú Chulainn's own fate (in the hero's death tale).[14]

The potential value of Patrick's charioteer as a sign is certainly acknowledged in hagiography, but it is always carefully circumscribed so as to make it as unthreatening as possible to the saint's own ability to control his significance. Thus the most "significant" charioteer is usually a dead or doomed charioteer. The Patrick of Tírechán's Life renders his dead charioteer in his grave a monument to the saint's commitment to return to Ireland in the Last Days and exercise the right to judge the Irish which he won from God on top of a mountain. In the story of the attempted assassination of Patrick by the incorrigible pagan Failge, the charioteer becomes Patrick, and thereby saves the saint's life, only as a prelude to becoming a model of Christian martyrdom.

13. Ibid., s.v. 1 *lorg* ii (c), and *slicht* (d).
14. See pp. 224–26.

Conspicuous Fénnidi

The hagiographic marginalization of the figure of the charioteer, a tactic that both utilized its capacity for reflecting and magnifying signification and limits the figure's access to central authority, is in fact hardly untraditional. Charioteers outside hagiography, we have seen, exhibit marginal characteristics as well. Relegating the charioteer (as well as other problematic companions of saints) to the outer limits of significance also proves something of a two-edged sword, for marginality confers its own special brand of authority in Irish tradition and even suggests a paradoxical intimacy with precisely those centers of authority which hagiography attempts to protect against possible undermining by the charioteer.

The classic example of this linking of the margins with the center of the social and cultural organism in medieval Irish literature is a figure we have already encountered, the *fénnid* 'brigand, hunter, warrior'. Like the charioteer, the fénnid looks for signs and interprets them as traces leading to his goal. In hunting for and gathering information he leaves his own traces, sometimes subtle and sometimes not, from which his own presence or absence can be read. The fénnid is a semiotician, living apart from society, yet well versed in the language of his culture. He himself emerges as a prominent signifier within the codes he so deftly interprets and generates.[15] Moreover, the fénnid, like the charioteer (another kind of tracker and dealer in signs), enjoys a special relationship with the hagiographic figure of the saint, who attempts to control him and to tap into his knowledge.

The compulsion of fénnidi to leave their mark behind, as well as their sensitivity to shades of meaning, emerges in an exemplary fashion from the Middle Irish text *Togail Bruidne Dá Derga* (Destruction of Dá Derga's hostel). The destruction to which the title refers is brought about by *fíana* (bands of fénnidi),[16] which upon landing in Ireland make it their first priority to signal their intentions and the hoped-for outcome of their expedition:

The brigands set out from Trácht Fuirbthin, and each of them brought a stone with which to build a cairn. For this was originally the distinction drawn among fiana between a slaughter or a defeat: they would plant pillars [on the site of the impending battle] when it was to be a defeat; when it was to be a slaughter, they would construct a cairn instead. At that time, they constructed a cairn, for there

15. The implications of these literary images of the identity and functions of fénnidi for our understanding of pre-Christian and early Christian social institutions are explored in McCone 1986b and 1987b.
16. Thus are they called in Knott 1936, lines 622, 1081, 1400, 1416, and 1427; see J. Nagy 1985, 43, 80–81. They are also called *díbergaig* 'brigands'. *Díberg* 'brigandage' and *díbergach* 'brigand' are often used to characterize the activities and the person of the fénnid (McCone 1990, 206–7).

was to be a slaughter. They did this far from the house [the hostel they were to destroy], lest they be heard or seen from the house.[17]

As they set out to ambush and slay the king of Ireland in the otherworldly guesthouse of Dá Derga, the fénnidi make sure to leave a sign that not only confidently predicts the story's denouement but also will serve as the verifying trace of a legendary event and of those who made it happen. It is worth noting, moreover, that the signifying cairn is built to announce what is to come to the fénnidi themselves and to us, the readers, but distinctly not to their soon-to-be-victims in Dá Derga's house. Along with the author/ storyteller, the brigands are aware of what is to happen in the story, and by signifying it, they control the story, as if they were projections of the author internalized within the text. Conaire, the king of Ireland, and his men are by now also aware of impending doom, but for them the awareness is a result of encountering and reading ominous signs over which they, prisoners of the story, have no control.[18] The fénnidi's production of signs to which they themselves assign meaning mirrors the authority behind the overarching sign of the text itself. It is that same textual authority in tandem with the oral performance of the intrusive cairn builders which produces the extended tour de force that takes the place of a climax in the text, namely, the famous description of the occupants of Dá Derga's hostel, including Conaire and the members of his retinue. This passage is presented as a dialogue among the fénnidi as they interpret and identify the visual images of the occupants as verbalized by the brigand chief, who has sent his single baleful eye into their midst to spy upon them.[19] Once again, the authorlike fénnidi construct signs—the fanciful descriptions of the occupants—to which they are able and free to assign meaning.[20]

Successful trackers though they may be, fénnidi with inquiring minds such as those in the *Togail* and other medieval texts have limited options in their search for knowledge. They construct and interpret signs far from their actual referents because fénnidi are by definition outsiders with limited access to the institutions, spaces, and people they seek. It is, however, precisely because they are viewing the interplay of cultural signs from the outside that they can play with the rules of the game.

A fénnid, as described in pre-thirteenth-century texts, is a male (sometimes

17. Tos-cuirther beadc na díbergaig a Trácht Fuirbthin ⁊ do-beraid cloich cach fir leó do chur chairn, ar ba sí deochuir lasna fianna i tosuch iter orcuin ⁊ maidm n-imairic, coirthi no clandaitis in tan ba maidm n-imairic. Carn immurgu fo-cerdaitis in tan ba n-orgun. Carn ro lásat íarum in tan sin húaire ba n-orgun. Hi cíanfoccus ón tigh ón, ar ná forclostais ⁊ ná aiccitis ón tigh (Knott 1936, lines 620–27).

18. Knott 1936, lines 229–373, 496–512, 524–79.

19. Ibid., lines 580–1394.

20. This dialogic situation resembles "watchman" scenes in the *Mesca Ulad* and in the medieval Welsh Second Branch of the *Mabinogi,* analyzed in Sims-Williams 1978a.

a female) in search of revenge, the righting of a wrong, or the opportunity to return to the social fold—in general, the missing pieces of his or her social identity. *Fénnidecht* 'being a fénnid' can be a temporary state, a prelude to the assumption of full adult status, responsibility, inheritance, and marriage. Or fénnidecht can become a permanent way of life, a deferral of adulthood as it is traditionally defined or an acknowledgment of the impossibility of obtaining adult status under a given set of circumstances. Fénnidi tend to band together into what is called a *fían* (with a *rígfhénnid* 'chief fénnid'), which forms a counterpoint to regular society and belies the seemingly antisocial and individualistic implications of fénnidecht. Thus, the deferral or absence of adulthood and social identity which life in the fían represents becomes a ghostly presence of social life seen through a prism of alternative possibilities. The "turf" of the fían, located beyond settled, politically defined territory, is in the wilderness of interstitial areas, where its members live by hunting, ravaging surrounding areas, or hiring themselves out as mercenaries.

It has long been observed that fénnidecht, whether ideological fiction or ethnographic fact, is clearly related to similar institutions in other parts of the Indo-European world for making boys into men and establishing male societies within or outside society proper. It has also been recognized that the fénnid/fían can, at least in the realm of story, play an important, even crucial, role in upholding cultural values, either by exemplifying them or by demonstrating what they are *not*. Moreover, the fénnid maintains social and political order by fighting on behalf of kings and by staving off unwelcome intrusions of "aliens" or otherworldly types. Most important of all, his marginality grants the fénnid a special, albeit hardly unique, perspective on "truth," an epistemological privilege that makes him a colleague of poets, seers, and others both within and outside society for whom marginality and wisdom prove to be synergistic characteristics. This "wisdom of the outlaw" is on particularly prominent display in the traditional cycle of stories centered on the longest-lived representatives of fénnidecht in Irish storytelling tradition. These are the rígfhénnid Finn mac Cumaill and the members of his fían, whose adventures and encounters with the otherworld often constitute explorations of the modes of enlightenment available to those who live such deferred lives.[21]

Signa Diabolica

The fénnid of early literature is frequently characterized as a determined hunter of supernaturally elusive prey and a seeker of magical, hard-to-find possessions.[22] Even in his capacity as a warrior, the fénnid is metaphorically a

---

21. J. Nagy 1985 is a general introduction to the mystique of the fénnid figure in this popular narrative tradition.

22. Various examples of these esoteric quests are presented in ibid., 164–92.

hunter and the enemy, the hunted. Fundamental to the fénnid's venery is his capacity to find and interpret traces or, more generally, information that leads to his prey. Therefore he is not only a seeker of the object of his quest but also a seeker of signs, the correct and subtle reading of which can determine the outcome of his quest and even of his "career" in fénnidecht.

The semantics formed of the metonymic vestiges, impressions, and effects left by whatever or whomever the fénnid is seeking does not engage him merely as an observing and interpreting subject. For just as the charioteer and his chariot leave tracks as well as following them, the fénnid leaves traces of himself. Indeed, in his transitional status he represents the social, often problematic identity and even the collective itself that he left behind, and he also anticipates the full-fledged adult responsibilities and roles he is to assume after his residency with the fian is over. The fénnid is therefore both a master of signification and a figure caught up in and defined by the process.[23]

Of course, fénnidi are not the only ones privileged with signification. It is possible, however, to signify more or less. And it is precisely those who experience a loss of significance and suffer from a concomitant powerlessness who tend to join the ranks of fénnidi. This move constitutes a quest for authority and control, which, as we have seen in the literary realm of hagiography and beyond, are most handily available in the form of signs and the act of signification itself. The semiotic quest of the fénnid is replayed in a variety of ways in medieval Irish literature, and it ultimately leads to an encounter and dialogue with the figure of the saint, who serves as the ultimate "reader" of the fénnid's significance.

In his groundbreaking exploration of the early Irish usages of Hiberno-Latin *laicus* and Irish *láech* 'layman, warrior, brigand', Richard Sharpe notes that the brigands so frequently featured in Irish saints' lives, most likely the fénnidi and fiana we find in other forms of literature, are sometimes described as wearing special insignia, *stigmata* or *signa diabolica*. In the hagiographic episodes in which these appear, the Christian holy man or woman undoes the evil significance of such signs, showing them or some other representation to be false, and thus winning the hearts of those who had previously been devoted to pagan ways.[24]

This pattern is of course familiar to us from Patrician hagiography, for

23. The notion of the hunter as trope master and seeker of knowledge is by no means limited in its application to the Irish fénnid. For instance, the metaphor of the hunt underlies the famous Old Irish poem in which the scribe-monk compares himself to his cat Pangur Bán, and his intellectual activities to the feline hunt for mice (edited and translated in Murphy 1962, 2–3; and Greene and O'Connor 1967, 81–83). Comparable applications of the metaphor are to be found in Boethius's *Consolation of Philosophy*, in the writings of the Anglo-Saxon king Alfred, and in those of his biographer Asser, all as discussed by Seth Lerer (1991, 77–81). Carruthers discusses classical and medieval comparisons between recollection and hunting (1990, 247).

24. Sharpe 1979, 82–85; and see Sharpe 1991, 319.

example, in Patrick's encounter with the *tyrannus* Mac Cuill.[25] An example of such undermining and subsequent redirecting of signification for the purpose of "enlightening" fénnidi comes from the earliest extant Irish saint's life, Cogitosus's seventh-century account of Brigit:

[The saint] saw nine men in a certain peculiar guise required by a godless and diabolical superstition, shouting in a grotesque tone of voice and showing signs of utter insanity, and in their paths lay destruction and misfortune. With the most wicked vows and oaths to the ancient enemy who reigned over them, they thirsted for bloodshed and planned the slaughter and murder of others before the kalends of the following month should arrive. The most reverent and affable Brigit preached to them with mellifluous eloquence, that they might abandon the deadly errors of their ways and blot out their crimes by compunction of heart and true repentance. But refusing in the blindness of their heart to do this until they had first fulfilled their godless vows, they continued on their way. But the illustrious virgin poured out unceasing prayers to the Lord for this intention, willing, after the Lord's example, all men to be saved and come to the knowledge of the truth. And, in consequence, the wicked men who were setting out beheld an apparition of the man whom they were to kill, and forthwith having killed him with their lances and beheaded him with their swords, they came back as they would after a triumph over their enemy and foe with weapons stained with blood and gore and appeared to many. In a strange way, although they had killed nobody, it seemed to them that they had fulfilled their vows. And since no one over whom they might have triumphed was missing from that province—and no one had any lingering doubt about that matter—the generous bestowal of the divine gift through Saint Brigit became known to all. Thus, those who hitherto were murderers were converted to the Lord through repentance.[26]

The clash between saint and brigand is encoded acoustically as well as visually, the noises made by the pagans versus the "mellifluous" preaching of Brigit. Here again, the narrated negotiation of authority between past and present and between pagan and Christian cultures takes on the form of a dialogue, a sequence of antiphonal verbal or, in the case of the brigands, subverbal performances.

Elsewhere in medieval Brigitine hagiography, another band of such supernaturally driven seekers of human prey, wearing *stigmata diabolica*, actually asks the saint to *bless* their upcoming murderous adventures, to be undertaken, our texts inform us, as a demonstration of the lethal proclivities of those who wear these signs or, alternatively, in an attempt to release the

25. See pp. 109–11.
26. C. 23, trans. Connolly and Picard 1987, 20–21. On the complex relationship between Brigit and brigands, see Coe 1989, 27–35.

brigands from the tyranny of their stigmata. Brigit miraculously arranges for both their liberation from the diabolic signs (which fall off) and the safekeeping of those the brigands had planned to attack.[27]

The motif of the maleficent signing of these reavers, who are held captive as well as empowered by their stigmata, is no hagiographic fantasy or misreading of cultural data. It derives from the traditional perception of fénnidi as living signs and bearers or seekers of authoritative signs, and as potential victims of those same signs, and from the hagiographic perception of saints as masters/ mistresses of signs, which they can confer or remove. Indeed, the saints do more than just remove or revalidate the brigands' emblems. These pagans become part of a tale very different from that which they seek to bring about in slaying their victims as the *stigmata* dictate they should. The saint brings their story to an unexpected, exemplary end, which imposes a surprising significance, as well as an irresistible constraint, on fénnidi in search of meanings quite different from those they come to bear themselves.

In regard to those undesirable signs that mysteriously exert maleficent control over those whom they make significant, Kim McCone, elaborating on Sharpe's findings concerning the use of the word *láech*, observes that the various physical disfigurements that mark fénnidi and other paragons of martial achievement in heroic story, such as the one-eyedness of Finn's perennial opponent Goll or the disfigurement of Cú Chulainn during his martial trance (*ríastrad*), may well be vernacular reflections of the *signa diabolica*.[28] These "trademarks" inscribed on the body are ambiguous signs. That is, they sug-

---

27. Cc. 64–65 of the *Vita prima* of Brigit (trans. in Connolly 1989, 31–32). "What the *stigmata* in the episode recounted in our text actually consisted of one can only conjecture," Connolly says. "In c. 67.1 the men are said to be wearing them on their heads. They may have been the images of their enemies. The word *stigma* itself may afford some clue. Originally a Greek noun formed from the verb *stizein* 'to prick' or 'pierce', it is tempting to connect it with the practice of making an image of wax or lead of a person whose death one wished and piercing it with a needle or nail so that the person in question suffered correspondingly. Such execratory or cursing tablets were commonly used all over the ancient world" (1989, 10–11). See also Sharpe 1979, 83–85.

The episode in the *Vita prima* has a remarkable sequel. Having saved Conall, son of Niall, from his stigmata and the commitment to brigandage, Brigit promises to protect him hereafter. Once, Conall and his men, having taken refuge for the night, are tracked down by those they have just attacked: "And when they drew near the fort where Conall was, they sent four men to reconnoitre the fort. The men went into the fort and there saw a whole throng of clerics sitting dressed in clerical garb around a fire with books open in front of them. For the army had arranged the heads of the slain in such a way that each one had a head lying in front of him. And so the men seemed as if they were closely examining the open books and the scouts went back and reported these matters. And a second time they sent three other men who were shrewder and they too saw the clerics with the books open, just as the first ones had seen" (trans. in Connolly 1989, 31–32). The conversion of these former fénnidi could not be more complete.

28. McCone notes these and other analogues to the conspicuous markings on brigands (1986b, 21–22). See also M. Ó Briain 1991, 101–2, and 112–13 n. 80, on horses' ears as possibly another kind of "diabolic sign."

gest a lack, an incompleteness, or even a vulnerability; yet, in fact, they are symbols and even instruments of supernatural power and control.

A Rígfhénnid's Head

The net result of the characteristic fénnid activities of tracking, bearing, and fighting over signs usually includes not only the gaining of booty or revenge but also a lesson in reading the signs of the past or a glimmer into the future. Alone and vulnerable in the face of overwhelming and devious signs, the fénnid himself is liable to become the sign of what he has experienced or learned, a synecdochic transformation of the person of the knower into a disembodied machine for communicating what he knows.

The saga of the celebrated rígfhénnid Fothad Canainne, a rival of the more famous fian leader Finn, presents us with a fénnid who dies in his prime during his quest for a possession that would set him apart from his fellow fénnidi.[29] With such a death he is guaranteed a place in tradition and even a strange kind of life after death, as a singing sign of himself. Fothad's story is told in the Middle Irish prose introduction to a lengthy Old Irish poem attributed to him.[30] He is one of three sons, all of whom are overmarked with a superfluity of names, as is, we are starting to see, not untypical for fénnidi. Yet these names strengthen the collective identity among them, since the members of each set of names contain the same core elements: Tréndia 'Strong God', Cáindia 'Fair God', and Óendia 'Singular God'; and Fothad Canainn(e) 'Of the Whelp [?]', Fothad Airgtech 'The Plunderer', and Fothad Cairpthech 'The Chariot-borne'.[31]

This triad of brothers is not described as fighting together in a fian, but we are told that the rhapsodizing Fothad was a rígfhénnid in the province of Connacht, and that he engaged in a long-standing feud with a Munster rígfhénnid, Ailill Flann Becc. The text alludes intriguingly to a particular issue of contention between them: "Fothad's appearance was more remarkable [(h)amru] than Ailill's, while Ailill's wife was more remarkable and more beautiful than Fothad's."[32] Although the fénnid may achieve fame or notoriety on his own, he is wont to seek persons or objects that will represent him

29. McQuillan 1990 sets out some of the links between Fothad and Finn.
30. Edited and translated in Meyer 1910a, 4–21. The prose introduction is also to be found in Hull 1936. My translation of the poetry is indebted to Meyer's, as well as to that of Greene and O'Connor (1967, 86–92).
31. The names are presented and analyzed in the introduction to the *Reicne* (Meyer 1910a, 4) and in the *Cóir Anmann* (Suitability of names) (Stokes 1897, 316). The canine element in Fothad's nickname is echoed in the alternative designation given to Fothad Canóine (Fothad "of the Canonical Text"), a historical figure whose name may punningly refer to the mythic hero: Cú Cruithne, 'Dog of the Picts' (Mac Airt 1951, 124 [A.D. 818], and note).
32. Ba hamru delb Fothaid ol bái Oilill, acht ba hamru ben Oilella 7 ba haille oldas ben Fhothaid (Meyer 1910a, 6).

authoritatively, signs that he can manipulate and call his own, but which are often beyond his control or even in the control of another. In this case, that sign, the acquisition of which would make Fothad even more famous or *amru*, is the wife of another fénnid.[33]

Fothad sends a negotiator to barter discreetly with Ailill's beloved, but the price she demands for agreeing to consort with Fothad instead of, or as well as, Ailill very graphically runs counter to the male relationships that have helped to make Fothad a successful and famous fénnid. From each spear of Fothad's men she is to be given three of the six rivets made of precious metals which bind it together. Such a loss will significantly reduce the splendor of his comrades' appearance, not to mention the durability of their spears in battle.

As soon as Fothad, having paid the price, meets with the woman and steals her away, he becomes remarkably conspicuous and vulnerable. The elopement brings disastrous results. Ailill pursues the pair, the fiana clash, Fothad's men are all slain, and their leader's head is cut off. Worth noting here is the traditional function of the severed head kept by the victor as a victory trophy, even though, according to the poem to follow, Ailill too is slain in battle, and so there would appear to be no one left to "use" the trophy. The object of contention, the woman, finds the head and while she is on her way to the grave to restore it to Fothad's body, the head speaks in verse to her.

As Fothad's poem makes clear, his final thoughts centered on the contrast between an active, heroic past informed by life among fellow fénnidi and a present shaped, so the head claims, by a conflict over a woman and marked by a living death. A gruesome synecdochic representation of the past, Fothad's head remembers or memorializes it and bequeaths its treasures to the woman. At one point in the text, Fothad identifies what he is saying as a *timna*, a word with very close links to *audacht* 'final words or testament'.[34] In that same stanza, the *timna* is equated with two other terms Fothad uses to describe his utterance, *reicne* and *cobra(d)*—the latter, we recall, occurs in compound form in *síaburchobra(e)*, the term used to describe the verse speech delivered by the dead Cú Chulainn to the mourning Ulsterwomen. What the dead hero has to say clearly will have a life of its own. The *timna / reicne / cobra* will always be remembered, provided the woman pays heed at its first telling, just as the treasures he bequeaths to the woman have already had lives of their own. Thus, complementing the woman's desire to reintegrate body and head, the promise of continuity between heroes of the past and those who carry on

---

33. Peter McQuillan notes that this is not the only narrative instance of Fothad's stealing a woman. He is said in *dindshenchas* literature to have abducted Medb Lethderg, "the Leinster sovereignty figure par excellence" (1990, 3).

34. Meyer 1910a, 16 (Mo c[h]obrad frit nī hinglae / má imraī te mo thimna, "My dialogue with you is not obscure if you remember my will"). On *audacht* and its meaning(s), see J. Nagy 1990c, 130–32, and references.

their memory beckons both the female protagonist and the audience of this story and of the poem it frames.

Yet, in disquieting counterpoint to the almost tender communicativeness of the head toward the beloved, we remain aware of the literal and metaphoric isolation of both the head and the intelligence it contains. Furthermore, the poem exudes Fothad's hostility toward the woman, which makes the communication one-sided and even suggests the possibility that it may be ignored. *Dúnad* 'closure', a typical feature of Irish poetry, comes by way of the negation of dialogue, namely, "Do not talk to me, woman,"[35] the phrase that begins and ends the poem.

Fothad would prefer to be alone, he explains, because his mind is still in the battle in which he fell. He even warns that talking with a dead man is dangerous.[36] Arguably, talking with a woman, which can lead to situations such as the one that deprived Fothad of a body, can be equally, if not even more, dangerous, as the pointed references to the sinister war goddess the Morrígan, "she who has stirred us up,"[37] make clear. Furthermore, in refusing to engage in dialogue with the woman, Fothad, who warns her not to talk to a "dead man," also appears to be rejecting his own value as a sign, namely, as a talking, disembodied head, which, as we have seen, is perhaps the most venerable supernatural source of statements that are to be heeded. A memorable demonstration of the compelling nature of the severed head's pronouncements occurs in the *Táin* when Cú Chulainn's father, Súaltaim, acting as messenger for his harried son, issues words of warning to the men of Ulster, but they are heard and acted on only after Súaltaim's head is detached from his trunk in a freak accident and yet continues to speak.[38] And in another corner of the literary tradition is the long-lasting skull of Cormac mac Airt, the king of Ireland traditionally noted for his wisdom.[39] This gigantic repository for one of the most celebrated intelligences from the pre-Christian era is found by Columba and speaks through the power of Columba's prayer, miraculously testifying to Cormac's anticipation of Christianity.[40]

As opposed to the statements of Súaltaim and Cormac, what Fothad's head has to say contains a defiant and even resentful note. Perhaps to speak *and* be spoken to in this situation would be to surrender his freedom of interpretative movement and to resign himself to being a mere remnant of the past, on display and available for questioning in the confines of the narrative tradition

35. A ben, náchamaicillé (Meyer 1910a, 10, 16).
36. Ni fiu cobraim fri fer marb (ibid., 12).
37. Isi cotanosoide (ibid., 16).
38. C. O'Rahilly 1976b, lines 3410–50; 1967, lines 3981–4047.
39. The various aspects of the mythological Cormac mac Airt, including his wisdom and kingliness, are the subject of Ó Cathasaigh 1977.
40. O'Kelleher and Schoepperle 1918, 128.

and the poem in which he speaks. Fothad, however, still has some things to say about his particular situation, and not just about a safe, abstracted past.

The ambivalence expressed toward the woman in Fothad's poetic utterance highlights the potentially deadly alternation between the freedom to signify and interpret signs (as in taking another's mate as one's own) and being reduced to a sign in the hands of others.

The dead hero refers in the last stanza of the poem to his *cobra* as well as his own appearance (*gné*) as *síabair* 'spectral' (recall Cú Chulainn's *síaburcho-brae*) shortly after he imparts a homiletic apothegm to his listener(s), expressing sentiments seemingly inconsistent with the rest of what he has had to say: "Love of this life is madness, except for worship of the King of Heaven."[41] Has Fothad's mind finally left behind the battlefield, strewn with the corpses of his slain comrades, and is he no longer concerned with what will happen to his treasures? Is he now divinely inspired? And is he imparting a newly found truth to the woman or just telling her what she already knows, or wants to hear? Whatever answers we propose to these questions, it is undeniable that the author of the poem appears to have modeled Fothad's testamentary utterance along the lines of the Christian scripting of the dialogue between saint and miraculously recovered hero from the past. It is precisely this kind of modeling that we see in the *Síaburcharpat Con Culainn,* although there, as I have observed, the interlocutor from the past in fact denies his spectrality. In the case of Fothad there is of course no saint but a woman. This is a curious substitution; yet it resonates with the image of the mourning band of women who try to stop Cú Chulainn from rushing to his doom and who subsequently receive his posthumous words, and with New Testament accounts of Christ's resurrection, according to which it is the faithful women who are first apprised of this, the greatest of Christ's miracles.[42] It is also possible to see the suddenly preaching head as transcending time altogether in its function as a lasting signifier, changing the signification of the woman from a figure who stands for the present into an antiquated denizen of a past still waiting to be enlightened. Thus, from this perspective, the head of Fothad lies closer to the stereotypical figure of the saint as he operates in such situations of cultural dialogue than does the woman. Still, her role in this scenario as the problematic link who evokes mutually incompatible affiliations and loyalties brings to mind the function of the sympathetic women who help the saint join forces with the native culture and with the social network in which it is grounded.

And so we see that the recasting of Fothad from reluctant battlefield relic/performance piece of the immediate past into prophet of the culture's future occurs within the poem along an axis of sexual polarization. This particular subtext to the Fothad saga takes on even larger proportions when

---

41. Serc bethu cé is miri / ingi adradh Rīgh nimi. . . . sī abra mo c[h]obra, mo gnē (Meyer 1910a, 16).
42. See p. 263.

we consider what otherwise might seem a stray bit of tradition. Some sources say Fothad's wife, either the recipient of the battlefield verses or another woman in his life, was the Caillech Bérre 'Old Woman of Beare.'[43] These paired figures, as revealed in the poem just discussed and the famous lament attributed to the Caillech,[44] share the characteristic of remarkable longevity—Fothad as a severed head and the Caillech as an ancient who has seen several generations and been the consort of many important men. In their noted rhapsodies, however, they both bid farewell to their pasts and their past affiliations. Yet Fothad and the Caillech elegize and thereby keep these memories alive in prosodic distillations, performed long after the performers should have been dead. Moreover, in declaring the past with its web of implicating relationships indeed the past, these nostalgists become promoters of a future of Christian salvation, which, however, calls into question the very authority the figures of fénnid and royal consort have accrued by way of accomplishment and memory.

The Mystery of Mongán

The fénnid Fothad when reduced to the synecdoche of a talking head becomes a reminder of what was and what will be, but the dialogue featured in his poem is decidedly one-sided, with Fothad virtually silencing his interlocutor and carrying on a conversation among the various strands of his own complex persona. There is, however, a remarkable case in early medieval Irish tradition in which not only does an ancient fénnid respond to the call of a "modern" collector of knowledge in search of information, but the representative of modernity is revealed to be a fénnid as well. An examination of this story (from the Old Irish cycle of stories about King Mongán) shows us that the fénnid, like the poet and the saint, is a master of signs who by following tracks left in time can revise his culture's formulations of its past and of its identity. These insights into the proper interpretation of old signs are paradoxically "old" and "new" at the same time.

Mongán, associated with the Dál nAraidi in northeastern Ulster and situated by the annals in the early seventh century, is, we recall, the young man from across the waves with whom Columba has an esoteric conversation about hidden truths, a dialogue hidden from Columba's fellow clerics and from us, the readers of the account.[45] That story constitutes a remarkable admission of the intimacy shared between Columba and representatives of native institutions and sources of knowledge, as well as a curious violation of

---

43. Dobbs 1930–32, 302, 176, 211. The mythological dimensions to the Caillech as she is featured in the poem attributed to her and in other medieval Irish texts are explored in Ó Cathasaigh 1989.
44. Edited and translated in Ó hAodha 1989.
45. See pp. 143–46.

the scribal tradition's chronological formulation of Irish cultural history. Columba here is the elder statesmen of the "young" religion engaging in dialogue and private epistemological negotiations with a youthful proponent of the "old" order. Characteristically, stories about Mongán, like the figure himself, question conventional expectations and assumptions about the passage of time and the putative traces of past events.

In one of the Old Irish Mongán tales preserved in the Labor na hUidre manuscript, a surprise link between the Dál nAraidi king and the Fenian tradition in the persons of Caílte (Finn's righthand man) and the rígfhénnid Finn himself is revealed in the course of a life-and-death struggle and dialogue over expertise between Mongán and a poet.[46] From the first of November to the first of May, the story tells us, Mongán and his court are entertained by the stories told by the visiting poet Forgoll, who is being handsomely paid for his performances. One day, Mongán asks the poet a question meant to elicit a story: How and where did the death of Fothad Airgthech come about? The topic already implicitly brings up the Fenian tradition, since the Fothads were fénnidi, like the Fenian heroes, and had dealings with Finn. Forgoll tells the story, presumably, and sets it in Leinster. Mongán responds that Fothad was in fact not slain in Leinster. Upon having his professional grasp of knowledge about the past so indelicately challenged, Forgoll furiously threatens to satirize Mongán, his kingship, and his kingdom into oblivion. Alarmed, Mongán gives the poet possession of anything he desires, short of Mongán's queen, in recompense for the slight, unless Mongán can prove he was right in three days' time. Forgoll, however, states that after those three days, if Mongán does not obtain proof, he, the poet, will accept nothing short of the queen. The king reluctantly agrees to this arrangement. On the third day, as the deadline draws near for surrendering the queen to the poet, she expresses her sorrow and anxiety to her husband, who is ill with anxiety himself but comforts her by claiming to hear the feet of someone who will vindicate him coming closer and closer as he fords the various rivers of Ireland (duly noted by Mongán). Finally, with the poet about to claim the queen, a stranger appears by the king's bedside. When he hears of what is being disputed, the stranger, who never identifies himself directly but is identified by the text as Caílte mac Rónáin, declares with an authority not questioned by the poet that Mongán was correct: "'It shall be proved. We were with you, Finn,' said the warrior. 'Hush!' said Mongán, 'that is not fair.'"[47]

Having been thus instructed not to divulge everything he knows, Caílte proceeds with his presentation of proof:

46. Best and Bergin 1929, lines 10938–98.
47. Proimfithir. Bámárni latsu la Find ol in t-óclach. Adautt ol Mongan ní maith sin (Best and Bergin 1929, lines 10983–84). The title assigned this tale in the manuscript also identifies Mongan as Finn in no uncertain terms (ibid., line 10938).

> "We were with Finn, then. We came from Scotland. We met with Fothad Airgthech over yonder on the Ollarba River. There we fought a battle. I made a cast at him, so that it passed through him and went into the earth beyond him and left its iron head in the earth. This here is the shaft that was in that spear. The bare stone from which I made that cast will be found, and the iron head will be found in the earth, and the tomb of Fothad Airgthech will be found a little to the east of it. A stone chest is about him there in the earth. There, upon the chest, are his two bracelets of silver, and his two arm-rings, and his neck-torque of silver. And by his tomb there is a stone pillar. And on the end of the pillar that is in the earth there is ogam. This is what it says: 'This is Fothad Airgthech. Caílte slew me in an encounter against Finn.'" They went with the warrior. Everything was found thus.[48]

With this testimony from an eyewitness to the past which also indicates the existence of yet another eyewitness and participant amidst the present of the performance of the narrative, Mongán's kingship, queen, and credibility are saved.

The king's credibility is at issue as well as the poet's because of Mongán's tendency here and elsewhere to usurp functions and authorities that at first do not appear to belong to him. True, in challenging the version of the story of the death of Fothad told by Forgoll, Mongán merely asserts his rights as the audience, which is entitled to receive an accurate product from the performer. Yet what Mongán initiates is a takeover, whereby he turns himself into the verbal performer and must be vindicated by another, even more authoritative performance. Mongán's accusation is that Forgoll has placed the killing, and the corpse of Fothad, in the wrong location—that he has in effect mismatched signifier and signified, not unlike the woman in the Patrician legend who places the cross on the wrong grave. Mongán's critique elicits the poet's threat to strip his critic of all the signs of his regal authority, including the most important of all, his queen. This threat refers to the beginning of the story, to what at first appears to be a negligible detail, that married couples had been complaining to Mongán about Forgoll's victimizing. It is as if the poet's power of satire, based on what are in his eyes impeccable knowledgeability and proper reading of the past and its memorials, enables him to

48. Bámárni la Find trá ol se dulodmar di Albae. Immarnacmár fri Fothud nAirgtech hi sund accut for Ollorbi. Fichimmir scandal n-and Fochartso erchor fair co sech trít co lluid hi talmain friss anall ⁊ co facab a iarnd hi tallam iss ed a ndíceltar so ro boí isin gai sin. Fugebthar in maelcloch día rolusa a roud sin ⁊ fogebthar a n-airiarnn isin talam fogebthar a ulad Fothaid Airgtig fris anair bic. Ata comrar chloche imbi and hi talam. Ataat a di foil airgit ⁊ a di bunne doat ⁊ a muintorc argit for chomrair. ⁊ atá coirthe oca ulaid. ⁊ atá ogom isin chind fil hi talam din corthi. Iss ed fil and. Eochaid Airgtech inso. ra mbí Caílte i n-imaeriuc fri Find. Éthe lasin n-óclaic aricht samlaid ule ⁊ fofrítha. Ba hé Caílte dalta Find dodánic. Ba hé Find dano inti Mongán acht nad leic a forndisse (ibid., lines 10984–98).

wrest away the authoritative signs of other males, among which women loom prominently here, as elsewhere in medieval Irish tradition.

Mongán's dilemma, in which his version of the past is pitted against that of a "historian" of unimpeachable authority, is resolved by means of a remarkable intrusion of the past into the present. A hero of old senses an emergency, or perhaps is summoned by Mongán, and transcends time in order to assist one who turns out to be equally of the past, and equally capable of stepping over the temporary boundaries that frame normal human existence. Appropriately, it is a fénnid who hears the "call" and tracks it down to its source, pointedly approaching through the rivers of Ireland, like some waterborne packet of knowledge sent from the otherworld. Caílte's beeline to the court is anticipated only by Mongán, whose hearing is as acute as a hunter's, and who can "hear" the past coming into the present, just as he knows the true facts of Fothad's death.

The revelation blurted out by the newly arrived fénnid and silenced by Mongán establishes an even more intimate link between modern amateur storyteller and ancient witness. With the news that Mongán could in fact tell the story as authoritatively as Caílte, Forgoll and his expertise are routed, in the same way that Lóegaire is outmaneuvered by the combination of Patrick and a rehabilitated, Christianized Cú Chulainn. In the case of the Mongán tale, however, it is not the present that has insinuated itself into the audience's expectations of the past but the past that is revealed to have its secret operators in the present. A seemingly autonomous reader or possessor of signs is revealed to be, in addition, the sign of someone else: Mongán is, it would appear, an avatar of Finn. In sum, then, by the end of the story of Mongán's contest with Forgoll, the details of the death of Fothad, originally a "signified" hard to signify, are crystal clear, and the relevant signs—the spear shaft, the spear head, the site of his burial, the treasures, the memorial stone, and the inscription—have been methodically read and witnessed. Yet perhaps the most important outcome of the story is the revelation that the audience-turned-performer can himself be read as a sign of the past, but a past whose full significance the story only barely traces. Questions concerning the link between Mongán and Finn remain tactfully unasked and unanswered.

There is at least one person in this story who knows the truth behind the confusing appearances, and the necessary ingredients for an enlightening dialogue are indeed present, including the figures of the verifying witness from the past and the poet who can pass the information on to posterity. Yet here as elsewhere in Mongán legendary, only a synecdochic bit of the knowledge to be had is let out of the bag, as teasing as the fragments divulged in the account of the dialogue between Mongán and Columba. It is by way of such mystifying refusal to disclose all there could be to tell that Mongán-Finn nurtures his charismatic authority, over the characters of the story and us, his readership, as well.

In his role as knowledgeable or unwitting summoner of the dead, Mongán stands out as unique in the gallery of nonclerical possessors of knowledge featured in medieval literary tradition. Otherwise, only saints are able to conduct dialogue with the dead which vindicates their formulation of the past or present, and only their once-dead informants evince such an intimacy and familiarity with their interrogators. The novel solution to the epistemological problem that has become a crisis of Mongán's kingship is of course not a mere borrowing from hagiography. The saint's summoning of the dead represents a coup for the present, but what happens to Mongán is very much a coup for the past, the unfathomable inner recesses of which are revealed to the eyes of the present as if in a flash of inspiration.

Marbán's Challenge to Poets

Cut from the same cloth as the story of Mongán's delivery from disgrace is the curious foretale associated with the *Táin Bó Cúailnge*. In this story-about-a-story, already discussed briefly in the Introduction,[49] we learn of how the poets of Ireland recovered the narrative of the cattle raid after being challenged to do so by an audience and clientele fast growing tired of the poets' arrogant claim to society's respect based on knowledge that they in fact no longer have. The tense situation featured in the account of the recovery of the *Táin* resonates strikingly with the cultural critique at the heart of the tale of Mongán and Forgoll, in which the Dál nAraidi king sets out to expose the hollowness of contemporary poetic authority within the sometimes treacherous confines of the performer-audience relationship. Moreover, the one who slyly offers a dilemma as well as its solution to the professional bearers of tradition, and the knowledgeable person of the past tracked down by poet and saint alike, are both denizens of the marginal world populated by fénnidi.

The version of the story of the finding of the *Táin* which dwells most extensively on the power struggle underlying the search is to be found in the late medieval text known as the *Tromdám Gúaire* (Heavy hosting of Gúaire).[50] The poets and other verbal performers who are preying upon the king are specifically said to belong to the generation succeeding those who were summoned to the epochal meeting with Columba at Druim Cet. En masse under the leadership of the *ollam* ('chief poet') Senchán Torpéist, this new generation descends upon the king of Connacht, Gúaire mac Colmáin, who is widely reputed for his generosity. The assembled artists, relying on the threat

---

49. See pp. 17–20.
50. Edited by Maud Joynt (1931). Carney (1955, 170–79) summarizes or translates the section of the text pertaining to the contention between the poets and Marbán, and the search for the *Táin*. Ó Coileáin 1977 provides background to the text (see also Ó Coileáin 1988; Carney 1955, 181–88). Shaw 1992 offers fascinating evidence for the persistence of the narrative tradition of the "heavy host" in twentieth-century Nova Scotia.

of satire, wish to test how far Gúaire's generosity extends. They finally meet their match in the person of Marbán, the king's brother, who becomes involved after his pet pig is demanded by and given over to the poetic extortionists. Marbán, whose name is based on the adjective *marb* 'dead' (perhaps in the Christian sense of "dead to the world"), is a hermit and as such does not normally participate in social affairs.[51] Despite, or perhaps precisely because of, this asocial streak, Marbán's range of talents proves to be extraordinary. In addition to being the king's swineherd, he is the "chief seer of heaven and earth,"[52] a poet, the mainstay of Gúaire's kingship, and the supplier of the various recherché foods and supplies requested of the king by the poets. These are items such as wild berries out of season, which only those well versed in the hiding places of nature can track down. While he is never described as a fénnid, Marbán occupies the same spatial and functional territory. He is, as I have already noted, a devotee of the wilderness, of which—and from which?—he has great knowledge. His self-imposed exile is so profound that, when Marbán approaches the gathering of the poets, no one recognizes him at first.[53] Moreover, what motivates Marbán to enter verbal combat with the poets, is, as he himself states, his wish to punish them in revenge for their destruction of his pet pig.[54] What brings the hermit back into contact with society, therefore, is a desire for vengeance, which is often the raison d'être for the fénnid's condition and actions.

Before demonstrating his impressive familiarity with the performers' crafts, the hermit uses the flimsiest pretext to claim his right to join them: "'I have my own family connection with poetry,' said Marbán. 'My servant's wife's grandmother was a poet's great-grandchild.'"[55] In this as well as in other respects, Marbán resembles Mongán, whose pedigree as a poet is questionable but whose authority is overwhelmingly convincing. Once he is allowed inside, Marbán proves to be unstoppable in his critique of the state of the verbal art. He proceeds to demand of the poets and other performers levels of performance they cannot achieve or information about the origins of their respective crafts they do not have, but he does. Thus, the amateur proves himself to be indubitably better informed about the legendary past and its performative manifestations than those whom society has designated, or who have designated themselves, as the purveyors of tradition to society.

The ultimate challenge Marbán sets for the verbal craftsmen pertains to the

51. One of the most famous "hermit" poems from early Irish tradition is an exchange between Marbán, praising the glories of his wilderness home, and Gúaire, attempting to win him back to the comfortable ways of civilization. Ed. and trans. in Murphy 1962, 10–19. On the literary persona of the hermit and the "genre" of nature poetry, see Ó Corráin 1989a.
52. Primfhaid nimhe 7 talman (Joynt 1931, line 387, and elsewhere).
53. Ibid., lines 811–41.
54. Ibid., lines 802–3.
55. "Ata mu charadrad fein re héicsi," ar Marban, ".i. senmháthair mhna mu ghilla iarmua fhiledh iside" (ibid., lines 822–25).

genre of storytelling. Can the men of art's best storyteller, he asks, tell him the tale of the cattle raid of Cúailnge? After an embarrassed silence, the confession is finally elicited that the story is, in fact, lost. With this professional scandal brought out into the open, Marbán forbids all the men of art to continue their various professional activities until they recover the story. Thus, he sends the poets and their colleagues on a hunt throughout the Gaelic-speaking world (Ireland and Scotland) and into the past.

According to an earlier telling of the story of the finding of the *Táin*, the poets had not simply lost the tale from their collective memory but had exchanged a written version of it for a manuscript containing Isidore of Seville's *Etymologiae*.[56] Hence, at least from the perspective afforded us by this twist to the story, the poets clearly are the nouveau intelligentsia, the literati of early Christian Ireland, or they have revamped themselves and their profession so thoroughly that they have become, as the story shows, hopelessly and helplessly "modern." The challenge to recollect the *Táin*, then, is not a contemporary questioning of the authority of traditional poets and other men of art corrupted by their status but an attempt to get them back to their roots, unwritten and based in the living context of performance.

In the *Tromdám* text it is performance indeed that punctuates and even fuels the poets' trip into their narratological past. Senchán and company set out for Scotland (where they hope to find the *Táin*) by way of Leinster, and they meet a hideous leper who insists that they take him along. Marbán's injunction has deprived them of the calling card they will need to gain access to the king of Leinster, that is, poetry. Fortunately, there is more to the leper than meets the eye, and he offers his poetic assistance.[57] And so it is thanks to the unseemly stranger, who composes a request in verse to the Leinster monarch, that the poets obtain the shipping and supplies necessary to cross the waters. As his price, the leper demands a kiss, which Senchán gives him most grudgingly. This curious demand harks back to two earlier episodes in the story, in which Senchán refused food served by servants in Gúaire's court because he remembered the servants' ancestors as having had unsightly, although minor, blemishes on their bodies. Subsequently, Gúaire imposes on his difficult guest the curse that he will be forced to kiss a leper sometime before he dies.[58] So, to find the *Táin*, Senchán must embrace what has become for him a nightmarish image of a corrupted past, accepting it as a salvific part of the present. It is precisely such an attitude of *pietas* which the poets are forced to rediscover as they search for the tradition they have lost. Furthermore, in embracing a nameless, servile figure, Senchán is forced to

56. See p. 18.
57. An examination of this figure and a translation of the lengthy entry in Cormac's Glossary which features an earlier incarnation of the helpful leper (Meyer 1912, 90–94) are offered in P. Ford 1990a, 30–35.
58. Joynt 1931, lines 650–82.

take seriously the tenuous channels of communication among different social classes which enable the marginal Marbán to contend with the poets and, in the long run, provide for the revitalization of the poetic profession as presented in this tale.

After leaving the Leinster court well stocked and refusing to permit the leper to accompany them on the sea voyage, the still haughty poets nonetheless find him on board at a key moment, just when they are issued a challenge from the shore. A female coastguard states that she will let them land only if they can finish the stanzas she recites to them. It is of course the leper who completes the verses, and having once again obtained passage for the poets, he disappears. Scotland, however, turns out to have been a false lead; no *Táin* is to be found, and Gúaire's prediction to the poets, that it would not be found where the actual events of the story did not take place, is realized.

Upon returning to Ireland with his fortunes and credentials at a low ebb, Senchán is met by his half-brother Caillín, a cleric who reveals that he in fact was the mysterious leper. He offers to go with Senchán and his colleagues to obtain from Marbán the secret of how the *Táin* can be recovered. Marbán reveals to them that no one living knows the tale anymore. Even of the dead, only one, Fergus mac Róich, could tell it. Marbán advises the poets to summon all the saints of Ireland together to fast against God and ask that Fergus be brought back to life for a short while, so he can tell the lost story. The assembly of the saints is arranged, God relents, and Fergus, whose size is notable and who must sit down in order to be heard by this postheroic audience, rehearses the story of the *Táin* for them. It is written down upon the hide of the cow of Ciarán of Clonmacnois, a precious relic upon which, we are told elsewhere, those who lay instantly went to heaven.[59] Thus the *Táin* is recaptured, fixed in a written form, which, this time, will presumably not be given away, and even symbolically "saved" and translated into heavenly terms, not unlike Cú Chulainn, the hero of the cattle raid in his Patrician chariot.[60]

The story of the search begins in a performance setting featuring a give-and-take dialogue between Marbán and the men of art. The search and the story of the search appear to gain momentum only to lose it in a wild-goose

---

59. See the Middle Irish notes to the Martyrology of Óengus (Stokes 1905b, 202, 204) and the Latin and Irish lives of this saint (Plummer 1910, 1:205 [c. 15]; Stokes 1890, 123 [lines 4116–17]). According to the legend implicit in the title Lebor na hUidre, assigned well after its production, Ciarán's *Odor* 'Dun [Cow]' provided the surface on which was written this famous late eleventh-century Irish manuscript (which includes, among other texts, the *Táin*). 60. Writing's potential authority as an extension of the witness of the dead is an issue in legal literature as well. See, e.g., *CIH* 596, lines 8–9, 13–15, 29–30, trans. Stacey 1986, 220, 221. On the evidentiary value of writing, see also McManus 1991, 162–64; and Carey 1992. And yet, writes Gearóid Mac Niocaill, "in sum, we may say that written evidence, though of its nature impugnable only with the greatest difficulty, held no more than a restricted place in early Irish law. Oral evidence, as in any largely non-literate society, was the norm, and the question of its admissibility figures in a number of texts" (Mac Niocaill 1972, 334).

chase of an episode featuring similar performance exchanges, the leper's poetic responses to the various requests. Then the tale struggles toward a solution through a sequence of negotiations, between Senchán and Caillín, Senchán and Marbán, the poets and the saints of Ireland, and the saints and God. This sequence climaxes in a spectacular confrontation between the living and the revived dead, who gives perhaps the most extensive and, significantly, the most comprehensive performance of any revenant featured in the tales we have examined so far. This untrammeled transmission of the past remembered, with no indication given here or in any variant of the story that Fergus's version of the *Táin* was in any way incomplete, goes hand in hand with the exceptional catholicity and synergy informing the picture of society which has developed by the end of the story. All previously polarized or unaccounted-for sectors have "talked out" their differences and are working together harmoniously toward the restitution of the past in a modern, written form. Everyone and everything, including past and present, prove ultimately compatible, and so the prize, the *Táin,* is won complete.

The key to this vision of universal harmony is the figure of the leper comparable to the lowly self-sacrificing performer numbered among Brendan's crew on his voyage in search of a paradise. This "nobody," however, offers not his life for a higher cause, like Brendan's crosán, but his poetic skill, which he puts at the disposal of the muted poets. He breaks ground and prepares the way for a rapprochement between past and present by way of performance and dialogue that turn alien into ally. In other words, he recreates himself, a figure who, despite his off-putting appearance, turns out to be indispensable and even closely akin to the prime beneficiary of his talents, Senchán. He guides, probes, knows, and completes, at first seemingly to no end, when it turns out that the *Táin* is not to be found in Scotland. Then, after his true identity as the brother of the poet and as a holy man is revealed, he guides the story and the quest to a spectacularly successful end. Caillín/the leper is also a producer of verbal signs that "deliver" on what they signify. His poem obtains for the poets what they want from the Leinstermen, supplies, which are precisely what his poem is about. Then, the completions of the stanzas he composes and recites to the female coastguard fill out the half signs she proposes and indicate his awareness of what her poetic metaphors "mean." Thanks to the leper-saint's efforts, the enemies Senchán and Marbán learn to cooperate, actually reflecting each other in their goal of ascertaining the *Táin,* and the company of poets is succeeded by and mirrored in the company of saints in a relationship both metaphoric and metonymic as it develops in the story. Most important of all, a synecdochic representation of the past is arranged with the reviving of Fergus, a participant in past events who in telling the story of those events is a miracle of reflexive hermeneutics. Here is a sign explaining, and luxuriantly elaborating upon, its signification.

Whereas in the *Tromdám Gúaire* the indefatigable and helpful interloper turns out to be not just Senchán's brother but also a cleric, the identity of a similar character in a version of the story of the poets' sea voyage told in an earlier source (Cormac's Glossary) is not so neatly resolved. After his disappearance is noted, the text tells us that he was the "Spirit of Poetry" itself.[61] The mysteriousness of this character, a quality compounded in the *Tromdám* by the detail of his being related to Senchán, can be construed as an expression of the uncertainty of the literary tradition concerning the relationship between its past and present and how the present can successfully make use of and incorporate the traditions of the past. It is noteworthy that the solution of Cormac's Glossary to the puzzle of who the repellent poetaster is, a solution according to which his authority stems not from his ecclesiastical connections but from a vague secular or even pre-Christian conceptualization of poetry personified, resists the further complication of his being a relation of the poet whom he guides and on whose behalf he performs. The identification of the leper as *Caillín,* in contrast, goes hand in hand with the revelation of a lost brother in Senchán's background, who actually facilitates the coming together of Senchán and his Christian archenemy Marbán. Caillín 'Little Forest[er]', who mediates between his poetic half-brother and his eremitical colleague, is himself reminiscent of the forest-dwelling, and doubtless wild-looking, Marbán.

The story as told in the *Tromdám* gives us the impression that the poet as represented by Senchán has in fact more in common with the cleric than with any pagan or nonecclesiastical purveyors of supernatural inspiration and knowledge. A variation on this theme of revitalized and revitalizing kinship is to be found in the rationale given in the Book of Leinster version of the story of the finding of the *Táin* for why particular saints were drawn into the search. The ones affected are said to descend from the seed of Fergus, an ancestor from whom, at the goading of Senchán, they are trying to recover their past, and with whom they are thus reaffirming their family connection.[62]

Senchán, according to yet another variant of the story, first fasts against a dead saint, Brendan, whose voyages I discussed in the previous chapter. Brendan, submitting to pressure, appears in a vision to a holy man and delivers a message to Senchán: it is Ciarán of Clonmacnois, yet another dead saint, whom Senchán should importune, since the *Táin* is to be found in *his* territory. Ciarán, communicating like his holy colleague through a third party, directs Senchán to Fergus's grave in Connacht, where, with the invocation of yet a third revenant (who, however, addresses Senchán directly), the *Táin* is

---

61. Poematis erat spiritus (Meyer 1912, 94).
62. Best and O'Brien 1967, lines 32897–98. According to another of the medieval Irish texts featuring this story, Senchán, on Brendan's advice, becomes along with his descendants a member of the spiritual family of Ciarán, and the affiliation is marked by a name change—no longer Senchán but Senchán Ciaráin (Meyer 1905b, 5).

finally captured.[63] Senchán's turning to saints, either living or dead, for help serves as further confirmation of an implicit bond between poet and cleric. Moreover, in other versions of this story, as well as in other legends featuring the motif of a holy man's fasting against someone in order to force him to do the holy man's will, the receiver of the message conveyed through the hunger strike is no stranger to the hunger striker.[64] In fact, their authorities reflect or complement each other, as in the case of Patrick fasting against God. Perhaps here as well, the fasting constitutes an attention-getting comment on a temporary breakdown of communication that normally flows unimpeded.

The poets' saintly allies are never said to fast against Fergus himself, only against God, to force God to bring Fergus back to life. Fergus and the poets/saints are too estranged from one another for such a gesture to be meaningful or effective, even if the saints ultimately descend from him. There are, however, some multiforms of the story in which one of the searching poets does attempt to find and control Fergus apart from saints and God— although not through fasting, which, as I have noted, assumes a relationship between contemporary and even compatible authorities. According to this denouement, Muirgein, the son of Senchán, finds the tombstone of Fergus and addresses a poem to it, as if it were a living patron who could repay the poet for his performance. Much to his surprise (or not?), Muirgein's poem elicits the gigantic Fergus, dressed, as the Book of Leinster text emphasizes, in a costume of old, who proceeds to recite the *Táin*.[65] This alternative strategy to gain access to Fergus, the past, and a recollection of the past, operates by way of reaction and improvisation, as opposed to the clear, premeditated plan of the saints converging on the grave of the old hero.

Muirgein's performance at the tombstone weaves together some of the fundamental concepts behind the institution of poetry and the function of praise in traditional Irish culture. The eulogy composed and sung by the *fili* to the patron serves the purpose of proclaiming the gratifying truth about the subject both to a present audience, composed primarily of the subject and his retinue, and to an audience of posterity, yet to be constituted but just as eager to hear of the deeds and virtues of great men, if not even more so. Praise in theory forms a lasting trace in sound, or in writing, of those it metaphorically

63. Ibid., 4–6.
64. For example, in the Middle Irish notes to the Martyrology of Óengus, it is said that the saints of Ireland fasted (successfully) to bring on the premature death of their colleague Ciarán of Clonmacnois, lest he become so preeminent that there be no room left in Ireland for the cults of other saints (Stokes 1905b, 202, 204). Perhaps not coincidentally, this remarkable instance of holy fasting for the purpose of containing a saint's potentially out-of-control posterity is associated with the saint responsible for the (re)writing down of the *Táin*, a lost metonym of posterity now fixed and rendered containable in manuscript form. The value and force of fasting, of both the native and the Christian variety, are discussed in Binchy 1982.
65. Best and O'Brien 1967, lines 32892–94; and Meyer 1905b, 5–6, in which this outcome to the story is offered as an alternative to one in which Senchán performs the *laíd* 'praise poem' for Fergus, as instructed by the dead Ciarán (ibid., 5).

represents. Such immortalization calls for, and is itself based on, reciprocation from the patron, with his generosity often constituting an important theme of praise poetry. His gift to the poet sustains the poetic institution and makes possible future performances of poetry, including the poem that makes him immortal. Thus the exchange of truthful "gifts" between poet and patron perpetuates the transmission of poetic representations of paradigmatic behavior which actually make possible the defeat of time itself. The patron's payment to the eulogizing poet redounds to his credit, confirming, nurturing, and propagating the adulatory "story" the poet has to tell, by way of the poem.

This interdependence of poetic efflorescence and patronal response is precisely what is illustrated in the story of Muirgein's encounter with Fergus. The poet does the ancient hero the truly thoughtful courtesy of reviving his memory and "performing" his heroic identity, although ever so privately. In return for the favor of treating him as an ongoing concern, even to a postheroic, Christian posterity, Fergus, or the memory of Fergus, transcends time itself and presents Muirgein with what is at the same time a gift, that which the poets had been seeking, and a story that inestimably enriches the praise and prominence awarded Fergus in the catalyst poem. Like Mongán, or even more like Mongán's secret friend Caílte, Fergus as moribund audience rises to the occasion when the contemporary poet exposes his gaps of knowledge about the past. Fergus turns performer himself in order to set the relationship between past and present aright. Thus it is the dynamics of poetry as it functions in society which sets the poetic institution and its practitioners back on the right track, poised, mediating between past and present, and renewed with the narrative stuff of which eulogy is made. Different indeed is the authority here behind the "miracle" of Fergus's revival and narration from the authority exhibited in those versions of the story according to which the dead hero and the story he has to tell are gifts God grants to his insistent saints.

In the versions of the tale featuring Muirgein, he is not said to have addressed Fergus with a poem but, very specifically, as if it were "the real thing," Fergus's tombstone. This detail brings out the semiotic experimentation behind what the desperate poet was doing, as well as the self-consciousness of poetic performance. The stone of Fergus serves the same purpose as a praise poem about Fergus. Both are means of memorializing him, albeit in different media. We should recall that tombstones often were inscribed in ogam, thus serving as textual as well as monumental signs of the presence, or absence, of a person of the past.

Given the similarity between eulogy and grave marker, for Muirgein to treat the stone as if it really were Fergus is to express the hope that his own, verbal representation is itself an efficient or even powerful device for framing, and thereby controlling, the bygone person and the events that made him noteworthy. We thus are witnessing two representations of the same reputed figure interacting or "conversing." Subsequently, they produce the figure himself along with a revelation about the past, which lies hidden behind its modern representations until these are integrated and allowed, as it were, to speak among themselves. The artifacts that meet and mingle to produce Fergus are the poet's projection, his poem, and Fergus's own funereal projection, a sign informing the landscape. In medieval Irish tradition, both verse and grave markers resist anonymity. Poems are usually ascribed to legendary poets, not recorded without attribution. And just as a poem conjures up not only its subject but also a poet who composed it, so too a grave marker entails a dead hero who gives meaning to the otherwise meaningless monument.

We should note how marked Fergus's appearance is said to be, wearing as he is the dress of a hero from a different age.[66] For Fergus, like any rigorously scrutinized "signified", turns out himself to be a sign, namely, of the past in which he played such a prominent role and which he continues to represent. In this case, thanks to the power underlying the link between eulogy and heroic prose narrative, the trace left by the past, once it is detected and interpreted for what it is, turns out to be far more than what the modern hunter of story bargained for. Here, commemoration is no mere snippet of what was or could have been. Fergus is fully himself, so tall, we are told in one text, that he had to sit down in order to be heard.[67] And as I have noted, the performance and story he gives are in no wise presented to us as lacking in detail.

Far from being a distracting supplement to an unrelated story, this account of the revival of the *Táin Bó Cúailnge* refurbishes some of the poetic reputation that grows so tarnished in the story of hospitality abused in Gúaire's court. With the revalorization of that reputation, poets are transformed from the pests they have become back into the pillars of the community. What remains, however, is the alienation of the framing figures who serve as paradoxically both attractive and repellent authorities for the peripatetic poets seeking justification in the eyes of society. Neither the *provocateur* who sends them off on their search, Marbán, nor the revenant who finally provides them with what they lack can be characterized as having social or stable identities. Although he is said in the text to be the sustaining force behind his brother's kingship and a holy man,[68] Marbán is hardly the institution-building sort of ecclesiastic. He clearly belongs to the peculiar breed of holy man which also

---

66. Perhaps in the emphasis placed on Fergus's appearance we have the vestige of what may be an Indo-European frame tale concerning the composition of epic. In a Latin account of Homer's life, as noted by Andrew Ford (1992, 170), the poet prays to the dead hero Achilles that he may see him in the full splendor of his armor. The request is granted, but at the cost of Homer's sight, which he loses on account of the brightness of the hero's armor. The Muses, however, take pity on Homer and grant him poetic inspiration in compensation for the loss of his vision. Thus, Homer composes his poems about Troy as a direct result of his confrontation with the central hero of the Trojan War, who is visually, if not verbally, overwhelming.
67. Meyer 1905b, 4.
68. Joynt 1931, lines 804–10.

includes figures such as Mac Dá Cherda, a cleric-fool famed for his outlandish, even foolish behavior as well as wisdom.[69]

Furthermore, we should note that no holy man of hagiography, not even
Columba, that aficionado of native arts, would interact with the poets so
much on their own terms, challenging them in tests and competitions involving performance skills. Marbán is an acutely marginal, and therefore mediating, figure, and his marginality is predicated on his self-imposed exile, which
he puts aside to deal with problems on the home front. In his artful manage-
ment of the crisis in his brother's kingship, Marbán perhaps reminds us that
he too could have been king. In a different narrative milieu, we can imagine
this marginal figure as a fénnid instead of a hermit. Even in his eremitical
incarnation he reminds us of fénnidi, exiles "dead" to the world. Hence it
does not come as a surprise to us that Marbán, in protecting his brother and
his kingdom from humiliation, evinces remarkable tracking skills, hunting
down the out-of-season foodstuffs that the company of the poets is demanding in order to show the court to be wanting. Marbán finds, or knows where
to find, these items on his own turf, the wilderness. When he finally obtains
the chance to demand that the poets procure something for him, a story
hidden in or lost from their repertoire, he demonstrates how unfamiliar they
have become with the lay of *their* land. He forces them to relearn the means of
accessing the information stored, or that should be stored, in poetic tradition.
Marbán is far more at home in this domain than are the poets, who ultimately
turn to him for guidance, or else find what they are looking for only by
accident.

Fergus too, the other framing figure, is emphatically characterized in his
own story tradition as an exile. He did once hold the kingship of Ulster,[70] and
he consistently maintains his intimate foster relationship with Cú Chulainn,
the hero of the sought-after *Táin*. Yet Fergus's key roles in that story are
those of leader of the Ulster exiles in Connacht, chief military adviser to the
army invading Ulster, and lover of Medb, the queen leading the expedition
against Cú Chulainn's province. Fergus's exile from Ulster is his self-imposed
response to his dishonoring at the hands of the king of Ulster.[71]

Surely it cannot be coincidence that the tale the poets are supposed to find
in order to win back their collective reputation—a tale the finding of which
takes them on a voyage that threatens to become perpetual exile—is pivoted
on the theme of displacement. Moreover, the figure from the tale itself who

69. Mac Dá Cherda is featured in various Middle and Early Modern Irish compositions,
including J. O'Keeffe 1911.
70. The Middle Irish text *Scéla Conchobair maic Nessa* (News of Conchobar mac Nessa), tells
how Fergus lost his kingship to Conchobar (Stokes 1910, 22, 24). In this text as elsewhere
Fergus is mac Rossa, and not mac Róich or mac Roich. See Ó hUiginn 1993, 32–34, on the
alternation of his patronymic/metronymic and on the story of Fergus's loss of kingship.
71. The details of Fergus's exile and uneasy alliance with Ailill and Medb are given in ibid.,
34–35.

finally supplies the poets with its text is perhaps the ultimately displaced person among the cast of conspicuously displaced characters. These include Medb, the queen playing the role of king; Cú Chulainn, who is his single-handed defense of the province grows more and more alienated from the various groups he must counter, manipulate, or protect; the men of Ireland, who find themselves invading and ransacking the "alien" province of Ulster; and the Ulstermen, who are prevented from fulfilling their martial function by a mysterious debilitating, emasculating disease.

Unlike Marbán, who is "dead" only in name, the Fergus of the *Tromdám* is truly deceased. He is once again in exile, but now from all the living, not just the province of Ulster. Death, however, does not prevent him from hearing Muirgein's message and responding to it heroically. This sensitivity is in character for the Fergus of the *Táin*, one of whose major functions is to "read" and interpret the tracks left by Cú Chulainn for the invading army.[72] Another of his important chores in the narrative is to tell, along with his fellow exiles, stories of Cú Chulainn's youthful deeds to the invaders and to the audience or readers of the story.[73]

Thus Fergus as an exiled "hired hand" comes very close in function, if not in his actual designation, to the figure of the fénnid. In fact, Cú Chulainn addresses and welcomes him in terms appropriate to a fellow warrior in no-man's-land.[74] Certainly, in the ways he glosses the traces of the most significant character in the *Táin* and provides him with a narrative background, Fergus demonstrates his potential as a fénnidlike source of arcane, dated information. This in turn is transmittable in the sign of a performance-turned-text culled by latter-day poets and clerics at least some of whom join the search for the *Táin* with gusto.

The Dialogue of the Ancients

So far in this chapter, we have seen fénnidi and related social and extrasocial figures, such as exiles, perennial outsiders, and even a seeming reincarnation of a famous fénnid, characterized in terms of their unusual abilities to read, produce, or function as traces, the signification of which does not necessarily depend on conventional authorities or systems of meaning. As trackers and track producers, the fénnid and his brethren exist, not always comfortably, in a literary tradition that also includes, indeed is grounded in, the institution of poetry, with its own authorization to read and produce signs, and the church, which brings with it not only a different semiotics but a new medium for signification. Many of the tales I have explored in this

72. C. O'Rahilly 1976b, lines 227–97.
73. Ibid., lines 341–824.
74. Ibid., lines 1312–16.

chapter constitute attempts to reconcile the literary mainstream with these troublesome marginalia or to eliminate such marginalia altogether. Reconciliation is the primary goal of the Fenian tradition, centered as it is on the figure of Finn, who is both fénnid and fully accredited poet. The hope is continually renewed in this cycle of stories that the potentially rivalrous systems of *filidecht* 'the craft of poetry' and *fénnidecht* 'the craft of the fénnid' can indeed "connect," through shared narrative motifs, and enter a productive dialogue.[75] It is therefore fitting that the Fenian tradition plays host to the most spectacular instance of confrontation leading to reconciliation between fénnid, on the one hand, and latter-day churchmen and poets, on the other. This meeting, as staged with a cast of Fenian characters, takes place in the twelfth- or thirteenth-century composition known as the *Acallam na Senórach* (Dialogue of the ancients), which has survived in many manuscripts, some as late as the nineteenth century. Such textual ubiquity attests to its long-lived popularity.[76]

An initially surprising characteristic of the *Acallam* as it survives in its various manuscript forms is that it is never complete and always lacks at least an end and often a beginning. Our surprise may wear away when we consider the nature of the text. This is essentially a frame tale, which by definition has a rather flexible structure and variable content. It is an account, we recall, of the adventures and primarily the storytelling of Caílte and, to a lesser extent, Oisín, prominent figures from the Fenian story cycle who live on into the post-Fenian era, well after the deaths of their leader Finn mac Cumaill and their other heroic companions. The bulk of the text consists of Caílte's responses, in narrative and/or poetic form to questions posed by people of this later era whom he meets, questions about the significance of various obscure place-names and about the lesser-known details of episodes from the Fenian cycle. These two topics are hard to distinguish in the *Acallam,* since most of the place-names about which Caílte is asked turn out to have something to do with Fenian adventures, and the heroic tales he recounts almost always include place-name lore. The ancient Fenian is therefore not only an unmistakable sign from the past which explains its significance but a valuable detective of antiquities who "performs" for his latter-day clients a sustained reading of nominal clues from, and of, the past.

Most of these clues, it seems, refer to Caílte's own past, or to the context that makes that Fenian past meaningful. In the course of his quite thorough

75. The delicate synergy between fénnid and poet in Fenian story, particularly in the cycle of tales centered on the boyhood of Finn, is the subject of J. Nagy 1985.

76. In the introduction to her edition of an Early Modern Irish recension of the text (1942), Nessa Ní Sheaghdha provides information concerning the manuscript sources and possible history of the *Acallam*. Stokes 1900 is an edition of the earliest extant recension of the text, datable to ca. 1200 or later. On the language of this text, see Nuner 1958–59 and Ó Cuív's endnotes to Dillon's edition of extracts (1970). Aspects of the *Acallam* are studied in J. Nagy 1989a and 1995, of which some of what follows is a revision.

travels throughout the provinces of Ireland as told in the *Acallam,* Caílte, with some help from his "now-you-see-him-now-you-don't" companion Oisín, maps out a specifically Fenian Ireland, previously buried in a collective amnesia but now revived in the memories of moderns. This thematically integrated terrain forms a contrast to the Ireland of the more catholic tradition of place-name lore presented in the better-known compilations of such information put together by the medieval literati.[77]

The reorientation of toponymical awareness which Caílte fosters entails a keen sensitivity to the passing of time, as does the genre of *dindshenchas* 'place-name lore' in general. Caílte and the author(s) of the *Acallam* frequently remind their audiences that many of the names mentioned, discussed, and explained are no longer used to designate these places in the here-and-now of the narrative. One of the most pointed of these references to changes in topical signification occurs at the beginning of the *Acallam,* directly before the old Fenians meet Patrick:

They went away from that place [where Caílte and company had been on blissful leave from the mortal world] onto the grassy field, where they held council. The decision they made was to leave one another, but it was like the soul leaving the body. But leave one another they did, with Oisín going to Síd Ochta Cleitig, where his mother Blái, daughter of Derg Dianscothach, lived, and Caílte going to Inber Bic Loingsig in Brega—now called Mainistir Droichit Átha—namely, the place where Becc Loingsech fell, the son of the king of the Romans who came to conquer Ireland but was drowned by a tidal wave there.[78]

Mainistir Droichit Átha is Mellifont, the first Cistercian monastery founded in Ireland (in 1142) and a vanguard of the twelfth-century reforms in the Irish church.[79] It was to a significant degree thanks to those reforms that the era of monastic patronage of vernacular literature came to an end in Ireland, and the era of secular families carrying on the literary tradition, as exemplified by the production and proliferation of the text of the *Acallam,* began in earnest.[80]

77. The lore of places as reflected in medieval Fenian literature, particularly in the *Acallam,* is the subject of Ó Coileáin 1993. On *dindshenchas* as esoteric knowledge, see Mac Cana 1988.
78. Is andsin táncatar rompu assan bhaile imach aran fhaithche bféraigh, ⁊ gníset comairle ann sin, ⁊ as í comhairle dorónad accu ann, scarad re chéile; ⁊ ba scaradh cuirp re hanmain a scarad. Ocus dorínset amhlaid sin, uair dochuaidh Oisín co Sídh Ochta Cleitigh, bhail a raibhe a mháthair .i. Bla inghen Déirc Dhianscothaig, ⁊ téit Cáilte roime co hIndber mBic Loingsigh a mBregaibh, risi-ráidter Mainistir Droichit Atha isin tan so .i. Bec Loingsech mac Airist itorchair ann .i. mac ríg Rómán táinic do ghabháil Eirenn co rus-báidh tonn tuile ann hé (Stokes 1900, lines 47–55).
79. Whitley Stokes observed that this passage, which features the monastery of Mellifont or Drogheda (established 1142), offers a seeming *terminus a quo* for the text (1900, 273, note on line 53). The sea changes wrought in the twelfth-century Irish church, and in its relationships with the church beyond Ireland, are chronicled in Hughes 1966, 253–74; and Watt 1972.
80. Characterizing the *Acallam* as a reaction to a changing world, Donnchadh Ó Corráin has

And so, Caílte, a pagan from the preliterate past, unwittingly advances toward Patrick and the written culture he represents by way of a notable sign of the future. Indeed, Mellifont would have represented to the audience of the *Acallam* a much more immediate turning point in the history of Irish literary tradition than the coming of Patrick and Christianity. Inber Loingsig Big, the older name of the site, which in typical fashion for the *Acallam* is the recipient of the narrative gloss, harks in its encoding back to a primeval situation with distinctly Fenian overtones, namely, the repelling of an invasion of Ireland.[81] The gloss concludes with what may have been construed as a much happier outcome to an invasion from outside than the death knell for the earlier literary milieu rung by the Cistercian reforms.

Caílte, as he approaches his epochal meeting with the missionary saint of Ireland, moves forward in time, but the text moves backward from Mellifont to Patrick. The itineraries of both character and text, moreover, contrast dramatically with the sojourn of Caílte's soul brother, Oisín. A poet in his own right, this normally outgoing Fenian regresses altogether into the comfortable past of his mother's otherworldly home, far away from clerics and their newfangled notions.

This pointed allusion to Mellifont confirms the implications of the Fenian bias informing the world mapped out in the text. The *Acallam* can be understood as what Jacques Derrida has called a *supplément,* an artifice defining the putative presence it supplements. That is, all *senchas* is now described in terms of the once-renegade Fenian tradition.[82] A soon-to-be-exiled scribal tradition that senses a challenge to its authority and the location of its authority picks up as a spokesman for its nostalgia a figure who is supplemental to the

said: "On another level, the texts from the *Acallam* cited above, betray an anxious preoccupation of the makers of traditional legend: their world, of reality and imagination, was under attack. . . . The *Acallam* is a rich record of their ambivalent position and response: they present Saint Patrick, the highest traditional ecclesiastical authority in the land, as approving enthusiastically of the cultivation of a literature which speaks lovingly and nostalgically of the pagan past (the imagined past of generations of composers of traditional legends). In the narratives cited above, the mandarins make a further concession: they mediate the conventional oppositions in that literary world, make Finn, the archetypical pagan warrior, a precocious deist (if not christian), and have the king of the Otherworld and his folk, submit to Saint Patrick and become true believers" (1987b, 36–37).

81. References in literature to Finn and his men as defenders of society, usually in the service of the High King of Ireland, can be found in J. Nagy 1985, 52–58.

82. Commenting on Rousseau's theory of the relation between writing and speech, Derrida says: "The concept of supplement . . . harbors within itself two significations whose cohabitation is as strange as it is necessary. The supplement adds itself, it is a surplus, a plenitude enriching another plenitude, the *fullest measure* of presence. . . . But the supplement supplements. It adds only to replace. It intervenes or insinuates itself *in-the-place-of;* if it fills, it is as if one fills a void. . . . As substitute, it is not simply added to the positivity of a presence, it produces no relief, its place is assigned in the structure by the mark of an emptiness. Somewhere, something can be filled up *of itself,* can accomplish itself, only by allowing itself to be filled through sign and proxy. The sign is always the supplement of the thing itself" (Derrida 1976, 144–45, trans. Spivak).

mainstream of heroic tradition, a vestige of a bygone era who is marginal to the present and conspicuously preliterate. It can even be suggested that the *Acallam* is a product of a scribal tradition already in exile and refashioning itself and its authority in the image of the supplemental relic from the past. Either way, in the fascinating rhetoric of this text, the interests and claims of a literary reflorescence converge with those of an oral past that it recreates.

Like the once-lost but now recovered lore they disseminate, the Fenian protagonists of the *Acallam* represent a fortuitous glitch in time. They should not still be alive and well in the era in which the *Acallam* places them, but in some unspecified way they are. Caílte and his companions transcend time and sequence, paralleling the innumerable anachronistic references to place-names which they and the text make, such as the Inber Bic Loingsig/Mellifont allusion. The key to this miracle, which both makes the miracle happen and provides its matter, is simply talk. This is, after all, an *acallam,* and each of the voices involved in this conversation has its own special authority. This situation makes for remarkable harmonies and disharmonies both in the situations the text presents and in the text itself. The most important of the several dialogues conducted at the same time is between Caílte, who, according to the chronological schema of medieval Irish historians, flourished along with his fellow Fenian heroes in the third century after Christ, and Patrick, who, we recall, is traditionally assigned to the fifth century. It can be argued that from the perspective of those who composed the *Acallam* Patrick himself was already an "ancient" (*senóir*). In the less sympathetic climate generated by the reformed church the preservation of his contribution to the dialogue, with its expression of saintly support for the project of maintaining the vernacular literary tradition, may have been just as important to the authors of the *Acallam* as the Fenian component.

Caílte the Revenant

Informative confrontations between bygone *fénnidi* and representatives of modernity can happen in later medieval Irish literature even without clerics or men of letters, as a thirteenth- or twelfth-century prose introduction to a poem on the place (name) Cnucha contained in the Book of Lismore makes clear.[83] In fact this text offers us a valuable counterpoint to those variations on the theme of the conversation with the dead, or the should-be-dead, which feature an ecclesiastical interlocutor. Here, the medium for communicating and keeping in touch with the past differs substantially from what hagiographically inclined accounts of similar situations present. This tale may even afford us a glimpse of what a secular, even pre-Christian version of the conceit of conversing with the past would have looked like.

83. Edited and translated in Power 1917. This text may well be contemporary with the twelfth- or thirteenth-century earliest extant recension of the *Acallam.*

The text in the Book of Lismore tells of three sons of a hospitaler of Meath who are deprived of their patrimony by the local king, and the youngest of whom (Aongus [Óengus in earlier Irish]) is seized by the king as a hostage. Hardly apathetic in the face of adversity, the two brothers at liberty rescue Aongus and flee to the uninhabited areas of neighboring Brega, from which, in fénnid fashion, they launch raids against the oppressive king. One evening, after they have returned from such a raid, the youngest of the exiles goes forth to commit even more depredation. When he returns, his brothers chide him for outdoing them. Aongus defends himself, and attacks them, by claiming that he is likely to be better at such activities than they, since he clearly resembles Caílte, their ancestor on their mother's side, more than his brothers do.

At this point in the argument, the three are joined, and greatly surprised, by an interloper who had been eavesdropping on them, Caílte himself. The old fénnid calms their fears, assuring them that he is not a dangerous specter,[84] just Caílte mac Rónáin of old. He invites them to visit his own *fianboth* (fían hut), which they find comfortably capacious. After a quarter of a year living with Caílte, the brothers are invited to claim their patrimony by the king of Ireland, Diarmait mac Cerbaill, who, it would appear, has succeeded to the throne of the disinheriting king. Learning of Caílte's whereabouts, Diarmait summons him to Tara, but Caílte refuses the invitation, opting instead to visit his sister. He is accompanied by a retinue from the king's court, and they pass by Cnucha in Leinster, where the presence of the "big man" attracts the local worthies and their musicians (*aos ciuil*), who seek information (*scéla*) from Caílte.[85] In particular, they inquire about the significance and history of Cnucha, the site of the battle in which Finn's father died. Caílte tells the story in verse and then enumerates the kings of Ireland prophesied by Finn and proclaims the remarkable age Finn attained (two hundred and thirty!). Caílte then proclaims to his audience that in an earlier time he had been converted by Patrick along with his fellow Fenian survivors, compared in the poem to Christ's apostles, and that they all took on new names at baptism. Caílte concludes with a prediction of his impending death: "My gravestone will be northwest of Tara, until Doomsday."[86]

Like the devil, Caílte appears when his name is spoken. Moreover, in this respect, he also brings to mind the figure of Fergus in the tale of the finding of the *Táin*, according to which it takes a poem of praise from the living to evoke the dead. In both cases, the name of the bygone hero is mentioned in a context of praise. The young overachiever Aongus is citing Caílte as a model of behavior, of special relevance to males in a state of alienation such as the one in which he and his brothers find themselves.

---

84. Ni harracht na urchóit mhisi (ibid., 40).
85. Ibid.
86. Biaidh mo lecht co laithi in luain re taobh Themhrach aniartuaidh (ibid., 44).

Another catalyst for the reappearance of Caílte is the realization of the paradigm, not just its verbal articulation. Aongus has acted, not just spoken, like a "new," reborn Caílte. Mongán, in the story in which he summons Caílte, seems to be a heroic fénnid reborn, but he reenacts Fenian heroism by what he knows and says, not by his own deeds, which in fact are hardly "heroic" in that particular story. In all three cases of evocation—namely, Caílte's surprise visit to the exiles, the revival of Fergus, and the rescue of Mongán—the audience within the story must somehow replicate the actions of the desired possessor of knowledge in order to gain his attention and his presence. What is being tested in these stories, then, is the iterability of the sign of the fénnid. Is it still meaningful in the era of the audience that wishes to have the opportunity to "read" the sign for itself, or to have the sign "read itself" aloud within their hearing? Recovering the past, according to this variation on the theme of reviving the dead, is a way of revitalizing the present, of removing the cap that marks off the past and making the past productively open-ended, a source of paradigm and inspiration for the future.

The coda to Caílte's poem, with its heavy air of approaching death, indicates the changes that the hagiographic utilization of the theme introduces into the process. As we have seen, the saint who summons forth the dead or serendipitously encounters them converts the traces of the past into signs of his own authority, which is often ineluctably intertwined with the authority of the written word. Caílte and company, on being converted, have new signs attached to them, their baptismal names, through which they are putatively contained. Caílte now knows his own end and his function, as a gravesite to mark Christian time and, by implication, the line of succession in the kingship of Ireland until Judgment Day. As such, he becomes a multiform of the figure of Patrick's charioteer, whose function is similarly to remain dead and dominated until the end of earthly time. Yet, as we have come to see, marginal types, such as the irrepressible Aongus and the extraordinary survivor Caílte, are hard to contain and keep down; they sometimes even violate the boundaries of their own or others' "definitive" readings of themselves.

conclusion

early on in the meandering course of the *Acallam na Senórach*
the mammoth fin-de-siècle text discussed in the last chapter,
Patrick finds himself in a quandary. He is experiencing pangs
of guilt for having neglected his missionary activities by listening to (and
enjoying) the fascinating lore freely offered to him by the old hero Caílte.
Fortunately for Patrick, unambiguous divine guidance on what to do about
this moral dilemma is forthcoming:

[Patrick and his retinue] stayed there until the morning of the next day, at
which time Patrick donned his vestments and went out onto the lawn. Following him were sixty priests, sixty psalmodists, and sixty bishops, sowing faith and
religion throughout Ireland. Two guardian angels came to Patrick at that time,
Aibelán and Solusbrethach. He asked them whether it was the wish of the King
of Heaven and Earth that he, Patrick, be listening to stories of the fían. The
angels responded in unison emphatically: "Dear holy cleric, no more than a
third of the stories that they used to know do the old warriors [Caílte and his
companions] tell you, on account of their forgetfulness. Let these be written
down by you on the stone tablets of poets and in the sayings of *ollamain* [the
highest order of poets], for it will be entertaining for both the masses and the
nobles of later times to listen to these tales." Then the angels left.[1]

---

1. Ocus do bhátur annsin co táinic maden arnamárach, 7 gabais Pátraic a eirredh uime, 7 táinic
ar in faithchi amach, 7 trí fichit sacart, trí fichit sailmchétlaid, 7 trí fichit naeimescub 'na fharrad
ac siladh creidmhe 7 crábaid sechnón Eirenn. Ocus doriachtadar a dhá aingel fhorcoiméta cum
Pátraic ann sin .i. Aibelán 7 Solusbreathach, 7 fiafraighios dibh in budh móid le rígh nime 7
talman beith dosom ag éisdecht re scéla na Féinne. Frecrait na haingil dosom co comnart
cubaidh: "A anum, a naeimchléirigh!" ar siat, "ní mó iná trian a scél innisit na senlaeich út ar
dáigh dermait 7 dichuimhne. Ocus scríbhthar letsa i támlorguibh filed 7 i mbriat[h]raibh

324

The saint, his curiosity about what Caílte has to say vindicated, proceeds to sate it, and thus the question-and-answer dialogue between Patrick and Caílte proceeds, eliciting from the hero of old a wealth of seasoned knowledge and remembrances.

Yet the heavenly approval so enthusiastically relayed to Patrick is conditional, and the condition imposed is to be dutifully observed. The saint is not simply to listen but to have Caílte's utterances recorded, preserved for a Christianized posterity, within the medium introduced to Ireland by the new religion: writing. And indeed, from this point on in the text, the tales told and the poems recited by the Fenian hero to the Christian saint are punctuated not only by Patrick's expression of pleasure but also by his command to his scribe Broccán to write down what has just been said. The *Acallam* itself is therefore the putative product of this series of "fieldwork" sessions. Its author(s)/ redactor(s) punctuate their composition with this dictational tag line, a recurring reminder of the project's inception. Thus the audience never loses sight of the conceit behind the text. Indeed, the conceit *is* the text. Writing could never encompass all of what the heroes of old could have said. And yet, as Patrick learns from his angels, those marvelous heroes are not what they used to be, their utterances now constitute but a faded synecdoche of their memories and experiences, but acts of writing sponsored by Patrick and sanctioned by God do measure up to the task of conveying those miraculously audible utterances, salvaged parts of an indescribable whole. There are now two angels visiting Patrick instead of one, the divine order given him is for Patrick to write instead of to read, and the saint's taste has grown more catholic. Otherwise, though, we can still recognize the Patrick of the *Confessio,* driven by guilt over language but compelled nonetheless to listen to and record a voice that is both within and outside of him.

Throughout the works I have been examining, from the beginnings of Irish literary tradition to its watershed in the twelfth-thirteenth centuries and beyond, from the realms of hagiography and vernacular literature predicated on hagiographic themes, talk with angels and ancients has provided the texts' legitimating core. Patrick, in the world of his lives and the world he inhabits in vernacular saga or metasaga, is sought out by an angel who speaks with him, and as a result of this conversion/conversation, Patrick returns to his "past," Ireland, and revives that past in order to speak with its representatives, convince them, and reform them in a Christian image. This talkative angel evolves out of a dream messenger described in Patrick's own words, a figure who pointedly does not speak but only delivers letters and stands by silently as the "voice of the Irish" speaks to Patrick.

---

ollaman, ór budh gairdiugudh do dronguibh ⁊ do degdáinibh deridh aimsire éisdecht frisna scéluib sin." Ocus do imt[h]igset na haingil iarsin (Stokes 1900, lines 290–303).

Columba is whipped into shape by an angel who both cajoles the saint and forces him to read an unwelcome text, and this private encounter is replicated, albeit with less violence, in the many sessions he is said to have had behind closed doors with Axal, his very own angel, or even with the Holy Spirit itself. To be added to the set of these esoteric, not altogether placid dialogues is Columba's illicit encounter with Saint Findén's copy of sacred Scripture, as fateful a coerced reproduction as is the imprinting of the import of the glass book upon the body of Columba, courtesy of the angel with a whip. It is by virtue of these authorizing and yet also isolating dialogues that Columba is cast in the role of holy and wise man in exile, who returns to the land of his youth to interview poets and bring them up to contemporary standards of expression and social function, and yet who is himself consulted as a venerable authority, or who returns from his self-imposed grave of exile in order to demonstrate the lasting validity of his word.

Meanwhile, from the vantage of the chariot, the saint, like his predecessor in that microcosmic space the pre-Christian *eirr* 'chariot warrior', observes, comments on, and shapes the unfolding scenery of medieval Ireland in conjunction with and occasionally in counterpoint to his charioteer, who provides a link with the past. In some cases, the driver even gives himself as a foundation sacrifice upon which to build the future envisioned by his angelically inspired passenger.

Roaming along the more desolate paths traveled by the saint is the seemingly timeless fénnid, haunted by a past the holy man want to know and record, and talented at finding and communicating with his "prey," in this case, a saint who can intercede for him. Patrick and Caílte, churchman and brigand of old, busy themselves with the task of commemorating the past, but meanwhile the past defers becoming the past, and literary activity is insinuated into a different cultural space, as the old space, provided by the monastery, fades away. A distillation of medieval Irish genres as they enter the early modern era, the adventures of saint and fénnid as documented in the *Acallam* chart a literary course marked by both conservative and innovative features.

These various dialogues with angels and ancients tend to be conducted interdependently. Both angels (including messengers from God and God himself) and ancients (including figures from the pre-Christian past and from an earlier Christian past) offer experiences and knowledge that are limitless in the actual event of the dialogue and fundamentally inexpressible beyond the event. What they say challenges their audience's ability to convey what they hear, and even shakes the audience's confidence in conventional systems of representation, whether oral or literary. Signifier is set adrift from signified in the course of such dialogue. Nevertheless, the auditor given the opportunity to converse with the angel or ancient manages to communicate enough of what he has heard to authorize his "voice" as the official representation of at least *some* of what the supernatural being had to say. Often this breakthrough is made possible through a supplemental dialogue with the other type of being, a second conversation in which the mortal interlocutor is implicated by the original conversation.

This is not to say, however, that the disruptive impact of the conversation(s) upon the epistemological and semantic assumptions of both the mortal interlocutor and the audience of the story itself is eradicated. In fact, it infuses the resultant communication by which we know that dialogue took place, and "scars" the authority of the communicator, leaving a wound that generates the desire as well as the need for further conversation. To put it in terms of one of our stories, Patrick, or rather, the legend of Patrick, does not simply put the spectacular nonconversation with Miliucc, a figure from his pagan past, behind him. It hovers over and even fuels his missionary endeavors, so many of which are in effect dialogues conducted by the hagiographer with paradigms of a pre-Christian past. Are not these proselytizing exchanges attempts to bridge the gap left by Miliucc's pyre?

Here, then, is one of the basic patterns, if not *the* basic pattern, underlying the various stories concerning the origins of medieval Irish culture. Key to this pattern, as to the very substance of medieval Irish literature, is the dialogic process. Within the auditorium of the text, voices, including the angelic and the ancient, are brought together, but they threaten either to speak in whispers, mockingly inaudible within the hapless text straining to hear and convey, or to ring out with enough volume to obliterate our sense of a fixed, closed, and efficient text. Internally, within the story, characters representing different epochs, worldviews, and semiotics engage in dialogues that reflect a struggle for mastery, and all the while, externally, the text itself engages in dialogue with those characters and with the story, a dialogue that is a struggle for a mastery of signs as well.

The only hope for continuity, for intelligibility, and for some correspondence between signifier and signified in the agonistic world of these sundry medieval Irish texts is the complementarity of angels and ancients in their shared capacity as informants. This seems to be the one solid, reliable link in a world where communication creates as much distance as closeness. It is as if the mortal interlocutor or writer were hopelessly at a loss until he realizes that he is not engaged in a single conversation but in two and that he is after all only mediating between two parties that never meet or converse face to face. Even in Patrick's *Confessio,* hardly representative of the Irish literary tradition, the encounters with the Spirit, the "inner man," and Victoricus ultimately return Patrick to the scene of his youth, and lead to a dialogue with the accusing ghosts of his past. Not only do the two dialogues (or sets of dialogues) form a sequence, but the "inexpressible" divine dialogue makes it possible for Patrick, or his text, to balance out or even contain the disturbing implications of the dialogue with the past. This interdependence is not very far from what we see in much later texts, the *Síaburcharpat Con Culainn* and the *Acallam,* in which the clerical need or desire to have a public audience with the hero of old stimulates a private conversation with an emissary from God. Simply put, angels, looking for new means of reflecting their own memorability, bring memories back to life, while memories create the need for angels to keep them alive and well.

Why speak with memorable ancients and reminding angels? And how do they form a pair? It would be a gross injustice to these texts and the tradition behind them to equate angels with "Christian present" or "literature," and ancients with "pagan past" or "oral tradition," although these concepts, fictional as they are in their monolithic proportions, were clearly as important to the authors of these texts as they are to latter-day scholars in search of literary origins.

Perhaps the most important characteristic of angels and ancients to keep in mind is that they can be differentiated through a variety of dichotomies, as Christian and pagan, present and past, living and dead, and so on. They constitute dramatically different and even divergent sources of information, and yet apparently both must be tapped in order for their interlocutor to obtain the authorization for what *he* has to say, or even for him to be able to say it. This ritual of legitimation points us in the direction of the dialogic nature of medieval Irish literature and the continuous dialogue in which the text engages the materials it proposes to contain and with which it attempts to lure extraneous materials inside. The author's act of bringing angels and ancients together in a text, not directly but indirectly as dialogic partners for those seeking to authorize themselves and their voices, is parallel to his absorbing into his text variants of what can be said about the subject in question. This strategy, endemic to medieval Irish vernacular literature, is exemplified in the inclusion in the Book of Leinster of two colophons for the *Táin Bó Cúailnge,* discussed in the Introduction. The Irish penchant for incorporating variation reflects a desire to make the text as comprehensive as possible a representation not only of the subject it claims to relay but also of the process of representation itself by which the subject was relayed to the text. Given the job cut out for the text, then, its very existence is a miracle of synthesis, even if its elements are not synthesized. And by the nature of its existence, the text mediates between the elements it herds together, so often left conspicuously disparate, almost in a display of authorial bravado. In fact, this balancing act is arguably what defined a text as "literature" in the world of the medieval Irish literati. Thus, the interdependence of what should be mutually exclusive dialogues within the text is perhaps an internalization of what is happening between the text and the elements within it, as well as between the text and the contextual, performative factors that threaten its textuality. Indeed, the dialogues, which paradoxically "speak" to each other, expose the artificiality of any discourse (whether written or spoken) as a self-sustaining entity, even as they authorize the voice of the interlocutor through or over whom the dialogues "speak." We cannot, any more than could the producers of medieval Irish literature, separate the authorized voice of the interlocutor from that of the author of the text himself, who allows competing dialogues into the literary space he is creating and, if he can, coaxes them into some semblance of control and cooperation.

In his account of the rise of the novel in the Western literary tradition, the literary theorist Mikhail Bakhtin focuses on what he calls "heteroglossia," which is both a staging and a babble of disparate voices and which, he claimed, permeates the textuality of the novel:

> Therefore, even when heteroglossia remains outside the novel, when the novelist comes forward with his own unitary and fully affirming language (without any distancing, refraction or qualifications) he knows that such language is not self-evident and is not in itself incontestable, that it is uttered in a heteroglot environment, that such a language must be championed, purified, defended, motivated. In a novel even such unitary and direct language is polemical and apologetic, that is, it interrelates dialogically with heteroglossia. It is precisely this that defines the utterly distinctive orientation of discourse in the novel—an orientation that is contested, contestable, and contesting—for this discourse cannot forget or ignore, either through naiveté or by design, the heteroglossia that surrounds it.
>
> Thus heteroglossia either enters the novel in person (so to speak) and assumes material form within it in the images of speaking persons, or it determines, as a dialogizing background, the special resonance of novelistic discourse.
>
> From this follows the decisive and distinctive importance of the novel as a genre: the human being in the novel is first, foremost and always a speaking human being; the novel requires speaking persons bringing with them their own unique ideological discourse, their own language.[2]

While it can hardly be said that we have been reading novels in these past five chapters, Bakhtin's heteroglossia is very similar to what we have been encountering again and again in texts from early medieval Ireland, from the inarticulate utterances heard by Patrick and his "inner man" to the yarns spun by the old Fenian heroes for the Christian scribe. No matter how much an exponent and a creation of reading, the early Irish author clung to the conceit that literature cannot afford to forget the voices that taught it how to speak, that the "natural" setting for literary performance, as for oral, is dialogue, and that, the more contentious the dialogue, the better it serves to stimulate and preserve memory.

2. Bakhtin 1981, 332 (trans. Emerson and Holquist).

bíblíography

Abbreviations

BBCS	*Bulletin of the Board of Celtic Studies*
CIH	*Corpus Iuris Hibernici* (= Binchy 1978)
CMCS	*Cambridge* [later *Cambrian*] *Medieval Celtic Studies*
DIAS	Dublin Institute for Advanced Studies
DIL	*Dictionary of the Irish Language, Based Mainly on Old and Middle Irish Materials,* gen. ed. E. G. Quin, Compact Edition (Dublin: RIA, 1983)
ÉC	*Études Celtiques*
IER	*Irish Ecclesiastical Record*
ITS	Irish Texts Society
JRSAI	*Journal of the Royal Society of Antiquaries of Ireland*
MMIS	Mediaeval and Modern Irish Series
PBA	*Proceedings of the British Academy*
PHCC	*Proceedings of the Harvard Celtic Colloquium*
PRIA	*Proceedings of the Royal Irish Academy*
RC	*Revue Celtique*
RIA	Royal Irish Academy
SC	*Studia Celtica*
SH	*Studia Hibernica*
ZcP	*Zeitschrift für celtische Philologie*

Aguirre, Manuel. 1990. "The Hero's Voyage in *Immram Curaigh Mailduin.*" *ÉC* 27:203–20.

Ahlqvist, Anders. 1983. Ed. and trans. *The Early Irish Linguist: An Edition of the Canonical Part of the Auraicept na nÉces.* Commentationes Humanarum Litterarum 73. Helsinki: Societas Scientiarum Fennica.

Anderson, Alan Orr, and Marjorie Ogilvie Anderson. 1991. Eds. and trans. *Adomnán's Life of Columba.* Rev. Marjorie Ogilvie Anderson. Orig. pub. 1961. Oxford: Clarendon Press.

Anscombe, Alfred. 1914. "St. Victoricus of Rouen and St. Patrick." *Ériu* 7:13–17.

d'Arbois de Jubainville, H. 1903. *The Irish Mythological Cycle and Celtic Mythology.* Trans. Richard I. Best. Dublin: Hodges, Figgis.

Babcock, Barbara A. 1987. "Reflexivity." In *The Encyclopedia of Religion,* ed. Mircea Eliade, 16:234–38. New York: Macmillan.

Bakhtin, Mikhail M. 1981. *The Dialogic Imagination: Four Essays,* ed. Michael Holquist. Trans. Caryl Emerson and Michael Holquist. Austin: University of Texas Press.

Bannerman, John. 1974. *Studies in the History of Dalriada.* Edinburgh: Scottish Academic Press.

Best, Richard I. 1905. Ed. and trans. "The Tragic Death of Cú Roí mac Dári." *Ériu* 2:18–35.

1910. Ed. and trans. "The Settling of the Manor of Tara." *Ériu* 4:121–72.

Best, Richard I., and Osborn Bergin. 1929. *Lebor na Huidre: Book of the Dun Cow.* Dublin: RIA.

Best, Richard I., M[ichael] A. O'Brien, and Anne O'Sullivan. 1954–83. Eds. *The Book of Leinster, formerly Lebar na Núachongbála.* 6 Vols. (Vol. 2, ed. Best and O'Brien [1956]; vol. 5, ed. Best and O'Brien [1967].) Dublin: DIAS.

Bhreathnach, Máire. 1982. "The Sovereignty Goddess as Goddess of Death?" *ZcP* 39:243–60.

Bieler, Ludwig. 1949. *The Life and Legend of St. Patrick.* Dublin: Clonmore and Reynold.

1952. Ed. *Libri epistolarum Sancti Patricii Episcopi.* 2 vols. Dublin: Stationery Office.

1958. "The Lives of St. Patrick and the Book of Armagh." In Ryan 1958, 53–66.

1963. Ed. and trans. *The Irish Penitentials.* Dublin: DIAS.

1971. Ed. *Four Latin Lives of St. Patrick: Colgan's Vita Secunda, Quarta, Tertia, and Quinta.* Scriptores Latini Hiberniae 8. Dublin: DIAS.

1975. "Ancient Hagiography and the Lives of St. Patrick." In *Forma futuri: Studi in onore del Cardinale Michele Pellegrino,* pp. 650–55. Turin: Bottega d'Erasmo.

1979. Ed. and trans. *The Patrician Texts in the Book of Armagh.* Scriptores Latini Hiberniae 10. Dublin: DIAS.

1986. *Studies on the Life and Legend of St. Patrick.* Ed. Richard Sharpe. London: Variorum Reprints.

Binchy, Daniel A. 1952. Ed. and trans. "The Saga of Fergus mac Léti." *Ériu* 16:33–48.

1958a. "The Fair of Tailtiu and the Feast of Tara." *Ériu* 18:113–38.

1958b. "Old Irish *Axal.*" *Ériu* 18:164.

1961. "The Background of Early Irish Literature." *SH* 1:7–18.

1962. "Patrick and his Biographers: Ancient and Modern." *SH* 2:7–173.

1963. Ed. *Scéla Cano Meic Gartnáin.* Dublin: DIAS.

1975–76. "The Pseudo-historical Prologue to the *Senchas Már,*" *SC* 10/11:15–28.

1978. Ed. *Corpus Iuris Hibernici.* 6 vols. Dublin: DIAS.

1982. "A Pre-Christian Survival in Mediaeval Irish Hagiography." In Whitelock et al. 1982, 165–78.

Bitel, Lisa M. 1984. "Women's Donations to the Churches in Early Ireland." *JRSAI* 114:5–23.

1990. *Isle of the Saints: Monastic Settlement and Christian Community in Early Ireland.* Ithaca: Cornell University Press.

Bloch, R. Howard. 1983. *Etymologies and Genealogies: A Literary Anthropology of the French Middle Ages.* Chicago: University of Chicago Press.

Bradley, D. R. 1983. "The *Rhetorici* in the *Confessio* of Patrick." *Journal of Theological Studies* 34:536–54.

Bray, Dorothy Ann. 1985–86. "Motival Derivations in the *Life of St. Samthann*." *SC* 20/21:78–86.

1992a. *A List of Motifs in the Lives of the Early Irish Saints*. Folklore Fellows Communications, no. 252. Helsinki: Academia Scientiarum Fennica.

1992b. "Saint Brigit and the Fire from Heaven." *ÉC* 29:105–13.

1992c. "*Secunda Brigida:* Saint Ita of Killeedy and Brigidine Tradition." In C. Byrne et al. 1992, 27–38.

Breathnach, Pól 1926. Ed. "Cath Cula Dremne." *Irisleabhar Muighe Nuadhat* 22:3–11.

Breatnach, Liam. 1981. Ed. and trans. "The Caldron of Poesy." *Ériu* 32:45–93.

1987. Ed. and trans. *Uraicecht na Ríar: The Poetic Grades in Early Irish Law*. Dublin: DIAS.

1989. "An Edition of *Amra Senáin*." In Ó Corráin et al. 1989, 7–31.

Breatnach, R. A. 1990. "Bunús an Fhocail *Fresabra*." *Celtica* 21:38–39.

Bromwich, Rachel. 1961. "Celtic Dynastic Themes and the Breton Lays." *ÉC* 9:439–74.

Brooks, Nicholas. 1982. Ed. *Latin and the Vernacular Languages in Early Medieval Britain*. Leicester: Leicester University Press; Atlantic Highlands, N.J.: Humanities Press.

Brown, Peter. 1981. *The Cult of the Saints: Its Rise and Function in Latin Christianity*. Chicago: University of Chicago Press.

1982. "Artifices of Eternity." In *Society and the Holy*, pp. 207–21. Berkeley: University of California Press.

Bruford, Alan. 1986–87. "Oral and Literary Fenian Tales." *Béaloideas* 54–55:25–56.

1989. "The Twins of Macha." *Cosmos* 5:125–41.

Bullock-Davies, Constance. 1978. *Menestrellorum Multitudo: Minstrels at a Royal Feast*. Cardiff: University of Wales Press.

Bullough, D. A. 1964–65. "Columba, Adomnan, and the Achievement of Iona." *Scottish Historical Review* 43 (1964):111–30; 44 (1965): 17–30.

Bury, J. B. 1905. *The Life of St. Patrick and His Place in History*. London: Macmillan.

Buttimer, Cornelius G. 1981. "Loegaire mac Néill in the *Bórama*." *PHCC* 1:63–78.

Byrne, Cyril J., Margaret Harry, and Pádraig Ó Siadhail. 1992. Eds. *Celtic Languages and Celtic Peoples: Proceedings of the Second North American Congress of Celtic Studies*. Halifax: D'Arcy Chair of Irish Studies, Saint Mary's University.

Byrne, Francis J. 1965. "The Ireland of St. Columba." *Historical Studies* 5:37–58.

1968. "Seventh-Century Documents." *IER* 108:164–82.

1973. *Irish Kings and High-Kings*. London: B. T. Batsford.

1974. "*Senchas:* The Nature of Gaelic Historical Tradition." In *Approaches to History*, ed. T. G. Barry, pp. 137–59. *Historical Studies* 9.

Byrne, Francis J., and Pádraig Francis. 1994. Trans. "Two Lives of Patrick: *Vita Secunda* and *Vita Quarta*." *JRSAI* 124:5–117.

Campanile, Enrico. 1989. "Zur Etymologie von altir. *arae* und *eirr*." *ZcP* 39:174–78.

Carey, John. 1984a. Ed. and trans. "Scél Tuáin meic Chairill." *Ériu* 35:94–111.

1984b. "Suibne Geilt and Tuán mac Cairill." *Éigse* 20:93–105.

1989. "*Visio Sancti Pauli* and the *Saltair*'s Hell." *Éigse* 23:39–44.

1990. "The Two Laws in Dubthach's Judgment." *CMCS* 19:1–18.

1992. "The Testimony of the Dead." *Éigse* 26:1–12.

1994. "An Edition of the Pseudo-historical Prologue to the *Senchas Már*." *Ériu* 45:1–32.

1995a. "Native Elements in Irish Pseudohistory." In Edel 1995, 45–60.

1995b. "On the Interrelationships of Some *Cín Dromma Snechtai* Texts." *Ériu* 46:71–92.

Carney, James. 1954. "The Impact of Christianity." In *Early Irish Society*, ed. Myles Dillon, pp. 66–78. Dublin: Three Candles.

1955. *Studies in Irish Literature and History*. Dublin: DIAS.

1961. *The Problem of St. Patrick*. Dublin: DIAS.

1976. "The Earliest Bran Material." In O'Meara and Naumann 1976, 174–93.

1987. "Literature in Irish, 1169–1534." In *A New History of Ireland II: Medieval Ireland, 1169–1534*, ed. Art Cosgrove, pp. 688–707. Oxford: Clarendon Press.

1990. "Early Irish Literature: The State of Research." In *Proceedings of the Sixth International Congress of Celtic Studies*, ed. Gearóid Mac Eoin with Anders Ahlqvist and Donnchá Ó hAodha, pp. 113–30. Dublin: DIAS.

Carruthers, Mary. 1990. *The Book of Memory: A Study of Memory in Medieval Culture*. Cambridge: Cambridge University Press.

Chadwick, Nora K. 1942. "Geilt." *Scottish Gaelic Studies* 5:106–53.

1961. *The Age of the Saints in the Early Celtic Church*. Repr. with corrections, 1963. London: Oxford University Press.

Charles-Edwards, Thomas M. 1976a. "Boundaries in Irish Law." In *Medieval Settlements: Continuity and Change*, ed. P. H. Sawyer, pp. 83–87. London: Edward Arnold.

1976b. "The Social Background to Irish *Peregrinatio*." *Celtica* 11:43–59.

1993. "Palladius, Prosper, and Leo the Great: Mission and Primatial Authority." In Dumville et al. 1993, 1–12.

Charles-Edwards, Thomas M., and Fergus Kelly. 1983. Eds. and trans. *Bechbretha*. Early Irish Law Series 1. Dublin: DIAS.

Clancy, Thomas Owen. 1993. "Fools and Adultery in Some Early Irish Texts." *Ériu* 44:105–24.

Clancy, Thomas Owen, and Gilbert Márkus O.P. 1995. Ed. and trans. *Iona: The Earliest Poetry of a Celtic Monastery*. Edinburgh: Edinburgh University Press.

Coe, Paula Powers. 1989. "The Severed Head in Fenian Tradition." *Folklore and Mythology Studies* 13:17–41.

Connolly, Seán. 1989. Trans. "Vita prima Sanctae Brigitae, Background and Historical Value." *JRSAI* 119:5–49.

Connolly, Seán, and Jean-Michel Picard. 1987. Trans. "Cogitosus's *Life of St. Brigit.*" *JRSAI* 117:5–27.

Corthals, Johan. 1989. "The *Retoiric* in *Aided Conchobuir*." *Ériu* 40:41–59.

1992. "A Reference to the Listener to Early Irish Prose Tales?" *CMCS* 23:25–27.

Crawford, O. G. S. 1933. "Iona." *Antiquity* 7:453–68.

Cross, Tom Peete. 1952. *Motif-Index of Early Irish Literature*. Indiana University Publications, Folklore Series, no. 7. Bloomington: Indiana University Publications.

Crowe, J. O'Beirne. 1871. Ed. and trans. "Siabur-charpat Con Culaind ['The Demoniac Chariot of Cu Chulaind']." *Journal of the Historical and Archaeological Society of Ireland* 1:371–448.

Curtius, Ernst Robert. 1953. *European Literature and the Latin Middle Ages*. Trans. Willard R. Trask. Bollingen Series 36. New York: Pantheon Books.

Czarnowski, Stefan. 1919. *Le culte des héros et ses conditions sociales: Saint Patrick, héros national de l'Irlande*. Paris: Librairie Félix Alcan.

Davidson, Olga M. 1985. "The Crown-Bestowers in the Iranian Book of Kings." In *Papers in Honour of Mary Boyce*, pp. 61–148. Leiden: E. J. Brill.

1994. *Poet and Hero in the Persian Book of Kings*. Ithaca: Cornell University Press.

Davies, Wendy. 1982. "Clerics as Rulers: Some Implications of the Terminology of Ecclesiastical Authority in Early Medieval Ireland." In Brooks 1982, 81–97.

Denny, Frederick, and Rodney Taylor. 1985. Eds. *The Holy Book in Comparative Perspective*. Columbia: University of South Carolina Press.

Derrida, Jacques. 1976. *Of Grammatology*. Trans. Gayatri Chakravorty Spivak. Baltimore: Johns Hopkins University Press.

Detienne, Marcel. 1967. *Les mâitres de vérité dans la Grèce archaïque*. Paris: François Maspéro.

Dillon, Myles. 1946. *The Cycles of Kings*. London: Geoffrey Cumberlege.

1953. Ed. and trans. *Serglige Con Culainn*. MMIS 14. Dublin: DIAS.

1970. Ed. *Stories from the Acallam*. MMIS 23. Dublin: DIAS.

Dinneen, Patrick S. 1908. Ed. and trans. *Foras Feasa ar Éirinn le Seathrún Céitinn: The History of Ireland by Geoffrey Keating*. Vols. 2, 3. ITS 8, 9. London: ITS.

Doan, James. 1983. "A Structural Approach to Celtic Saints' Lives." In P. Ford 1983b, 16–28.

Dobbs, Margaret C. 1930. Ed. and trans. "Altromh Tighi Da Medar." *ZcP* 18:189–230.

1930–32. Ed. and trans. "The Ban-Shenchus." *RC* 47:283–339; 48:163–234; 49:437–89.

Doherty, Charles. 1987. "The Irish Hagiographer: Resources, Aims, Results." In Dunne 1987, 10–22.

1991. "The Cult of St. Patrick and the Politics of Armagh in the Seventh Century." In Picard 1991, 53–94.

Dronke, Peter. 1981. "St. Patrick's Reading," *CMCS* 1:21–38.

Dumville, David N. 1976. "*Echtrae* and *Immram*: Some Problems of Definition." *Ériu* 27:73–94.

Dumville, David N., et al. 1993. *Saint Patrick, A.D. 493–1993*. Woodbridge, Eng.: Boydell Press.

Dunne, Tom. 1987. Ed. *The Writer as Witness: Literature as Historical Witness*. Historical Studies 16. Cork: Cork University Press.

Edel, Doris. 1995. Ed. *Cultural Identity and Cultural Integration: Ireland and Europe in the Early Middle Ages*. Black Rock, Ireland: Four Courts Press.

Enright, Michael J. 1985a. "Royal Succession and Abbatial Prerogative in Adomnán's *Vita Columbae*." *Peritia* 4:83–103.

1985b. *Iona, Tara, and Soissons: The Origin of the Royal Anointing Ritual*. Berlin: Walter de Gruyter.

Flower, Robin. 1947. *The Irish Tradition*. Oxford: Clarendon Press.

Foley, John Miles. 1986. Ed. *Oral Tradition in Literature: Interpretation in Context*. Columbia: University of Missouri Press.

Ford, Andrew. 1992. *Homer: The Poetry of the Past*. Ithaca: Cornell University Press.

Ford, Patrick K. 1974. "The Well of Nechtan and 'La Gloire Lumineuse.'" In *Myth in Indo-European Antiquity*, ed. Gerald Larson, C. Scott Littleton, and Jaan Puhvel, pp. 67–74. Berkeley: University of California Press.

1977. Trans. *The Mabinogi and Other Medieval Welsh Tales*. Berkeley: University of California Press.

1983a. "Aspects of the Patrician Legend." In P. Ford 1983b, 29–49.

1983b. Ed. *Celtic Folklore and Christianity*. Santa Barbara: McNally and Loftin; Los Angeles: Center for the Study of Comparative Folklore and Mythology, University of California, Los Angeles.

1987. "The Death of Aneirin." *BBCS* 34:42–50.

1990a. "The Blind, the Dumb, and the Ugly: Aspects of Poets and Their Craft in Early Ireland and Wales." *CMCS* 19:27–40.

1990b. "A Highly Important Pig." In Matonis and Melia 1990, 292–304.

1994. "The Idea of Everlasting Fame in the *Táin*." In *Ulidia: Proceedings of the First International Conference on the Ulster Cycle of Tales*, ed. James P. Mallory and Gerald Stockman, pp. 255–61. Belfast: December Publications.

Fox, Robin Lane. 1988. *Christians and Pagans*. San Francisco: Harper and Row.

Frame, Douglas. 1978. *The Myth of Return in Early Greek Epic*. New Haven: Yale University Press.

Freeman, Philip M. 1994a. "The Earliest Classical Sources on the Celts: A Linguistic and Historical Study." Diss., Harvard University.

1994b. "Visions from the Dead in Herodotus, Nicander of Colophon, and the *Táin Bó Cúailnge*." *Emania* 12:45–48.

Geary, Patrick J. 1994. *Living with the Dead in the Middle Ages*. Ithaca: Cornell University Press.

Gellrich, Jesse M. 1985. *The Idea of the Book in the Middle Ages: Language Theory, Mythology, and Fiction*. Ithaca: Cornell University Press.

Gerriets, Marilyn. 1991. "Theft, Penitentials, and the Compilation of the Early Irish Laws." *Celtica* 22:18–32.

Graham, William. 1987. *Beyond the Written Word: Oral Aspects of Scripture in the History of Religion*. Cambridge: Cambridge University Press.

Greene, David. 1972. "The Chariot as Described in Irish Literature." In *The Iron Age in the Irish Sea Province*, ed. Charles Thomas, pp. 59–73. Council for British Archaeology Research Report 9. London: CBA.

1976. "The 'Act of Truth' in a Middle-Irish Story." *Saga och Sed*, 30–37.

Greene, David, and Frank O'Connor. 1967. Ed. and trans. *A Golden Treasury of Irish Poetry*, A.D. 600 to 1200. London: Macmillan.

Greenwood, E. M. 1992. "Manchín's Cowl in 'Aislinge Meic Con Glinne.'" *Seanchas Ard Mhacha* 15:36–49.

Grosjean, P., S.J. 1927. Ed. and trans. "S. Columbae Hiensis cum Mongano Heroe Colloquium." *Analecta Bollandiana* 45:75–83.

1934. Ed. "Notes on the Original Names of Irish Saints." *Irish Texts* 4:99.

1937. Ed. and trans. "Textes hagiographiques irlandais." *ÉC* 2:269–303.

1958. "The Confession of St. Patrick." In Ryan 1958, 81–94.

Gwynn, Aubrey, S.J. 1966. "The Cult of Saint Martin in Ireland." *IER* 105:353–64.

Gwynn, Edward J. 1913. Ed. and trans. *The Metrical Dindshenchas*. Vol. 3. RIA Todd Lecture Series, 10. Dublin: Hodges, Figgis and Williams and Norgate.

1927. Ed. and trans. *The Rule of Tallaght*. Dublin: Hodges, Figgis.

Gwynn, John. 1913. Ed. *Liber Ardmachanus: The Book of Armagh*. Dublin: Hodges, Figgis.

Gwynn, Lucius. 1911. Ed. and trans. "Life of St. Lasair." *Ériu* 5:73–109.

Hamp, Eric P. 1982. "Varia VII.1. *Fer Diad*." *Ériu* 33:178.

1991. "Varia." *Celtica* 22:33–47.

Hanson, Richard P. C. 1968. *Saint Patrick: His Origins and Career*. Oxford: Clarendon Press.

1975. "The Omissions in the Text of the Confession of St. Patrick in the Book of Armagh." *Studia Patristica* 12:91–95.

1977. "The D-Text of Patrick's *Confession:* Origin or Reduction?" *PRIA* 77C:251–56.

1983. *The Life and Writings of the Historical Saint Patrick.* New York: Seabury Press.

Hanson, Richard P. C., and Cécile Blanc. 1978. Ed. and trans. *Saint Patrick: Confession et Lettre à Coroticus.* Sources chrétiennes 249. Paris: Cerf.

Harland, Richard. 1987. *Superstructuralism: The Philosophy of Structuralism and Poststructuralism.* London: Methuen.

Harrison, Alan. 1984. Ed. and trans. "Séanadh Saighre," *Éigse* 20:136–48.

1989. *The Irish Trickster.* Sheffield, Eng.: Sheffield Academic Press.

Harvey, Anthony. 1992. "Latin, Literacy, and the Celtic Vernaculars around the Year A.D. 500." In C. Byrne et al. 1992, 11–27.

Havelock, Eric A. 1986. *The Muse Learns to Write: Reflections on Orality and Literacy from Antiquity to the Present.* New Haven: Yale University Press.

Haycock, Marged. 1990. "The Significance of the 'Cad Goddau' Tree-List in the Book of Taliesin." In *Celtic Linguistics/Ieithyddiaeth Geltaidd: Readings in the Brythonic Languages, Festschrift for T. Arwyn Watkins,* ed. Martin J. Ball, James Fife, et al., pp. 297–331. Amsterdam Studies in the Theory and History of Linguistic Science 68. Amsterdam: John Benjamins.

Heist, William W. 1965. Ed. *Vitae sanctorum hiberniae ex Codice olim Salmanticensi nunc Bruxellensi.* Brussels: Société des Bollandistes.

Henken, Elissa R. 1987. *Traditions of the Welsh Saints.* Cambridge: D. S. Brewer.

1991. *The Welsh Saints: A Study in Patterned Lives.* Cambridge: D. S. Brewer.

Hennessy, W. M., and D. H. Kelly. 1875. Ed. (Hennessy) and trans. (Kelly). *The Book of Fenagh.* Dublin: Alexander Thom.

Hennig, John. 1949–51. "The Literary Tradition of Moses in Ireland." *Traditio* 7:233–61. Also in *Medieval Ireland, Saints and Martyrologies,* ed. Michael Richter. Northampton: Variorum Reprints, 1989.

Henry, P. L. 1978. *Saoithiúlacht na Sean-Ghaeilge: Bunú an Traidisiúin.* Dublin: Oifig an tSoláthair.

1979–80. Ed. and trans. "The Caldron of Poesy." *SC* 14–15:114–28.

1982. "*Furor Heroicus.*" *ZcP* 39:235–42.

Herbert, Máire. 1988a. *Iona, Kells, and Derry: The History and Hagiography of the Monastic Familia of Columba.* Oxford: Clarendon Press.

1988b. "The World, the Text, and the Critic of Early Irish Heroic Narrative." *Text and Context* 3:1–9.

1989. "The Preface to *Amra Coluim Cille.*" In Ó Corráin et al. 1989, 67–75.

Herbert, Máire, and Martin McNamara M.S.C. 1989. Ed. and trans. *Irish Biblical Apocrypha.* Edinburgh: T & T Clark.

Herbert, Máire, and Pádraig Ó Riain. 1988. Ed. and trans. *Betha Adamnáin: The Irish Life of Adamnán.* ITS 44. Cork: ITS.

Herren, Michael. 1976. "The Pseudonymous Tradition in Hiberno-Latin: An Introduction." In O'Meara and Naumann 1976, 121–31.

Hiltebeitel, Alf. 1976. *The Ritual of Battle: Krishna in the Mahābhārata.* Ithaca: Cornell University Press.

1982. "Brothers, Friends, and Charioteers: Parallel Episodes in the Irish and Indian Epics." In *Homage to Georges Dumézil,* ed. Edgar Polomé, pp. 85–111. Journal of Indo-European Studies Monograph, no. 3. Washington, D.C.: Journal of Indo-European Studies.

Howlett, David. 1989. "Ex Saliva Scripturae Meae." In Ó Corráin et al. 1989, 86–101.

——— 1994. Ed. and trans. *Liber Epistolarum Sancti Patricii Episcopi: The Books of Letters of Saint Patrick the Bishop.* Black Rock, Ireland: Four Courts Press.

——— 1995. *The Celtic Latin Tradition of Biblical Style.* Black Rock, Ireland: Four Courts Press.

Hughes, Kathleen. 1966. *The Church in Early Irish Society.* Ithaca: Cornell University Press.

Hull, Vernam. 1936. Ed. and trans. "The Death of Fothadh Cananne." *ZcP* 19:174–76.

——— 1949. Ed. and trans. *Longes Mac n-Uislenn: The Exile of the Sons of Uisliu,* New York: Modern Language Association; London: Oxford University Press.

——— 1960–61. "Amra Choluim Chille." *ZcP* 28:242–51.

Hyde, Douglas. 1915. Coll. and trans. *Legends of Saints and Sinners.* Dublin 1915; rpt. New York: Barnes and Noble, 1973.

Ireland, Colin. 1995. Review of Wright 1993. *Peritia* 9:446–54.

Jackson, Kenneth Hurlstone. 1953. *Language and History in Early Britain: A Chronological Survey of the Brittonic Languages, First to Twelfth Century A.D.* Edinburgh: University of Edinburgh Press.

——— 1990. Ed. *Aislinge Meic Con Glinne.* Dublin: DIAS.

Jager, Eric. 1993. *The Tempter's Voice: Language and the Fall in Medieval Literature.* Ithaca: Cornell University Press.

James, J. W. 1967. Ed. and trans. *Rhigyfarch's Life of St. David.* Cardiff: University of Wales Press.

Jarman, A. O. H. 1991. "The Merlin Legend and the Welsh Tradition of Prophecy." In *Arthur of the Welsh: The Arthurian Legend in Medieval Welsh Literature,* ed. Rachel Bromwich, Jarman, and Brynley F. Roberts, pp. 117–45. Cardiff: University of Wales Press.

Joynt, Maud. 1928. "Airbacc Giunnae." *Ériu* 10:130–34.

——— 1931. Ed. *Tromdámh Guaire.* MMIS 2. Dublin: Stationery Office.

Kelber, Werner H. 1983. *The Oral and the Written Gospel: The Hermeneutics of Speaking and Writing in the Synoptic Tradition, Mark, Paul, and Q.* Philadelphia: Fortress Press.

Kelleher, John V. 1971. "The Táin and the Annals." *Ériu* 22:107–27.

Kelly, Fergus. 1976. Ed. and trans. *Audacht Morainn.* Dublin: DIAS.

——— 1986. Ed. and trans. "An Old-Irish Text on Court Procedure." *Peritia* 5:74–106.

——— 1988. *A Guide to Early Irish Law.* Early Irish Law Series 3. Dublin: DIAS.

Kelly, Joseph F. 1979. "Books, Learning, and Sanctity in Early Christian Ireland." *Thought* 54 (September):253–61.

Kenney, James F. 1929. *The Sources for the Early History of Ireland: Ecclesiastical. An Introduction and Guide.* New York: Columbia University Press. Reprinted with corrections, New York: Octagon Books, 1966.

Knott, Eleanor. 1936. Ed. *Togail Bruidne Da Derga.* MMIS 8. Dublin: DIAS.

Koch, John T. 1987. "Llawr en Assed- (CA 932) 'The Laureate Hero in the War Chariot': Some Recollections of the Iron Age in the *Gododdin*." *ÉC* 24:253–78.

Koep, Leo. 1952. *Das Himmlische Buch in Antike und Christentum: Eine religionsgeschichtliche Untersuchung zur altchristlichen Bildersprache.* Bonn: P. Hanstein.

Krause, David. 1982. *The Profane Book of Irish Comedy.* Ithaca: Cornell University Press.

Kugel, James L. 1990a. "David the Prophet." In Kugel 1990b, 45–55.

——— 1990b. Ed. *Poetry and Prophecy: The Beginnings of a Literary Tradition.* Ithaca: Cornell University Press.

Lambert, Pierre-Yves. 1991. "Le vocabulaire du scribe irlandais." In Picard 1991, 157–67.

Lambkin, Brian K. 1987. "Patrick, Armagh, and Emain Macha." *Emania* 2:29–31.

Lapidge, Michael. 1982. "The Study of Latin Texts in Late Anglo-Saxon England: [1] The Evidence of Latin Glosses." In Brooks 1982, 99–140.

——— 1990. "A New Hiberno-Latin Hymn on St. Martin." *Celtica* 21:240–51.

Lapidge, Michael, and Richard Sharpe. 1985. *A Bibliography of Celtic-Latin Literature, 400–1200*. RIA Dictionary of Medieval Latin from Celtic Sources, Ancillary Publications 1. Dublin: RIA.

Lawlor, H. J. 1916. "The Cathach of St. Columba." *PRIA* 33 C, 241–443.

Lehmann, Paul. 1955. Ed. *Die Admonitio S. Basilii ad filium spiritualem*. Sitzungsberichte der Bayerische Akademie der Wissenschaften. Philosophisch-historische Klasse, 7. Munich: Bayerische Akademie der Wissenschaften.

Lerer, Seth. 1991. *Literacy and Power in Anglo-Saxon Literature*. Lincoln: University of Nebraska Press.

Leupin, Alexandre. 1982. *Le Graal et la littérature: Étude sur la Vulgate arthurienne en prose*. Lausanne: L'Age d'Homme.

Levi, Peter. 1971. Trans. *Pausanias, Guide to Greece*. 2 vols. Harmondsworth, Eng.: Penguin.

Lévi-Strauss, Claude. 1962. *La pensée sauvage*. Paris: Librairie Plon.

——— 1985. "An Anatomical Foreshadowing of Twinship." In *The View from Afar*, trans. Joachim Neugroschel and Phoebe Hoss, pp. 201–9. New York: Basic Books.

Lord, Albert B. 1960. *The Singer of Tales*. Harvard Studies in Comparative Literature 24. Cambridge: Harvard University Press.

——— 1986. "The Merging of Two Worlds: Oral and Written Poetry as Carriers of Ancient Values." In Foley 1986, 19–64.

Lucas, A. T. 1986. "The Social Role of Relics and Reliquaries in Ancient Ireland." *JRSAI* 116:5–37.

Lyle, Emily. 1985. "The Place of the Hostile Twins in a Proposed Theogonic Structure." *Cosmos* 1:1–14.

Mac Airt, Seán. 1951. Ed. and trans. *The Annals of Inisfallen (Ms. Rawlinson B. 503)*. Dublin: DIAS.

——— 1958. "The Churches Founded by Saint Patrick." In Ryan 1958, 67–80.

Mac Airt, Séan, and Gearóid Mac Niocaill. 1983. Ed. and trans. *The Annals of Ulster (to A.D. 1131)*. Part 1, Text and Translation. Dublin: DIAS.

Mac an Luain, Pádraig Eoghain Phádraig. 1985. *Uair an Chloig cois Teallaigh/An Hour by the Hearth: Stories Told by Pádraig Eoghain Phádraig Mac an Luain*. Coll., ed., and trans. Séamas Ó Catháin. Dublin: Comhairle Bhéaloideas Éireann.

Mac Cana, Proinsias. 1958. *Branwen Daughter of Llŷr: A study of the Irish Affinities and of the Composition of the Second Branch of the Mabinogi*. Cardiff: University of Wales Press.

——— 1970. "The Three Languages and the Three Laws." *SC* 5:62–78.

——— 1975. "On the 'Prehistory' of *Immram Brain*." *Ériu* 26:33–52.

——— 1976. "The Sinless Otherworld of *Immram Brain*." *Ériu* 27:95–115.

——— 1979. "*Regnum* and *Sacerdotium*: Notes on Irish Tradition." *PBA* 65:443–79.

——— 1980a. *The Learned Tales of Medieval Ireland*. Dublin: DIAS.

——— 1980b. *Literature in Irish*. Dublin: Department of Foreign Affairs, Ireland.

——— 1984. "The Rise of the Later Schools of *Filidheacht*." *Ériu* 25:126–46.

1986. "Christianisme et paganisme dans l'Irlande ancienne." In *Rencontres de religions: Actes du Colloque du Collège des irlandais tenu sous les auspices de l'Académie royale irlandaise (Juin 1981)*, ed. Mac Cana and Michel Meslin, pp. 57–74. Paris: Les Belles Lettres.

1988. "Placenames and Mythology in Irish Tradition: Places, Pilgrimages, and Things." In MacLennan 1988, 319–41.

1989. "Notes on the Combination of Prose and Verse in Early Irish Narrative." In *Early Irish Literature—Media and Communication/Mündlichkeit und Schriftlichkeit in der frühen irischen Literatur,* ed. Stephen N. Tranter and Hildegard L. C. Tristram, pp. 125–47. ScriptOralia 10. Tübingen: Gunter Narr.

1992. "*Laíded, Gressacht* 'Formalized Incitement'." *Ériu* 43:69–92.

McCone, Kim. 1984a. "Clones and Her Neighbours in the Early Period: Hints from Some Airgialla Saints' Lives." *Clogher Record* 11:305–25.

1984b. "An Introduction to Early Irish Saints' Lives." *Maynooth Review* 11:26–59.

1986a. "Dubthach maccu Lugair and a Matter of Life and Death in the Pseudo-historical Prologue to the *Senchas Már.*" *Peritia* 5:1–35.

1986b. "Werewolves, Cyclopes, *Díberga,* and *Fíanna:* Juvenile Delinquency in Early Ireland." *CMCS* 12:1–22.

1987. "Hund, Wolf, and Krieger bei den Indogermanen." In *Studien zum Indogermanischen Wortschatz,* ed. Wolfgang Meid, pp. 101–54. Innsbrucker Beiträge zur Sprachwissenschaft 52. Innsbruck: Institut für Sprachwissenschaft der Universität Innsbruck.

1989. "A Tale of Two Ditties: Poet and Satirist in *Cath Maige Tuired.*" In Ó Corráin et al. 1989, 122–43.

1990. *Pagan Past and Christian Present in Early Irish Literature.* Maynooth Monographs 3. Maynooth: An Sagart.

Mac Craith, Mícheál. 1990. "Gaelic Ireland and the Renaissance." In *The Celts and the Renaissance: Tradition and Innovation,* Proceedings of the Eighth International Congress of Celtic Studies, 1987, ed. Glanmor Williams and Robert Owen Jones, pp. 57–89. Cardiff: University of Wales Press.

Mac Eoin, Gearóid S. 1968. "The Mysterious Death of Loegaire mac Néill." *SH* 8:21–48.

Mackey, J. P. 1992. "Christian Past and Primal Present." *ÉC* 29:285–97.

MacLennan, Gordon W. 1988. Ed. *Proceedings of the First North American Congress of Celtic Studies.* Ottawa: University of Ottawa.

McLeod, Neil. 1982. "The Concept of Law in Ancient Irish Jurisprudence." *Irish Jurist* 17:356–67.

McManus, Damian. 1988. "Irish Letter-Names and Their Kennings." *Ériu* 39:127–68.

1991. *A Guide to Ogam.* Maynooth Monographs 4. Maynooth: An Sagart.

MacNeill, Máire. 1962. *The Festival of Lughnasa: A Study of the Survival of the Celtic Festival of the Beginning of Harvest.* London: Oxford University Press.

MacNickle, Sister Mary Donatus. 1934. "Beasts and Birds in the Lives of the Early Irish Saints." Diss., University of Pennsylvania.

Mac Niocaill, Gearóid. 1969. "Admissible and Inadmissible Evidence in Early Irish Law." *Irish Jurist* 4:332–37.

1972. *Ireland before the Vikings.* Dublin: Gill and Macmillan.

McQuillan, Peter. 1990. "Finn, Fothad, and *Fian:* Some Early Associations." *PHCC* 8:1–10.

Mallory, James P. 1992. "The World of Cú Chulainn: The Archaeology of the *Táin Bó*

Cúailnge." In *Aspects of the Táin,* ed. Mallory, pp. 103–59. Belfast: December Publications.

Marstrander, Carl. 1911a. Ed. and trans. "Bídh Crínna." *Ériu* 5:126–41.

    1911b. Ed. and trans. "A New Version of the Battle of Mag Rath." *Ériu* 5:226–47.

Matonis, A. T. E., and Daniel F. Melia. 1990. Eds. *Celtic Language, Celtic Culture: A Festschrift for Eric P. Hamp.* Van Nuys, Calif.: Ford and Bailie.

Meid, Wolfgang. 1974. "Dichtkunst, Rechtspflege, und Medizin im alten Irland." In *Antiquitates indogermanicae: Studien zur indogermanischen Altertumskunde und zur Sprach- und Kulturgeschichte der indogermanischen Völker: Gedenkschrift für Hermann Güntert,* ed. M. Mayrhofer, Meid, B. Schlerath, and R. Schmitt, pp. 21–34. Innsbrucker Beiträge zur Sprachwissenschaft 12. Innsbruck: Institut für Sprachwissenschaft der Universität Innsbruck.

    1985. "Die irische Literatur des 7. bis 12. Jahrhunderts." In *Neues Handbuch der Literaturwissenschaft,* vol. 6, *Europäisches Frühmittelalter,* ed. Klaus von See, pp. 125–50. Wiesbaden: AULA.

Melia, Daniel F. 1978. "The *Grande Troménie* at Locronan: a Major Breton Lughnasa Celebration." *Journal of American Folklore* 91:528–42.

    1979. "Some Remarks on the Affinities of Medieval Irish Saga." *Acta antiqua Academiae scientiarum Hungaricae* 27:255–61.

    1983. "Law and the Shaman-Saint." In P. Ford 1983b, 113–28.

Merdrignac, Bernard. 1985–86. *Recherches sur l'hagiographie armoricaine du VIIeme au XVeme siecle.* Vol. 1: *Les saints bretons, temoins de Dieu ou temoins des hommes?* Vol. 2: *Les hagiographes et leur publics en Bretagne au Moyen Âge.* Saint-Malo: Centre Régional Archéologique d'Alet.

    1987. "Folklore and Hagiography: A Semiotic Approach to the Legend of the Immortals of Landevennec." *CMCS* 13:73–86.

Meroney, Howard. 1958a. "The Alphabet of the World." *Journal of Celtic Studies* 2:173–88.

    1958b. Review of MMIS 14–17. *Journal of Celtic Studies* 2:242–60.

Meyer, Kuno. 1892. Ed. and trans. "Scél Baili Binnbérlaig." *RC* 13:220–27.

    1893. Ed. and trans. "Anecdotes of St. Moling," *RC* 14:188–94.

    1899. Ed. and trans. "The Colloquy of Colum Cille and the Youth at Carn Eolairg." *ZcP* 2:313–20.

    1905a. Ed. and trans. *Cain Adamnáin: An Old-Irish Treatise on the Law of Adamnan.* Anecdota Oxoniensa, Medieval and Modern Series, 12. Oxford: Clarendon Press.

    1905b. Ed. "Neue Mitteilungen aus irischen Handschriften." *Archiv für celtische Lexikographie* 3:1–7.

    1906a. Ed. and trans. *The Death-Tales of the Ulster Heroes.* RIA Todd Lecture Series 14. Dublin: Hodges, Figgis; London: Williams and Norgate.

    1906b. Ed. and trans. *The Triads of Ireland.* RIA Todd Lecture Series 13. Dublin: Hodges, Figgis.

    1910a. *Fianaigecht.* RIA Todd Lecture Series 16. Dublin: Hodges, Figgis.

    1910b. "The Irish Mirabilia in the Norse 'Speculum Regale'." *Ériu* 4:1–16.

    1910c. Ed. "Síaburcharpat Conculaind." *Anecdota from Irish Manuscripts* 3, ed. Osborn J. Bergin et al. Halle: Max Niemeyer.

    1911a. Ed. and trans. *Betha Colmáin maic Lúacháin: Life of Colmán son of Lúachan.* RIA Todd Lecture Series 17. Dublin: Hodges, Figgis.

    1911b. "The Bodleian MS. Laud 615." *Ériu* 5:7–14.

1912. Ed. *Sanas Cormaic: An Old-Irish Glossary. Anecdota from Irish Manuscripts* 4, ed. Osborn J. Bergin et al. Halle: Max Niemeyer; Dublin: Hodges, Figgis.

1918. Ed. "Mitteilungen aus irischen Handschriften." *ZcP* 12:358–97.

Miller, Jacqueline T. 1986. *Poetic License: Authority and Authorship in Medieval and Renaissance Contexts.* Oxford: Oxford University Press.

Minnis, A. J. 1988. *Medieval Theory of Authorship: Scholastic Literary Attitudes in the Later Middle Ages.* 2d ed. Aldershot, Eng.: Scolar Press.

Mohrmann, Christine. 1961. *The Latin of Saint Patrick: Four Lectures.* Dublin: DIAS.

Mulchrone, Kathleen. 1939. Ed. *Bethu Phátraic: The Tripartite Life of Patrick.* Vol. 1: *Text and Sources.* Dublin: Hodges Figgis.

Murphy, Gerard. 1962. Ed. and trans. *Early Irish Lyrics, Eighth to Twelfth Century.* Rev. ed. Orig. pub. 1956. Oxford: Clarendon Press.

1971. *The Ossianic Lore and Romantic Tales of Medieval Ireland.* Rev. Brian Ó Cuív. Cork: Mercier Press.

Myrick, Leslie Diane. 1993. *From the De Excidio Troiae Historia to the Togail Troí: Literary-Cultural Synthesis in a Medieval Irish Adaptation of Dares' Troy Tale.* Anglistische Forschungen 223. Heidelberg: Winter.

Nagy, Gregory. 1979. *The Best of the Achaeans: Concepts of the Hero in Archaic Greek Poetry.* Baltimore: Johns Hopkins University Press.

1982. "Theognis of Megara: The Poet as Seer, Pilot, and Revenant." *Arethusa* 15:109–28.

1990. *Pindar's Homer: The Lyric Possession of an Epic Past.* Baltimore: Johns Hopkins University Press.

1992a. "Homeric Questions." *Transactions of the American Philological Association* 122:17–60.

1992b. "Sêma and Nóēsis: The Hero's Tomb and the 'Reading' of Symbols in Homer and Hesiod." In G. Nagy, *Greek Mythology and Poetics,* pp. 202–22. Ithaca: Cornell University Press.

Nagy, Joseph Falaky. 1981a. "Demne Mael." *Celtica* 14:8–14.

1981b. "Shamanic Aspects of the *Bruidhean* Tale." *History of Religions* 20:302–22.

1981–82. "Liminality and Knowledge in Irish Tradition." *SC* 16–17:134–43.

1982. "The Wisdom of the *Geilt.*" *Éigse* 19:44–60.

1983a. "Beowulf and Fergus: Heroes of Their Tribes?" In *Connections between Old English and Medieval Celtic Literature,* ed. Patrick K. Ford and Karen Borst, pp. 31–44. Old English Colloquium Series 2. Berkeley: University of California, Berkeley, Old English Colloquium.

1983b. "Close Encounters of the Traditional Kind in Medieval Irish Literature." In P. Ford 1983b, 129–49.

1985. *The Wisdom of the Outlaw: The Boyhood Deeds of Finn in Gaelic Narrative Tradition.* Berkeley: University of California Press.

1985–86. "Otter, Salmon, and Eel in Traditional Gaelic Narrative," *SC* 20–21:123–44.

1986. "Orality in Medieval Irish Literature: An Overview." *Oral Tradition* 1:272–301.

1986–87. "Fenian Heroes and Their Rites of Passage." *Béaloideas* 54–55:161–82.

1987a. "In Defense of Rómánsaíocht." *Ériu* 38:9–26.

1987b. "The Sign of the Outlaw: Multiformity in Fenian Narrative." In *Comparative Research on Oral Traditions: A Memorial for Milman Parry,* ed. John Foley, pp. 465–92. Columbus, Ohio: Slavica Press.

1988. "Oral Life and Literary Death in Medieval Irish Tradition." *Oral Tradition* 3:368–80.

1989a. "Compositional Concerns in the *Acallam na Senórach*." In Ó Corráin et al. 1989, 149–58.

1989b. "Representations of Oral Tradition in Medieval Irish Literature." *Language and Communication* 9:143–58.

1990a. "The Herons of Druim Ceat Revisiting, and Revisited." *Celtica* 21:368–76.

1990b. "Hierarchy, Heroes, and Heads: Indo-European Structures in Greek Myth." In *Approaches to Greek Myth*, ed. Lowell Edmunds, pp. 200–38. Baltimore: Johns Hopkins University Press.

1990c. "Sword as *Audacht*." In Matonis and Melia 1990, 131–36.

1995. "Oral Tradition in the *Acallam na Senórach*." In *Oral Tradition in the Middle Ages*, ed. W. F. H. Nicolaisen, pp. 77–95. Binghamton, N.Y.: Medieval and Renaissance Texts and Studies.

1996. Introduction. In J. O'Keeffe 1910, 1–32 (reissued 1996).

Nerney, D. S., S. J. 1949. "A Study of Saint Patrick's Sources." *IER* 71:497–507; 72:14–26, 97–110, 265–80.

Ní Chatháin, Próinséas. 1976. "Some Early Irish Hymn Material." In *Famulus Christi: Essays in Commemoration of the Thirteenth Centenary of the Birth of the Venerable Bede*, ed. Gerald Bonner, pp. 229–38. London: SPCK.

1979–80. "Swineherds, Seers, and Druids." *SC* 14/15:200–211.

Ní Chatháin, Próinséas, and Michael Richter. 1984. Eds. *Irland und Europa: Die Kirche im Frühmittelalter/Ireland and Europe: The Early Church*. Stuttgart: Klett-Cotta.

1987. Eds. *Irland und die Christenheit: Bibelstudien und Mission/Ireland and Christendom: The Bible and the Missions*. Stuttgart: Klett-Cotta.

Nichols, Stephen G. 1991. "Voice and Writing in Augustine and in the Troubador Lyric." In *Vox Intexta: Orality and Textuality in the Middle Ages*, ed. A. N. Doane and Carol Braun Pasternack, pp. 137–61. Madison: University of Wisconsin Press.

Ní Shéaghdha, Nessa. 1942–45. Ed. *Agallamh na Seanórach*. 3 vols. Leabhair ó Láimhscríbhnibh 7, 10, 15. Dublin: Oifig an tSoláthair.

Nuner, Robert D. 1958–59. "The Verbal System of the Agallamh na Senórach." *ZcP* 27:230–309.

Ó hAodha, Donncha. 1978. Ed. and trans. *Bethu Brigte*. Dublin: DIAS.

1989. Ed. and trans. "The Lament of the Old Women of Beare." In Ó Corráin et al. 1989, 308–31.

Ó Briain, Felim, O. F. M. 1945. "Miracles in the Lives of the Irish Saints." *IER* 56:331–42.

1947. "Saga Themes in Irish Hagiography." In *Féilscríbhinn Torna: Essays and Studies presented to Professor Tadhg Ua Donnchadha (Torna)*, ed. Séamus Pender, pp. 33–42. Cork: Cork University Press.

Ó Briain, Máirtín. 1989. "Some Material on Oisín in the Land of Youth." Ó Corráin et al. 1989, 181–99.

1991. "The Horse-Eared Kings of Irish Tradition and St. Brigit." In *Crossed Paths: Methodological Approaches to the Celtic Aspect of the European Middle Ages*, ed. Benjamin T. Hudson and Vickie Ziegler, pp. 83–113. Lanham, N.Y.: University Press of America.

O'Brien, M. A. 1962. Ed. *Corpus Genealogiarum Hiberniae*. Vol. 1. Reprinted with intro. by John V. Kelleher. Dublin: DIAS, 1976.

1973. "Old Irish Personal Names. M. A. O'Brien's 'Rhŷs Lecture' Notes." Ed. Rolf Baumgarten. *Celtica* 10:211–36.

Ó Buachalla, Breandán. 1989. "Aodh Eanghach and the Irish King-Hero." In Ó Corráin et al. 1989, 200–32.

Ó Cathasaigh, Tomás. 1977. *The Heroic Biography of Cormac mac Airt*. Dublin: DIAS.
    1984. "Pagan Sources: The Evidence of Early Irish Narrative." In Ní Chatháin and Richter 1984, 291–307.
    1989. "The Eponym of Cnogba." *Éigse* 23:27–38.
    1993. "Mythology in *Táin Bó Cúailnge*." In Tristram 1993, 114–32.

Ó Coileáin, Seán. 1973. "The Structure of a Literary Cycle." *Ériu* 24:88–125.
    1977. "The Making of *Tromdám Guaire*." *Ériu* 28:32–67.
    1977–78. "Oral Or Literary? Some Strands of the Argument." *SH* 17–18:7–35.
    1988. "Tromdhámh Ghuaire: An Aoir agus an Insint." *Léachtaí Cholm Cille* 18:20–38.
    1993. "Place and Place name in *Fianaigheacht*." *SH* 27:45–60.

O'Connor, Frank. 1959. Trans. *Kings, Lords, and Commons: An Anthology from the Irish*. New York: Knopf.

Ó Corráin, Donnchadh. 1972. *Ireland before the Normans*. Dublin: Gill and Macmillan.
    1978. "Nationality and Kingship in Pre-Norman Ireland." In *Nationality and the Pursuit of National Independence*, ed. T. W. Moody, pp. 1–35. *Historical Studies* 11. Belfast: Appletree Press.
    1987a. "Irish Vernacular Law and the Old Testament." In Ní Chatháin and Richter 1987, 284–307.
    1987b. "Legend as Critic." In Dunne 1987, 23–38.
    1989a. "Early Irish Hermit Poetry?" In Ó Corráin et al. 1989, 251–67.
    1989b. "Prehistoric and Early Christian Ireland." In *The Oxford Illustrated History of Ireland*, ed. R. F. Foster, pp. 1–52. Oxford: Oxford University Press.

Ó Corráin, Donnchadh, Liam Breatnach, and Kim McCone. 1989. Eds. *Sages, Saints, and Storytellers: Celtic Studies in Honour of Professor James Carney*. Maynooth Monographs 2. Maynooth: An Sagart.

Ó Cróinín, Dáibhí. 1995. *Early Medieval Ireland 400–1200*. London: Longman.

Ó Cuív, Brian. 1961–63. Review of *ÉC* 9, Fascicule 2 (1961). *Éigse* 10, 337–39.
    1964–66. "Some Items from Irish Tradition." *Éigse* 11:167–87.
    1967–68. Ed. and trans. "A Colam Cille Dialogue." *Éigse* 12:165–72.
    1980. "Irish Words for 'Alphabet.'" *Ériu* 31:100–110.
    1982. "Acallam na Senórach." In *Dictionary of the Middle Ages*, ed. in chief Joseph R. Strayer, pp. 33–34. Vol. 1. New York: Charles Scribner's Sons.
    1986. "Varia VII: The Two Herons of Druim Ceat." *Ériu* 37:194–96.

Ó Fiannachta, Pádraig. 1985. "Betha Choluimb Chille." *Léachtaí Cholm Cille* 15:11–33.

O'Flaherty, Wendy Doniger. 1988. *Other Peoples' Myths: The Cave of Echoes*. New York: Macmillan.

O'Grady, Standish H. 1892. Ed. and trans. *Silva Gadelica*. 2 vols. London: Williams and Norgate.

O'Keeffe, J. G. 1910. Ed. and trans. *Buile Suibhne (The Frenzy of Suibhne), Being the Adventures of Suibhne Geilt: A Middle-Irish Romance*. ITS 12. London: David Nutt.
    1911. Ed. and trans. "Mac Dá Cherda and Cummaine Foda." *Ériu* 5:18–44.
    1931. Ed. *Buile Shuibhne*. MMIS 1. Dublin: DIAS.

O'Keeffe, Katherine O'Brien. 1990. *Visible Song: Transitional Literacy in Old English Verse*. Cambridge: Cambridge University Press.

O'Kelleher, A., and G. Schoepperle. 1918. Ed. and trans. *Betha Colaim Chille: Life of*

Columcille, compiled by Manus O'Donnell in 1532. Urbana: University of Illinois Press.

O'Leary, Philip. 1986. "A Foreseeing Driver of an Old Chariot: Regal Moderation in Early Irish Literature." *CMCS* 11:1–16.

———. 1987. "*Fír Fer:* An Internalized Ethical Concept in Early Irish Literature?" *Éigse* 22:1–14.

Olrik, Axel. 1965. "Epic Laws of Folk Narrative." Trans. Jeanne P. Steager. In *The Study of Folklore,* ed. Alan Dundes, pp. 129–41. Englewood Cliffs, N.J.: Prentice-Hall.

O'Meara, John J., and Bernd Naumann. 1976. Eds. *Latin Script and Letters, A.D. 400–900: Festschrift Presented to Ludwig Bieler on the Occasion of His 70th Birthday.* Leiden: E. J. Brill.

Ong, Walter J., S. J. 1982. *Orality and Literacy: The Technologizing of the Word.* London: Methuen.

———. 1986. "Text as Interpretation: Mark and After." In Foley 1986, 147–69.

Ó hÓgáin, Dáithi. 1985. *The Hero in Irish Folk History.* Dublin: Gill and Macmillan; New York: St. Martin's Press.

O'Rahilly, Cecile. 1962. Ed. *Cath Finntrágha.* MMIS 20. Dublin: DIAS.

———. 1967. Ed. and trans. *Táin Bó Cúalnge from the Book of Leinster.* Dublin: DIAS.

———. 1976a. Ed. and trans. "Cathcharpat Serda." *Celtica* 11:194–202.

———. 1976b. Ed. and trans. *Táin Bó Cúailnge: Recension I.* Dublin: DIAS.

O'Rahilly, Thomas F. 1946. *Early Irish History and Mythology.* Dublin: DIAS.

———. 1957. *The Two Patricks.* Dublin: DIAS.

Ó Raifeartaigh, T. 1978. "Silva Focluti, Quae Est Prope Mare Occidentale (Patrick's Confession, 23): A New Approach." *Maynooth Review* 4:25–27.

———. 1983/84. "St. Patrick and the *Defensio.*" *Seanchas Ard Mhacha* 11(1):22–31.

———. 1984. "The Censuring of St. Patrick by the *Seniores.*" *Celtica* 16:13–33.

Orchard, Andy. 1993. Ed. and trans. "Audites Omnes Amantes: A Hymn in Patrick's Praise." In Dumville et al. 1993, 153–73.

Ó Riain, Pádraig. 1972. "A Study of the Irish Legend of the Wild Man." *Éigse* 14:179–206.

———. 1974. "The Materials and Provenance of 'Buile Shuibhne'," *Éigse* 15:173–88.

———. 1977. "St. Finnbarr: A Study in a Cult." *Journal of the Cork Historical and Archaeological Society* 82:63–82.

———. 1978. Ed. *Cath Almaine.* MMIS 25. Dublin: DIAS.

———. 1983. "Cainnech *alias* Colum Cille, Patron of Ossory." In *Folia Gadelica: Essays Presented by Former Students to R. A. Breatnach,* ed. Pádraig de Brún, Seán Ó Coileáin, and Ó Riain, pp. 20–35. Cork: Cork University Press.

———. 1984. "Finnian or Winniau?" In Ní Chatháin and Richter 1984, 52–57.

———. 1992a. "Adamnán's Age at Death: Fact or Symbol?" *Studia Celtica Japonica* 5:7–17.

———. 1992b. "Early Irish Literature." In *The Celtic Connection,* ed. Glanville Price, pp. 65–80. Gerrards Cross, Eng.: Colin Smythe.

———. 1994. Ed. and trans. *Beatha Bharra. Saint Finbarr of Cork: The Complete Life.* ITS 57. London: ITS.

———. 1995. "Pagan Example and Christian Practice: A Reconsideration." In Edel 1995, 144–56.

Ó Súilleabháin, Seán. 1945. "Foundation Sacrifices." *JRSAI* 75:45–52.

———. 1970. "Etiological Stories in Ireland." In *Medieval Literature and Folklore Studies: Essays in Honor of Francis Lee Utley,* ed. Jerome Mandel and Bruce A. Rosenberg, pp. 257–74. New Brunswick: Rutgers University Press.

O'Sullivan Sean (= Seán Ó Súilleabháin). 1977. Trans. *Legends from Ireland*. London: B. T. Batsford.

Ó hUiginn, Ruairí. 1993. "Fergus, Russ, and Rudraige: A Brief Biography of Fergus mac Róich." *Emania* 11:31–40.

Paor, Liam de. 1979. "Saint Mac Creiche of Liscannor." *Ériu* 30:93–121.

———. 1993. Trans. *Saint Patrick's World: The Christian Culture of Ireland's Apostolic Age*. Blackrock, Ireland: Four Courts Press.

Picard, Jean-Michel. 1981. "The Marvelous in Irish and Continental Saints' Lives of the Merovingian Period." In *Columbanus and Merovingian Monasticism*, ed. H. B. Clarke and Mary Brennan, pp. 91–103. BAR International Series 113. Oxford: British Archaeological Reports.

———. 1985. "Structural Patterns in Early Hiberno-Latin Hagiography." *Peritia* 4:67–82.

———. 1989. "The Strange Death of Guaire mac Aedáin." In Ó Corráin et al. 1989, 367–75.

———. 1991. Ed. *Ireland and Northern France, A.D. 600–850*. Blackrock, Ireland: Four Courts Press.

———. 1992. "Les celticismes des hagiographes irlandais du VIIe siècle." *ÉC* 29:355–73.

Piggott, Stuart. 1986. "Horse and Chariot: The Price of Prestige." In *Proceedings of the Seventh International Congress of Celtic Studies, Oxford, 1983*, ed. D. Ellis Evans, John G. Griffith, and E. M. Jope, pp. 25–30. Oxford: Jesus College.

Plummer, Charles. 1883–85. Ed. and trans. "Irish Miscellanies: The Conversion of Loegaire, and His Death." *RC* 6:162–72.

———. 1910. Ed. *Vitae sanctorum Hiberniae*. 2 vols. Oxford: Clarendon Press.

———. 1922. Ed. and trans. *Bethada Náem nÉrenn: Lives of Irish Saints*. 2 vols. Oxford: Clarendon Press.

———. 1925. *Miscellanea hagiographica Hibernica*. Brussels: Société des Bollandistes.

———. 1926. "On the Colophons and Marginalia of Irish Scribes." *PBA* 12:11–44.

Pokorny, Julius. 1913. Ed. "Altirische Texte." *ZcP* 9:235–41.

Poli, Diego. 1986–89. "La metafora di Babele e le *partitiones* nella teoria grammaticale irlandese dell' *Auraicept na n-Éces*." In *Episteme: In ricordo di Giorgio Raimondo Cardona*, ed. Poli, pp. 179–97. Quaderni Linguistici e Filologici 4. Macerata: Università di Macerata.

———. 1989. "Biblioteca dell'oralità, codice miscellaneo e grammatica come mezzo di trasmissione dei saperi nell'Irlanda antica." In *La trasmissione del sapere: Aspetti linguistici e antropologici*, ed. Giorgio R. Cardona, pp. 223–34. Rome: Bagatto Libri.

———. 1992. "Le divin porcher: Un essai de comparaison." *ÉC* 29:375–81.

Poppe, Erich. 1985. Ed. and trans. "A Middle Irish Poem on Eimíne's Bell." *Celtica* 17:59–72.

Powell, T. G. E. 1963. "Some Implications of Chariotry." In *Culture and Environment: Essays in Honour of Sir Cyril Fox*, ed. I. L. Foster and L. Alcock, pp. 153–69. London: Routledge and Kegan Paul.

Power, Maura. 1917. Ed. and trans. "Cnucha Cnoc os Cionn Life." *ZcP* 11:39–55.

Puhvel, Jaan. 1987. *Comparative Mythology*. Baltimore: Johns Hopkins University Press.

Quin, E. G[ordon]. 1981a. "The Early Irish Poem *Isucán*." *CMCS* 1:39–52.

———. 1981b. Ed. and trans. "Ochtfochlach Choluim Chille." *Celtica* 14:125–53.

Radner, Joan Newlon. 1982. "'Fury Destroys the World': Historical Strategy in Ireland's Ulster Epic." *Mankind Quarterly* 23:41–60.

———. 1983. "The Significance of the Threefold Death in Celtic Tradition." In P. Ford 1983b, 180–99.

1990. "'Men Will Die': Poets, Harpers, and Women in Early Irish Literature." In Matonis and Melia 1990, 172–86.

Raftery, Barry. 1993. "Fahren und Reiten in Irland in der Eisenzeit: Die archäologischen Belege." In Tristram 1993, 173–91.

Rank, Otto. 1932. "The Myth of the Birth of the Hero." Trans. F. Robbins and Smith Ely Jeliffe. In Rank, *The Myth of the Birth of the Hero and Other Writings*, pp. 3–96. Ed. Philip Freund. New York: Alfred A. Knopf.

Rees, Alwyn, and Brinley Rees. 1961. *Celtic Heritage: Ancient Tradition in Ireland and Wales.* London: Thames and Hudson.

Reeves, William. 1874. Ed. and trans. *Life of Saint Columba, Founder of Hy, Written by Adamnan.* Historians of Scotland 6. Edinburgh: Edmonston and Douglas.

Richter, Michael. 1994. *The Formation of the Medieval West: Studies in the Oral Culture of the Barbarians.* Black Rock, Ireland: Four Courts Press.

Robinson, F[red] N[orris]. 1913. "Human Sacrifice among the Irish Celts." In *Anniversary Papers by Colleagues and Pupils of George Lyman Kittredge,* pp. 185–97. Boston: Ginn.

Ross, Anne. 1967. *Pagan Celtic Britain: Studies in Iconography and Tradition.* London: Routledge and Kegan Paul.

Ryan, John, S.J. 1946. "The Convention of Druim Ceat (AU. 575)." *JRSAI* 76:35–55.

——— 1972. *Irish Monasticism.* 2d ed. Orig. pub. 1931. Ithaca: Cornell University Press.

Saussure, Ferdinand de. 1972. *Cours de linguistique générale.* Ed. Charles Bally and Albert Séchehaye, with the collaboration of Albert Riedlinger. Critical ed. by Tullio de Mauro. Paris: Payot.

Sayers, William. 1981. "Varia IV. Three Charioteering Gifts in *Táin Bó Cúailnge* and *Mesca Ulad:* Immorchor nDelend, Foscul nDiriuch, Léim Dar Boilg." *Ériu* 32:163–67.

——— 1991a. "*Airdrech, Sirite,* and other Early Irish Battlefield Sprites." *Éigse* 25:45–55.

——— 1991b. "Early Irish Attitudes toward Hair and Beards, Baldness and Tonsure." *ZcP* 44:154–89.

Snowcroft, R. M. 1987. "*Leabhar Gabhála,* Part I: The Growth of the Text." *Ériu* 38:79–140.

——— 1995. "Abstract Narrative in Ireland." *Ériu* 46:121–58.

Sharpe, Richard. 1979. "Hiberno-Latin *Laicus,* Irish *Láech,* and the Devil's Men." *Ériu* 30:75–92.

——— 1982a. "Palaeographical Considerations in the Study of the Patrician Documents in the Book of Armagh." *Scriptorium* 36:3–28.

——— 1982b. "The Patrician Documents." *Peritia* 1:363–69.

——— 1982c. "St. Patrick and the See of Armagh." *CMCS* 4:33–59.

——— 1985. "Latin and Irish Words for 'Book-Satchel.'" *Peritia* 4:152–56.

——— 1989. "Quatuor Sanctissimi Episcopi: Irish Saints before St. Patrick." In Ó Corráin et al. 1989, 376–99.

——— 1990a. "Maghnus Ó Dohmnaill's Source for Adomnán's *Vita S. Columbae* and Other *Vitae.*" *Celtica* 21:604–7.

——— 1990b. "Saint Mauchteus, *Discipulus Patricii.*" In *Britain, 400–600: Language and History,* ed. Alfred Bammesberger and Aldred Wollmann, pp. 85–93. Heidelberg: Carl Winter/Universitätsverlag.

——— 1991. *Medieval Irish Saints' Lives: An Introduction to Vitae Sanctorum Hiberniae.* Oxford: Clarendon Press.

——— 1995. Trans. *Adomnán of Iona, Life of St. Columba.* London: Penguin.

Shaw, John. 1992. "Scottish Gaelic Traditions of the *Cliar Sheanchain*." In C. Byrne et al. 1992, 141–58.

Sims-Williams, Patrick. 1978a. "'Is It Fog or Smoke or Warriors Fighting?': Irish and Welsh Parallels to the *Finnsburg* Fragment." *BBCS* 27:505–14.

———. 1990. "Some Celtic Otherworld Terms." In Matonis and Melia 1990, 57–81.

Sinos, Dale S. 1980. *Achilles, Patroklos, and the Meaning of Philos.* Innsbrucker Beiträge zur Sprachwissenschaft 29. Innsbruck: Institut für Sprachwissenschaft der Universität Innsbruck.

Slotkin, Edgar M. 1977–79. "Medieval Irish Scribes and Fixed Texts." *Éigse* 17:437–50.

Smyth, Alfred P. 1984. *Warlords and Holy Men: Scotland, A.D. 80–1000.* London: Edward Arnold.

Speyer, Wolfgang. 1992. "Das Buch als magisch-religiöser Kraftträger im griechischen und römischen Altertum." In *Das Buch als magische und als Repräsentationsobjekt,* ed. Peter Ganz, pp. 59–86. Wolfenbütteler Mittelalter-Studien 5. Wiesbaden: Otto Harrassowitz.

Stacey, Robin Chapman. 1986. Trans. "*Berrad Airechta*: An Old Irish Tract on Suretyship." In *Lawyers and Laymen: Studies in the History of Law Presented to Professor Dafydd Jenkins,* ed. T. M. Charles-Edwards, Morfydd E. Owen, and D. B. Walters, pp. 210–33. Cardiff: University of Wales Press.

Stancliffe, Clare. 1982. "Red, White, and Blue Martyrdom." In Whitelock et al. 1982, 21–46.

———. 1983. *St. Martin and His Hagiographer: History and Miracle in Sulpicius Severus.* Oxford: Clarendon Press.

———. 1992. "The Miracle Stories in Seventh-Century Irish Saints' Lives." In *Le septieme siécle: Changements et continuités / The Seventh Century: Change and Continuity,* ed. Jacques Fontaine and J. N. Hillgarth, pp. 87–115. Studies of the Warburg Institute 42. London: Warburg Institute and University of London.

Stevenson, Jane. 1989. "The Beginnings of Literacy in Ireland." *PRIA* 89C:127–65.

———. 1990. "Literacy in Ireland: The Evidence of the Patrick Dossier in the Book of Armagh." In *The Uses of Literacy in Early Mediaeval Europe,* ed. Rosamond McKitterick, pp. 11–35. Cambridge: Cambridge University Press.

———. 1995. "Literacy and Orality in Early Medieval Ireland." In Edel 1995, 11–22.

Stock, Brian. 1983. *The Implications of Literacy: Written Language and Models of Interpretation in the Eleventh and Twelfth Centuries.* Princeton: Princeton University Press.

Stokes, Whitley. 1887. Ed. and trans. *The Tripartite Life of Patrick, with Other Documents Relating to That Saint.* 2 vols. London: Her Majesty's Stationery Office.

———. 1890. Ed. and trans. *Lives of the Saints from the Book of Lismore.* Oxford: Clarendon Press.

———. 1897. Ed. and trans. *Cóir Anmann: The Fitness of Names.* In *Irische Texte,* ed. Stokes and Ernst Windisch. pp. 285–444. 3d ser., vol. 2. Leipzig: S. Hirzel.

———. 1899–1900. Ed. and trans. "The Bodleian Amra Choluimb Chille." *RC* 20 (1899):30–55, 132–83, 249–87, 400–437; 21 (1900):133–36.

———. 1900. Ed. *Acallamh na Senórach.* In *Irische Texte,* ed. Stokes and Ernst Windisch. 4th ser., vol. 1. Leipzig: S. Hirzel.

———. 1905a. Ed. and trans. "The Colloquy of the Two Sages." *RC* 26:4–64.

———. 1905b. Ed. and trans. *Félire Oengusso Céli Dé: The Martyrology of Oengus the Culdee.* London: Henry Bradshaw Society.

1906–7. Ed. and trans. "The Birth and Life of St. Moling." *RC* 27 (1906):257–312; 28 (1907):70–72.

1908. Ed. "Poems Ascribed to S. Moling." In *Anecdota from Irish Manuscripts* 2, ed. Osborn J. Bergin et al., pp. 20–41. Halle: Max Niemeyer; Dublin: Hodges, Figgis.

Svenbro, Jesper. 1993. *Phrasikleia: An Anthropology of Reading in Ancient Greece.* Trans. Janet Lloyd. Ithaca: Cornell University Press.

Swift, Catherine. 1994. "Tírechán's Motives in Compiling the *Collectanea:* An Alternative Interpretation." *Ériu* 45:53–82.

Szövérffy, Josef. 1957. *Irisches Erzählgut im Abendland: Studien zur vergleichenden Volkskunde und Mittelalterforschung.* Berlin: Eric Schmidt.

Thurneysen, Rudolf. 1918. "Zu irischen Texten." *ZcP* 12:398–407.

1921. *Die irischen Helden- und Königsage bis zum siebzehnten Jahrhundert.* Halle: Max Niemeyer.

Tierney, J. J. 1960. "The Celtic Ethnography of Posidonius." *PRIA* 60C:189–275.

Tohall, Patrick. 1948. "The Dobhar-Chú Tombstones of Glenade, Co. Leitrim." *JRSAI* 78:127–29.

Tristram, Hildegard L. C. 1989. "Early Modes of Insular Expression." In Ó Corráin et al. 1989, 427–48.

1990. "Warum Cenn Faelad sein 'Gehirn des Vergessens' Verlor—Wort und Schrift in der älteren irischen Literatur." In *Deutschen, Kelten, und Iren: 150 Jahre deutsche Keltologie (Gearóid Mac Eoin zum 60. Geburtstag gewidmet)*, ed. Tristram, pp. 207–48. Hamburg: Helmut Buske.

1993. Ed. *Studien zur Táin Bó Cuailnge.* Tübingen: Gunter Narr.

Tymoczko, Maria. 1981. Trans. *Two Death Tales from the Ulster Cycle: The Death of Cu Roi and the Death of Cu Chulainn,* Dublin: Dolmen Press; Atlantic Heights, N.J.: North America Humanities Press.

1985–86. "Animal Imagery in *Loinges Mac nUislenn.*" *SC* 20–21:145–66.

Vance, Eugene. 1987. *From Topic to Tale: Logic and Narrativity in the Middle Ages.* Theory and History of Literature 47. Minneapolis: University of Minnesota Press.

van Hamel, A. G. 1933. Ed. *Compert Con Culainn and Other Stories.* MMIS 3. Dublin: DIAS.

1941. Ed. *Immrama.* MMIS 10. Dublin: Stationery Office.

Walsh, Maura, and Dáibhí Ó Cróinín. 1988. Ed. and trans. *Cummian's Letter De Controversia Paschali and the De Ratione Conputandi.* Toronto: Pontifical Institute of Mediaeval Studies.

Ward, Donald. 1968. *The Divine Twins: An Indo-European Myth in Germanic Tradition.* Folklore Studies 19. Berkeley: University of California Press.

Watkins, Calvert. 1976. "The Etymology of Irish *Dúan.*" *Celtica* 11:270–77.

Watson, J. Carmichael. 1941. Ed. *Mesca Ulad.* MMIS 13. Dublin: Stationery Office.

Watt, John. 1972. *The Church in Medieval Ireland.* Dublin: Gill and Macmillan.

Whitelock, Dorothy, Rosamond McKitterick, and David Dumville. 1982. Eds. *Ireland in Early Mediaeval Europe: Studies in Memory of Kathleen Hughes.* Cambridge: Cambridge University Press.

Williams, J. E. Caerwyn. 1971. "The Court Poet in Medieval Ireland." *PBA* 57:85–135.

1979–80. "Posidonius's Celtic Parasites." *SC* 14/15:313–43.

1983. "Welsh *Drythyll, Trythyll;* Irish *Drettel, Treitell.*" *Celtica* 15:150–57.

Williams, J. E. Caerwyn, and Patrick K. Ford. 1992. *The Irish Literary Tradition.* Cardiff: University of Wales Press; Belmont, Mass.: Ford and Bailie.

Winterbottom, Michael. 1976. "Variations on a Nautical Theme." *Hermathena* 120:55–58.

Wormald, Patrick. 1977. "*Lex Scripta* and *Verbum Regis:* Legislation and Germanic Kingship, from Euric to Cnut." In *Early Medieval Kingship,* ed. P. H. Sawyer and I. N. Wood, pp. 105–38. Leeds: School of History, University of Leeds.

Wright, Charles D. 1993. *The Irish Tradition in Old English Literature.* Cambridge: Cambridge University Press.

Youngson, A. J. 1974. Ed. *Beyond the Highland Line. Three Journals of Travel In Eighteenth Century Scotland: Burt, Pennant, Thornton.* London: Collins.

Zimmer, Heinrich. 1888. "Keltische Beiträge I." *Zeitschrift für deutsches Alterthum* 32:249–55.

Ziolkowski, Jan M. 1990. "The Nature of Prophecy in Geoffrey of Monmouth's *Vita Merlini.*" In Kugel 1990b, 151–62.

——— 1994. Ed. and trans. *The Cambridge Songs (Carmina Cantabrigiensia).* New York: Garland.

index

Joseph Falaky Nagy, Professor of English, teaches Celtic Studies at the University of California, Los Angeles.